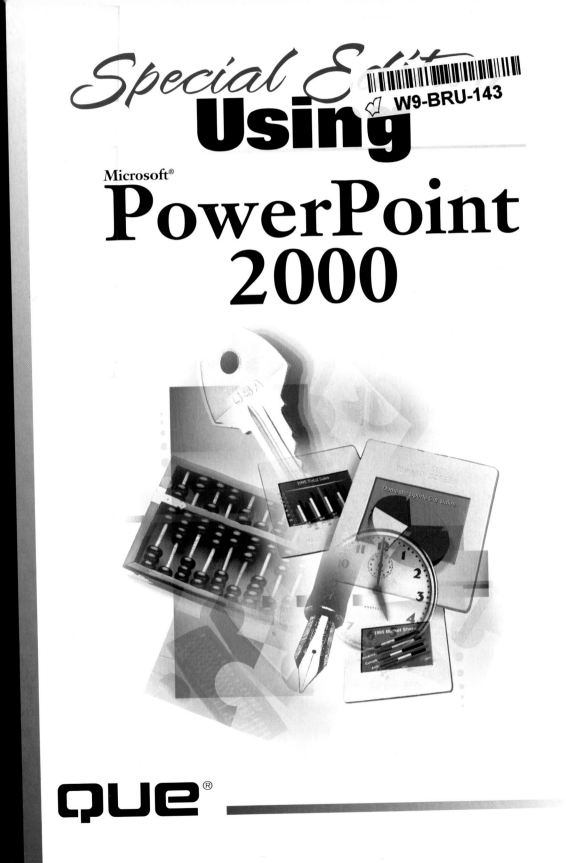

Special Edition

Using

Microsoft® PowerPoint 2000

W9-BRU-143

que®

VISUALLY SPEAKING

By Tom Mucciolo

The world is composed of a growing number of visual creatures. They get most of their information from a visual source called television. This medium provides two critical elements that all visual creatures crave—action and eye contact. On TV, the images move and the characters look at one another or directly at the camera. Planned movements and timely eye contact are the staples of any visual diet. Presenting is no different.

Many studies have been done about the way we communicate in various situations. The statistics may shock you, as Figure 1 indicates. Some studies suggest that 55% of everything you say is seen and understood from what you look like when you speak. Another 38% is conveyed by how you actually deliver the information and only 7% is from what you say. Some may argue that the percentages are different, but most agree that the delivery style of the messenger can surely affect the interpretation of the message.

Figure 1

The majority of your presentation is judged from how you look and sound rather than the what you actually say.

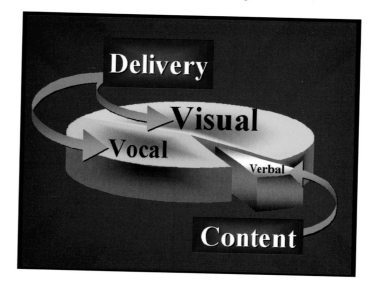

Having spent the last 15 years coaching presenters, I am convinced that the greatest percent of communication rests with the delivery skill of the person carrying the message. This is not to say that content needs to be ignored; rather, it needs to be streamlined and well planned, because it only filters through a small funnel into the ear of the listener. The rest of the story is very visual.

The three components of a presentation shown in Figure 2 are the message (script), the media (visual support), and the mechanics (delivery). Because 93% of the communication is physical, the actions of the presenter, from a physical delivery standpoint, affect the value derived from the event. Actions speak louder than words and in many cases, poor delivery skills become the noticeable distractions that an audience translates into a waste of time. If you want to master the skill of presenting, you will need to concentrate mostly on your delivery mechanics.

Special Edition

Using

Microsoft®
PowerPoint®
2000

Patrice-Anne Rutledge

Tom Mucciolo

Timothy Dyck

Robert Fuller

Read Gilgen

Laurie Ulrich

que®

A Division of Macmillan Computer Publishing, USA
201 W. 103rd Street
Indianapolis, Indiana 46290

SPECIAL EDITION USING MICROSOFT® POWERPOINT® 2000

International Standard Book Number: 0-7897-1904-5

Library of Congress Catalog Card Number: 98-87632

Printed in the United States of America

First Printing: May 1999

02   01   00   4   3   2

TRADEMARKS

WARNING AND DISCLAIMER

Executive Editor
Angela Wethington

Acquistions Editor
Jamie Milazzo

Development Editor
Brian-Kent Proffitt

Managing Editor
Thomas Hayes

Project Editor
Damon Jordan

Copy Editor
Suzanne Rose

Proofreader
Mary Ellen Stephenson

Indexer
Angie Bess

Technical Editors
Connie Grey
Jim Grey
Michelle Hileman

Layout Technician
Eric S. Miller

Cover Designers
Dan Armstrong
Ruth Lewis

Book Designers
Lousia Klucznik
Ruth Lewis

CONTENTS

About the Authors

Patrice-Anne Rutledge writes about technology from her home outside San Francisco and is the author or co-author of 17 computer books including *Special Edition Using Microsoft Office 97 Professional, Bestseller Edition* and *Sams Teach Yourself Quicken Deluxe 99 in 24 Hours*, also by Macmillan Computer Publishing. She has used—and has trained others to use—PowerPoint for many years, designing presentations for meetings, seminars, trade shows, and worldwide audiences.

Tom Mucciolo, founder and president of MediaNet, is an accountant, turned actor, turned author and acclaimed speaker on presentation skills. He is an expert at enhancing the key components of communication including the message (scripting), the media (visual design), and the mechanics (delivery). His seminars and workshops have been rated as "exceptional" and "entertaining" and many consider Tom one of the country's top presentation specialists. His one-to-one coaching sessions, ranging from basic to advanced, develop individual style and prepare a person for presenting in a very visual world.

Timothy Dyck has been using, supporting, and developing Microsoft Office applications since 1984 (when he was blown away seeing Microsoft Word for DOS's on-screen italics for the first time). He is a Microsoft Certified Systems Engineer and has an honors degree in Computer Science from the University of Waterloo, Ontario, Canada. He is now a contributing editor for *PC Week Labs*, specializing in databases and Web development tools.

Robert Fuller has employed PowerPoint for the last five years to design and edit marketing materials for one of America's most successful multinationals. A film student in New York City and Web designer at his own small firm of MacIntyre & Company, Robert spends his waking hours attempting to break free of obscurity (screenwriting), communing with fellow digit-heads (Web development), and trying to maintain his sanity (sleeping, eating, etc.).

Read Gilgen is the director of Learning Support Services at the University of Wisconsin, Madison, and is currently the president of the International Association for Language Learning Technology. He holds a Ph.D. in Latin American Literature and Linguistics from the University of California, Irvine, and has taught and written extensively on DOS, Windows, and WordPerfect. He authored Que's *WordPerfect for Windows Hot Tips* and contributed to *Special Edition Using WordPerfect Suite 8* and *Special Edition Using Microsoft Office 97 Professional, Bestseller Edition*.

Laurie Ulrich has been teaching computer classes for universities and corporate training centers for over 10 years. She also runs her own firm, Limehat & Company, Inc., an organization that specializes in technical documentation, software education, Web page design, and Web site hosting. Her firm's primary focus is helping businesses to make the most of their computer investment by shedding their fears of computerization, and remaining on the cutting edge of business software. Laurie has authored four books for Macmillan Computer Publishing: *Using Word 97, Using PowerPoint 97, The Office 97 Productivity Pack*, and *The Complete Idiot's Guide to Running a Small Office with Microsoft Office*.

PATRICE-ANNE RUTLEDGE'S ACKNOWLEDGMENTS

I'd like to thank everyone who contributed to the creation of *Special Edition Using Microsoft PowerPoint 2000*. Jamie Milazzo, for suggesting I write this book and providing enthusiasm, support, and encouragement during the many months of this project. Tom Mucciolo, Read Gilgen, Tim Dyck, Laurie Ulrich, and Robert C. Fuller for contributing many great chapters. Brian-Kent Proffitt for his many organizational and editorial contributions. And, Michelle Hileman, Suzanne Rose, Jim Grey, Connie Grey, and Brian Reilly for their attention to detail. Finally, special thanks to my mom, Phyllis Rutledge, for both her editorial expertise and her encouragement throughout the creation of this book.

DEDICATION

To my family with thanks for their love and support.

—PR

TOM MUCCIOLO'S ACKNOWLEDGMENTS

I'd like to thank my brother, Rich, for his support and advice, along with his creative talents in designing, capturing, and printing all the figures used in my chapters. My thanks to Patrice Rutledge for shaping the main content of this book; Read Gilgen, Tim Dyck, Laurie Ulrich, and Robert C. Fuller for lending such quality expertise to specific areas; the editorial team, from copy to technical to production, in being so adept at bringing this project to fruition. In addition, I would like to thank Jamie Milazzo for keeping me on task, for allowing me the luxury of putting my own personality into each chapter, and for just making this book so much fun to write. On the personal side, I want to thank my mom and dad for always supporting everything I attempted, regardless of success or failure. On the technical side, I owe a debt of gratitude to my notebook computer for accepting every keystroke throughout the entire project, without complaint; and a really important thank you goes to my friend, the backspace key, without which my words would loofk ljke thyss. Oh, and finally, I want to thank everyone on the island of Crete, mainly because no one ever thanks those people for anything and this has to stop right now!

DEDICATION

To my wife, Joan, and my son, Peter. They tolerate my travel, inspire my creativity, and motivate my performance. Their love, their patience, and their willingness to let me spend valuable weekend hours writing made my efforts on this book so much easier.

—TM

TELL US WHAT YOU THINK!

As the reader of this book, *you* are our most important critic and commentator. We value your opinion and want to know what we're doing right, what we could do better, what areas you'd like to see us publish in, and any other words of wisdom you're willing to pass our way.

As the Executive Editor for the General Desktop Applications team at Que Corporation, I welcome your comments. You can fax, email, or write me directly to let me know what you did or didn't like about this book—as well as what we can do to make our books stronger.

Please note that I cannot help you with technical problems related to the topic of this book, and that due to the high volume of mail I receive, I might not be able to reply to every message.

When you write, please be sure to include this book's title and authors, as well as your name and phone or fax number. I will carefully review your comments and share them with the authors and editors who worked on the book.

Fax: 317-581-4666

Email: office_que@mcp.com

Mail: Angela Wethington, Executive Editor
          General Desktop Applications
          Que Corporation
          201 West 103rd Street
          Indianapolis, IN 46290 USA

INTRODUCTION

by Patrice-Anne Rutledge

Microsoft PowerPoint 2000 is the latest version of this powerful presentation graphics software program, and is part of the Microsoft Office 2000 family. Using PowerPoint, you can quickly create a basic slideshow or you can delve into sophisticated features to create a customized presentation. Because it's part of the Microsoft Office suite of products, you'll find PowerPoint intuitive and very familiar if you already use any other Office applications, such as Word or Excel.

Because creating a successful presentation is more than just becoming a PowerPoint power user, we've included a special section in this book on presentation skills. After you master PowerPoint, you can master presentation techniques such as creating a script, evaluating the use of multimedia and color, reaching your audience, rehearsing your speech, speaking in public, and dealing with the technicalities of presentation. This information combines with a thorough discussion of all PowerPoint's many features to create a complete reference manual for anyone who makes presentations using PowerPoint.

WHY YOU SHOULD USE THIS BOOK

Special Edition Using Microsoft PowerPoint 2000 is created for experienced computer users who want to be able to use PowerPoint's more sophisticated features, as well as its basic ones. The focus of this book is to get you up and running quickly, and then spend more time exploring the advanced features PowerPoint has to offer—customization, Web interface, animation, and multimedia. If you want to become a PowerPoint power user, this book is for you.

HOW THIS BOOK IS ORGANIZED

Special Edition Using Microsoft PowerPoint 2000 is divided into seven parts and includes three appendixes.

Part I, "PowerPoint Basics," introduces the fundamentals of using PowerPoint, such as navigation, using views, getting help, creating a basic presentation, and saving and opening files. If you're an experienced computer user but are new to PowerPoint, these chapters will get you up and running quickly. If you've used PowerPoint extensively in the past, they can serve as a quick review and introduce you to the new, exciting features of PowerPoint 2000.

In Part II, "Editing and Formatting Presentations," you continue on to the most essential, and universally used, features of PowerPoint—formatting, organizing, and adding content to your slides. You'll learn to work with text and tables, organize with Outline view, as well as customize and format your presentation.

Part III, "Making Presentations," takes you to the logical next step—the actual delivery of a presentation. You'll learn how to easily set up a slideshow, customize it to work with a particular projector, create timings and narrations, preview your work, and even create portable PowerPoint presentations to display from another computer. Finally, you'll learn how to create a variety of printed material, such as notes and handouts, to go with your slideshow.

Next, you can start exploring some of PowerPoint's more advanced capabilities. Part IV, "Working with Graphics, Charts, and Multimedia," introduces you to techniques that can add a creative flair to your slideshows. For example, you can add charts—including organization charts—to provide additional information in a presentation. Or you can add clip art, photos, movies, sounds, and animation for a complete multimedia effect. For a finishing touch, you can format, customize, and add a variety of special effects to these multimedia objects.

From here, you can check out PowerPoint's Web capabilities in Part V, "Working with PowerPoint on the Web." Many of these are new to PowerPoint 2000. From saving PowerPoint presentations as Web pages to designing Web scripts to creating online broadcasts and meetings, you can integrate all the latest Web technologies with your PowerPoint presentation.

Part VI, "Advanced PowerPoint," explores other sophisticated uses of PowerPoint. You can embed and link Office objects, create macros to automate procedures, utilize the power of VBA (the programming language Visual Basic for Applications), and extensively customize PowerPoint's features and interface.

Part VII, "From Concept to Delivery," takes you out of PowerPoint and into the world of presentation design. Written by a presentations expert, this section offers detailed information and advice about actually creating a presentation specifically for PowerPoint. It covers topics such as scripting a concept, choosing a visual design, developing presentation skills, and using technology in your presentation.

And finally, the appendixes cover areas such as troubleshooting and using PowerPoint 2000's new foreign language features.

CONVENTIONS USED IN THIS BOOK

Special Edition Using Microsoft PowerPoint 2000 uses a number of conventions to provide you with special information. These include

Tip #1 from *Patricia-Anne Rutledge*	Tips offer suggestions for making things easier or provide alternate ways to do a particular task.

Note	Notes provide additional, more detailed information about a specific PowerPoint feature.

Caution	Cautions warn you about potential problems that may occur and offer advice on how to avoid these problems.

Cross-references refer you to other sections of the book in which you find more detailed explanations of a particular function, such as the following:

→ To learn more about preparing yourself to present, **see** "Developing Internal Presentation Skills," **p. xxx** (Chapter 24).

Inline indexes are a new feature in Special Edition books. They provide an easy way for you to find the definition of a term or concept explained elsewhere in the book, without having to consult the actual index itself.

Most chapters end with two specific elements: Troubleshooting and a Design Corner. The Troubleshooting section provides tips on common problems you may encounter using the PowerPoint features presented in the chapter. Design Corners provide a before and after look at a specific feature explained in that chapter. Design Corners take you one step further than the typical example in this book by showing you common design tasks you may perform and their end results.

PART

I

POWERPOINT BASICS

CHAPTER 1

INTRODUCING POWERPOINT 2000

In this chapter

by Patrice-Anne Rutledge

POWERPOINT OVERVIEW

PowerPoint is a powerful, yet easy-to-use presentation software package that is part of the Microsoft Office 2000 suite of products. You can use PowerPoint to create presentations for a wide variety of audiences and for a wide variety of purposes. A presentation communicates information, and a good presentation can truly convince, motivate, inspire, and educate its audience. PowerPoint offers the tools both to create a basic presentation, as well as enhance and customize it to truly meet its goals.

In this chapter you learn about

- *New PowerPoint features*   PowerPoint 2000 includes dozens of new features—small, but useful user interface enhancements, as well as major new features such as online broadcasting and online meetings.

- *Using menus and toolbars*   The menus and toolbars in PowerPoint function in much the same way as other Office programs, so that any previous Office or PowerPoint experience will have you up and running with PowerPoint 2000 in no time.

- *Working with PowerPoint views*   PowerPoint's new Normal view combines the outline, slide, and notes panes. Four other view also provide greater usability.

- *Using PowerPoint help features*   You can use the Office Assistant to ask questions in plain English, do extensive searching in the Microsoft PowerPoint Help window, or go to the Web for the latest updates.

UNDERSTANDING WHAT POWERPOINT CAN DO

One of PowerPoint's strengths is its flexibility. Using wizards and other automated features, you can quickly create a basic presentation with little or no design skills. And if you are a designer, PowerPoint's advanced features and customization options enable you to have complete creative control. With PowerPoint you can

- Create a presentation using a wizard, using a design template, or from scratch.
- Add content to your presentation with text and tables.
- Use different views to outline, organize, add content, revise, and preview your presentation.
- Format a presentation by customizing color schemes, background, and templates.
- Make a presentation onscreen using a computer, with overheads and a projector, or via the Web.
- Create and print notes and handouts for you and your audience.
- Add additional content with charts, pictures, clip art, and other shapes or objects.
- Bring multimedia into the picture through the use of sound, video, and animation.
- Use PowerPoint's powerful Web features to create online broadcasts, Web discussions, online meetings, Web scripts, and even complete Web pages.

- Explore advanced features such as linking, embedding, and macros to create customized PowerPoint applications.

EXPLORING NEW POWERPOINT 2000 FEATURES

PowerPoint 2000 includes many new features that users of previous versions will enjoy. This new version of PowerPoint focuses particularly on user productivity and integration with the Web. Some new features that may interest you include

- *Normal View* The default Normal View now combines three panes—slide, outline, and notes—for easier use.

→ To learn about each of these views, **see** "Understanding PowerPoint Views," **p. 16**.

- *AutoNumbered and Graphical Bullets* Bullet enhancements now include the capability to create a numbered, bulleted list automatically, as well as to use graphic images instead of circles and squares for bullets.

→ For detailed information on using a variety of bullet types, **see** "Using Bullets," **p. 66**

- *Built-In Table Creation* You can now create tables directly in PowerPoint, rather than having to use the features of Word or Excel to do this.

→ To learn more about the variety of table options PowerPoint provides, **see** "Working with Tables," **p. 79**

- *HTML Formatting and Publishing* In PowerPoint 2000, you can save your presentation in an HTML format while maintaining PowerPoint features and optimizing Web graphics. You can also easily present and preview in a browser.

→ For more details on HTML formatting and publishing, **see** "Using PowerPoint's Web Features," **p. 337**

- *Online Collaboration/Meetings* PowerPoint now integrates with Microsoft NetMeeting Internet conferencing software.

→ To learn more about PowerPoint's collaborative tools, **see** "Interactive Online Meetings," **p. 398**

Tip #1 from *Patricia-Anne Rutledge*	Check out the NetMeeting Web site for more information on this product. You can find it at www.microsoft.com/netmeeting.

- *Online Broadcast* This new feature enables you to display a PowerPoint presentation over a company intranet using audio and video.

→ To learn more about delivering PowerPoint presentations over the Internet, **see** "Setting the Broadcast Time," **p. 391**

EXPLORING THE POWERPOINT DESKTOP

The PowerPoint 2000 desktop is very similar to that of other Office 2000 applications. If you're familiar with one Office program, you should be able to navigate the others as well.

USING MENUS AND SHORTCUT MENUS

You use PowerPoint menus to perform specific actions. The PowerPoint *menu bar (p. xxx)* includes nine menu categories, each displaying a list of related commands. Figure 1.1 illustrates the menu bar.

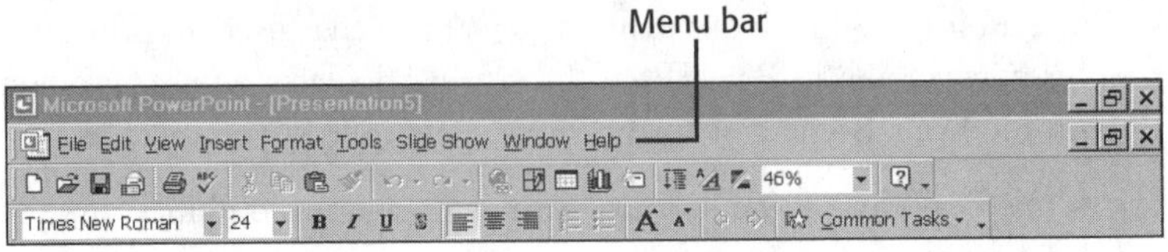

Menu bar

Figure 1.1
Use menus to navigate PowerPoint.

In PowerPoint, only the most commonly used menu commands display when you first install the program. To see additional menu commands, click the double down arrows at the bottom of the list. After you use a menu command, it becomes part of the regular menu and you don't need to select the down arrows to locate it.

Tip #2 from
Patrice-Anne Rutledge

To open a menu using the keyboard, press the Alt key plus the underlined letter in the menu category you want to open. For example, pressing Alt+D opens the Slide Show menu. This is called a *hotkey*.

Tip #3 from
Patrice-Anne Rutledge

You can automatically display all menu commands if you want to. To do this, choose Tools, Customize and go to the Options tab of the Customize dialog box. Remove the check mark from the Menus Show Recently Used Commands First check box and click Close.

Several PowerPoint menus also include submenus, identified with a right arrow next to the menu command itself. Figure 1.2 illustrates a submenu.

Figure 1.2
Submenus are a second menu-level of navigation in PowerPoint.

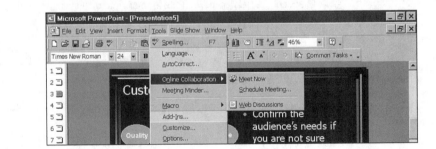

PowerPoint also includes shortcut menus, specific menus that are context-sensitive and relate to a selected object. To view a shortcut menu, right-click the mouse. Figure 1.3 displays a shortcut menu.

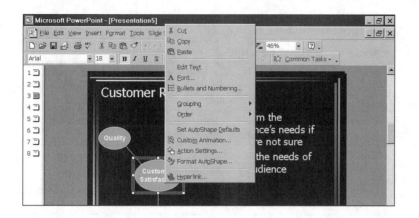

Figure 1.3
To see specific menu
options, right-click
the mouse.

→ To learn more about the many ways you can customize PowerPoint menus, **see** "Customizing Menu Commands," **p. 459**

USING TOOLBARS

A toolbar is similar to a menu in that it categorizes related commands to make it easier for you to perform a specific task. But toolbars use a graphical representation, or button, rather than a menu-based text representation. Even though toolbars use buttons rather than text, you can still display a text description of what the button does by pausing the mouse over it. A *ScreenTip (p. 348)* appears, identifying the button's function. Figure 1.4 illustrates a ScreenTip.

⚡ **ScreenTips don't appear?** See the Troubleshooting section at the end of the chapter.

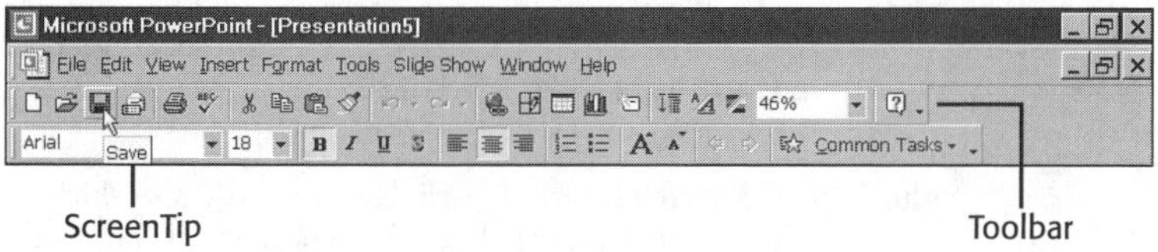

Figure 1.4
ScreenTips identify
toolbar buttons.

ScreenTip   Toolbar

The Standard and Formatting toolbars are the two most commonly used PowerPoint toolbars. Table 1.1 describes the buttons on the Standard toolbar, which you'll use frequently in PowerPoint.

Tip #4 from
Patrice-Anne Rutledge

If you want to save screen space, check the Standard and Formatting toolbars share one row check box on the Options tab of the Customize dialog box. This moves these toolbars to one row. Open this dialog box by selecting Tools, Customize.

→ To view a table of the buttons on the Formatting toolbar, **see** "Using the Formatting Toolbar," **p. 62**

TABLE 1.1   STANDARD TOOLBAR BUTTONS

Button	Name	Description
	New	Creates a new presentation and opens the New Slide dialog box from which you can choose from a variety of slide layouts.
	Open	Opens the Open dialog box from which you can open an existing presentation.
	Save	Opens the Save As dialog box in which you can save your open presentation.
	E-mail	Displays fields in which you can enter an email recipient to whom you want to send the open presentation.
	Print	Prints the presentation on the default printer.
	Spelling	Checks the spelling and style of the open presentation.
	Cut	Cuts the selected text or object, which is deleted from the presentation, and places it on the Clipboard.
	Copy	Copies the selected text or object, which remains on the presentation, and places it on the Clipboard.
	Paste	Pastes the most recently cut or copied object into the selected location in the presentation.
	Format Painter	Copies the format of the selected text or object and applies this formatting to the next object you click.
	Undo	Undoes the last action.
	Redo	Does the previous action again.
	Insert Hyperlink	Opens the Insert Hyperlink dialog box from which you can insert a hyperlink to a Web page, email address, or another document or presentation.
	Tables and Borders	Displays the Tables and Borders toolbar.
	Insert Table	Displays a palette in which you can choose the size of table you want to insert.
	Insert Chart	Activates Microsoft Graph with which you can insert a chart in your presentation.
	New Slide	Displays the New Slide dialog box in which you can add a new slide to the open presentation.
	Expand All	Expands the outline pane to display all titles and body text for each slide.
	Show Formatting	Displays text formatting in the outline pane.

Button	Name	Description
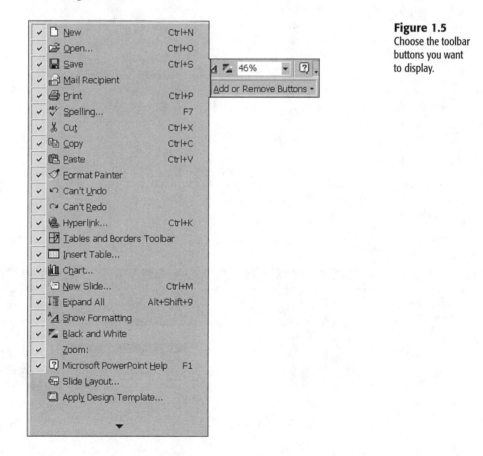	Grayscale Preview	Previews the presentation in grayscale.
1 pt ▾	Zoom	Enables you to select a zoom percentage from the drop-down list—from 25% to 400%.
?	Microsoft PowerPoint Help	Activates the Office Assistant.

DISPLAYING TOOLBARS

Other toolbars appear automatically when you select a certain command. For example, when you choose Insert, Comment from the menu, the Reviewing toolbar automatically displays.

To the right of each toolbar is a down arrow. Click this arrow and then click Add or Remove Buttons. In the drop-down menu that appears, you can choose which buttons you want to appear on the toolbar, reset the toolbar to its default, or customize the toolbar even further (see Figure 1.5).

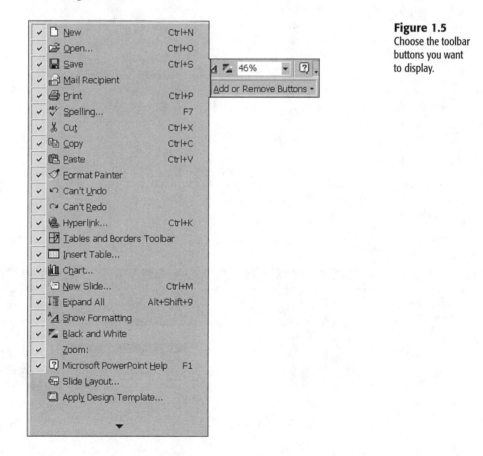

Figure 1.5
Choose the toolbar buttons you want to display.

→ To learn how to customize and modify PowerPoint toolbars to fit your needs, **see** "Customizing Toolbars," **p. 446**

To open and close toolbars manually, choose <u>V</u>iew, <u>T</u>oolbars and select or deselect toolbars from the list of available options. Figure 1.6 illustrates this menu and the available toolbars.

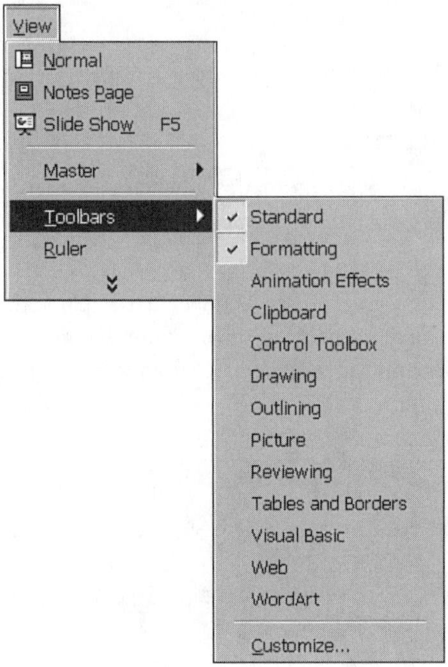

Figure 1.6
Select a toolbar
from this menu
to display it.

MOVING TOOLBARS

You can easily move a toolbar to a new location. How you do this depends on whether the toolbar is *docked (p. 446)* or is a *floating toolbar (p. 446)*. Figure 1.7 illustrates both types of toolbars.

Move handle   Docked toolbar

Figure 1.7
You can move
PowerPoint toolbars
to make the program
easier to use.

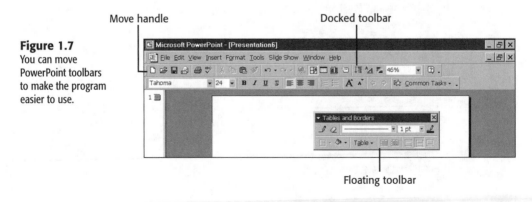

Floating toolbar

To move a docked toolbar, drag the move handle on its left side to a new location. To move a floating toolbar, drag its title bar. You can easily switch a toolbar from docked to floating, and vice versa. Drag a docked toolbar to a central location on the screen to float it. Drag a floating toolbar to the edge of the window to dock it.

Tip #5 from
Patrice-Anne Rutledge

You can resize a floating toolbar by dragging on any side. This way you can display the buttons straight across in one row or in several rows, depending on which way it's easier to view your presentation.

Can't find a toolbar button you've used before? See the Troubleshooting section at the end of the chapter.

USING THE CLIPBOARD TOOLBAR

Multiple clipboard functionality is new to PowerPoint 2000 and is shared with other Office 2000 applications such as Word or Excel. This collect-and-paste feature enables you to copy multiple items and then paste them selectively, rather than simply copying and pasting a single item as you could in past Office versions. In Office 2000, you can collect up to 12 items—text, objects, graphics, documents, Web pages, and so forth—and then selectively paste these as needed. The *Clipboard toolbar (p. 448)* enables you to view and manage the 12 items you have most recently copied. Figure 1.8 illustrates this toolbar, which you can open by selecting View, Toolbars, Clipboard.

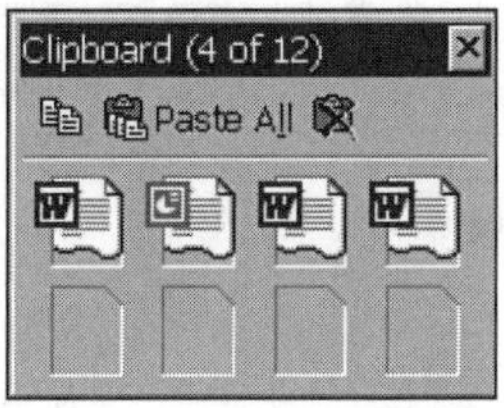

Figure 1.8
You can more easily manage and share information using the Clipboard toolbar.

The toolbar displays up to 12 items, leaving empty spaces if you have fewer than this number of collected items. If you pause the mouse over the button that represents each individual item, the initial text of that item displays as a ScreenTip. Click on the button to paste its data into your presentation. Table 1.2 lists the buttons on this toolbar.

TABLE 1.2   CLIPBOARD TOOLBAR BUTTONS

Button	Name	Description
	Copy	Copies selected object to the Clipboard.
	Paste All	Pastes all collected objects into the open presentation or document.
	Clear Clipboard	Deletes all collected items from the Clipboard.

UNDERSTANDING POWERPOINT VIEWS

PowerPoint includes five different kinds of views. A view is a way you see and work with the software; which one you use depends on what you're doing at any particular time.

To display a particular view, click its view button in the lower-left portion of the PowerPoint window (see Figure 1.9).

Figure 1.9
PowerPoint includes
five different views.

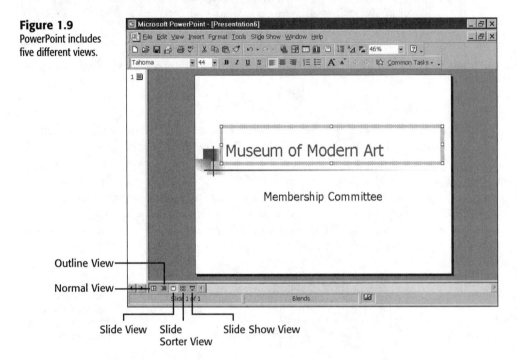

PowerPoint's five views are

- *Normal View* This is the default view and displays three different panes: slide, outline, and notes. Figure 1.10 illustrates Normal View.
    - The slide pane is the largest of the three. You can add text, graphics, tables, charts, and other objects to your presentation on the slide pane.

Note
Use the drop-down list next to the Zoom button on the Standard toolbar to make the magnification larger or smaller than the default.

    - The outline pane is on the left side of the window and displays an outline of your presentation. You can use this pane to enter the text content, to rearrange and organize slides, or to move to another slide.

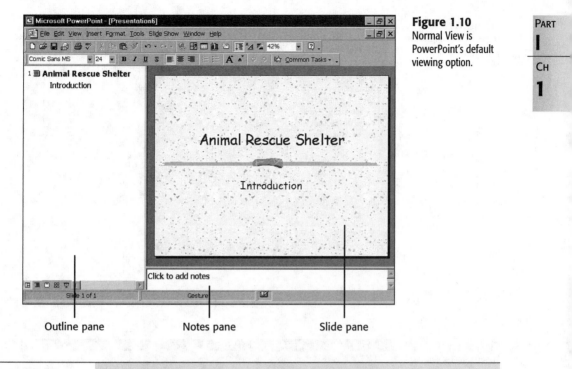

Figure 1.10
Normal View is
PowerPoint's default
viewing option.

PART

I

CH

1

Outline pane   Notes pane   Slide pane

Tip #6 from
Patricia-Anne Rutledge

You can also use the scrollbar on the right side of the slide pane to navigate between presentation slides. The Page Up and Page Down keys can also enable you to navigate.

- The notes pane includes space for you to write speaker's notes or notes to yourself about your presentation.

→ To get suggestions about creating effective speaker's notes, **see** "Creating Notes and Handouts," **p. 178**

■ *Outline View* Outline View also includes the outline, slide, and notes panes, but in different sizes. The focal point in this view is the outline pane and it provides you more space in which to create a detailed outline. The slide pane includes a slide miniature in which you can still see the basic format of your slide as well as a notes pane for detailed notes. Figure 1.11 illustrates Outline View.

■ *Slide View* This view provides a close-up look at your slide. The notes pane doesn't display at all, and the outline pane only includes slide numbers, not a detailed outline. Figure 1.12 displays this view.

■ *Slide Sorter View* This view, shown in Figure 1.13, displays miniature views of all the slides in your presentation, making it easier for you to organize them.

■ *Slide Show View* Slide Show View displays your slides as they would appear in a slide show, full-screen without any PowerPoint menus, toolbars, or other features. Figure 1.14 illustrates this view.

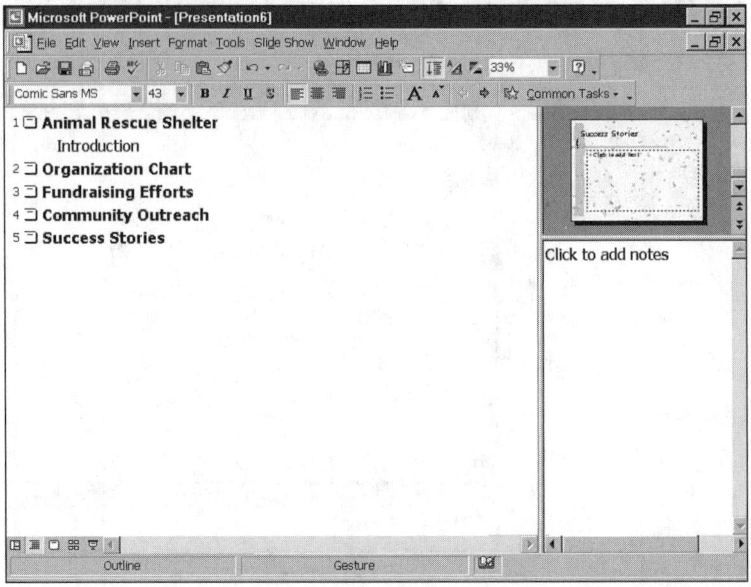

Figure 1.11
Outline View helps you organize your presentation.

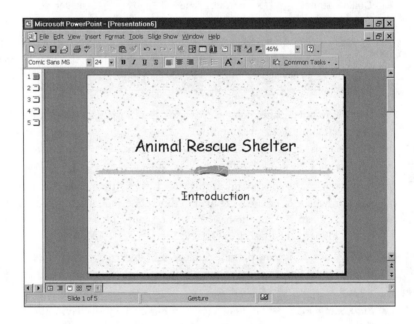

Figure 1.12
To enlarge the slide pane, choose Slide View.

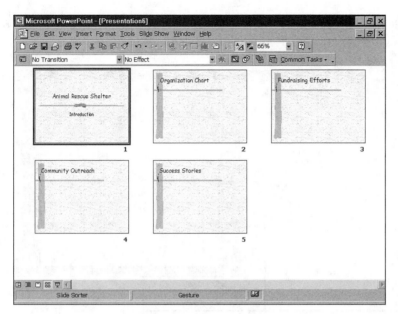

Figure 1.13
Seeing miniature
versions of your
slides can help you
rearrange them.

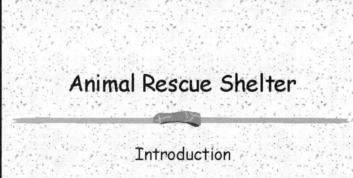

Figure 1.14
Slide Show View
demonstrates how
your presentation
will look.

You can easily resize the panes in Normal, Outline, or Slide View. To do so, drag the border between panes to a new location. Figure 1.15 illustrates a resized pane.

Figure 1.15
You can resize Normal View to suit your needs.

Drag these borders to resize

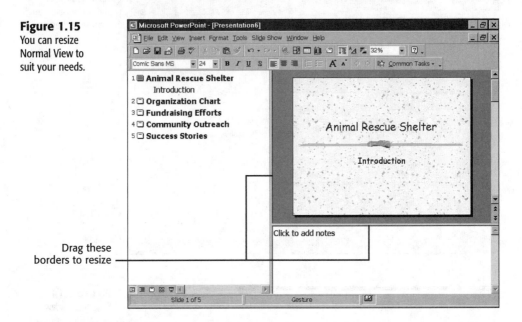

GETTING HELP

PowerPoint includes a wide variety of help options, one of which should suit your needs and the way you use information. Options include the Office Assistant, a full-search Help window, and help on the Web.

Tip #7 from	At times, PowerPoint may not behave as expected, or deliver an error message when none is needed. To automatically find and fix repairs to PowerPoint at these times, choose <u>H</u>elp, Detect and <u>R</u>epair.
Patricia-Anne Rutledge	

USING THE OFFICE ASSISTANT

The *Office Assistant* lets you ask natural language questions—such as "How do I insert WordArt?"—and provides help topics that answer these questions. Click the assistant when you need help, and a balloon appears that asks you what you want to do (see Figure 1.16).

Enter your question—or just a word or phrase if you like—and click the <u>S</u>earch button. The balloon offers a list of topics related to the question. Figure 1.17 illustrates this.

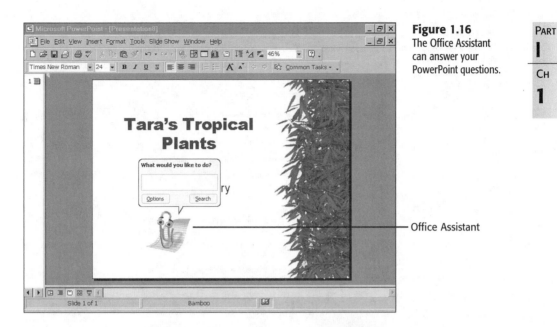

Figure 1.16
The Office Assistant can answer your PowerPoint questions.

Office Assistant

Figure 1.17
PowerPoint gives you several topics based on your questions.

Tip #8 from
Patrice-Anne Rutledge

Click See More at the bottom of the Help caption to view additional help topics.

Click the topic that is most relevant. The Microsoft PowerPoint Help window opens, shown in Figure 1.18.

Figure 1.18
The Help window displays detailed help on your selected topic.

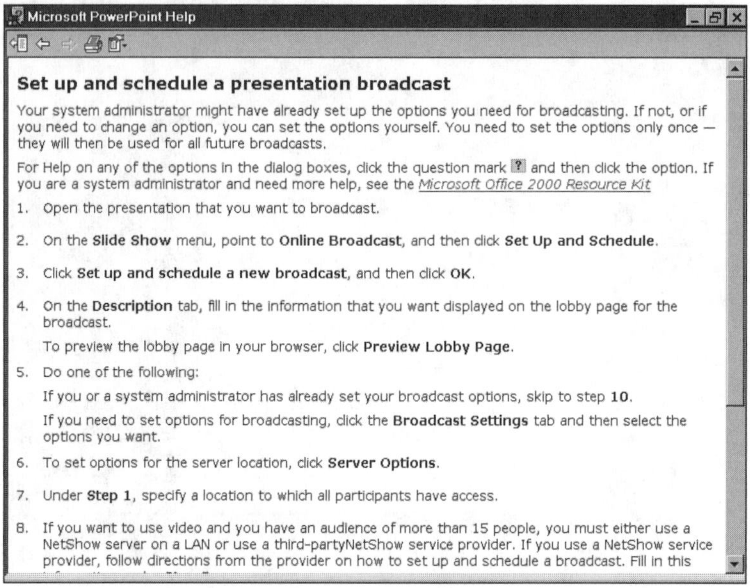

Set up and schedule a presentation broadcast

Your system administrator might have already set up the options you need for broadcasting. If not, or if you need to change an option, you can set the options yourself. You need to set the options only once — they will then be used for all future broadcasts.

For Help on any of the options in the dialog boxes, click the question mark [?] and then click the option. If you are a system administrator and need more help, see the *Microsoft Office 2000 Resource Kit*.

1. Open the presentation that you want to broadcast.

2. On the **Slide Show** menu, point to **Online Broadcast**, and then click **Set Up and Schedule**.

3. Click **Set up and schedule a new broadcast**, and then click **OK**.

4. On the **Description** tab, fill in the information that you want displayed on the lobby page for the broadcast.

   To preview the lobby page in your browser, click **Preview Lobby Page**.

5. Do one of the following:

   If you or a system administrator has already set your broadcast options, skip to step **10**.

   If you need to set options for broadcasting, click the **Broadcast Settings** tab and then select the options you want.

6. To set options for the server location, click **Server Options**.

7. Under **Step 1**, specify a location to which all participants have access.

8. If you want to use video and you have an audience of more than 15 people, you must either use a NetShow server on a LAN or use a third-partyNetShow service provider. If you use a NetShow service provider, follow directions from the provider on how to set up and schedule a broadcast. Fill in this

Note

You can change to a different Office Assistant if you don't like the default. Click the Options button in the assistant balloon and choose the Gallery tab. The Gallery offers alternative assistant images, including Rocky, the Genius, Mother Nature, and the Dot. Be sure to have your Office 2000 CD on hand when you do this, for it will be needed to switch assistants.

USING MICROSOFT POWERPOINT HELP

You can access Microsoft PowerPoint Help either through the Office Assistant or directly from the Help menu if the assistant is turned off. To turn off the assistant, click the Options button in the assistant balloon, go to the Options tab, and remove the check mark next to the Use the Office Assistant check box. You can turn the Office Assistant back on again by choosing Help, Show the Office Assistant.

Tip #9 from
Patrice-Anne Rutledge

Temporarily hide the Office Assistant by choosing Help, Hide the Office Assistant. This isn't the same as turning off the assistant because it's temporary. The assistant returns again the next time you ask for help by clicking the Microsoft PowerPoint Help button or another dialog box help button.

After you turn off the Office Assistant, you can open the Microsoft PowerPoint Help window by clicking the button of the same name on the Standard toolbar. You can also press F1 to do this.

The Microsoft PowerPoint Help window includes three main tabs, as seen in Figure 1.19:

- *Contents* Lists a table of contents for the help system based on specific tasks you may want to perform.

- *Answer Wizard* Enables you to ask a question in plain English, much like the Office Assistant.

- *Index* Includes a list of words and phrases you can search to find the appropriate help topic.

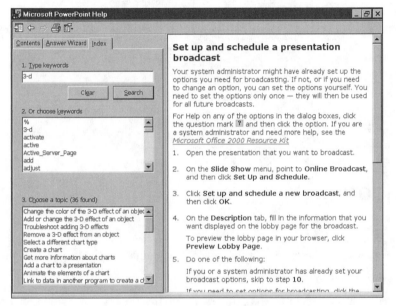

Figure 1.19
This screen lets you search Microsoft PowerPoint Help by keyword.

From each help topic, you can click the Back button to return to the previous screen, click the Print button to print the topic, or click the Hide button to display the help topic full-windows without the search tabs.

GETTING HELP FROM THE WEB

You can also search for the latest information and news about PowerPoint on Microsoft's Office 2000 Web site. To access it, select Help, Office on the Web. Figure 1.20 illustrates this Web site.

Figure 1.20
The Web is an alternative source for PowerPoint help.

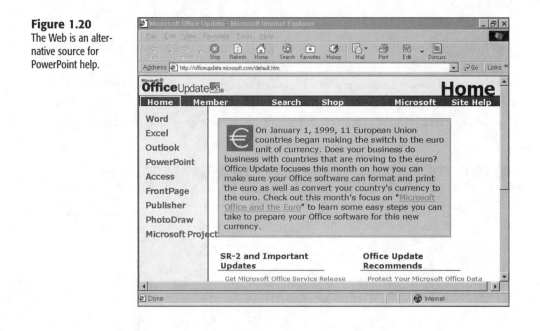

TROUBLESHOOTING

A ScreenTip doesn't appear when I pause the mouse over a toolbar button.

Verify that the Show ScreenTips on Toolbars check box is checked on the Options tab of the Customize dialog box. Access this dialog box by selecting View, Toolbars, Customize.

I can't find a button I need on the toolbar.

If you've moved your toolbars or placed two toolbars on the same row, not all buttons may be visible. Click the More Buttons button at the far right of the toolbar to display additional buttons.

DESIGN CORNER

You can arrange toolbars to make working with PowerPoint easier for you.

BEFORE

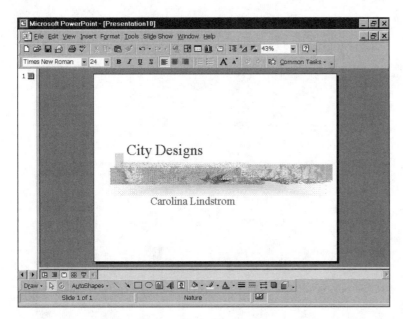

AFTER

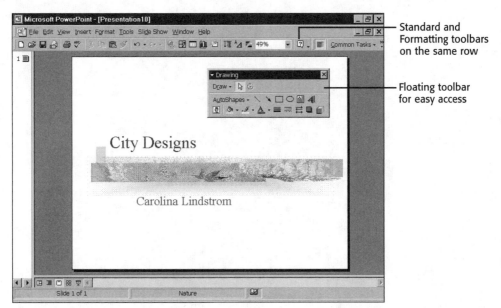

Standard and
Formatting toolbars
on the same row

Floating toolbar
for easy access

CREATING A BASIC PRESENTATION

In this chapter   *by Patrice-Anne Rutledge*

UNDERSTANDING POWERPOINT PRESENTATIONS

Once you learn—or refresh your memory of—how to navigate PowerPoint, you can create a basic presentation. This chapter gets you up and running on presentation basics so you can quickly move forward to more advanced and sophisticated PowerPoint techniques.

In PowerPoint, you can create a presentation in several different ways, depending on the amount of content and design assistance you require. You can create

- *A presentation using the AutoContent Wizard* The wizard selects a design template that matches your presentation type and creates a series of slides with content and slide layout suggestions. Using the AutoContent Wizard can help you save time and provide detailed design assistance if you aren't yet design-savvy.
- *A presentation using a design template* This lets you add your own slides and content, but still have a consistent design scheme (layout, colors, fonts, and so on).
- *A blank presentation* This type of presentation includes no preset design, colors, or content suggestions. Create a blank presentation only when you are very experienced with PowerPoint and know you want to create a custom design rather than use one of PowerPoint's existing designs.

Tip #10 from	Even if you want to create a custom presentation, it often saves you time to start with an existing design and then customize it.
Patrice-Anne Rutledge	

UNDERSTANDING DESIGN TEMPLATES

A *design template (p. 40-41)* includes preformatted layouts, fonts, and colors that blend together to create a consistent look and feel for your presentation. Figures 2.1 and 2.2 illustrate two sample design templates that you might use for totally different audiences and purposes.

→ To learn how to apply design templates, **see** "Working with Design Templates," **p. 550**

The AutoContent Wizard automatically selects a design template that is suited to the type of presentation you want to make. If you don't use the AutoContent Wizard and instead select your own design template, be sure that the template you select matches your audience and fits the message you want to convey.

UNDERSTANDING SLIDE LAYOUTS

In addition to a design template, the other important design feature you need to consider is a slide layout. PowerPoint includes 24 different types of layouts, called *AutoLayouts (p. 199)*:

- Title Slide
- Bulleted List
- Two Column Text
- Table
- Text & Chart
- Chart & Text
- Organization Chart
- Chart
- Text & Clip Art

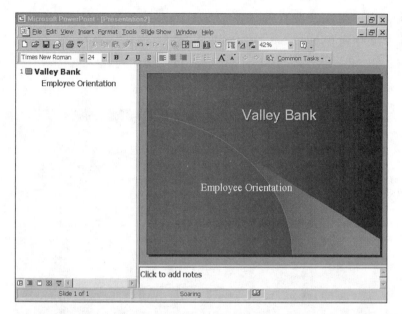

Figure 2.1
A conservative design template such as Soaring suits a corporate audience.

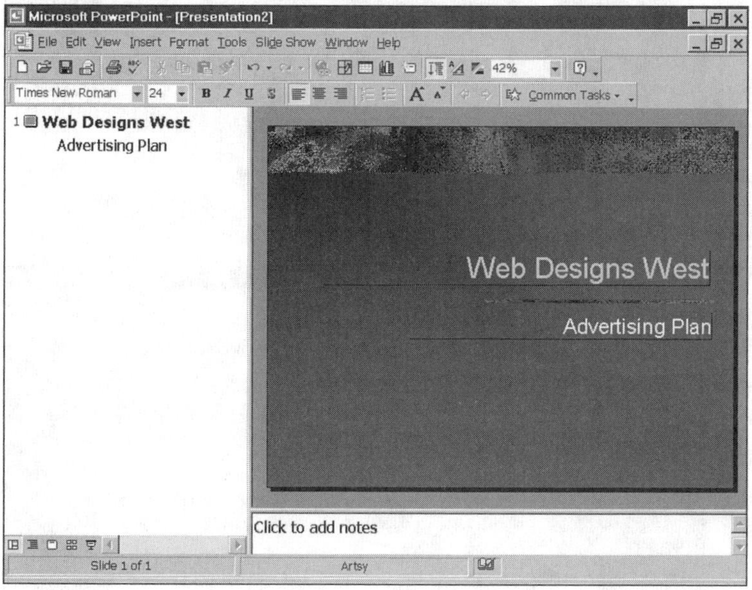

PART

I

CH

2

Figure 2.2
A more creative design template such as Artsy works better for an artsy audience.

- Clip Art & Text
- Title Only
- Blank
- Text & Object
- Object & Text

- Large Object
- Object
- Text & Media Clip
- Media Clip & Text
- Object over Text

- Text over Object
- Text & Two Objects
- Two Objects & Text
- Two Objects over Text
- Four Objects

Even though PowerPoint provides a multitude of layout combinations from which to choose, these layouts only contain a total of eight different elements. These elements are

■ *Titles*   Inserts a text box in which you can enter a title. Figure 2.3 illustrates a title slide.

Figure 2.3
Every presentation should have a title slide.

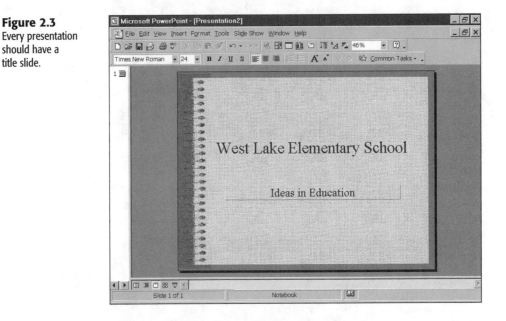

■ *Lists*   Inserts a bulleted list on a slide. Figure 2.4 illustrates such a list.

Figure 2.4
Bulleted lists make it easier to read a series of items.

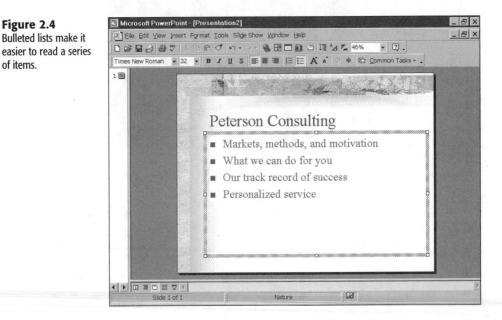

■ *Tables*   Inserts a table that you can format and customize. Figure 2.5 illustrates a table.

→ To explore the ways you can work with tables even more, **see** "Working with Tables," **p. 79**

Note

This procedure inserts a PowerPoint table. For more advanced formatting options, you may want to insert a Microsoft Word table in your presentation. To do so, select Insert, Picture, Microsoft Word Table.

→ If you want to learn more about inserting Word tables into PowerPoint presentations, **see** "Inserting a Word Table," **p. 94**

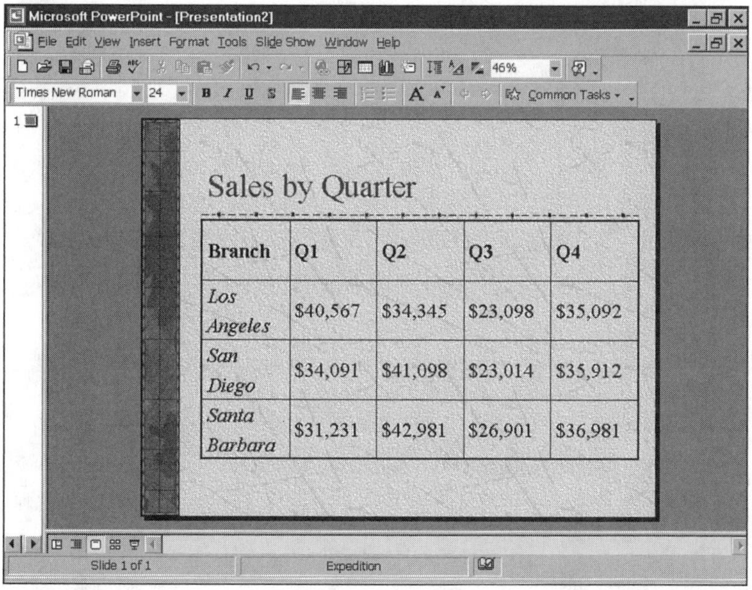

Figure 2.5
Tables enable you to more easily present detailed information.

■ *Text*   Inserts a text placeholder on a slide in which you can add the desired text (see Chapter 3, "Working with Text"). Figure 2.6 illustrates a text placeholder.

■ *Charts*   Inserts a chart (bar, column, pie, and so on) that you create with Microsoft Graph. Figure 2.7 illustrates a chart.

→ For more information about using charts in PowerPoint, **see** "Working with Charts, **p. 195**

■ *Organization Charts*   Includes an organization chart that you create with Microsoft Organization Chart (see Chapter 10, "Working with Organization Charts"). Figure 2.8 illustrates such a chart.

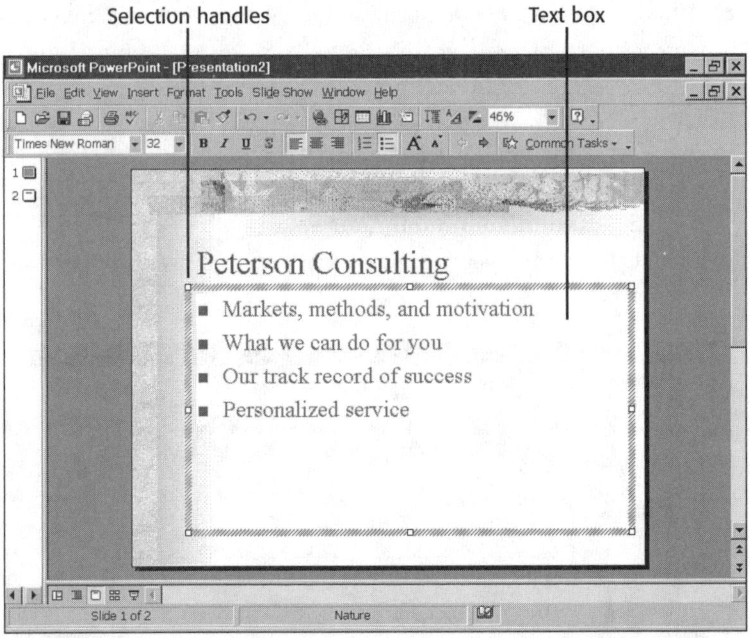

Selection handles   Text box

Figure 2.6
The way you present
text can affect how
your presentation is
perceived.

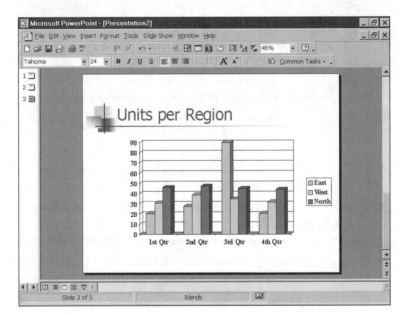

Figure 2.7
Charts can add visual
punch to a presen-
tation.

■ *Clip Art*   Inserts a clip art image you choose from the Clip Gallery. Figure 2.9 illustrates a slide that contains clip art.

Tip #11 from
Patrice-Anne Rutledge

Before inserting your own art here, you can first import it into the Clip Gallery.

➔ To learn how to import graphic images into the Clip Gallery, **see** "Importing Clips," **p. 258**

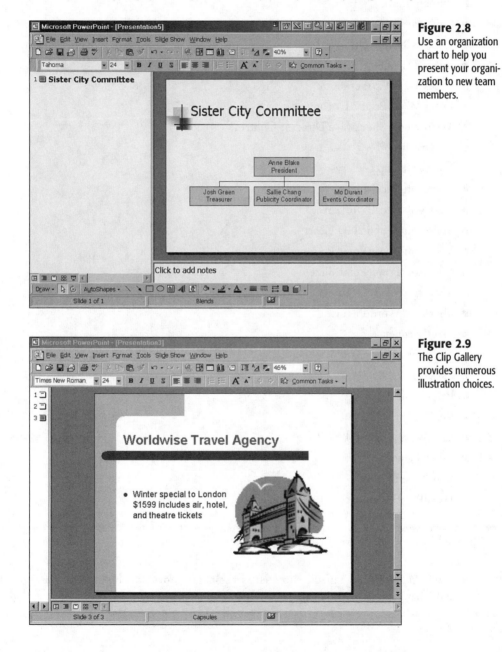

Figure 2.8
Use an organization chart to help you present your organization to new team members.

Figure 2.9
The Clip Gallery provides numerous illustration choices.

When you double-click an object placeholder, the Insert Object dialog box displays. From this dialog box, you can select or create a variety of objects (see Figure 2.10). Some examples include

- Adobe Control for ActiveX
- Adobe Acrobat Object
- Bitmap Image
- Calendar Control 9.0
- Comic Chat Room
- Image Document
- Lotus 1-2-3 97 Workbook
- Lotus Word Pro 97 Document
- Macromedia Shockwave Director Control
- Media Clip
- Microsoft Clip Gallery
- Microsoft Excel Chart
- Microsoft Excel Worksheet
- Microsoft Graph 2000 Chart
- Microsoft PowerPoint Presentation
- Microsoft PowerPoint Slide
- Microsoft Word Document
- Microsoft Word Picture
- MIDI Sequence
- Netscape Hypertext Document
- Package
- Paintbrush Picture
- RegWizCtrl
- Sax Webster Control V2.2
- Video Clip
- Wave Sound
- WordPad Document

→ For more information about using objects in PowerPoint presentations, **see** "Creating and Formatting Objects," **p. 267**

- *Media Clips*   Inserts a media clip such as a sound or movie file. Figure 2.11 illustrates a slide that includes a media clip.

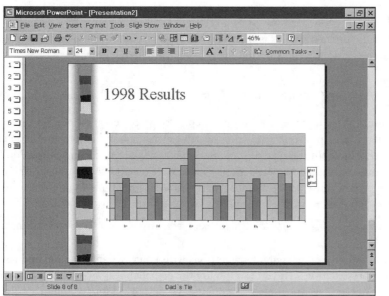

Figure 2.10
You can insert a variety of different objects into a PowerPoint presentation, such as this Excel chart.

Note

A media clip is a special kind of object that you use specifically to insert a sound or movie file. You can choose an AutoLayout that includes an Object to insert a media clip as well, but it's usually easier to select a layout that specifies Media Clip if this is what you want.

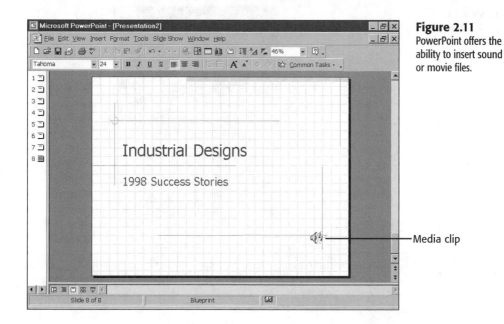

Figure 2.11
PowerPoint offers the ability to insert sound or movie files.

Media clip

→ To learn more about inserting media clips, **see** "Adding Movies and Sound," **p. 299**

If none of these predefined layouts is what you want, you can modify a blank slide or customize one of the existing layouts by adding, moving, or deleting objects.

USING THE AUTOCONTENT WIZARD

The AutoContent Wizard guides you step-by-step through the creation of a PowerPoint presentation and is the option that provides the most assistance and automation. You answer a few basic questions about the type of presentation you need to make and PowerPoint does the rest. The end result is a complete series of slides with content suggestions based on the presentation type you chose. PowerPoint also applies a design template suitable to the type of presentation you need to make and applies a layout to each individual slide.

→ To learn techniques for adding dynamic content to your presentations, **see** "The Message—Scripting the Concept," **p. 493**

From there you can revise the content suggestions with your own information and you're ready to do the presentation. Or, you can modify the actual appearance of the presentation by applying a different design template, modifying the design, adding or removing slides, and so forth.

To use the wizard when you first start PowerPoint, follow these steps:

1. Select Start, Programs, Microsoft PowerPoint. The PowerPoint dialog box displays, as shown in Figure 2.12.

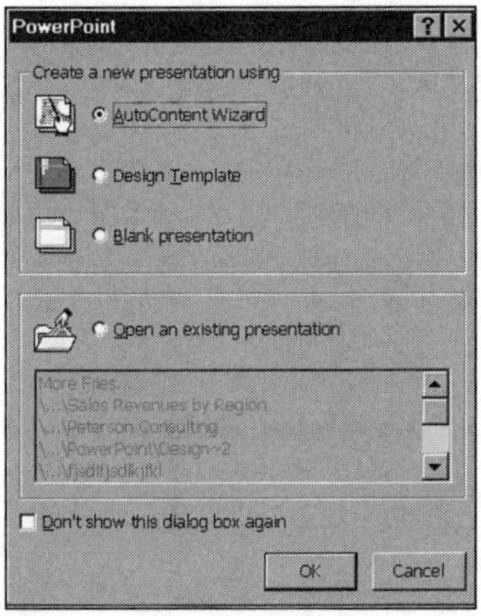

Figure 2.12
You can choose what you want to do when you first start PowerPoint.

Tip #12 from

You can also start the AutoContent Wizard from within PowerPoint. To do so, select File, New to display the New Presentation dialog box. Select AutoContent Wizard on the General tab and click OK.

2. Select the AutoContent Wizard option button and click OK. The wizard displays (see Figure 2.13).

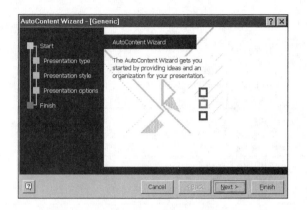

Figure 2.13
The AutoContent Wizard offers detailed guidance on creating a presentation.

3. Click **Next** to continue to the next step, as shown in Figure 2.14.

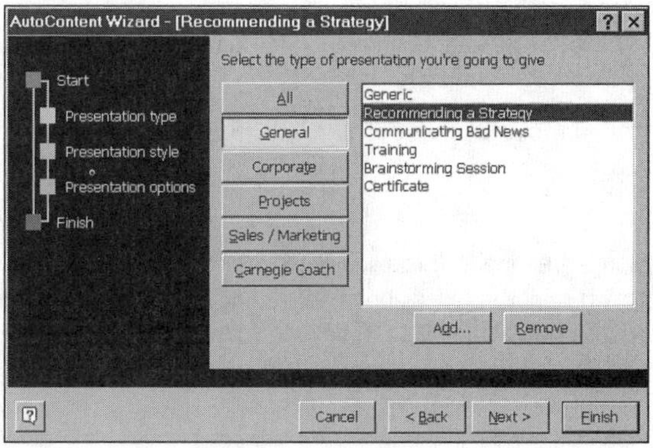

Figure 2.14
You can choose from a variety of presentations in specific category groups.

4. Click the category button that represents the type of presentation you want to create. The adjacent box displays the available presentations, listed in Table 2.1.

TABLE 2.1   POWERPOINT PRESENTATION TYPE

Presentation Type	Options
General	Generic Recommending a Strategy Communicating Bad News Training Brainstorming Session Certificate
Corporate	Business Plan Financial Overview Company Meeting

continues

TABLE 2.1   CONTINUED

Presentation Type	Options
Corporate (cont'd)	Employee Orientation Group Home Page Company Handbook
Projects	Project Overview Reporting Progress or Status Project Post-Mortem
Sales/Marketing	Selling a Product or Service Marketing Plan Product/Services Overview
Carnegie Coach	Selling Your Ideas Motivating a Team Facilitating a Meeting Presenting a Technical Report Managing Organizational Change Introducing and Thanking a Speaker

5. Select the presentation you want to use and click Next. Figure 2.15 illustrates the next step.

Caution

Not all presentations are initially installed. PowerPoint lets you know if you choose a presentation that isn't currently installed and asks if you want to install it. You must have your Office 2000 installation CD in the CD-ROM drive to do this.

Tip #13 from
Patrice-Anne Rutledge

To add your own presentation to the AutoContent Wizard, click the Add button. To remove a presentation, click Remove.

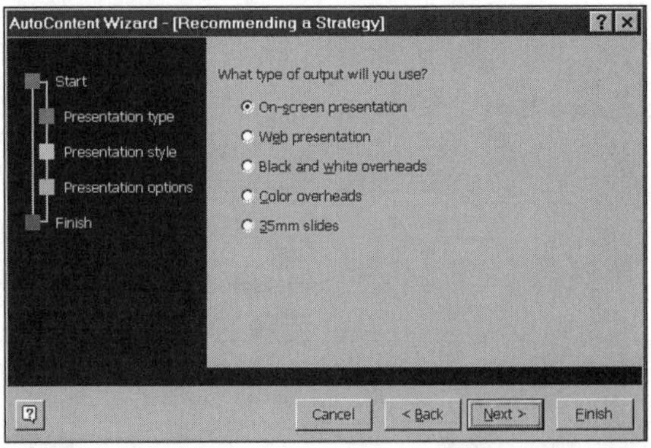

Figure 2.15
The type of output you choose affects the presentation background the wizard applies.

6. Select the type of output to use. Choices include

- On-screen presentation
- Web presentation
- Black-and-white overheads
- Color overheads
- 35mm slides

PowerPoint chooses a background and color scheme suited to the output you select.

PART

I

CH

2

Tip #14 from	To change this background after you've created your presentation, select Format, Slide Color Scheme to open the Color Scheme dialog box.
Patrice-Anne Rutledge	

7. Click **Next** to continue, shown in Figure 2.16.

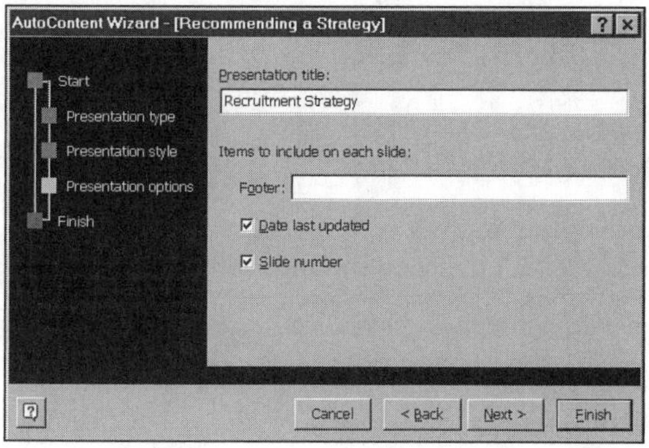

Figure 2.16
In the final step, you enter a title and choose optional footers, numbers, and dates.

8. Enter a presentation title.

9. If you want to include a footer on each slide, enter it.

10. Select Date last updated or Slide number to include this information in the presentation.

11. Click Finish.

PowerPoint displays a sample presentation with slides you can view from the outline section of the window. Figure 2.17 illustrates a sample presentation for facilitating a meeting.

You can then replace the existing text with content that reflects your own needs. You can also delete images and slides that you don't need, change the design of your presentation, and otherwise modify it to your satisfaction.

Figure 2.17
The AutoContent Wizard includes content suggestions for facilitating a meeting.

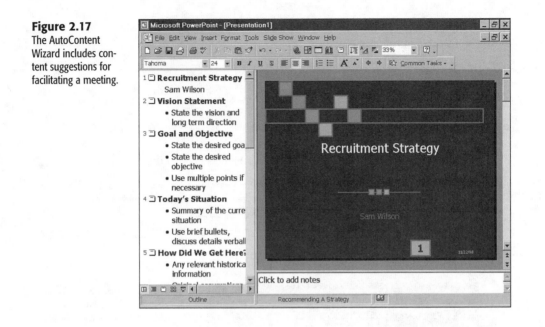

CREATING A PRESENTATION USING A DESIGN TEMPLATE

If you don't need the assistance of the AutoContent Wizard to create sample slides and content for you, you can start with a design template and then add your own slides and content.

To create a presentation with a design template when you first start PowerPoint, follow these steps:

1. Select the Design Template option in the PowerPoint dialog box that displays when you first start PowerPoint. The New Presentation dialog box appears with the Design Templates tab selected, illustrated in Figure 2.18.

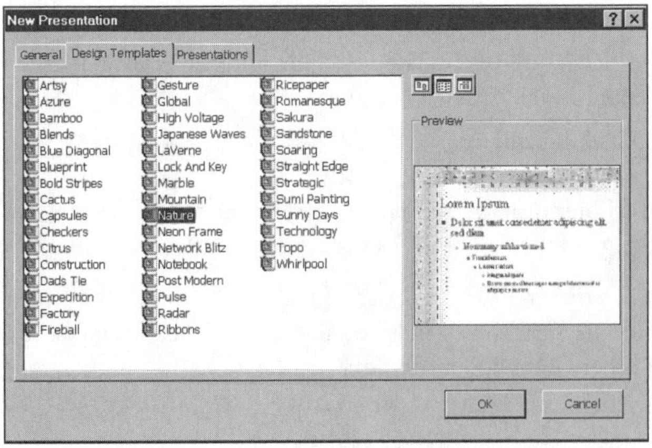

Figure 2.18
PowerPoint includes several design templates from which to choose.

Tip #15 from
Patrice-Anne Rutledge

To access this dialog box from within PowerPoint, select File, New. You can then select the Design Templates tab to access the various templates.

2. Select the template you want to use; the Preview box lets you see what it looks like.

Caution

Not all design templates are already installed. If PowerPoint displays a warning that you need to install a template, be sure to have the program CD in your CD-ROM drive, and then follow the installation instructions in the warning.

3. Click OK to apply the selected template.
4. The New Slide dialog box appears, shown in Figure 2.19.

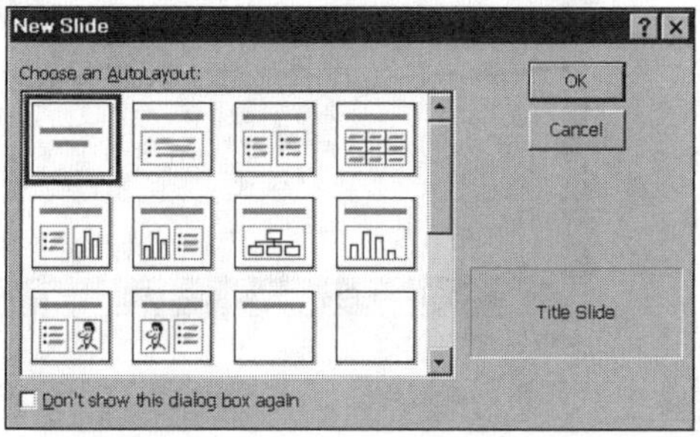

Figure 2.19
The New Slide dialog box lets you choose the layout for your slide.

5. Select the AutoLayout that you want to use in your first slide and then click OK. Each layout option includes a preview box that shows you approximately what the layout will look like onscreen.

6. Click OK.

Tip #16 from
Patrice-Anne Rutledge

You can also create your own design templates and save them for future use. To save a presentation as a design template, choose Design Template in the Save As Type field in the Save As dialog box.

CREATING A BLANK PRESENTATION

You can create a blank presentation in one of two ways:

- Select the Blank Presentation option in the initial PowerPoint dialog box that appears when you first start PowerPoint.
- Select File, New and choose Blank Presentation from the New Presentation dialog box General tab.

The New Slide dialog box appears. Choose the AutoLayout you want to use in your presentation and click OK.

Figure 2.20 illustrates a sample blank presentation.

Figure 2.20
To have complete design control you can use a blank presentation.

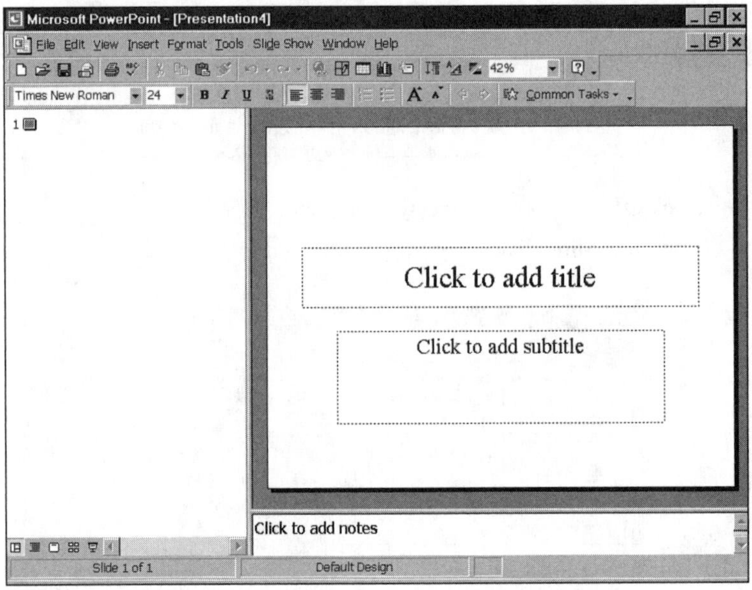

Remember that a blank presentation doesn't include a design template unless you attach one manually.

Caution

Creating a blank presentation takes more time and is really recommended only if neither the AutoContent Wizard nor any of the existing design templates suits your needs.

SAVING A PRESENTATION

To save a PowerPoint presentation you created, follow these steps:

1. Click the Save button on the Standard toolbar. The Save As dialog box displays, shown in Figure 2.21.

Tip #17 from
Patrice-Anne Rutledge

You can also press Ctrl+S to open this dialog box.

2. Select the folder in which you want to save your presentation from the Save in drop-down list.

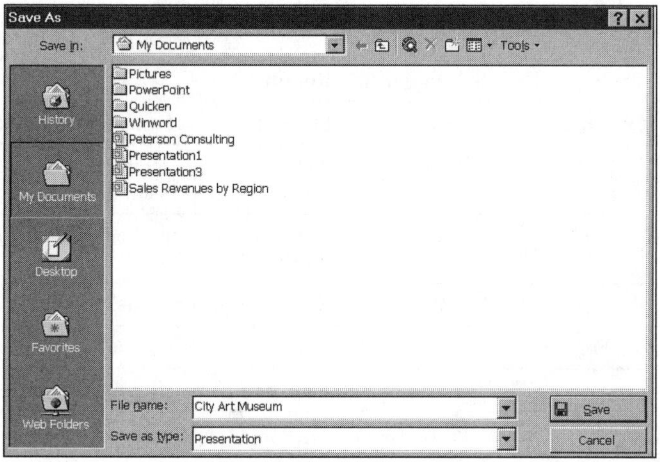

Figure 2.21
Specify save parameters in this dialog box.

Tip #18 from
Patrice-Anne Rutledge

The default folder in which to save your presentations is My Documents. You can customize the default folder in the Options dialog box.

3. Enter a name for the presentation in the File name field.

Caution

The drop-down list in the File Name field includes previously saved presentations. Be sure not to choose one of these file names and accidentally overwrite an existing presentation.

4. Choose the file format from the Save as type drop-down list.

   Presentation is the default file type, but you can also save your PowerPoint presentation as a Web page, a design template, or in a previous PowerPoint version format such as PowerPoint 97 or PowerPoint 95. Table 2.2 lists the available options for saving your presentation:

TABLE 2.2   POWERPOINT FILE TYPES

File Type	Extension	Result
Presentation	PPT	Saves as a regular PowerPoint presentation
Web Page	HTM	Saves as a presentation that opens in a Web browser
PowerPoint 95	PPT	Saves in this previous version of PowerPoint
PowerPoint 97-2000 & 95 Presentation	PPT	Saves as a presentation you can open in PowerPoint 95, 97, or 2000

continues

TABLE 2.2   CONTINUED

File Type	Extension	Result
PowerPoint 4.0	PPT	Saves as a PowerPoint 4.0 presentation
Design Template	POT	Saves as a design template that you can use for future presentations
PowerPoint Show	PPS	Enables you to run the presentation directly as a slide show
PowerPoint Add-In	PPA	Saves as a custom add-in
GIF Graphical Interchange Format	GIF	Saves as a graphic for use on the Web
JPEG File Interchange Format	JPG	Saves as a graphic for use on the Web
PNG Portable Network Graphic Format	PNG	Saves as a graphic for use on the Web
Device Independent Bitmap	BMP	Saves as a bitmap graphic image
Windows Metafile	WMF	Saves as a graphic image
Outline/RTF	RTF	Saves as an outline
Tag Image File Format	TIF	Saves as a TIFF graphic image

5. Click **Save** to save the file.

Tip #19 from
Patrice-Anne Rutledge

After you've saved a presentation, clicking the Save button once saves your changes without opening the Save As dialog box. To access this dialog box from a presentation that you've already saved, choose File, Save As.

Note

To set and modify save options such as fast saves and AutoRecovery, choose Tools, Options and go to the Save tab of the Options dialog box.

→ To learn more about advanced save options, **see** "Setting Save Options," **p. 472**

OPENING A PRESENTATION

You can open an existing presentation in several different ways:

- Select the Open an existing presentation option when you first start PowerPoint.

Tip #20 from
Patrice-Anne Rutledge

You can also directly open one of the last four PowerPoint files you used by selecting it in the text box at the bottom of the dialog box. From within PowerPoint, the bottom of the File menu lists previously opened presentations.

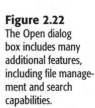

- Click the Open button on the standard toolbar if PowerPoint is already open.
- Press Ctrl+O from within PowerPoint.
- Double-click a PowerPoint presentation from the Windows Explorer.
- Choose File, Open from the menu within PowerPoint.

The Open dialog box appears, shown in Figure 2.22.

PART

I

CH

2

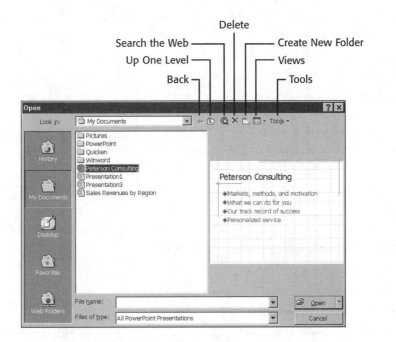

Figure 2.22
The Open dialog box includes many additional features, including file management and search capabilities.

Select the folder and then the file that you want to open and click Open. PowerPoint opens the selected presentation.

Tip #21 from
Patrice-Anne Rutledge

You can use wildcard such as an asterisk (*) to locate multiple characters or the question mark (?) to locate specific characters in the File Name field.

The down arrow to the right of the Open button provides several other options. You can also

- *Open Read-Only* Opens the file as read-only. To make changes and save this file, choose File, Save As from the menu and save with another name.
- *Open as Copy* Opens the presentation as a copy of the original.
- *Open in Browser* Opens a presentation saved in a Web page format (.HTM, .HTML, .HTX, or .ASP) in your default browser.

→ If you want to save a presentation as a Web page, **see** "Saving a Presentation as a Web Page," **p. 353**

Exploring the Open Dialog Box

The top portion of the Open dialog box includes several buttons that assist with both opening files as well as with file management. These include

- *Back*   This button returns you to previous folders or drives you have viewed. It lists the name of the folder as the button name.
- *Up One Level*   Moves up one level in the directory structure.
- *Search the Web*   Opens the Pick a Search Engine page on the Microsoft Web site.
- *Delete*   Deletes the selected file.
- *Create New Folder*   Opens the New Folder dialog box in which you can enter a Name for a new folder.
- *Views*   Includes several options for displaying your files as well as the ability to arrange icons by name, type, size, and date.
- *Tools*   Displays a menu that enables you to find, rename, delete, or print files as well as add them to your favorites folder, map to a network drive to find a file, or display file properties.

Setting View Options

You can view files in four different ways in the Open dialog box. Click the down arrow next to the Views button and choose the view option you prefer:

- *List*   Lists all files without any detail
- *Details*   Lists file size, type, and date last modified
- *Properties*   Displays a property sheet for the selected file
- *Preview*   Displays a preview of the actual presentation for the selected file

Searching for a File

Sometimes you won't be able to immediately find a presentation you want to open. You may have so many saved presentations that it's difficult to find files whose names you've forgotten. Or you may have saved the file you're looking for in another folder and can't locate it. Using the Find dialog box you can conduct sophisticated searches based on presentation properties to help you find the exact file you need.

These properties align to the information you see in the Properties dialog box. To access this dialog box, choose File, Properties. Figure 2.23 illustrates the Summary tab of the Presentation Properties dialog box.

→ If you want to know the exact definition of each file property, **see** "Setting Presentation Properties," **p. 475**

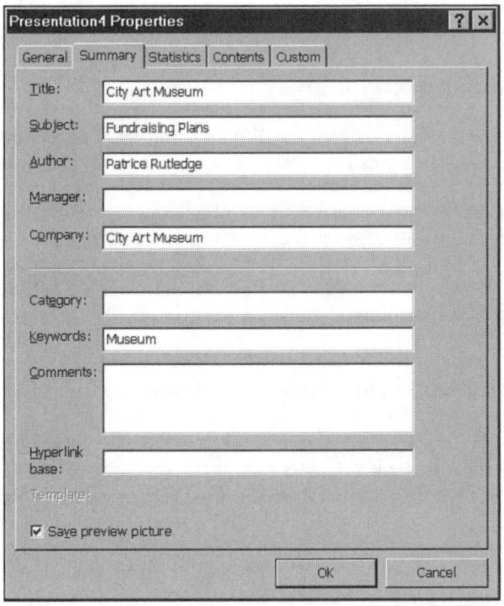

Figure 2.23
You can search on the properties that display in this dialog box.

Table 2.3 lists all the properties you can search in the Find dialog box as well as the conditions available for each, which fall into three main categories: text, numbers, and dates.

TABLE 2.3   FIND DIALOG BOX PROPERTIES AND CONDITIONS

Properties	Available Conditions
Application Name	Includes words, Includes phrase, Begins with phrase, Ends with phrase, Includes near each other, Is (exactly), Is not
Author	Includes words, Includes phrase, Begins with phrase, Ends with phrase, Includes near each other, Is (exactly), Is not
Category	Includes words, Includes phrase, Begins with phrase, Ends with phrase, Includes near each other, Is (exactly), Is not
Comments	Includes words, Includes phrase, Begins with phrase, Ends with phrase, Includes near each other, Is (exactly), Is not
Company	Includes words, Includes phrase, Begins with phrase, Ends with phrase, Includes near each other, Is (exactly), Is not
Contents	Includes words, Includes phrase, Includes near each other
Creation date	Yesterday, Today, Last week, This week, Last month, This month, Any time, Anytime between, On, On or after, On or before, In the last
File Name	Includes, Begins with, Ends with
File of type	All files, All PowerPoint presentations, Presentations and shows, Web pages, Design templates, Freelance Windows, All outlines, PowerPoint add-ins

continues

TABLE 2.3   CONTINUED

Properties	Available Conditions
Format	Includes words, Includes phrase, Begins with phrase, Ends with phrase, Includes near each other, Is (exactly), Is not
Hyperlink base	Includes words, Includes phrase, Begins with phrase, Ends with phrase, Includes near each other, Is (exactly), Is not
Keywords	Includes words, Includes phrase, Begins with phrase, Ends with phrase, Includes near each other, Is (exactly), Is not
Last modified	Yesterday, Today, Last week, This week, Last month, This month, Any time, Anytime between, On, On or after, On or before, In the last
Last printed	Yesterday, Today, Last week, This week, Last month, This month, Any time, Anytime between, On, On or after, On or before, In the last
Last saved by	Includes words, Includes phrase, Begins with phrase, Ends with phrase, Includes near each other, Is (exactly), Is not
Manager	Includes words, Includes phrase, Begins with phrase, Ends with phrase, Includes near each other, Is (exactly), Is not
Number of characters	Equals, Does not equal, Any number between, At most, At least, More than, Less than
Number of characters and spaces	Equals, Does not equal, Any number between, At most, At least, More than, Less than
Number of hidden slides	Equals, Does not equal, Any number between, At most, At least, More than, Less than
Number of lines	Equals, Does not equal, Any number between, At most, At least, More than, Less than
Number of multimedia clips	Equals, Does not equal, Any number between, At most, At least, More than, Less than
Number of notes	Equals, Does not equal, Any number between, At most, At least, More than, Less than
Number of pages	Equals, Does not equal, Any number between, At most, At least, More than, Less than
Number of paragraphs	Equals, Does not equal, Any number between, At most, At least, More than, Less than
Number of slides	Equals, Does not equal, Any number between, At most, At least, More than, Less than
Number of words	Equals, Does not equal, Any number between, At most, At least, More than, Less than
Revision	Includes words, Includes phrase, Begins with phrase, Ends with phrase, Includes near each other, Is (exactly), Is not
Size	Equals, Does not equal, Any number between, At most, At least, More than, Less than

Properties	Available Conditions
Subject	Includes words, Includes phrase, Begins with phrase, Ends with phrase, Includes near each other, Is (exactly), Is not
Template	Includes words, Includes phrase, Begins with phrase, Ends with phrase, Includes near each other, Is (exactly), Is not
Text or property	Includes words, Includes phrase, Includes near each other
Title	Includes words, Includes phrase, Begins with phrase, Ends with phrase, Includes near each other, Is (exactly), Is not
Total editing time	Equals, Does not equal, Any number between, At most, At least, More than, Less than

Depending on your selection in the Condition field, the Value field may activate. If you search the Last Printed property and choose Yesterday as your condition, no further value is required. However, if you choose to search the Title property and select Includes words as the condition, you have to enter a Value to indicate the exact words to include.

For example, let's say you want to find a specific presentation whose file name you've forgotten. You do remember, however, that you created the presentation sometime last week. To find this file, you could search the Creation Date property for the Last Week condition. Based on this information, you can locate all presentations created within the past week, which should narrow your search considerably.

As another example, let's say you entered a keyword in the Keywords field in the Properties dialog box. You can now search for this word to help you locate an elusive presentation. In this case, you would select Keywords as your property, use the condition Is, and enter the exact Value, such as *Budget* or *Orientation*.

There are several things to keep in mind as you set criteria. You can

- Use wildcards with text conditions such as Is or Includes. A question mark (?) matches a single character and an asterisk (*) matches multiple characters. For example, pr* would mach both presentation and present. Pr? would match pro, but not presentation or present, because it only looks for single characters.

- Specify the Any Number Between condition by using the following format in the Value field: 1 and 2, 10 and 20, and so forth. Be sure to use the word AND to separate the two conditions.

- Use the operators AND and OR to indicate whether to search for files that meet all criteria or only one of the selected criteria.

- Specify the Any Time Between condition by using the following format in the Value field: 11/1/98 AND 11/30/98, 1/1/99 AND 12/31/99, and so forth.

To use the Find dialog box, follow these steps from the Open dialog box:

1. Select Tools, Find to display the Find dialog box (see Figure 2.24).

Figure 2.24
You can search for a presentation in the Find dialog box.

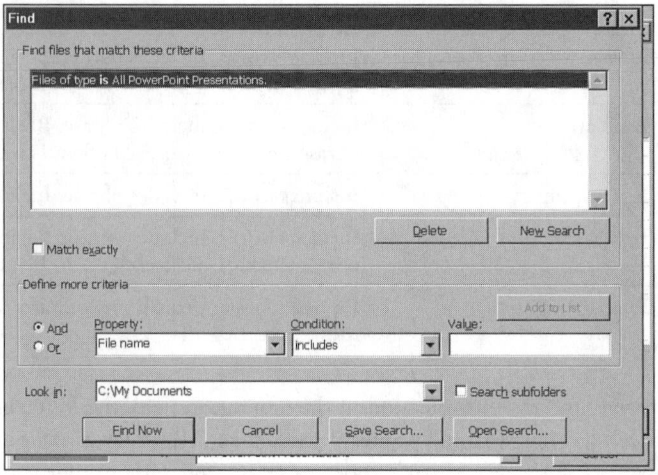

2. By default, *Files of Type is All PowerPoint Presentations* is listed as a criterion in the top portion of the dialog box. You can leave this criterion in the list, or select it and click the Delete button to remove it.

3. You can add your own criteria in the Define More Criteria group box by selecting a Property and Condition.

4. If required, enter a Value that matches the criterion for which you're searching.

5. Choose either the And or Or option button to specify whether the search should look for this criterion *and* other specified criteria or whether it should look for this criterion *or* other specified criteria.

6. Click the Add to List button to add this search criterion to the list above.

7. Continue adding search criteria in the Define More Criteria group box as needed.

8. In the Look In field, select the folder you want to search from the drop-down list.

9. Click the Search Subfolders check box if you want to search all subfolders of the folder you selected in the previous step.

10. Click Find Now to begin the search.

Tip #22 from
Patrice-Anne Rutledge

Click the New Search button to delete the criteria you've added and start again.

PowerPoint finds matching presentations and includes them in the Open dialog box.

Tip #23 from
Patrice-Anne Rutledge

To locate all PowerPoint presentations on your computer don't enter anything in the Value field, select C:\ in the Look in field, and click Find Now.

If you want to save these search criteria for a future search, click the Save Search button. Figure 2.25 illustrates the Save Search dialog box which opens.

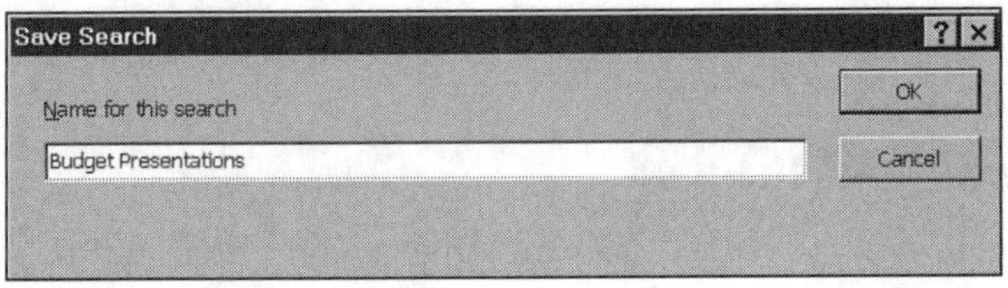

Figure 2.25
Save a search so you don't have to enter it again.

Enter a Name for this Search and click OK.

To open this search later on without having to enter all the search criteria again, click the Open Search button in the Open dialog box. Figure 2.26 illustrates the Open Search dialog box, which appears.

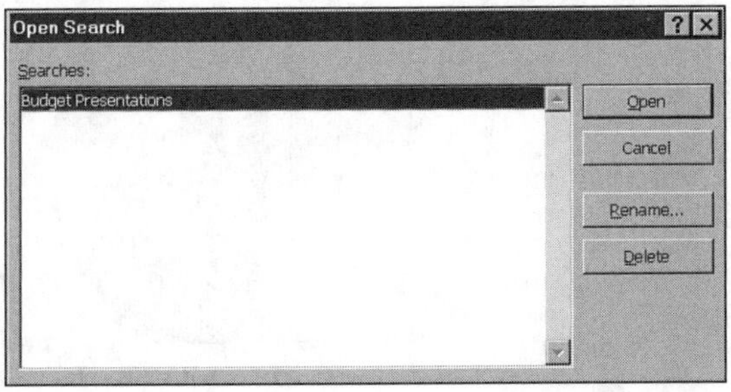

Figure 2.26
You can open and reuse a saved search.

Select the search you want and click Open. The saved search criteria appear in the Open dialog box.

Tip #24 from
Patrice-Anne Rutledge

You can also Rename and Delete saved searches in the Open Search dialog box.

DELETING A PRESENTATION

To delete a PowerPoint presentation you no longer want, select it in the Open dialog box and click the Delete key. A warning dialog box displays, verifying that you want to delete the file and send it to the Recycle Bin. Figure 2.27 illustrates this dialog box. Click Yes to confirm the deletion.

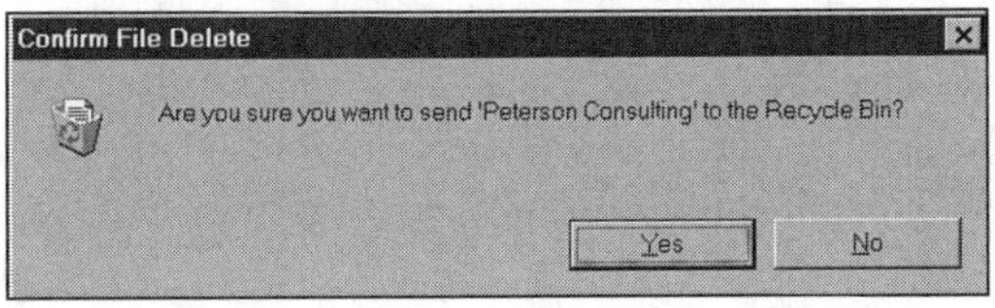

Figure 2.27
PowerPoint confirms you want to delete a presentation.

Tip #25 from
Patrice-Anne Rutledge

You can also delete a PowerPoint presentation in Windows Explorer. To do so, click on the presentation file in Explorer and press the Delete key to remove the file to the Recycle Bin.

RENAMING A PRESENTATION

To rename a PowerPoint presentation, select it in the Open dialog box, right-click, and choose Rename from the menu that displays. PowerPoint converts the filename to an edit box in which you can overwrite the filename, as shown in Figure 2.28.

Figure 2.28
Rename a presentation to something more meaningful.

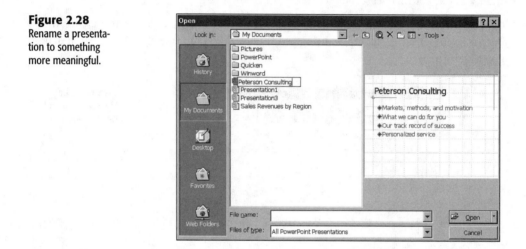

Tip #26 from
Patrice-Anne Rutledge

You can also convert the field to an edit box by slowly clicking the file you want to rename two times.

Tip #27 from
Patrice-Anne Rutledge

Again, you can also rename a PowerPoint presentation in Windows Explorer. To do so, select the file in Explorer, right-click, choose Rename from the menu, and enter a new name for the presentation.

TROUBLESHOOTING

My presentation didn't save in the folder I thought it would.

By default, your presentation is saved in the My Documents folder unless you manually specify another location in the Save As dialog box. To change this default, choose Tools, Options and choose a different Default File Location in the Save tab.

I can't find a PowerPoint presentation I saved.

In the Open dialog box, verify that you made the appropriate selection from the Files of Type drop-down list. For example, if you're looking for a PowerPoint Presentation or a Web page, be sure you've selected that option. Also, verify that you're searching in the right folder. If you still can't find your presentation, do a search using the Find dialog box (Tools, Find from within the Open dialog box).

I want to open my presentation in a browser, but the Open in Browser option isn't available from the menu next to the Open button in the Open dialog box.

You must have saved the presentation in a Web format (such as .HTM, .HTML, .HTX, or .ASP) in order to open it in a browser. To save as a Web page, choose File, Save as Web Page.

I don't like any of the existing design templates. What can I do?

You can create your own design template and then save it for future use. Start by modifying an existing template and then save it as a design template in the Save As dialog box.

DESIGN CORNER

By using the Text & Chart AutoLayout, you can quickly create a slide that includes a title, bulleted list, and chart. The new slide includes placeholders and prompts to help guide you in creating your content.

BEFORE

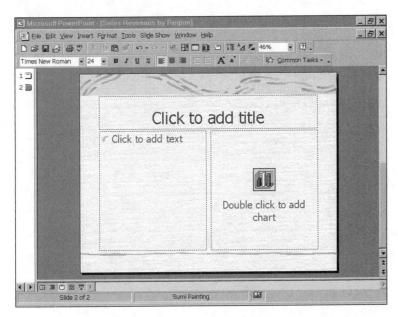

AFTER

Title

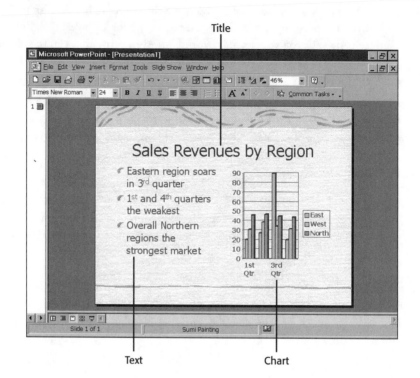

Text   Chart

Editing and Formatting Presentations

CHAPTER 3

WORKING WITH TEXT

In this chapter   *by Patrice-Anne Rutledge*

UNDERSTANDING POWERPOINT'S TEXT CAPABILITIES

Adding and formatting text is a fairly straightforward task in PowerPoint. What's often more difficult is choosing the appropriate fonts, colors, and effects for your presentation. PowerPoint offers sophisticated text formatting and customization options, yet also provides a great deal of automation if you're in a hurry or have limited design skills. And when you're done adding text to your presentation, you can verify that both its spelling and style are error-free with PowerPoint's spelling checker.

In this chapter you learn:

- *How to add and format text*   You can add text in either text placeholders or text boxes and then apply formatting such as bold, italics, and underlining using the Font dialog box and Formatting toolbar.

- *When to create a bulleted or numbered list*   PowerPoint enables you to use traditional bullets or numbers as well as more creative picture and character bullets.

- *How to check spelling and text styles*   Using PowerPoint's spelling and style checkers, you can automatically proof your presentation as well as customize what to check.

ADDING TEXT

In PowerPoint, you add text in a text placeholder or in a text box. Figure 3.1 illustrates an example of a text placeholder.

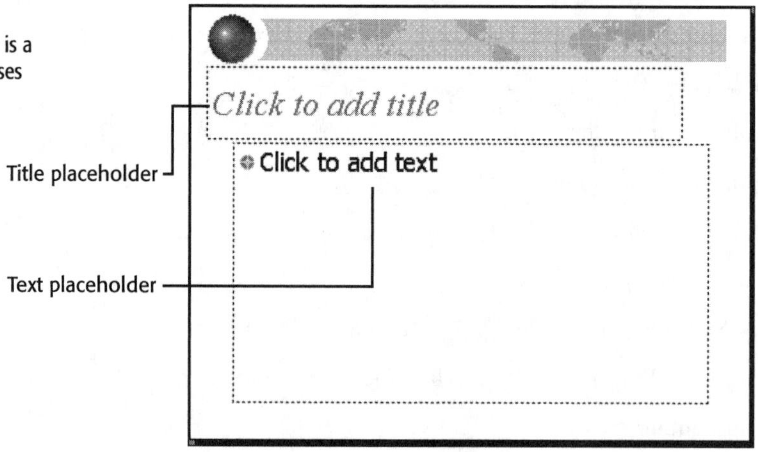

Figure 3.1
A text placeholder is a tool PowerPoint uses for entering text.

Title placeholder ⌐

Text placeholder ───

Click to add title

⚙ Click to add text

If you use the AutoContent Wizard or add a slide that includes a text or title *placeholder (p. 31)* from the New Slide dialog box, you can immediately start creating text.

If you want to add your own *text box (p. 286)* to a blank slide, choose Insert, Text Box and draw a text box on the slide using the mouse. As you add text, the box expands. Figure 3.2 displays a text box.

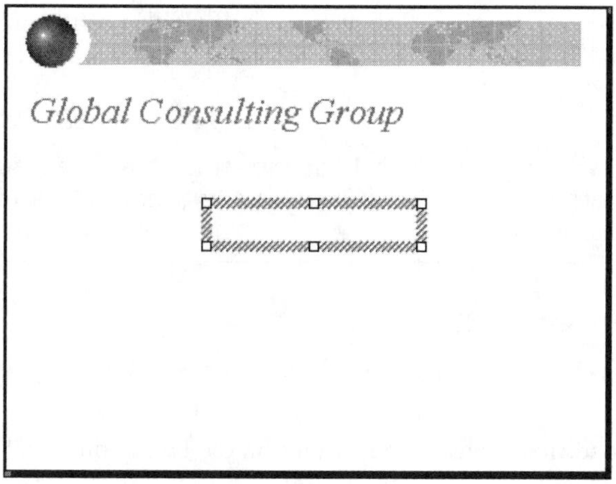

Figure 3.2
A text box is another tool that PowerPoint uses to enter text.

Global Consulting Group

Tip #28 from
Patrice-Anne Rutledge

You can also add create a text box by clicking the Text Box button on the Drawing toolbar.

What should you do if your text doesn't fit in the text box? *See the Troubleshooting section at the end of the chapter.*

FORMATTING TEXT

PowerPoint's design templates include preselected colors, fonts, font sizes, and other formatting parameters that are designed to work well together—a real timesaver and also very useful for people who are new to presentation design.

→ To learn more about how typefaces and fonts affect your presentation, **see** "Choosing Typefaces and Fonts," **p. 559**

→ To learn more about how to modify text and formatting on Slide Masters, rather than on individual slides, **see** "Modifying the Slide Master," **p. 481**

You'll only need to apply extensive text formatting if you create a text box in a blank slide in a presentation without an attached design template. In most cases, you'll either use the formatting that the design template suggests or make only minor modifications to it.

Some changes you may consider:

■ *Enlarge or reduce font size to fit the page*   For example, if your title is too long to fit across one line, you may want to slightly reduce the font size. Or, if you have only a few bullet points on a slide, you may want to increase their size to fill the page.

■ *Replace one font with another*   You may have a particular font you prefer to use in presentations. Be careful, however, not to be too creative with unusual fonts. You want to be sure everyone can clearly read your presentation.

- *Add boldface, italics, or color*   Use these to emphasize a point with a certain word or words.

> **Caution**
>
> Unless you have experience in graphic design, you're better off using the preselected fonts, colors, and font sizes included in one of PowerPoint's design templates or making only very minor modifications.

You can format text in two different ways:

- Use the Font dialog box to make a number of changes in one place and to set font defaults.
- Apply text formatting individually using the buttons on the Formatting toolbar.

USING THE FONT DIALOG BOX

To use the Font dialog box to format text, follow these steps:

1. Select the text you want to format and choose Format, Font. The Font dialog box appears, shown in Figure 3.3.

Figure 3.3
Make numerous font changes quickly in the Font dialog box.

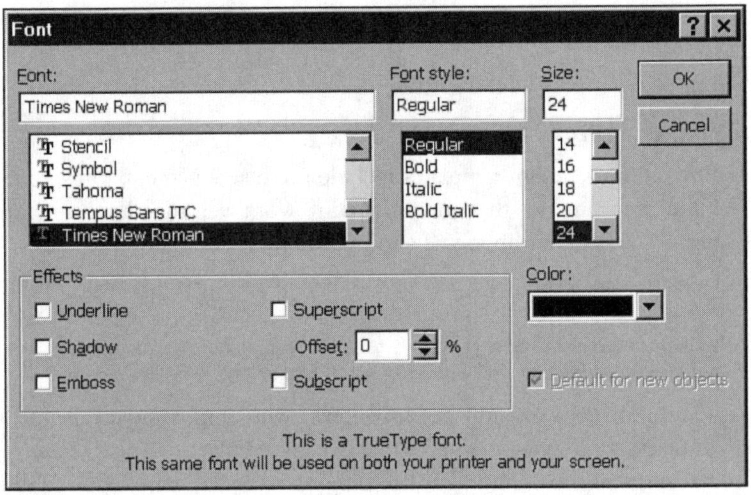

2. Select the font you want to use from the Font drop-down list. Scroll down the list to see additional font selections.
3. Select a Font style—Regular, Bold, Italic, or Bold Italic.
4. Choose a Size—from 8 to 96 points, or enter an exact size in the edit box.

5. Apply additional desired effects by checking the check box next to any of the following:
   - *Underline*   Underlines the selected text.
   - *Shadow*   Applies a slight shadow to the lower right of the text.
   - *Emboss*   Creates an embossed effect on the selected text.
   - *Superscript*   Raises the text above the baseline and reduces the font size. Sets the Offset to 30%, which you can adjust.
   - *Subscript*   Lowers the text below the baseline and reduces the font size. Sets the Offset to –25%, which you can adjust.

Figure 3.4 illustrates examples of these text effects.

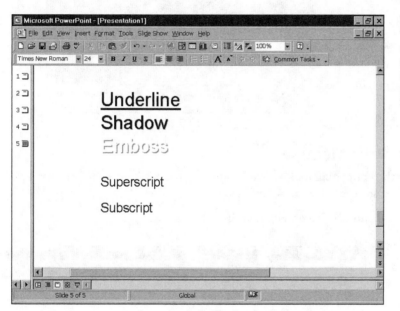

Figure 3.4
Text effects such
as underlining and
shadowing can add
emphasis to your
presentation, but use
them sparingly.

→ To learn how PowerPoint WordArt can also create innovative text objects, **see** "Inserting WordArt,"
p. 245

6. Choose a color from the palette that displays from the <u>C</u>olor drop-down list.

→ To learn more about color theory and how it relates to emotions, **see** "Understanding Background
Colors and Emotions," **p. 580**

7. If you want to see additional colors, click <u>M</u>ore Colors, and the Colors dialog box appears. Figure 3.5 illustrates the dialog box, which offers you very precise color selections.

8. By moving the hexagonal cursor, choose the color you want and click OK to return to the Font dialog box.

9. Click OK to close and apply the font formatting.

Figure 3.5
Choose from a wide variety of color variations.

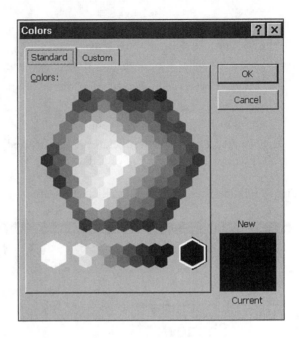

USING THE FORMATTING TOOLBAR

You can use the Formatting toolbar (see Figure 3.6) to apply individual formatting elements to selected text such as bold, italics, and shadows.

Table 3.1 lists the formatting options on this toolbar.

Figure 3.6
The Formatting toolbar includes buttons for commonly used text effects.

TABLE 3.1 FORMATTING TOOLBAR BUTTONS

Button	Name	Description
 Comic Sans MS	Font	Applies a font to the selected text.
 24	Font Size	Sets the size of the font—from 8 to 96 points or any size you enter in the edit box.
 B	Bold	Bolds the selected text.
 I	Italic	Italicizes the selected text.

Button	Name	Description
U	Underline	Underlines the selected text.
S	Text Shadow	Applies a shadow to the selected text.
≣	Align Left	Aligns text to the left margin of the object.
≣	Center	Centers text across the slide.
≣	Align Right	Aligns text to the right margin.
≣	Numbering	Applies numbering to the selected text.
≣	Bullets	Applies bullets to the selected text.
A▲	Increase Font Size	Increases the font size of selected text by one increment.
A▼	Decrease Font Size	Decreases the font size of selected text by one increment.
⬅	Promote	Outdents the selected bullet point.
➡	Demote	Indents the selected bullet point.
☆	Animation Effects	Opens the Animation Effects dialog box, which enables you to apply animation to selected text or objects.
	Common Tasks	Enables you to add a new slide, adjust slide layout, or apply a design template.

To apply specific formatting, select the text you want to format and click the toolbar button. Clicking the Bold, Italic, Underline, Text Shadow, Numbering, or Bullets button a second time acts as a toggle and removes the formatting.

With the Font drop-down list, you can preview a sample of what each font actually looks like. Figure 3.7 illustrates some sample fonts in the list.

Tip #29 from
Patrice-Anne Rutledge

To justify selected text, choose Format, Alignment, Justify.

REPLACING FONTS

If you want to replace all occurrences of one type of font in your presentation with another font, you can easily do so by following these steps:

1. Choose Format, Replace Fonts to open the Replace Font dialog box (see Figure 3.8).

Figure 3.7
Being able to preview
a font before applying
it can be a timesaver.

Figure 3.8
Replace fonts
throughout your
presentation with
this dialog box.

2. Select the font that you want to replace from the Replace drop-down list. Only those fonts that currently exist in your presentation display.

3. Select the replacement font from the With drop-down list. All available fonts in PowerPoint display.

4. Click Replace to automatically replace all matching fonts in your presentation.

5. Click Close to return to the presentation.

→ To learn how to change fonts on the Master Slide, **see** "Modifying the Master Slide," **p. 481**

CHANGING CASE

You can also automate a change of case in your presentation, by following these steps:

1. Select the text that you want to change.

2. Select Format, Change Case to open the Change Case dialog box, shown in Figure 3.9.

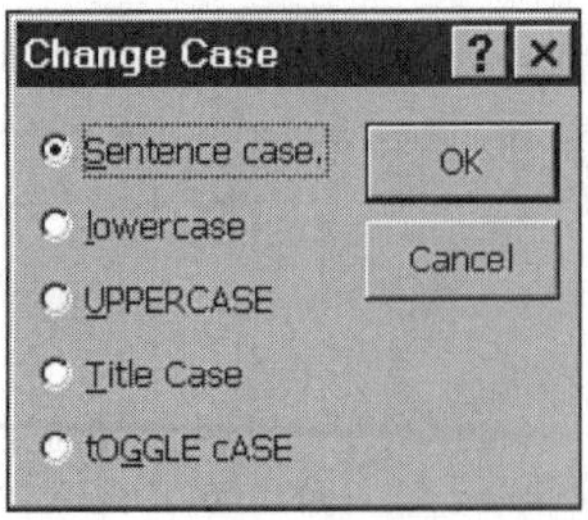

Figure 3.9
You can quickly
change case if
something doesn't
look right.

3. Choose the case to which you want to change. Options include

- <u>S</u>entence case   Only the first word in a sentence is capitalized.
- <u>l</u>owercase   All letters appear in lowercase.
- <u>U</u>PPERCASE   All letters appear in UPPERCASE.
- <u>T</u>itle Case   The first letter of every title word is capitalized. Exceptions include words such as *the*, *and*, *to*, and so on, which remain lowercase in titles.
- t<u>O</u>GGLE c<u>A</u>SE   Toggles all existing cases. For example, lowercase becomes uppercase and uppercase becomes lowercase.

4. Click OK to apply the case changes to the selected text.

Tip #30 from
Patrice-Anne Rutledge

| If you can't find this menu option, select the down arrow at the bottom of the menu list, and more menu options display. |

Caution

| Remember that an unusual use of case may be difficult to read, particularly uppercase and toggle case. With text, you need to strive for readability and clarity. |

Only part of your text changes? *See the Troubleshooting section at the end of the chapter.*

SETTING LINE SPACING

To set line spacing, follow these steps:

1. Select the text you want to format and choose F<u>o</u>rmat, Line <u>S</u>pacing. Figure 3.10 illustrates the Line Spacing dialog box, which appears.

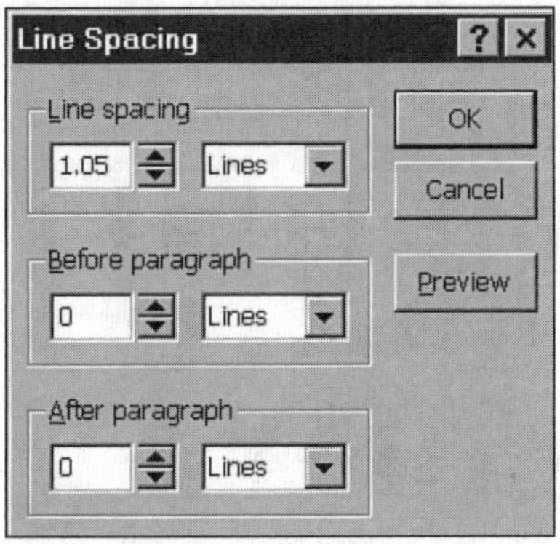

Figure 3.10
Appropriate line spacing can enhance a presentation.

In this dialog box you can set either lines or points for line spacing, space before paragraphs, and space after paragraphs.

PART
II
CH
3

2. Select the numeric amount from the first field and then choose either Lines or Points from the second drop-down list.

3. Click the Preview button to view the suggested changes in your presentation before accepting them.

4. Click OK to apply the changes.

USING BULLETS

Creating a bulleted list of text is a very common PowerPoint task. If you use the AutoContent Wizard, your presentation probably already contains a *bullet list (p. 30)* slide. You also can add a new bullet list slide by selecting Common Tasks, New Slide from the Formatting toolbar, and choosing the Bulleted List AutoLayout.

Tip #31 from
Patrice-Anne Rutledge

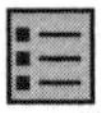

Click the Bullets button on the Formatting toolbar to automatically add bullets to selected paragraph.

The default style for the bullets comes from the design template applied to the presentation. You can change this if you want, however. To do so, select the bulleted list that you want to change and choose Format, Bullets and Numbering. Figure 3.11 shows the Bullets and Numbering dialog box that appears.

Figure 3.11
You can choose from many different bullet types.

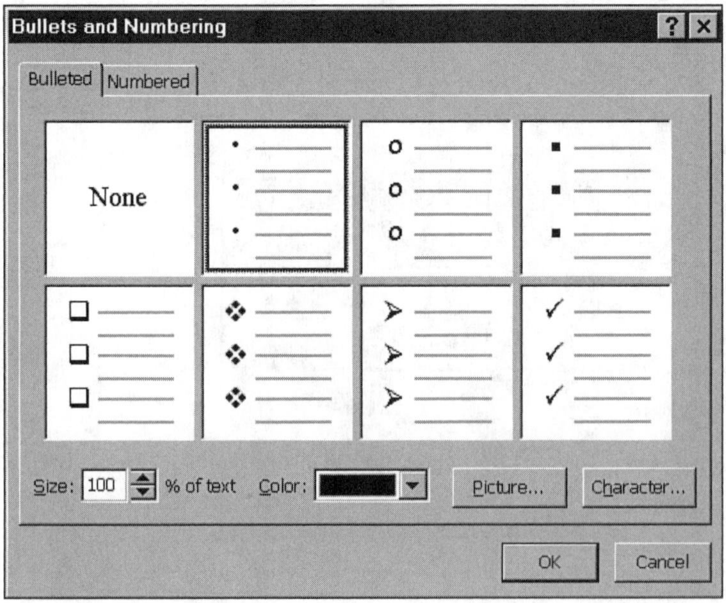

Bullets and Numbering	? X

Bulleted | Numbered

None	• • •	o o o	▪ ▪ ▪
☐ ☐ ☐	❖ ❖ ❖	➤ ➤ ➤	✓ ✓ ✓

Size: 100 % of text   Color: ▼   Picture...   Character...

OK   Cancel

On the Bulleted tab of this dialog box you can choose from among the seven displayed bullet styles or you can choose None to remove bullets. In the Size field you can scroll to enlarge or reduce the bullet size from the default 100%.

To change the color of a bullet, select a new color from the Color drop-down list. Click More Colors at the bottom of the Color drop-down list to open the Colors dialog box (refer to Figure 3.5), in which you can specify the exact color for your bullets. Click OK to apply the color.

Tip #32 from *Patrice-Anne Rutledge*	To change the bullets in your entire presentation, do so on the master slide (View, Master, Slide Master).

→ To learn how to change bullets on the master slide, **see** "Modifying the Master Slide," **p. 481**

You can also create picture or character bullets, if none of the seven default bullet styles suits your needs.

CREATING PICTURE BULLETS

To apply a picture bullet, click the Picture button to open the Picture Bullet dialog box which is a variation of the Clip Gallery. Figure 3.12 illustrates this dialog box, which enables you to choose from a wide variety of more creative bullet styles.

Select your desired bullet and click OK to apply. Figure 3.13 depicts a presentation that uses picture bullets.

Note	You can also add a motion clip as a picture bullet by choosing a clip from the Motion Clips tab on the Picture Bullet dialog box.

→ To learn more about motion clips, **see** "Understanding Sound and Video Files," **p. 300**

Tip #33 from *Patrice-Anne Rutledge*	You can also use your company logo as a bullet if you want—and if its style and design would work well as a bullet. To do so, add the logo to the Picture Bullet dialog box as you would any other external image to the Clip Gallery. To add the logo, click the Import Clips button in the Picture Bullet dialog box.

→ For step-by-step instructions on importing a logo or other clip art image, **see** "Importing Clips," **p. 258**

PART

II

CH

3

Figure 3.12
You can choose a
picture bullet that
matches the theme
of your presentation.

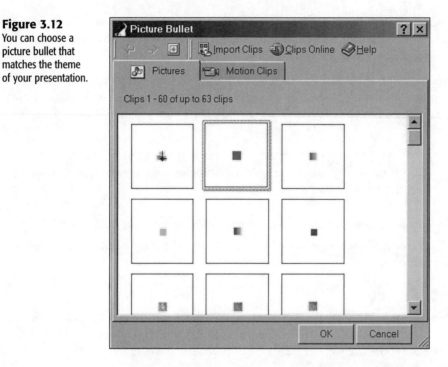

Figure 3.13
A picture bullet can
enhance a creative
presentation.

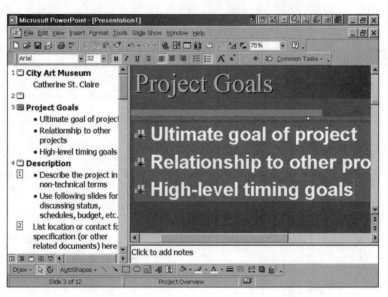

CREATING CHARACTER BULLETS

You can also choose a character bullet for your bulleted list if you want something a little different. In the Bullet dialog box you can choose from a variety of fonts. Each font displays its character set below; you can then choose your new character bullet from among the characters and symbols that display.

To apply a character bullet, click the Character button in the Bullets and Numbering dialog box to open the Bullet dialog box, shown in Figure 3.14.

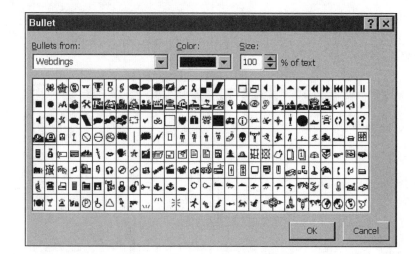

Figure 3.14
Use a font like Webdings for character bullets.

PART

II

CH

3

Select the bullet category from the Bullets From drop-down list, choose the bullet you want from the display area, and click OK.

Tip #34 from	Click a bullet in the Bullet dialog box to enlarge it for easier viewing.
Patrice-Anne Rutledge	

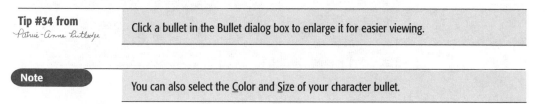

Note

You can also select the Color and Size of your character bullet.

USING NUMBERED LISTS

For a sequence of items, creating a numbered list is a good alternative to a bulleted list. For example, a procedural series of steps or a list of dollar amounts from highest to lowest would work well in a numbered list. You can create numbered lists with actual numbers, roman numerals, or letters of the alphabet.

To change a bulleted list or other text to a numbered list, select the text and click the Numbering button on the Formatting toolbar.

Tip #35 from
Patrice-Anne Rutledge

You can also create a numbered list by pressing the Backspace key at the beginning of a bulleted list, typing the number **1** (or the letter **a** if you're using letters instead of numbers), pressing the Tab key, and entering your first list item. PowerPoint then continues the numbering series when you press Enter to move to the second line.

To change the numbering style, follow these steps:

1. Choose Format, Bullets and Numbering and go to the Numbered tab, shown in Figure 3.15.

Figure 3.15
A numbered list can put a series of items in order.

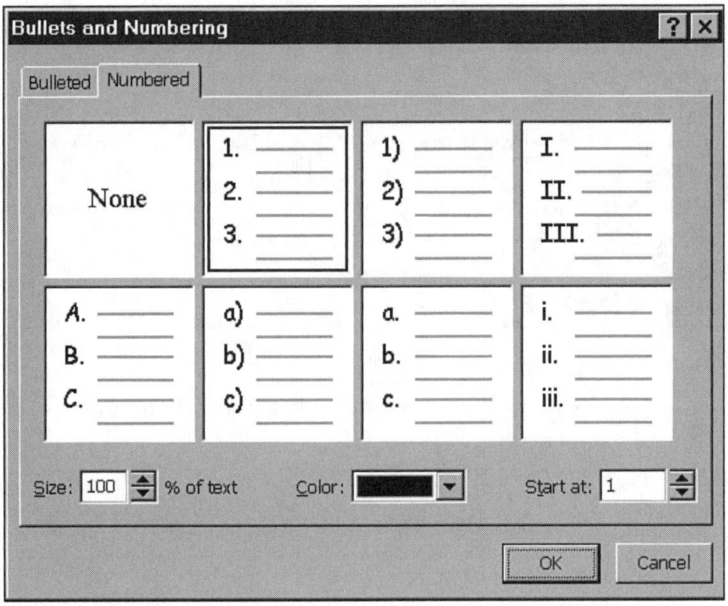

Bullets and Numbering	? X

Bulleted | Numbered

None

1. ———
2. ———
3. ———

1) ———
2) ———
3) ———

I. ———
II. ———
III. ———

A. ———
B. ———
C. ———

a) ———
b) ———
c) ———

a. ———
b. ———
c. ———

i. ———
ii. ———
iii. ———

Size: 100 % of text   Color: Start at: 1

OK   Cancel

2. Select one of the seven number styles that display.

Tip #36 from
Patrice-Anne Rutledge

Choosing None removes the numbered list.

3. Choose the Size as a percentage of the text—100% (or the same size as text) is the default. Lower the number to reduce the size, increase the number to enlarge the size.

4. Choose a color from the Color drop-down list.

Tip #37 from
Patrice-Anne Rutledge

Click <u>M</u>ore Colors on bottom of the <u>C</u>olor drop-down list to open the Color dialog box, which offers many additional color choices.

5. If you want the numbering to start at a number other than 1, enter that number in the S<u>t</u>art at field.

6. Click OK to apply the numbering.

CHECKING SPELLING AND STYLE

PowerPoint's spelling and style checkers can help ensure a quality presentation that is error-free and easy to read. To set options for spelling and style checks, select <u>T</u>ools, <u>O</u>ptions and go to the Spelling and Style tab. Figure 3.16 illustrates this tab.

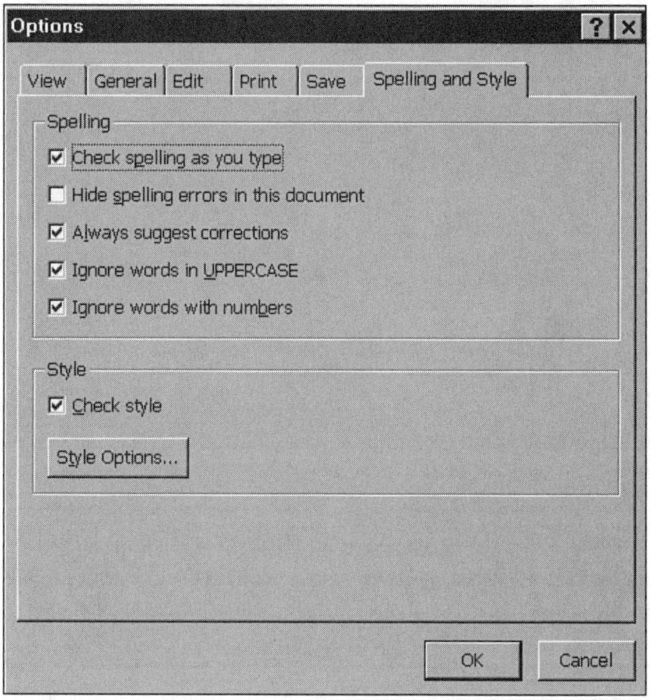

Figure 3.16
You can automate spell checking in PowerPoint.

PART
II

CH
3

You can choose any of the following spelling options:

- *Check spelling as you type*   Underlines each suspected spelling error as you type it.
- *Hide spelling errors in this document*   Doesn't display underlining for suspected spelling errors.
- *Always suggest corrections*   Suggests possible correct spelling options.

- *Ignore words in UPPERCASE*   Skips any word that is all uppercase in the spell-check process.

- *Ignore words with numbers*   Skips any word that includes a number in the spell-check process.

SETTING STYLE OPTIONS

If you also want to check style, select the Check style check box and click the Style Options button. This opens the Style Options dialog box, shown in Figure 3.17.

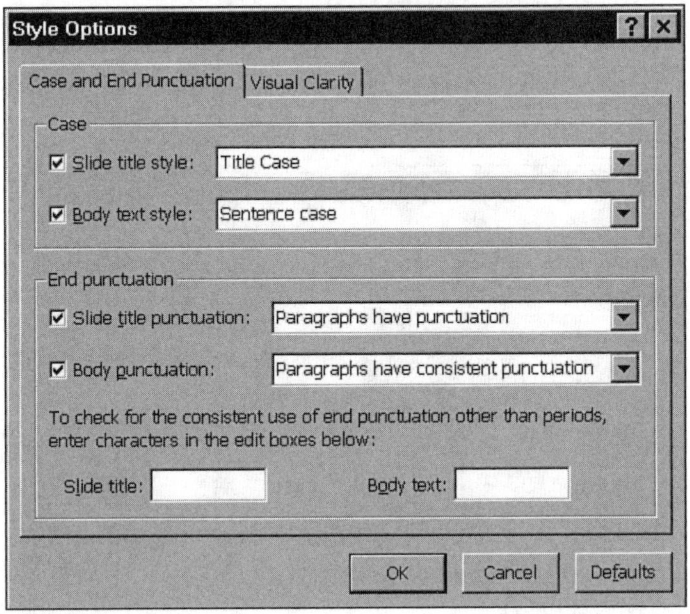

Figure 3.17
Set default case and
punctuation on
this tab.

> **Caution**
>
> Although having PowerPoint search for potential style errors can help you find mistakes you wouldn't otherwise notice, be careful to look closely at the changes it suggests rather than just automatically accepting all style changes. Sometimes automation can yield unusual results.

On the Case and End Punctuation tab, you can select the default case and end punctuation styles for your presentation slide titles and body text. Options include the capability to:

- Set Slide title style to Sentence case, lowercase, UPPERCASE, or Title Case (the default).

- Set Body text style to Sentence case (the default), lowercase, UPPERCASE, or Title Case.

- Set Slide title punctuation to either Paragraphs have punctuation (the default) or Paragraphs do not have punctuation.

- Set Body punctuation to Paragraphs have punctuation, Paragraphs do not have punctuation, or Paragraphs have consistent punctuation (the default).

Select the check boxes next to all options for which you want PowerPoint to search and choose the default from the drop-down list.

Tip #38 from
Patricia-Anne Rutledge

> If you want to place a character other than a period at the end of the slide title or body text, enter the appropriate characters in the Slide Title or Body Text Edit boxes in the End Punctuation group box. For example, you may want to use a colon instead of a period in some cases.

On the Visual Clarity tab (see Figure 3.18), you can view and revise the existing defaults for font clarity and presentation legibility.

In this tab you can set the

- Maximum number of fonts
- Minimum point size for title text
- Minimum point size for body text
- Maximum number of bullets
- Maximum number of lines per title and per bullet

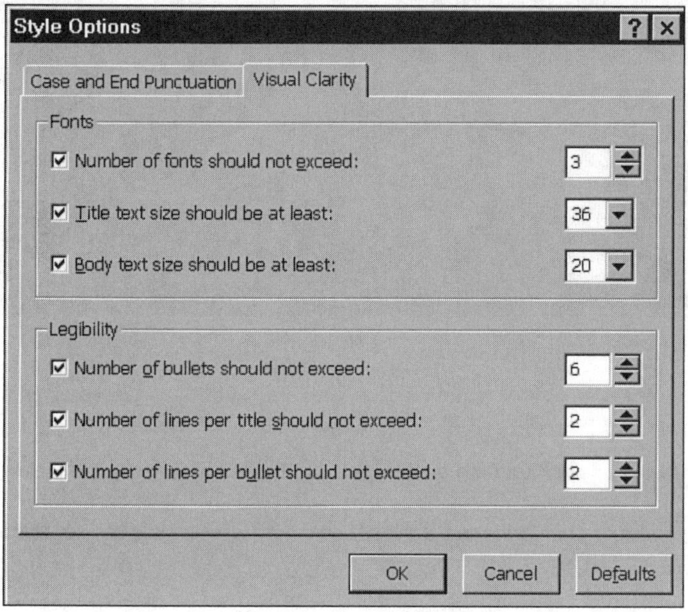

Figure 3.18
PowerPoint also can look for common style errors.

The Visual Clarity tab already includes default selections for these options that are based on basic design principles, but you can change any settings in the adjacent drop-down lists. When you run PowerPoint's spelling checker, it looks for violations of these constraints.

Caution

Even though you can change these defaults to suit your needs, consider carefully before doing so. Exceeding the recommended number of fonts and bullets and changing to overly small or overly large fonts can make your presentation difficult to read.

RUNNING A SPELLING AND STYLE CHECK

After you've set the spelling and style options you want, you can check your presentation.

If you set the option to have PowerPoint check spelling as you type, you immediately know when you've potentially misspelled a word. PowerPoint underlines all suspected misspellings, as shown in Figure 3.19.

Figure 3.19
Underscored text indicates a potential spelling error.

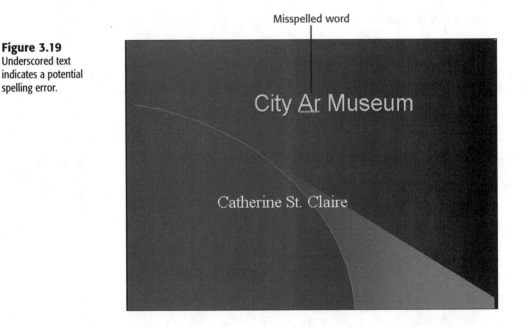

You can either fix the error yourself, or right-click to see some suggested alternatives from which to choose. Figure 3.20 illustrates some suggestions.

Is PowerPoint missing some of your spelling errors? See the Troubleshooting section at the end of the chapter.

Is PowerPoint missing some of your grammar errors? See the Troubleshooting section at the end of the chapter.

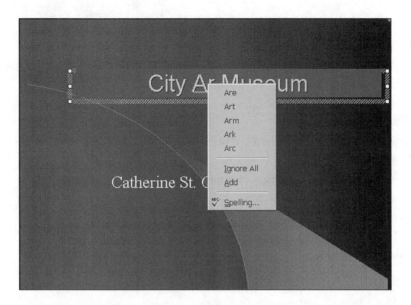

Figure 3.20
PowerPoint offers suggested spellings for you.

You can also spell-check your entire presentation all at once. To do so, follow these steps:

1. Click the Spelling button on the Standard toolbar, or choose Tools, Spelling.

2. When PowerPoint encounters an error, it displays the Spelling dialog box, shown in Figure 3.21.

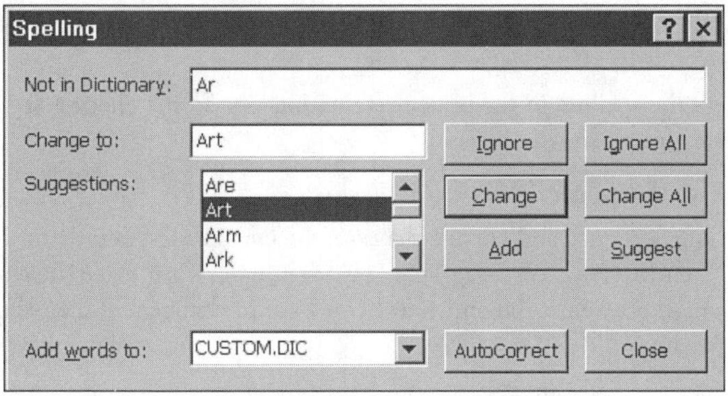

Figure 3.21
The Spelling dialog box offers several options for handling potential misspellings.

3. The Not in Dictionary field highlights the misspelled word and the Change To field suggests the most likely alternative. The Suggestions box also provides additional alternatives.

4. Select the correct spelling or enter it manually in the Change To field.

5. The Spelling dialog box also includes several buttons that provide other options:

- Ignore   Ignores the individual suggested change and continues checking spelling.
- Ignore All   Ignores all instances of the suggested change in the presentation and continues checking spelling.
- Change   Changes the individual misspelled word to the spelling offered in the Change To field.
- Change All   Changes all instances of the misspelled word to the spelling offered in the Change To field.
- Add   Adds the suspect word to the custom dictionary as a correctly spelled word.
- Suggest   Provides additional spelling suggestions.
- AutoCorrect   Adds the misspelled word and its corrected version to the AutoCorrect list.

Note

> PowerPoint also targets unknown words as spelling errors, such as a person's name, a company name, or a product. Be sure to check carefully for these and add the names and words you commonly use in presentations to the dictionary.

When PowerPoint finishes checking spelling, it informs you with another dialog box.

TROUBLESHOOTING

The spelling checker didn't find all the spelling errors in my presentation.

PowerPoint only checks the spelling in the basic presentation—it doesn't check text in charts, WordArt objects, or embedded objects.

I tried to change the case of my text, but only part of it changed.

If you only select part of a sentence and change the case, the change applies only to the selected text, not to the entire sentence/paragraph. It isn't enough to just place the cursor in the specified line or paragraph. Select the entire text you want to change and then choose Format, Change Case again.

I ran the spelling check and it didn't find my grammar errors.

PowerPoint's spelling checker only looks for actual spelling errors and the style flaws you specified on the Spelling and Style tab on the Options dialog box (Tools, Options). It doesn't check for any other grammatical or style errors.

My text doesn't fit in my text box.

Select the text box and then choose Format, Text Box to open the Format Text Box dialog box. Be sure that you've checked the Resize AutoShape to Fit Text check box.

DESIGN CORNER

You can use PowerPoint's text formatting options to create a more aesthetically pleasing presentation.

BEFORE

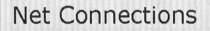

AFTER

New font —

Character bullets —

Underlining removed
from unknown word
found by spelling
checker

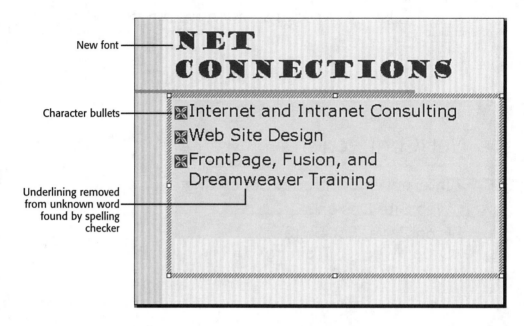

CHAPTER 4

WORKING WITH TABLES

In this chapter   *by Patrice-Anne Rutledge*

UNDERSTANDING TABLES IN POWERPOINT

You can include a table in a PowerPoint presentation in several ways. PowerPoint itself offers two options for table creation (inserting a table and drawing a table); you can also insert a table created in another Office 2000 application such as Word, Excel, or Access. You can

- *Insert a table in PowerPoint*   PowerPoint's basic table insertion feature places a table into a PowerPoint slide based on the number of rows and columns you specify. You can then format, customize, and add data into this table.

- *Draw a table in PowerPoint*   This option is most useful if PowerPoint's regular table insertion feature doesn't meet your needs. It takes longer to draw your own table, so use this option only if what you want to create is too complex for the automated table feature.

- *Create a table in Word and use it in PowerPoint*   If you've already created a table in Word, you can insert it in PowerPoint. Or if you need to use Word's advanced table formatting options such as bulleted text, numbered lists, or diagonal formats, you can create a table in Word and then use it in PowerPoint.

- *Create a worksheet in Excel and use it in PowerPoint*   You can insert a table you've already created in Excel into a PowerPoint presentation. If you want to create a table that has detailed calculations or charts, you may want to create it in Excel first and then use it in PowerPoint.

- *Create a table in Access and use it in PowerPoint*   You can insert a table that includes data from an Access database into PowerPoint.

Tip #39 from
Patrice-Anne Rutledge

Creating a table directly in PowerPoint is usually easier. Use a table created in another application only if the table already exists in that format and you don't want to re-create it or you need to use table features that PowerPoint can't provide.

→   To learn more about using Word and Excel within PowerPoint, **see** "Integrating with Office 2000," **p. 415**

ADDING A TABLE

The easiest way to add a table to your PowerPoint presentation is to select the *Table AutoLayout (p. 31)* from the New Slide dialog box.

 To access this dialog box, shown in Figure 4.1, click the New Slide button on the Standard toolbar or select <u>C</u>ommon Tasks, <u>N</u>ew Slide from the Formatting toolbar.

Tip #40 from
Patrice-Anne Rutledge

You can also press Ctrl+M to open the New Slide dialog box.

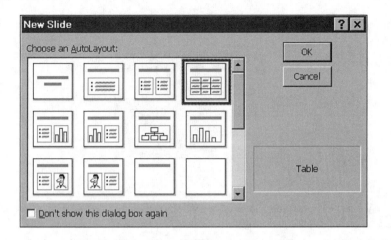

Figure 4.1
The New Slide dialog box includes Table AutoLayout options.

→ To learn more about the New Slide dialog box, **see** "Understanding Slide Layouts," **p. 28**

Tip #41 from
Patrice-Anne Rutledge

If you use the AutoContent Wizard to create your presentation, it may already have a slide that contains a table.

PART

II

CH

4

→ For more information about creating ready-made presentations with the AutoContent wizard, **see** "Using the AutoContent Wizard," **p. 36**

Figure 4.2 illustrates the start of a sample table slide.

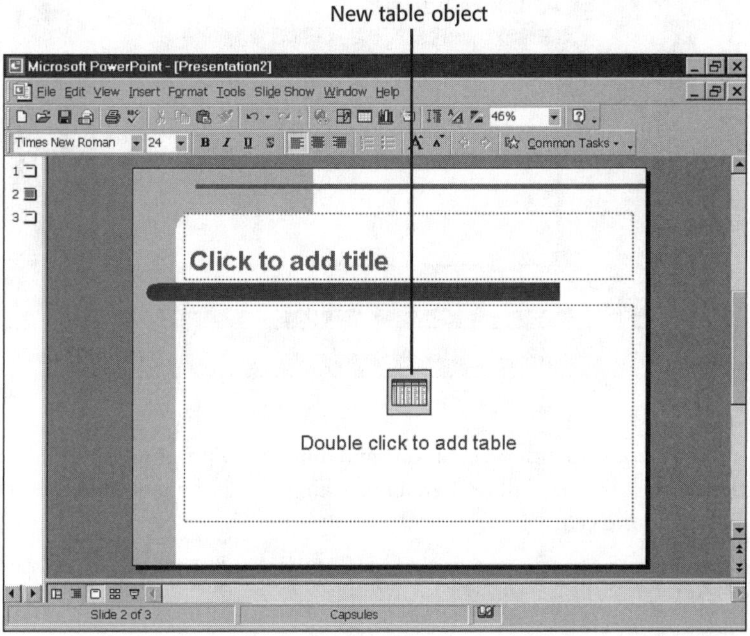

New table object

Figure 4.2
You can start adding a table by double-clicking the table object.

Double-click the Table object to open the Insert Table dialog box, illustrated in Figure 4.3.

Figure 4.3
Choose the number of rows and columns you want to include.

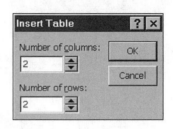

Tip #42 from
Patrice-Anne Rutledge

You can also insert a table into an existing slide by clicking the Insert Table button on the Standard toolbar or by selecting Insert, Table.

Choose the Number of Columns and Number of Rows to display and click OK.

A blank table displays in your slide, shown in Figure 4.4.

Figure 4.4
Enter the title and table text to complete your table.

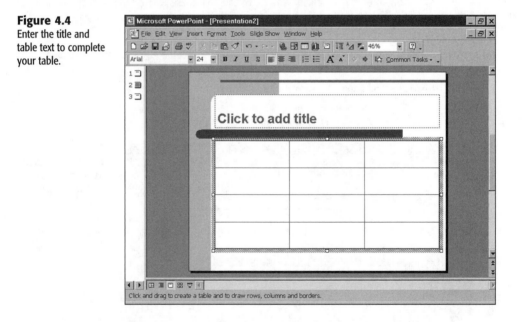

Click the title area to remove the directional text and enter an appropriate title for the slide. Next, add the desired text in each cell of the table clicking inside the table and then tabbing to the cell or clicking in the cell.

→ To learn more about adding text to your presentations, **see** "Working with Text," **p. 57**

Table text doesn't appear in the outline pane, only in the slide title.

You can format this text as you would any other text. For example, you may want to bold the first row or column or add other special formatting.

FORMATTING A TABLE

PowerPoint enables you to apply a variety of formats and borders to your tables including the ability to

- Apply different styles, widths, and colors
- Insert and delete rows and columns
- Merge and split cells
- Align cell text to the top, bottom, or center

You want to use the Tables and Borders toolbar to access all PowerPoint's table formatting options. If this toolbar doesn't currently display, you can open it by clicking the Tables and Borders button on the Standard toolbar or by selecting View, Toolbars, Tables and Borders. Table 4.1 lists all the buttons on this toolbar.

PART

II

CH

4

TABLE 4.1   TABLES AND BORDERS TOOLBAR BUTTONS

Button	Name	Description
	Draw Table	Draws a custom table
	Eraser	Erases column and row lines in a custom table
	Border Style	Applies one of several table border styles
1 pt	Border Width	Applies a selected table border width
	Border Color	Applies a selected table border color
	Outside Borders	Sets outside and inside border lines
	Fill Color	Applies a fill color to the interior of selected table cells
Table ▾	Table	Lists a variety of menu options for table formatting
	Merge Cells	Merges selected cells into one cell
	Split Cell	Splits the selected cell into two cells
	Align Top	Aligns cell text to the top of the cell
	Center Vertically	Aligns cell text in the center of the cell
	Align Bottom	Aligns cell text to the bottom of the cell

MERGING AND SPLITTING CELLS

In PowerPoint you can merge and split cells if you don't want to have the same number of rows or columns throughout your table. For example, you may want to merge all the cells across the top row of your table to serve as a title. Or, you may want to split one cell into two if the content of that cell includes two separate sets of information.

 To merge cells, select the cells you want to merge and click the Merge Cells button on the Tables and Borders toolbar. Figure 4.5 illustrates two cells that were merged into one.

Figure 4.5
Merging cells is one way to add a title row to your table.

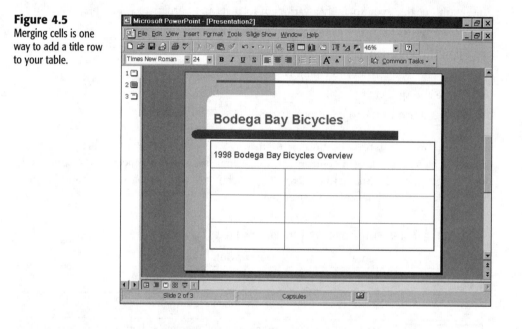

Caution

If you already have text in each of the cells you merge, each cell text becomes a line of text in the new single cell.

Tip #43 from
Patrice-Anne Rutledge

To undo a merge, click the Undo button on the Standard toolbar; choose Edit, Undo Merge Cells; or press Ctrl+Z.

To split a cell, select the cell you want to split and click the Split Cell button on the Tables and Borders toolbar. Figure 4.6 illustrates a cell that was split into two.

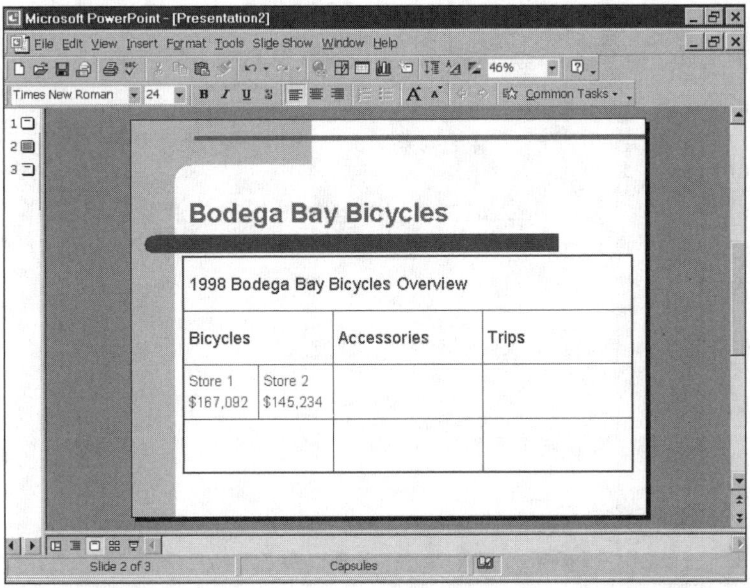
Microsoft PowerPoint - [Presentation2]
File Edit View Insert Format Tools Slide Show Window Help
Times New Roman 24
46%
Common Tasks
Bodega Bay Bicycles
1998 Bodega Bay Bicycles Overview
Bicycles
Accessories
Trips
Store 1
$167,092
Store 2
$145,234
Slide 2 of 3
Capsules

Figure 4.6
Use split cells to create columns within columns.

Tip #44 from *Patrice-Anne Rutledge*

To undo a split, click the Undo button on the Standard toolbar; choose Edit, Undo Split Cell; or press Ctrl+Z.

ALIGNING TABLE TEXT

You can align table text to the top, bottom, or center of the cell. To do so, select the cell that you want to align and click the Align Top, Center Vertically, or Align Bottom button on the Tables and Borders toolbar. Figure 4.7 illustrates examples of each kind of alignment.

Tip #45 from *Patrice-Anne Rutledge*

You can also select multiple cells and apply the alignment in one step.

To align table text to the left, right, or center, you can use the Align Left, Center, or Align Right buttons on the Formatting toolbar. To do so, select the table cells you want to align and click the appropriate button.

Figure 4.7
Align table text to the
top, center, or bottom
of a cell.

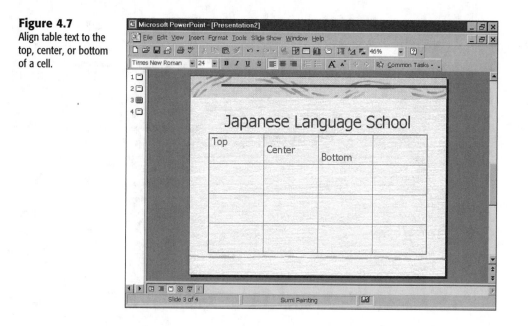

CREATING A BORDER

Borders can add to the visibility of your table and can also add to its dramatic flair.
PowerPoint tables include a solid line, black border by default, but you can change this. To
apply border formatting options, select the table and then click the appropriate Tables and
Borders toolbar button.

SETTING BORDER STYLE

To set the border style, click the Border Style drop-down list on the Tables and Borders
toolbar and choose the style of border you prefer. The list includes the option to apply no
border, a solid line, or a variety of dashed line styles, shown in Figure 4.8.

Figure 4.8
Choose the border
style that suits your
table.

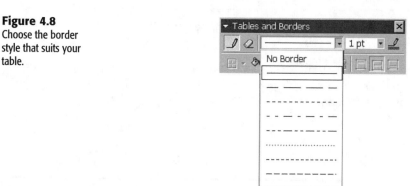

SETTING BORDER WIDTH

To set the border width, click the Border Width drop-down list on the Tables and Borders toolbar and choose the width you prefer. Options include point sizes from ¼ point (a very thin line) to 6 points (a thick line), shown in Figure 4.9.

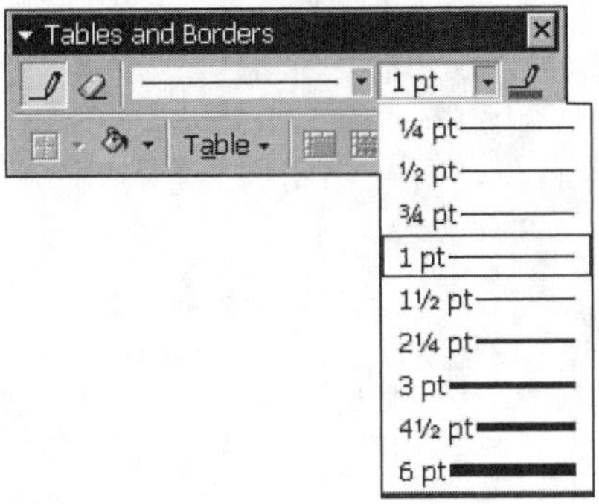

Figure 4.9
Use a thick border to create more emphasis, a thin border to create less.

SETTING BORDER COLORS

To set the color for the table border, click the Border Color button. The box that displays (see Figure 4.10) offers several possible colors from which to choose based on the presentation's color scheme.

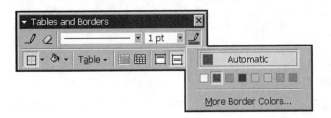

Figure 4.10
Choose one of the default colors for your border.

PART

II

CH

4

Or you can select More Border Colors to open the Colors dialog box in which you can choose from a multitude of color options or even create your own custom color as shown in Figure 4.11.

Choose the color you prefer and click OK.

If you want to create a custom color, go to the Custom tab in the Colors dialog box. On this tab you can click the color you prefer in the Colors box. The level of hue, saturation, and luminance display as well as the amounts of red, green, and blue that make up the selected color. To modify these levels, you can adjust the numbers from 0 to 255 to increase or decrease the desired color effect.

Figure 4.11
The Colors dialog box enables you to make more sophisticated color choices.

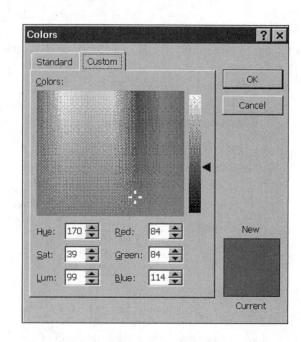

 Note

If you're not familiar with color theory, *hue* refers to the actual color, *saturation* refers to the intensity of the color, and *luminance* refers to the brightness of the color. In general, the lower the number, the lighter or less intense it is.

→ To learn more about color and color theory, **see** "Using Color," **p. 569**

CREATING OUTSIDE BORDERS

You can specify which parts of your table contain a border—all of it or only specific outside or inside areas.

 To set options for outside borders, click the down arrow to the right of the Outside Borders button on the Tables and Borders toolbar. A palette displays with several outside border options, shown in Figure 4.12.

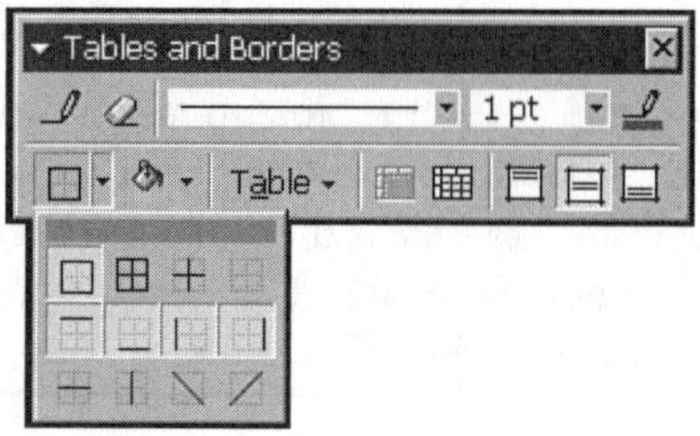

Figure 4.12
You can have both inside and outside borders on your table.

Select the option you prefer to apply. Choices include

- Outside Borders
- All Borders
- Inside Borders
- No Border
- Top Border
- Bottom Border
- Left Border
- Right Border
- Inside Horizontal Border
- Inside Vertical Border
- Diagonal Down Border
- Diagonal Up Border

You can also specify table border options in the Format Table dialog box. Open it by choosing Table, Borders and Fill from the Tables and Borders toolbar. Figure 4.13 illustrates this dialog box.

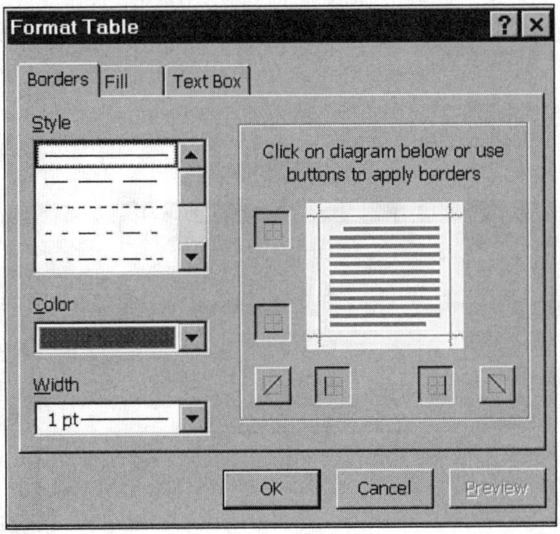

Figure 4.13
The Format Table dialog box offers alternative ways to format your table.

SETTING TABLE FILL COLOR

You can change the fill color of an individual cell or cells in your table if you want.

Caution

Be sure that your table is still readable if you change a cell's fill color.

→ To learn more about color and color theory, **see** "Using Color," **p. 569**

→ For more information about changing fill color, **see** "Specifying Fill Color," **p. 274**

 To change fill color, select the cell or cells that you want to change and click the down arrow next to the <u>F</u>ill Color button on the Tables and Borders toolbar. Figure 4.14 illustrates the palette that appears.

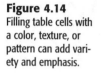

Figure 4.14
Filling table cells with a color, texture, or pattern can add variety and emphasis.

You can

■ Choose from one of the colors that display or the palette.

■ Click <u>M</u>ore Fill Colors to display the Colors dialog box. You can choose from a large number of colors in this dialog box or create a custom color.

■ Click <u>F</u>ill Effects to choose from a number of gradients, textures, patterns, and pictures.

Figure 4.15 illustrates the use of a textured fill.

Figure 4.15
Carefully chosen, a textured fill can add a creative flair to a table.

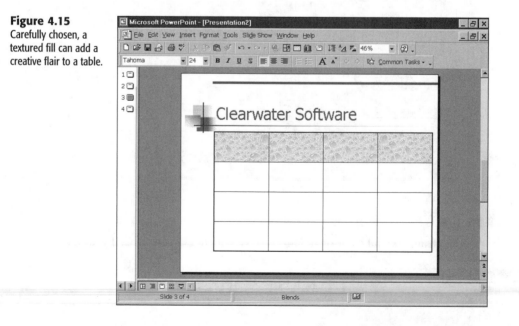

Tip #46 from
Patrice-Anne Rutledge

To remove a fill you no longer want, click the down arrow next to the Fill Color button and choose No Fill from the palette.

WORKING WITH COLUMNS AND ROWS

After you create a table, you may decide that you need to add additional information or that you want to remove some of the data it currently contains.

INSERTING ROWS AND COLUMNS

To insert a new row into your table, select an existing table row by inserting the cursor in the row and choosing Table, Select Row from the Tables and Borders toolbar. You can also select a row by clicking the first cell in the row and dragging across with the mouse. Then choose Table, Insert Rows Above or Insert Rows Below from the Tables and Borders toolbar. PowerPoint inserts a row either above or below the selected row, depending on your menu choice. Figure 4.16 illustrates a table with an added row.

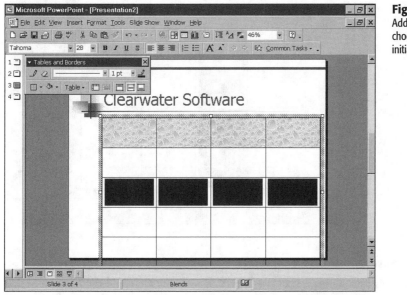

Figure 4.16
Add rows if you didn't choose enough during initial table creation.

PART

II

CH

4

Tip #47 from
Patrice-Anne Rutledge

You can resize the height or width of any row or column by selecting the row or column separator with the mouse and dragging it to the new location.

Caution

When you add or delete rows and columns, your table may no longer fit well on the slide. You then need to resize the table by dragging a corner with the mouse. Be careful, however, that you don't hide existing text by making the cells too small during resizing.

Tip #48 from

Patrice-Anne Rutledge

If you want to insert multiple rows, select that number of rows before selecting the insert command. For example, if you select two table rows and then choose Table, Insert Rows Above in the Tables and Borders toolbar, two rows are inserted above the selected rows.

To add a new column to your table, select an existing table column by inserting the cursor in the column and choosing Table, Select Column from the Tables and Borders toolbar. You can also select a column by clicking the first cell in the column and dragging down with the mouse. Then choose Table, Insert Columns to the Left or Insert Columns to the Right from the Tables and Borders toolbar. PowerPoint inserts a column either to the right or the left of the selected column, depending on your menu choice. Figure 4.17 illustrates a table with added columns.

Figure 4.17
You can add columns if your table design changes.

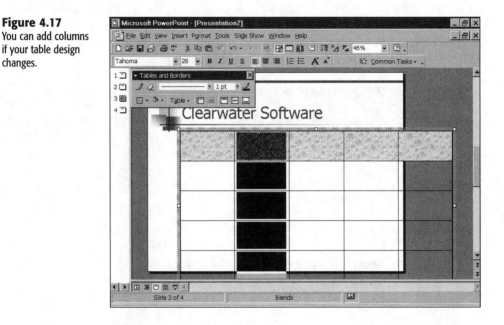

DELETING ROWS AND COLUMNS

To delete rows or columns, select the areas you want to delete and then choose Table, Delete Rows or Delete Columns from the Tables and Borders toolbar. PowerPoint deletes the entire column or row of the cell(s) you select.

Tip #49 from
Patrice-Anne Rutledge

Click the Undo button to undo any row/column insertion or deletion if you make a mistake.

CHANGING ROW AND COLUMN WIDTH AND HEIGHT

To change the width or height of a table row or column, select the object you want to change by clicking with the mouse and drag the column or row separator to resize.

DELETING TABLES AND TABLE CONTENTS

To delete specific text in a table cell, select the text (not just the cell), and press the Delete key.

Caution

You must select the actual text or cell—not just place the cursor in the cell—in order to delete the text.

To delete an entire table, choose Table, Select Table from the Tables and Borders toolbar and then press the Delete key. The table disappears and is replaced by the initial "Double-click to Add a Table" directive that displays when you first create a table slide.

Tip #50 from
Patrice-Anne Rutledge

You can also click the outside border of the table and press the Delete key.

DRAWING A TABLE

If the default table options don't provide you with what you need in a table, you can create a custom table. Drawing your own table enables you to make columns and rows of varying widths, for example. For some people, drawing a table is faster than using the table place-holder method.

 To draw a table, select the Draw Table button on the Tables and Borders toolbar. The mouse pointer becomes a pencil. Drag the mouse diagonally across the slide to create the basic table. Then use the mouse to draw lines representing columns and rows. Figure 4.18 illustrates a table created using this method.

Figure 4.18
Drawing your own table provides more flexibility in table design.

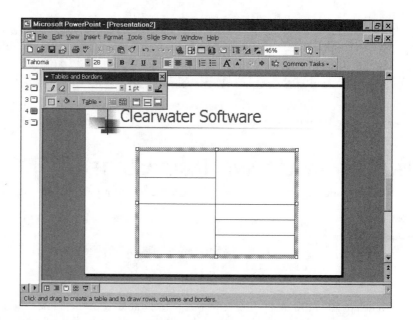

If you make mistakes or want to imitate the merge and split cells features, click the Eraser button on the Tables and Borders toolbar. Use this eraser to remove the lines between rows and cells as necessary.

To make it easier to create your rows and columns, you can display rulers and guides on your slide. Select View, Ruler to display a ruler. Select View, Guides to create an invisible grid across your slide. These lines are invisible when you print or display a slide show.

Tip #51 from
Patrice-Anne Rutledge

To create your own guide line, select an existing guide, press the Ctrl key, and drag it to a new location. Delete a guide by dragging it off the slide.

INSERTING A WORD TABLE

If you want to take advantage of Word's powerful formatting capabilities, you should consider creating a Word table within your PowerPoint presentation.

To do so, choose Insert, Picture, Microsoft Word Table. The Insert Table dialog box appears, shown in Figure 4.19.

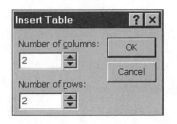

Figure 4.19
Specify the number of columns and rows in this dialog box.

Choose the Number of Columns and Number of Rows to display and then click OK. PowerPoint inserts a blank Word table in your presentation (see Figure 4.20).

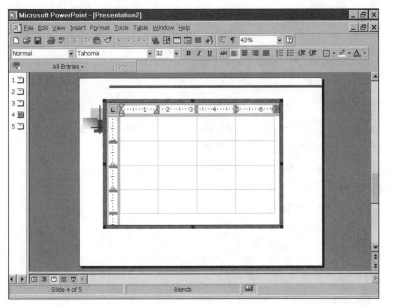

Figure 4.20
You can now format this embedded Word table.

PART

II

CH

4

When you select the Word table, Word menu options and toolbars appear within PowerPoint that enable you to enter data and to format this table as you would using Microsoft Word.

To return to the standard PowerPoint menus and tools, click outside the table. Double-click the table to return to the Word menus and tools for further modification.

FORMATTING A WORD TABLE

With an embedded Word table, you can apply all of the formatting options that are available in PowerPoint as well as those available in Microsoft Word. This gives you a lot of added flexibility and functionality for creating sophisticated and complex tables.

The Word Tables and Borders toolbar includes several additional options that the PowerPoint version doesn't contain. Table 4.2 lists these additional buttons and their functions.

TABLE 4.2   WORD TABLES AND BORDERS TOOLBAR BUTTONS

Button	Name	Description
	Distribute Rows Evenly	Resizes rows to make them equal in size.
	Distribute Columns Evenly	Resizes columns to make them equal in size.
	Table AutoFormat	Opens the Table AutoFormat dialog box in which you can apply special preset formatting to your table.
	Change Text Direction	Toggles the text direction between vertical and horizontal.
	Sort Ascending	Sorts selected table text in ascending (A-Z) order.
	Sort Descending	Sorts selected table text in descending (Z-A) order.
	AutoSum	Automatically sums number table text.

ADDING BULLETED AND NUMBERED LISTS WITHIN TABLES

To create a bulleted list within a table cell, select the cell you want to format and click the Bullets button on the Formatting toolbar.

To create a numbered list within a selected table cell, click the Numbering toolbar button.

Tip #52 from *Patricia-Anne Rutledge*	For additional bullet and numbering options, select the text you want to format and then choose F**o**rmat, Bullets and **N**umbering to open the Bullets and Numbering dialog box. This dialog box offers many additional options including the ability to create alphabetical lists as well as picture bullets.

AUTOFORMATTING A TABLE

You can use the Table AutoFormat feature to apply special formatting to your table such as borders, fonts, and colors.

 Click the Table AutoFormat button on the Tables and Borders toolbar. The Word Table AutoFormat dialog box appears (see Figure 4.21).

Choose the format you want to apply from the available list. The Preview box displays what the formatting looks like.

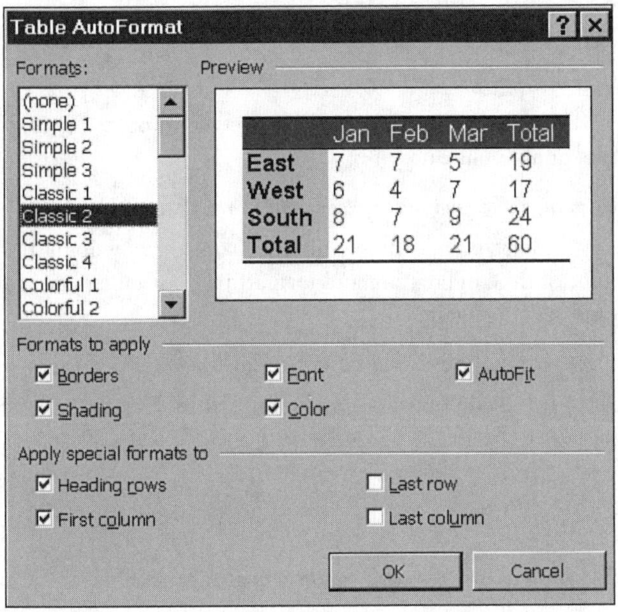

Figure 4.21
Choose from a variety
of preset formats.

PART

II

CH

4

You can apply formatting changes to one or all of the following:

- Borders
- Shading
- Font
- Color
- AutoFit

You can also differentiate specific columns and row by applying special formatting to any of the following:

- Heading Rows
- First Column
- Last Row
- Last Column

Click OK to apply the selected AutoFormats.

TROUBLESHOOTING

I can't access the Word table formatting tools and menus from within PowerPoint.

The Word table in the PowerPoint presentation must be selected in order to view these options. To select this table, double-click it.

I added some additional rows to my table, and now it doesn't fit in the slide.

You can resize your table to fit, but you may hide table text from view by doing this. If you haven't already invested a lot of time in creating and formatting your table, you may be better off deleting the table and starting again.

I applied several formatting options to my table, and I don't like the results.

Click the down arrow next to the Undo button on the Standard toolbar to see a list of formatting tasks you can undo.

DESIGN CORNER

By using PowerPoint's table design features, you can create attractive tables to include in your presentations.

BEFORE

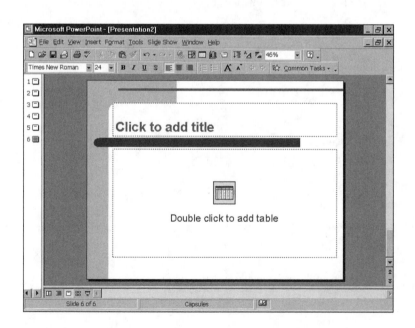

AFTER

Slide title   Patterns   Bolding

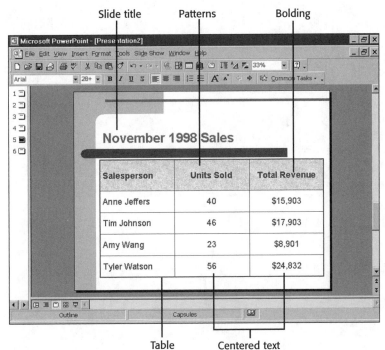

Table   Centered text

CHAPTER 5

ORGANIZING YOUR PRESENTATION IN OUTLINE VIEW

In this chapter

by Patrice-Anne Rutledge

EXPLORING POWERPOINT'S OUTLINING FEATURES

PowerPoint's outlining features make it easy to create a well-organized presentation. Using the outline pane in Outline view or Normal view, you can create a basic outline as well as revise, rearrange, and reorganize it. The Outlining toolbar includes buttons that provide even more options and flexibility in outlining, such as the ability to collapse and expand your outline, design a summary slide, or display text formatting. And if you create outlines in other programs such as Word 2000, you can quickly import these into PowerPoint and automatically create a presentation.

In this chapter you learn about specific ways in which PowerPoint organizes your presentation, such as:

- *How to organize your presentation*   You have several ways that you can organize a presentation in PowerPoint, depending on how you work best and whether you've already created an outline in another program.

- *Exploring Outline View*   Both Outline view and Normal view display the outline pane, in which you can easily organize and rearrange your presentation.

- *How to use the Outlining toolbar*   The Outlining toolbar enables you to promote and demote outline points as well as move, collapse, and expand them. You can also create a summary slide or display font formatting as well.

- *Importing outlines from other programs*   If you create outlines in Word or another program, you can import them into PowerPoint. PowerPoint also imports other common file formats such as RTF and TXT.

ORGANIZING PRESENTATIONS

Before you actually create a PowerPoint presentation, you should determine the presentation's purpose, organize your ideas, and establish the flow of what you're going to say. Essentially, you need to create an outline.

→ To learn some useful outlining techniques, **see** "Creating an Outline and Storyboard," **p. 507**

You can create an outline for a PowerPoint presentation in one of four ways:

- Create a presentation in PowerPoint using the outline pane in Outline View or Normal View.

- Create a presentation in PowerPoint using the AutoContent Wizard to design a basic outline and suggest appropriate content.

→ To learn what this wizard does, **see** "Using the AutoContent Wizard," **p. 36**

- Create a presentation in PowerPoint by entering information directly on the slides. This information then displays in the outline pane.

- Create an outline in another application, such as Word 2000, and import it into PowerPoint.

→ To learn how to import existing outlines, **see** "Importing Outlines from Microsoft Word and Other Programs," **p. 112**

As you create your basic outline, keep several things in mind:

- You'll want to start nearly every presentation with a title slide that introduces your topic and its presenter.

- Think of several main points to cover and design your presentation around these talking points.

- Try not to cover more than one main topic or concept in an individual slide.

- Remember that a PowerPoint outline is usually designed to accompany a verbal presentation. Keep in mind what you want your audience to see versus what you want them to listen to during your presentation.

- If you're going to use bulleted lists extensively, try to keep them balanced and consistent. For example, a single bullet on a slide doesn't really make sense; a list should contain at least two bullets. Too many bullets on one slide and very few on another also may not work well.

- Consider using a summary slide to summarize the points you made during your presentation and conclude it.

UNDERSTANDING OUTLINE VIEW

No matter which method you use to create your outline, you need to use PowerPoint's outline pane to organize this information at some point. The outline pane appears in both Normal view and Outline view in PowerPoint. In Normal view, the outline appears on the left side of the window and shares the desktop with the slide itself and related notes. In Outline view, the outline pane takes up two-thirds of the window space, with smaller panes for viewing the slide and notes.

PART

II

CH

5

Tip #53 from
Patrice-Anne Rutledge

You can change the size of a pane by dragging its border to a new location. This can be done when the cursor changes to a double-headed arrow.

To switch to Outline view, click the Outline View button in the lower-left corner of the PowerPoint window. You can switch back to Normal view, the default, by clicking the Normal View button.

Figure 5.1 shows Outline view.

Figure 5.1
Outline view offers a
flexible approach to
creating an outline.

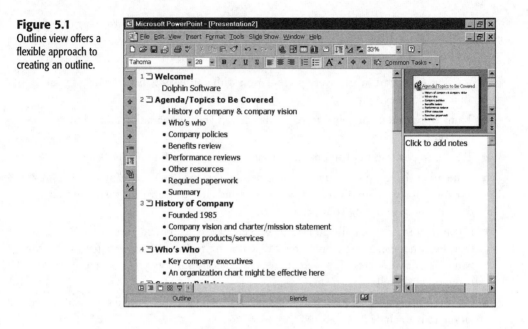

Each slide in your presentation is numbered and is followed by a slide icon and the title text. The body text is listed under each slide, up to five levels. This body text includes bulleted and indented lists, as well as other text information. The title text is also referred to as the outline heading and each individual point in the body text as a subheading. Clip art, tables, charts, and other objects don't appear in the outline pane.

> **Note**
>
> Any text that you enter other than in the Click to Add Title or the Click to Add Text placeholders doesn't display in the outline either.

Adding new outline information is simple. Enter the content and press the Enter key to move to the next point. To delete a point you no longer need, select it and press the Delete key.

USING THE OUTLINING TOOLBAR

You can use the Outlining toolbar to help organize and rearrange your slides in the outline pane. To display the toolbar, choose View, Toolbars, Outlining. It appears vertically on the left side of the outline pane. Table 5.1 lists the buttons on this toolbar.

TABLE 5.1   OUTLINING TOOLBAR BUTTONS

Button	Name	Description
	Promote	Applies the style/formatting of the level that is one step above the level of the selected text.
	Demote	Applies the style/formatting of the level that is one step below the level of the selected text. Demoting a slide title moves the text of the selected slide to the previous slide.
	Move Up	Moves the selected text ahead of the previous item in the outline.
	Move Down	Moves the selected text beneath the next item in the outline.
	Collapse	Hides all body text for the selected slides.
	Expand	Displays all body text for the selected slides.
	Collapse All	Hides all body text in the outline.
	Expand All	Displays all body text in the outline.
	Summary Slide	Creates a slide that summarizes the presentation by listing slide titles.
	Show Formatting	Shows the actual presentation font formatting in the outline pane.

Tip #54 from
Patrice-Anne Rutledge

> You can move the Outlining toolbar to another location on the screen by dragging the move handle (above the Promote button) to another location.

PROMOTING AND DEMOTING OUTLINE POINTS

You can demote outline headings and promote and demote subheadings to reorganize and rearrange your presentation. Promoting a first level subheading makes it become a heading (slide title) in a new slide. Promoting a secondary level subheading (such as indented text or lower level bullet) moves it up to the next level.

For example, if you select the text of a second level bullet in the outline and click the Promote button, the bullet becomes a first level bullet. (See Figures 5.2 and 5.3.)

Figure 5.2
The bulleted list item you want to change is currently indented.

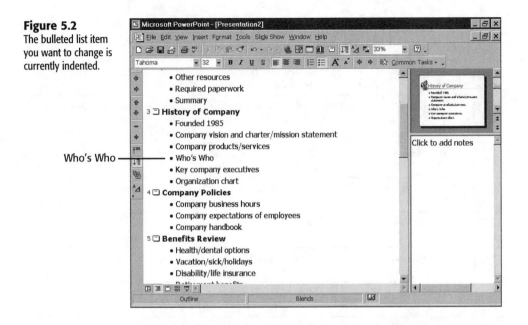

Figure 5.3
Promoting the bul-leted list item moves it up one level, but doesn't change its location.

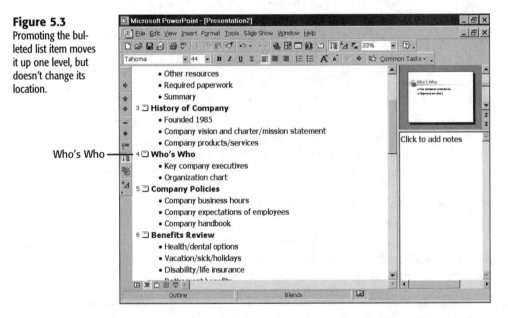

If you promote a first level bullet, it becomes a slide title and PowerPoint inserts a new slide into the presentation.

Note

Promoting indented text outdents it.

The Demote button works in much the same way as the Promote button. Demoting a sub-heading such as a first level bullet moves the bullet point to a second level bullet. Demoting other text indents the text.

Tip #55 from
Patrice-Anne Rutledge

You can also easily demote a specific heading by selecting it and pressing the Tab key.

Demoting an outline heading (slide title) deletes the slide and moves its text content to the bottom of the previous slide. PowerPoint verifies this action before doing it if your slide contains notes or graphics.

Do you lose notes and graphics when demoting? See the Troubleshooting section at the end of the chapter.

MOVING OUTLINE POINTS UP AND DOWN

In addition to promoting and demoting outline points, you can also move the location of each point. For example, to move a numbered list item from the second to the first position in the list, select that second item and click the Move Up button.

Or, let's say you want to move the first of three bulleted list items from one slide to the top of the list in the following slide. To do this, click the Move Down button three times. (See Figures 5.4 and 5.5.)

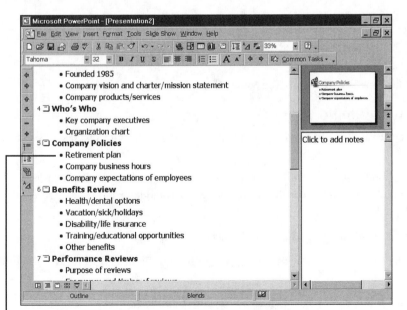

Figure 5.4
The original bullet position.

Retirement plan

Figure 5.5
Its position after clicking the Move Down button three times.

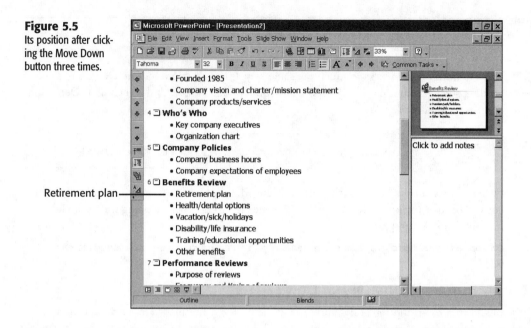

Retirement plan

Tip #56 from
Patrice-Anne Rutledge

To undo moves of more than one position, you should click the Undo button the same number of times that you clicked the Move Up or Move Down button.

→ To learn more about the different ways you can organize slides in PowerPoint, **see** "Rearranging Slides," **p. 120**

Tip #57 from
Patrice-Anne Rutledge

Use Slide Sorter view to view your actual slides as you rearrange them.

→ For details on this view, **see** "Using the Slide Sorter View," **p. 123**

COLLAPSING AND EXPANDING OUTLINE POINTS

To make things easier to read in a long outline, you can collapse and expand slides and their body text.

To collapse the body text of an individual slide, select it and click the Collapse button. The slide number and title remain, but the related body text is hidden from view. Figure 5.6 shows a collapsed slide.

Select the slide again and click Expand to display the hidden text.

To collapse the entire outline, click the Collapse All button. Figure 5.7 illustrates an outline that is entirely collapsed.

To display the outline details again, click the Expand All button.

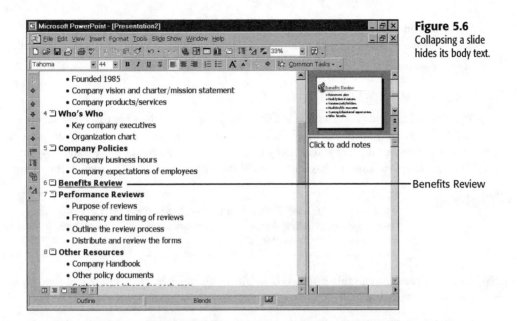

Figure 5.6
Collapsing a slide hides its body text.

Benefits Review

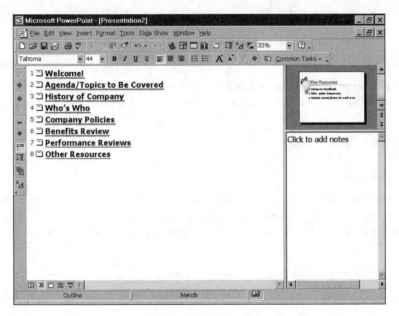

Figure 5.7
Collapsing an entire presentation creates a presentation outline summary.

PART

II

CH

5

Tip #58 from
Patrice-Anne Rutledge

If you want to collapse and expand more than one slide, but not all slides, press Shift, choose the consecutive slides, and then click the Collapse or Expand button. Note that the slides you select must be consecutive.

Collapsing and expanding your outline make it easier to print as well. You can print an entire outline in detail; only certain sections in detail; or only a collapsed, summary outline.

→ To learn how to print outlines, **see** "Printing an Outline," **p. 184**

CREATING A SUMMARY SLIDE

You can create a slide that summarizes the outline headings (the slide titles) for all, or selected, slides in your presentation. You can then use this slide to introduce your presentation, to highlight the areas you're going to discuss, or to close your presentation by summarizing it. To create a summary slide, select all the slides you want to include in the summary.

> **Note**
>
> You need to either choose all slides or a series of consecutive slides when you create a summary slide in Outline View. Create a summary slide from Slide Sorter view if you want to choose multiple, non-consecutive slides.

Usually it's easier to do this if you collapse all the headings by clicking the Collapse All button on the Outlining toolbar.

> **Tip #59 from**
> *Patrice-Anne Rutledge*
>
> You can easily select all slides in the presentation by selecting the first slide and dragging the mouse down to the last slide or by pressing Ctrl+A.

Next, click the Summary Slide button. PowerPoint automatically creates a summary slide that contains a bulleted list of all the selected slide titles in your presentation. The summary slide is inserted before the first selected slide, but you can move it to another location if you want.

Figure 5.8 shows a sample summary slide.

SHOWING SLIDE FORMATTING

By default, the outline pane displays each heading and subheading in the same font, bolding the headings for emphasis. If you want the outline to display using the actual fonts and formatting of the presentation itself, click the Show Formatting button on the Outlining toolbar.

Figure 5.9 displays a sample outline that shows formatting.

The specific font and attributes such as size, bolding, italics, underlining, and shadow now display in the outline pane. The font color, however, does not display.

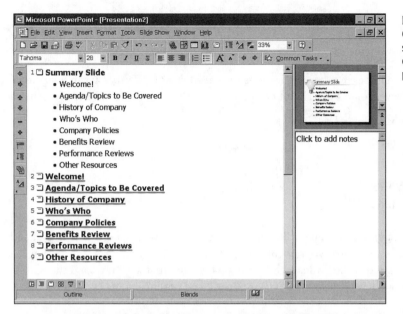

Figure 5.8
Create a summary slide to introduce or close your presentation.

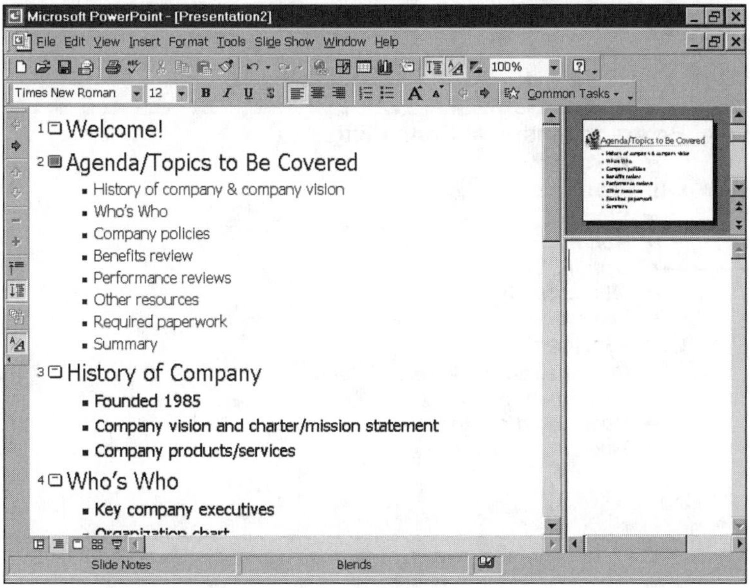

Figure 5.9
This outline displays text formatting.

IMPORTING OUTLINES FROM MICROSOFT WORD AND OTHER PROGRAMS

If you create outlines in other applications such as Microsoft Word, you can easily import them into PowerPoint. PowerPoint can import outlines from many different formats such as:

- Word documents (.DOC)
- Rich Text Format (.RTF)
- Text files (.TXT)
- Excel worksheets (.XLS)
- HTML (.HTM)

For example, if you create an outline in Word 2000, you use heading 1, heading 2, and heading 3 styles to format your document. When PowerPoint imports your outline, each heading 1 becomes a slide title, each heading 2 becomes first level text, and each heading 3 becomes second level text. Figure 5.10 shows a Word outline and its components.

Figure 5.10
Outline in Word and then import your outline into PowerPoint.

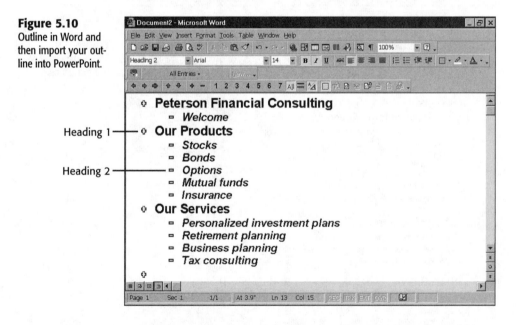

If the file you import doesn't contain these heading styles, PowerPoint uses paragraph indentations and tabs to determine the structure of the outline. Use the Outlining toolbar buttons to reorganize the outline if the initial format isn't correct.

To import the outline into PowerPoint, follow these steps:

1. Click the Open button on the Standard toolbar or choose File, Open to display the Open dialog box, shown in Figure 5.11.

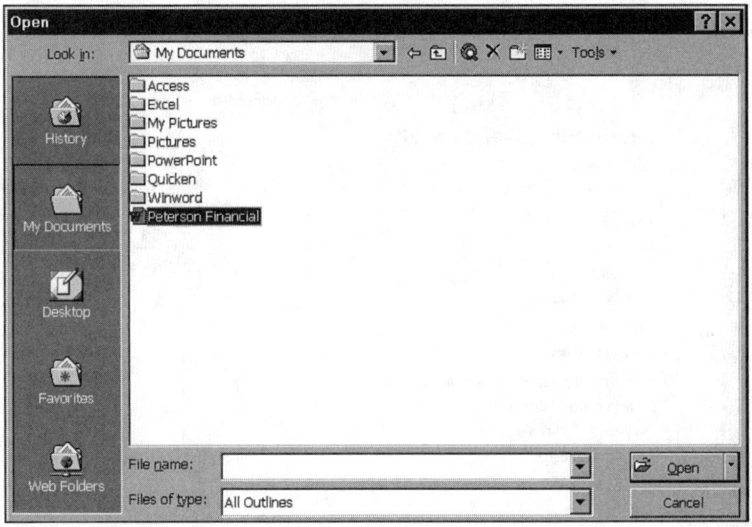

Figure 5.11
Select the outline you want to import in the Open dialog box.

2. Select All Outlines from the Files of Type drop-down list.
3. Navigate to the outline you want to import and select it.
4. Click Open.

Caution

The first time you import an outline, PowerPoint may display a warning dialog box telling you that it needs to install a converter. Some converters are tagged as install upon first use if you chose the default setup when you installed Office 2000. Be sure to have your installation CD in your CD-ROM drive before clicking Yes.

Tip #60 from
Patrice-Anne Rutledge

If you are creating your outline in Word 2000, choose File, Send To, and then Microsoft PowerPoint. PowerPoint automatically creates a presentation from this information. Apply a design template, graphics, and other pizzazz and your presentation is complete.

Does your imported outline look strange? See the Troubleshooting section at the end of the chapter.

PowerPoint imports the outline and creates a presentation from it. Figure 5.12 illustrates an example of an imported outline.

After PowerPoint imports your outline, you should apply a design template and make any other necessary formatting changes.

→ For more information about using these templates in your presentation, **see** "Understanding Design Templates," **p. 28**

Figure 5.12
The outline now displays in a PowerPoint presentation.

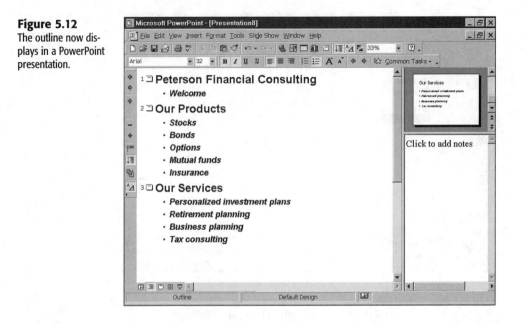

Note

You can also import an outline into an existing presentation. To do this, select the slide in the outline pane after which you want to insert the new outline. Choose Insert, Slides from Outline to open the Insert Outline dialog box. Choose the outline you want to import and click Insert.

Tip #61 from
Patrice-Anne Rutledge

You can also just copy the outline text from the source application, paste into PowerPoint, and reformat to quickly create a basic outline.

TROUBLESHOOTING

I imported an outline and it doesn't look right.

Remember that PowerPoint imports an outline from another application "as is." Before importing, be sure that the existing document makes a suitable outline. For example, importing a lengthy text file or detailed spreadsheet might not make sense as an outline.

I demoted a slide and the text moved to the previous slide, but the notes and graphics disappeared.

When you demote a slide using the Demote button on the Outlining toolbar, the text content remains and carries over to the previous slide, but any graphics or notes are deleted.

DESIGN CORNER

Use an outline to ensure a logical flow of thought through your presentation. Often creating an initial outline can call attention to such problems. PowerPoint's outlining features make it easy to correct and perfect your outline.

BEFORE

Demote these two bullet points, which are part of the project introduction.

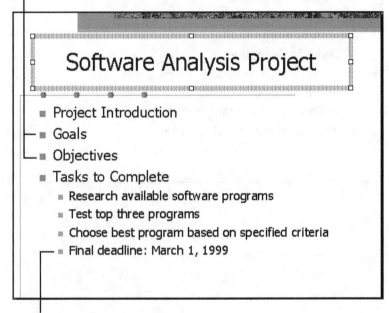

Promote this bullet point, which is its own topic.

AFTER

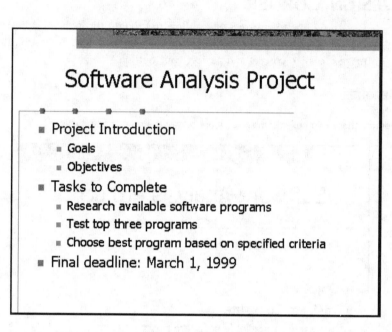

CHAPTER 6

FORMATTING SLIDES AND PRESENTATIONS

In this chapter

by Patrice-Anne Rutledge

EXPLORING POWERPOINT FORMATTING OPTIONS

After you create a presentation, you may want to make some changes to it. Adding, deleting, rearranging, copying, and moving slides are simple tasks in PowerPoint. You can also make more detailed changes to the original format of your presentation. For example, you can apply a new design template, change colors and color schemes, and apply a special effects background. When it's time to review your presentation, PowerPoint includes a comment utility that lets others provide input and suggestions on each slide.

In this chapter you learn about:

- *Manipulating slides*   You can add, delete, and rearrange slides easily in PowerPoint.

- *Using comments*   Comments are a good way to get feedback on your presentation from a number of people. After receiving comments, you can review them and update your presentation as needed.

- *Using Slide Sorter*   You can use the Slide Sorter View to organize and analyze your presentation while viewing multiple slides. This view also makes it easier to rearrange large numbers of slides.

- *Copying and moving slides to another presentation*   If you want to reuse work you've already done, you can copy or move slides from an existing presentation to a new one.

- *Applying a new design template*   You can apply a new design template to change the appearance of your presentation. If the existing templates don't suit your needs, you can download more from the Web or create your own.

- *Using color schemes*   Each design template includes several possible color schemes that coordinate with it. Choose any of these or customize a color scheme.

- *Applying a background*   As an alternative to a solid color background, you can apply textures, patterns, gradients, and pictures as background images.

ADDING SLIDES

After you create a presentation, you may want to add new slides. To open the New Slide dialog box, click the New Slide button on the Standard toolbar. This adds a new slide right after the slide you are working on. Figure 6.1 shows this dialog box.

Tip #62 from	You can also open the New Slide dialog box by pressing Ctrl+M or by choosing Common Tasks, New Slide from the Formatting toolbar.
Patrice-Anne Rutledge	

Choose the AutoLayout you want to use and click OK. PowerPoint creates a new slide using the selected layout (see Figure 6.2).

→ To learn more about each layout type, **see** "Understanding Slide Layouts," **p. 28**

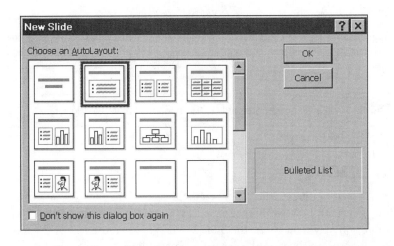

Figure 6.1
Choose from many different slide types from the New Slide dialog box.

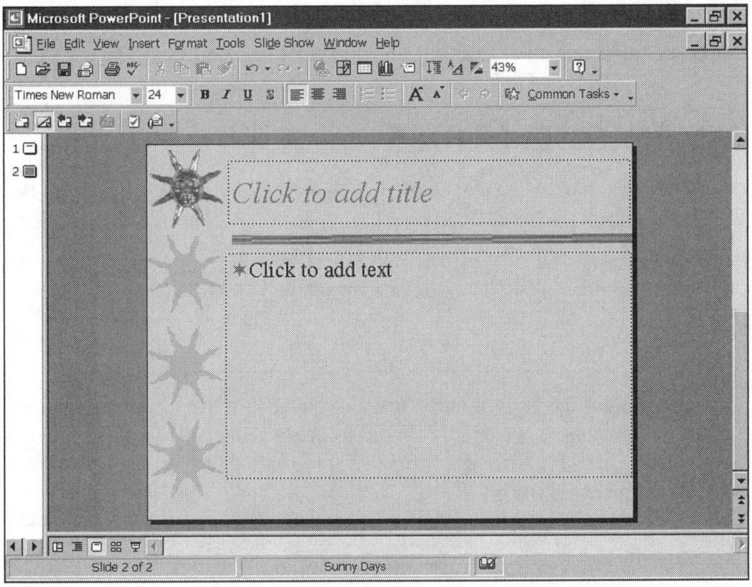

Figure 6.2
Enter your own content in a new slide.

PART
II

CH
6

DELETING SLIDES

If you no longer need a slide or make a mistake and want to start again, you can delete it. Select the slide in the outline pane and press the Delete key.

To delete multiple consecutive slides, press the Shift key and select the slides you want to delete before pressing the Delete key.

Tip #63 from
Patricia-Anne Rutledge

> You can delete multiple nonconsecutive slides in Slide Sorter View by holding the Ctrl key, selecting the slides you want to delete, and pressing the Delete key.

Tip #64 from
Patricia-Anne Rutledge

> Click the Undo button on the Standard toolbar to reverse a mistaken deletion.

REARRANGING SLIDES

You can rearrange slides using the outline pane. Select the icon of the slide you want to move and drag it to a new location within that pane. If you have major reorganization to do on your presentation, you may want to use the Slide Sorter View because it provides more flexibility and the ability to actually view the contents of your slides as you rearrange them.

→ To learn more about using this view to organize your slides, **see** "Using the Slide Sorter View," **p. 123**

→ To discover more outlining techniques, **see** "Moving Outline Points Up and Down," **p. 107**

ADDING COMMENTS TO SLIDES

The ability to add *comments (p. 178)* to slides is a useful reviewing utility that is shared with other Office 2000 applications such as Word and Excel. For example, if associates or co-workers need to provide feedback or approve your presentation, you can request they enter comments on each individual slide so that you can see exactly what they're referring to in their commentary.

Caution

> Comments aren't the same as notes. You add comments within a presentation to provide input on specific slides. Comments are usually deleted after you read them and update your presentation. Notes are information you keep with your presentation to provide additional information as you speak.

→ For details on creating these notes, **see** "Creating Notes and Handouts," **p. 178**

To add a comment to a slide, choose <u>I</u>nsert, Co<u>m</u>ment. A yellow box appears at the top-left corner of your slide; your name appears as the reviewer. Figure 6.3 illustrates a sample comment box.

Note

> You can't add a comment in Slide Sorter View; this option is dimmed on the menu. And although you can add a comment in Outline View, it's usually too difficult to see the comment in the slide pane. Normal View and Slide View are the best views for adding comments.

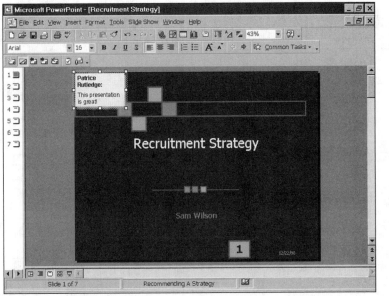

Figure 6.3
Comments provide a way to get feedback on your presentation.

PowerPoint places all comments in the upper-left corner of the slide by default. If you add more than one comment to the slide, it is placed on top of the existing slide, covering most of it. You can move the comment from its default location by selecting it and dragging it with the mouse.

Tip #65 from
Patrice-Anne Rutledge

To change the reviewer name, choose Tools, Options, and enter a new Name in the User Information group box on the General tab.

Enter your comments in the yellow box, which expands based on the length of the comments. The Reviewing toolbar displays when you insert a comment. Table 6.1 describes these toolbar buttons.

Tip #66 from
Patrice-Anne Rutledge

You can also display and hide the Reviewing toolbar by selecting View, Toolbars, Reviewing.

PART

II

CH

6

TABLE 6.1   REVIEWING TOOLBAR BUTTONS

Button	Name	Description
	Insert Comment	Inserts a comment box on a slide
	Show/Hide Comments	Toggles the display of comments on and off
	Previous Comment	Cycles back to the previous comment in a presentation
	Next Comment	Cycles forward to the next comment in a presentation
	Delete Comment	Deletes a selected comment
	Create Microsoft Outlook Task	Creates an Outlook task related to this comment
	Send to Mail Recipient	Emails this presentation to someone for review

REVIEWING COMMENTS

To review comments in a presentation, select the Show/Hide Comments button on the Reviewing toolbar if comments don't display.

In general, comments should be very apparent because of their bright yellow color. But in a long presentation, it can be easier to simply jump to the next comment, rather than look at each slide. To do this, click the Next Comment button on the Reviewing toolbar.

Tip #67 from
Patrice-Anne Rutledge

To jump back to previous comments and look at them again, click the Previous Comment button.

Tip #68 from
Patrice-Anne Rutledge

When you reach the end of a presentation, clicking the Next Comment button brings you back to the first comment of the presentation again.

After you read a comment, you may want to delete it. To do that, select it and click the Delete Comment button on the Reviewing toolbar.

FORMATTING COMMENTS

You can format both the text in a comment and the comment box itself. For example, using the Formatting toolbar, you can change the font or font size or choose to bold, italicize, or underline the text in your comment for specific emphasis.

 To learn more about how to use these toolbar buttons to format a PowerPoint presentation, **see** "Using the Formatting Toolbar," **p. 62**

Note

Because the comment itself is considered text, spell checking your presentation also finds spelling errors in comments.

The comment box is similar to any other PowerPoint object, and you can format it using the Format dialog box. In this dialog box, you can change the color, border, shape, size, and position of the comment box based on your preference.

Caution

Be sure you have a solid reason for customizing a comment box before doing so. In general, it's not worth the effort to make extensive changes to the appearance of a comment.

→ To learn how to use this dialog box to format a comment, **see** "Using the Format Dialog Box," **p. 282**

⚠️ *Are comments displaying in your slide shows?* See the Troubleshooting section at the end of the chapter.

USING THE SLIDE SORTER VIEW

You can use the *Slide Sorter (p. 17)* view to help you organize and rearrange your slides. To open this view, click the Slide Sorter View button on the lower-left corner of the PowerPoint window or select <u>V</u>iew, Sli<u>d</u>e Sorter. Figure 6.4 displays this view.

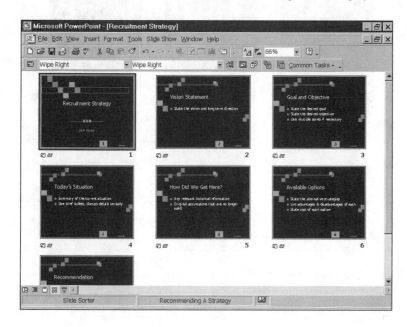

Figure 6.4
Analyze and organize slides in Slide Sorter view.

PART

II

CH

6

In this view, you see smaller versions of your slides in several rows and columns. By viewing the basic content of each slide, you can more easily rearrange their order.

To move a slide in the Slide Sorter, select it and drag it to a new location.

Tip #69 from
Patrice-Anne Rutledge

Click the Undo Drag and Drop button to undo a move you made by mistake.

To view a particular slide in more detail, click on the desired slide and select the Normal View button at the lower-left corner of the PowerPoint window (see Figure 6.5).

Figure 6.5
Choose how you want to view your presentation.

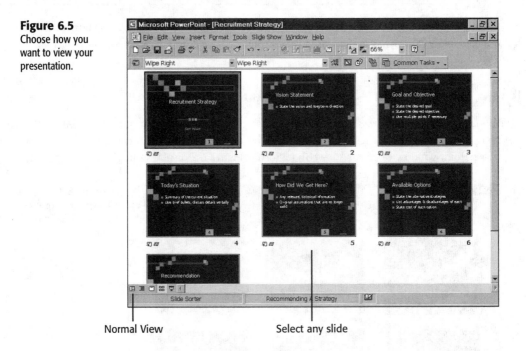

Normal View   Select any slide

Tip #70 from
Patrice-Anne Rutledge

You can also rearrange slides in the outline pane by selecting their icons with the mouse and dragging them to a new location.

To delete a slide in Slide Sorter View, select it and press the Delete key. To select multiple slides to delete, press Ctrl, select the slides, and then press the Delete key.

Occasionally, you may also want to hide slides from view during an onscreen presentation, but not delete them from the presentation itself.

To do that, select the slide or slides you want to hide and click the Hide Slide button on the Slide Sorter toolbar. The slides remain in the presentation, but they don't display when you run your slide show.

The Slide Sorter toolbar also includes buttons for applying optional effects, such as transitions, animation effects, and speaker's notes, which we discuss later in this book.

→ To learn why you might want to use speaker's notes, **see** "Creating Notes and Handouts," **p. 178**

→ For details on using this form of animation in your presentation, **see** "Using Preset Animation," **p. 322**

→ To learn how to create transitional effects, **see** "Setting Slide Transitions," **p. 319**

MOVING AND COPYING SLIDES FROM ONE PRESENTATION TO ANOTHER

Using the Slide Sorter View, you can either copy or move slides from one PowerPoint presentation to another. To do this, open both the source and destination presentations in Slide Sorter View. Choose Window, Arrange All. PowerPoint displays both presentations in Slide Sorter View, in two different window panes, shown in Figure 6.6.

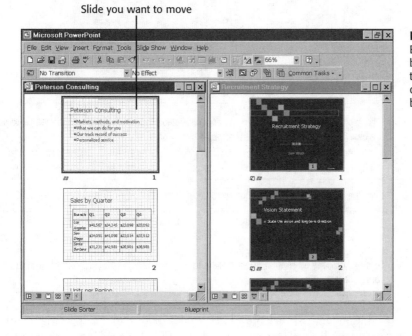

Slide you want to move

Figure 6.6
By splitting panes between two presentations, you can copy or move slides between them.

PART

II

CH

6

To copy a slide, select it, click the Copy button on the Standard toolbar, position the mouse in the new destination location, and click the Paste button. PowerPoint places the slides in the destination presentation, but they also remain in the source.

To move a slide, select it and drag it with the mouse to the desired location in the other presentation. The slide is removed from the source presentation and inserted in the destination presentation as shown in Figure 6.7.

The slide moves from the source presentation...   ...to the target presentation.

Figure 6.7
Moving a slide
removes it from its
original location.

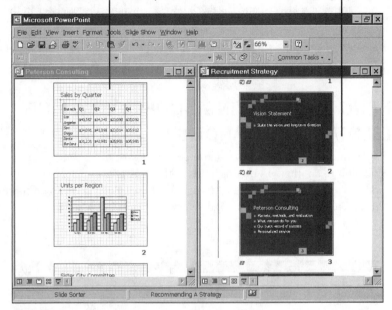

Note

If each presentation uses a different design template, the slide changes to the template of the new presentation. The content remains the same.

Tip #71 from
Patrice-Anne Rutledge

Click the Undo Drag and Drop button to undo a move.

Tip #72 from
Patrice-Anne Rutledge

To move or copy more than one slide at a time, press Ctrl as you drag slides from the source presentation.

To remove the dual window view, click the Close Window button in the upper-right corner of the presentation you no longer want to view and then the Maximize button in the upper-right corner of the presentation you want to keep active.

If arranging both presentations in one window is too distracting, you can also do this same task in separate windows.

1. Open the presentation from which you want to copy or move slides.

2. Click the Slide Sorter View button at the lower-left side of the screen to display the presentation in this view.

3. Select the slides you want to copy or move. To select multiple noncontiguous slides, press the Ctrl key and then choose slides.

4. Press Ctrl+C to copy the slides; Ctrl+X to cut the slides if you would rather move them.

5. Open the presentation in which you want to place the selected slides.

6. Click where you want to insert these slides and press Ctrl+V to paste them.

Tip #73 from
Patrice-Anne Rutledge

> If more than one presentation is open at a time, and each is in a maximized window, you can press Ctrl+F6 to cycle through each one. This helps when you want the full-screen view and want to copy/move from one presentation to the next without having to use the Window menu.

APPLYING A NEW DESIGN TEMPLATE

You can easily change the *design template (p. 28)* originally applied to your presentation. To do so, choose Format, Apply Design Template or Common Tasks, Apply Design Template from the Formatting toolbar. The Apply Design Template dialog box appears, as shown in Figure 6.8.

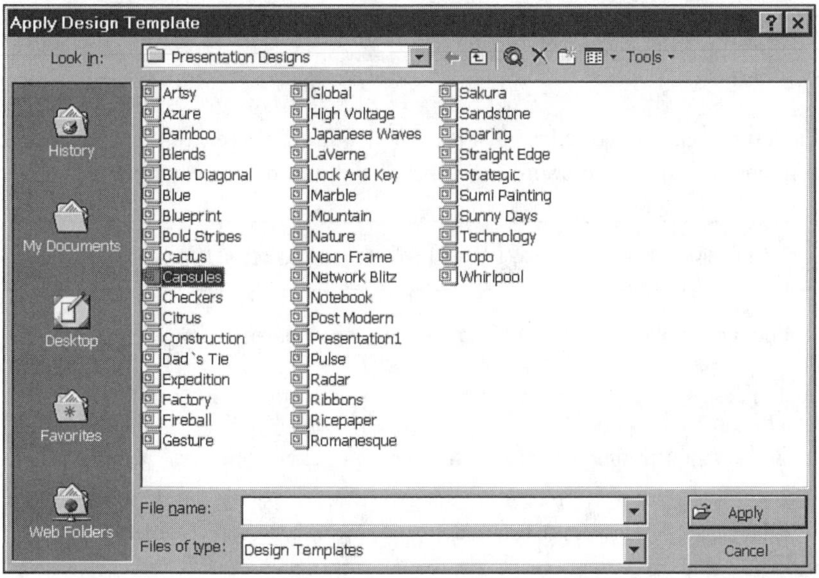

Figure 6.8
Choose a design template that matches the mood and goals of your presentation.

PART
II

CH
6

Tip #74 from
Patrice-Anne Rutledge

> The default location for design templates can vary based on where you choose to install the program, but it's usually c:\Program Files\Microsoft Office\Templates\ Presentation Designs. To apply just the design template attached to one of PowerPoint's existing presentations, look in the c:\Program Files\Microsoft Office\Templates\1033 folder.

Click the down arrow to the right of the Views button and choose Preview. The right side of the dialog box previews what each design template looks like, as shown in Figure 6.9, helping you choose the appropriate one.

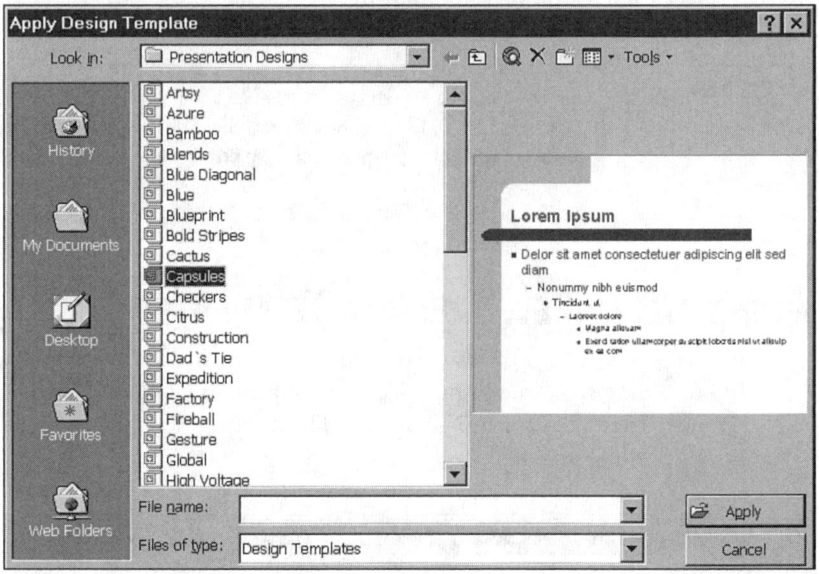

Figure 6.9
Preview lets you see what a presentation looks like before you apply it.

When you find a design template you like, click the Apply button. PowerPoint applies this design template to your entire presentation, changing all slides to this new template.

Tip #75 from
Patrice-Anne Rutledge

Click the History button to display the most recently selected design templates.

→ To learn more about design templates and how to best use them, **see** "Understanding Design Templates," **p. 28**

→ To learn how to apply a design template to a presentation when you create it, **see** "Creating a Presentation Using a Design Template," **p. 40**

→ For more advanced design template information, **see** "Working with Design Templates," **p. 550**

Tip #76 from
Patrice-Anne Rutledge

To download additional design templates from the Web, choose Help, Office on the Web.

CREATING YOUR OWN DESIGN TEMPLATE

Sometimes none of the existing design templates offers exactly what you're looking for. In this case, you can either modify an existing template or create one of your own. Some ideas of things you might want to do to customize, or add, to a blank slide:

- Change the master title or text style to a different font (View, Master, Slide Master).
- Change the background color (Format, Background).
- Change the slide color scheme (Format, Slide Color Scheme).
- Change the bullet styles (Format, Bullets and Numbering).
- Add additional objects such as a logo, picture, or WordArt image.

To save a customized design template for future use, follow these steps:

1. Choose File, Save As to open the Save As dialog box (see Figure 6.10).

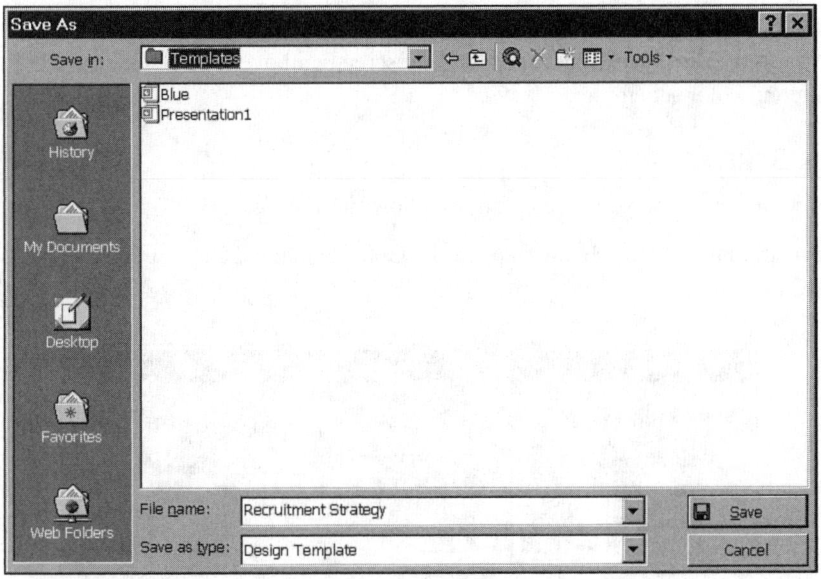

Figure 6.10
Save a new design template in this dialog box by choosing the Design Template file type.

2. In the Save As Type drop-down list, choose Design Template. The Save In drop-down list selects the folder in which you store design templates by default (usually `C:\Windows\Application Data\Microsoft\Templates`).

3. Enter a name for your design template in the File Name box.

4. Click the Save button.

The saved design template is available the next time you open the Apply Design Template dialog box.

CHOOSING A NEW SLIDE COLOR SCHEME

Each design template includes several *color schemes (p. 39)* from which you can choose. A color scheme is a set of eight coordinated colors that apply to the following parts of your slides:

- Background
- Text and lines
- Shadows
- Title text
- Fills
- Accent
- Accent and hyperlink
- Accent and followed hyperlink

For example, you may like a basic design template, but prefer to use different colors. Or you may want to use the same presentation for both onscreen and overhead delivery, but they require different color schemes.

APPLYING A COLOR SCHEME

To apply a new color scheme to your presentation, follow these steps:

1. Choose Format, Slide Color Scheme to open the Color Scheme dialog box, shown in Figure 6.11.

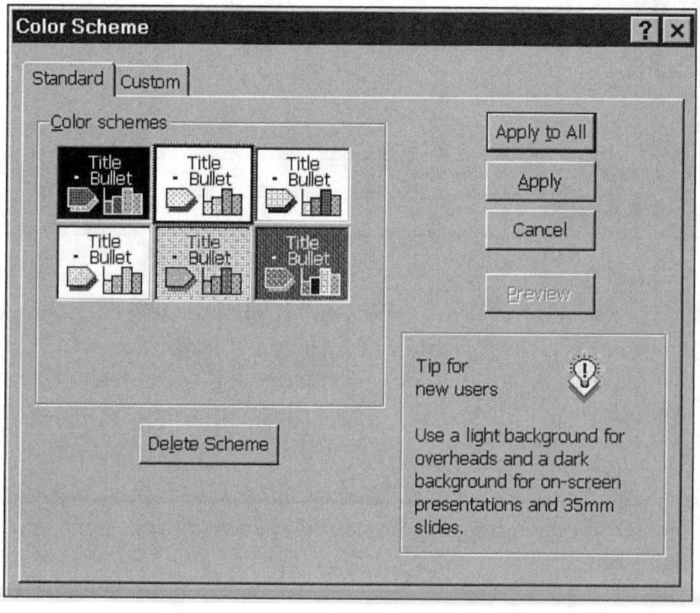

Figure 6.11
Use this dialog box to modify your presentation's color scheme.

2. In the Color Scheme group box, select the new color scheme that you want to apply. To preview what it will look like, click the Preview button.

Tip #77 from
Patrice-Anne Rutledge

You may have to move the Color Scheme dialog box by dragging it to preview your presentation.

3. Click Apply to apply the color scheme to the current slide.

Click Apply to All to apply the color scheme to the entire presentation.

→ For more information about color theory, **see** "Using Color," **p. 569**

CREATING A CUSTOM COLOR SCHEME

Occasionally you may want to customize the individual colors in a color scheme. For example, you may like a particular scheme, but want to modify only the background color. To do this, follow these steps from within the Color Scheme dialog box:

1. Click the Custom tab, displayed in Figure 6.12.

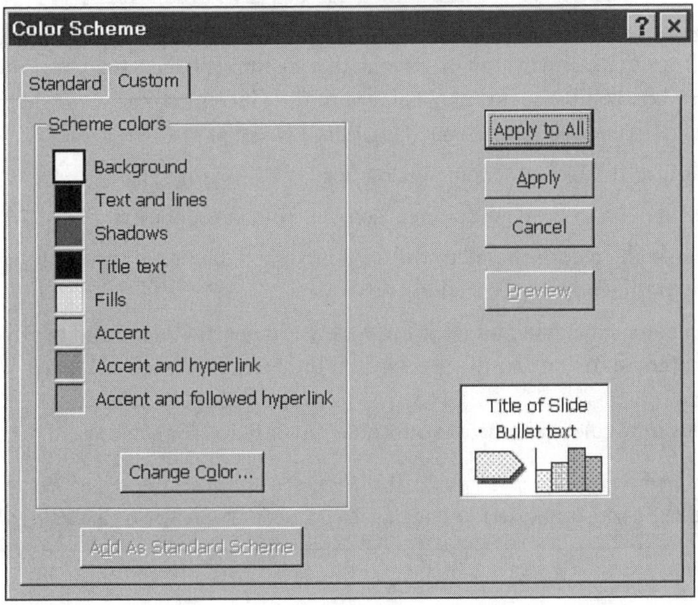

Figure 6.12
Change the color of certain areas of your presentation to customize it.

2. Choose the object whose color you want to change, such as the background or title text.

3. Click the Change Color button, which displays the Background Color dialog box. Figure 6.13 shows this dialog box.

PART

II

CH

6

Figure 6.13
Choose a standard
color or specify a
custom color.

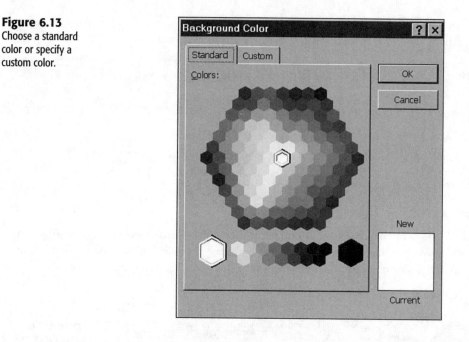

4. Choose a color from the Standard tab or formulate a custom color on the Custom tab.
   The New preview box compares this new color with the Current color.

→ For more details on color selection dialog boxes, **see** "Specifying Colors," **p. 274**

5. Click OK to return to the Color Scheme dialog box.

6. Click the Preview button to preview this new color in your presentation.

7. Click Apply to apply the color scheme to the current slide. Click Apply to All to apply
   the color scheme to the entire presentation.

8. Open the custom color tab again and click the Add As Standard Color Scheme if you
   want to add this scheme to your basic selections on the Standard tab (see Figure 6.14) .

You can now apply this new color scheme as you would any other color scheme.

Tip #78 from
Patrice-Anne Rutledge

To delete a color scheme, select it and click the Delete Scheme button on the Standard tab.

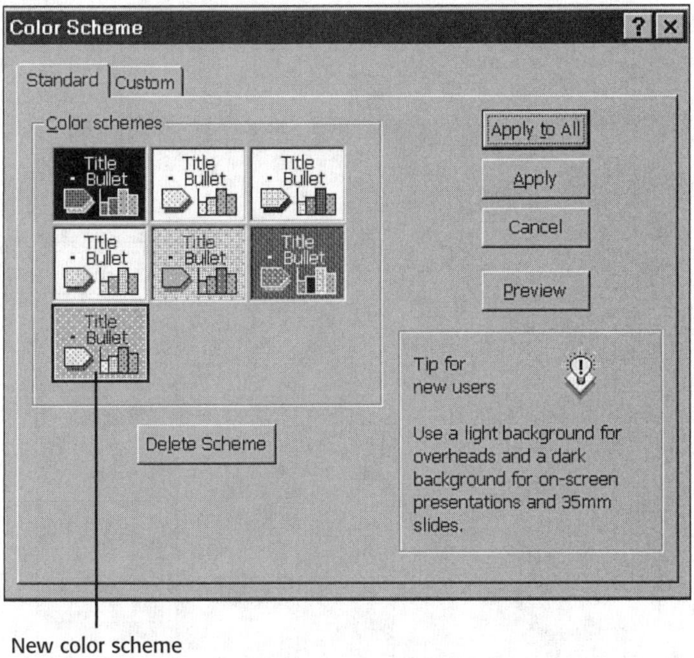

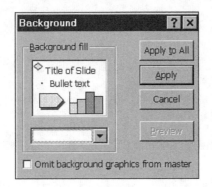

Figure 6.14
The color scheme you created is now a standard selection.

New color scheme

APPLYING A BACKGROUND

In addition to specific color backgrounds, you can also add special background effects such as shading, patterns, textures, and pictures. To apply a special background, choose Format, Background to open the Background dialog box, illustrated in Figure 6.15.

Figure 6.15
You can apply a special effects background to your presentation.

PART

II

CH

6

From the drop-down list in the Background Fill group box, choose one of the compatible colors under the Automatic color box.

Or click More Colors to open the Colors dialog box, in which you can select from many other colors or even specify your own custom color.

To apply a special background effect, choose Fill Effects from the drop-down list to open the Fill Effects dialog box, shown in Figure 6.16.

Figure 6.16
Choose from Gradient, Texture, Pattern, and Picture effects.

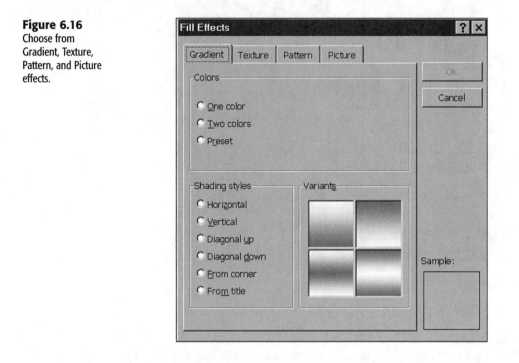

This dialog box includes four different tabs—Gradient, Texture, Pattern, and Picture—that guide you in selecting special effects backgrounds. After you select the fill effect you want, you can return to the Background dialog box where you can select Preview to see the effects before applying them, Apply to the current slide only, or Apply to All the slides in your presentation.

APPLYING A GRADIENT BACKGROUND

To apply a *gradient (p. 277)* (shading) effect, follow these steps:

1. Choose Format, Background to open the Background dialog box.

2. From the drop-down list in the Background Fill group box, choose Fill Effects to open the Fill Effects dialog box.

3. Select the Gradient tab (see Figure 6.17).

4. Choose one of the following Colors options:

    • *One color* Applies a gradient effect with just one color. You choose the base color from the Color 1 drop-down list and specify how dark or light to make the contrast.

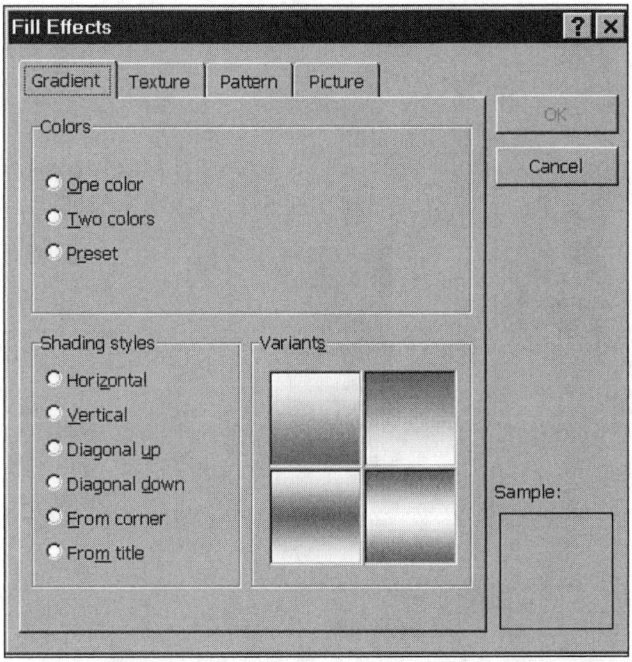

Figure 6.17
A gradient can add an interesting visual effect to your presentation.

- *Two colors*   Choose the two colors you want to use from the Color 1 and Color 2 drop-down lists.
- *Preset*   Displays a drop-down list of preset color combination options such as Daybreak, Peacock, or Rainbow.

5. Next, choose how to apply the gradient in the Shading Styles group box. Options include Horizontal, Vertical, Diagonal Up, Diagonal Down, From Corner, and From Title.

   The Variants and Sample boxes preview your selections.

6. Click OK to return to the Background dialog box.

7. In the Background dialog box, you can select Preview to see the effects before applying them, Apply to the current slide only, or Apply to All the slides in your presentation.

8. Click OK to close the dialog box.

APPLYING A TEXTURE BACKGROUND

To apply a *texture (p. 278)*:

1. Choose Format, Background to open the Background dialog box.

2. From the drop-down list in the Background Fill group box, choose Fill Effects to open the Fill Effects dialog box.

3. Select the Texture tab. Figure 6.18 shows this tab.

Figure 6.18
Textures can add
variety to a
presentation.

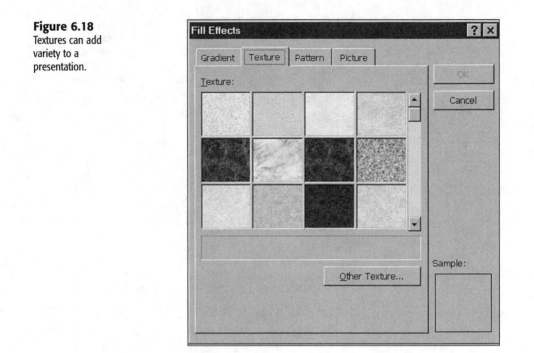

4. Scroll down the available textures until you find one you like. Select it and click OK to return to the Background dialog box.

5. In the Background dialog box, you can select Preview to see the effects before applying them, Apply to the current slide only, or Apply to All the slides in your presentation.

6. Click OK to close the dialog box.

If the existing textures don't suit your needs, you can use an external texture file such as a bitmap, Windows metafile, or other graphic image for which you installed an import filter. To choose an external texture graphic file that you have on your computer, click the Other Texture button on the Texture tab of the Fill Effects dialog box. The Select Texture dialog box, shown in Figure 6.19, opens.

Navigate to the image you want to use as a textured fill, select it, and click Insert. The fill is added to the Texture area of the dialog box, and you can use it as you would any of the existing fills.

APPLYING A PATTERN BACKGROUND

To apply a *pattern (p. 278)*, follow these steps:

1. Choose Format, Background to open the Background dialog box.

2. From the drop-down list in the Background Fill group box, choose Fill Effects to open the Fill Effects dialog box.

3. Select the Pattern tab on the Fill Effects dialog box (see Figure 6.20).

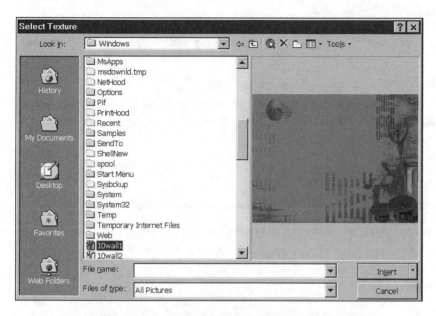

Figure 6.19
Choose an external texture image from this dialog box.

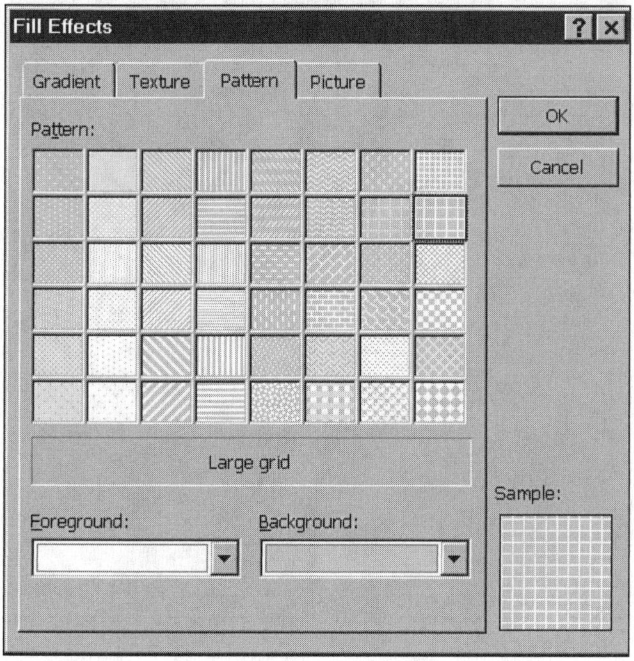

Figure 6.20
PowerPoint offers many different pattern effects.

PART

II

CH

6

4. Choose <u>F</u>oreground and <u>B</u>ackground colors and then select from the many available patterns.

> **Note**
>
> The default foreground and background colors coordinate with your existing color scheme.

5. Click OK to return to the Background dialog box.

6. In the Background dialog box, you can select Preview to see the effects before applying them, Apply to the current slide only, or Apply to All the slides in your presentation.

7. Click OK to close the dialog box.

Applying a Picture Background

To apply a picture to the background of your presentation, follow these steps:

1. Choose Format, Background to open the Background dialog box.

2. From the drop-down list in the Background Fill group box, choose Fill Effects to open the Fill Effects dialog box.

3. Select the Picture tab. (See Figure 6.21.)

Figure 6.21
Use your own image, such as a custom graphic or logo, as a background.

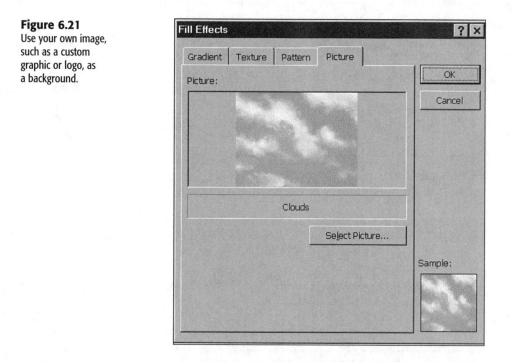

4. Click the Select Picture button to open the Select Picture dialog box, shown in Figure 6.22.

5. Select the folder that contains the picture you want from the Look in drop-down list.

6. Select the graphic image you want to use and click Insert to return to the Fill Effects dialog box.

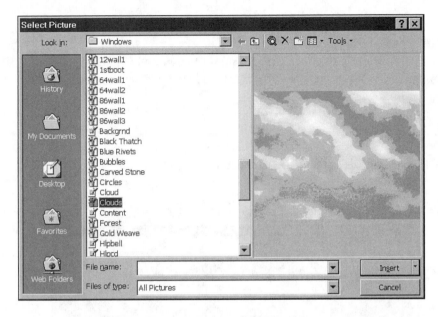

Figure 6.22
Choose a picture of
your own to apply
as a background.

Tip #79 from
Patrice-Anne Rutledge

To preview the picture on the right side of the dialog box, click the down arrow next to the
Views button and choose Pre<u>v</u>iew.

---

7. Click OK to return to the Background dialog box.

8. In the Background dialog box, you can select <u>P</u>review to see the effects before applying
   them, <u>A</u>pply to the current slide only, or Apply <u>t</u>o All the slides in your presentation.

9. Click OK to close the dialog box.

Caution

Although selecting a picture or graphic file of your own can definitely personalize and customize your presentation, be sure that it works as an effective background. Some images
are simply too confusing or "busy" to use as a slide background.

TROUBLESHOOTING

Comments display in my slide show.

If you don't want to delete your comments, you can hide them so they don't appear in a
show. To do so, click the Show/Hide Comments button on the Reviewing toolbar.

I thought I copied slides from one presentation to another, but now they've disappeared from my original presentation.

Be sure to use Ctrl+C (copy) rather than Ctrl+X (cut) if you want to keep the original slides in place. Moving slides removes them from their original location; copying just creates duplicates.

Design Corner

You can modify an existing design template to create a new one.

Before

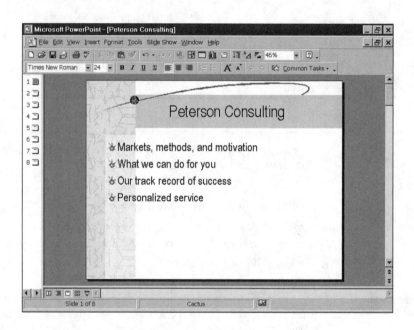

AFTER

Font changes

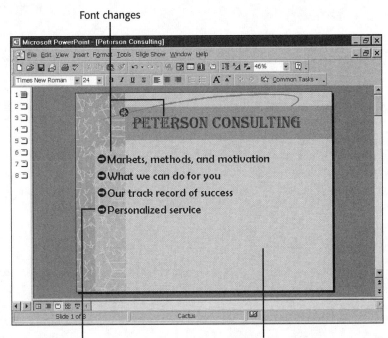

New bullet styles   Color scheme modification

MAKING PRESENTATIONS

PRESENTING A SLIDE SHOW

In this chapter   *by Patrice-Anne Rutledge*

PLANNING A SHOW

After you create all the slides you want to include in your presentation, you'll want to plan how you're going to present them in a slide show. Fortunately, PowerPoint makes it easy to set up and rehearse your presentation, as well as to configure it to work with a projector.

You can deliver a PowerPoint presentation in three different ways. You can

- *Present it live with a speaker*   This is the most common method of delivering a PowerPoint presentation, in front of an audience.
- *Browse it individually through the PowerPoint browser*   This option enables someone to view your presentation at any convenient time.
- *Browse it at a kiosk*   This method enables you to create a self-running presentation such as you would use at a tradeshow booth.

SETTING UP A SHOW

Before you deliver a PowerPoint presentation, you should think through its entire visual flow. This is the time to rehearse in your mind what you want to present and how you want to present it, as well as to plan for the technical aspects of your presentation.

→ To learn more about how to prepare yourself to present, **see** "The Mechanics of Function—Developing Internal Presentation Skills," **p. 623**

→ To learn about staging, projectors, overheads, and using laptops, **see** "Techniques and Technicalities," **p. 645**

After you've mentally rehearsed your presentation, you can start to set it up within PowerPoint. To do this, follow these steps:

1. Choose Slide Show, Set Up Show to open the Set Up Show dialog box (shown in Figure 7.1).

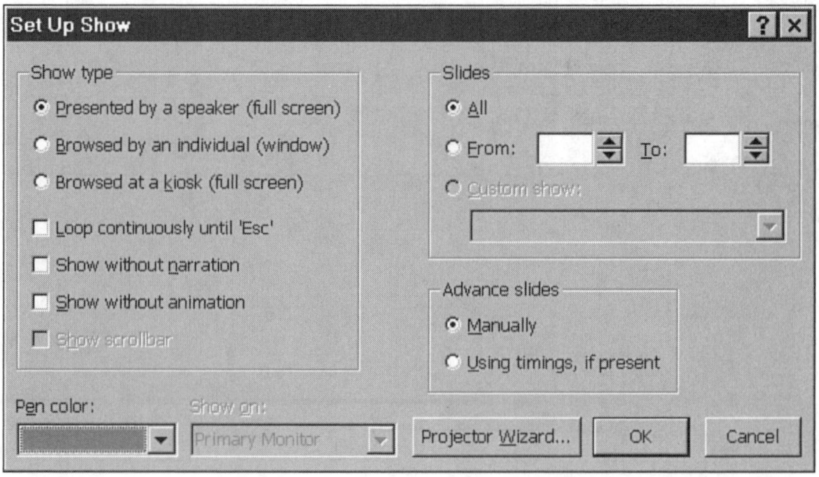

Figure 7.1
Specify the type of presentation you want to make in this dialog box.

2. Select a Show Type. Options include a show

- *Presented by a Speaker (Full Screen)*   This is the default viewing option for slide shows that you present full screen (using your computer, for example). Figure 7.2 shows this view.

Figure 7.2
Having a speaker present a slide show is the most common way to deliver a presentation.

- *Browsed by an Individual (Window)*   This option enables an individual to control and view the presentation in PowerPoint's browser. (See Figure 7.3.)

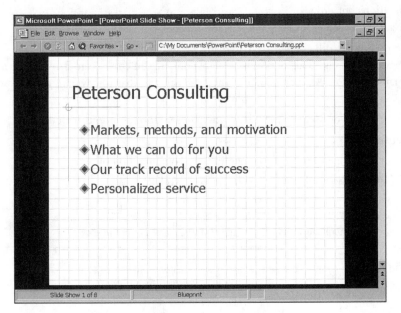

Figure 7.3
Choosing the Browsed by an Individual option enables users to view your presentation on demand.

- *Browsed at a Kiosk (Full Screen)* This option enables you to create a self-running show that displays without user or presenter intervention. Its appearance is full screen, similar to a presentation presented by a speaker, but it runs without any human intervention. This show type automatically loops continuously.

Note

A tradeshow demonstration is one example of when you might want to set up your show to be browsed at a kiosk. Using automatic timings and continuous looping, you can continually display the same show over and over for new viewers. You can add a voice narration if you want, but be sure that your show plays in a location where the narration will be audible.

⚡ ***Your presentation won't browse at a kiosk?*** *See the Troubleshooting section at the end of the chapter.*

→ If you want to learn how to use the Slide Transition dialog box, **see** "Setting Slide Transitions," **p. 319**

→ To learn about the advantages of rehearsing timings, **see** "Rehearsing Timings," **p. 152**

3. Check the <u>L</u>oop Continuously Until 'Esc' check box if you want your presentation to play over and over again until you press the Esc key. This check box is available only if you select the Presented by a Speaker or Browsed by an Individual options. A presentation loops continuously by default if browsed at a kiosk.

4. Check the Show Without <u>N</u>arration check box to temporarily deactivate any accompanying narrations. For example, if you are presenting at a show, narrations may be either inaudible or distracting.

→ For more details about creating narrations, **see** "Recording a Voice Narration," **p. 150**

5. Check the <u>S</u>how Without Animation check box to temporarily deactivate any accompanying slide animations. For example, you may want to include animations to use in some situations but not all.

→ If you want to add animation to your presentation, **see** "Working with Animation," **p. 317**

6. Check the S<u>h</u>ow Scrollbar check box to display a scrollbar on the right side of the browser when viewing. This option is available only if you choose the Browsed by an Individual show type. An individual can then use the scrollbar to navigate your presentation.

7. Specify the slides you want to include in your presentation. Options include
   - <u>A</u>ll slides
   - A certain range of slides, indicated in the <u>F</u>rom and <u>T</u>o boxes
   - A <u>C</u>ustom Show selected from the drop-down list

Note

The <u>C</u>ustom Show field is active only if you've created a custom show.

→ To learn how to create a custom show, **see** "Working with Custom Shows," **p. 153**

8. You can choose to advance slides either <u>M</u>anually or <u>U</u>sing Timings, If Present. To advance the slide manually, you need to press a key or click the mouse.

> **Caution**
>
> You can't advance slides manually if it is to be browsed at a kiosk because this type of show is self-running.

> **Note**
>
> Choosing <u>M</u>anually in this field overrides any timings you previously set.

→ For more information about slide transitions, **see** "Setting Slide Transitions," **p. 319**

→ To learn more about timings, **see** "Rehearsing Timings," **p. 152**

9. If you choose to present by a speaker, you can choose a P<u>e</u>n Color to use if you're going to utilize the pen function when presenting.

From the Show <u>O</u>n drop-down list, you can choose the monitor on which to display the commentary you write with the pen if there is a second monitor.

> **Note**
>
> You can only use two monitors if you are running Windows 98 or Windows NT 5.0 and have installed dual-monitor hardware. This feature enables you to display a full-screen presentation on one monitor for your audience, while you see your presentation with accompanying notes on a second monitor.

→ To learn how to preview and present your show, **see** "Previewing Your Show," **p. 159**

10. Click OK to close the dialog box.

USING THE PROJECTOR WIZARD

If you want to automate the connection of your laptop computer with an external projector, you can use the Projector Wizard. To do this, simply click the Projector <u>W</u>izard button on the Set Up Show dialog box. The Projector Wizard then displays, as shown in Figure 7.4.

First, turn off the projector; next, connect it to the computer, turn it on again, and wait for the computer to try to automatically detect your projector. If this doesn't work, the Projector Wizard provides alternative steps and advice for choosing and configuring your computer/projector combination. Follow the steps and guidance of the wizard until you complete the projector setup.

> **Note**
>
> Because there are many possible configurations of projectors and monitors, you should consult system hardware and projector manuals before trying this. You can blow a monitor if your drivers are not set up correctly.

PART

III

CH

7

Figure 7.4
The Projector Wizard automates projector configuration.

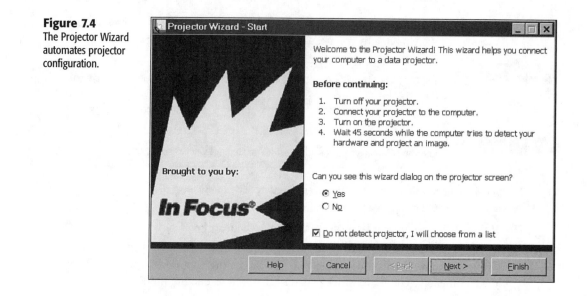

RECORDING A VOICE NARRATION

A voice narration is useful for many reasons. You can record your own voice-over to accompany

- A Web-based presentation.

- An on-demand presentation that people can listen to at any time.

- An automated presentation, such as one you run continuously at a tradeshow booth.

- A presentation delivered by a speaker that includes special recorded commentary by a particular individual. A human resources representative delivering an employee orientation that includes a voice narration from the CEO would be an example of this.

Before recording your narration, you should create a script and rehearse it several times until it flows smoothly and matches your presentation.

Caution

You need to have a microphone and a sound card to record a narration.

Tip #80 from
Patrice-Anne Rutledge

In addition to pre-recording a narration, you can record while you're presenting to have a record of the live presentation. To do so, choose Slide Show, Voice Narration and click OK to start running the slide show while recording.

⚡ **You can't hear your other sound files after recording a voice narration?** *See the Troubleshooting section at the end of this chapter.*

To record a voice narration, follow these steps:

1. Choose Slide Show, Record Narration to open the Record Narration dialog box, shown in Figure 7.5.

Figure 7.5
Add voice narrations to your slideshows.

2. Before you record your narration, you can verify that your microphone is set up properly. To do this, click the Set Microphone Level button. The Microphone Check dialog box appears (see Figure 7.6).

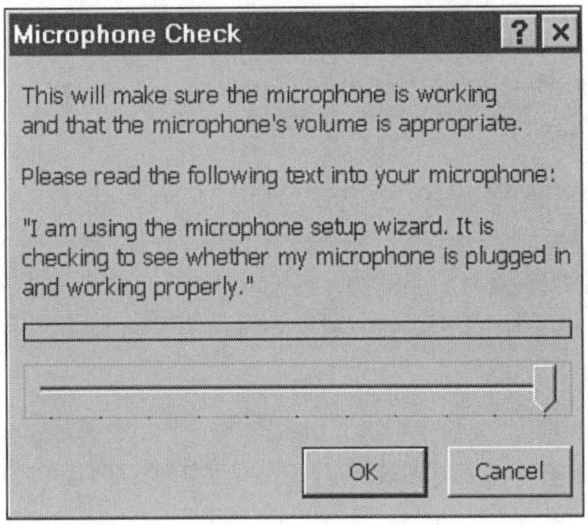

Figure 7.6
Set your microphone level to record properly.

3. Read the sentence that displays into the microphone, and the microphone wizard automatically adjusts your microphone level. Click OK to return to the main dialog box.

Note

To change the sound quality to CD, radio, or telephone quality, click the Change Quality button to open the Sound Selection dialog box. The better the sound quality, however, the larger the file size.

4. To store the narration as a separate file, click the <u>L</u>ink Narrations In check box. Your narration will be stored in a separate .WAV file in the same folder as your presentation.

Tip #81 from *Patrice-Anne Rutledge*	If you want to store your narration in another folder, click the <u>B</u>rowse button and choose the appropriate folder in the dialog box that appears.

5. If you want to embed the narration in the presentation, be sure the <u>L</u>ink Narrations In check box is cleared.

6. Click OK to start recording. PowerPoint displays your presentation in Slide Show View.

7. Continue narrating as the slide show displays.

8. When you reach the end of the presentation, a dialog box asks you if you want to save the timings with each slide. If you do, click <u>Y</u>es.

The presentation displays in Slide Sorter View, with the slide timings appearing below each slide if you chose to save them with the presentation.

Tip #82 from *Patrice-Anne Rutledge*	To delete the narration from a slide while in Normal view or Slide view, select the sound icon that displays in the lower right corner and press the Delete key. You need to repeat this for each slide that has a corresponding narration.

REHEARSING TIMINGS

PowerPoint enables you to set both fixed slide transition timings, as well as to rehearse the time it takes to deliver your presentation. After you rehearse a presentation, you can save those timings to deliver automatically.

You may not always want to automatically move from slide to slide, however. For example, it can sometimes take you more or less time to discuss a slide in person, or an audience member may interrupt your presentation with a question. Even if you don't want to automate your slide transitions, rehearsing timings can be useful because it helps you adjust your presentation to fit into an allotted time.

To rehearse timings, choose Sli<u>d</u>e Show, <u>R</u>ehearse Timings. The presentation displays in Slide Show View, opening a Rehearsal toolbar in the upper-left corner, shown in Figure 7.7.

Begin talking through your presentation, clicking the Next button in the toolbar to advance to the next slide. If you need to stop temporarily, click the Pause button. If you make a mistake and want to start over, click the Repeat button.

The elapsed time of the current slide displays in the white Slide Time box in the center of the toolbar. You can also enter a time in this box manually. The time field on the right side of the toolbar shows you the elapsed time of the entire presentation.

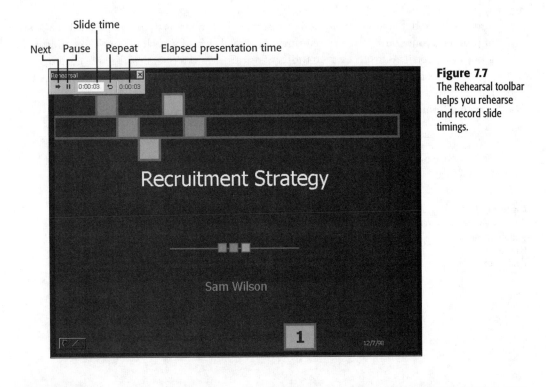

Next   Pause   Slide time   Repeat   Elapsed presentation time

Figure 7.7
The Rehearsal toolbar helps you rehearse and record slide timings.

> **Note**
>
> You can enter timings manually in the Slide Transition dialog box as well.

→ To learn more about slide transitions, **see** "Setting Slide Transitions," **p. 319**

After you rehearse the last slide, PowerPoint displays a dialog box that asks if you want to save the timings. If you click Yes, the presentation opens in Slide Sorter View with the timings displayed under each slide.

Tip #83 from
Patrice-Anne Rutledge

> If you record and save timings but don't want to use them to automatically, advance your presentation, you can select the Advance Slides, <u>M</u>anually option for advancing slides in the Set Up Show dialog box.

→ To help you set up your show, **see** "Planning a Show," **p. 146**

WORKING WITH CUSTOM SHOWS

Custom shows enable you to create customized PowerPoint presentations designed for different audiences or purposes without having to create multiple, nearly identical presentations.

For example, you may want to create a sales presentation that you can use with three different types of prospective clients. Let's say the first seven slides of your show cover information about your company and its history, which remains the same for all three types of prospects. But you've also created three individual slides for each of your three prospect groups that detail your successes in those industries. You can then design three custom shows, each of which includes the seven main slides, plus the three specific slides that pertain only to that prospect type. This helps save you time and effort when you need to update information in the seven main slides; this way, you need only do it once.

To create a custom show, follow these steps:

1. Choose Slide Show, Custom Shows to open the Custom Shows dialog box, shown in Figure 7.8.

Figure 7.8
Customizing your slideshows saves time and reduces duplication.

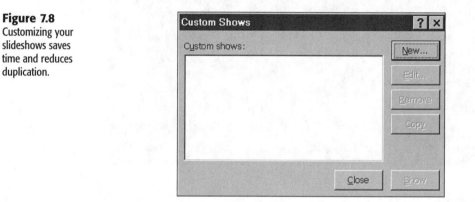

2. Click the New button to open the Define Custom Show dialog box, shown in Figure 7.9.

Figure 7.9
Add a new custom show in this dialog box.

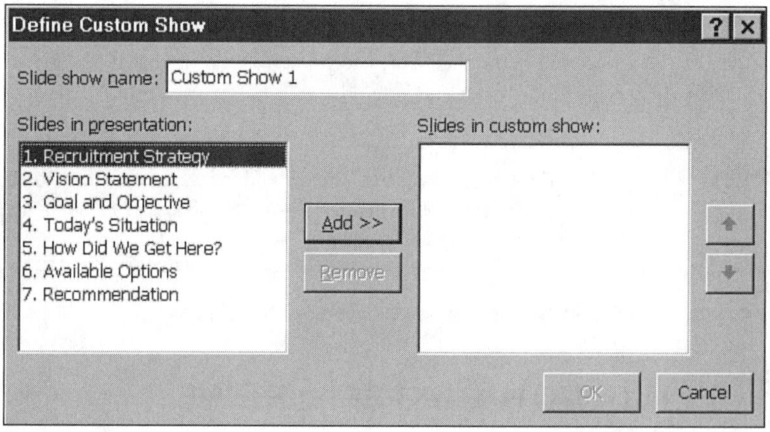

3. Enter a Slide Show Name for this custom show by replacing the default name.

4. From the Slides in Presentation list, choose the first slide you want to include in your custom show.

5. Click the Add button to copy this slide to the Slides in Custom Show list.

6. Repeat steps 4 and 5 until you've copied all the required slides to this list.

Tip #84 from
Patrice-Anne Rutledge

To remove a slide from the Slides in Custom Show list, select it and click the Remove button.

Tip #85 from
Patrice-Anne Rutledge

Use the up and down button on the right side of the dialog box to rearrange slides you highlighted.

7. Click OK to save the custom show and return to the Custom Shows dialog box.

8. From this dialog box you can now Edit, Remove, or Copy any selected custom show. Copying is useful if you want to create several similar versions of a custom show and don't want to repeat the same steps over and over.

9. To preview what the show will look like, click the Show button. The show previews in Slide Show View.

10. Click the Close button to close the Custom Shows dialog box.

To play a custom show, select it from the Custom Show drop-down list in the Set Up Show dialog box. Then either press the F5 key or select Slide Show, View Show menu command.

→ To select a presentation to play a custom show, **see** "Planning a Show," **p. 146**

INSERTING SLIDES FROM OTHER PRESENTATIONS

As an alternative to creating a custom show, you can also insert slides from another presentation. This helps save time and redundancy as well.

Note

A major difference between custom shows and inserting slides is that inserting makes a copy of the slide and, if you change the original, the copy isn't affected. Custom shows "link" to the slides, so they are stored only once.

1. Choose Insert, Slides from Files to open the Slide Finder dialog box, shown in Figure 7.10.

2. From the Find Presentation tab, click the Browse button to open the Browse dialog box (see Figure 7.11).

Tip #86 from
Patrice-Anne Rutledge

You can also enter the filename and path directly in the File edit box.

PART

III

CH

7

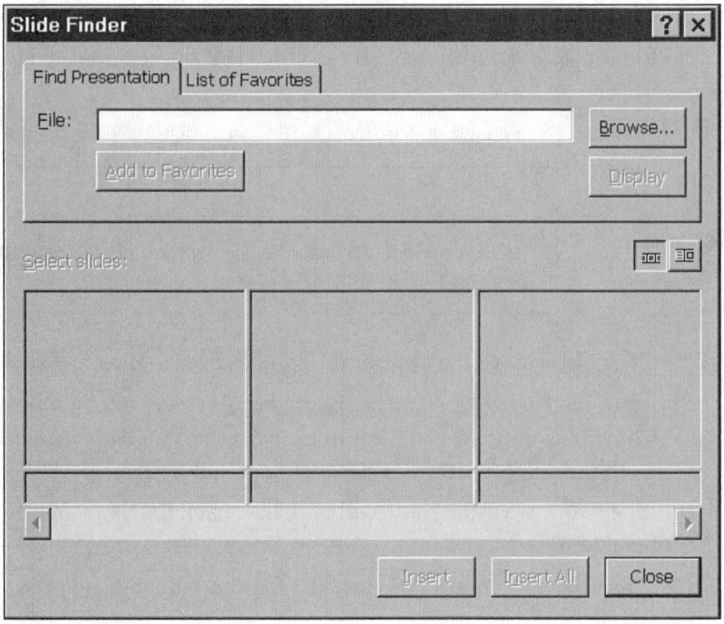

Figure 7.10
The Slide Finder helps you add slides from other presentations.

Figure 7.11
Browse to find your source presentation.

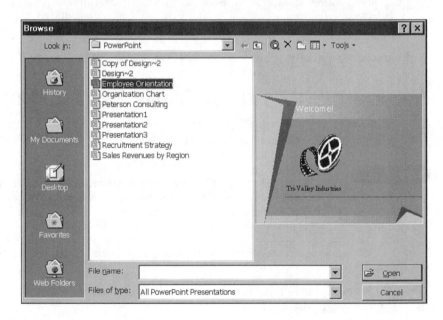

3. Click the <u>D</u>isplay button to display the presentation in the lower portion of the dialog box, as shown in Figure 7.12.

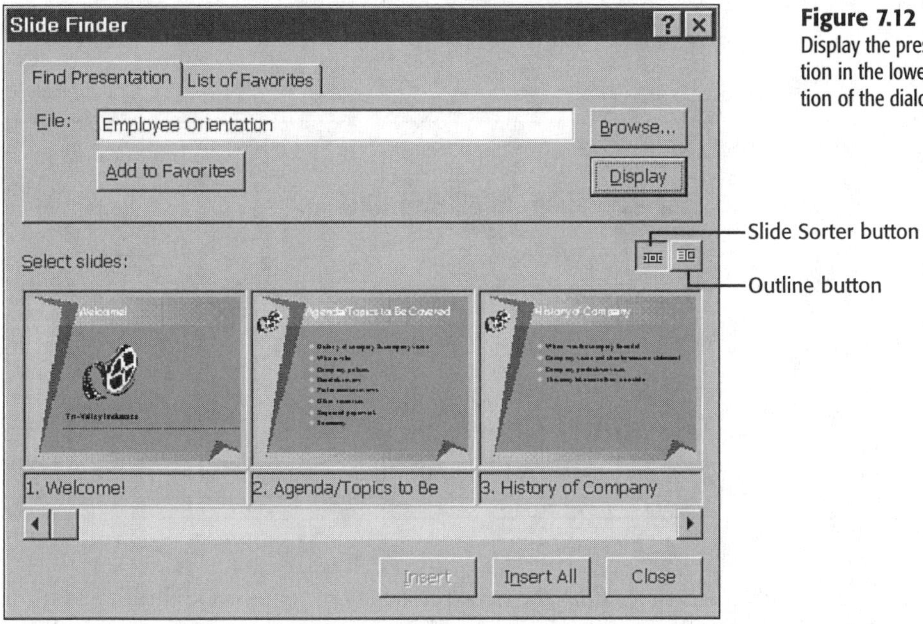

Figure 7.12
Display the presentation in the lower portion of the dialog box.

4. To display all the slides in a view similar to Slide Sorter View, click the Slide Sorter button to the far right of the <u>S</u>elect Slides part of the dialog box. Use the scrollbar at the bottom of the dialog box to navigate and select slides.

5. To display an outline list of all slides on the left side and the slide itself on the right, as shown in Figure 7.13, click the Outline button to the far right of the <u>S</u>elect Slides part of the dialog box.

6. Select the slide you want to insert and click <u>I</u>nsert.

7. Continue selecting and inserting slides until you finish. The slides are inserted in the order you selected them, following the active slide in the current presentation.

Tip #87 from
Patrice-Anne Rutledge

Click the <u>I</u>nsert All button to insert all slides in the current presentation.

8. Click the Close button to exit the dialog box.

Note

The inserted slides take on the design template of the presentation in which they are inserted, not the template of their source presentation.

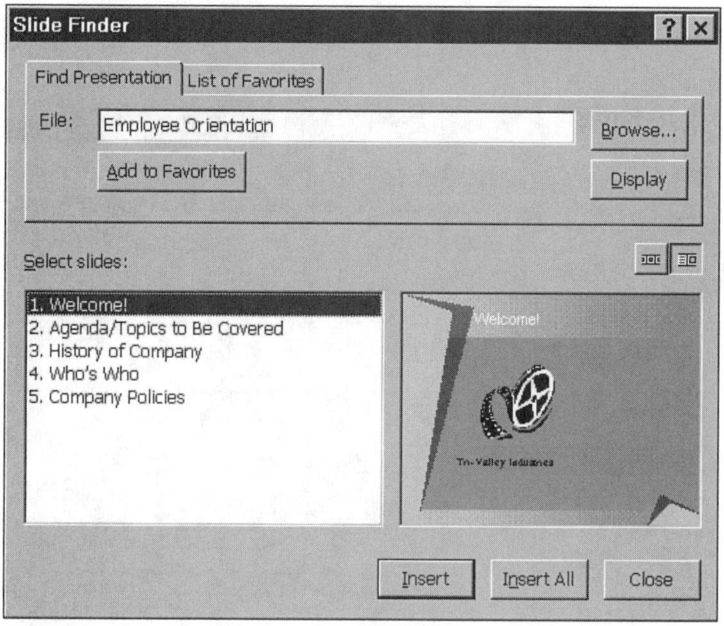

Figure 7.13
Use an outline to find the slide you want to insert.

If you frequently insert slides from the same presentation, you can add them to a favorites list. Click the Add to Favorites button to do so. The next time you want to insert slides from this presentation, you can go to the List of Favorites tab in the Slide Finder dialog box (see Figure 7.14) to easily locate them.

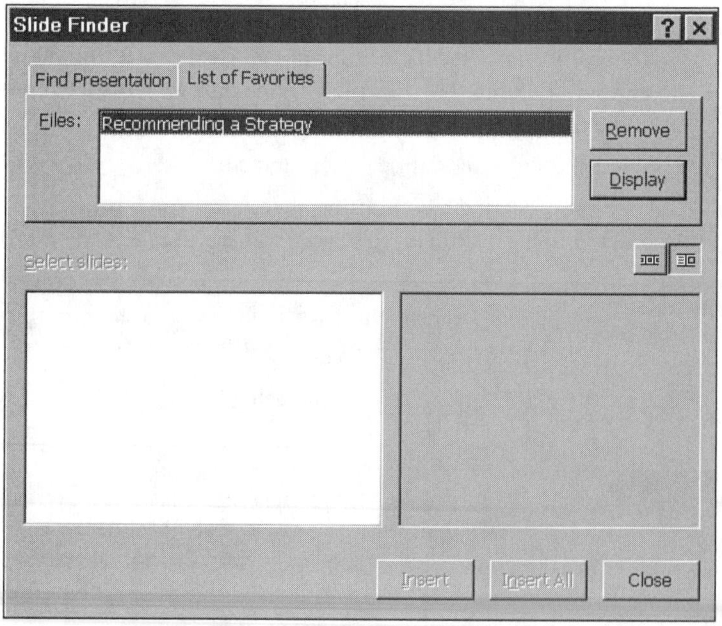

Figure 7.14
Using the List of Favorites tab makes it easier to find commonly used slides.

Note

In addition to inserting slides, you can also hide them. To hide a selected slide or slides, choose Slide Show, Hide Slide. This doesn't delete the slide; it simply prevents it from displaying in the show.

PREVIEWING YOUR SHOW

After you plan and set up your PowerPoint presentation, you should preview it. To do this, select Slide Show, View Show, or press F5. Figure 7.15 illustrates a sample slide show preview.

Figure 7.15
Preview your show to see what it will look like.

PowerPoint previews a show using the settings you enter in the Set Up Show dialog box. For example, you can preview in a browser or full screen, depending on what you entered in this dialog box. Whether you need to advance each slide manually also depends on your choices in this dialog box. How you navigate the presentation also depends on how you view it:

- *Full screen* You'll preview full screen if you choose the Presented by a Speaker or the Browsed at a Kiosk option in the Set Up Show dialog box. The major difference between the two is that, when you present by a speaker, you have numerous navigation options available, because a person is in control of the presentation. When you browse at a kiosk, these navigation options aren't available, because this type of show is self-running.

PART

III

CH

7

Tip #88 from
Patrici-Anne Rutledge

If you set up your show to be browsed by an individual, you can view the presentation full screen by choosing Browse, Full Screen.

- *PowerPoint Browser* You'll preview in the PowerPoint browser if you chose Browsed by an Individual in the Set Up Show dialog box. This browser is similar to other browsers such as Internet Explorer or Netscape Navigator. You can use the scrollbar to scroll through the presentation if it's available, or you can use the Page Up or Page Down keys to navigate manually.

Tip #89 from
Patrici-Anne Rutledge

Specify whether to display a scrollbar in the Set Up Show dialog box.

→ For more information about the Set Up Show dialog box, **see** "Setting Up a Show," **p. 146**

Tip #90 from
Patrici-Anne Rutledge

To preview the show starting with the current slide, click the Slide Show button in the lower-left corner of the window.

NAVIGATING A SHOW FULL SCREEN

If you chose to present your PowerPoint slide show by a speaker, you'll display your presentation full screen. In this slide show type, you have several ways to advance each slide manually if you chose this method of advancing slides rather than by automatic timing.

You can left-click the mouse, press the spacebar, press the letter N, press the right arrow, press the down arrow, press the Page Down key, or press the Enter key. Table 7.1 lists other ways to navigate a slide show.

TABLE 7.1   SLIDE SHOW ACTIONS

Slide Show Action	Method
Advance to next slide	Left-click the mouse Press the spacebar Press the letter N Press the right-arrow key Press the down-arrow key Press the Enter key Press the Page Down key
Return to previous slide	Press the Backspace key Press the letter P Press the left-arrow key Press the up-arrow key Press the Page Up key
Go to a specific slide	Enter the number of the slide and press the Enter key

Slide Show Action	Method
Black/unblack the screen (toggle)	Press the letter B Press the period key
White/unwhite the screen (toggle)	Press the letter W Press the comma (,)
Display/hide the arrow (toggle)	Press the letter A Press the equal sign (=)
Stop/restart the show (toggle)	Press the letter S Press the plus sign (+)
End the show	Press the Esc key Press Ctrl+Break Press the minus (–) key
Erase screen drawing	Press the letter E
Advance to hidden slide	Press the letter H
Rehearse using new timing	Press the letter T
Rehearse using original timing	Press the letter O
Return to the show's beginning	Press both mouse keys
Activate the pen	Press Ctrl+P
Activate the arrow pointer	Press Ctrl+A
Hide pointer/button	Press Ctrl+H
Automatically show/hide pointer	Press Ctrl+U

Tip #91 from
Patrice-Anne Rutledge

Right-click and choose <u>H</u>elp from the menu to display this list of shortcuts within your presentation.

Note

The capability to toggle a black or white screen is a useful tool. For example, if you want to explain a detailed concept and want your audience to focus on what you're saying and not on the slide, you can temporarily make the screen either black or white. This is also useful during breaks for long presentations.

You have other ways to navigate a PowerPoint show. Right-click the mouse and from the <u>G</u>o menu you can choose any of the following navigational options:

■ *Slide <u>N</u>avigator*   Displays the Slide Navigator dialog box (see Figure 7.16), in which you can choose the <u>S</u>how and the <u>S</u>lide title you want to view. Simply select the slide you want and click the <u>G</u>o To button.

PART

III

CH

7

Note

The Show field is available only in presentations that include custom shows and enables you to choose the custom show that contains the slides you want to view.

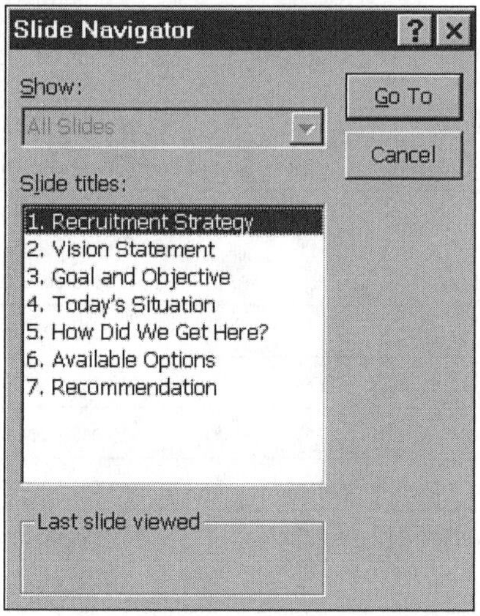

Figure 7.16
The Slide Navigator dialog box helps you find slides.

- *By Title*   Displays a menu listing all slides in your presentation. Click the one you want to view.

- *Custom Show*   Displays a menu listing available custom shows. Click the one you want to view.

- *Previously Viewed*   Displays the previously viewed slide again.

Tip #92 from
Patrice-Anne Rutledge

Although these options are useful for finding a specific slide you want to display, you'll probably want to avoid using them during an actual presentation because a break in your flow can be distracting. One case in which you may want to use these features during a presentation would be when you have to go back to previous slides to answer questions or clarify a point and don't want to page through numerous slides to do so.

SETTING POINTER OPTIONS

You can use an arrow pointer during a PowerPoint presentation, write with a pen, or hide all pointers. To choose these options, right-click the mouse, choose Pointer Options, and select Arrow, Pen, or Hidden from the menu that displays.

Figure 7.17 shows an arrow pointer. This is the standard type of pointer you're probably very familiar with.

Figure 7.17
Use a pointer during your slide presentation.

Pointer

If you choose the pen option, you can make notes on your presentation as you deliver it. Figure 7.18 illustrates sample comments written with the pen.

Figure 7.18
Use a pen to add comments or illustrations to the presentation.

Pen

PART
III

CH
7

You can choose your pen color in the Set Up Show dialog box, or you can set it by right-clicking the mouse, choosing Pointer Options, and selecting a color from the list that displays.

➔ To set up the pen color, **see** "Setting Up a Show," **p. 146**

Tip #93 from *Patrice-Anne Rutledge*

To erase your pen markings, right-click the mouse and choose Screen, Erase Pen, or press the letter E. Annotations are also erased when you advance to the next slide.

USING THE MEETING MINDER

With the *Meeting Minder (p. 175)*, you can take meeting minutes, assign action items, and export these to Outlook and Word. To use the Meeting Minder, right-click the mouse and choose Meeting Minder. Figure 7.19 illustrates the Meeting Minder dialog box.

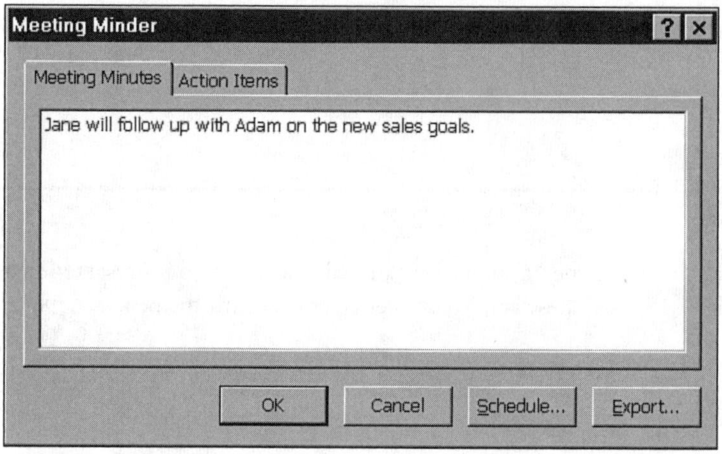

Figure 7.19
The Meeting Minder enables you to keep track of what happens during a meeting.

In the Meeting Minutes tab, you can enter detailed minutes from your presentation.

In the Action Items tab (see Figure 7.20), you can enter multiple action items for specific people.

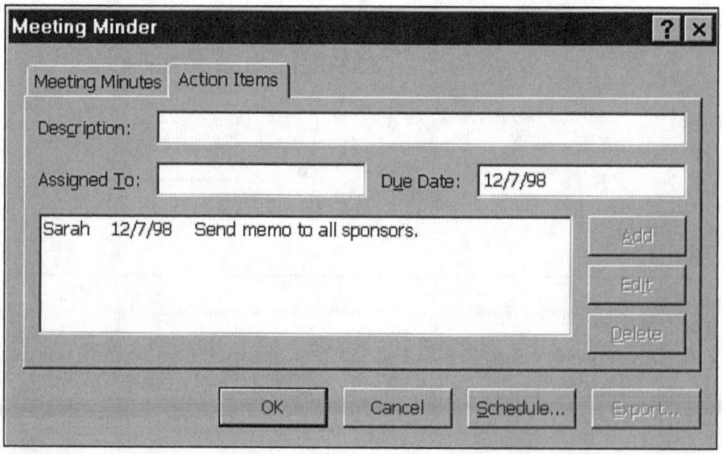

Figure 7.20
Record action items in the Action Items tab.

To add an item, enter its Description, the name of the person to whom it's assigned, and a Due Date. Then click the Add button to add this item to action item list below.

Tip #94 from
Patrice-Anne Rutledge

You can also Edit and Delete selected action items by clicking these buttons.

To export the meeting minutes and action items to Outlook or Word, click the Export button. Figure 7.21 shows the Meeting Minder Export dialog box, which displays.

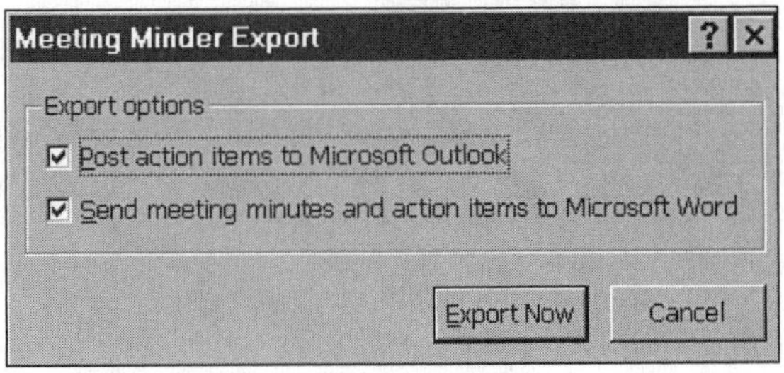

Figure 7.21
Export meeting minutes to Word or Outlook.

You can

- Post Action Items to Microsoft Outlook
- Send Meeting Minutes and Action Items to Microsoft Word

Choose either one or both options and click the Export Now button. Figure 7.22 shows a sample export to Microsoft Word.

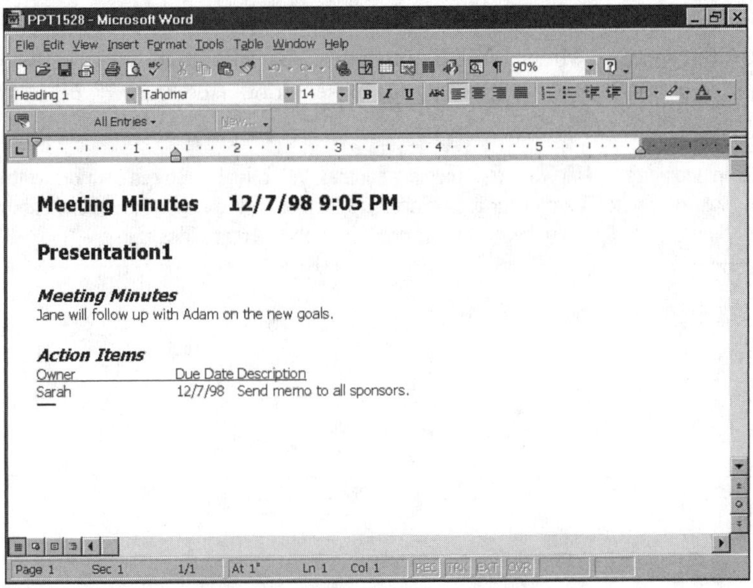

Figure 7.22
When in Word, you can format meeting minutes.

You can't see the Post Action Items to Microsoft Outlook option? See the *Troubleshooting section at the end of the chapter.*

Click the Schedule button to open Outlook 2000 and display an appointment (see Figure 7.23).

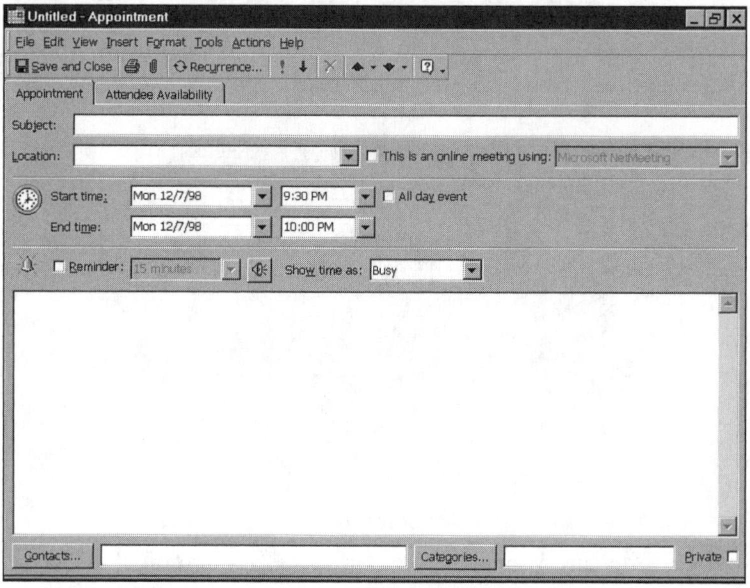

Figure 7.23
You can post action items in Outlook 2000.

Note

If you haven't installed Microsoft Outlook, the Outlook 2000 Startup dialog box appears.

Click OK to exit the Meeting Minder. You'll notice that PowerPoint adds a slide that contains your recorded action items to the end of this presentation (see Figure 7.24).

Note

In addition to taking your own meeting minutes, you can also refer to your prewritten speaker's notes during your presentation. To do this, right-click the mouse and choose Speaker's Notes from the menu. The notes from the current slide display.

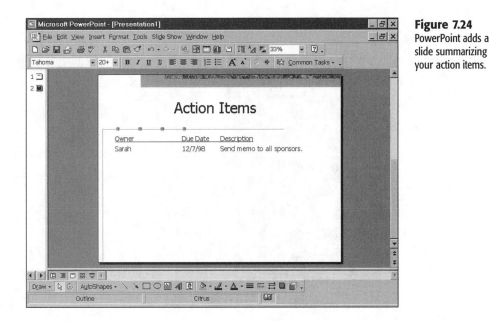

Figure 7.24
PowerPoint adds a slide summarizing your action items.

USING THE PACK AND GO WIZARD

The Pack and Go Wizard enables you to package your presentation for delivery on another computer. You can also simply copy your presentation to a disk or move it to a network location and then present it on another computer (if you're sure that the other computer has the same version of PowerPoint and the same fonts as your original computer). But if you're not sure, the Pack and Go Wizard can verify that you have everything you need.

1. Choose File, Pack and Go to open the Pack and Go Wizard, shown in Figure 7.25.

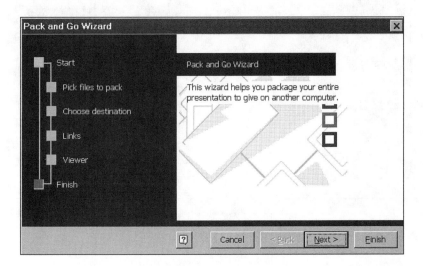

Figure 7.25
With the Pack and Go Wizard, you can deliver your presentation on another computer.

PART

III

CH

7

2. Click the <u>N</u>ext button to continue to the next step of the wizard (see Figure 7.26).

Figure 7.26
You can package the active presentation or choose another.

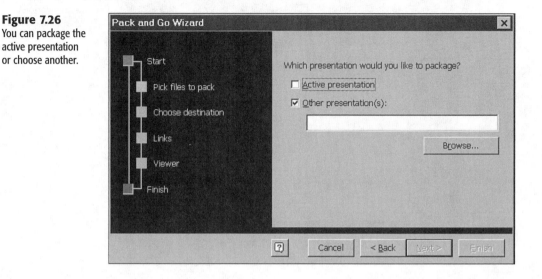

3. Specify whether you want to package the <u>A</u>ctive Presentation or another presentation.

4. If you select <u>O</u>ther Presentation(s), you can enter its name in the edit box or click the B<u>r</u>owse button to locate it in the Select a Presentation to Package dialog box (see Figure 7.27).

Figure 7.27
Choose the presentation you want to package in this dialog box.

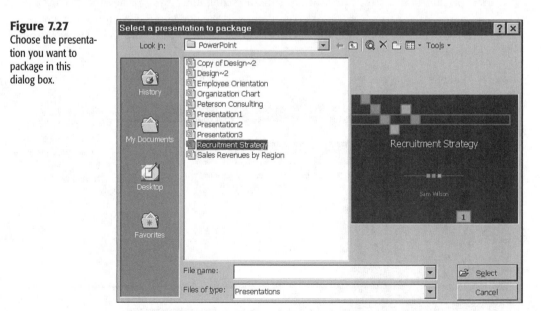

5. If you use the Select a Presentation to Package dialog box to locate your presentation, choose it and click the Select button to return to the wizard. The path name you selected displays in the edit box.

6. Click Next to continue to the next step, shown in Figure 7.28.

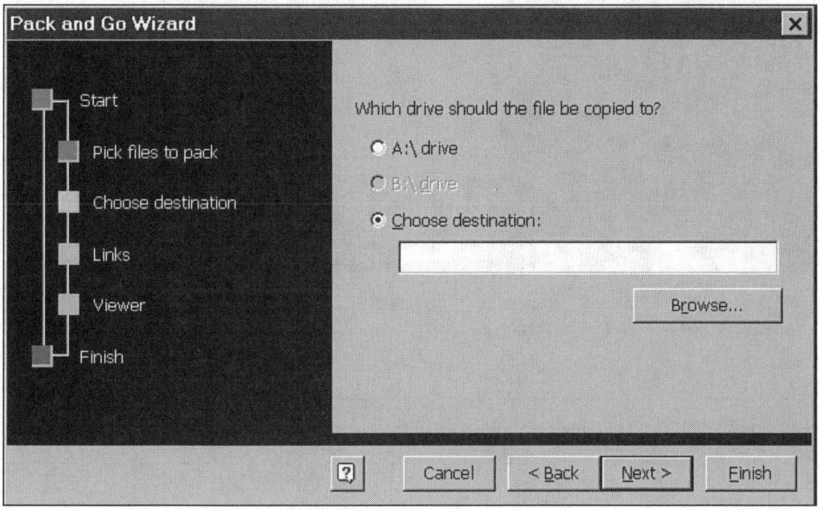

Figure 7.28
Save the file to any drive you specify.

7. Specify where to save the packaged presentation. Options include drive A:, drive B:, or another drive.

Caution

The Pack and Go Wizard compresses numerous additional files with your presentation. If the final presentation package is too large for a single disk, you'll receive a message prompting you to insert additional disks.

Tip #95 from
Patrice-Anne Rutledge

If you want to save on another drive—one on a network, for example—you can click the Browse button and choose this drive from the Specify Directory dialog box.

---

8. Click Next again to continue (see Figure 7.29).

9. Indicate whether you want to Include Linked Files and to Embed TrueType Fonts. Choosing both these options ensures that all external clip art images, media clips, sounds, and special fonts are included in the package.

Tip #96 from
Patrice-Anne Rutledge

You can embed TrueType fonts that come with Windows. You can embed other TrueType fonts that you install only if they aren't license- or copyright-restricted. You'll receive an error message if you try to embed a restricted font. To embed fonts directly in a presentation before using the Pack and Go Wizard, choose File, Save As and then choose Tools, Embed TrueType Fonts from the Save As dialog box.

PART

III

CH

7

Figure 7.29
Include linked files and fonts to form a complete package.

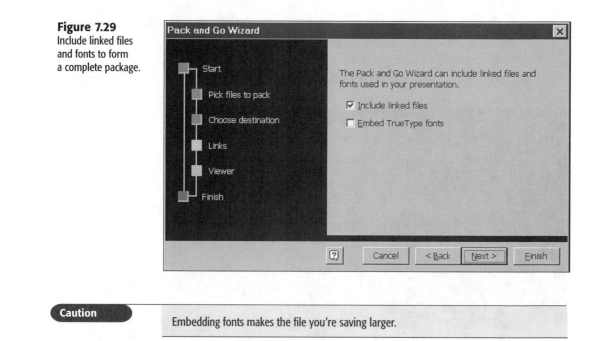

Caution

Embedding fonts makes the file you're saving larger.

10. Click Next to continue to the final step, as shown in Figure 7.30.

Figure 7.30
You can also include the PowerPoint Viewer.

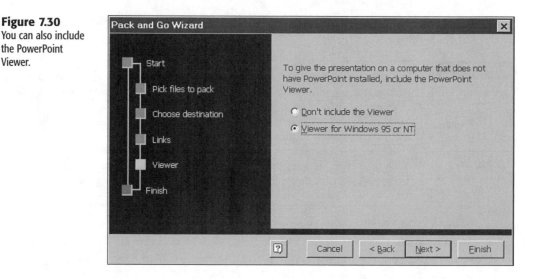

11. If you're going to present on a computer that doesn't have PowerPoint installed, you can include the PowerPoint Viewer within the package. Choose either Don't Include the Viewer or Viewer for Windows 95 or NT, as appropriate.

→ To learn what this viewer is and how it works, **see** "Using the PowerPoint Viewer," **p. 171**

12. Click Next to advance to the summary step (see Figure 7.31).

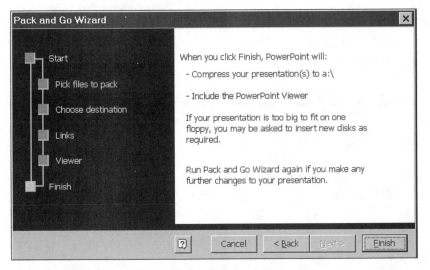

Figure 7.31
The final step summarizes your actions.

13. This step summarizes what the wizard will do, such as compress the files to a specific drive and potentially include the PowerPoint Viewer. Click Finish to complete.

PowerPoint compresses your file to its target destination in a file called PRES0.PPZ. It also includes an application file called PNGSETUP.EXE. When you're ready to deliver your presentation on the new computer, run PNGSETUP.EXE, which extracts the presentation and runs it.

USING THE POWERPOINT VIEWER

The PowerPoint Viewer is an application that enables people who don't have PowerPoint installed on their computers to view a PowerPoint presentation. You can freely distribute the viewer without any license fee. Using the Pack and Go Wizard, you have the option of including this viewer in your presentation package.

→ To learn more about how to use this wizard and how it works with the PowerPoint Viewer, **see** "Using the Pack and Go Wizard," **p. 167**

The PowerPoint Viewer's filename is PPVIEW32.EXE. If you installed the viewer on your computer, it should be located in the `\Program Files\Microsoft Office\Office\Xlators` folder. From the CD-ROM, you can access it in the `\Pfiles\Msoffice\Office\Xlators` folder. Finally, you'll also find this application on the PowerPoint Web site (`www.microsoft.com\office\powerpoint`).

Tip #97 from
Patrice-Anne Rutledge

PPVIEW32.EXE is also compressed when you use the Pack and Go Wizard and is extracted to the folder you indicate when you run PNGSETUP.EXE to decompress your presentation.

PART

III

CH

7

To run the viewer, follow these steps:

1. Double-click PPVIEW32.EXE from within Windows Explorer. Figure 7.32 illustrates the Microsoft PowerPoint Viewer dialog box.

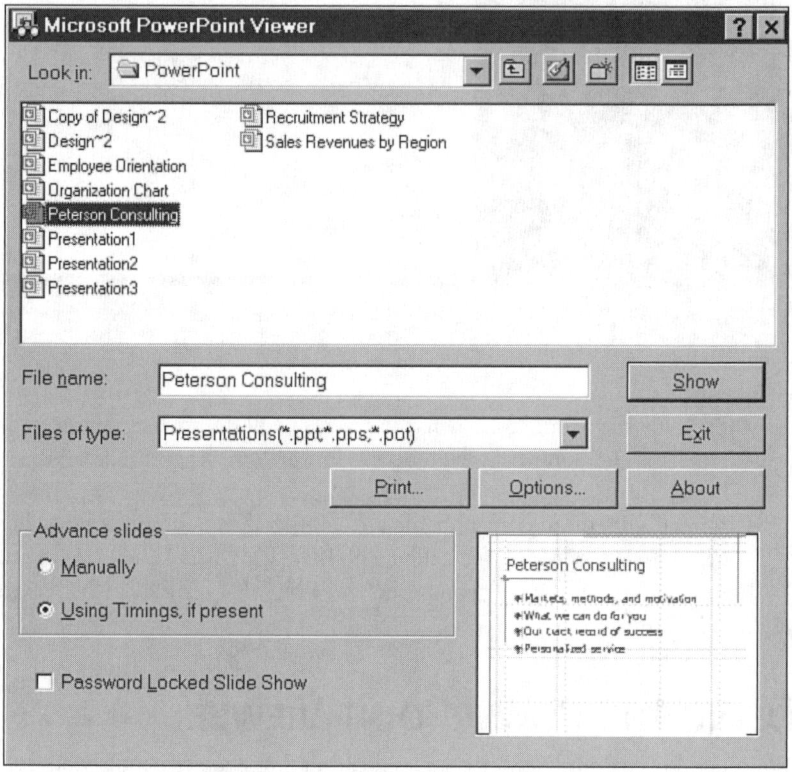

Figure 7.32
The PowerPoint Viewer enables you to deliver slideshows on computers without PowerPoint.

2. Navigate to the presentation you want to view or enter its name in the File Name field.
3. Specify whether you want to advance slides Manually or Using Timings, If Present.
4. Click the Print button if you want to print this presentation. The standard Print dialog box displays, in which you can set print options.
5. Click the Options button to set presentation and viewer settings, shown in Figure 7.33.
6. You can select Use Settings Saved with File or Override Saved Settings.

Note

These are the settings you specified in the Set Up Show dialog box.

→ For more information on the Set Up Show dialog box, **see** "Setting Up a Show," **p. 146**

7. If you want to override, you have the following options:
   - *Loop Continuously Until 'Esc'*   Plays the presentation over and over again until you press the Esc key.

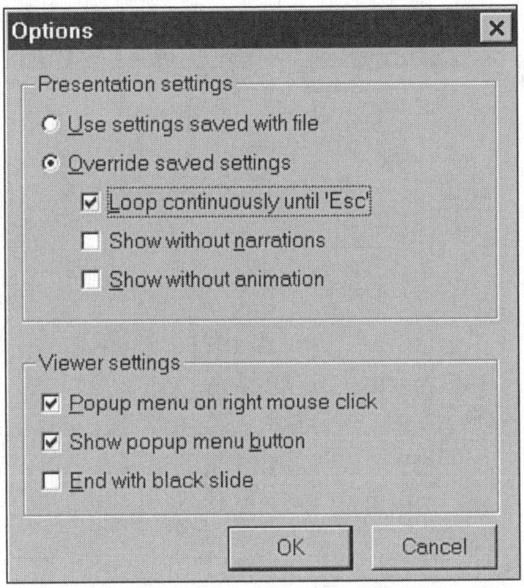

Figure 7.33
Specify settings in this dialog box.

- *Show without Narrations*   Temporarily deactivates any accompanying narrations.
- *Show without Animation*   Temporarily deactivates any accompanying animations.

8. You can also set the following Viewer Settings:

- *Popup Menu on Right Mouse Click*   Displays a subset of the menu options that are available within PowerPoint during a slide show.

→ To learn how to use these options, **see** "Previewing Your Show," **p. 159**

- *Show Popup Menu Button*   Displays the pop-up menu button in the lower-left corner.
- *End with Black Slide*   Finishes the show with a black slide.

9. Click OK to return to the main dialog box.

10. Click the Show button to run the show with the parameters you set.

11. Click Exit to close the PowerPoint Viewer.

You can also play multiple shows with the viewer by creating a playlist file with Notepad. To do this, follow these steps:

1. Open Notepad by choosing Programs, Accessories, Notepad from the Start button.

2. Enter each presentation and its path on a single line in Notepad, avoiding any spaces between lines. Figure 7.34 provides an example.

PART

III

CH

7

Figure 7.34
Enter multiple presentations files in Notepad.

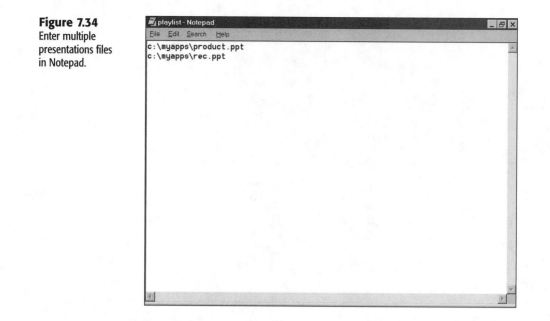

3. Choose File, Save to open the Save As dialog box, shown in Figure 7.35.

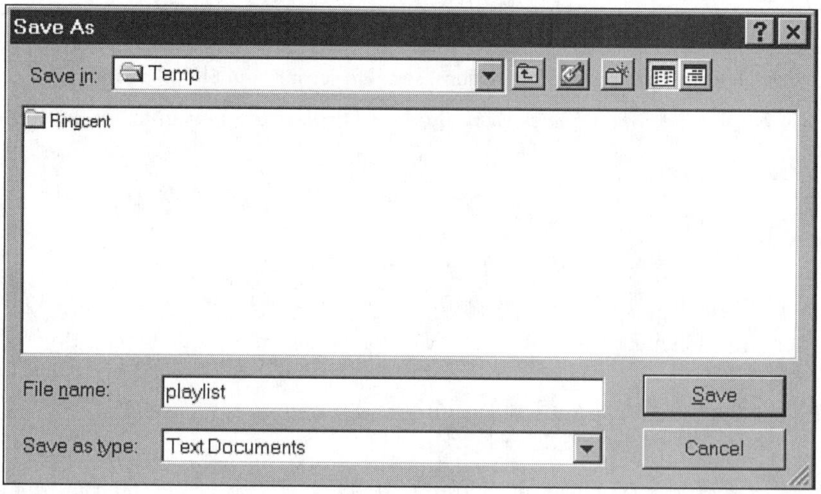

Figure 7.35
Save your playlist.

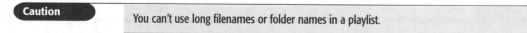

4. Enter a name for the file in the File Name field and click Save.

Caution

You can't use long filenames or folder names in a playlist.

5. Choose File, Exit to close Notepad.

Next, you have to rename the playlist with the extension .LST. The playlist must have the extension .LST or it won't run. Then you can return to the PowerPoint Viewer and run the playlist. Be sure to select playlist in the Files of Type field.

Tip #98 from	For more information about the parameters you can use in setting up a playlist, click the About button in the Microsoft PowerPoint Viewer dialog box.
Patrice-Anne Rutledge	

TROUBLESHOOTING

My presentation doesn't display all the slides I created.

Be sure you don't have any hidden slides. To verify this, open your presentation in Slide Sorter view and verify that none of the slide numbers has a strikethrough, which indicates it's hidden. To unhide a slide, select it and choose Slide Show, Hide Slide.

I want to browse my presentation at a kiosk, but the slides don't advance.

Be sure you set automatic timings if you want to browse at a kiosk because you can't do this manually. Also verify that you chose the Using Timings, If Present option in the Set Up Show dialog box.

I added a voice narration, and now I can't hear other sound files I've included.

If you insert media clips such as sounds and then add a voice narration, the narration takes precedence over the media clips. As a result, you'll hear only the narration. To resolve this, delete the narration if the media clips are of more importance, or find a way to include the other sounds in the narration you record.

I want to export an action item from the Meeting Minder to Microsoft Outlook, but that option isn't available in the Meeting Minder Export dialog box.

You must click the Add button to add at least one action item to the Action Items tab before you can export that item. If you just enter one action item without clicking the Add button, the Post Action Items to Microsoft Outlook option won't be available.

DESIGN CORNER

Export from the Meeting Minder to instantly create minutes and action items in Microsoft Word.

BEFORE

Meeting Minutes and Action Items come directly from the Meeting Minder dialog box in PowerPoint

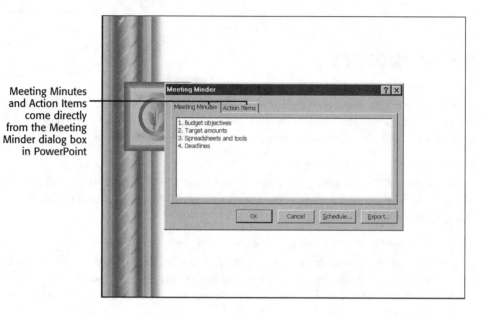

AFTER

CHAPTER 8

CREATING AND PRINTING PRESENTATION MATERIALS

In this chapter   *by Patrice-Anne Rutledge*

EXPLORING PRESENTATION OUTPUT OPTIONS

You can create a variety of printed output from PowerPoint—slides, notes, handouts, and outlines. You can use these materials to proof your slide content, to remind yourself of what you want to say while presenting, or to give to audience members who attend your presentation. If you don't have a color printer, you can print your presentation in either grayscale or pure black and white. PowerPoint also includes numerous customization options for printing auxiliary materials. You can export these to Microsoft Word for even more flexibility. And finally, PowerPoint offers a special wizard that helps you send your presentation to a service bureau to create 35mm slides or overheads.

In this chapter you learn about:

- *Using notes and handouts*   Notes provide a way to remind yourself what to say as well as to give detailed content to the people who attend your presentation. Handouts provide an easy way to print multiple slides on one page.

- *Setting page options*   The Page Setup dialog box enables you to set page orientation and size for printing.

- *Printing a presentation*   The Print dialog box includes many options for how and what you want to print. You can choose the slides to print, the desired type of output, and a color scheme.

- *Understanding grayscale and black and white*   Even if you don't have a color printer, you can still print a color presentation in either a combination of black, white, and gray, or pure black and white.

- *Customizing printed output in Word*   For the most flexibility and customization, you can send your handouts, slides, outlines, and notes to Word for final formatting and printing.

- *Using a service bureau*   If you want to print 35mm slides or overheads, PowerPoint includes a wizard to simplify this procedure.

CREATING NOTES AND HANDOUTS

In addition to slides and outlines, notes and *handouts (p. 553)* are two of the most common forms of printed output. You create notes in the notes pane, which is visible in both Normal view and Outline view. Figure 8.1 illustrates a notes pane in the lower-right corner of the window in which you can create detailed speaker's notes about your presentation.

Caution

Notes are not the same as comments. A comment displays in a yellow box on top of your presentation and provides commentary about its content. You use comments most often during the review process to get feedback from others and usually delete them later. Notes are designed to be kept with a presentation, as a reference for the speaker or audience members.

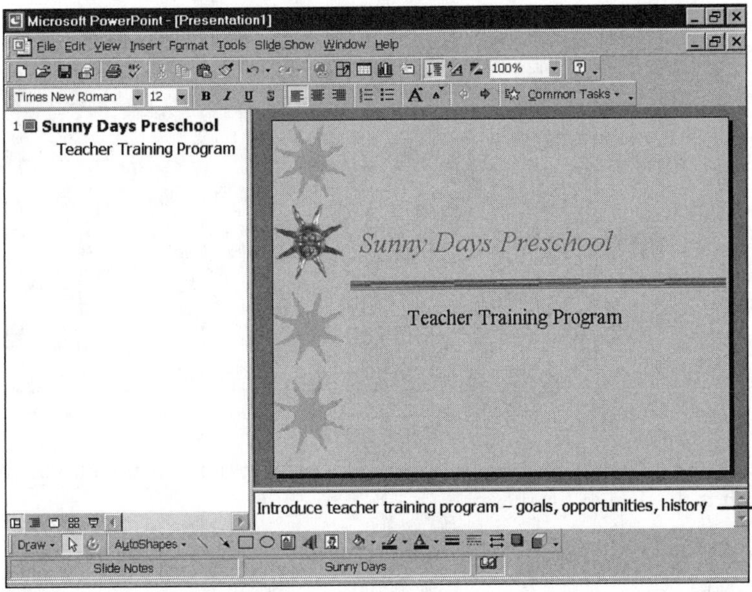

Figure 8.1
Add notes for yourself
or your audience in
the notes pane.

→ For details about the use of comments, **see** "Adding Comments to Slides," **p. 120**

You can use notes to remind yourself about what you're going to present, to create an entire script for your presentation in the notes pane, or to provide information you print out for audience members.

Creating handouts is very similar to printing slides, except that with handouts you can print from two to nine slides on a page. This can greatly reduce the number of pages and amount of printer toner required to print your presentation. When you print handouts you only see the slides, not the accompanying notes.

→ To learn more about when and how to use handouts, **see** "Creating Handout Materials," **p. 553**

SETTING PAGE SETUP OPTIONS

Before you print, you'll want to set up page options such as a default output and orientation. To do this, follow these steps:

1. Choose File, Page Setup to open the Page Setup dialog box, shown in Figure 8.2.

2. Select your output from the Slides Sized For drop-down list. Options include Onscreen Show, Letter Paper, A4 Paper (international standard), 35mm Slides, Overhead, Banner, or Custom.

3. If you choose Custom, enter the exact Width and Height in inches.

4. In the Number Slides From field, select the starting number to use on the first slide.

5. Choose either a Portrait or Landscape orientation for your slides. Landscape is the default.

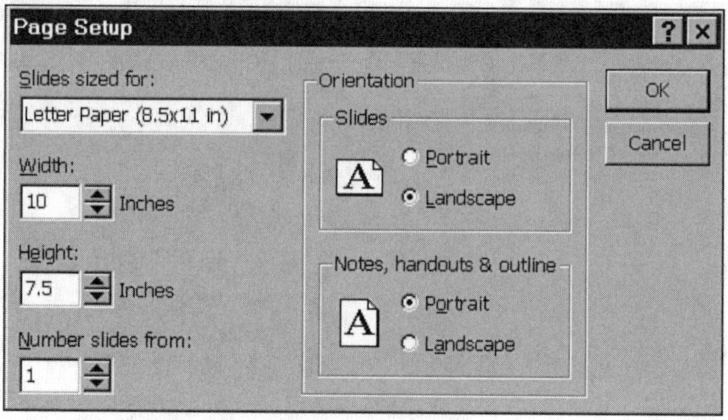

Figure 8.2
Set up page orientation and other defaults in this dialog box.

6. Choose either a Portrait or Landscape orientation for your notes, handouts, and outline. Portrait is the default for these.

7. Click OK to close this dialog box.

PRINTING POWERPOINT PRESENTATIONS

To print an open PowerPoint presentation, follow these steps:

1. Choose File, Print to open the Print dialog box, shown in Figure 8.3.

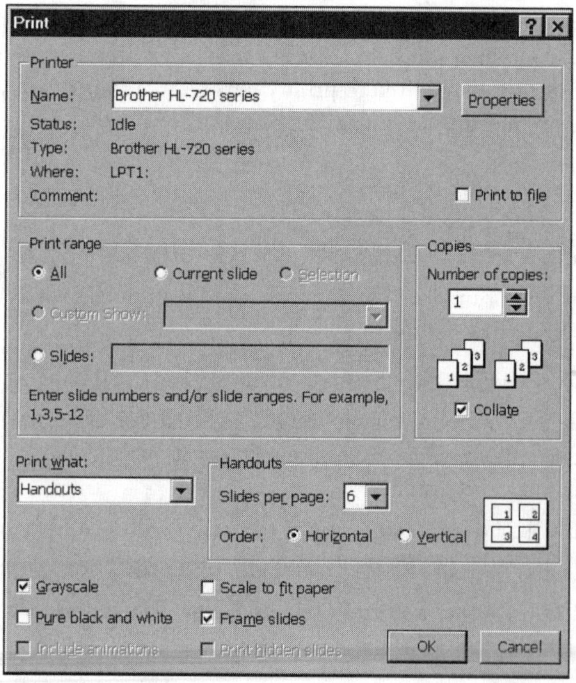

Figure 8.3
You can specify numerous print parameters in the Print dialog box.

Tip #99 from
Patrice-Anne Rutledge

Click the Print button on the Standard toolbar if you want to automatically print with the defaults rather than setting options in the Print dialog box. Be sure that your default settings match your desired output, such as grayscale or black and white. You can set these defaults in the Print dialog box.

2. Select the printer you want to use from the <u>N</u>ame drop-down list.

Tip #100 from
Patrice-Anne Rutledge

Click the <u>P</u>roperties button to change the properties and print parameters of the selected printer.

3. In the Print Range group box, select the slides you want to print. Choices include

   - *All* Prints all slides in the presentation.
   - *Curre<u>n</u>t Slide* Prints only the currently selected slide.
   - *Selection* Prints the selected slides. For example, if you select specific slides in the Outline pane, only these slides print.
   - *Cust<u>o</u>m Show* Enables you to select a custom show to print. This option isn't available if you haven't created at least one custom show.

→ For more information on Custom Shows, **see** "Working with Custom Shows," **p. 153**

   - *Sl<u>i</u>des* Enter the numbers of the slides you want to print. For example, you could enter 1-4, 10 to print slides 1, 2, 3, 4, and 10. Page numbers must be selected in ascending order.

4. Enter the Number of <u>C</u>opies you want to print. If you choose to print more than one copy, specify whether or not to Colla<u>t</u>e. Collating keeps multiple copies in sequence. If you were to print five copies of a presentation without collating, for example, you would print five copies of page one first, then five copies of page two, and so on.

5. Specify what you want to print in the Print <u>W</u>hat drop-down list. Options include Slides, Handouts, Notes Pages, or Outline View.

6. If you choose to print handouts, the Handouts group box displays. Indicate how many slides you want to print per page—up to nine— in the Slides pe<u>r</u> Page field and choose either a Hori<u>z</u>ontal or <u>V</u>ertical Order for the flow of slides on a page.

7. Next, choose any of the following print options that apply:

   - *<u>G</u>rayscale* Prints the presentation as grayscale (using shades of black, white, and gray) which optimizes a color presentation for a black-and-white printer.
   - *P<u>u</u>re Black and White* Prints the presentation in black and white only, without any gray.

Tip #101 from
Patrice-Anne Rutledge

To print in color on a color printer, be sure to clear the Grayscale and Pure Black and White check boxes.

- *Include Animations* Displays animated graphics in your presentation as icons on the printed page.
- *Scale to Fit Paper* Changes the size of slides to fit the paper, making them either larger or smaller as appropriate.
- *Frame Slides* Includes a border around the slides. Not available when you print Outline View.
- *Print Hidden Slides* This option is available only if your presentation includes hidden slides.

8. Click OK to print.

Tip #102 from
Patrice-Anne Rutledge

You can customize printing defaults for the existing presentation in the Options dialog box. To access it, choose Tools, Options and go to the Print tab.

→ For more information about printing, **see** "Changing Print Options," **p. 470**

PREVIEWING IN GRAYSCALE AND BLACK AND WHITE

If you don't have a color printer, you can print a color presentation in two different ways—grayscale or black and white. Table 8.1 illustrates how each PowerPoint object appears when printed in grayscale or black and white.

TABLE 8.1 GRAYSCALE AND BLACK-AND-WHITE OBJECTS

Object	Grayscale	Black-and-White
Bitmaps	Grayscale	Grayscale
Charts	Grayscale	Grayscale
Embossing	None	None
Fill	Grayscale	White
Frames	Black	Black
Lines	Black	Black
Patterns	Grayscale	White
Shadows (object)	Grayscale	Black
Shadows (text)	None	None
Slide backgrounds	White	White
Text	Black	Black

To preview what your color presentation will look like in grayscale, click the Grayscale Preview button on the Standard toolbar. Figure 8.4 illustrates a presentation in grayscale.

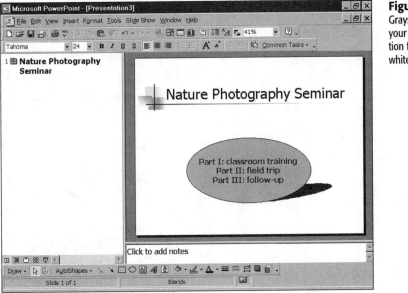

Figure 8.4
Grayscale optimizes your color presentation for a black-and-white printer.

To preview the same presentation in black and white, press the Shift key, which converts the Grayscale Preview button to the Pure Black and White Preview button. Click this button to see the differences in this color scheme. Figure 8.5 illustrates a pure black-and-white version of the same slide.

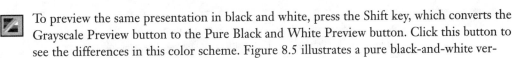

Tip #103 from
Patrice-Anne Rutledge

The Grayscale Preview button must be unselected before you press the Shift key. Then click Grayscale Preview button to convert it to Pure Black and White Preview.

You can manually change how an object prints in either grayscale or black and white when you are viewing in Grayscale Preview or Pure Black and White Preview. To do so, select the object, right-click, and choose Black and <u>W</u>hite from the shortcut menu. You can then choose from the following color options:

- <u>A</u>utomatic
- <u>G</u>rayscale
- L<u>i</u>ght Grayscale
- <u>I</u>nverse Grayscale
- Gra<u>y</u> with White Fill
- Blac<u>k</u> with Grayscale Fill
- Blac<u>k</u> with White Fill
- <u>B</u>lack
- <u>W</u>hite
- <u>D</u>on't Show

Figure 8.5
Printing in pure black
and white is another
option.

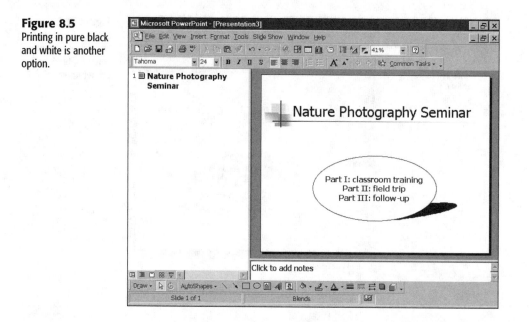

PRINTING AN OUTLINE

In the Print dialog box you can choose to print a presentation's outline by selecting the
Outline View option in the Print <u>W</u>hat drop-down list.

→ For more detailed information about printing, **see** "Printing PowerPoint Presentations," **p. 180**

Before you do this, however, you may want to set up your outline for printing.

 To display the entire contents of each slide, click the Expand All button on either the
Standard or Outlining toolbar.

Tip #104 from
Patrice-Anne Rutledge

To print only the title of each slide, click the Collapse All button on the Outlining
toolbar.

 To print an outline with the same formatting (font styles and sizing, line spacing, and the
like) as the presentation itself, click the Show Formatting button on the Standard or
Outlining toolbar.

→ To better understand outlines, **see** "Collapsing and Expanding Outline Points," **p. 108**

CUSTOMIZING HEADERS AND FOOTERS

You can also add headers and footers to your outline, notes, and handouts when you print them. To do this, choose View, Header and Footer, and go to the Notes and Handouts tab on the Header and Footer dialog box. Figure 8.6 illustrates this dialog box.

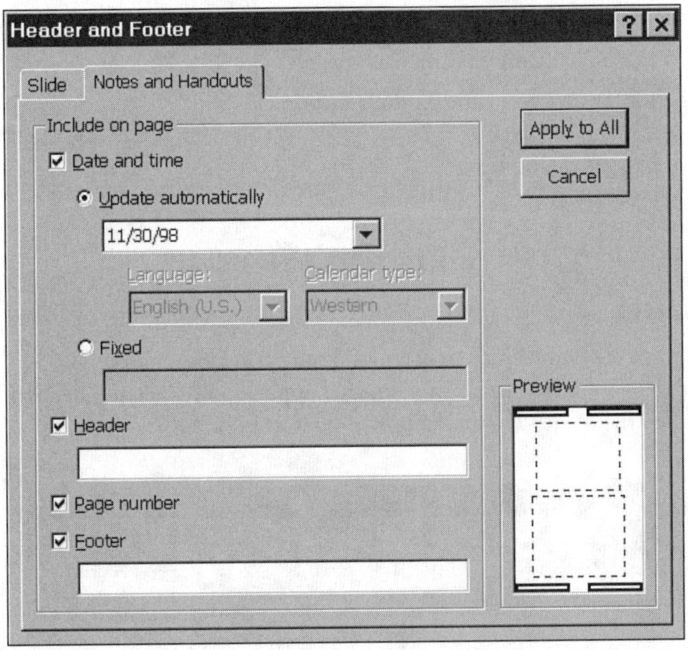

Figure 8.6
Indicate the headers and footers you want to print.

You can choose to add any or all of the following when you print notes, handouts, or outlines:

- *Date and Time*   Select this check box and then choose to either update the date automatically or enter a fixed date. If you choose to Update automatically, you can pick a format from the drop-down list. Options include displaying the date only, the time only, or the date and time in up to 13 different ways. You can also choose your base Language and Calendar type (depending on the language selection). If only English is enabled, the calendar and language buttons in headers and footers are dimmed out.

Note

In order to change Language settings, you must have more than one language enabled. Languages are enabled by selecting Start, Programs, Office Tools, Language Settings.

→ For details on multilingual presentations, **see** "Using PowerPoint's Foreign Language Capabilities,"
p. 733

> **Note**
>
> The date options you can choose from the Update automatically drop-down list are based on your choice of language/country. For example, choosing English (UK) results in date options that display a dd/mm/yy format rather than the mm/dd/yy format that is used in the United States.

- *Header*   Prints the header text you enter in the text box.
- *Page Number*   Prints the page number on each page.
- *Footer*   Prints the footer text you enter in the text box.

Click Apply to All to close the dialog box.

PRINTING A POWERPOINT PRESENTATION IN MICROSOFT WORD

If you want to make more customizations than PowerPoint provides, you can also send your presentation to Word, customize it, and print from that application. Choose File, Send To, Microsoft Word to open the Write-Up dialog box, shown in Figure 8.7.

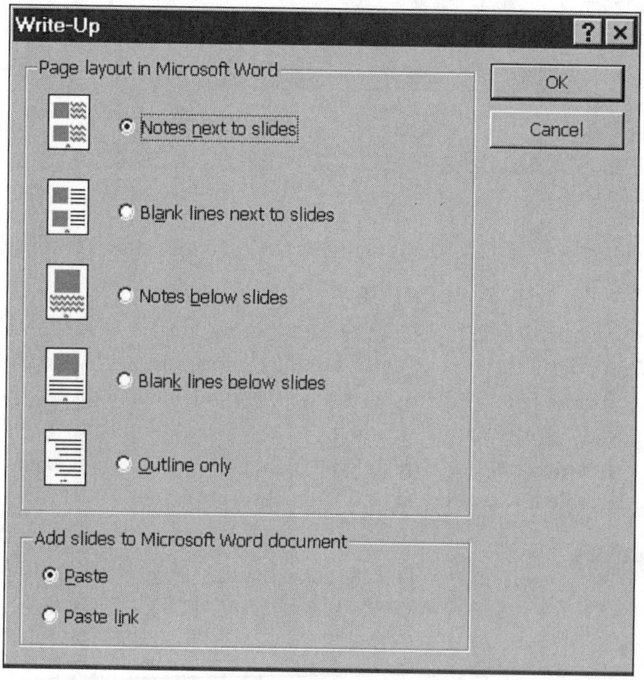

Figure 8.7
The Write-Up dialog box includes several options for what you want to export to Word.

This dialog box includes the following choices on how to display the PowerPoint presentation in Word:

- Notes Next to Slides
- Blank Lines Next to Slides
- Notes Below Slides
- Blank Lines Below Slides
- Outline Only

You can either Paste or Paste Link the slides into Word. Pasting is the equivalent of embedding. If you embed a PowerPoint presentation into Word and later change that presentation, those changes won't display in the Word document. If you paste link the PowerPoint presentation into Word and later make changes in PowerPoint, these changes display the next time you open the document in Word.

→ To learn more about linking objects, **see** "Linking Office Objects," **p. 416**

→ For more information on embedding, **see** "Working with Embedded Office Objects," **p. 422**

Click OK to send to Word and open in that application. After your presentation is in Word, you can use all its features to customize your notes and handouts.

CREATING OVERHEADS AND 35MM SLIDES

If you want to create overheads and 35mm slides from your PowerPoint presentation, you can use a service bureau to produce these materials for you. Most service bureaus accept files submitted electronically.

PowerPoint includes a special feature that enables you to send your presentation files to the Genigraphics service bureau for producing 35mm slides, digital color overhead transparencies, large display prints, and posters. PowerPoint provides a wizard to help you make your request and transmit it.

To open the Genigraphics Wizard, choose File, Send To, Genigraphics. Figure 8.8 illustrates the first step of this wizard.

Caution

If the Genigraphics menu option doesn't display, reinstall PowerPoint specifying to run the Genigraphics Wizard from your computer.

Tip #105 from
Patrice-Anne Rutledge

For more information about Genigraphics and its services, click the Genigraphics on the Web button to jump to the Genigraphics Web site.

You can order presentation material, such as slides and overheads (see Figure 8.9).

Figure 8.8
Use the Genigraphics Wizard to easily transmit your PowerPoint files to this service bureau.

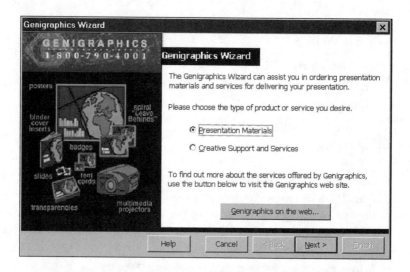

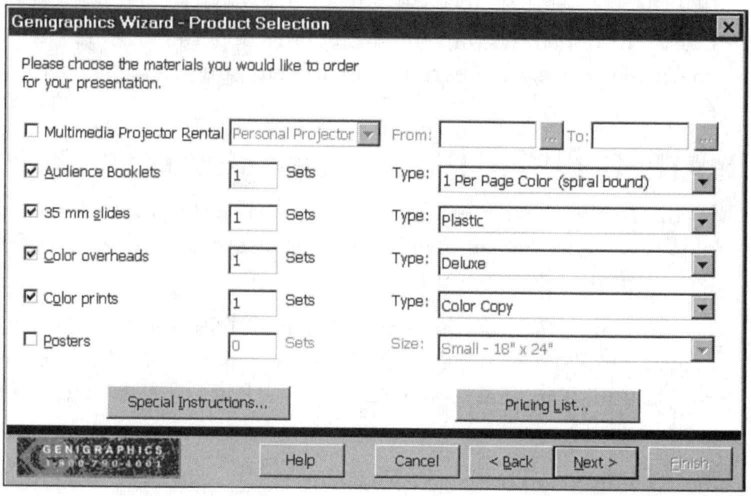

Figure 8.9
Specify the kinds of slides, overheads, prints, and posters you want to order.

Or, you can request creative support and services, such as a creative facelift of your design, custom design templates, animations, or digitized videos and sounds (see Figure 8.10).

Follow the steps of the wizard to choose the exact items you want to order and their quantity as well as to specify which presentations you want to submit.

To enter special instructions for your order, click the Special Instructions button and enter this information in the box that appears.

Tip #106 from
Patrice-Anne Rutledge

To get a price quote on the work you want to have done, click the Pricing List button to display a detailed price list.

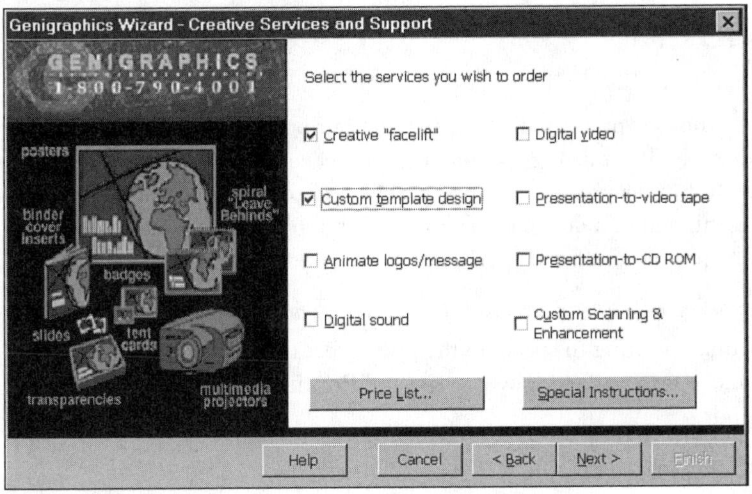

Figure 8.10
Genigraphics can also provide a facelift or custom designs for your presentation.

ENSURING A SMOOTH PRINT PROCESS

The following are some tips to help ensure a smooth process in printing your PowerPoint presentation:

- If you want to continue working with PowerPoint while printing a large presentation, choose Tools, Options and select Background Printing on the Print tab.

- If your print job is moving too slowly, turn off background printing.

- Proof your presentation carefully before printing it to save time and money. Run the spelling and grammar checker, verify the content, look at the placement of all graphics, and ensure that the color scheme and design templates are appropriate. When you're confident about your presentation, then print.

- If the fonts in your presentation don't print out properly, try substituting other fonts. In particular, if you don't use TrueType fonts and your printer can't recognize a font, it prints a different font.

- If you're going to distribute notes or handouts to audience members, carefully consider the quality and color of paper you use. Although a heavier paper stock may make attractive handouts, not all printers are equipped to handle the heavier weight. Specialty paper is also more expensive. In terms of color, light colors other than white can work well, but be wary of paper that's too dark or bright. It can make your presentation hard to read.

TROUBLESHOOTING

I can't print. What should I do?

If you're having problems printing, first verify that your printer is turned on, you selected the right printer in the Print dialog box, and that you checked for error messages in the Printers Folder. To further isolate a printing problem, check to see if you can print another PowerPoint presentation or a document from another application. If not, the problem is probably with the printer and not PowerPoint or your presentation.

My print job is printing too slowly. How can I speed up the print process?

Turn off background printing to speed up the print process. To do so, choose Tools, Options and remove the checkmark by Background Printing on the Print tab of the Options dialog box.

My graphics don't print completely. How do I fix this?

First, verify that a document without graphics prints properly. If so, your printer may not have enough memory to complete a print job with complex graphics. Refer to your printer manual for information about memory and memory upgrades.

DESIGN CORNER

By utilizing the advanced formatting features in Microsoft Word, you can create a custom PowerPoint handout for printing. Just choose the page layout options you want in the Write-Up dialog box (File, Send To, Microsoft Word) and then customize the output in Word.

BEFORE

AFTER

Custom fonts and font sizes

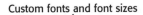

Bodega Bay Bicycles ——————————— Header
November 1998 Meeting

Slide 1

November 1998 Sales

Provide info about sales this month.

Salesperson	Units Sold	Total Revenue
Anne Jeffers	40	$15,903
Tim Johnson	46	$17,903
Amy Wang	23	$8,901
Tyler Watson	56	$24,832

Working with Graphics, Charts, and Multimedia

WORKING WITH CHARTS

EXPLORING POWERPOINT CHART POSSIBILITIES

PowerPoint *charts (p. xxx)* can be as simple or as complex as you like. You can create a basic chart using the Microsoft Graph application from within PowerPoint or insert a chart you create using Microsoft Excel. You can choose from common chart types such as column, bar, line, or pie charts; try something out of the ordinary such as a doughnut or radar chart; or create a chart type of your own. PowerPoint charts are preformatted based on the attached design template, but you can also make extensive modifications to nearly every aspect of a chart if you like—its color, text, labels, and more.

In this chapter, you learn

- *Chart terminology*   Before you create your first chart, learn the basics of chart object terminology including the meaning of terms such as *plot area*, *axis*, and *data series*.

- *How to add a chart*   Adding a chart in PowerPoint can be done in two ways—by using Microsoft Graph from within PowerPoint or by inserting a Microsoft Excel chart.

- *How to choose a chart type*   You need to choose from many different chart types such as *column*, *bar*, *pie*, and *doughnut* to determine which best suits the message you want to convey.

- *How to enter data in a datasheet*   PowerPoint uses a datasheet to store a chart's actual data. A *datasheet* is similar to an Excel worksheet, and you enter information in it in much the same way as you would in a worksheet.

- *How to format your chart*   After you create a basic chart, you may want to modify it by formatting its *legend*, *axes*, *data labels*, *data table*, and other objects.

- *When to use trendlines*   If you want to predict the future based on your existing chart information, you can use a *trendline*.

UNDERSTANDING CHARTS IN POWERPOINT

In PowerPoint, you can use the Microsoft Graph application to create powerful charts in your presentation or you can insert charts created in another application such as Excel. Using Microsoft Graph from within PowerPoint is the easiest alternative if you need to create a chart from scratch and don't need to apply Excel's calculation and formula capabilities to your chart data. If you've already created a chart in Excel or you need to analyze complex data, then inserting an Excel chart is the best solution.

In addition to the common chart types such as column, bar, line, and pie, you can also create doughnut, radar, cone, bubble, stock, and other chart types.

Tip #107 from
Patrice-Anne Rutledge

For help in using Microsoft Graph, choose Help, Microsoft Graph Help. This opens the help file specific to this application.

Before you start creating a chart using Microsoft Graph from within PowerPoint, you should become familiar with the terms associated with charts. Table 9.1 lists these terms and their definitions.

TABLE 9.1   CHART OBJECT TERMINOLOGY

Term	Definition
Axis	A line that frames one side of the plot area. The two most common axes are the value axis and the category axis.
Datasheet	A sheet with rows and columns that resembles a spreadsheet, in which you can enter data for your chart.
Data label	A label that describes a specific data marker or series of data markers. This label can be a numerical value, text, percent, or combination of these items.
Data marker	A value that represents a single cell or data point in a datasheet.
Data series	Data series are the main categories of information in a chart and are usually reflected in a chart's legend and in the first cell of each datasheet row or column.
Data table	A table that displays in the chart listing the exact data in the datasheet.
Gridlines	Lines that display across the category or value axes, which enhance a chart's readability. By default, major gridlines are in increments of 10 and minor gridlines in increments of 2.
Legend	A box that lists and color-codes all data series.
Trendline	A line that forecasts future values based on current data. definitions.

Figure 9.1 shows some of these chart objects.

To determine what each object is in a chart, place the mouse on that object or part of the chart and a chart tip displays its name. Figure 9.2 shows an example of a chart tip with the name and value for a data series.

Note   Only the data series displays a numeric value.

If the chart tip doesn't display, activate Microsoft Graph by double-clicking the chart; choose Tools, Options; and verify that the Show Names and Show Values check boxes are selected on the Chart tab of the Graph Options dialog box (see Figure 9.3).

Figure 9.1
Learn the basic objects of a chart before you create one.

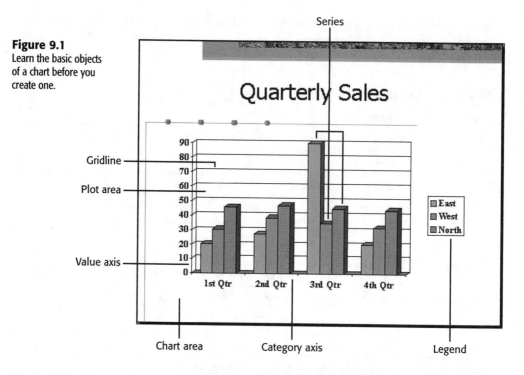

Series

Gridline

Plot area

Value axis

Chart area

Category axis

Legend

Figure 9.2
This chart tip lets you know the name of the chart object as well as its value.

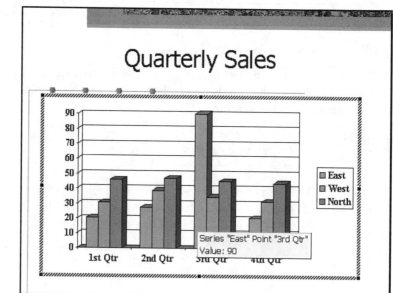

Series "East" Point "3rd Qtr"
Value: 90

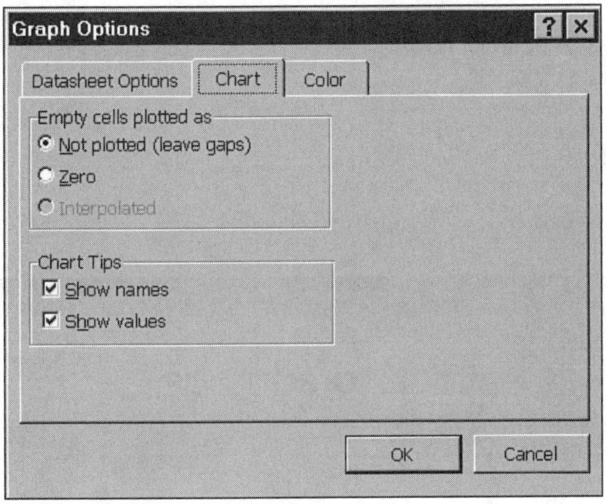

Figure 9.3
PowerPoint displays names and values in chart tips by default.

PART

IV

CH

9

ADDING A CHART

The fastest way to add a chart to your PowerPoint presentation is to select one of the AutoLayouts from the New Slide dialog box, such as Chart, Text & Chart, and Chart & Text. To access this dialog box, shown in Figure 9.4, select the New Slide button from the Standard toolbar or choose Common Tasks, New Slide from the Formatting toolbar.

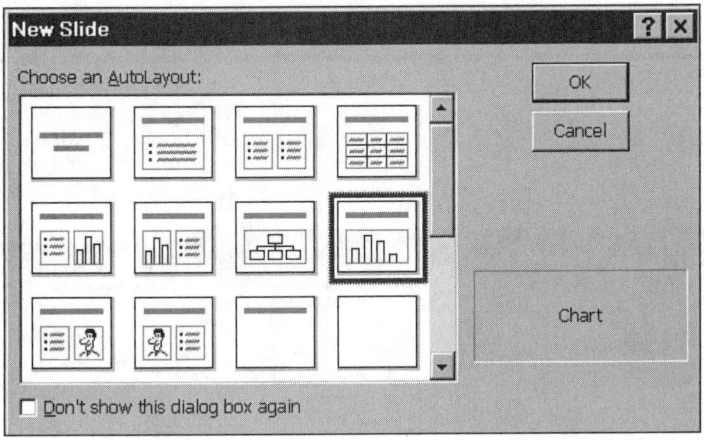

Figure 9.4
The New Slide dialog box includes several AutoLayouts that include charts.

→ To learn more about how slide layouts affect your presentation, **see** "Understanding Slide Layouts," **p. 28**

Tip #108 from
Patrice-Anne Rutledge

> If you use the AutoContent Wizard to create your presentation, it may already have a slide that contains a chart.

→ For details on automating presentation creation with this wizard, **see** "Using the AutoContent Wizard," **p. 36**

Figure 9.5 shows a sample chart slide with a chart placeholder.

Figure 9.5
You can start adding a chart by double-clicking the placeholder.

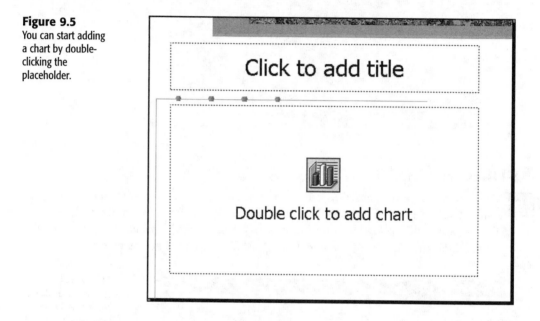

Double-click the chart placeholder to activate the chart in Microsoft Graph, as shown in Figure 9.6.

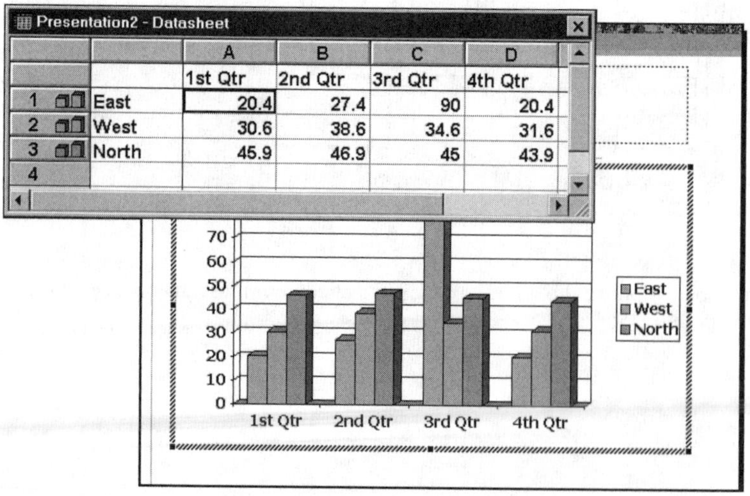

Figure 9.6
PowerPoint displays a chart with sample data.

Tip #1001 from

Patrice-Anne Rutledge

You can also insert a chart into an existing slide by clicking the Insert Chart button on the Standard toolbar or by selecting Insert, Chart.

A sample 3D clustered column chart displays by default and the related datasheet opens. The menu bar and toolbars are also customized for Microsoft Graph. The menu bar now includes Data and Chart menu items, and the toolbar includes several new selections including:

- *Chart Objects*   Enables you to select the chart object you want to format or work with such as plot area, chart area, legend, axis, or series.

- *Format*   Opens a Format dialog box tailored to the selected chart object.

→ To learn more about object-formatting options in PowerPoint, **see** "Using the Format Dialog Box," **p. 282**

- *Import File*   Opens the Import File dialog box from which you can import another file into your chart, such as an Excel worksheet.

- *View Datasheet*   Displays the datasheet if it's no longer in view; otherwise, closes it.

Caution

You must double-click the chart in PowerPoint to view the Chart menu and chart toolbar options.

You can create a basic chart very quickly in PowerPoint or you can make numerous enhancements and formatting changes. After you activate Microsoft Graph to create a chart, it's easiest to proceed in the following order:

- Enter a title for the chart slide.
- Change the chart type if you don't want to use the default (a 3D column chart).
- Edit the datasheet data (the text and numbers for your chart).
- Modify and format chart objects as needed.

Tip #110 from

Patrice-Anne Rutledge

Before creating an actual chart, you should be sure you understand chart object terminology and know the types of charts you can create in PowerPoint. Sometimes, designing a paper sketch of the chart you want to create can help as well.

SELECTING A CHART TYPE

PowerPoint offers numerous chart types and chart subtypes for almost every kind of graphic representation you could want to create. Subtypes offer variations on the basic chart type, such as 3D options. PowerPoint includes the following basic chart types:

- *Column* Creates vertical columns to compare the values of categories of data. Column, bar, and line charts work well if you want to compare values over a time period such as months or quarters. Figure 9.7 illustrates a sample column chart.

Figure 9.7
A column chart makes it easy to compare series of information.

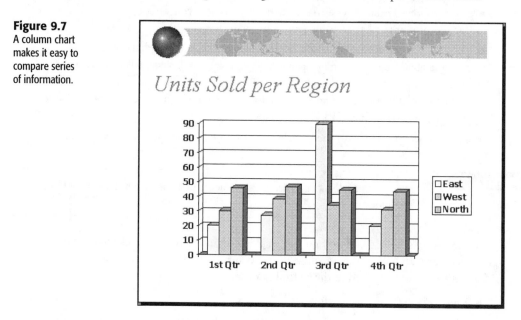

- *Bar* Creates horizontal bars to compare the values of categories of data.
- *Line* Creates a line with markers for each data value.
- *Pie* Creates a pie that analyzes percentages of a total number. Use a pie chart if you want to see the contribution of each item to a total. For example, you might want to see how much each line of items you sell contributed to total revenues for the year. Figure 9.8 displays an example of a pie chart.
- *XY (Scatter)* Creates a chart that compares sets of values.
- *Area* Creates a chart displaying the trend of values in a single solid area.
- *Doughnut* Creates a pie chart that can contain more than one series.
- *Radar* Creates a radar image with markers for each data point.
- *Surface* Creates a single 3D surface that analyzes trends in value.
- *Bubble* Creates a comparison of three sets of values displayed as bubbles.

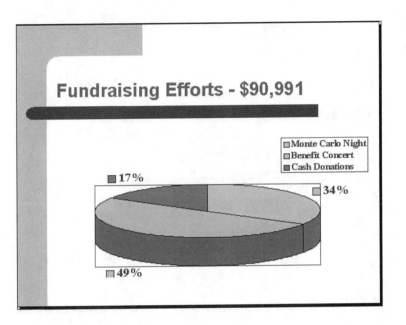

Figure 9.8
Use pie charts to
show percentages
of a total amount.

- *Stock*   Creates a chart displaying a stock's high, low, and close figures.
- *Cylinder*   Creates columns shaped like cylinders.
- *Cone*   Creates columns shaped like cones. Figure 9.9 shows a sample cone chart.
- *Pyramid*   Creates columns shaped like pyramids.

Note   To get a visual example of what each of these chart types looks like, you can select the type you want to learn more about in the Chart Type dialog box (Chart, Chart Type) and then click the Example of the selected chart type option from the Office Assistant that displays. This takes you to a Microsoft Graph Help window that provides details and examples of each chart type.

If you already know that you want to create a 3D clustered column chart, the PowerPoint default, you don't need to do anything to select a chart type. But if you want to use a different chart type, you should select it before you enter any data or make any other modifications.

To apply a new chart type, follow these steps:

1. In Microsoft Graph, choose Chart, Chart Type from the menu. The Chart Type dialog box displays, as shown in Figure 9.10.

Tip #111 from
Patrice-Anne Rutledge

To quickly apply a new chart type, click the down arrow to the right of the Chart Type button on the Standard toolbar in Microsoft Graph. Choose from one of the chart type buttons on the palette that displays.

Figure 9.9
Use a cone chart as
an alternative to a
basic column or
bar chart.

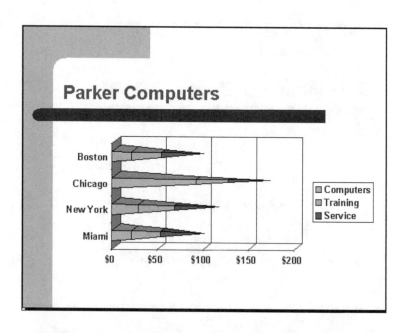

Figure 9.10
PowerPoint offers
many different
chart types.

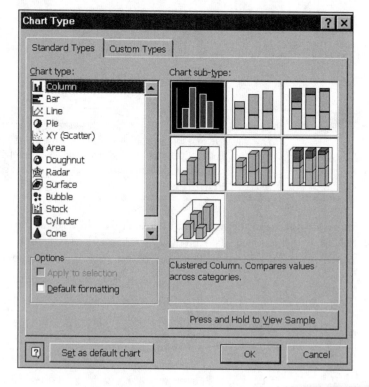

2. On the Standard Types tab, select the type of chart you want from the Chart Type list. A variety of subtypes appear in the Chart Sub-Type box.

3. Click the image of the subtype you want. The text box below provides detailed information about this subtype.

4. To preview what an actual chart of this type looks like, click the Press and Hold to View Sample button. A sample chart temporarily replaces the Chart Sub-Type box, as shown in Figure 9.11.

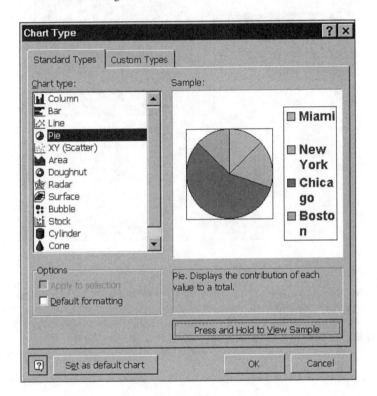

Figure 9.11
You can preview changes before making them.

5. If you want to change this to your default, select the Set as Default Chart button.

6. If none of the chart types in the Standard Types tab suits your needs, click the Custom Types tab to view more options. Figure 9.12 illustrates this tab.

Note
Custom charts include detailed formatting and some are customized specifically for a certain kind of output, such as onscreen presentations. The text box beneath the sample indicates these details.

7. Click the Built-In option button to display PowerPoint's ready-made custom charts.

Figure 9.12
Custom charts
provide variety
and options.

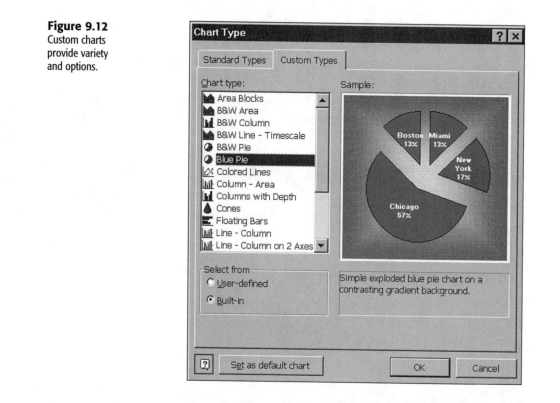

You can also add an active chart in your current presentation to the list of chart types. Simply select the User-Defined option button on the Custom Types tab, click the Add button, and enter details about this active chart to the Add Custom Chart Type dialog box that displays. Microsoft Graph adds this chart to its list of custom chart types.

8. Select the chart type you want to use from the Chart Type list. A sample displays in the Sample box.

9. Click OK to apply the chart type and return to your presentation.

ENTERING DATA IN THE DATASHEET

The default datasheet that opens when you first create a chart includes four columns and three rows. This is a common chart format—comparing specific categories over periods of time—but only one of the hundreds of possible formats. Figure 9.13 illustrates this datasheet.

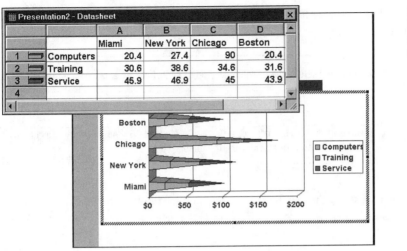

Figure 9.13
Enter chart data in a
datasheet, similar to
an Excel worksheet.

Note

If the data you need is already in an Excel spreadsheet, you can import directly from Excel
without re-entering this information in the datasheet. To do so, choose Edit, Import File
from within Microsoft Graph to open the Import File dialog box. Choose the Excel file you
want to import and click Open. The Import Data Options dialog box guides you through
this process. Note that you can import from Lotus 1-2-3 and text file formats as well.

The first row and first column of a datasheet serve as headers for the information in the
datasheet. Therefore, the second row begins with the number 1 and the second column
with the letter A. In this example, the columns display as the category axis, the rows display
as the data series listed in the legend, and the cell data (A1:D3) represents the value axis.

Tip #112 from
Patrice-Anne Rutledge

To reverse the chart and use the column data as the data series instead of the row data,
choose Data, Series in Columns. Microsoft Graph redesigns the chart based on this change.
For example, if you changed the default chart to display as in columns, the quarters would
appear in the legend and the locations in the category axis.

To modify the default data, you can simply overwrite the existing information in each cell.

⚡ ***Does your chart have extra spaces?*** *See the Troubleshooting section at the end of the chapter.*

INSERTING AND DELETING DATASHEET ROWS AND COLUMNS

To delete a row or column, place the cursor within the appropriate row or column and
choose Edit, Delete from the menu. To remove the contents of a cell rather than the cell
itself, choose Edit, Clear, Contents. Clearing the contents is best when you want to remove

existing data and replace it with new data. If you no longer need the row or column, you should delete it.

Tip #113 from
Patrice-Anne Rutledge

You can also delete a row or column by selecting its heading and pressing the Delete key.

Tip #114 from
Patrice-Anne Rutledge

You can also cut (Ctrl+X), copy (Ctrl+C), and paste (Ctrl+V) data in the datasheet by using keyboard commands or by choosing the toolbar buttons.

To insert a new row, select the row below where you want to place the new row and choose Insert, Cells from the menu. Microsoft Graph inserts a new row directly above the selected row.

To insert a new column, select the column heading to the right of where you want to place the new column and choose Insert, Cells. Microsoft Graph inserts a new column directly to the left of the selected column.

If you want to insert a new cell, rather than a complete row or column, select the cell adjacent to where you want to insert; choose Insert, Cells; and choose either Shift Cells Right or Shift Cells Down in the Insert dialog box (see Figure 9.14).

Figure 9.14
Determine the direction to move the existing cells in the Insert dialog box.

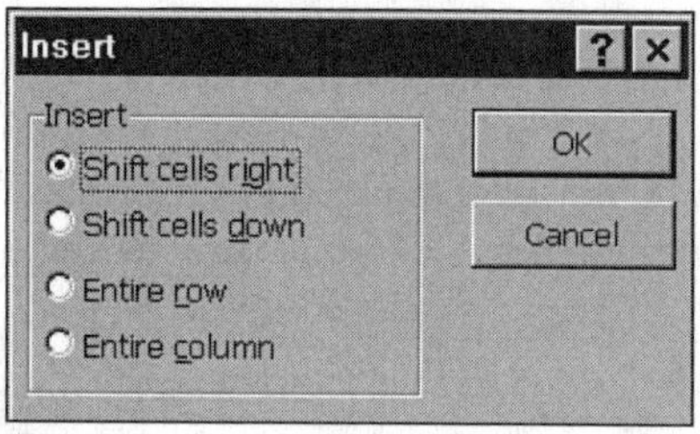

PowerPoint inserts a new cell and shifts the row to the right or shifts the column down, depending on your selection.

Tip #115 from
Patrice-Anne Rutledge

You can undo insertions and deletions by clicking the Undo button or pressing Ctrl+Z.

FORMATTING DATASHEET COLUMN WIDTH

To format the datasheet's column width, follow these steps:

1. Select the column heading of the column whose width you want to adjust.

2. Choose Format, Column Width. Figure 9.15 shows the Column Width dialog box, which displays.

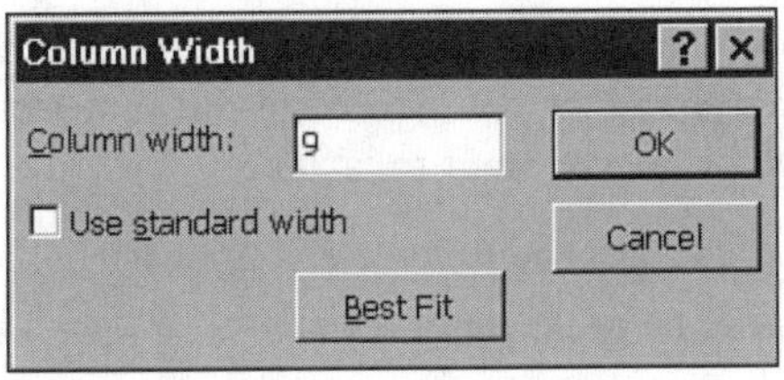

Figure 9.15
You can customize the width of a datasheet column.

3. Enter the number of spaces you want to include in the Column Width field. To adjust to the standard width, select the Use Standard Width check box.

4. Click the Best Fit button to have the columns adjust automatically based on the existing data.

5. Click OK to return to the datasheet.

FORMATTING DATASHEET NUMBERS

You can format the text and numbers in your datasheet if you want. To format numerical data, select the cell or cells you want to format and choose Format, Number. The Format Number dialog box displays, as shown in Figure 9.16.

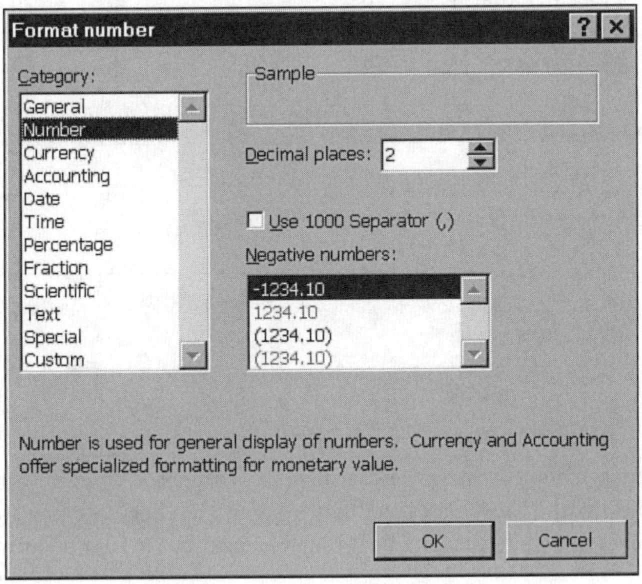

Figure 9.16
Customize the way numbers display in this dialog box.

Select the type of number you want from the Category list, such as date, time, or currency format. Based on your category selection, the right side of the dialog box offers additional formatting options related to the category.

For example, if you choose Currency, the right side of the dialog box lets you choose the currency symbol such as the dollar, pound, or yen. Several of the numeric categories also let you choose the number of decimal places you want to include.

Click OK to accept the formatting changes and to update your chart.

⚠ **Do your datasheet numbers display in an exponential format?** See the Troubleshooting section at the end of the chapter.

INCLUDING AND EXCLUDING ROWS AND COLUMNS

You can include rows and columns in your datasheet, but temporarily hide them in your presentation. To do that, select the column or row that you want to hide, and choose Data, Exclude Row/Column. The row or column appears shaded in your datasheet and temporarily disappears from your presentation. Figure 9.17 shows an example of a hidden column in a datasheet.

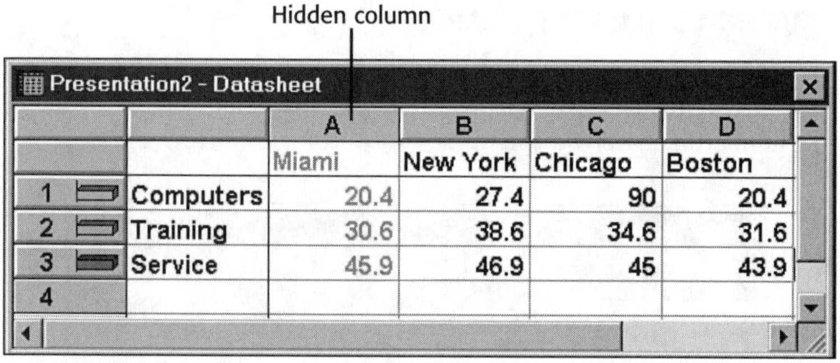

Hidden column

Figure 9.17
This hidden column will temporarily be removed from the chart.

Presentation2 - Datasheet		A	B	C	D
		Miami	New York	Chicago	Boston
1	Computers	20.4	27.4	90	20.4
2	Training	30.6	38.6	34.6	31.6
3	Service	45.9	46.9	45	43.9
4					

To include this information again, choose Data, Include Row/Col.

Tip #116 from
Patrice-Anne Rutledge

You can also double-click the row or column head to include or exclude the rows. In this case, the action serves as a toggle.

RETURNING TO THE PRESENTATION FROM THE DATASHEET

When you finish formatting and modifying the datasheet, you can close it and return to the presentation itself by clicking the View Datasheet button on the toolbar. Or, you can return to working on the presentation while the datasheet remains open by clicking on any section of the presentation.

Tip #117 from
Patrice-Anne Rutledge

To open the datasheet again after closing, click the View Datasheet button again.

FORMATTING A CHART

You can set overall chart options or format specific objects in a chart. Microsoft Graph offers detailed precision in chart creation and the opportunity to make numerous formatting changes. Before making major changes to the chart default, be sure to carefully consider your reason for customizing. Different isn't always better, unless it adds value or clarity to your chart.

PART

IV

CH

9

> **Caution**
>
> If the chart isn't active, you won't see the chart menu and toolbar options. Double-click the chart to select it and display the appropriate options.

SETTING OVERALL CHART OPTIONS

You can set overall chart options for the chart type you selected in the Chart Options dialog box. In Microsoft Graph, choose Chart, Chart Options to display this dialog box, shown in Figure 9.18.

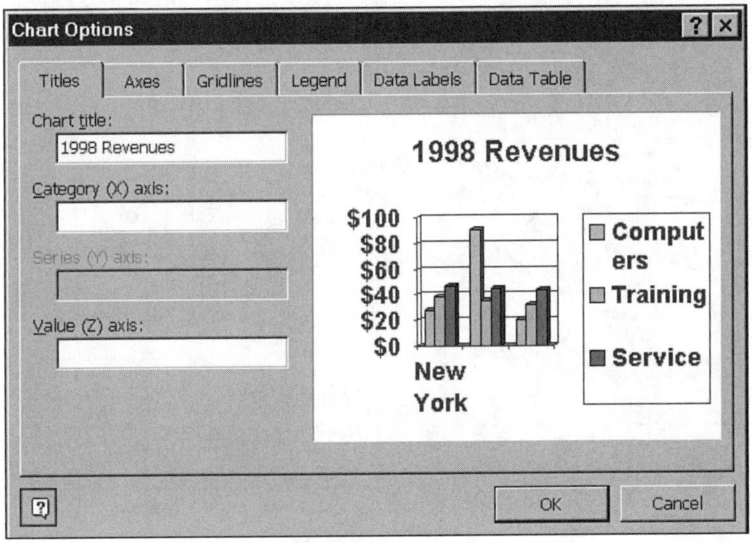

Figure 9.18
Set a variety of chart-formatting options in this dialog box.

We'll use the clustered 3D columnar chart type as an example as we explore the tabs of this dialog box. Remember, however, that if you select a different chart type (such as a pie), the options and tabs may differ slightly.

Make any necessary changes within the tabs of this dialog box, and then click OK to apply them to your presentation.

ENTERING CHART TITLES

On the Titles tab you can enter titles for the overall chart and the available axes such as category, value, or series. The sample to the right previews these changes in your chart.

> **Caution**
>
> The chart title isn't the same as a slide title. If you create a chart title, your chart will have two separate titles, one for the slide and one for the chart.

FORMATTING AXES

On the Axes tab, shown in Figure 9.19, you can choose whether or not to display category, series, and value axes. If a particular axis isn't available, you won't be able to choose it. In this example, the category axis displays the data you entered in the first row of cells in your datasheet. The value axis displays a numerical series based on the values you entered in the datasheet.

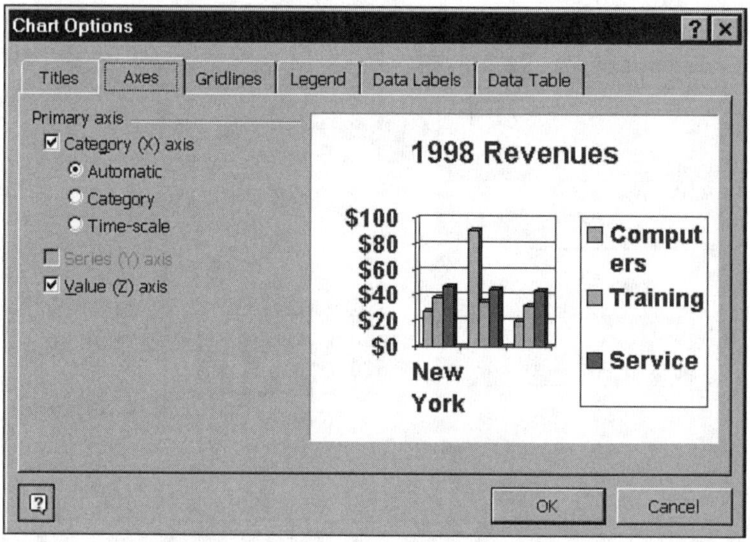

Figure 9.19
Specify whether or not to display a particular axis.

FORMATTING GRIDLINES

In the Gridlines tab (see Figure 9.20), you can choose whether or not to display major and minor gridlines for all available axes.

> **Note**
>
> Pie and doughnut charts don't have gridlines.

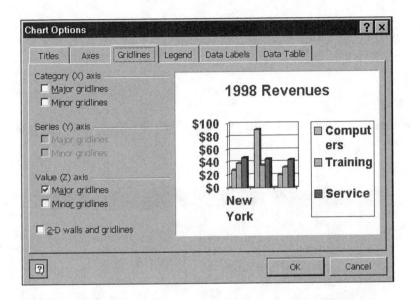

Figure 9.20
Major gridlines, selected by default, can make values easier to read.

DISPLAYING A LEGEND

On the Legend tab, shown in Figure 9.21, you can choose to display a legend by selecting the Show Legend check box.

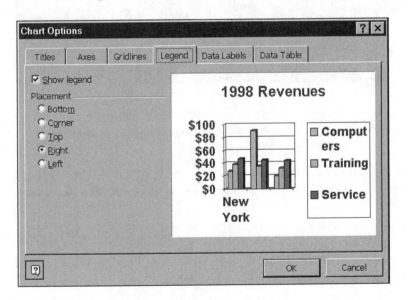

Figure 9.21
A legend makes a chart easier to understand.

You can place your legend at the bottom, corner, top, right, or left of your chart.

Tip #118 from
Patricie-Anne Rutledge

After you place a legend on your chart, you can select it and drag with the mouse to a new location as well.

DISPLAYING DATA LABELS

A data label can make data in your chart easier to identify. You can display a value, percent, text label, text label and percent, a bubble size, or no label at all. Figure 9.22 shows the Data Labels tab.

Figure 9.22
Data labels are optional means of identifying chart information.

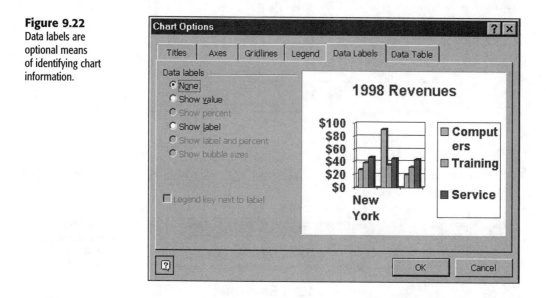

Caution

Depending on the chart type you select, not all data label options are available.

If you do choose to display a data label, the Legend Key Next to Label check box appears. Check this box if you want to display a color-coded box next to the data label to associate it with the legend.

DISPLAYING A DATA TABLE

If you want to include a table with all your datasheet data in your chart, you can choose the Show Data Table check box in the Data Table tab (see Figure 9.23).

If you do select this option, you also have the choice to Show Legend Keys, if you want to display a color-coded box in the table columns to associate them with the legend.

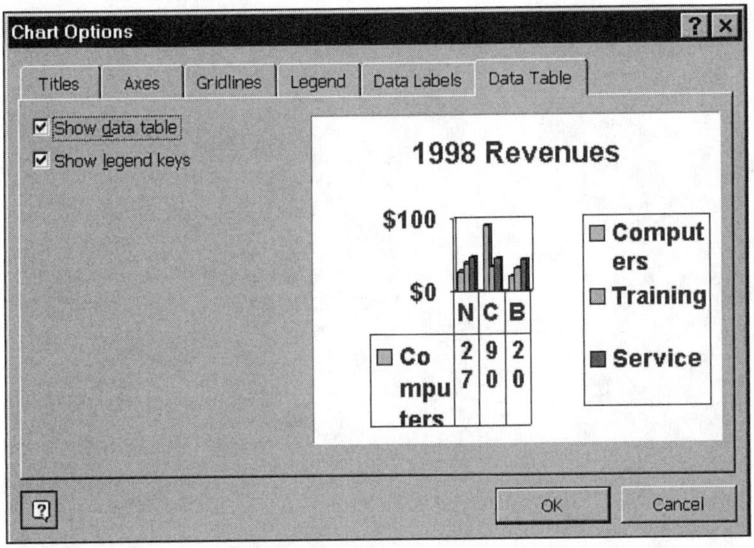

Figure 9.23
If your chart contains complex numerical data, a data table can make this information more meaningful.

FORMATTING CHART OBJECTS

You can also format individual chart objects such as the chart area, axes, series, legend, and gridlines. To format a specific chart object, select it from the Chart Objects drop-down list on the toolbar, and then click the Format button to the right of the drop-down list. A Format dialog box specifically for the type of object you select appears.

Caution

If the Format button isn't available, no formatting options exist for the selected chart object.

You can modify a multitude of formatting options from the Format dialog boxes including pattern, font, placement, scale, alignment, and shape. Remember though, that numerous changes don't always enhance a chart and you may want to make only a small number of formatting enhancements on a regular basis.

→ To learn more about the available options in this dialog box, **see** "Using the Format Dialog Box," **p. 282**

Some things you may want to consider changing:

- Apply a different color to the data series fill areas. To do this, select the data series you want to modify from the Chart Objects drop-down list and click the Format button. Figure 9.24 illustrates the Format Data Series dialog box.

- Choose a new color from the Area group box and click OK. PowerPoint updates the color in the presentation.

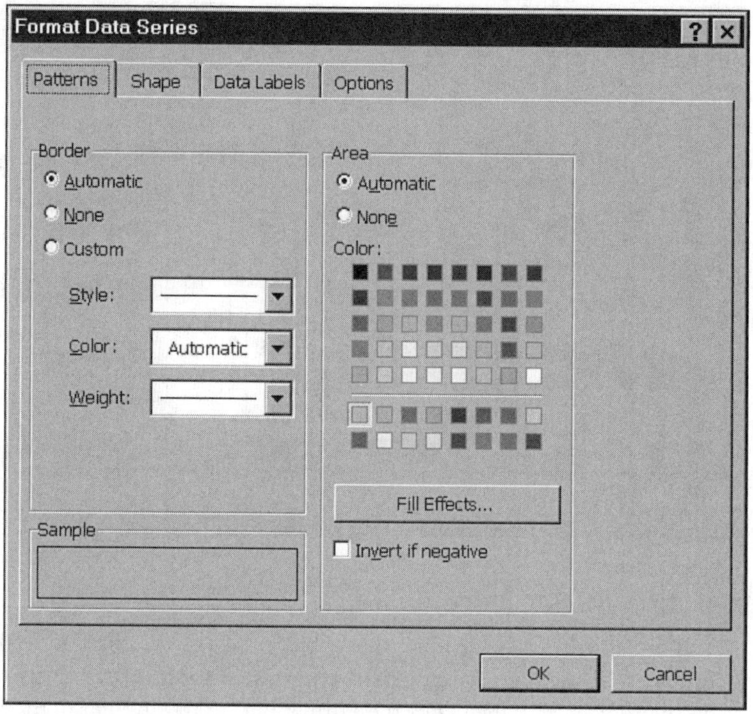

Figure 9.24
Change fill color in
this dialog box.

- Increase or decrease font size to make text more readable or to make it fit a specific area. For example, to change the font size of the legend, select the legend in the Chart Objects drop-down list and click the Format Legend button to display the dialog box of the same name (see Figure 9.25).

- From the Font tab, you can increase or decrease the font size as needed.

- Adjust the value axis scale. To do this, select the value axis from the Chart Objects drop-down list and click the Format Axis button. Figure 9.26 shows the Scale tab in the Format Axis dialog box.

- You can change the minimum and maximum values or the major and minor gridline units on the Scale tab. For example, you could change the minimum value from 0 to 100 if all the values in your chart are more than 100 and you want to see the variations in the existing values more clearly. PowerPoint updates the presentation, making the differences between the three data series much more apparent.

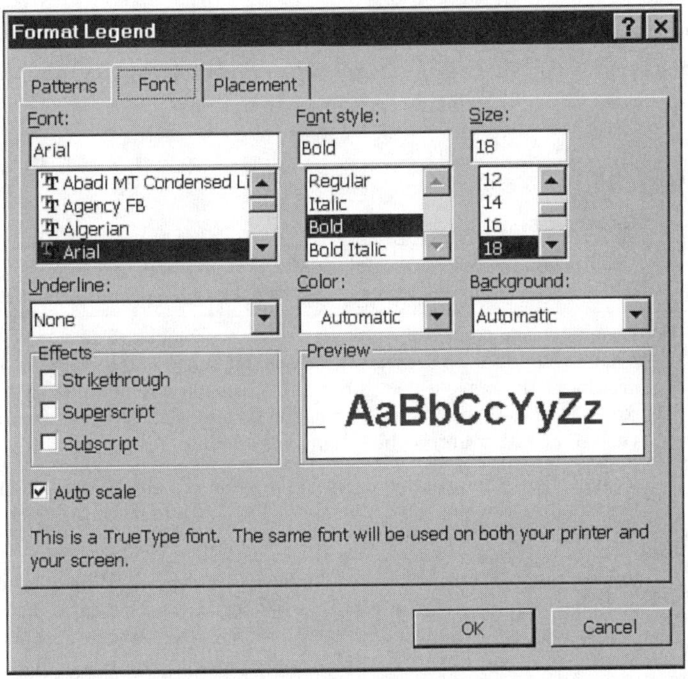

Figure 9.25
Adjusting font size is
a common formatting
change.

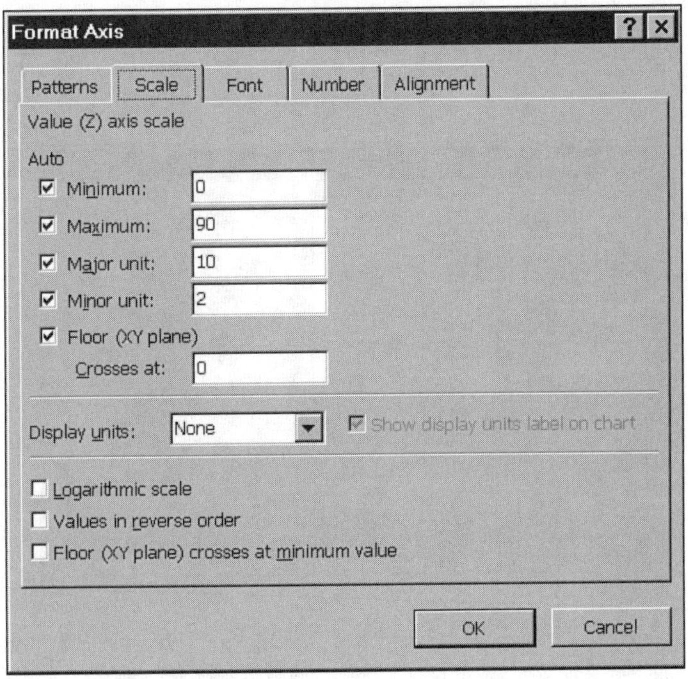

Figure 9.26
You can adjust the
axes and gridlines
in the Format Axis
dialog box.

FORMATTING 3-D VIEW

If you choose a 3D chart type, you can format 3D viewing options such as elevation, rotation, height, and perspective. Table 9.2 explains each of these options.

TABLE 9.2 3-D VIEW OPTIONS

3-D View Option	Description
Elevation	Enables you to control the elevation level from which you view the chart. The range is from –90 degrees to 90 degrees with a default of 15 degrees.
Rotation	Enables you to control the plot area rotation around a vertical axis. The default rotation is 20 degrees with a possible range of 0 to 360. On 3D bar charts, the range is up to only 44 degrees. Be careful not to overdo rotation, however. A 90-degree rotation on a typical column chart will yield some rather unreadable results, for example.
Height	Enables you to control the height of the value axis as a percentage of the length of the category axis. A height of 150% would make the chart height one and a half times the length of the category axis.
Perspective	Enables you to control the chart depth view in degrees. With a default of 30 degrees, the range is from 0 to 100 degrees and measures the ratio of the chart front to back. This option is unavailable when the Right Angle Axes check box is selected or when the chart type is a 3D bar.

To format these options, follow these steps:

1. In Microsoft Graph, choose Chart, 3-D View. Figure 9.27 displays the 3-D View dialog box.

Figure 9.27
Modify the way your chart displays 3D objects in this dialog box.

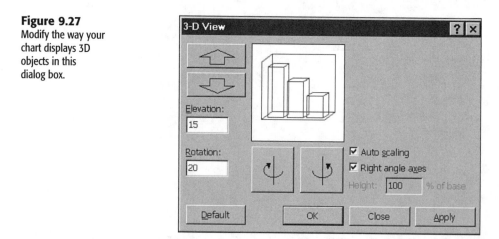

Caution

Again, the default settings for 3D options are designed to work with this chart. Carefully consider any changes you make. Major modifications to a chart's elevation, rotation, height, or perspective can make it unreadable.

→ To learn more about 3D, **see** "Adding Shadow and 3D Effects," **p. 289**

2. Enter a new elevation in the Elevation field or click the up and down arrow buttons above this field to adjust elevation. The box to the right displays an example of what the selected change looks like.

3. Enter a new Rotation or click the left and right arrow buttons to the right of the field to change the rotation. The sample box previews this change.

4. Click the Auto Scaling check box to automatically scale the chart to fit the slide.

5. If you remove the check mark from the Auto Scaling check box, the Height field appears. In it, you can set height as a specific percentage of the base.

6. If you remove the check mark from the Right Angle Axes check box, the Perspective field appears. Set the perspective manually or use the buttons to modify perspective.

7. Click the Apply button to view the effects of potential changes to chart.

8. Click the Default button to set the 3D changes you've made as your new default.

PART
IV
CH
9

Tip #119 from
Patrice-Anne Rutledge

If you make a mistake, click Close to exit the dialog box without saving changes.

---

9. Click OK to apply the changes and return to your presentation.

ADDING A TRENDLINE

You can display a trendline in unstacked area, bar, column, line, stock, XY (scatter), and bubble charts that don't have a 3D effect. A trendline creates a forecast of future trends based on existing data. For example, you can use a trendline to predict future revenues based on existing revenue data in a chart. This is also referred to as regression analysis.

Caution

You can use trendlines to make basic forecasts, but a solid understanding of regression analysis and statistics is necessary to make the best use of this feature.

To create a trendline, follow these steps:

1. Choose Chart, Add Trendline to open the Add Trendline dialog box, shown in Figure 9.28.

⚠ **Can't access the Add Trendline menu option?** See "Chart Types and Trendlines," the Troubleshooting section at the end of the chapter.

2. Choose the Trend/Regression Type, such as Linear or Moving average, from the group box.

3. Select the series on which you want to base the trend from the Based on Series list.

4. Click the Options tab for more options, shown in Figure 9.29.

5. You can enter your own custom name for the trendline or accept the default. The default uses the type of trendline you selected in the Type tab followed by the series name in parentheses.

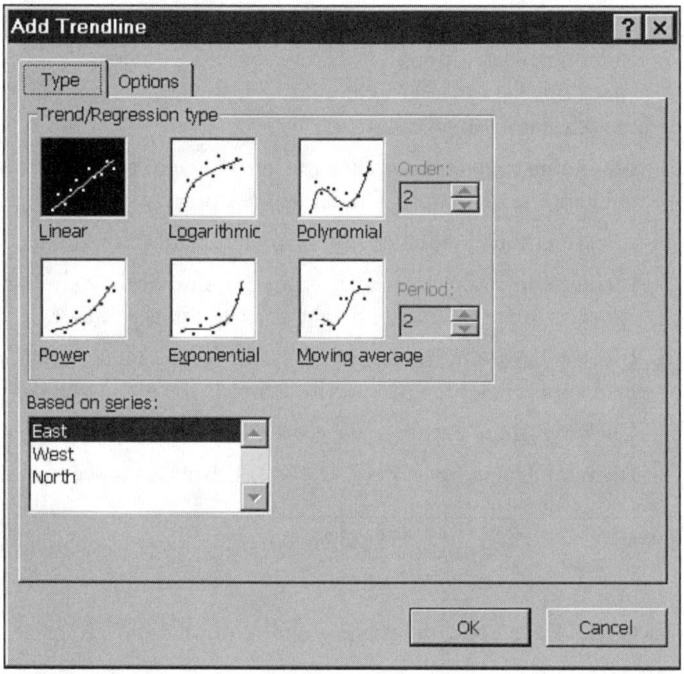

Figure 9.28
Predict future values
by creating a
trendline.

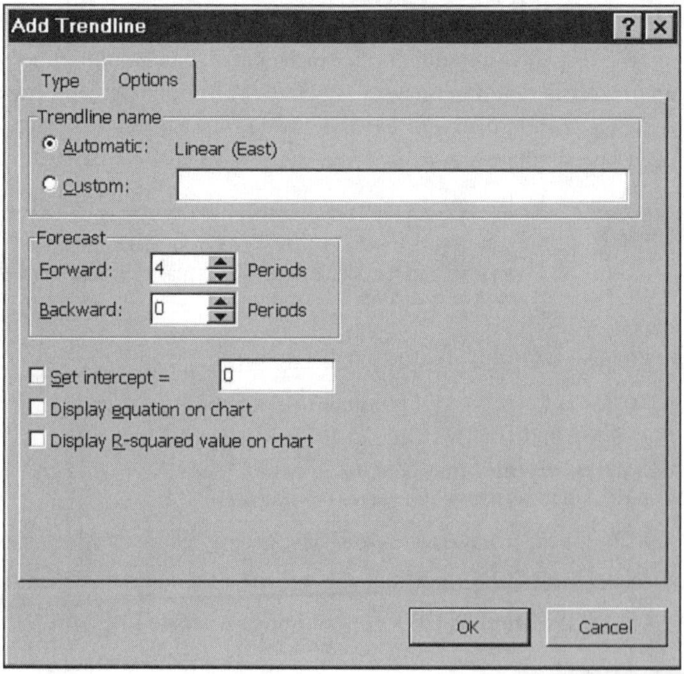

Figure 9.29
Specify the period
of time you want
to forecast.

6. Indicate how many periods you want to forecast either forward or backward. For example, if your chart displays data for four quarters and you choose to forecast four periods forward, PowerPoint displays trends for the next full year in quarterly increments.

7. Click OK to apply the trendline.

Figure 9.30 shows a sample trendline forecasting sales for the next year for a specific region based on its actual data for the current year.

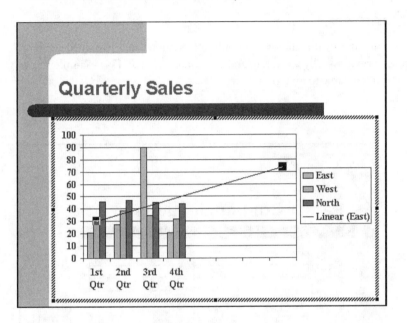

Figure 9.30
This chart illustrates both current values and future predictions.

TROUBLESHOOTING

I can't find the menus or toolbar buttons you mention.

Be sure that Microsoft Graph is active if the text mentions that this menu or toolbar button is part of that application. If you're in PowerPoint, the Graph options won't display. To activate Microsoft Graph, double-click your chart and it appears within PowerPoint.

My datasheet numbers display in exponential formatting.

You need to apply a formatting category other than the default General formatting if your numbers exceed 11 characters. To do so, choose Format, Number from within Microsoft Graph and change to a Category such as Number or Currency.

I can't see the Add Trendline option from the Chart menu.

You can only create a trendline with unstacked area, bar, column, line, stock, XY (scatter), and bubble charts that don't have a 3D effect. Otherwise, this menu option won't be available.

My chart has empty spaces where there should be a data series.

If you don't need one of the existing datasheet rows or columns, you need to remove it entirely from the datasheet, not just the contents. Otherwise, it can display as an empty space on your chart and disrupt formatting. If a series you entered is missing, verify that none of your columns or rows is hidden. To include a hidden row/column, choose Data, Include Row/Col from within Microsoft Graph.

DESIGN CORNER

PowerPoint, in combination with Microsoft Graph, offers numerous chart-formatting options to help you create visually appealing and memorable charts. This example shows how even minor changes can enhance your chart.

BEFORE

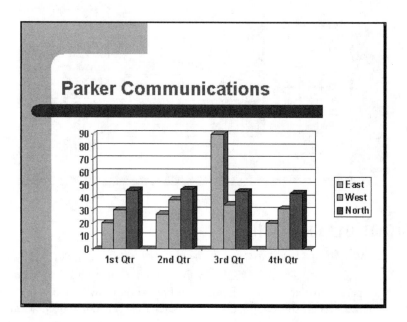

AFTER

Added chart title

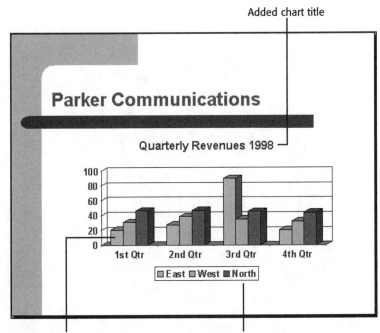

PART

IV

CH

9

Increased 3D rotation to 30%   Moved legend to bottom

CHAPTER 10

WORKING WITH ORGANIZATION CHARTS

In this chapter

by Patrice-Anne Rutledge

UNDERSTANDING ORGANIZATION CHARTS

In PowerPoint you can insert detailed organization charts that you create in Microsoft Organization Chart 2.0, an application that interfaces directly with PowerPoint. Although the application's terminology—manager, subordinate, and so forth—is directed to a corporate environment, you can use an organization chart anywhere you need to set up a hierarchy of people. For example, an organization chart could describe a volunteer committee, school organization, club, or nonprofit group. You can even use Microsoft Organization Chart to organize ideas and projects, not just people.

Organization Chart isn't part of PowerPoint—it's an external application. As such, its features and functions don't necessarily work the same as in PowerPoint. Drawing, formatting, and font options are all slightly different, for example, and aren't as powerful as those found in PowerPoint itself.

Tip #1001 from *Patricia-Anne Rutledge*	If you need to create more flexible or customizable organization charts, you can do so in PowerPoint using the features of the Drawing toolbar or in other external applications such as Visio.

In this chapter you learn

- How to create an organization chart using Microsoft Organization Chart
- How to add staff members
- Why and how to format an organization chart
- How to save and modify organization charts

CREATING AN ORGANIZATION CHART

The fastest way to add an organization chart to your PowerPoint presentation is to select the *Organization Chart AutoLayout (p. 31)* option from the New Slide dialog box.

 To access this dialog box, shown in Figure 10.1, click on the New Slide button on the Standard toolbar.

Tip #121 from *Patricia-Anne Rutledge*	You can also access this dialog box by pressing Ctrl+M or by selecting Common Tasks, New Slide from the Formatting toolbar.

→ For more information about using the New Slide dialog box, **see** "Understanding Slide Layouts," **p. 28**

Tip #122 from *Patricia-Anne Rutledge*	If you use the AutoContent Wizard to create your presentation, it may already have a slide that contains an organization chart.

→ To learn more about the AutoContent Wizard, **see** "Using the AutoContent Wizard," **p. 36**

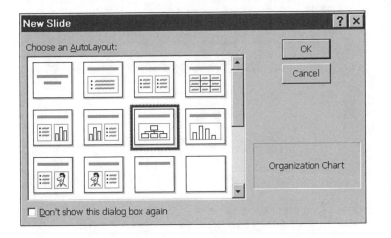

Figure 10.1
Choose the
Organization Chart
AutoLayout option
in the New Slide
dialog box.

Figure 10.2 illustrates a sample organization chart slide.

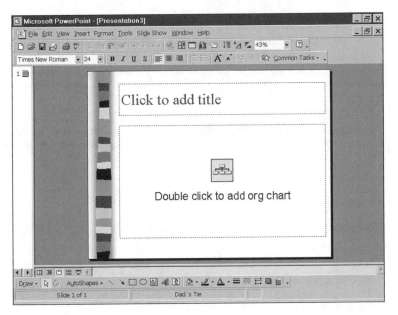

Figure 10.2
You can make your
organization charts
as detailed—or as
simple—as you want.

Double-click the organization chart to open the Microsoft Organization Chart window, illustrated in Figure 10.3.

Tip #123 from
Patrice-Anne Rutledge

You can also insert an organization chart into an existing slide by choosing Insert, Object and selecting MS Organization Chart 2.0 from the Insert Object dialog box.

Figure 10.3
Microsoft
Organization Chart
2.0 displays a blank
chart.

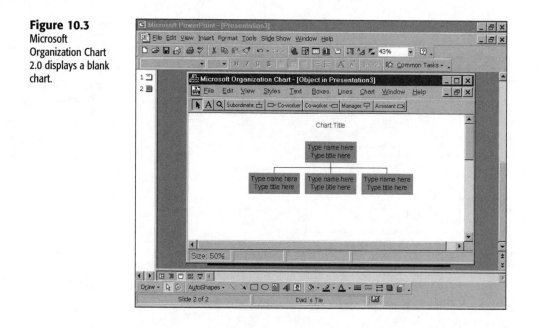

Caution

If this is the first time you're using Org Chart, it may not activate right away because it may not have been installed with the default installation. PowerPoint will prompt you to install it at this point, allowing you to install it now or later. The installation CD-ROM may be needed.

Tip #124 from
Patrice-Anne Rutledge

You should design your organization chart on paper first, particularly if you're not familiar with this application. This enables you to focus on creating the chart rather than on content.

CHOOSING A STYLE

The default organization chart style includes a manager box with horizontal subordinate boxes. If this style doesn't suit your needs, however, you can change it. Other options include grouped boxes, vertical boxes, and styles that omit boxes altogether. Based on your original paper design, determine which style works best.

To change your organization chart to another style, select the entire chart—or a portion of the chart—with the mouse, choose Styles from the menu, and then click the new style on the palette. Figure 10.4 illustrates this palette. PowerPoint redesigns the default style.

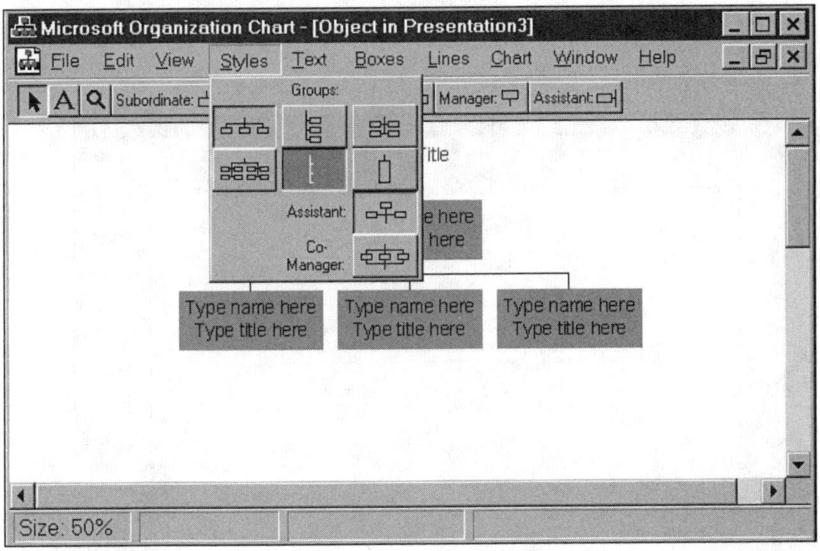

Figure 10.4
You can use the
default style in your
organization chart or
choose another style.

Note

You might want to apply the style to an entire chart, but in some cases you may only want to apply a style to a certain part of a chart. Grouping subordinates vertically rather than horizontally is an example.

Figure 10.5 illustrates an organization chart with subordinates displayed vertically.

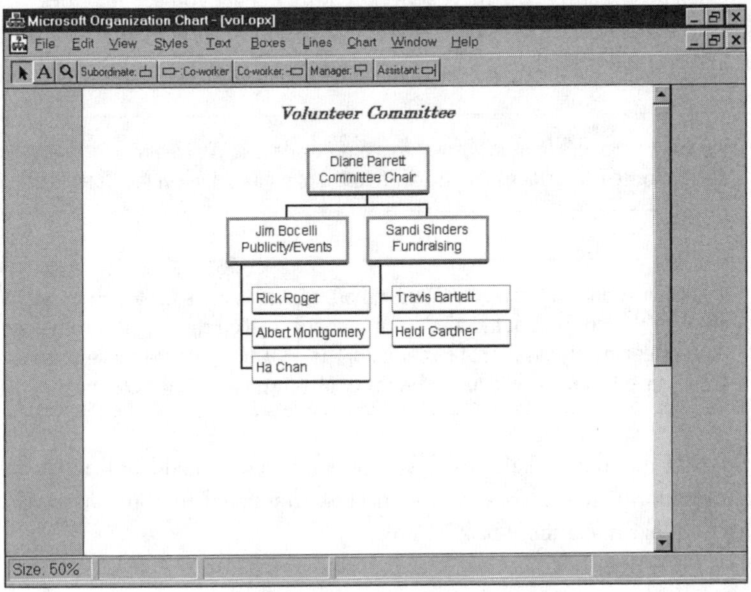

Figure 10.5
A vertical alignment
works well for
a group of
subordinates.

To save space, you can eliminate subordinate boxes entirely if you want. Figure 10.6 illustrates an example of this.

Figure 10.6
Eliminating boxes is a space-saving technique.

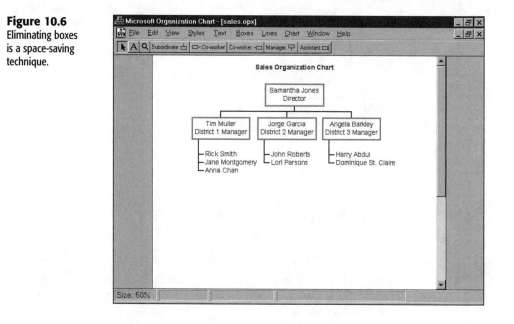

ADDING STAFF MEMBERS

If you choose the default organization chart style, the initial chart you see includes boxes for a manager and three subordinates. In each box you can enter a person's name and title as well as two optional comment lines.

Tip #125 from
Patrice-Anne Rutledge

You can change this four-box default to a one-box default. While in Microsoft Organization Chart, choose Edit, Options and specify to use a one-box default in the Options dialog box.

Caution

If you don't want to include titles in your chart, be sure to erase the text that says "Type title here"; otherwise, that text displays in your organization chart. If for some reason you don't enter a name, this default text also displays on your actual chart unless you delete it. The comment lines are optional and won't display if you don't enter comments.

After you enter data in the four default boxes, you probably need to add additional staff members including subordinates, assistants, co-workers, and managers. Buttons on the organization chart toolbar make these tasks simple.

Tip #126 from
Patrice-Anne Rutledge

You can delete a staff member you added by choosing Edit, Undo Insert before saving. You can also select a box or boxes to delete and press the Delete key.

ADDING AN ASSISTANT

To add an assistant, click the Assistant button on the toolbar, and then select the box of the person to whom the assistant reports. Microsoft Organization Chart adds a box for the assistant, shown in Figure 10.7.

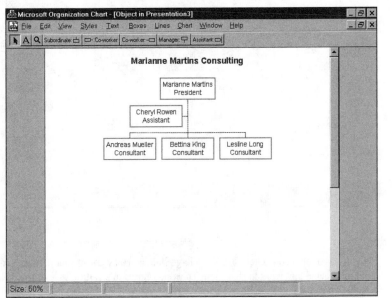

Figure 10.7
Use the Assistant button to quickly add an assistant.

ADDING SUBORDINATES

To add subordinates to an organization chart, click the Subordinate button on the toolbar, and then select the box of the person to whom the subordinate reports. PowerPoint adds the subordinate box.

ADDING MANAGERS

To add a manager to an existing subordinate, click the Manager button on the toolbar and select the box of the subordinate. PowerPoint inserts a box between the subordinate and the previously designated manager.

ADDING CO-WORKERS

You can add a co-worker box to the left or right of an existing box. To do this, select either the Left Co-worker or Right Co-worker button on the toolbar and click the box of the existing staff member. PowerPoint adds a box to either the left or right, depending on your selection. Figure 10.8 illustrates an example of added co-worker boxes.

Figure 10.8
You can format co-workers in several ways.

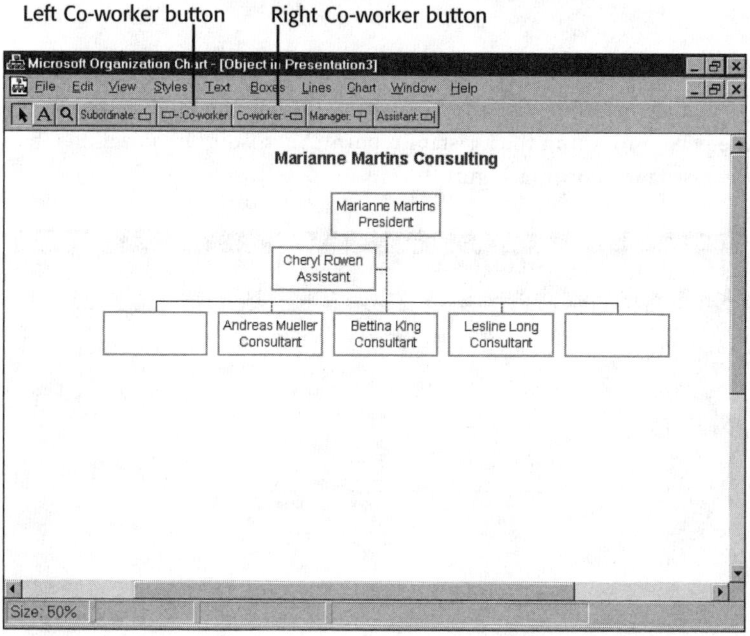

Left Co-worker button   Right Co-worker button

Caution

If you add a lot of co-worker boxes for a large staff, you may crowd your organization chart. To avoid this, you can change the co-worker boxes to a vertical style or to a style without boxes from the Styles menu.

FORMATTING YOUR CHART

You can quickly create an organization chart by using the default formatting options, or you can make modifications to a chart's text, colors, boxes, and lines.

Caution

Remember to consider readability and visual clarity when you modify an organization chart's defaults. Some formatting can enhance a chart's appearance, but too much formatting can make it confusing or worse—unreadable.

Tip #127 from
Patrice-Anne Rutledge

To copy formatting and apply it to another box or text area, select the area you want to copy and choose Edit, Copy Setup. Then select the new area to which you want to apply the formatting and choose Edit, Paste Setup (or Ctrl+V).

FORMATTING TEXT

The default text font is Arial, but you can modify this. Microsoft Organization Chart enables you to change the font, color, and alignment of organization chart text.

Caution

Because Microsoft Organization Chart is an external application, not all the PowerPoint formatting options apply. For example, Ctrl+B bolds text in PowerPoint, but doesn't have this same function in Organization Chart.

CHANGING FONTS

1. Select the text you want to change—an individual box or the entire chart.
2. Choose Text, Font. The Font dialog box opens, shown in Figure 10.9.

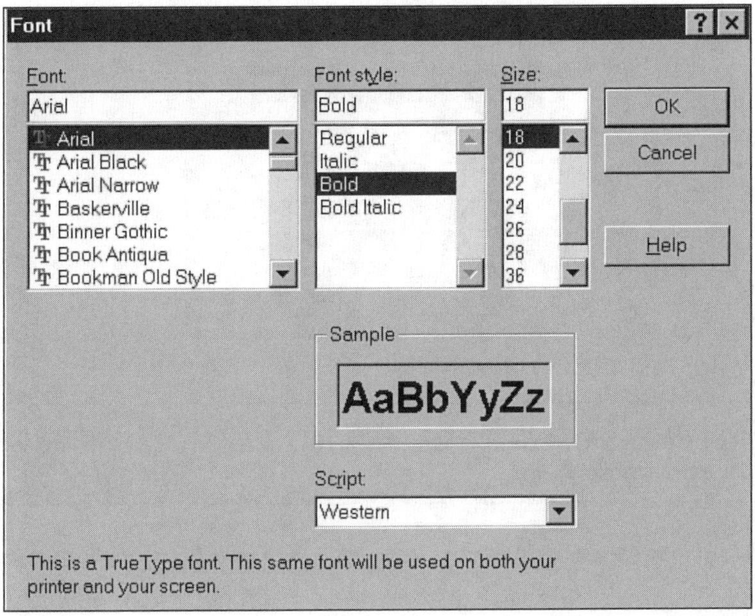

Figure 10.9
Apply a variety of font formatting changes in this dialog box.

PART
IV

CH
10

3. Select the new font from the Font drop-down list.
4. Select the new font style from the Font style drop-down list. Options include regular, bold, italic, and bold italic.
5. Select the new font size, ranging from 8 to 72 points.
6. Verify that Western is selected in the Script drop-down list. Other options such as Greek, Turkish, or Baltic won't display your text properly unless, of course, you are creating an organization chart in another language.

→ To learn how to deal with foreign language fonts, **see** "Using PowerPoint's Foreign Language Capabilities," **p. 733**

Tip #128 from
Patricia-Anne Rutledge

> The Sample box previews what your font changes look like in the chart.

7. Click OK to apply the font changes.

Caution

> Be sure that the font changes you make are still readable.

CHANGING TEXT COLOR

Select the text you want to change and choose <u>T</u>ext, C<u>o</u>lor. The Color dialog box appears, shown in Figure 10.10.

Figure 10.10
The Color dialog box includes a wide variety of colors from which to choose.

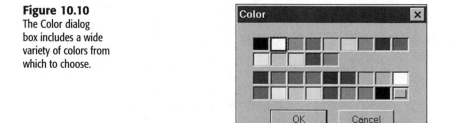

Note

> This Color dialog box isn't the same as the PowerPoint Colors dialog box, which provides many additional color choices.

Choose the new color from the available options and click OK. PowerPoint applies the new color.

→ For additional details on the use of color in your presentations, **see** "Using Color," **p. 569**

CHANGING TEXT ALIGNMENT

By default, organization chart text is centered in each box. You can also left- or right-align this text if you want.

To left-align selected text, choose <u>T</u>ext, <u>L</u>eft. To right-align selected text, choose <u>T</u>ext, <u>R</u>ight. And to center selected text, choose <u>T</u>ext, <u>C</u>enter.

Note

> You can only align text to the left, right, or center in Microsoft Organization Chart and not to the top, middle, or bottom.

FORMATTING BOXES

You can change the colors, shadowing, and borders on organization chart boxes.

CHANGING BOX FILL COLOR

To change the fill color of selected boxes, choose Boxes, Color to display the Color dialog box (identical to the Color dialog box for text). Select the new color and click OK.

Tip #129 from	To change the fill color of the entire organization chart background, choose Chart, Background Color and select the appropriate color from the Color dialog box.
Patrice-Anne Rutledge	

APPLYING A BOX SHADOW

If you want to add a shadow to selected boxes, choose Boxes, Shadow. Figure 10.11 shows the palette that displays. You can choose from seven different shadow options.

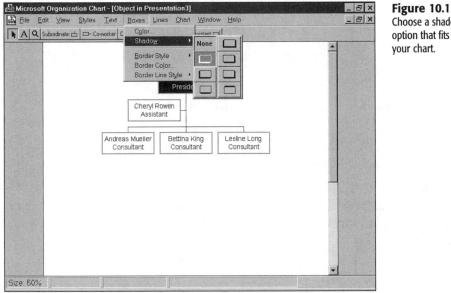

Figure 10.11
Choose a shadow option that fits your chart.

Tip #130 from	You can use a shadow and colors to differentiate between managers and staff, highlight teams or departments, and so forth.
Patrice-Anne Rutledge	

CHANGING BOX BORDERS

You can change the style, color, and line style of organization chart box borders.

To change the border style, select the boxes you wish to change and choose Boxes, Border Style. Figure 10.12 illustrates the border style palette that displays.

Figure 10.12
This palette enables you to choose the exact width and style of a border.

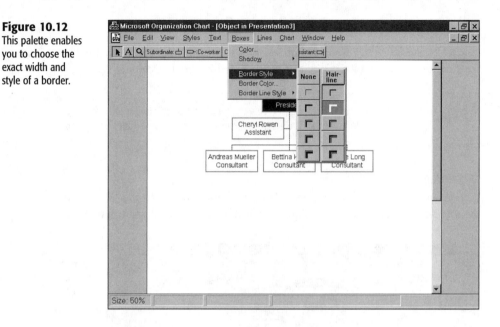

You can choose from a number of border styles—both single and double—ranging from hairline to thick widths.

To change the border color of selected boxes, choose Boxes, Border Color to open the Color dialog box. Select the new color and click OK to apply.

To change the border line style of selected boxes, choose Boxes, Border Line Style and select from the three options that display—a solid line, a broken line with wide spaces, and a broken line with narrow spaces.

Figure 10.13 illustrates an organization chart with border modifications.

FORMATTING LINES

Finally, you can format the lines that connect organization chart boxes.

> **Caution**
> These lines are not the same as the lines that frame box borders.

In Microsoft Organization Chart, select the chart you want to format by dragging the mouse to cover the entire chart area. Alternately, select the area of the chart you want to format.

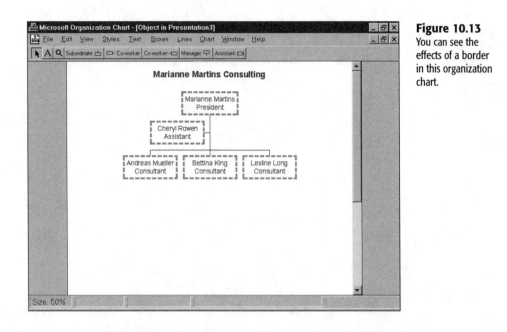

Figure 10.13
You can see the effects of a border in this organization chart.

Tip #131 from
Patrice-Anne Rutledge

Choose Edit, Select, All or press Ctrl+A to select the entire organization chart (except the chart title). You can also select specific areas of the chart from the Edit, Select menu as well.

To change the thickness of the connecting lines, choose Lines, Thickness and select from the options that display—from a thick line to no line at all.

To change the style of connecting lines, choose Lines, Style and select from the three options that display—a solid line, a broken line with wide spaces, and a broken line with narrow spaces.

To change the color of these lines, choose Lines, Color and select the appropriate color from the Color dialog box.

Figure 10.14 illustrates an organization chart with modifications to these connecting lines.

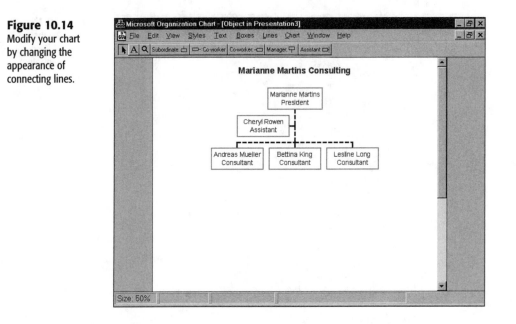

Figure 10.14
Modify your chart by changing the appearance of connecting lines.

VIEWING AN ORGANIZATION CHART

The View menu includes several options for viewing the organization chart. Options include

- *Size to Window*   Displays the chart in a complete window
- *50% of Actual*   The default (and best) size for creating a chart
- *Actual Size*   Enlarges the organization chart to 100% for easier viewing, but part of chart is obscured from view
- *200% of Actual*   Zooms the organization chart so you can view details of a particular section at 200%

Tip #132 from
Patrice-Anne Rutledge

You can also click the Zoom button on the toolbar to zoom in on a particular part of the chart.

USING DRAW TOOLS

Microsoft Organization Chart includes several drawing tools that can provide even greater formatting control. You can use these tools to actually draw your own organization chart, rather than rely on existing features. To view these tools, select View, Show Draw Tools. Buttons that enable you to draw your own lines and boxes appear on the toolbar (see Figure 10.15).

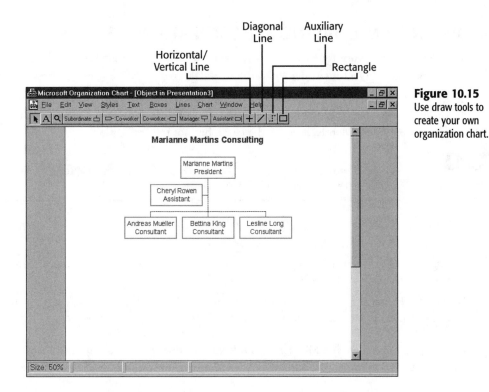

Figure 10.15
Use draw tools to create your own organization chart.

Table 10.1 describes the four available tools.

Button	Name	Description
$+$	Horizontal/Vertical Line	Draws a horizontal or vertical line.
/	Diagonal Line	Draws a diagonal line.
⠿	Auxiliary Line	Draws a connecting line from the edge of one box to the edge of another box.
▢	Rectangle	Creates a rectangular-shaped box.

TABLE 10.1 MICROSOFT ORGANIZATION CHART DRAW TOOLS

These draw tools are specific to the tasks you need to create organization charts and aren't the same as the drawing tools on the Drawing toolbar within PowerPoint, which includes a far greater array of options.

Tip #133 from
Patrice-Anne Rutledge

To hide these draw tools, choose View, Hide Draw Tools or press Ctrl+D.

MODIFYING AND SAVING ORGANIZATION CHARTS

After you complete your organization chart, you need to save it. Organization Chart includes several options for closing and exiting. You can

- *Close and Return to Presentation* If you opened Microsoft Organization Chart from within PowerPoint, this closes the chart and exits Organization Chart. If you open the application independently, it closes the chart, but not the application.

Note

If you created a new organization chart or modified an existing one, a warning box asks you if you want to update your PowerPoint presentation.

- *Update Presentation* Updates the PowerPoint presentation with the new chart, but doesn't exit Microsoft Organization Chart.
- *Save Copy As* Opens the Save Chart dialog box, in which you can save your organization chart outside of PowerPoint.
- *Exit and Return to Presentation* Closes the chart and exits Organization Chart regardless of whether you started the application from within PowerPoint or independently.

For example, you can choose File, Close and Return to Presentation to save the chart and return to PowerPoint. PowerPoint asks whether you want to update this chart (see Figure 10.16).

Figure 10.16
Verify that you want to save and close this presentation.

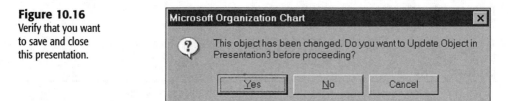

Click Yes to save and close Microsoft Organization chart.

PowerPoint displays the chart you created on your presentation slide, as illustrated in Figure 10.17.

When you save an organization chart in a PowerPoint presentation, you can later modify that chart by double-clicking it within PowerPoint. Microsoft Organization Chart opens, and you can make any desired changes before saving again.

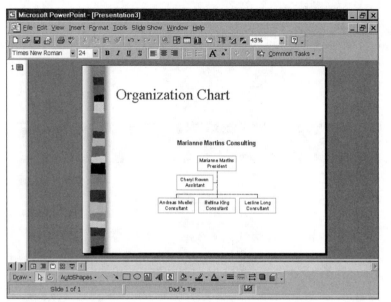

Figure 10.17
Your organization chart now displays in a PowerPoint presentation.

TROUBLESHOOTING

I tried italicizing text in my org chart by pressing Ctrl+I, but it didn't work.

Organization Chart is a separate application from PowerPoint; therefore, not all PowerPoint functions work in Organization Chart. To italicize text, select it and choose Text, Font from the menu. In the Font dialog box you can apply italics.

I saved my chart, but the changes don't display in PowerPoint.

If you save your chart using the File, Save Copy As command, you will save your chart externally, but not update it in PowerPoint. To update PowerPoint, choose File, Update Presentation.

DESIGN CORNER

You can use Microsoft Organization Chart to create a variety of organizational or hierarchical charts.

BEFORE

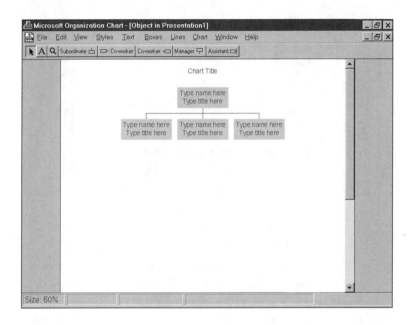

AFTER

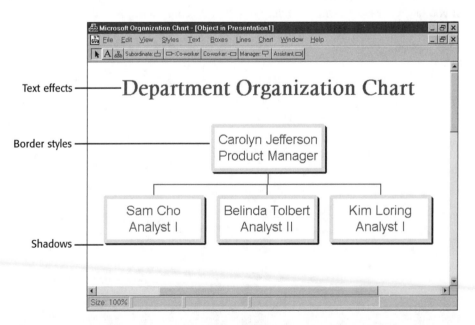

CHAPTER 11

WORKING WITH WORDART AND CLIP ART

In this chapter   *by Patrice-Anne Rutledge*

EXPLORING THE CAPABILITIES OF WORDART AND CLIP ART

Office 2000 incorporates two additional applications that can enhance the design quality of your presentation: *WordArt* and the Microsoft *Clip Gallery*. WordArt enables you to create text-based graphic images that include special effects such as shadowed, reshaped, and rotated text. WordArt is particularly useful for logos and titles, but should be used judiciously for best effect. The Microsoft Clip Gallery offers thousands of clip art images that you can use to enliven your presentations. Microsoft's Web site includes even more images. After you insert clip art into your presentation, you can reformat, recolor, and redesign it to suit your needs.

In this chapter, you learn how to:

- *Insert WordArt pictures*   WordArt combines text with images to create words with special effects such as shadowing, shapes, and rotation.
- *Format WordArt*   After you insert a WordArt image, you can format it by changing its color, reshaping it, or even adding 3D effects.
- *Use the Microsoft Clip Gallery*   The Microsoft Clip Gallery stores hundreds of ready-made pictures, photos, sounds, and videos you can add to your PowerPoint presentation.
- *Import clip art*   If you already have clip art images from another source, you can import them into the clip gallery.
- *Download clip art online*   Microsoft's Clip Art Live Web site contains hundreds of additional clip art images you can download free of charge. Choose a single image or a basket of images to add to the clip gallery.
- *Format clip art*   You can resize, recolor, and reformat clip art images after you place them in a presentation.

UNDERSTANDING WORDART

WordArt 3.0 is an application you can use within PowerPoint to create special text effects such as shadowed, rotated, stretched, or multicolored text. PowerPoint treats WordArt pictures as drawing objects, not text, so the properties that apply to other drawing objects—such as formatting, the use of 3D, and the like—also apply to WordArt.

→ To learn how to apply 3D effects to WordArt, **see** "Adding Shadow and 3D Effects," **p. 289**

Caution

Spell check doesn't work with WordArt because it's a drawing object, not text. You must check spelling manually in WordArt pictures.

Figure 11.1 provides some samples of the type of text formatting you can do with WordArt.

Figure 11.1
WordArt provides numerous options for creating words with special graphic effects.

PART

IV

CH

11

Caution

Be careful not to overuse WordArt in your presentation or it can become cluttered and confusing. WordArt should be used for emphasis only.

INSERTING WORDART

To insert a WordArt image in your slide, follow these steps:

1. Select Insert, Picture, WordArt to open the WordArt Gallery dialog box, shown in Figure 11.2.

Tip #134 from
Patrice-Anne Rutledge

You can also open the WordArt Gallery dialog box by clicking the WordArt button from the Drawing toolbar.

2. Select the WordArt style you want and click OK. The Edit WordArt Text dialog box appears, as shown in Figure 11.3.

3. Enter the text that you want to format using WordArt.

4. Format this text by choosing an appropriate Font and Size and by clicking the Bold and Italic buttons if you want to add these effects.

5. Click OK to place the WordArt drawing on your slide.

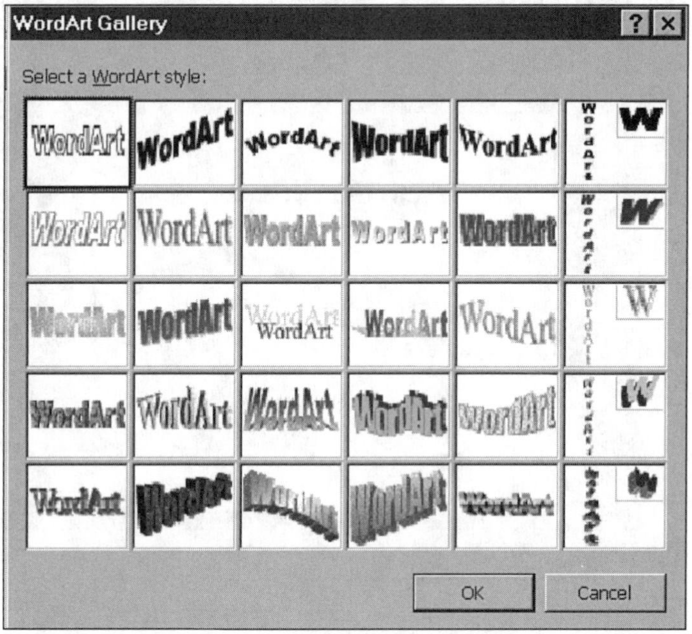

Figure 11.2
Preview WordArt
styles before you
choose one.

Figure 11.3
Enter the word
or words you want
to format in this
dialog box.

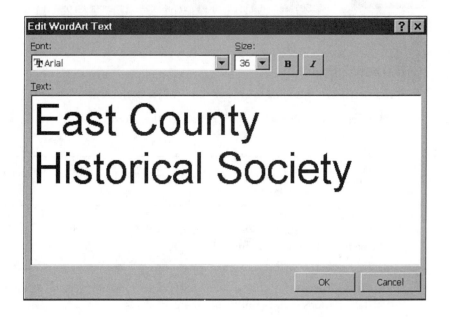

FORMATTING WORDART

After you insert a WordArt image, the WordArt toolbar appears. You can use this toolbar to apply additional formatting options. Table 11.1 describes the WordArt toolbar buttons.

TABLE 11.1   WORDART TOOLBAR BUTTONS

Button	Name	Description
	Insert WordArt	Opens the WordArt Gallery so that you can add an additional WordArt image
Edit Text...	Edit Text	Opens the Edit WordArt Text dialog box so that you can revise the text of the existing WordArt image
	WordArt Gallery	Opens the *WordArt Gallery (p. XXX)* so that you can apply a new style to the existing WordArt image
	Format WordArt	Opens the Format WordArt dialog box in which you can format color, lines, size, and position
Abc	WordArt Shape	Displays a palette of additional shapes that you can apply to your WordArt picture
	Free Rotate	Enables you to rotate a WordArt picture
Aa	WordArt Same Letter Heights	Makes all letters in a WordArt picture the same height
Ab bJ	WordArt Vertical Text	Rotates a WordArt picture to make it vertical
	WordArt Alignment	Enables you to set WordArt alignment including left, right, center, and justified alignments
AV	WordArt Character Spacing	Enables you to make character spacing looser or tighter than normal or to set a specific spacing percentage

Tip #135 from
Patricia Anne Rutledge

Use the buttons on the Drawing toolbar for other formatting options such as changing the fill color of a WordArt picture, adding a shadow, or applying a 3D perspective.

→ For more details on the powerful design capabilities of this toolbar, **see** "Using the Drawing Toolbar," **p. 268**

FORMATTING WORDART CHARACTERS

You can customize several aspects of character spacing and orientation using WordArt.

Click the WordArt Character Spacing button on the WordArt toolbar to choose from a menu that displays the following spacing options:

- Very tight
- Tight

- Normal
- Loose
- Very Loose

You can also set a Custom percentage for character spacing. The default is 100%—a higher percentage loosens the text; a lower percentage tightens the text. Select the Kern Character Pairs option if you want to adjust sets of characters together.

 Click the WordArt Same Letter Heights button to make all the letters in your WordArt picture the same height as the highest character.

 Click the WordArt Vertical Text button to change the WordArt picture from a horizontal to a vertical orientation. You may have to resize the picture to make it fit properly by dragging the bottom side with the mouse.

Figure 11.4 illustrates examples of text spacing modifications.

Figure 11.4
Spacing and orientation make WordArt adjust to your presentation needs.

Text the same height

Vertical text

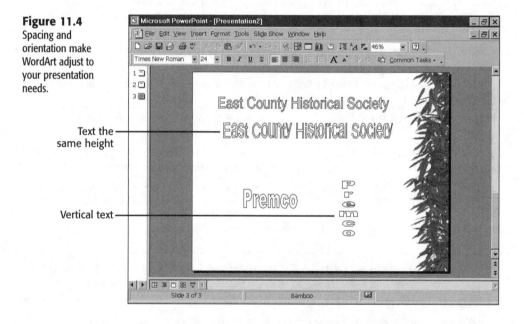

Tip #136 from
Patrice-Anne Rutledge

Click the Undo button to undo any WordArt formatting option that you apply.

MODIFYING WORDART

To modify an existing WordArt picture, select it. The WordArt toolbar appears again. Use the toolbar buttons to change or further customize the WordArt picture.

UNDERSTANDING CLIP ART

The Microsoft Clip Gallery, available from within Office 2000, includes thousands of ready-made illustrations, photographs, sound files, and video clips to use in your presentations. You can search the gallery by keyword or category to find the right clip, import your own clips to the gallery, or download clips from the Microsoft Clip Gallery Live Web site.

→ To learn about adding sound clips in PowerPoint, **see** "Inserting Your Own Sound File," **p. 311**

→ For details on including movie clips in your presentation, **see** "Inserting Your Own Movie File," **p. 312**

The Microsoft Clip Gallery includes clip art images in the following formats:

- Windows Metafile (WMF)
- Computer Graphics Metafile (CGM)
- Graphics Interchange Format (GIF)
- Joint Photographic Experts Groups (JPEG)

Tip #137 from *Patrice-Anne Rutledge*	You can also add images in the Portable Network Graphics (PNG) and Bitmap (BMP) formats.

INSERTING CLIP ART

The quickest way to add clip art to your PowerPoint presentation is to select one of the AutoLayouts from the New Slide dialog box that includes clip art such as Text & Clip Art or Clip Art & Text.

 To access this dialog box, shown in Figure 11.5, select the New Slide button or choose Common Tasks, <u>N</u>ew Slide from the Formatting toolbar.

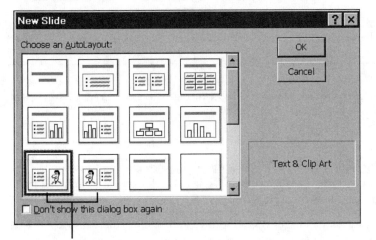

Clip art layouts

Figure 11.5
The New Slide dialog box includes two AutoLayouts that include clip art.

→ To learn more about the kinds of available slide layouts in PowerPoint, **see** "Understanding Slide Layouts," **p. 28**

Tip #138 from
Patrice-Anne Rutledge

> If you use the AutoContent Wizard to create your presentation, it may already have a slide that contains a placeholder for clip art.

→ For further explanation on how to use this wizard and why you might want to use it, **see** "Using the AutoContent Wizard," **p. 36**

Figure 11.6 shows a sample slide with a clip art placeholder.

Figure 11.6
You can start adding clip art by double-clicking the placeholder.

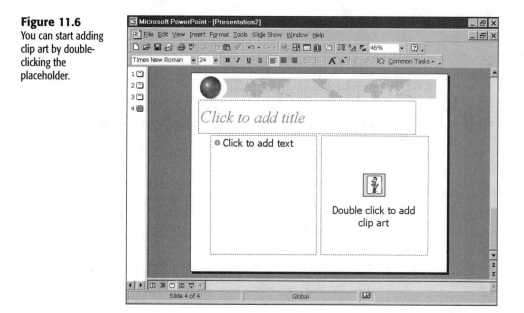

Double-click the clip art placeholder to open the Microsoft Clip Gallery, shown in Figure 11.7.

Tip #139 from
Patrice-Anne Rutledge

> You can also insert clip art into an existing slide by clicking the Insert Clip Art button on the Drawing toolbar or by selecting Insert, Picture, Clip Art. If you use either of these ways to insert clip art, the dialog box is called Insert Clip Art, rather than Microsoft Clip Gallery.

The Microsoft Clip Gallery contains 51 categories of clip art, ranging from animals to backgrounds to photographs to Web elements. To insert a clip art image from the gallery into your presentation, follow these steps:

1. Click the category whose images you want to view. The clip gallery displays a series of individual images relating to that category, as shown in Figure 11.8.

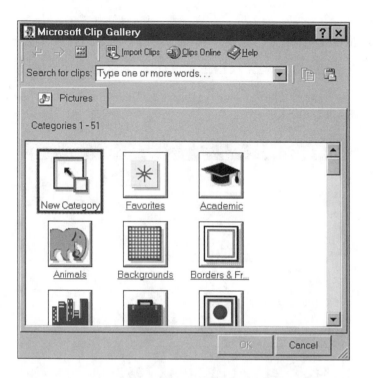

Figure 11.7
PowerPoint opens the
Microsoft Clip Gallery.

Figure 11.8
You can display
clip art by category.

Tip #140 from
Patrice-Anne Rutledge

Use the navigation buttons, Back and Forward, to go back and forth between categories you've selected.

2. Click the image you want to insert in your presentation. A menu with several buttons appears, as shown in Figure 11.9.

Figure 11.9
This menu provides several clip art options.

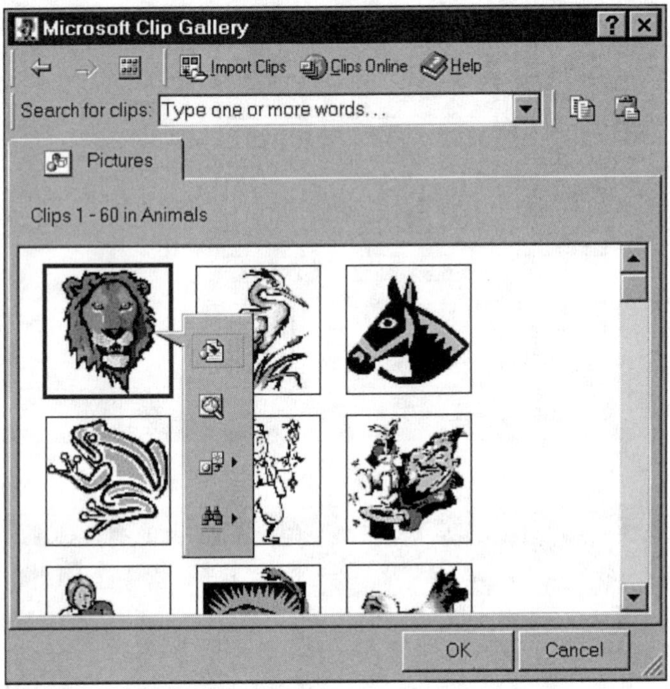

![Microsoft Clip Gallery dialog box showing Search for clips field, Pictures tab, and Clips 1-60 in Animals with various animal clip art images and OK/Cancel buttons.]

3. Click the top button, Insert Clip, to insert the clip into your PowerPoint presentation, closing Microsoft Clip Gallery.

Clip art images don't display in the Microsoft Clip Gallery? See the Troubleshooting section at the end of the chapter.

Figure 11.10 shows a sample clip art image in a presentation.

WORKING WITH THE MICROSOFT CLIP GALLERY

After you are in a clip gallery category, you can find out additional information about each image, recategorize it, or add it to a favorites folder.

To determine the file format of a specific clip art image, place the mouse over it to display a tip that lists the image's file format as well as related keywords, as displayed in Figure 11.11.

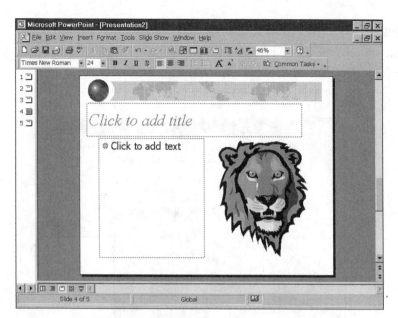

Figure 11.10
Using clip art
can enliven a
presentation.

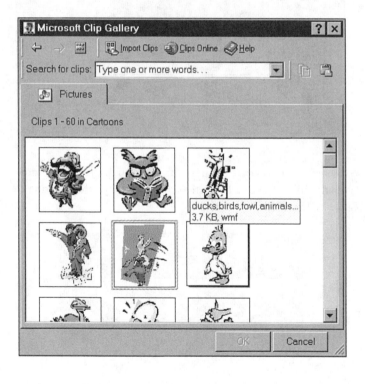

Figure 11.11
Use the mouse to get
information about
file format.

Click the image to display a floating menu using the following four buttons.

- *Insert Clip* Inserts the selected clip into the PowerPoint presentation and closes Microsoft Clip Gallery.

- *Preview Clip* Previews the clip in a preview window, shown in Figure 11.12.

Figure 11.12
Use the preview window to see what a clip art image looks like up close.

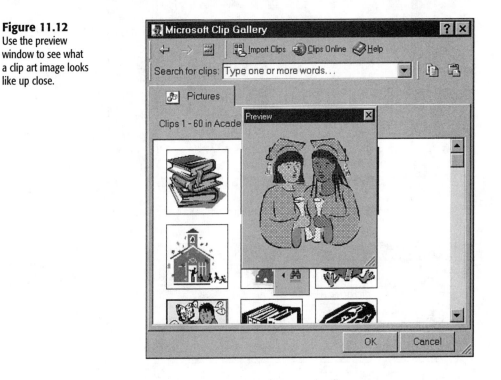

- *Add Clip to Favorites or Other Category* Enlarges the menu to display a drop-down list that enables you to add this image to a Favorites category or any other existing category (see Figure 11.13). Click Add to close.

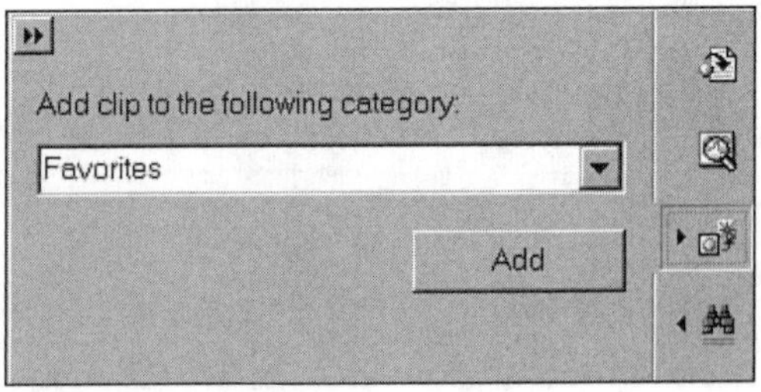

Figure 11.13
You can add clip art to other categories or a favorites list.

PART

IV

CH

11

> **Note**
>
> After you add a clip to the Favorites category, it's available under this category button when you open Microsoft Clip Gallery.

- *Find Similar Clips* Enlarges the menu, shown in Figure 11.14.

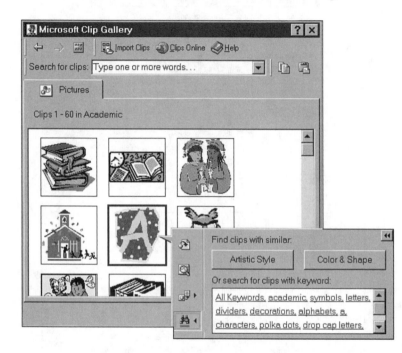

Figure 11.14
If one image isn't quite right, look for other similar images.

Click the Artistic Style or Color & Shape button to have Microsoft Clip Gallery search for related clips and display them. Or, select one of the related keywords to display images that match that keyword.

> **Tip #141 from**
> *Patrice-Anne Rutledge*
>
> You can also search for clips by entering a keyword in the Search for Clips field at the top of Microsoft Clip Gallery and pressing Enter. When you use this feature, you can select previous entries from the drop-down list.

CREATING A NEW CATEGORY

To create a new category, click the New Category button in the main Microsoft Clip Gallery window. The New Category dialog box displays, shown in Figure 11.15.

Enter a new category name in the Enter New Category field and click OK. This category now displays as its own category button, as shown in Figure 11.16, with an icon matching that of the Favorites category.

Figure 11.15
Create your own categories to organize images.

Figure 11.16
You can easily identify new categories you've created.

Tip #142 from *Patrice-Anne Rutledge*

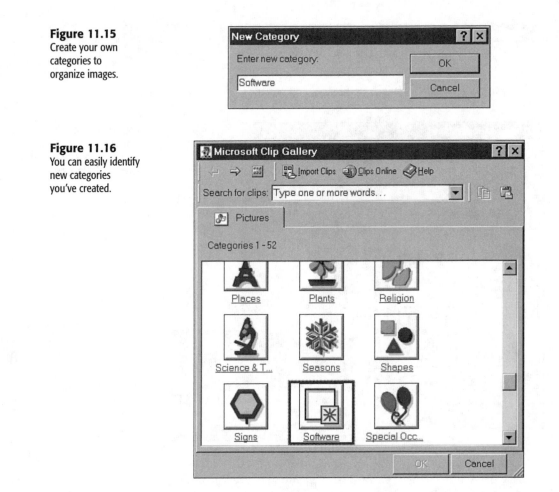

To delete or rename this or any other category icon, right-click and choose either Delete Category or Rename Category from the menu.

RECATEGORIZING CLIP ART IMAGES

1. To recategorize a clip art image, right-click it and choose Clip Properties from the menu. Click the Categories tab, shown in Figure 11.17.
2. Scroll down the available categories, placing and removing check marks as necessary to appropriately categorize the image.
3. Click the Keywords tab, illustrated in Figure 11.18, to change the keywords associated with the image.
4. To add a keyword, click the New Keyword button, which opens the New Keyword dialog box (see Figure 11.19).

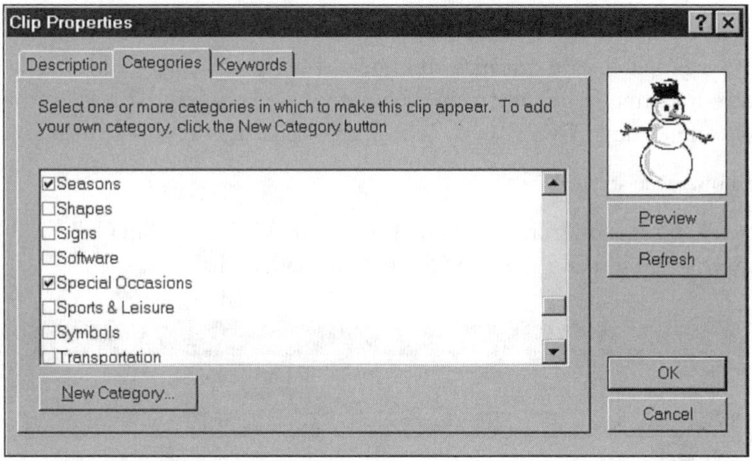

Figure 11.17
Recategorizing clip art images makes them easier to find.

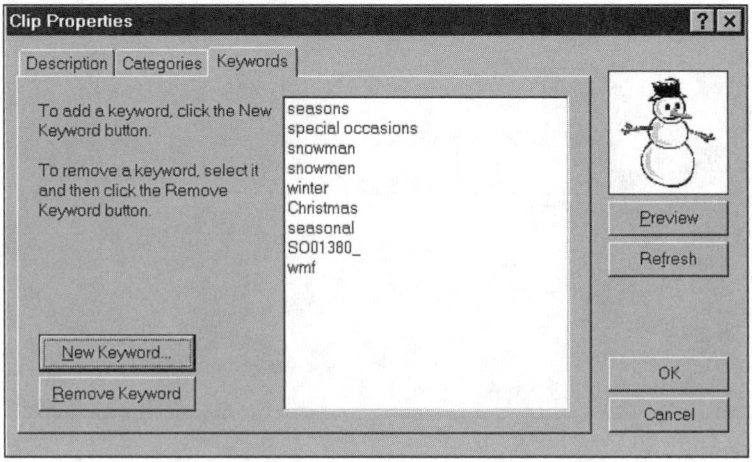

Figure 11.18
Associate keywords with clip art to make them easier to retrieve.

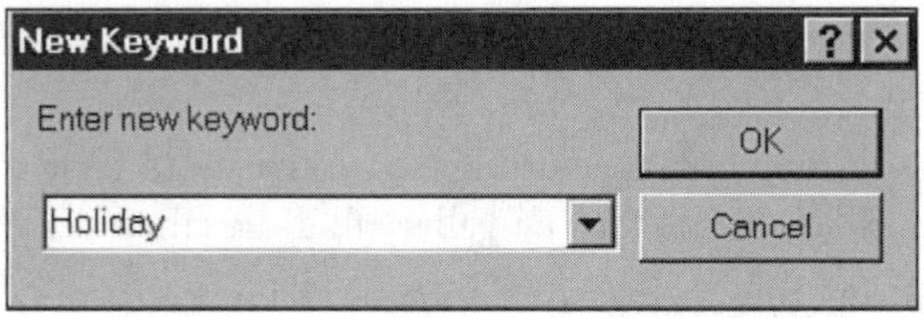

PART
IV
CH
11

Figure 11.19
You can add and remove keywords if you want.

5. Enter a new keyword and click OK.

6. To remove a keyword, select it in the list and click the Remove Keyword button.

7. Click OK to close the Clip Properties dialog box.

IMPORTING CLIPS

PowerPoint also has the capability to organize and categorize clip art images you already store elsewhere on your computer by importing them into the clip gallery. The Microsoft Clip Gallery supports importing WMF, CGM, GIF, JPEG, BMP, and PNG file formats.

To import a file, follow these steps:

1. Click the Import Clips button from the Insert Clip Art or Microsoft Clip Gallery dialog box. Figure 11.20 displays the Add Clip to Clip Gallery dialog box.

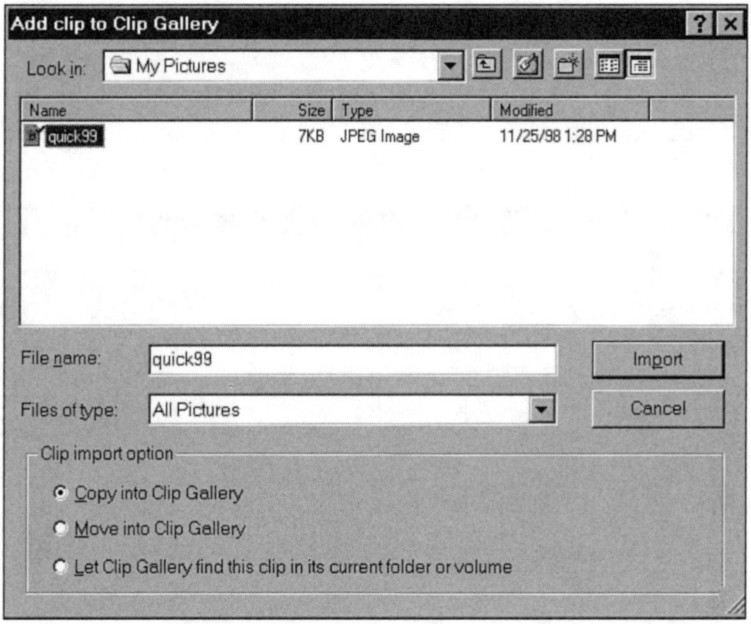

Figure 11.20
Select an image
to import in this
dialog box.

Add clip to Clip Gallery				? X
Look in:	My Pictures			

Name	Size	Type	Modified	
quick99	7KB	JPEG Image	11/25/98 1:28 PM	

File name: quick99   Import

Files of type: All Pictures   Cancel

Clip import option
- Copy into Clip Gallery
- Move into Clip Gallery
- Let Clip Gallery find this clip in its current folder or volume

2. Select the folder where the image is located from the Look In drop-down list.
3. Select the file you want to import. You can narrow your choices in the Files of Type drop-down list.
4. In the Clip Import Option group box, specify whether you want to copy the file, actually move it into the clip gallery, or let the clip gallery find the clip in its current folder.
5. Click Import. The Clip Properties dialog box displays (see Figure 11.21).
6. On the Description tab, you can enter a descriptive word or phrase about the image.
7. On the Categories tab, you can select the categories in which to display the image.

Tip #143 from
Patrice-Anne Rutledge

Click New Category to add another category if none of the existing categories suits your needs.

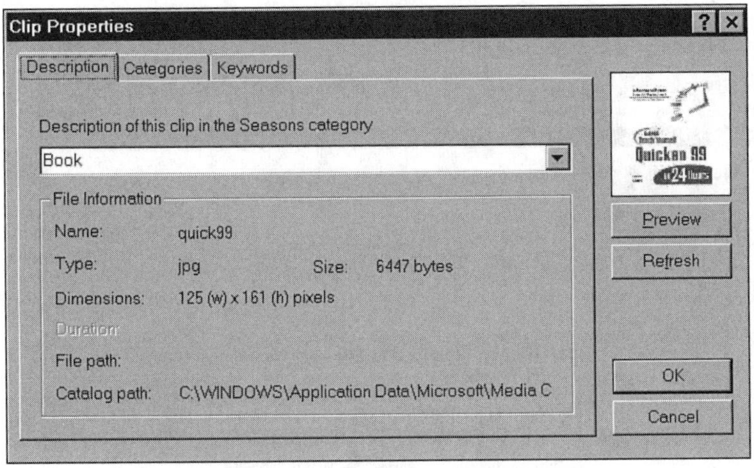

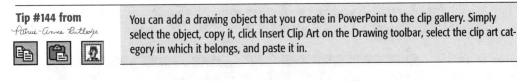

Figure 11.21
Describe the clip
in this tab.

8. On the Keywords tab, you can add or delete keywords associated with this image.

9. Click OK to add to the clip gallery.

→ For more details about categorizing your images, **see** "Recategorizing Clip Art Images," **p. 256**

Tip #144 from
Patrice-Anne Rutledge

You can add a drawing object that you create in PowerPoint to the clip gallery. Simply select the object, copy it, click Insert Clip Art on the Drawing toolbar, select the clip art category in which it belongs, and paste it in.

Tip #145 from
Patrice-Anne Rutledge

To delete a clip art image, select it and press the Delete key.

GETTING CLIP ART IMAGES ONLINE

If the existing clip art images don't suit your needs, you can download additional clip art from Microsoft's online library of images on the Web.

To download online clips, follow these steps:

1. From the Microsoft Clip Gallery, click the Clips Online button. PowerPoint displays a dialog box which verifies that you can connect to the Internet.

Tip #146 from
Patrice-Anne Rutledge

To access online clips and other Web-connected PowerPoint features, you must have Internet access either through a company intranet site or through your own account with an Internet service provider.

---

2. Click OK to proceed. The licensing agreement for the Microsoft Clip Gallery Live Web site opens (see Figure 11.22).

Figure 11.22
Download new and seasonal clip art images from this Web site.

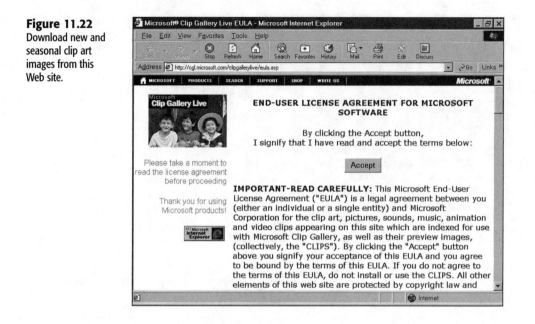

3. Click the Accept button to accept the licensing agreement and continue. Under the Clip Art tab, the Clip Gallery Live displays groups of clip art as well as a search engine that lets you Search Clips by Keyword or Browse Clips by Category (see Figure 11.23).

Figure 11.23
You can download images into the selection basket.

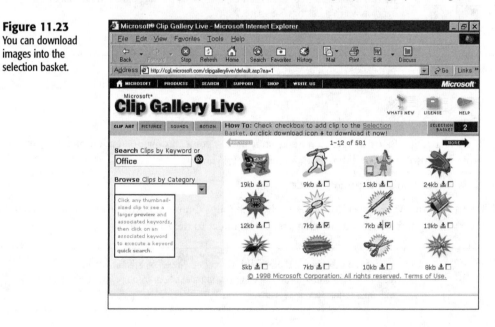

Tip #147 from
Patrice-Anne Rutledge

The Microsoft Clip Gallery Live Web site also includes photographs, sounds, and videos.

4. To download clips, select the check box beneath each image to place it in the selection basket.

5. Click the Selection Basket hyperlink when you're done to display the basket of selected images.

6. Click the Download hyperlink to continue to the next page.

Tip #148 from
Patrice-Anne Rutledge

Click the Empty hyperlink to delete images from the selection basket.

7. Click Download Now!, shown in Figure 11.24.

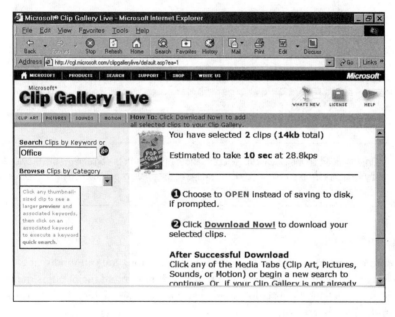

Figure 11.24
You can choose whether to open or download the clip.

The clips are downloaded and displayed in the Microsoft Clip Gallery (see Figure 11.25).

Figure 11.25
Select your new downloaded images from the Microsoft Clip Gallery.

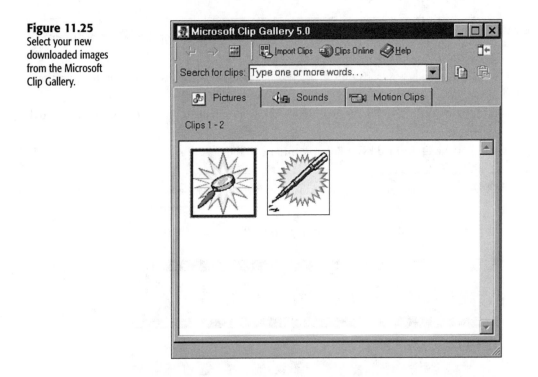

> **Note**
>
> To download an individual clip, select it, and it previews in the box below the Browse Clips by Category drop-down list. Click the image in the preview box to open the File Download dialog box.

MODIFYING CLIP ART IMAGES

After you insert a clip art image into a PowerPoint presentation, you can modify it to suit your needs. Using the Picture toolbar, you can make both minor and major adjustments to an inserted clip such as changing its color or adjusting its contrast. Table 11.2 describes each button on the Picture toolbar.

TABLE 11.2   PICTURE TOOLBAR BUTTONS

Button	Name	Description
	Insert Picture from File	Opens the Insert Picture dialog box from which you can choose another image
	Image Control	Enables you to convert the image to grayscale, black-and-white, or watermark images
	More Contrast	Enhances the contrast of the selected image

Button	Name	Description
	Less Contrast	Reduces the contrast of the selected image
	More Brightness	Increases the image's brightness
	Less Brightness	Decreases the image's brightness
	Crop	Enables you to crop the image to another size
	Line Style	Displays a list of varying line widths and styles from which to choose
	Recolor Picture	Enables you to change the color of a clip art image
	Format Picture	Offers numerous options for formatting an image's lines, color, size, and position
	Set Transparent Color	Converts a single color to a transparent image
	Reset Picture	Returns the image to its original state

RECOLORING A CLIP ART IMAGE

You can recolor a Windows metafile image (WMF), such as a clip art image, after you place it in a PowerPoint presentation. This can be very useful, particularly if you want the image to match the colors of a selected design template.

Can't recolor your image? See the Troubleshooting section at the end of the chapter.

To recolor a WMF image, follow these steps:

1. Select the image you want to recolor and click the Recolor Picture button on the Picture toolbar. The Recolor Picture dialog box opens, as shown in Figure 11.26.

2. Select the Colors option button to change the actual image colors or the Fills option button to change background colors.

Note

Selecting Fills doesn't affect line colors.

3. Place a check mark next to the Original color you want to change.

4. Select a New color from the drop-down list of colors.

Tip #149 from
Patrice-Anne Rutledge

Click More Colors from the drop-down list of colors to open the Colors dialog box, which offers a wide array of custom colors from which to choose.

Figure 11.26
Change the color of a
WMF image to match
your presentation.

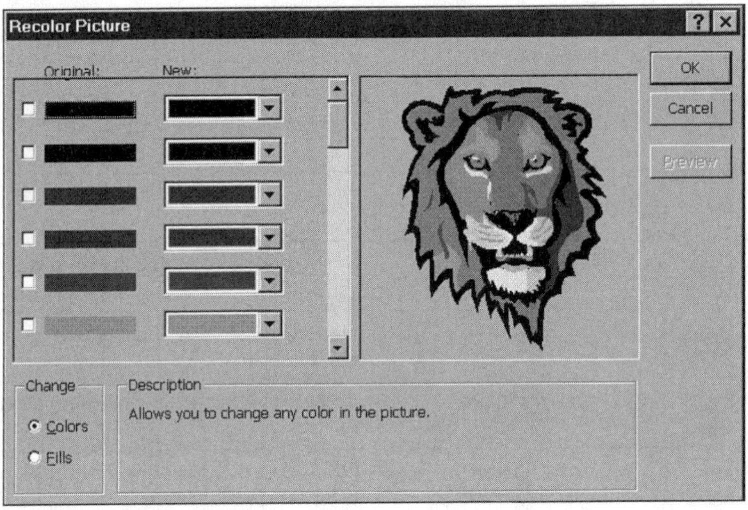

→ To learn more about applying colors to objects, **see** "Specifying Color," **p. 274**

→ For details on color theory, **see** "Using Color," **p. 569**

    5. Click the Preview button to view the suggested color changes before you make them.

    6. Click OK to apply the changes to the presentation.

FORMATTING CLIP ART IMAGES

When you place a clip art image in your presentation, you can make changes to its lines, size, and position in the Format dialog box. Chapter 12, "Creating and Formatting Objects," describes how to use this dialog box in detail.

You can also combine clip art with WordArt pictures to create a complete graphic image such as a logo, an example of which is shown in Figure 11.27.

To create this image, place both a WordArt picture and clip art on the slide and adjust their position to create the image you want. You should also group these two images together to make them one.

→ For instructions on how to group PowerPoint objects, **see** "Grouping Objects," **p. 294**

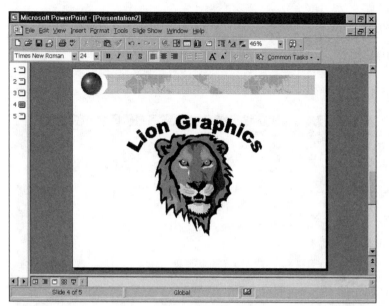

Figure 11.27
Combine WordArt and clip art to make an interesting logo or title.

TROUBLESHOOTING

I can't recolor my clip art image.

You can't recolor BMP, JPG, GIF, or PNG images. Instead, you have to use an external program, such as Microsoft Photo Editor, to convert the color of these images.

I'm having trouble modifying an animated GIF image with the Picture toolbar buttons.

You can't use many of the Picture toolbar and Format Picture dialog box formatting options with an animated GIF. You need to use an animated GIF editing program to make these changes.

The Microsoft Clip Gallery doesn't contain any clip art images.

Reinstall Office 2000, selecting the Clip Art option under Office Tools.

DESIGN CORNER

The appropriate use of WordArt and clip art can enliven a presentation.

BEFORE

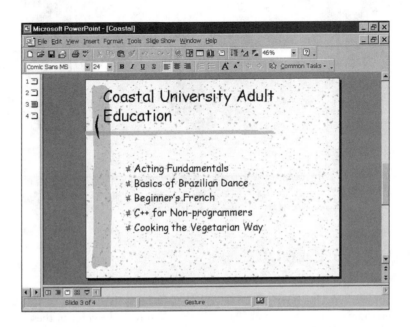

AFTER

WordArt——

Clip art——

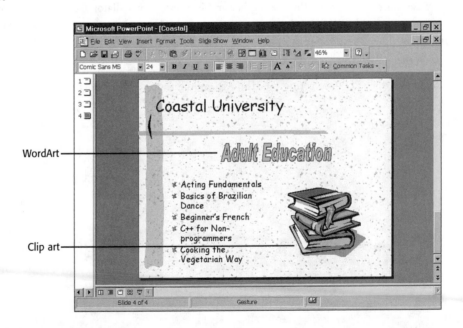

CHAPTER 12

CREATING AND FORMATTING OBJECTS

In this chapter

by Patrice-Anne Rutledge

EXPLORING OBJECT CREATION AND FORMATTING

PowerPoint includes more drawing and object formatting options than you'll probably ever use. These features are simple enough to meet the needs of the casual user, yet powerful enough to handle the customization requirements of a sophisticated PowerPoint designer. The Drawing toolbar is the centerpiece of PowerPoint's suite of drawing tools and includes buttons that enable you to insert images, shapes, WordArt, and clip art. This toolbar also provides access to detailed and varied options for coloring, positioning, formatting, and manipulating the drawing objects you create.

In this chapter you learn

- *How to use the Drawing toolbar* PowerPoint's Drawing toolbar enables you to place a variety of different shapes and images on your presentation slides.
- *Applying colors* The effective use of color can really make your presentation stand out. Using the Drawing toolbar, you can apply fill, font, and line color as well as patterns.
- *When to use the Format dialog box* The Format dialog box enables you to make a multitude of formatting changes all in one place. You can adjust the color, size, position, and other characteristics of a selected object.
- *Manipulating objects* PowerPoint makes cutting, copying, pasting, moving, and resizing objects a simple and straightforward task.
- *Applying shadow and 3D effects* You can apply a variety of shadow and 3D effects to a selected object and can even adjust the lighting, surface, and exact position using special settings toolbars.
- *Aligning and adjusting objects* Setting alignment, nudging, snapping to a grid or shape, grouping, setting order, rotating, and flipping are all additional modifications you can make to a PowerPoint object.

USING THE DRAWING TOOLBAR TO CREATE OBJECTS

You can use the Drawing toolbar to add a variety of visual objects to your PowerPoint presentation such as rectangles, ovals, AutoShapes, WordArt, and clip art. You can also modify existing objects using the toolbar buttons to apply shading, 3D, color, and other effects.

To open this toolbar, choose <u>V</u>iew, <u>T</u>oolbars, Drawing. Table 12.1 lists all the buttons on this toolbar.

TABLE 12.1   DRAWING TOOLBAR BUTTONS

Button	Name	Description
Dr<u>a</u>w ▾	Draw	Displays a menu with a variety of drawing options such as placement and formatting
▚	Select Objects	Activates a pointer that enables you to select drawing objects

Button	Name	Description
	Free Rotate	Enables you to rotate an object
AutoShapes ▾		
	AutoShapes	Displays a menu of AutoShape types from which to choose
	Line	Enables you to draw a line
	Arrow	Enables you to draw an arrow
	Rectangle	Enables you to place a rectangular shape on your slide
	Oval	Enables you to place an oval shape on your slide
	Text Box	Enables you to place a text box on your slide
	Insert WordArt	Opens the WordArt Gallery
	Insert Clip Art	Opens the Microsoft Clip Gallery
	Fill Color	Displays the Fill Color palette from which you can choose a fill color or pattern
	Line Color	Displays the Line Color palette from which you can choose a line color or pattern
	Font Color	Displays the Font Color palette from which you can choose a font color
	Line Style	Displays a series of line styles you can apply to a selected line
	Dash Style	Displays a series of dash styles you can apply to a selected line
	Arrow Style	Displays a series of arrow styles you can apply to a selected arrow
	Shadow	Displays a Shadow palette from which you can choose a shadow to apply to a selected object
	3D	Displays a 3D palette from which you can choose a 3D effect to apply to a selected object

PART

IV

CH

12

Adding Lines and Arrows

You can add *lines (p. 236)* and *arrows (p. 569)* to your presentation for emphasis. For example, you may want to add a line beneath a word or phrase to draw attention to it. You could also use an arrow to point to text or an object of special importance.

Tip #150 from
Patrice-Anne Rutledge

To underline selected text, you can also click the Underline button on the Formatting toolbar. The line drawing feature, however, provides more flexibility in terms of the color, position, and width of line you use.

CREATING A LINE

To draw a line on your presentation, click the Line button on the Drawing toolbar. Use the mouse to draw a line in the exact location you want to place it. If the line looks crooked or is the wrong length, select it and adjust the ends.

Tip #151 from
Patrice-Anne Rutledge

Press the Shift key as you drag the mouse to create perfectly straight horizontal or vertical lines. Press the Ctrl key as you drag the mouse to draw a line from a center point, lengthening the line in both directions as you drag.

To specify line style, select the line and click the Line Style button on the toolbar. The Line Style palette displays, shown in Figure 12.1.

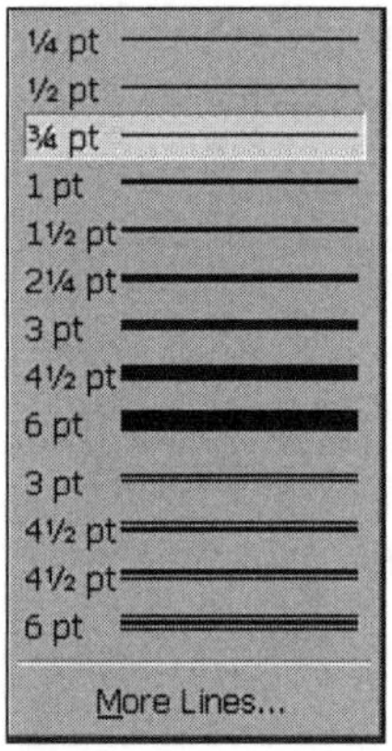

Figure 12.1
Create either single or double lines in your presentation.

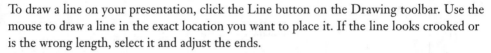

You can choose from a variety of single and double lines from ¼ point to 6 points in width. For additional options, select <u>M</u>ore Lines, which opens the Format AutoShapes dialog box where you can set additional line options.

Tip #152 from
Patrice-Anne Rutledge

You can also open this dialog box by right-clicking the mouse and choosing Format Aut<u>o</u>Shape.

→ To learn more about this dialog box, **see** "Using the Format Dialog Box," **p. 282**

→ For more details about coloring lines, **see** "Specifying Line Color," **p. 280**

You can use the Line Style palette for more than just formatting lines. You can use this palette to format lines associated with arrows, rectangles, ovals, AutoShapes, and other objects as well.

Tip #153 from
Patricia-Anne Rutledge

You can also change your line to a dashed line or an arrow by clicking the Dash Style or Arrow Style button.

CREATING AN ARROW

To draw an arrow on your presentation, click the Arrow button on the Drawing toolbar. Use the mouse to draw an arrow in the location you want to place it.

To specify an arrow style, select the arrow and click the Arrow Style button on the toolbar. The Arrow Style palette displays, shown in Figure 12.2.

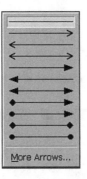

Figure 12.2
Arrows can point to areas you want to emphasize.

You can choose from a variety of arrow types—both single and double arrows. For additional options, select More Arrows, which opens the Format AutoShapes dialog box.

→ For details on the available options in this dialog box, **see** "Using the Format Dialog Box," **p. 282**

Figure 12.3 shows a slide that utilizes both lines and arrows.

PART

IV

CH

12

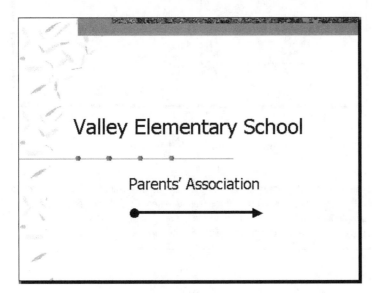

Figure 12.3
Use lines and arrows to add clarity and visual effect.

ADDING RECTANGLES AND OVALS

You can draw rectangular and oval shapes directly on your PowerPoint presentation.

 To draw a rectangle, click the Rectangle button on the Drawing toolbar and use the mouse to draw a rectangular (or square) shape.

Tip #154 from	To draw a square, press the Shift key while drawing your shape.
Patricia-Anne Rutledge	

 To draw an oval or circular shape, click the Oval button on the Drawing toolbar and use the mouse to draw the desired shape.

Tip #155 from	Pressing the Shift key while creating an oval shape forms a perfectly shaped circle.
Patricia-Anne Rutledge	

Figure 12.4 shows the use of rectangular and oval shapes in a slide.

Figure 12.4
You can add images such as squares and circles to your presentation.

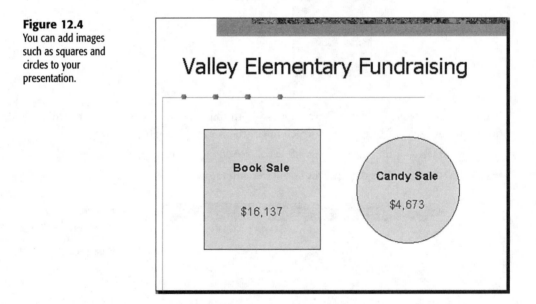

You can then reshape and resize this image or apply other formatting to it.

Tip #156 from	You can add text to a rectangular or oval shape. If you only want to add a word or two, select the object and type in the text you want to enter. Or click the Text Box button on the Drawing toolbar and create a text box inside the original object. Be sure, however, that the text box fits into the object without overlapping its borders.
Patricia-Anne Rutledge	

ADDING TEXT BOXES

You can create a *text box (p. 58)* to add text to your slide other than in your original text placeholders or to frame special text. Click the Text Box button on the Drawing toolbar and click where you want to place the text box on the slide. Start entering text to create the box. Figure 12.5 illustrates the use of a text box.

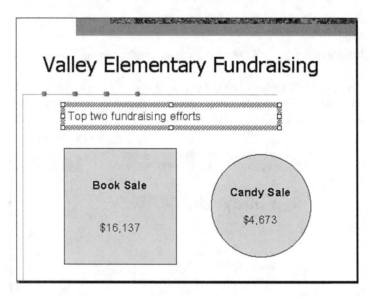

Figure 12.5
A text box calls attention to something you want to say in your presentation as well as enables you to place text exactly where you want it.

You can format the text in a text box as you would any other text, including formatting the font, font size, color, and style.

→ For more details on ways to format text in PowerPoint, **see** "Formatting Text," **p. 59**

→ To learn how to make changes to a text box you add, **see** "Formatting a Text Box," **p. 286**

ADDING AUTOSHAPES

An *AutoShape* is a drawing object such as a rectangle or oval. AutoShapes make creating callouts, flowcharts, block arrows, and other special objects much easier.

To insert an AutoShape, click the AutoShapes button on the Drawing toolbar and choose the type of AutoShape you want from the menu. Options include

- *Lines*   Includes special line forms such as curves, scribbles, and freeform.

- *Connectors*   Offers three different kinds of connectors to connect objects—straight, elbow, or curved. Even if you move one of the connected objects, its connector stays attached and moves with it.

Tip #157 from
Patrice-Anne Rutledge

> To ensure that the connection between two objects is the shortest possible distance, you can reroute connectors. To do this, click the Draw button from the Drawing toolbar and choose Reroute Connectors.

- *Basic Shapes*   Includes shapes such as a hexagon, moon, triangle, box, arc, and plaque.
- *Block Arrows*   Offers large block arrows similar to regular line arrows, but much thicker.
- *Flowcharts*   Offers flowchart images such as process, document, input, and terminator.
- *Stars and Banners*   Offers waves, scrolls, explosions, and pointed stars.
- *Callouts*   Includes several types of callout images that you can use to call attention to a particular part of the slide.
- *Action Buttons*   Includes several action button options such as beginning, forward, and next.

Choose the specific AutoShape you want from the palette that displays when you select a menu option and place it on the slide by dragging the mouse. You can then format the AutoShape as you would any other object. Figure 12.6 shows some sample AutoShapes.

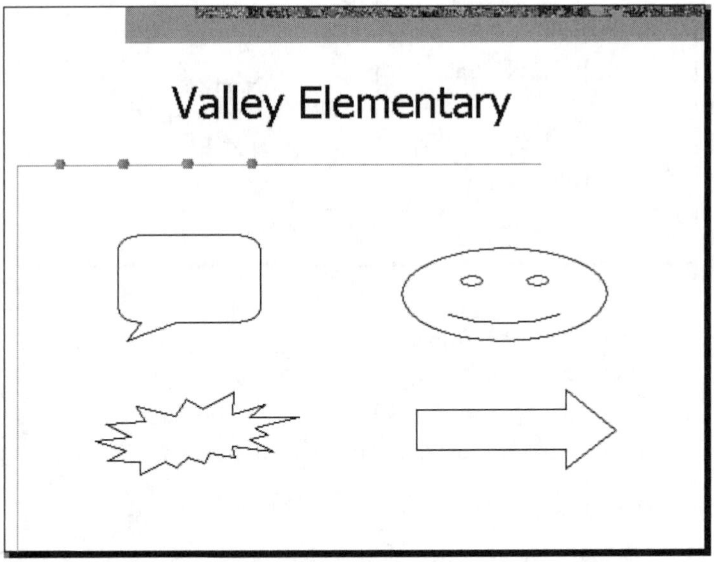

Figure 12.6
Callouts are just one example of an AutoShape.

Tip #158 from
Patrice-Anne Rutledge

Choose More AutoShapes from the AutoShapes menu to open the More AutoShapes dialog box, which offers even more options. This dialog box works in much the same way as the Microsoft Clip Gallery.

→ To learn how to insert clip art images, **see** "Using the Microsoft Clip Gallery," **p. 252**

SPECIFYING COLORS

You can apply color to objects, text, and lines using three different Drawing toolbar buttons. The Fill Color, Font Color, and Line Color buttons all operate in basically the same way, with slight differences based on the object they are coloring. To select the default color, click the button directly. To select another color, click the arrow to the right of the button to display a palette with additional options.

Tip #159 from
Patricé-Anne Rutledge

You can also set color in the Format dialog box.

→ To learn more about formatting options, **see** "Using the Format Dialog Box," **p. 282**

SPECIFYING FILL COLOR

To set an object's fill color, select it, and click the arrow next to the Fill Color button. The Fill Color palette displays, shown in Figure 12.7.

Figure 12.7
You can add colors or patterns to fill an object.

You can do one of the following in this palette:

- Click No Fill to remove the existing fill color. The object becomes transparent and displays the color of the existing slide background.
- Choose one of the compatible colors under the Automatic color box.
- Click More Fill Colors to open the Colors dialog box in which you can select from many other colors or even create your own custom color.
- Click Fill Effects to open the Fill Effects dialog box in which you can apply gradient, texture, pattern, and picture effects.

USING THE COLORS DIALOG BOX

Click More Fill Colors on the palette to open the Colors dialog box, illustrated in Figure 12.8.

Select the new color from the palette. It displays in the New section of the preview box to contrast with the Current color.

Tip #160 from
Patricé-Anne Rutledge

Choose the Semitransparent check box to add an alternate look to the selected color.

Click the Preview button to preview what the color will look like in your presentation. Click OK to return to the presentation, or Cancel if you do not want to apply the color changes.

PART

IV

CH

12

Figure 12.8
The Colors dialog box provides numerous options for color selection.

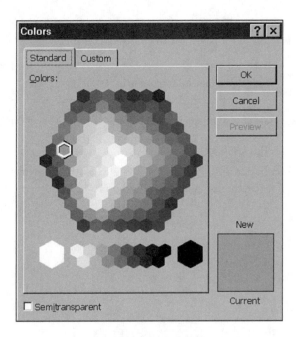

USING A CUSTOM COLOR

To add a custom color, click the Custom tab on the Colors dialog box, shown in Figure 12.9.

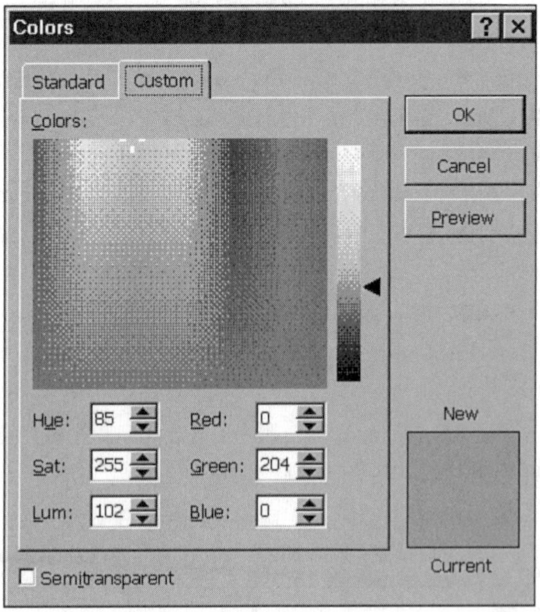

Figure 12.9
Create a custom color to suit your exact needs.

On the Custom tab, you can create a custom color by adjusting its hue, saturation, and luminance or by specifying the level of red, green, and blue. Chapter 22, "The Media—Designing Visual Support," provides more information about color theory to help you make intelligent choices in this dialog box. Click the Preview button to preview your suggested changes and then click OK to save.

→ For more information about color theory, **see** "Using Color," **p. 569**

SPECIFYING FILL EFFECTS

To specify fill effects, select the object you want to format and click the arrow next to the Fill Color button. From the palette that displays, choose Fill Effects to open the Fill Effects dialog box. Figure 12.10 illustrates this dialog box, in which you can choose effects such as gradients, textures, patterns, and pictures.

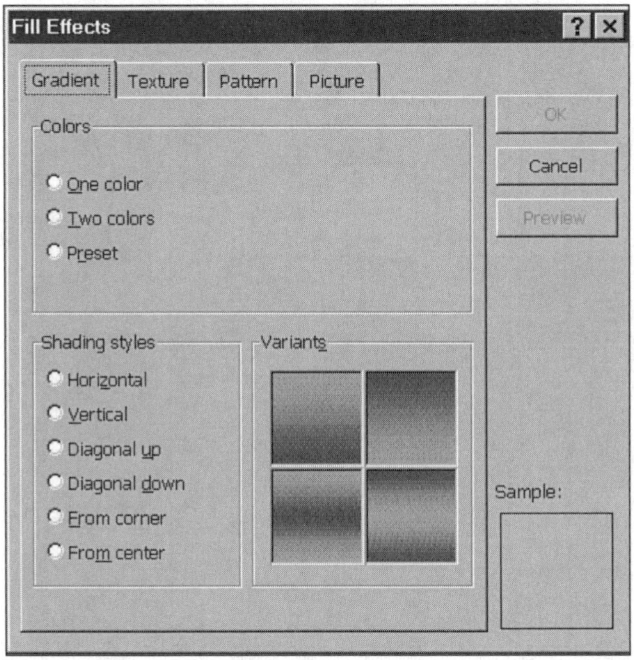

Figure 12.10
Choose from gradient, texture, pattern, and picture effects.

This dialog box includes four different tabs—Gradient, Texture, Pattern, and Picture—that guide you in selecting special effects fills.

APPLYING A GRADIENT FILL   To apply a gradient (shading) effect, select the Gradient tab on the Fill Effects dialog box. In the Colors group box, choose one of the following:

- *One color*   Applies a gradient effect with just one color. You choose the base color from the Color 1 drop-down list and specify how dark or light to make the contrast.

- *Two colors*   Choose the two colors you want to use from the Color <u>1</u> and Color <u>2</u> drop-down lists.

- *Preset*   Displays a drop-down list of preset color combination options such as Daybreak, Peacock, and Rainbow.

Next, you can choose how to apply the gradient in the Shading Styles group box. Options include Hori<u>z</u>ontal, <u>V</u>ertical, Diagonal <u>up</u>, Diagonal <u>d</u>own, <u>F</u>rom corner, and Fro<u>m</u> center. Pick the option you prefer in the Variant<u>s</u> group box; it displays in the Sample box. Click Preview to view the selection in your actual presentation and then click OK to apply.

APPLYING A TEXTURED FILL   To apply a texture, select the Texture tab on the Fill Effects dialog box and scroll down the available textures until you find one you like. Select it and click OK. Figure 12.11 illustrates the Texture tab.

Figure 12.11
Textures can provide variety to a presentation.

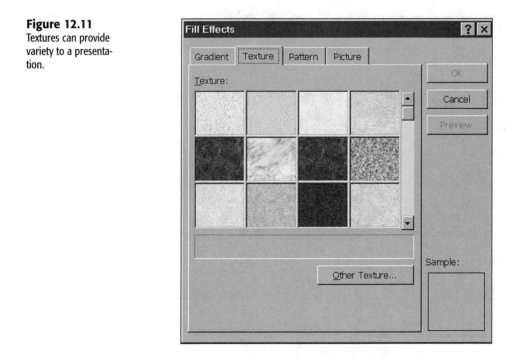

To choose an external texture graphic file that you have on your computer, click the <u>O</u>ther Texture button to open the Select Texture dialog box. In this dialog box, you can choose the texture you would like to use and click the In<u>s</u>ert button to display it in your selected object. You can choose to search among all pictures or specify a particular graphic format such as a Windows metafile or bitmap image.

APPLYING A PATTERNED FILL   To apply a pattern, select the Pattern tab on the Fill Effects dialog box (see Figure 12.12).

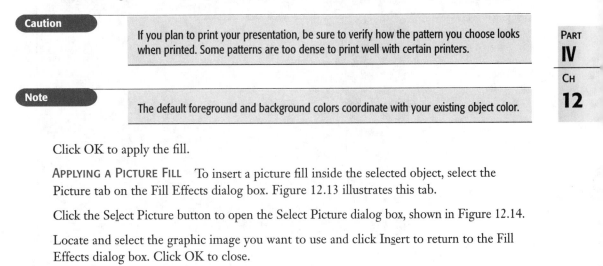

Figure 12.12
PowerPoint provides
many different pattern
effects.

Choose Foreground and Background colors and then select from the many available patterns.

Caution

If you plan to print your presentation, be sure to verify how the pattern you choose looks when printed. Some patterns are too dense to print well with certain printers.

Note

The default foreground and background colors coordinate with your existing object color.

PART
IV
CH
12

Click OK to apply the fill.

APPLYING A PICTURE FILL   To insert a picture fill inside the selected object, select the Picture tab on the Fill Effects dialog box. Figure 12.13 illustrates this tab.

Click the Select Picture button to open the Select Picture dialog box, shown in Figure 12.14.

Locate and select the graphic image you want to use and click Insert to return to the Fill Effects dialog box. Click OK to close.

Caution

Although selecting a picture or graphic file of your own can definitely personalize and customize your presentation, be sure that it works as an effective fill.

Figure 12.13
Use your own image,
such as a logo, as a
fill.

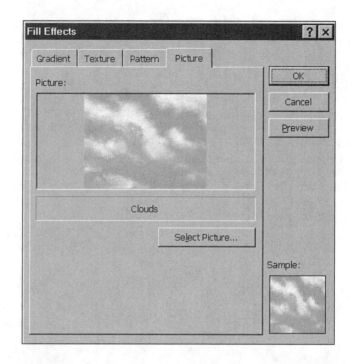

Figure 12.14
Choose a picture of
your own to apply as
a fill.

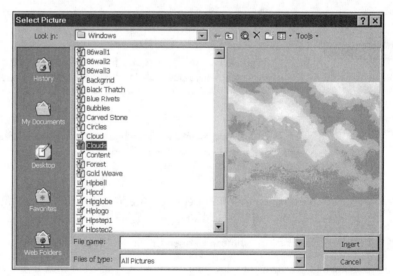

SPECIFYING LINE COLOR

To add color to a selected line, choose the arrow to the right of the Line Color button on the Drawing toolbar. The Line Color palette displays, shown in Figure 12.15.

Figure 12.15
Format or remove lines in the Line Color palette.

Choose from the following options:

- Click No Line to hide the existing line.
- Choose one of the compatible colors under the Automatic color box.
- Click <u>M</u>ore Line Colors to open the Colors dialog box in which you can select from a variety of other colors or even create your own custom color.

→ To learn more about color options, **see** "Using the Colors Dialog Box," **p. 275**

→ For details on expanding your color options, **see** "Using a Custom Color," **p. 276**

- Click <u>P</u>atterned Lines to open the Patterned Lines dialog box. This dialog box is almost identical to the Pattern tab on the Fill Effects dialog box.

Caution

Unless you create a very thick line, patterns in a line probably won't be visible.

→ To learn how patterns work as fill colors, **see** "Applying a Patterned Fill," **p. 278**

SPECIFYING FONT COLOR

To add color to selected text, choose the arrow to the right of the Font Color button on the Drawing toolbar. The Font Color palette displays, shown in Figure 12.16.

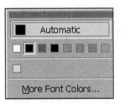

Figure 12.16
Specify the color of your text here.

You can either choose one of the compatible colors under the Automatic color box or click <u>M</u>ore Font Colors to open the Colors dialog box in which you can select from a variety of other colors.

→ To learn more about what's available in this dialog box, **see** "Using the Colors Dialog Box," **p. 275**

→ To learn how to insert a custom color, **see** "Using a Custom Color," **p. 276**

PART
IV
CH
12

USING THE FORMAT DIALOG BOX

You can use the Format dialog box to apply numerous object formatting changes all in one place. The Format dialog box duplicates some of the functions of the Drawing toolbar, but also has some special features of its own.

To open the Format dialog box for a selected object, double-click that object or right-click and choose Format from the menu that displays. Figure 12.17 shows a sample Format dialog box—Format AutoShape.

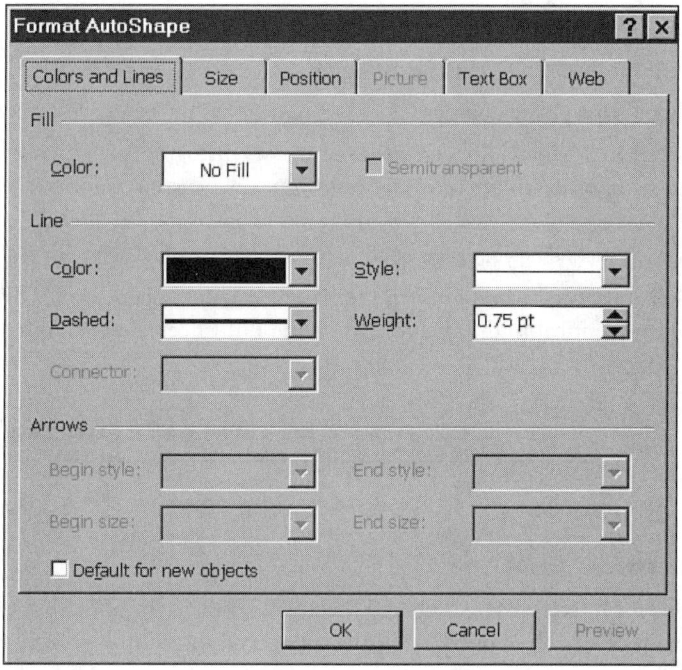

Figure 12.17
The Format AutoShape dialog box enables you to make many changes in one place.

Depending on the type of object you're formatting, only the tabs and fields that pertain are available.

FORMATTING COLORS AND LINES

On the Colors and Lines tab, you can set colors and styles for fill, lines, and arrows. Most of these options duplicate what the Line Color, Line Style, Dash Style, and Arrow Style Drawing toolbar buttons also achieve. The drop-down lists provide palettes that are very similar to the ones you access from these buttons. The effect is the same whichever method you use to apply a specific color or line format. The only difference is the way you choose to apply the formatting.

→ To learn the best way to use these objects in your presentation, **see** "Adding Lines and Arrows," **p. 269**
→ To learn how to use the Line Color button, **see** "Specifying Line Color," **p. 280**

Click the Preview button to preview the changes in your presentation. Click the Default for New Objects check box to make these customizations your default for future objects you create in this presentation.

FORMATTING SIZE

On the Size tab (see Figure 12.18), you can manually set size, rotation, and scaling options.

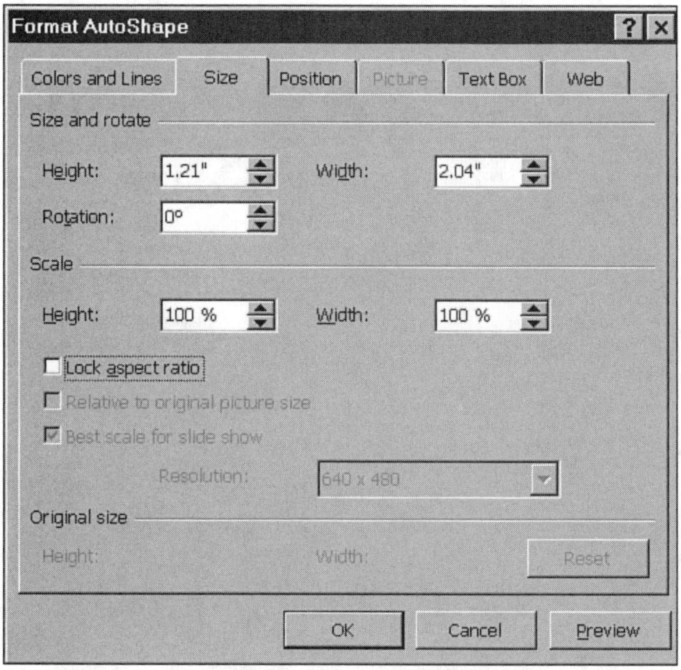

Figure 12.18
Specify the exact size of the selected object on this tab.

You can specify the exact height and width of an object, rather than resizing it with the mouse, if you want. This is useful if you want to create several objects of the same size and need greater precision than what you can achieve by resizing with the mouse. You can also specify an exact rotation percentage, rather than rotate using menu options.

Tip #162 from
Patrice-Anne Rutledge

Another quick way to create multiple objects of the same size is to copy and paste from the same master object.

→ For details on rotation and flipping, **see** "Rotating and Flipping Objects," **p. 294**

To resize the selected object by scale, you can adjust the percentages in the Scale Height and Width fields. For example, you may want to reduce an object to 50% of its original size.

⚠️ **Is your rescaled object distorted?** *See the Troubleshooting section at the end of the chapter.*

You can also set the object's size as Relative to Original Picture Size or as Best Scale for Slide Show to automatically set the proper proportions.

FORMATTING POSITION

On the Position tab, shown in Figure 12.19, you can specify the exact position of the object on the slide.

Figure 12.19
With this dialog box, you can easily set an exact position.

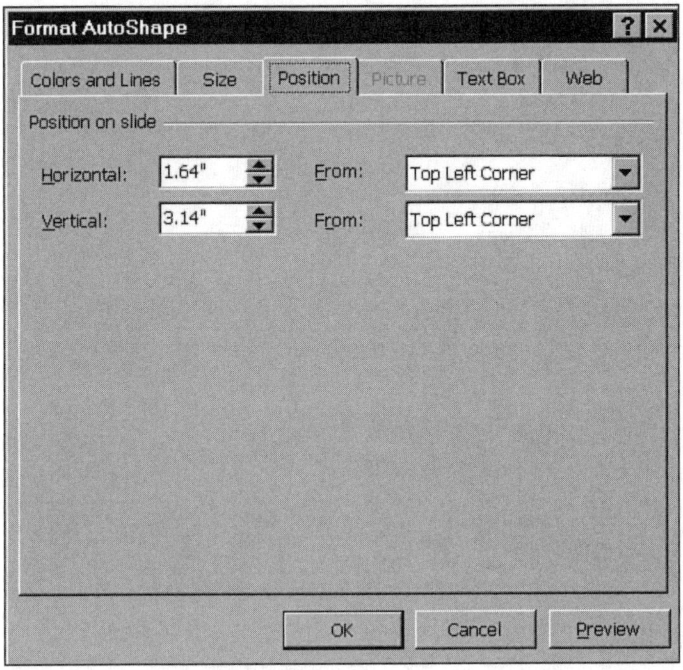

Enter the exact Horizontal and Vertical position for the object. For example, to move an object currently 2.75 inches from the margin one inch to the left, you would enter 1.75 in the Horizontal field. You can also set the position at either Top Left Corner or Center.

FORMATTING A PICTURE

If the selected object is a picture, the Picture tab (see Figure 12.20) offers several formatting options.

You can crop a picture if you don't want to include the entire image in your presentation. Select the inches to crop in the Left, Right, Top, and Bottom fields. The inches you select are removed from the picture.

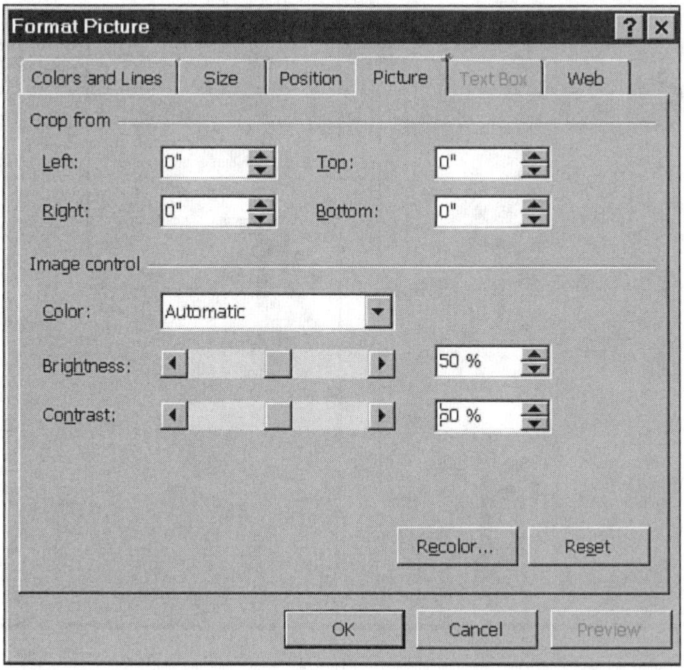

Figure 12.20
Set options for a picture, such as a clip art image, on the Picture tab.

Tip #163 from
Patrice-Anne Rutledge

You can also crop a picture using the Crop button on the Picture toolbar if you prefer cropping by using the mouse.

Select a coloring format from the Color drop-down list. Options include Automatic, Grayscale, Black & White, and Watermark. Figure 12.21 illustrates examples of each for the same picture.

→ For interesting information about color theory, **see** "Using Color," **p. 569**

You can also specify brightness and contrast for this selected picture.

Click Recolor to open the Recolor Picture dialog box in which you can change the color of a PowerPoint object or a WMF clip art image.

→ To learn more about the types of images you can recolor, **see** "Recoloring a Clip Art Image," **p. 293**

Click Preview to see what the changes would look like in your presentation before you save them. Click Reset to restore everything to its original setting.

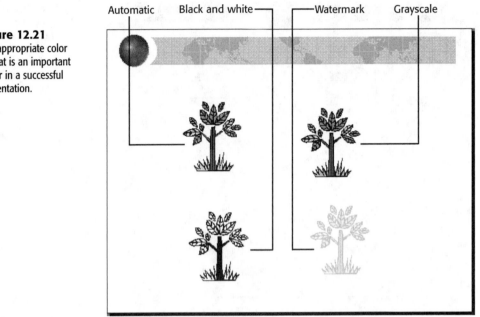

Figure 12.21
The appropriate color format is an important factor in a successful presentation.

FORMATTING A TEXT BOX

If the selected object is a text box, you can specify additional formatting options in the Text Box tab. Figure 12.22 illustrates this tab.

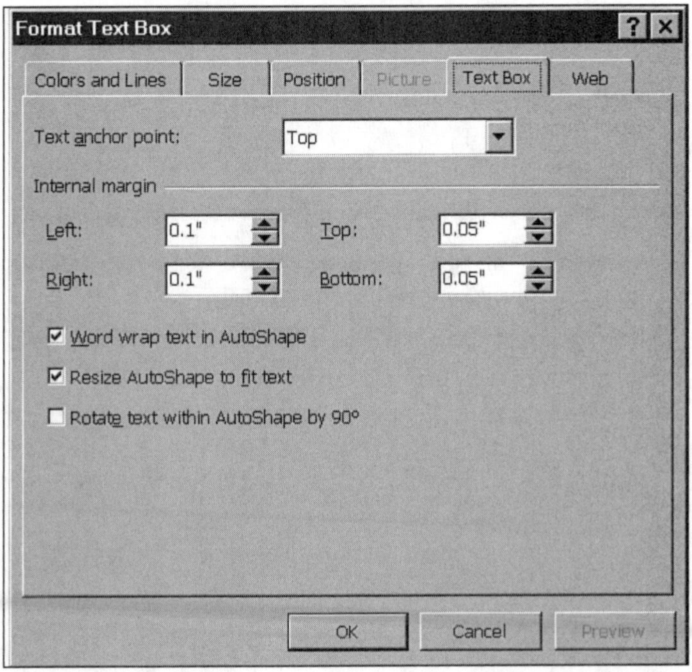

Figure 12.22
You can make several text box customizations.

You can set a Text Anchor Point to align your text in the text box. Options include Top, Middle, Bottom, Top Centered, Middle Centered, and Bottom Centered.

The Internal Margin section enables you to determine how much open space—or internal margin—to display within the text box. You can select fractions of inches in the Left, Right, Top, and Bottom fields.

Other options include

- *Word Wrap Text in AutoShape*   You should choose this option if you want to place text within an AutoShape object; otherwise, the text displays straight across the shape, rather than neatly inside it.

- *Resize AutoShape to Fit Text*   Resizes the AutoShape object to fit the text exactly. For example, if you have one word inside an AutoShape, it reduces the shape to a size that precisely surrounds that word.

- *Rotate Text Within AutoShape by 90°*   Rotates horizontal text to a vertical format.

FORMATTING WEB INFORMATION

On the Web tab (see Figure 12.23), you can enter the text you want to display while this image is loading on the Web. This information is useful only if you're going to give a Web presentation.

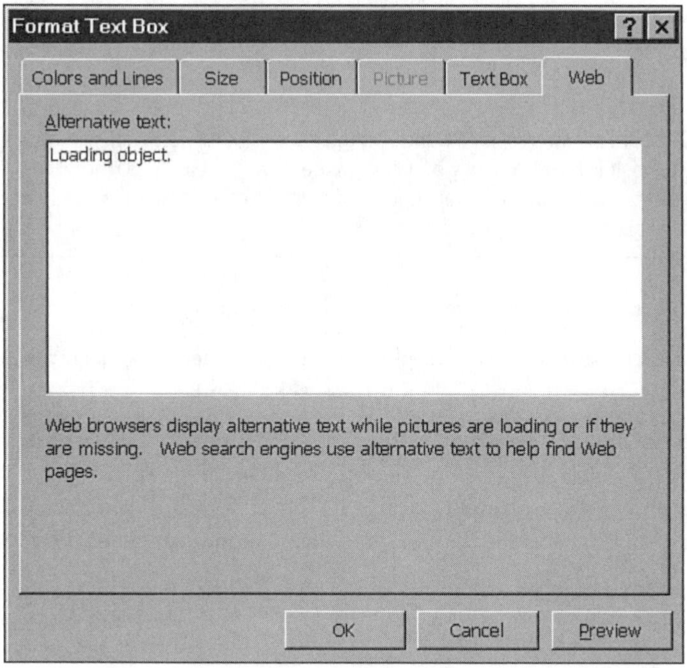

Figure 12.23
In this dialog box, indicate what you want people to see while your Web graphic is loading.

MANIPULATING OBJECTS

You can easily cut, copy, paste, move, and resize PowerPoint objects.

To cut a selected object, click the Cut button on the Standard toolbar or press Ctrl+X.

Tip #164 from
Patrice-Anne Rutledge

To select more than one object, hold down the Shift key while selecting objects or drag a rectangular shape around all the objects with the mouse.

Tip #165 from
Patrice-Anne Rutledge

Click the Undo button to undo cutting an object.

To copy a selected object, click the Copy button or press Ctrl+C.

Tip #166 from
Patrice-Anne Rutledge

To copy the attributes of a particular object and apply them to another object, use the Format Painter button on the Standard toolbar. For example, selecting an object with 3D effects, clicking the Format Painter button, and then selecting another object would apply 3D effects to the new object as well.

To paste a cut or copied object to another location, such as another slide, click the Paste button or press Ctrl+V.

Note

The Clipboard in PowerPoint 2000 includes the capability to store 12 different copies. To see what the Clipboard currently contains, choose View, Toolbars, Clipboard. The Clipboard dialog box displays graphic icons of available clips. To view the initial text of each clip, place the mouse over the icon.

To move a selected object, use the mouse to drag the object to a new location.

Resizing an existing object is also an easy procedure. When you select an object, resizing handles display around its edges. Figure 12.24 illustrates these handles.

Drag the handles with the mouse to make the object smaller, larger, or a different shape. Notice that depending on which sizing handle you select—a corner or interior handle—you can either enlarge the entire object or totally change its shape. To resize the selected object proportionately from a corner, press the Shift key and drag a corner handle to the appropriate size.

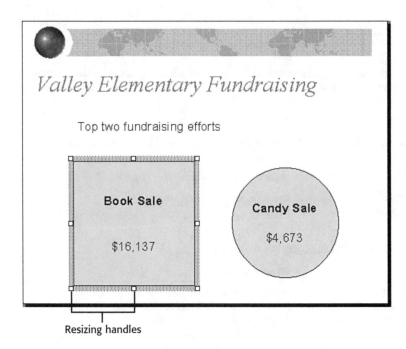

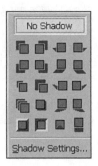

Figure 12.24
Resizing handles make it easier to adjust the size and shape of your object.

Resizing handles

ADDING SHADOW AND 3D EFFECTS

You can add shadow and 3D effects to objects including AutoShapes, WordArt, and clip art.

→ To learn more about adding an AutoShape object to a slide, **see** "Adding AutoShapes," **p. 273**

→ For details on how to effectively use WordArt to enhance your presentation, **see** "Inserting WordArt," **p. 245**

→ To learn what clip art images are available and how to use them, **see** "Inserting Clip Art," **p. 249**

 Select an object and click the Shadow button on the Drawing toolbar to display the Shadow palette, shown in Figure 12.25.

Figure 12.25
Shadows can add a dramatic effect to a presentation.

PART

IV

CH

12

Choose the shadow style you want to apply from the available palette options.

Tip #167 from
Patrice-Anne Rutledge

> To immediately remove a shadow, click the Undo button. To remove a shadow later on, select the shadowed object, click the Shadow button on the Drawing toolbar, and choose No Shadow.

You can also customize the shadow by specifying its exact position and color. To do this, select Shadow Settings from the Shadow palette. The Shadow Settings toolbar displays, as described in Table 12.2. Figure 12.26 shows several objects with shadows.

→ To learn how to nudge an object to move it slightly, **see** "Nudging Objects," **p. 294**

→ For details on the effects of this dialog box, **see** "Using the Colors Dialog Box," **p. 275**

TABLE 12.2 SHADOW SETTINGS TOOLBAR BUTTONS

Button	Name	Description
	Shadow On/Off	Acts as a toggle to remove and replace the shadow
	Nudge Shadow Up	Moves the shadow up slightly
	Nudge Shadow Down	Moves the shadow down slightly
	Nudge Shadow Left	Moves the shadow slightly to the left
	Nudge Shadow Right	Moves the shadow slightly to the right
	Shadow Color	Enables you to select a standard color, apply a semitransparent image, or go to the Colors dialog box for additional color choices

To add 3D effects, select the object you want to modify and click the 3D button on the Drawing toolbar. The 3D palette displays, illustrated in Figure 12.27.

Choose the 3D style you want to apply from the available palette options.

⚠️ *Can't apply 3D effects?* See the Troubleshooting section at the end of the chapter.

Tip #168 from
Patrice-Anne Rutledge

> To immediately remove a 3D effect, click the Undo button. To remove 3D later, select the object, click the 3D button on the Drawing toolbar, and choose No 3D.

You can also customize the 3D effect by specifying its tilt, depth, direction, lighting, surface, and color. To do this, select 3D Settings from the 3D palette. The 3D Settings toolbar displays, described in Table 12.3.

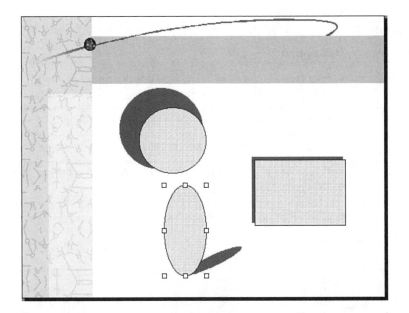

Figure 12.26
Get dramatic with shadows.

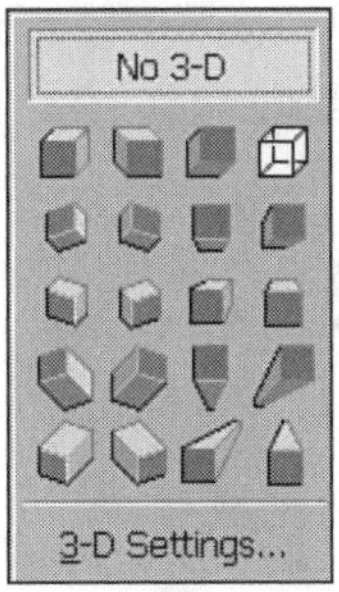

Figure 12.27
Get creative with 3D, but be sure your object doesn't become too distorted.

TABLE 12.3   3D SETTINGS TOOLBAR BUTTONS

Button	Name	Description
	3D On/Off	Acts as a toggle to turn the 3D off and on
	Tilt Down	Turns the object slightly downward
	Tilt Up	Turns the object slightly upward
	Tilt Left	Turns the object slightly to the left
	Tilt Right	Turns the object slightly to the right
	Depth	Enables you to adjust the depth from 0 points to infinity

continues

TABLE 12.3   CONTINUED

Button	Name	Description
	Direction	Enables you to set the direction, using either perspective or parallel options
	Lighting	Enables you to set the direction and intensity of the lighting
	Surface	Enables you to choose from a wire, matte, plastic, or metal surface
	3D Color	Enables you to select a standard color, apply a transparent image, or go to the Colors dialog box for additional color choices

→ To learn more about the options available in this dialog box, **see** "Using the Colors Dialog Box," **p. 275**

Figure 12.28 shows several objects with 3D effects.

Figure 12.28
Properly used, 3D can enhance a presentation.

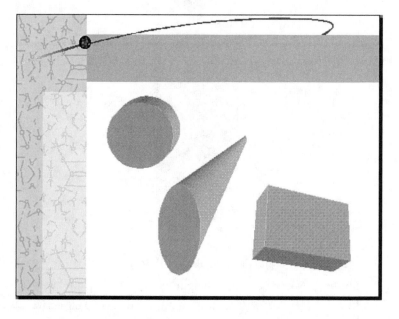

SETTING OBJECT ORDER

Sometimes you may want to layer objects in a presentation to create a special visual effect. To rearrange the order that an object appears in this layer, choose it, select the D<u>r</u>aw button on the Drawing toolbar, and choose O<u>r</u>der from the menu. You can also right-click the mouse and choose O<u>r</u>der from the shortcut menu.

Tip #169 from
Patrice-Anne Rutledge

If the object you want to select is hidden from view, press the Tab key to cycle through all objects to find the one you want.

This menu includes four options:

- *Bring to Front*   Brings the selected object to the front layer of the stack, placing all other objects behind it.
- *Send to Back*   Sends the selected object to the back layer of the stack, bringing all other objects closer to the front.
- *Bring Forward*   Brings the selected object one layer closer to the front. This is most useful with more than two objects.
- *Send Backward*   Sends the selected object one layer to the back. Also most useful when you have more than two objects.

Figure 12.29 includes two examples of the same layered objects.

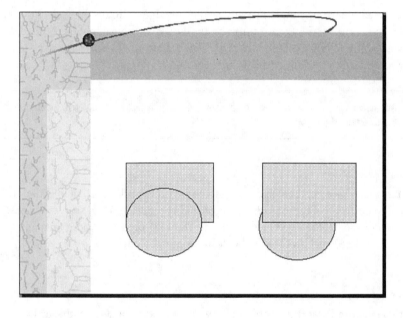

Figure 12.29
You can layer objects for a special effect.

In the left example, the oval shape has been brought to the front. In the right example, the rectangle shape is in the front.

ALIGNING OBJECTS

You can align objects much in the same way that you align text. Select the objects you want to align, click the Draw button on the Drawing toolbar, choose Align or Distribute from the menu, and then select one of the following menu options:

- *Align Left*   Aligns selected objects by their left edge.
- *Align Center*   Aligns selected objects horizontally by their center.
- *Align Right*   Aligns selected objects by their right edge.

- *Align Top*   Aligns selected objects by their top edge.
- *Align Middle*   Aligns selected objects vertically based on their middle point.
- *Align Bottom*   Aligns selected objects by their bottom edge.
- *Distribute Horizontally*   Aligns three or more selected objects horizontally across the slide.
- *Distribute Vertically*   Aligns three or more selected objects vertically across the slide.
- *Relative to Slide*   Aligns selected objects relative to the slide, rather than the other objects. For example, if you choose Relative to Slide and Align Left, all objects align to the left of the slide itself, rather than to the object that is farthest to the left.

NUDGING OBJECTS

If you want to move an object only incrementally, you can nudge it. To do this, select the object you want to nudge, click the Draw button on the Drawing toolbar, choose Nudge, and then select one of the following directions: Up, Down, Left, or Right. You may need to nudge an object several times to achieve the desired results.

Tip #170 from
Patrice-Anne Rutledge

> Alternatively, you can also select an object and use the arrow keys to nudge the object in the direction of the arrow.

SNAPPING TO A GRID OR SHAPE

When you align or move objects, the objects snap to an invisible grid, which guides their positioning. If you want to use other objects as a positioning guide, you can snap to shapes. To choose these options, click the Draw button on the Drawing toolbar, choose Snap, and then select To Grid or To Shape. To Grid is the default option.

GROUPING OBJECTS

You can group two or more PowerPoint objects in order to treat them as one object. For example, if you combine WordArt with a clip art image to create a logo, you might want to group these objects so that they stay together when you move them. A grouped set of objects moves in unison, always remaining in the same position in relation to each other as when you grouped them. When you format grouped objects, the formatting applies to all the objects. For example, let's say you have two grouped objects that were originally different colors. If you now recolor them, the new color applies to both objects, not just one. To make individual changes, you have to ungroup the objects.

To group selected objects, click the Draw button on the Drawing toolbar and choose Group. The object handles now treat the objects as one, shown in Figure 12.30.

You can ungroup selected objects by clicking the Draw button on again and choosing Ungroup.

Figure 12.30
Group objects to treat them as one.

Tip #171 from
Patrice-Anne Rutledge

Choose Regroup from the Draw menu to regroup items you just ungrouped.

ROTATING AND FLIPPING OBJECTS

Many times when you add an AutoShape or clip art image, it ends up facing the wrong direction. For example, you may add a callout to draw attention to specific text, but the callout is pointing the wrong way.

Tip #172 from
Patrice-Anne Rutledge

To rotate or flip a single object in a group, you need to ungroup it first and then regroup after changing its direction.

To rotate or flip a selected object, click the Draw button on the Drawing toolbar, choose Rotate or Flip, and then select one of the following menu options:

- *Free Rotate*   Enables you to openly rotate the object
- *Rotate Left*   Moves object counterclockwise
- *Rotate Right*   Moves object clockwise
- *Flip Horizontal*   Turns object horizontally
- *Flip Vertical*   Turns object vertically

PART
IV
CH
12

TROUBLESHOOTING

I want to add 3D effects to a selected object, but the effects on the 3D palette are dimmed and unavailable.

If you can't apply 3D effects to the selected object, the 3D palette won't be active. For example, you can't apply 3D effects to pictures or text boxes, because it wouldn't make sense to do so.

I tried to rescale an object in the Format dialog box, but it became distorted.

To preserve the ratio of height to width in an object that you're rescaling, be sure to check the Lock Aspect Ratio check box. Otherwise, the object may become distorted.

DESIGN CORNER

By adding special formatting effects such as AutoShapes, shadows, and line styles, you can greatly enhance your presentation.

BEFORE

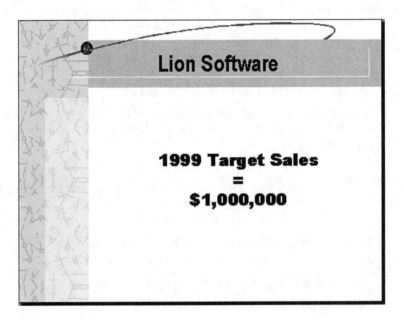

AFTER

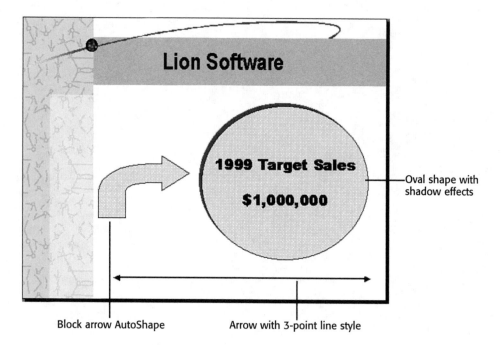

Lion Software

1999 Target Sales

$1,000,000

Oval shape with shadow effects

Block arrow AutoShape

Arrow with 3-point line style

CHAPTER **13**

ADDING MOVIES AND SOUND

In this chapter

by Patrice-Anne Rutledge

EXPLORING MOVIES AND SOUND IN POWERPOINT

You can insert media clips—sound and movie files—into your PowerPoint presentation for a full multimedia effect. You can insert clips from a variety of sources—clips from the *Microsoft Clip Gallery (p. 244)*, clips you download from the Microsoft Web site, or your own sound and video clips. A PowerPoint presentation can play a clip automatically during a slide show, or you can customize the clip to play only by a mouse action. Other multimedia options include recording your own sounds or playing a CD track as a slide show background. In this chapter you learn how to

- *Insert media clips* The Microsoft Clip Gallery includes numerous sound and movie clips you can insert into your presentation. You can also download Web clips and import your own clips into the gallery.

- *Insert your own media clips* If you have your own media clips on your computer, you can directly insert them into a PowerPoint presentation as well.

- *Record a sound file* If you want to add a sound file to a particular slide, you can record it yourself with a microphone.

- *Play a CD audio track* Use music or other CD content as a background sound for a PowerPoint slide show.

UNDERSTANDING SOUND AND VIDEO FILES

PowerPoint includes the capability to insert media clips into your presentations. To use these features, you need to have a sound card, microphone, and speakers installed on your computer.

Media clips work in much the same way as clip art illustrations and photographs, and are also available through the Microsoft Clip Gallery. Common *media clip file formats (p. 34)* include

- *MIDI* Musical Instrument Digital Interface.
- *WAV* Microsoft Windows audio format.
- *MPEG* A standard video format.
- *AVI* Microsoft Windows video format.
- *GIF* Graphical Interchange Format. Animated GIFs (a series of GIF images that appear animated) are stored with other video files.

Media clips can greatly enhance the multimedia effect of your presentation, but remember that, as with clip art and other images, overuse of media clips can also clutter a presentation.

→ To learn more about ways to include multimedia content in your presentations, **see** "Incorporating Multimedia," **p. 667**

INSERTING MEDIA CLIPS

The quickest way to add a *media clip (p. 34)* to your PowerPoint presentation is to select one of the AutoLayouts from the New Slide dialog box that includes a media clip such as Text & Media Clip or Media Clip & Text.

To access this dialog box, shown in Figure 13.1, select the New Slide button or choose Common Tasks, New Slide from the Formatting toolbar.

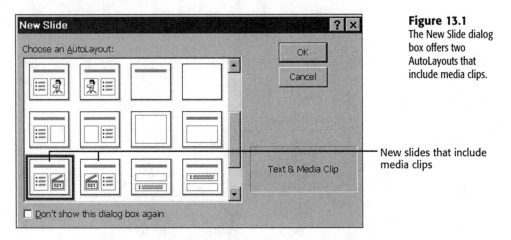

Figure 13.1
The New Slide dialog box offers two AutoLayouts that include media clips.

New slides that include media clips

→ For details on choosing and using layouts, **see** "Understanding Slide Layouts," **p. 28**

Figure 13.2 shows a sample slide with a media clip placeholder.

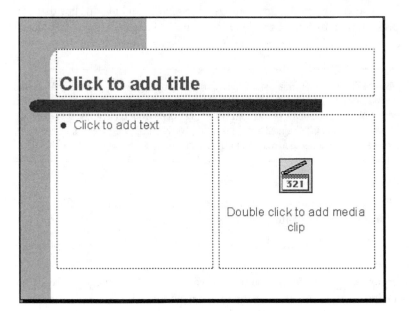

Figure 13.2
You can add a media clip by double-clicking the placeholder.

PART

IV

Cн

13

Double-click the media clip placeholder to open the Microsoft Clip Gallery, shown in Figure 13.3.

Figure 13.3
PowerPoint opens the
Microsoft Clip Gallery.

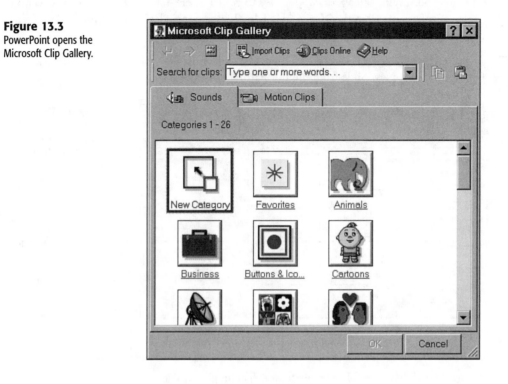

The Microsoft Clip Gallery stores clip art, photographs, sounds, and movie clips that you can use in your presentation. Accessing the Microsoft Clip Gallery from the placeholder displays only the Sounds and Motion Clips tabs, not the Pictures tab.

Tip #173 from
Patrice-Anne Rutledge

You can also insert a media clip into an existing slide by clicking the Insert Clip Art button on the Drawing toolbar and choosing the Sounds or Motion Clips tab. Alternatively, select Insert, Movies and Sound, Movie from Gallery, or Sound from Gallery. If you use any of these methods to insert a media clip, the dialog box is called Insert Clip Art, Insert Movie, or Insert Sound rather than Microsoft Clip Gallery.

→ For more detailed explanations on using clip art, **see** "Inserting Clip Art," **p. 249**

The Microsoft Clip Gallery contains numerous categories of sound and video files. To insert a media clip from the gallery into your presentation, follow these steps:

1. Click either the Sounds tab or the Motion Clips tab, depending on the type of media clip you want to add.

2. Click the category whose selections you want to view. The Clip Gallery displays a series of individual clips relating to that category, shown in Figure 13.4.

Figure 13.4
Narrow down your
media clip search
by category.

Tip #174 from
Patrice-Anne Rutledge

Use the navigation buttons, Back and Forward, to navigate the Clip Gallery if the first category of selections doesn't suit your needs.

3. Click the selection you want to insert in your presentation. A menu with several buttons appears, as shown in Figure 13.5.

4. Click the Insert Clip button to insert the media clip into your PowerPoint presentation, closing Microsoft Clip Gallery.

5. A message box asks if you want to play the file automatically in the slide show. Click Yes if you do. Otherwise, you need to click the file to play it.

To later change how the clip is played, you can choose Slide Show, Action Settings to specify mouse click and mouse over effects. You can set additional play options on the Multimedia Settings tab of the Custom Animation dialog box. Access this dialog box by choosing Slide Show, Custom Animation.

→ For details on using action settings to animate your presentation, **see** "Using Action Settings," **p. 329**

→ To learn about the advanced options in the Custom Animation dialog box, **see** "Creating Custom Animations," **p. 323**

PART

IV

CH

13

Figure 13.5
This menu provides
several media clip
options.

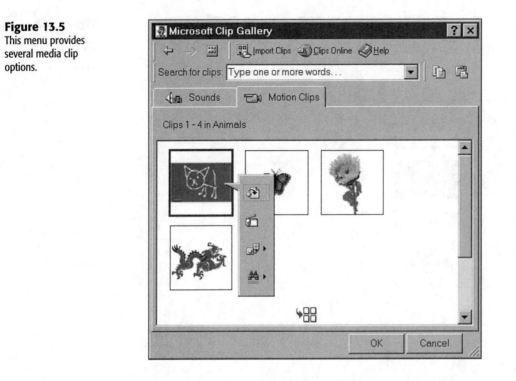

Tip #175 from
Patrice-Anne Rutledge

You can also insert a sound or video file by choosing Insert, Object and choosing the appropriate object from the Insert Object dialog box. This uses the Windows Media Player to play the clip rather than the PowerPoint Player. In general, use this method of inserting a media clip only when PowerPoint doesn't support the clip format you want.

WORKING WITH MEDIA CLIPS IN THE MICROSOFT CLIP GALLERY

When you are in a Clip Gallery category, you can find out additional information about each clip, recategorize it, or add it to a Favorites folder.

Click the media clip to display a floating menu with four buttons. These buttons are

- *Insert Clip*   Inserts the selected clip into the PowerPoint presentation and closes Microsoft Clip Gallery.

- *Play Clip*   Plays a sound file or previews a video clip in a preview window, as shown in Figure 13.6.

Figure 13.6
Use the preview
window to see what a
movie clip looks like.

- *Add Clip to Favorites or Other Category* Enlarges the menu to display a drop-down list that lets you add this clip to a Favorites category or any other existing category (see Figure 13.7). Click OK to close.

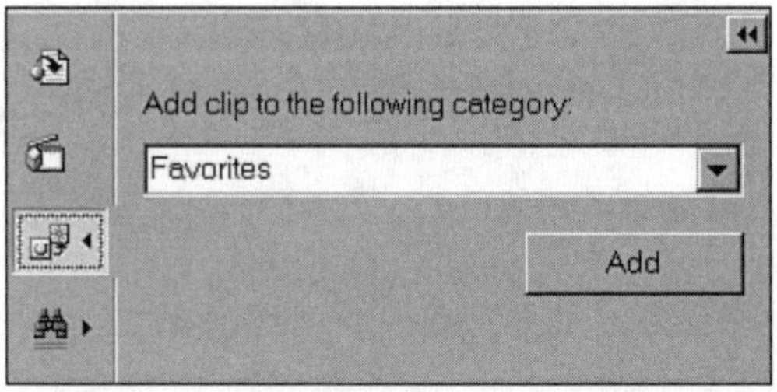

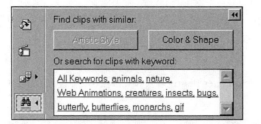

Figure 13.7
You can add media clips to other categories or a favorites list.

Whenever you add a clip to the Favorites category, it's available under this category button when you start Microsoft Clip Gallery.

- *Find Similar Clips* Enlarges the menu, as shown in Figure 13.8.

Figure 13.8
If one clip isn't quite right, look for other similar clips.

Click the Artistic Style or Color & Shape button to find and display clips that match these criteria. Or select one of the related keywords to display clips that match that keyword.

IMPORTING MEDIA CLIPS

PowerPoint also includes the capability to organize and categorize media clips you already store elsewhere on your computer by importing them into the Clip Gallery. To import a file, follow these steps:

1. Click the Import Clips button from the Microsoft Clip Gallery. Figure 13.9 displays the Add Clip to Clip Gallery dialog box.
2. Select the folder in which the clip is located from the Look In drop-down list.
3. Select the file you want to import. You can narrow your choices in the Files of Type drop-down list.

PART
IV

CH
13

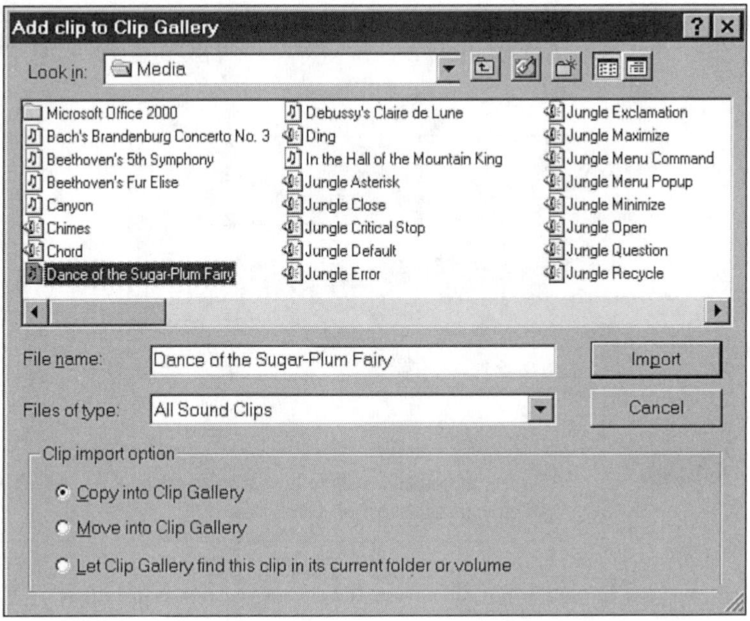

Figure 13.9
Select a clip to import
into this dialog box.

4. In the Clip Import Option group box, specify whether you want to copy the file, actually move it into the Clip Gallery, or let the Clip Gallery find this clip in its current folder.

5. Click Import. The Clip Properties dialog box displays (see Figure 13.10).

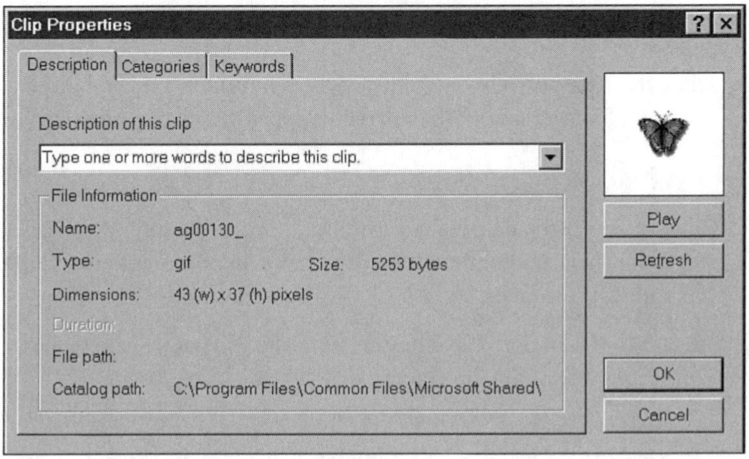

Figure 13.10
Describe the clip
in this tab.

6. On the Description tab, you can enter a descriptive word or phrase about the clip.

7. On the Categories tab, you can select the categories in which to display the clip.

Tip #176 from	Click New Category to add another category if none of the existing categories suits your needs.
Patrie-Anne Rutledge	

→ To learn how to set up a new category for clips, **see** "Creating a New Category," **p. 255**

8. On the Keywords tab, you can add or delete keywords associated with this clip.

9. Click OK to add to the clip gallery.

→ For information about how to organize your images, **see** "Recategorizing Clip Art Images," **p. 256**

Tip #177 from	To delete a media clip, select it and press the Delete key.
Patrie-Anne Rutledge	

GETTING MEDIA CLIPS ONLINE

If the existing media clips don't suit your needs, you can download additional clips from Microsoft's Web site.

To download online clips, follow these steps:

1. From the Microsoft Clip Gallery, click the Clips Online button. PowerPoint displays a dialog box verifying that you can connect to the Internet.

Tip #178 from	To access online clips and other Web-connected PowerPoint features, you must have Internet access—either through a company intranet site or through your own account with an Internet service provider.
Patrie-Anne Rutledge	

2. Click OK to proceed. The licensing agreement for the Microsoft Clip Gallery Live Web site opens (see Figure 13.11).

3. Click the Accept button to accept the licensing agreement and continue (see Figure 13.12).

4. Click the Sounds or Motion tab in the upper-left corner to access sound or movie files.

Note	Note that downloading other media clips from the Web can violate copyright laws. Be sure to verify that you are using clips legally in your presentation before distributing to a wide audience. Clips that you retrieve from the Microsoft Clip Gallery are approved for use in any PowerPoint presentation, but you can't resell them as part of another clip collection.

5. To download clips, select the check box beneath each clip to place it in the selection basket, as shown in Figure 13.13.

PART

IV

CH

13

Figure 13.11
Download sound and movie clips from the Microsoft Clip Gallery Live Web site.

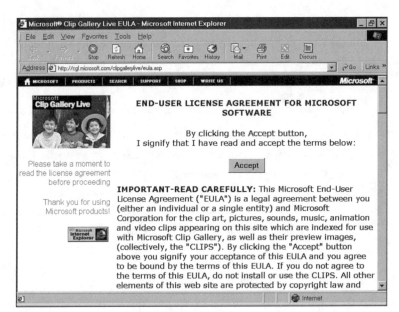

Figure 13.12
Click on the appropriate tab to display sounds, motion, clip art, or pictures.

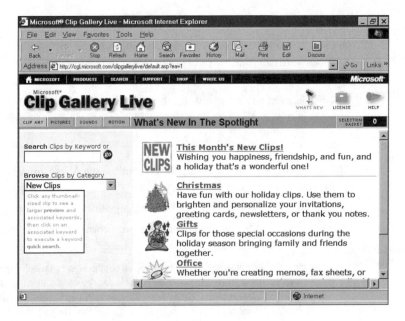

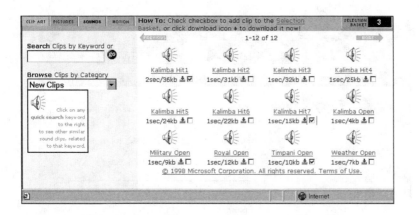

Figure 13.13
Choose the clips you
want to download.

6. Click the Selection Basket hyperlink when you're done to display the basket of selected clips (see Figure 13.14).

Tip #179 from
Patrice-Anne Rutledge

Click the Empty hyperlink to delete clips from the selection basket.

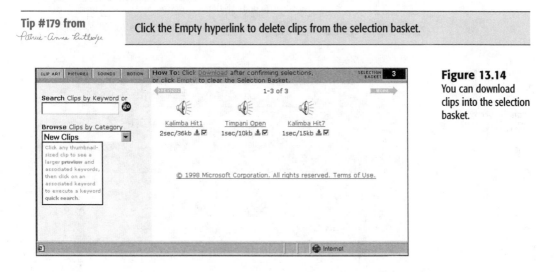

Figure 13.14
You can download
clips into the selection
basket.

7. Click the Download hyperlink to continue to the next step (see Figure 13.15).
8. Click the Download Now! hyperlink.

Microsoft Clip Gallery Live downloads the clips and displays them in the Microsoft Clip Gallery (see Figure 13.16).

PART

IV

CH

13

Figure 13.15
You can choose whether to open or download the clip.

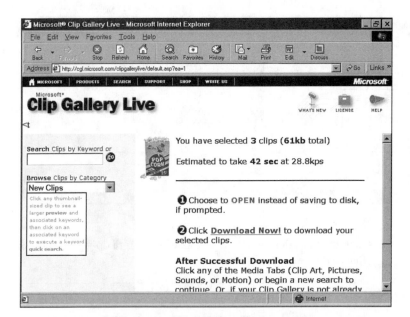

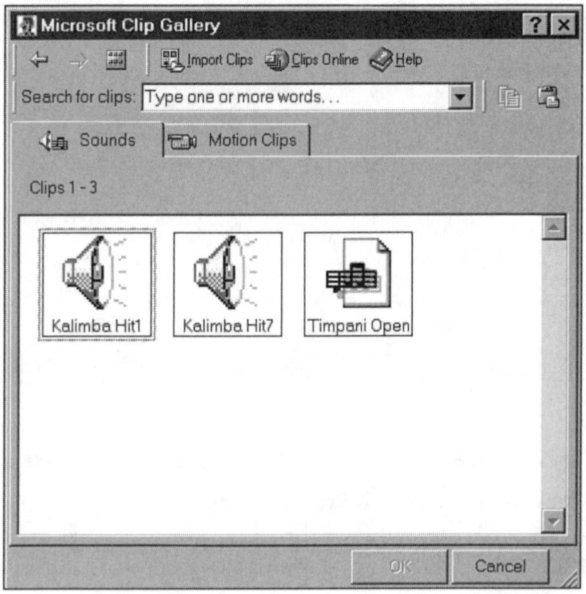

Figure 13.16
Select your new downloaded clips from the Microsoft Clip Gallery.

Note

To download an individual clip, select it to preview in the box below the Browse Clips by Category drop-down list. Click the clip in the preview box to open the File Download dialog box and download the file.

Tip #180 from
Patrice-Anne Rutledge

You can locate additional media clips in the \Windows\Media folder.

INSERTING YOUR OWN SOUND FILE

You can also insert your own sound file into a PowerPoint presentation. To do this, simply follow these steps:

1. Choose Insert, Movies and Sound, Sound from File. The Insert Sound dialog box displays, as shown in Figure 13.17. Sound Files displays in the Files of Type field by default.

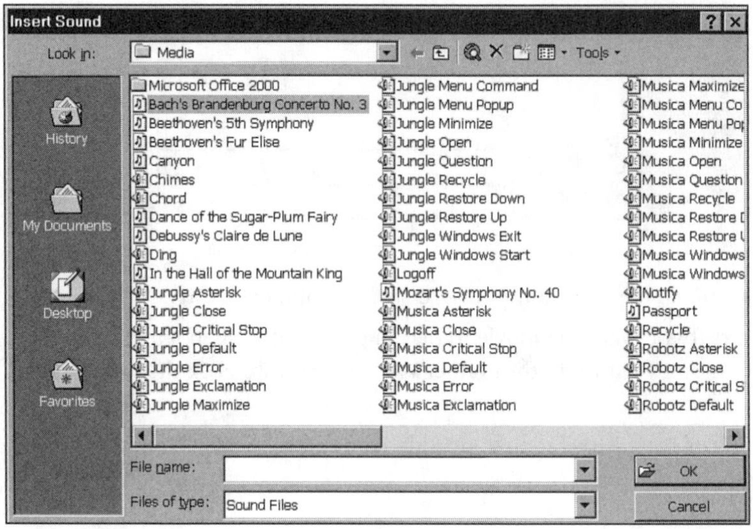

Figure 13.17
You can insert your own sound file and have it play automatically.

2. Navigate to the sound file you want to insert, select it, and click OK.

3. A dialog box asks if you want the sound to play automatically when you display the slide. Click Yes if you want to do this. Otherwise, you need to click the sound file to play it.

   The sound file displays as an icon on your slide. You can move this icon to another part of the slide if you want to.

INSERTING YOUR OWN MOVIE FILE

You can insert your own movie file into a PowerPoint presentation as well. To do this, follow these steps:

1. Choose Insert, Movies and Sound, Movie from File. The Insert Movie dialog box displays, as shown in Figure 13.18. Movie Files displays in the Files of Type field by default.

Figure 13.18
Inserting your own movie file is easy, too.

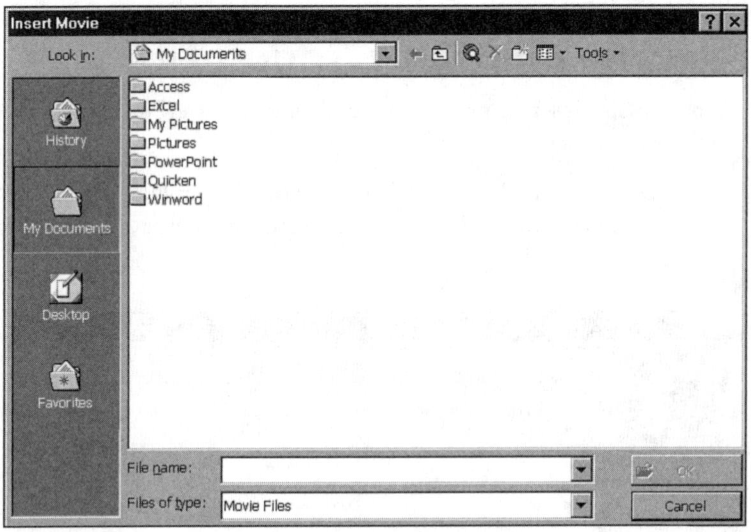

2. Navigate to the movie file you want to insert, select it, and click OK.
3. A dialog box asks if you want the movie to play automatically when you display the slide. Click Yes if you want to do this. Otherwise, you need to click the movie file to play it.

   The movie file displays as an icon on your slide. You can move this icon to another part of the slide if you want to.

RECORDING SOUND FILES

You can record your own sound clips to insert in your PowerPoint presentation. You need to have a microphone and sound card to do this.

Tip #181 from
Patrice-Anne Rutledge

In addition to adding a sound clip to a single slide, you can record a narration for your entire presentation by choosing Slide Show, Record Narration.

→ To learn how to narrate your presentations, **see** "Recording a Voice Narration," **p. 150**

To record a sound, follow these steps:

1. Choose Insert, Movies and Sound, Record Sound to open the Record Sound dialog box, which appears in Figure 13.20.

Play   Stop   Record

Figure 13.20
Record a sound to play with a particular slide.

2. Enter a description for this sound in the Name field.

3. Click the Record button to begin recording your sound.

4. Click the Stop button when you finish recording.

Tip #182 from
Patrice-Anne Rutledge

To play back the sound, click the Play button.

5. Click OK to save the sound with the presentation; click Cancel to exit and start over.

The sound now displays as an icon in your presentation, and you can use it anywhere in that slide show. For example, you can play the sound when you click a specific object using PowerPoint's action settings.

→ To learn how to play sounds with action settings, **see** "Using Action Settings," **p. 329**

PLAYING A CD AUDIO TRACK

You can also play an audio track from a CD during a PowerPoint presentation. For example, you might want to include music from a CD as a background or to introduce your presentation. To do this, follow these steps:

1. Choose Insert, Movies and Sound, Play CD Audio Track to open the Movie and Sound Options dialog box, shown in Figure 13.21.

2. Select the Loop until Stopped check box if you want the track to play continuously during your presentation.

3. In the Play CD Audio Track group box, choose the Start and End Tracks to play.

4. If you want to play only part of a track, indicate the timespans in the Start At and End At fields. For example, you may only want to play the first two minutes of a track.

5. Click OK to close.

Figure 13.21
Music from a CD
can serve as a
background sound.

PowerPoint displays a CD icon on the open slide. These steps insert the CD clip into the slide, but you must use the Custom Animation dialog box to set up your presentation to play this file during the slide show.

→ For details on setting up custom animation options, **see** "Creating Custom Animations," **p. 323**

TROUBLESHOOTING

My sound file won't play.

Your computer must have correctly configured speakers and sound card to play music and sounds. Also be sure to check the volume if the sound is too low.

My sound and movie files don't behave as expected during a presentation.

Check the Custom Animation dialog box to verify the settings in place for each media object such as when to start it, whether or not to loop, and so forth. Access this dialog box by choosing Slide Show, Custom Animation.

DESIGN CORNER

By inserting a simple motion clip into your PowerPoint presentation, you can easily add animation effects.

In this motion clip, the snowman takes off his hat.

BEFORE

AFTER

CHAPTER **14**

WORKING WITH ANIMATION

In this chapter *by Patrice-Anne Rutledge*

UNDERSTANDING ANIMATION

PowerPoint includes a multitude of animation options. You can use *animation (p. 323-327)* to transition from one slide to another in your presentation or to introduce objects and text on a slide. You can also customize these basic animations in a variety of ways. Additional animation options include the capability to have action buttons or other objects perform a specific action in your presentation, such as opening a Web page on the Internet.

In this chapter you learn how to:

- *Set transitions* Automating transitions from one slide to another in your PowerPoint presentation is easy when you use one of many available slide transition techniques.

- *Use preset animation* Introduce new objects and text onto a slide by using preset animation. This feature enables you to have objects appear using techniques such as wiping, dissolving, flying, or flashing.

- *Create custom animations* For more complex animations, you can use the Custom Animation dialog box. This dialog box also includes options for animating media clips and embedded objects.

- *Use action settings and buttons* If you want to jump to another slide or to an external application while presenting, you can easily do so using action settings. You can apply action settings to objects you create or to predesigned action buttons.

- *Use the Animation Effects toolbar* If you want to animate text, this toolbar provides a handy way to access all the features you need in one place.

Like most of PowerPoint's capabilities, animation can be either very simple or detailed and complex. It all depends on how creative and sophisticated you want to make your presentation.

Caution

Animation can definitely enliven any presentation, but as with any special effect, be careful not to overdo.

→ To learn more about animation and visual design, **see** "The Media—Designing Visual Support," **p. 537**

PowerPoint includes a variety of animation options, which can be overwhelming if you're not sure about what each one does. Depending on what you want to animate (slide, text, drawing object, chart, media clip, and so forth) and what type of animation you want to use (a direction or an action), you have several ways to create the desired animation effect in PowerPoint. Your basic choices include

- *Slide transitions* Enables you to determine how to transition from one slide to the next in your presentation.

- *Preset animation* Enables you to animate PowerPoint objects such as text or drawing objects using directional effects similar to slide transitions. For example, you can use preset animation to dissolve or wipe title text into your presentation.

- *Custom animation*   Enables you to set more sophisticated animation options such as the order and timing of multiple animation objects in one slide. You can also use custom animation to animate charts and media clips such as sound and movie files.

- *Action settings*   Enables you to attach a mouse action to a PowerPoint object. For example, you can open a Web page, go to another slide, or start an external program by clicking the mouse or even just passing the mouse pointer over the selected object. An action setting differs from the previous types of animation in that it performs an action rather than defines how to directionally introduce an object or slide.

- *Action buttons*   Enables you to attach an action to a specific button. An action button is a predefined object that includes an action setting. You can attach an action setting to an object you create or you can use one of the pre-existing action buttons instead.

SETTING SLIDE TRANSITIONS

Setting slide transitions is one of the most common PowerPoint animation effects. You can set slide transitions that apply to the entire presentation or just to the current slide. Transition options include:

- Blinds
- Box
- Checkerboard
- Cover
- Cut
- Dissolve

- Fade
- Random bars
- Split
- Strips
- Uncover
- Wipe

Within each of these main categories, you have other directional choices. For example, you can wipe up, down, left, or right.

Caution

It's best to use a limited number of slide transition effects for your entire slide show unless you have a good reason for applying many different transitions. Too many transitions can make your presentation confusing.

Tip #183 from
Patrice-Anne Rutledge

If you're not sure which transition effect to use or what each looks like, go to Slide Sorter view where you can attach slide transitions and preview them all in the same window.

→ To understand more about using transitions in this view, **see** "Setting Transitions in Slide Sorter View," **p. 321**

PART
IV

CH
14

SETTING TRANSITIONS IN THE SLIDE TRANSITION DIALOG BOX

To set slide transitions, follow these steps:

1. Choose Slide Show, Slide Transition. Figure 14.1 shows the Slide Transition dialog box.

Figure 14.1
You can specify how you want to move from this slide to another slide during a presentation.

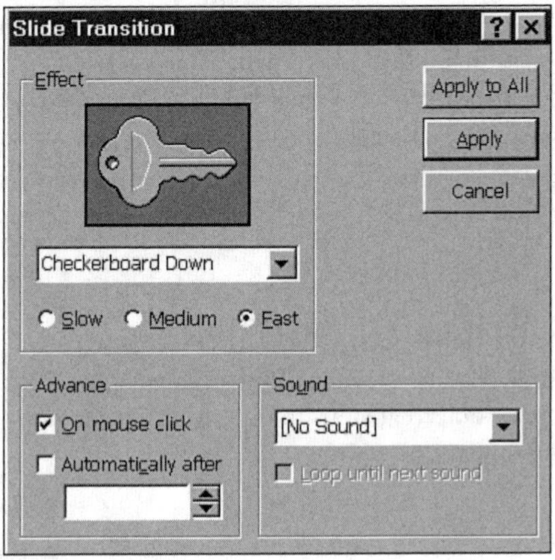

2. From the drop-down list in the Effect group box, select the transition you want to apply.

3. Choose a transition speed of Slow, Medium, or Fast, depending on how quickly you want the transition to occur in a slide show.

4. Select the On Mouse Click check box to advance to the next slide when you click the mouse or press a key such as the spacebar, Enter, Page Up, or Page Down keys. This is selected by default.

5. If you would rather have PowerPoint automatically transition to the next slide after a specified amount of time, select the Automatically After check box, and then enter a specific time in the field below.

6. To add sound effects to your transition, select a Sound from the drop-down list.

Can't hear your sound files? See the Troubleshooting section at the end of the chapter.

Tip #184 from
Patrice-Anne Rutledge

To add a sound other than one of the default WAV files, select Other Sound from the drop-down list. This opens the Add Sound dialog box, from which you can choose another sound.

→ To learn how to add WAV and other sound files, **see** "Inserting Your Own Sound File," **p. 311**

Note

Use the Loop Until Next Sound check box to continually play a selected sound until the presentation encounters another sound file.

7. Click the Apply to All button to apply these transition effects to your entire presentation.

Click the Apply button to apply these transition effects only to the current slide.

To preview what the animation will look like in a slide show, choose Slide Show, Animation Preview. A preview window displays the actual animation effect, shown in Figure 14.2.

Animation preview window

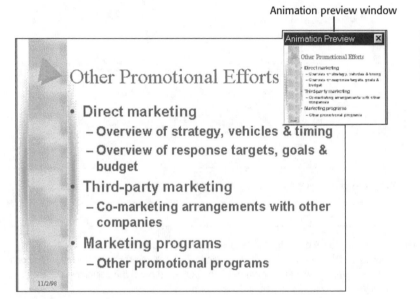

Figure 14.2
Preview your animation to make sure it has the desired effect.

SETTING TRANSITIONS IN SLIDE SORTER VIEW

You can also set slide transitions in Slide Sorter view, which enables you to view all your slides at the same time. Figure 14.3 illustrates this view.

→ For more details on this view, **see** "Using the Slide Sorter View," **p. 123**

Click the Slide Sorter View button in the lower-left corner of the PowerPoint window to open the presentation in Slide Sorter view. Select the slide or slides to which you want to set the transition, and then choose the transition from the Slide Transition Effects drop-down list on the Slide Sorter toolbar. These transitions are identical to the ones you can apply from the Slide Transition dialog box.

PART
IV

CH
14

Slide Transition Effects drop-down list

Figure 14.3
Setting slide transitions in Slide Sorter View is another option.

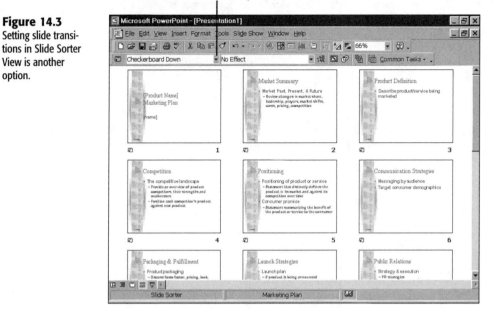

Tip #185 from
Patrice-Anne Rutledge

To select non-contiguous slides, press the Ctrl key and click the slides you want.

Tip #186 from
Patrice-Anne Rutledge

The best way to get a real-time view of your slide transitions is to view your actual slide show. To do this, click the Slide Show button in the lower-left corner of the screen to open your show starting with the current slide. To open the show at the beginning, choose Slide Show, View Show from the Standard menu or press F5.

→ To get more information about previews, **see** "Previewing Your Show," **p. 159**

USING PRESET ANIMATION

In addition to animating the transitions of your slides, you can also animate specific slide objects such as a title, text, or drawing object. You do this using *preset animation (p. 333)*. Options include:

- Drive-In
- Flying
- Camera
- Flash Once
- Laser Text
- Typewriter
- Reverse Order

- Drop-In
- Fly from Top
- Wipe Up
- Wipe Right
- Dissolve
- Split Vertical Out
- Appear

To add a preset animation effect, select the object you want to animate and choose Slide Show, Preset Animation. The menu displays a list of available animation options.

⚡ *You can't get preset animation to work?* See the Troubleshooting section at the end of the chapter.

Depending on whether you choose text or another kind of object, not all options are available. For example, the typewriter preset animation, which displays text as if you were typing it letter by letter, is available only for text objects.

Choose the preset animation from the menu, which closes. To preview what this animation effect looks like, choose Slide Show, Animation Preview or view the actual slide show.

Tip #187 from *Patrice-Anne Rutledge*	To remove a preset animation effect from a selected object, choose Slide Show, Preset Animation, Off.

Tip #188 from *Patrice-Anne Rutledge*	You can also specify preset animation in Slide Sorter view.

→ For more information about this view, **see** "Using the Slide Sorter View," **p. 123**

CREATING CUSTOM ANIMATIONS

The Custom Animation dialog box includes more advanced animation options such as the capability to set order and timings. You also use this dialog box to set animation effects for charts and media clips.

Note	Using custom animation, you can perform many of the same animation tasks as you can with preset animation. Custom animation offers more advanced functionality, however.

Choose Slide Show, Custom Animation to open the Custom Animation dialog box, shown in Figure 14.4.

As you set animation effects in this dialog box, you can use the Preview button to get an idea of what your animation will look like before saving these changes. PowerPoint displays the animations in the preview box to the left of the Preview button. When you're satisfied with your changes, click OK.

SETTING ORDER AND TIMING

On the Order & Timing tab, you can specify the order in which to animate multiple objects on a single slide as well as how long to wait between animations.

In the box in the upper-left corner of the dialog box, select the check box to the left of all objects that you want to animate.

PART

IV

CH

14

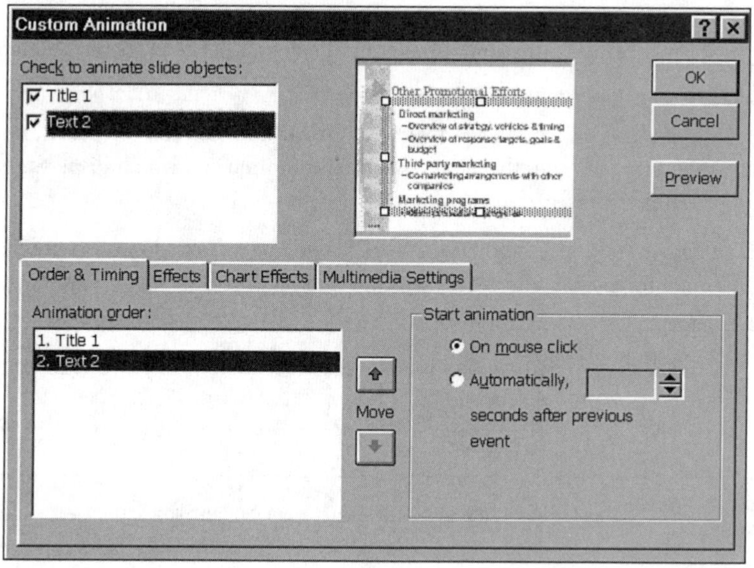

Figure 14.4
The Custom Animation offers more complex animation options.

The order in which the selected objects are animated appears in the Animation Order box. To change this order, select an animation object, and then click the up or down Move button.

Select the On Mouse Click option in the Start Animation group box to activate the animation effect by clicking the mouse during the slide show.

If you want to automate the timing of the animation effect, select the Automatically option and enter the desired time lapse in seconds in the adjacent field.

Note

On Mouse Click is the default method of starting animation. If you want to automate animation for multiple objects, you need to select each object individually and apply this option.

SPECIFYING EFFECTS

Click the Effects tab to set other special effects. Figure 14.5 shows this tab.

In this tab, you can add transition and sound effects to the animation of individual objects.

Select the object to which you want to apply special effects in the box in the upper-left corner of the dialog box.

In the Entry Animation and Sound group box, select the animation effect in the first drop-down list, its direction in the adjacent drop-down list, and finally its sound effect, if any.

→ To learn more about sound effects in PowerPoint, **see** "Inserting Your Own Sound File," **p. 311**

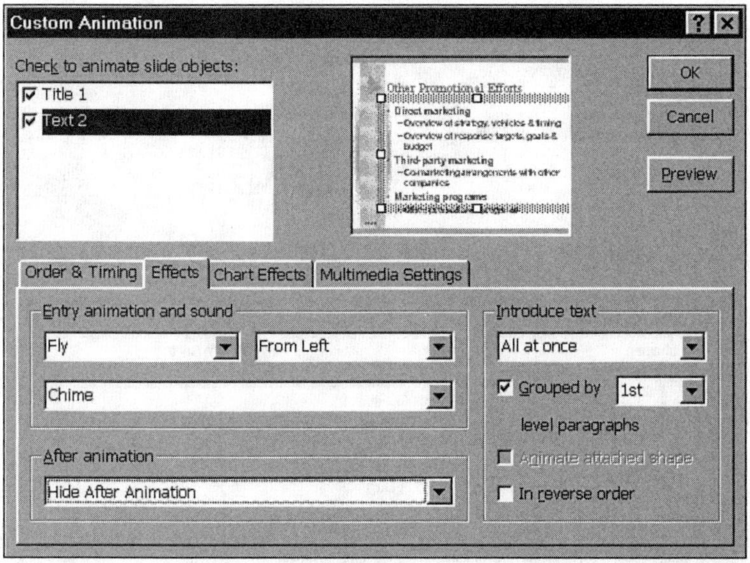

Figure 14.5
Add entry animations and sounds in this tab.

These animation effects are in many ways similar to the slide transition and preset animation effects. In addition, you can specify how to end your animation in the After Animation drop-down list. Options include:

- *Standard Colors* Enables you to choose a color from the default palette, which changes the object's color after animation.

- *More Colors* Displays the Colors dialog box in which you can choose from a variety of other color options.

→ To learn more about this dialog box, **see** "Using the Colors Dialog Box," **p. 275**

- *Don't Dim* Continues to display a static image of the object after animation.

- *Hide After Animation* Hides the object after animation.

- *Hide on Next Mouse Click* Hides the object when you click the mouse.

If the object you select is a text object, the Introduce Text group box is active. From the drop-down list choose a method for introducing text: All at Once (the default), By Word, or By Letter.

You can also specify to group the text by paragraph levels, animate an attached shape, or animate in reverse order.

SPECIFYING CHART EFFECTS

In the Chart Effects tab, you can add special animation effects to charts you create. Figure 14.6 shows this tab.

PART

IV

CH

14

Figure 14.6
Animating a chart is
another possibility.

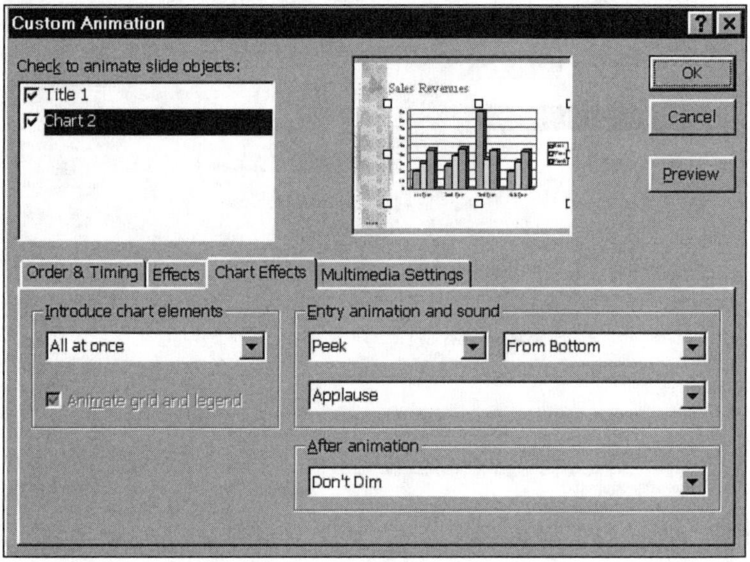

→ For more details on chart capabilities, **see** "Working with Charts," **p. 195**

To animate a chart object, follow these steps:

1. Select the check box next to the chart you want to animate in the upper-left corner of the dialog box.

2. From the Introduce Chart Elements drop-down list, choose a method for animating the chart. Options include All at Once, By Series, By Category, By Element in Series, or By Element in Category.

Tip #189 from
Patrice-Anne Rutledge

> If you choose any option other than All at Once, the Animate Grid and Legend check box activates, enabling you to include the chart grid and legend in the animation effect.

3. Next, choose an entry animation method, such as Box, Checkerboard, or Crawl from the drop-down list in the Entry Animation and Sound group box.

4. In the adjacent drop-down list, choose a direction for this animation method. For example, if you choose the Box animation method, you can direct this animation either In or Out.

Note

> Only those directions that apply to the selected animation method will appear in this drop-down list.

5. If you want to add sound effects to this chart animation, select the sound file to use from the bottom drop-down list in the Entry Animation and Sound group box. To insert a sound file that isn't in the list of options, choose Other Sound from the drop-down list, which opens the Insert Sound dialog box.

Tip #190 from

If you don't want to include a sound, choose No Sound, the default option.

→ To understand how to work with sound effects, **see** "Inserting Your Own Sound File," **p. 311**

6. Finally, you can specify how to end your animation in the <u>A</u>fter Animation drop-down list. Options include converting the object to another color, continuing to display it without dimming, hiding it immediately, or hiding it upon a mouse click. The <u>A</u>fter Animation drop-down list in the Chart Effects tab is identical to the drop-down list of the same name in the Effects tab.

→ For more details, **see** "Specifying Effects," **p. 324**

SPECIFYING MULTIMEDIA SETTINGS

Use the Multimedia Settings tab to activate media clips—such as sounds and movies—that you insert into your presentation. Figure 14.7 shows this tab.

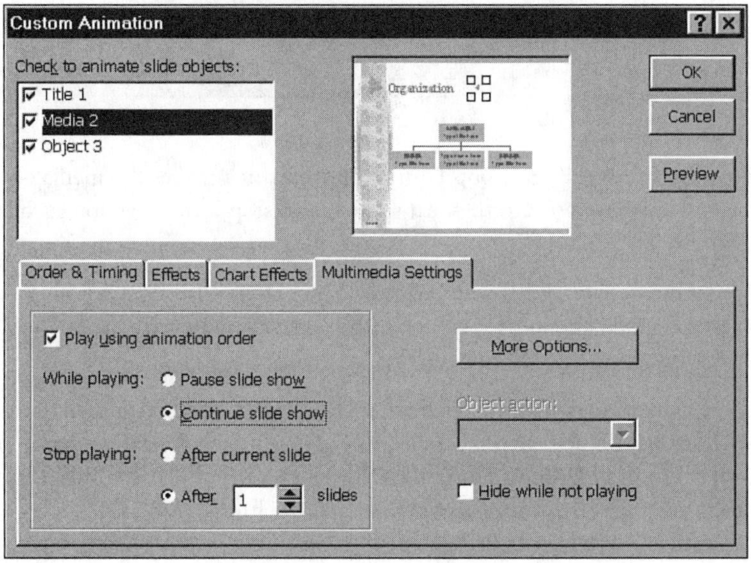

Figure 14.7
The Multimedia Settings tab enables you to work with media clips such as sounds and movies.

Select the Play <u>U</u>sing Animation Order check box to play the media clip in this presentation.

Caution

If you don't select this check box, your media clip won't play.

While you're playing the media clip, you can choose to either Pause Slide Sho<u>w</u> or <u>C</u>ontinue Slide Show. If you pause the show, any timings you set are put on hold.

→ To learn how to set timings, **see** "Rehearsing Timings," **p. 152**

PART
IV

CH

14

If your media clip is long, it's a good idea to pause the show; otherwise, it may proceed before the clip finishes.

If you do choose to continue the show, more options are available. You can stop playing After the Current Slide or After a certain number of Slides. Stopping after the current slide forces the media clip to stop as soon as it's time to move to the next slide.

To view additional options, click the More Options button. The Sound Options dialog box displays (see Figure 14.8).

Figure 14.8
Set additional media clip options in this dialog box.

In this dialog box, you can specify to Loop Until Stopped, which makes the media clip continue playing until it's time to move to the next slide or you stop it by an action such as a mouse click.

If the media clip is a movie, you can Rewind Movie When Done Playing. Choosing this option enables you to display the movie's initial image when it's done playing.

→ To learn more about using media clips, **see** "Adding Movies and Sound," **p. 299**

If the object you're animating is an embedded object, such as an organization chart or Word file, the Object Action field is activated. Use this field to specify whether to play, edit, or open the object during the slide show. For example, if you want to open an organization chart and edit it during a presentation, you would attach the Edit action to it.

→ To understand how to include an org chart in a presentation, **see** "Working with Organization Charts," **p. 225**

→ To learn more about embedded objects, **see** "Working with Embedded Office Objects," **p. 422**

This is similar to the Object Action field in the Action Settings dialog box.

→ For details on this dialog box, **see** "Using Action Settings," **p. 329**

Tip #191 from
Patrice-Anne Rutledge

Click Hide While Not Playing to hide an object, such as a sound icon, which has no real visual value.

USING ACTION SETTINGS

Use the *Action Settings (p. 348-350)* dialog box to start an action by clicking an object with the mouse or by simply passing the mouse pointer over it.

For example, you can place an object such as a rectangle in your presentation and have it connect to the Web, play a sound, run a macro, or open another program when you click it or pass the mouse over it. This can be useful when you want to demonstrate other applications during your presentation, but don't want to take the time to try to locate and open them in the middle of a slide show.

To add an action to a PowerPoint object, follow these steps:

1. Select the object to which you want to add an action.

2. Choose Slide Show, Action Settings to open the Action Settings dialog box, shown in Figure 14.9.

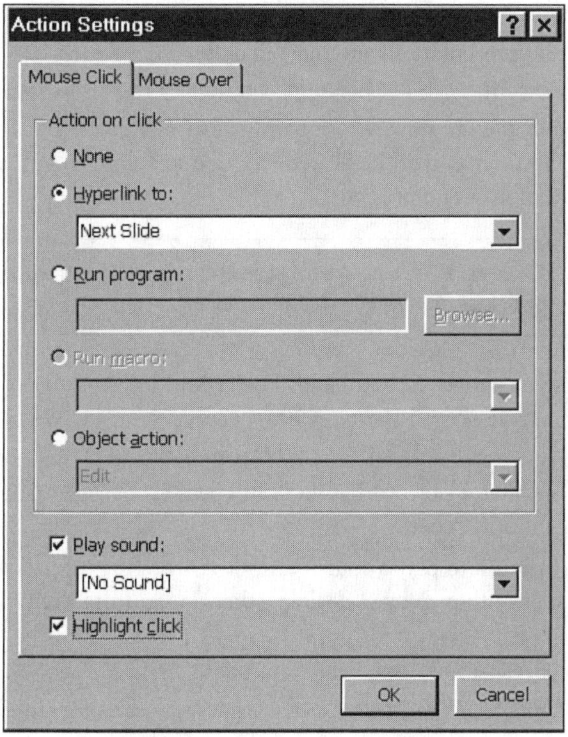

Figure 14.9
Use a mouse click or touch to perform actions in your presentation.

Tip #192 from
Patrice-Anne Rutledge

You can also select an object, right-click the mouse, and choose Action Settings from the shortcut menu.

3. Choose the Mouse Click tab if you want to start the action with a mouse click; choose the Mouse Over tab to start the action by passing the mouse over the object.

Caution

Passing the mouse over an object to start an action is the easier method, but be careful not to get too close to the object too soon or you may start the action before you intend to.

Note

The Mouse Click and Mouse Over tabs are nearly identical. The only real difference is the method by which you start the action.

4. PowerPoint provides five main action choices in this dialog box, as well as the capability to activate a sound. Choose one of the following:

- *None* No action occurs. Choose this option to remove a previously placed action.

- *Hyperlink To* Creates a hyperlink to a selected slide within your presentation, another PowerPoint presentation, another file on your computer, or a Web page.

→ For further explanation about using hyperlinks in PowerPoint, **see** "Adding Hyperlinks," **p. 338**

- *Run Program* Runs the program whose path you specify in the text box. You can click the Browse button to open the Select Program to Run dialog box where you can search for the appropriate program.

Tip #193 from
Patrice-Anne Rutledge

You can also use Run Program to open a file in another program. For example, entering c:\budget.xls would open Excel and the Budget worksheet.

- *Run Macro* Lets you choose from a list of PowerPoint macros you've created.

→ To learn how to create macros, **see** "Running a Macro," **p. 441**

- *Object Action* Enables you to open, edit, or play an embedded object. This option is available only for objects that you can open, edit, or play, such as a media clip or organization chart.

- *Play Sound* Enables you to play a sound you select from the drop-down list. You can select other sounds to play by choosing Other Sound from the drop-down list.

→ For details on sound files, **see** "Inserting Your Own Sound File," **p. 311**

- *Highlight Click/Highlight When Mouse Over* Highlights the selected object when you perform the mouse action.

5. Click OK to close the Action Settings dialog box.

USING ACTION BUTTONS

Action buttons are another alternative for using PowerPoint objects to perform certain actions. PowerPoint includes 12 different action buttons:

- Custom
- Home
- Help
- Information
- Back or Previous
- Forward or Next
- Beginning
- End
- Return
- Document
- Sound
- Movie

These buttons function in much the same way as applying an action setting to an existing object. In fact, when you place an action button on a slide, the Action Settings dialog box appears. You can then specify mouse actions for the action button. Many action buttons perform common tasks such as moving to a previous slide; this action is already defined by default in the Action Settings dialog box.

To place an action button on a PowerPoint slide, choose Slide Show, Action Buttons. The Action Buttons palette displays, shown in Figure 14.10.

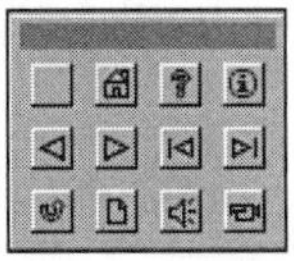

Figure 14.10
This palette includes several ready-made action buttons.

Tip #194 from
Patrice-Anne Rutledge

You can also create an action button from the Drawing toolbar by choosing AutoShapes, Action Buttons.

The Action Settings dialog box appears, in which you can accept the default action setting or specify the action to attach to this button. Enter the required information and click OK. The action button now displays on your PowerPoint slide, as illustrated in Figure 14.11.

Figure 14.11
Use action buttons in your presentation for added flexibility and convenience in transitioning to other slides or applications.

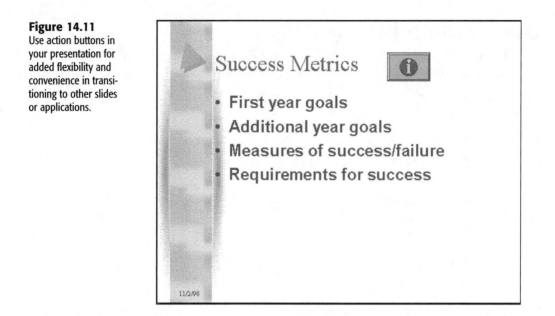

Tip #195 from	An action button is similar to other PowerPoint objects—you can easily move, resize, copy, delete, and format it.
Patrice-Anne Rutledge	

→ To learn how to move, resize, copy, delete, and format an object, **see** "Creating and Formatting Objects," **p. 267**

USING THE ANIMATION EFFECTS TOOLBAR

The Animation Effects toolbar provides another means for accessing many of PowerPoint's animation capabilities for text. Table 14.1 illustrates the buttons on this toolbar.

TABLE 14.1   ANIMATION EFFECTS TOOLBAR BUTTONS

Button	Name	Description
	Animate Title	Applies a default animation effect to the slide title
	Animate Slide Text	Applies a default animation effect to the slide text
	Drive-In Effect	Displays a drive-in effect on the selected text, which enters from the right
	Flying Effect	Displays a flying effect on the selected text, which enters from the left
	Camera Effect	Makes object appear through a camera shutter with accompanying camera click sound effect

Button	Name	Description
	Flash Once	Flashes the selected text once
	Laser Text Effect	Displays the selected text as if it were printed by a laser printer
	Typewriter Text Effect	Displays the selected text as if it were entered on a type-writer
	Reverse Text Order Effect	Displays the selected text in reverse order
	Drop-In Text Effect	Drops in the selected text from the top of the slide
Edit Te_xt...	Animation Order	Displays a drop-down list for setting the order in which slide objects are animated
	Custom Animation	Opens the Custom Animation dialog box
	Animation Preview	Previews the slide animation in a small preview window

To view the Animation Effects toolbar, click the Animation Effects button on the Formatting toolbar. These buttons all duplicate animation features we've already discussed, but their placement on one toolbar can be very useful for animating text objects.

TROUBLESHOOTING

I can't hear sound files I embedded in my presentation.

You must have a sound card and speakers to hear sounds that you add to your presentation. Also verify that your volume is turned up sufficiently to hear the sounds.

Why can't I see the preset animation options?

You can't use preset animation with an entire slide. You need to select an object to animate before the selections from the Preset Animation menu are available.

PART

IV

CH

14

DESIGN CORNER

With PowerPoint's animation features, you can enliven presentations using transitions, action buttons, or preset animation.

BEFORE

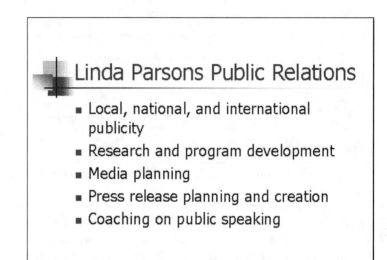

AFTER

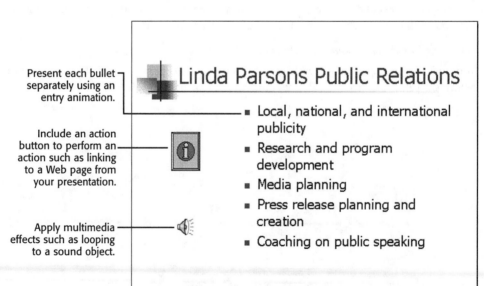

Present each bullet separately using an entry animation.

Include an action button to perform an action such as linking to a Web page from your presentation.

Apply multimedia effects such as looping to a sound object.

PART

V

WORKING WITH POWERPOINT ON THE WEB

CHAPTER 15

USING POWERPOINT'S WEB FEATURES

In this chapter   *by Read Gilgen*

WORKING WITH HYPERLINKS

If you've ever surfed the World Wide Web, you're already familiar with *hyperlinks (p. 352)*. Simply put, by clicking your mouse on linked objects you can jump somewhere else: to another location in your slide show, to another program, or even to a location on the Web.

Unlike a book or a typical slide show where you must proceed sequentially through the material, a hyperlinked PowerPoint presentation enables you to go where you need to go and to present what you need to present when you want to present it.

Suppose, for example, you are making a presentation to the board of directors of your entertainment company. You suspect some board members will want to know more about current promotions by a rival company. You can create a hyperlink in your slide show that opens up your Web browser, connects to the Internet, and displays your competitor's Web site. Of course, if no one asks or if time is running short, you need not even use the link. But you know it's there just in case it's needed.

ADDING HYPERLINKS

The first step in creating an Internet hyperlink is to identify the object to be linked. Any object including text, clip art, WordArt, charts, AutoShapes, and more can be linked. To create a link, follow these steps:

1. While in the Normal (tri-pane) or Slide view, select the text or object you want to link (see Figure 15.1).

Figure 15.1
Select text, or any other object, to which you want to add a hyperlink.

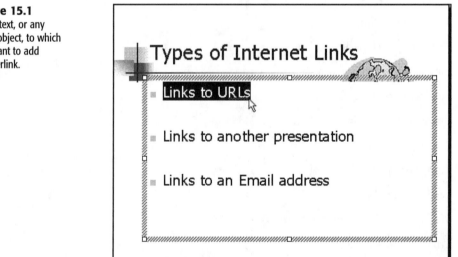

Types of Internet Links

- Links to URLs
- Links to another presentation
- Links to an Email address

Note

You can also select text, but not other objects, in the Outline view or the outline pane of the Normal view.

2. Click the Insert Hyperlink icon. Alternatively, you can choose Insert, Hyperlink; or press Ctrl+K. PowerPoint displays the Insert Hyperlink dialog box (see Figure 15.2).

Note

When you create a hyperlink for the first time, you use the Insert Hyperlink dialog box. If you change the hyperlink, you use the Edit Hyperlink dialog box. However, both are identical except for the Remove Link button found in the Edit Hyperlink dialog box.

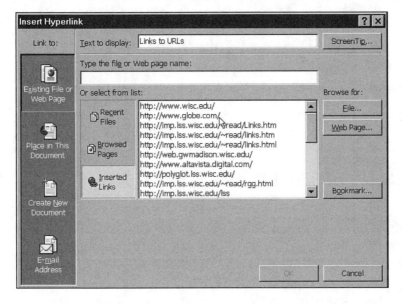

Figure 15.2
Use the Insert Hyperlink dialog box to specify the location you want to link to the selected text or object.

3. Type the Internet URL in the Type the File or Web Page Name box.

Note

URL stands for *uniform resource locator* and it is the standard method for describing World Wide Web addresses. For example, in the following address you find three distinct components:

`http://www.mycompany.com/sales/june/report.html`

The first part of the URL is the protocol being used to "serve" you the information (`http://`). The second section is the name of the Internet computer or "Web server," which consists of at least the domain name (`mycompany.com`), along with any other names that distinguish more than one server in that domain. The final component is the "path" to the specific document you want, ending in the actual filename (`/sales/june/report.html`).

Caution

Be sure to carefully type the URL, including all special characters (such as the tilde ~). Generally, you should use lowercase characters. Some Web servers distinguish between upper- and lowercase characters, and using an uppercase character in the URL may not work.

4. Click OK.

If you added a link to text, that text now appears underlined and in a different color (see Figure 15.3). The actual color you see depends on the PowerPoint design template you are using. If you added the link to any other object, you do not see any difference in the appearance of the object, but the object is linked, nonetheless.

Figure 15.3
Linked text appears underlined and in a highlighted color.

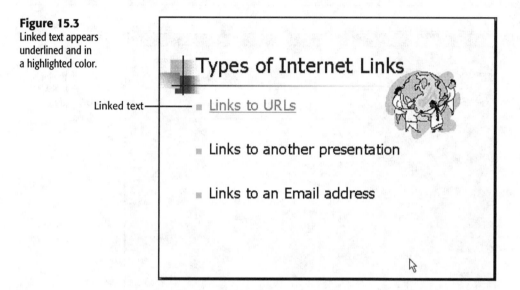

Linked text ⟶

CREATING INVISIBLE HYPERLINKS FOR TEXT

Linked text appears markedly different from the non-linked text around it. You may not like the look this creates, but you still want to be able to click on that text and have it linked.

The solution is really quite simple: Draw an AutoShape, such as a rectangle, that covers the text you want to link, link the AutoShape, and then make it invisible.

To create an invisible hyperlinked object, follow these steps:

1. Use the Drawing toolbar to draw a rectangular box that covers the text you want to link (see Figure 15.4).

2. With the AutoShape selected, click the Insert Hyperlink icon (or choose Insert, Hyperlink; or press Ctrl+K).

3. Type the Internet URL in the Type the File or Web Page Name box.

4. Click OK. This creates the link to the AutoShape image.

5. Right-click the AutoShape, and choose Format AutoShape; or choose Format, AutoShape. PowerPoint displays the Format AutoShape dialog box (see Figure 15.5).

6. Click the Fill Color drop-down menu and choose No Fill.

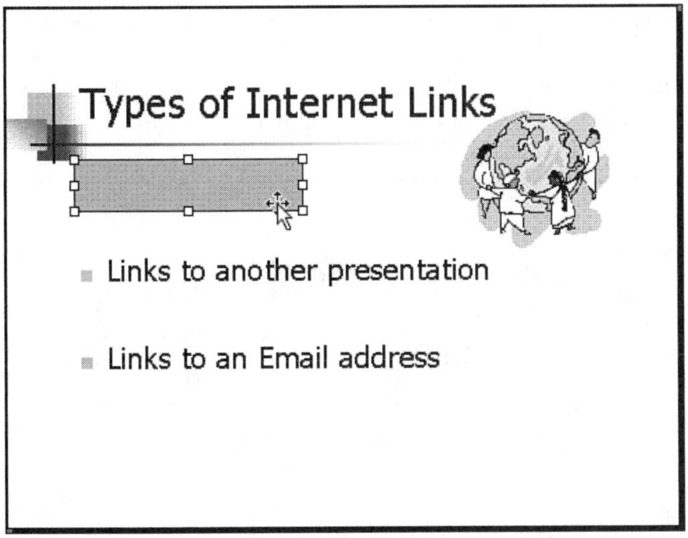

Figure 15.4
To create the effect of
linked text without
making it look linked,
use an AutoShape
graphic image to
create the link, then
make the image
invisible.

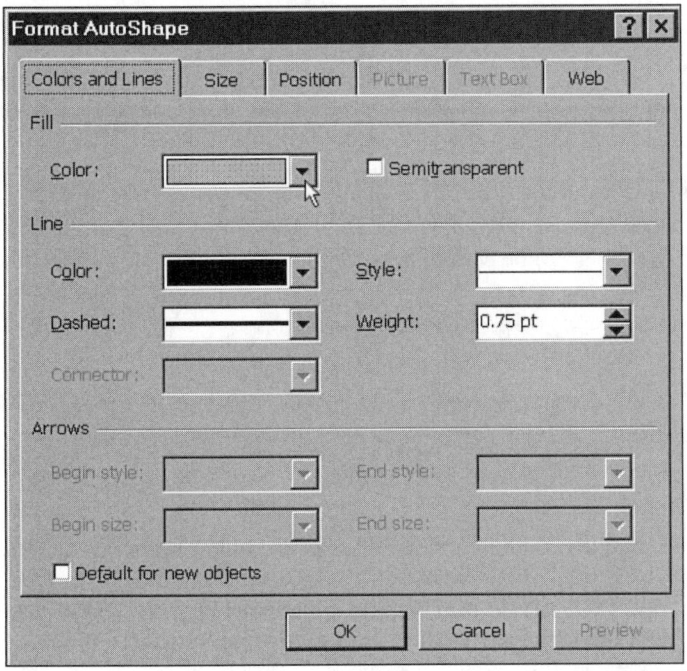

Figure 15.5
Use the Format
AutoShape dialog
box to remove fill
color and line color,
thus making the
AutoShape invisible.

7. Click the Line Color drop-down menu and choose No Line.

8. Click OK.

An invisible, linked object now appears over the text you want linked (see Figure 15.6). When you play your slide show, you simply move the mouse pointer to that text area and click when the mouse pointer changes to a hand. To the audience, it appears you are clicking on text, although you are really clicking a linked, invisible graphic shape.

Figure 15.6
An invisible AutoShape can be linked, making it appear that the text beneath it is linked.

Linked AutoShape——

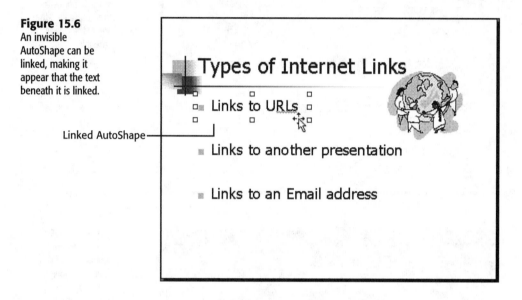

An additional benefit to using an invisible link is that no one except you has to know the link is there. If you choose not to use it, no one will ever know. Text linked in the normal manner, on the other hand, begs to be clicked because the text around it is so obviously different.

MODIFYING HYPERLINKS

The Insert Hyperlink dialog box is a powerful tool for quickly and efficiently creating and modifying your hyperlinks.

CHANGING URL LOCATIONS

For example, to change the URL for a hyperlink you created, follow these simple steps:

1. Click or select the linked object.
2. Right-click the object and choose Hyperlink, Edit Hyperlink; or choose Insert, Hyperlink; or press Ctrl+K. PowerPoint displays the Edit Hyperlink dialog box (see Figure 15.7)
3. Type the new URL or use one of the dialog box tools to select what you want to link to.
4. Choose OK to update the hyperlink.

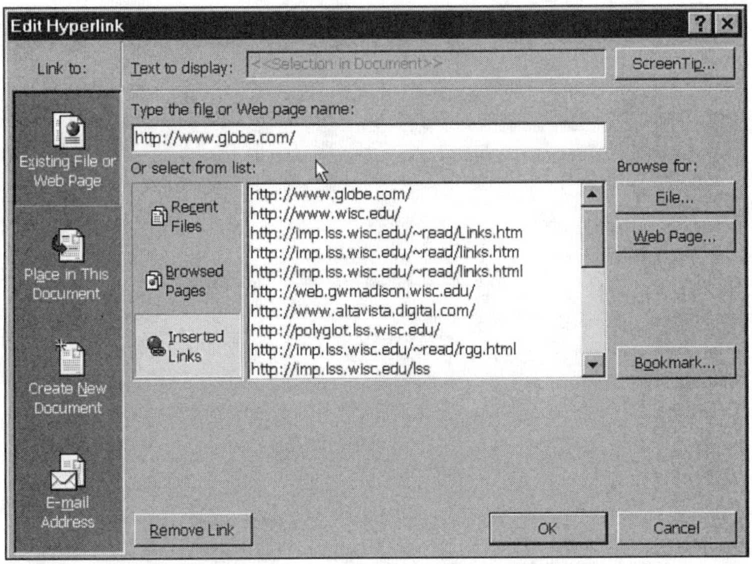

PART

V

CH

15

Figure 15.7
The Edit Hyperlink
dialog box offers
several tools for
locating what you
want to link to.

When you access the Insert Hyperlink (or Edit Hyperlink) dialog box, by default, PowerPoint displays the Link to Existing File or Web Page view (refer to Figure 15.7). This view enables you to find the URL you want in these ways:

- If you know the URL, simply type it in the Type the File or Web Page Name box.

- If the link is to a location that you have visited recently, you can select it from the list of displayed URLs.

- If you don't remember the location by its URL, you can click the Browsed Pages button, and choose the location from a list of location titles (see Figure 15.8).

- You can click the Web Page button to take you to your browser, enabling you to browse for the Internet location you want. When you find the location, you switch back to PowerPoint (use the Windows taskbar, or press Alt+Tab), and the URL from your browser appears automatically in the dialog box.

Note

Don't forget that you must be connected to the Internet if you wish to browse for a URL. Generally, those connected directly to a network need not be concerned; those using dial-up connections must first make sure they are connected.

- If you want to jump to a specific location within a Web page after inserting the URL, click the Bookmark button. PowerPoint displays a list of all bookmarks found in the Web page (see Figure 15.9). Select a Bookmark in the Web Page and choose OK. PowerPoint adds the pound sign (#) and the bookmark name to your URL.

Figure 15.8
The Browsed Pages button displays URLs by their titles, making them easier to find.

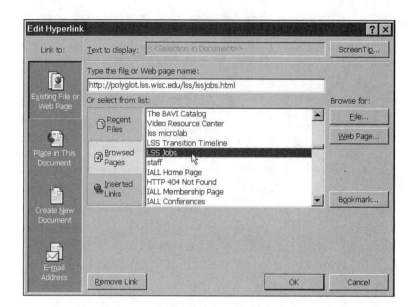

Figure 15.9
If you need to link to a bookmark, PowerPoint can connect to the Web site and return a list of bookmarks in the target Web page.

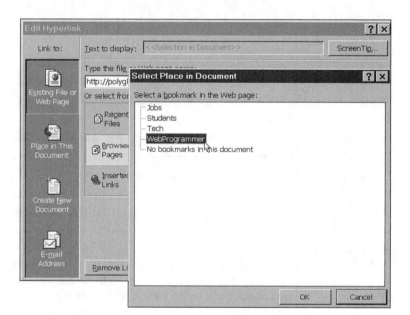

CREATING LINKS TO OTHER SLIDES

In addition to Web sites—and perhaps of more practical use—you can also create links that enable you to jump to other slides within your presentation, or even to a slide within another PowerPoint presentation.

Creating links to other slides helps you customize your slide show so that you can go quickly to those slides you need. For example, after your opening title slide, you might want to include a table of contents slide, with hyperlinks from each topic to a specific location in the slide show. On the last slide for each topic, you could include a link back to the table of contents slide. To create this type of internal link, follow these steps:

1. Select the object to be linked and access the Insert Hyperlink dialog box.

2. Click the Place in This Document button. PowerPoint displays a list of slides in the current slide show (see Figure 15.10).

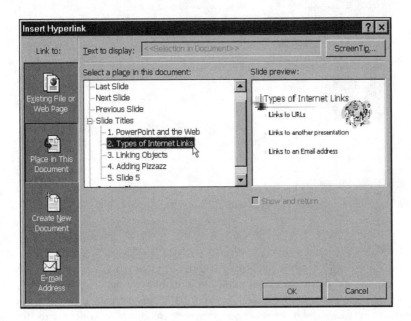

Figure 15.10
To link to a slide in your current presentation, click Place in This Document and select the slide you want.

3. Select the slide to which you want to jump.

4. Click OK.

To create a link to another slide show:

1. Select the object to be linked and access the Insert Hyperlink dialog box.

2. Click the Existing File or Web Page button.

3. Click the Recent Files button.

4. Choose the PowerPoint slide show you want to jump to. Use the Browse for File button if necessary.

5. Click the Bookmark button. PowerPoint displays the Select Place in Document dialog box.

6. Expand the list of Slide Titles (see Figure 15.11).

Figure 15.11
You can link to a specific slide in an entirely different PowerPoint presentation.

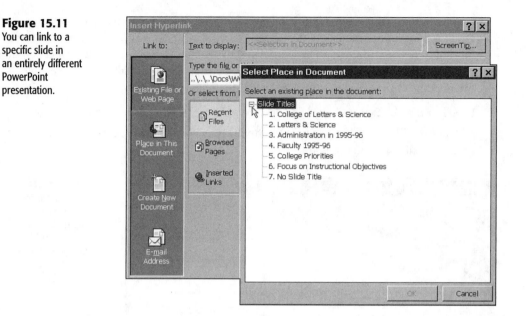

7. Select the slide to which you want to jump.

8. Click OK twice to return to the PowerPoint editing screen.

LINKING TO ANOTHER FILE

PowerPoint also enables you to create a hyperlink to another document, either on your own computer or on the network, if you are connected to one. When you jump from your PowerPoint presentation to another file, the application that displays that file automatically starts. Other PowerPoint files display, of course, in PowerPoint. But Word documents display in Word, HTML files display in your browser, and so on.

To link to a file, you can

- Type the name of the file, including its full path name (for example, `c:\my documents\ sales.xls`).

- Click the Recent Files button to display a list of recently accessed files.

- Click the Browse for File button and browse your computer or your network files for the file you want.

CREATING OTHER TYPES OF LINKS

Finally, you can create links to files you haven't even created, as well as links to send electronic mail (see Figure 15.12).

To create a link to an electronic mail address, click the E-mail Address button. Type the address in the E-mail Address box and enter a Subject. You can even select the email address from a list of recently used email addresses (see Figure 15.13).

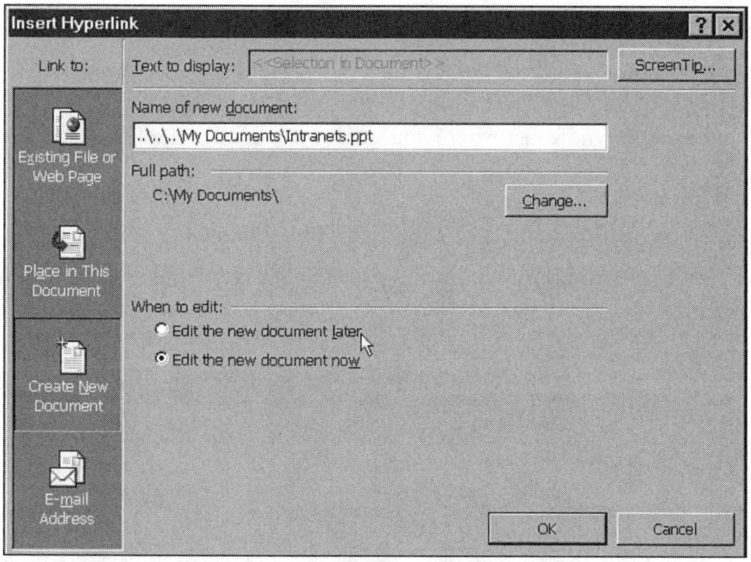

Figure 15.12
You can even link to
a yet-to-be-created
document.

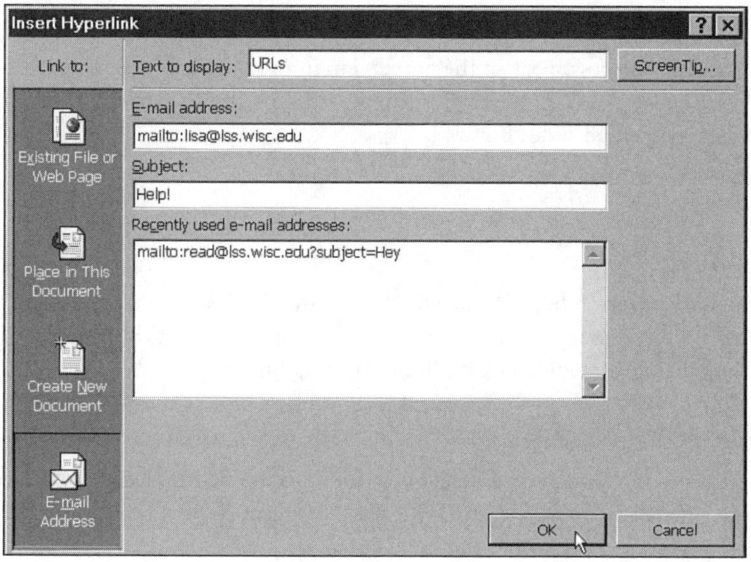

Figure 15.13
Create a link to
an email address,
enabling a viewer
to send a message.

Note

Traditionally, PowerPoint presentations were designed to be presented to an audience by a speaker. PowerPoint is now designed so that viewers can also be allowed to run the presentation by themselves. PowerPoint presentations placed on a company network or on a Web site can be designed so that the viewer can navigate and even interact with the presentation at his or her own pace.

CHANGING THE SCREEN TIP

When you point your mouse at a linked object during a presentation, a *ScreenTip (p. 24)* appears detailing the location of the link. You can customize the ScreenTip to make it easier for you (or the audience) to know just where you will go if you click the linked object.

To change the ScreenTip:

1. Select the object to be linked and access the Edit Hyperlink dialog box.

2. Click the ScreenTip button. PowerPoint displays the Set Hyperlink ScreenTip dialog box (see Figure 15.14).

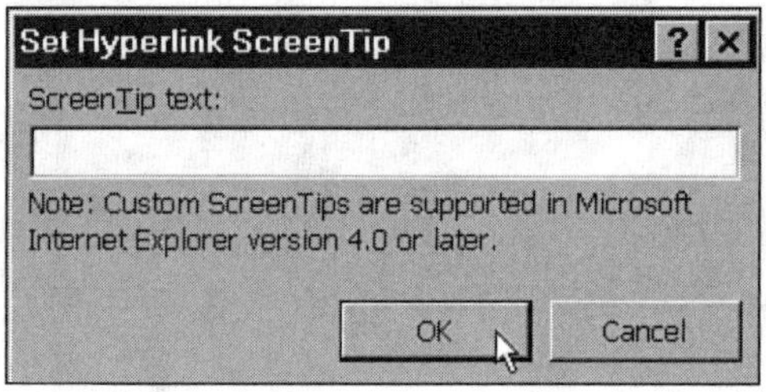

Figure 15.14
Customize the ScreenTip that appears when you move the mouse pointer to a linked object.

3. Type the text you want to appear in the ScreenTip in the ScreenTip Text box. The note about ScreenTips in Internet Explorer refers to slide shows viewed in the browser, not to normally presented slide shows.

4. Click OK twice to return to the PowerPoint editing screen.

REMOVING HYPERLINKS

After inserting a hyperlink, you may decide you don't want that link or that you need to link it to another object on the screen. To remove a hyperlink, simply select the object, access the Edit Hyperlink dialog box, and click the Remove Link button.

CHANGING A HYPERLINKED OBJECT'S ACTION SETTINGS

The most important action for a linked object is to jump to the desired location. However, using PowerPoint's *Action Settings (p. 329-330)* feature, you can control how you activate the hyperlink, and also add some pizzazz to the linked object.

To access the Action Settings dialog box:

1. Select the linked object.

2. Right-click and choose Action Settings, or choose Slide Show, Action Settings. PowerPoint displays the Action Settings dialog box.

If you've created a hyperlink, Hyperlink To is already selected, and the location of the link is listed. Note that the action is displayed on the Mouse Click tab, which means that you have to click the linked object to activate the hyperlink. The Mouse Over tab offers the same options, but actions are activated merely by passing the mouse pointer over the linked object, without clicking.

Tip #196 from
Read Gilgen

You may be able to save some time by selecting an object and using the Action Settings dialog box both to create the hyperlink, and also to set any actions you want.

Caution

You don't want surprises during your slide presentation. Unfortunately, the Mouse Over option for activating hyperlinks can take you places before you're really ready to go there. Generally, you should activate hyperlinks only by clicking the mouse.

You can add some pizzazz to your presentation by creating actions that produce sound effects or that highlight linked objects. For example, you can require a mouse click to activate a hyperlink, but can highlight the object (graphic objects only) or add a sound effect when the mouse pointer is passed over the object.

To add Mouse Over sound and highlighting effects:

1. Select the object to which you want to add the effects.

2. Right-click and choose <u>A</u>ction Settings, or choose Sli<u>d</u>e Show, <u>A</u>ction Settings. PowerPoint displays the Action Settings dialog box.

3. Click the Mouse Over tab (see Figure 15.15).

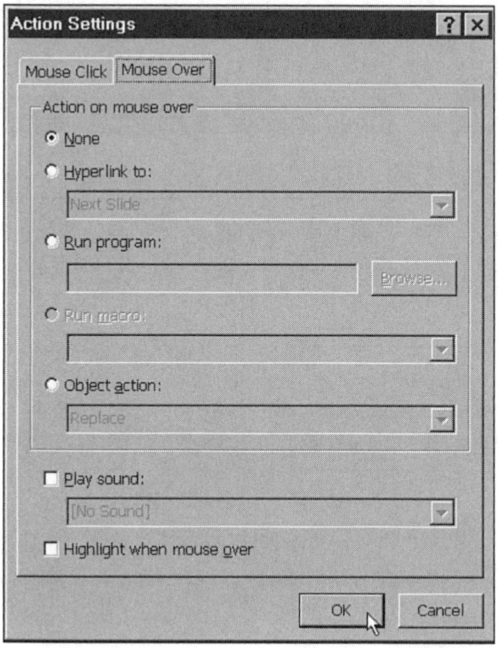

Figure 15.15
Add Action Settings to a link that are activated when you pass the mouse pointer over the linked object.

4. Click the Highlight When Mouse Over check box (you cannot select this option if the object you have selected is text).

5. Click the Play Sound check box.

6. Click the Play Sound drop-down list, and select the sound effect you want to use (see Figure 15.16).

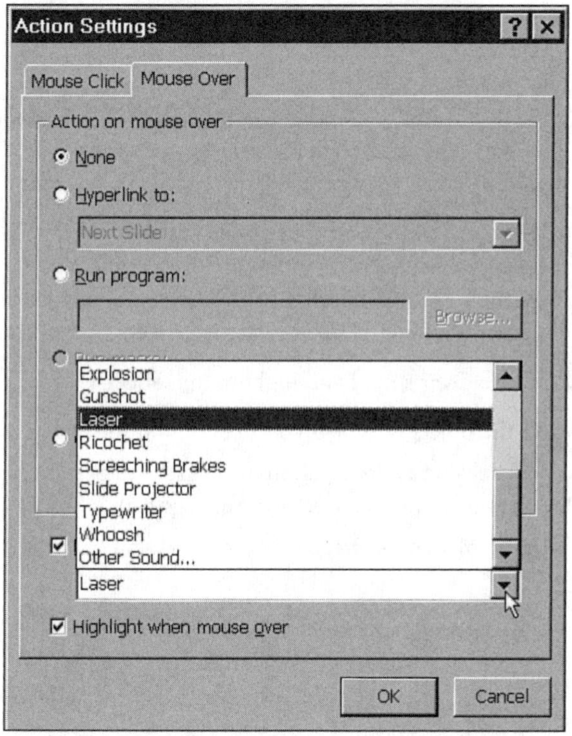

Figure 15.16
Add pizzazz to your presentation by adding sounds or highlighting to a link.

Tip #197 from
Read Gilgen

You can associate any .WAV–formatted sound file with the object. Simply choose Other Sound from the drop-down list, and browse until you find the sound you want.

Note

If you add Action Settings to an object, when you try to access the Edit Hyperlink dialog box, you see instead the Action Settings dialog box. You can still edit the URL, but you have to remove any Action Settings if you want to access the Edit Hyperlink dialog box.

TESTING HYPERLINKS

More likely than not, you will test your hyperlinks as you go. Nevertheless, before you take your presentation before an audience, you'll want to test all your hyperlinks to verify that you set them up correctly.

Note

Don't forget that you must be connected to the Internet, either via a network or through a dial-up connection, if you want to test links to the Web.

To test a hyperlink:

1. Go to the slide you want to test.

2. Click the Slide Show view. Choosing Slide Show, View Show (or pressing F5) starts you at the beginning of your presentation, not at the currently selected slide.

3. Move the mouse pointer to the linked object.

4. Check that the ScreenTip displays properly.

5. Note whether Action Settings work properly (such as sound effect on Mouse Over).

6. Click the linked object and verify that you are taken to the appropriate Web location, slide, or file.

7. Return to your slide show by closing the linked location. Usually, this involves closing the application, although you can also just minimize the application if you want it to start more quickly the next time you use it.

When you complete your slide show, you should test all the links in the entire presentation. This means starting the slide show at the beginning and trying out each hyperlink. (We'll talk about how to do that in the next section.) Stop and fix any hyperlink that doesn't work the way you expect it to.

NAVIGATING A HYPERLINKED PRESENTATION

You would probably never get lost in a sequential slide presentation, but in a hyperlinked presentation, you can become disoriented—and even get lost—very easily.

You can minimize the likelihood of getting lost by rehearsing your presentation many times, trying out various links, and learning what will happen and how to get back on track.

Some typical techniques for returning to the right place in your presentation include:

■ If you go to a browser, you can use the browser's "Back" button to return to PowerPoint. Generally, this doesn't close the browser, but keeps it open in case you need to use it again during the presentation.

■ If you jump to another PowerPoint presentation, you can right-click the slide in the new presentation, and choose Go, Previously Viewed to return to the original presentation. If your browser was open prior to opening a second slide show, the browser may get closed.

■ If you link to another document that opens up another program, such as Word, you can switch back to PowerPoint without closing the application you jumped to by pressing Alt+Tab.

■ If you are linking primarily to other slides within your own presentation, you can also add navigational links, such as linked Action Buttons, that help you stay on course.

LINKING TO THE WEB DURING A PRESENTATION

The more elements you add to your presentation, the more complex it becomes, thus increasing the chances that something will go wrong. This can be particularly true when you link to the Internet during a presentation. Try to determine what parts of your presentation are most critical, and have a backup plan in case things don't work the way you hope they will. Make allowances that minimize your risk, and consider the following:

- Test links thoroughly. Remove dead links and update incorrect ones.

- Consider the time of day you'll be giving the presentation. Internet traffic tends to be heavier in the afternoon. Morning Internet connections are usually a bit faster.

- Test your links for speed relative to other sites. If the linked URL contains a lot of graphics, uses Java, or is served by a slower Web server, you may not want to patiently wait during your presentation for the site to display.

- Always evaluate and reevaluate just how important the link is. If you don't need it, don't use it. What takes a few seconds to load in your office will seem like an eternity when you're standing in front of your audience.

- Have a backup plan, in case your hyperlinks don't work. One method is to copy the files from the URL to your local computer (or network) and display them from there. However, the complexity of some sites, as well as copyright considerations, may make this impractical.

- Consider creating other slides that convey the same information as the Web site you wanted to connect to. They may not measure up to the actual Web site, but then again, you won't stand there waiting for the URL to come up, only to find that network congestion prevents you from doing so.

PUBLISHING TO THE INTERNET

The World Wide Web has taken the world by storm. Everyone either wants to receive or disseminate information via the Web. PowerPoint makes it easier than ever to convert your presentation into a format that can be viewed by Web browsers, such as Internet Explorer or Netscape Navigator.

Before doing so, however, you should consider the following:

- A Web version of your presentation can be viewed by anyone who has access to your Web server. Unless your server is limited to your company (such as a corporate intranet), anyone from anywhere in the world can look in.

- A Web version enables your viewers to see the presentation at their convenience. This can be particularly important for global audiences who live in vastly different time zones.

- You have less control over a Web version of your presentation. No longer can you dictate the sequence of the slides, nor can you add clarifying comments if they are needed.

- In the case of classroom presentations, will a Web version encourage students to skip class, knowing they can get the presentation off the Web at another time?
- Will your potential Web audience have the necessary computer hardware and software to view your presentation the way you intended it to appear?

After you determine that you really want to publish your presentation to the Web, you next need to make sure that the slide show is well-designed for Web use. Consider the following:

- Use good presentation design principles. If the slide show works for an audience that sits before you, it will probably work well on the Web.
- Because the presentation will be viewed unattended, make sure you have abundant navigational aids so viewers don't get lost. Include a table of contents, or Home, Back, and Forward buttons to assist the viewer.
- Be more judicious in your use of graphics, animations, and other multimedia effects. What works well from a hard disk or over a local area network might be deadly slow over a modem connection. Keep such elements small or eliminate them altogether, if they don't really add to the presentation.
- Be aware of issues related to accessibility for disabled users. For example, consider whether you need an alternative text-based page for the visually impaired who use special voice readers.

Caution

Be careful to understand and follow copyright laws and guidelines when publishing your slide show to the Web. If any of your material is copyrighted by someone else, you may be required to limit access to the material or not even use it at all if you don't first obtain permissions.

SAVING A PRESENTATION AS A WEB PAGE

PowerPoint not only enables you to save your work directly in HTML format, but also allows you to open your HTML slide shows directly into PowerPoint, edit them, and save them again in HTML. As you will see, this is not only easy, but it saves lots of time and space because you don't have to keep an original PowerPoint show and convert it each time.

Publishing your show to the Internet involves two steps: saving the presentation in HTML format and transferring the resulting files to a Web server. If you're lucky enough to be connected directly to your Web server over a company intranet, you don't even have to worry about transferring files because you can save the show directly at the Web site.

Note

HTML stands for *Hypertext Markup Language*. Although much of HTML is standard, some of the markup commands have been enhanced by Microsoft and other companies to provide added functionality. With HTML as the base technology, *Cascading Style Sheets* (CCS) provide enhanced formatting of the file, and *eXtensible Markup Language* (XML) is used to store nonviewing information that enables PowerPoint to read, edit, and save presentations without losing any of PowerPoint's advanced presentation features.

To save a slide show as a Web page, follow these steps:

1. Choose File, Save as Web Page, and PowerPoint displays a somewhat modified Save As dialog box (see Figure 15.17).

Figure 15.17
Saving a PowerPoint presentation as a Web page can be quite simple, or you can customize the Web page.

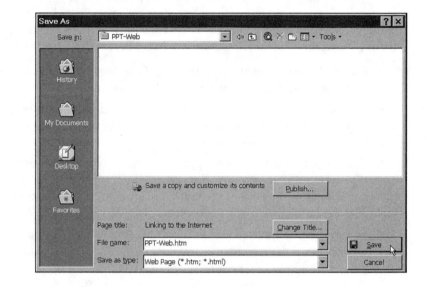

2. Browse to the location where you want to save your presentation, making sure that location appears in the Save In edit box.

Tip #198 from
Read Gilgen

Saving your show as a Web page generates several separate files. To make it easier to locate these files, to delete them, or to transfer them to a Web server, it's a good idea to create a separate folder for the Web version of your slide show. Click the Create New Folder button and supply the name of the folder for your Web files.

---

3. Edit the filename if you want. Note that the filename ends in .htm, a standard extension for HTML files.

4. Click Change to change the page title. Otherwise, PowerPoint simply uses the title of the first slide as the title of the Web page.

5. Click Save to save your presentation as a Web page.

Tip #199 from
Read Gilgen

If you know that PowerPoint's Web options are set the way you want them, you can save time by choosing Save. By default, this gives you a frame-based Web page that includes an outline, navigation buttons, and other tools, along with the slide. The HTML file is also optimized for use with Internet Explorer 4.0 or later.

If you want to customize the way you present your slide show as a Web page, follow these steps:

1. Choose File, Save as Web Page.

2. In the Save As dialog box (refer to Figure 15.17), click Publish to customize the Web page display. PowerPoint displays the Publish as Web Page dialog box (see Figure 15.18).

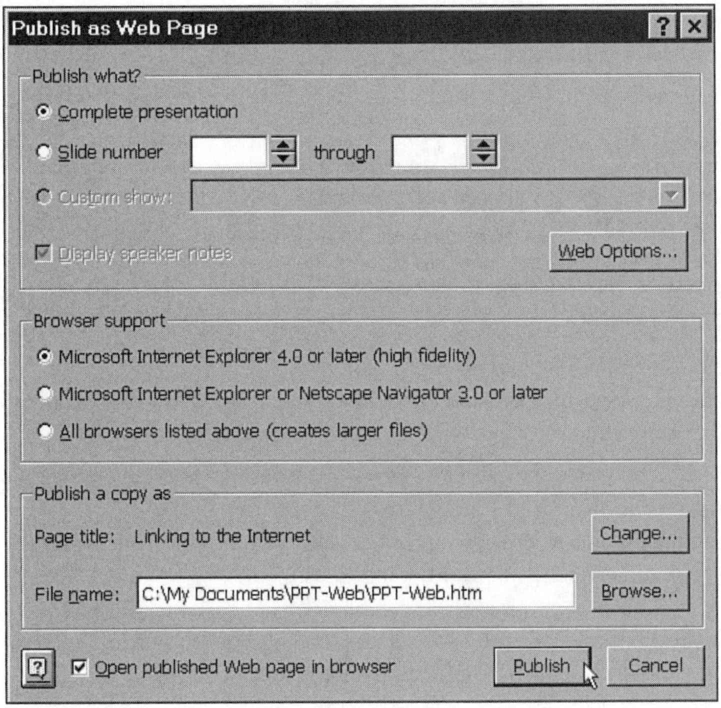

Figure 15.18
Publishing a presentation as a Web page enables you to customize how the page will appear on the Web.

3. Choose the options you want (see "Customizing a Web Presentation" in the next section).

4. Click Publish to save your presentation as a series of HTML files that work together to display your slides on the Web.

CUSTOMIZING A WEB PRESENTATION

The many options for saving your presentation as a Web page enable you to tailor your Web page to match the needs of your viewers. For example, some browsers won't be able to view animations, while others can.

To customize a Web presentation, you must first decide exactly what you want to publish to the Web page, based on these options (shown in Figure 15.18):

- Publish a Complete Presentation
- Publish a range of slides (Slide Number... Through)

- Publish only selected slides (Custom Show) based on slides you designated using PowerPoint's Custom Show feature

- Display Speaker Notes, if you have them

You can also optimize the Web presentation for browsers that audience members are likely to use by selecting the following options under Browser Support:

- To attain the highest fidelity to your original presentation, publish the presentation for use by selecting Microsoft Internet Explorer 4.0 or Later (High Fidelity). This option enables viewers with the latest browsers to see animations and to experience other multimedia features.

Caution

> You must decide whether to ignore users who may be using older browsers or to force them to upgrade to view your Web page. If you're pretty sure that most browsers are up-to-date, optimize for the highest quality. Otherwise, you may want to choose an option that allows all browsers to view the Web page.

- To enable users of older Web browsers to view your Web page content, choose Microsoft Internet Explorer or Netscape Navigator 3.0 or Later. Some of the pizzazz of your PowerPoint presentation may be lost with this conversion.

- All Browsers Listed Above is a special dual-HTML feature that enables viewers to see the best presentation they can, based on the browser they use. This option creates larger files, which means slower downloads, but it helps you avoid having to guess which browser your audience members are going to use.

The Web Options button takes you to the Web Options dialog box (shown in Figure 15.19) where you have many other options. On the General tab, you can choose

- *Add Slide Navigation Controls*   Controls include a hyperlinked outline list of the slides, and Forward and Back buttons that aid the viewer in moving through the slide show.

- *Colors*   Enables you to choose combinations for the Slide Outline navigation menu. The default is white text on a black background, but several other preset color combinations are also available on the drop-down menu.

- *Show Slide Animation While Browsing*   Turn this off if you want static slide transitions.

- *Resize Graphics to Fit Browser Window*   This handy option eliminates the need to guess what size screen or resolution will be used in the browser. Some audience members may use a standard VGA screen (640×480 pixels), whereas others may use Super VGA (800×600). With this option turned on, the slide automatically sizes itself to display as large as possible.

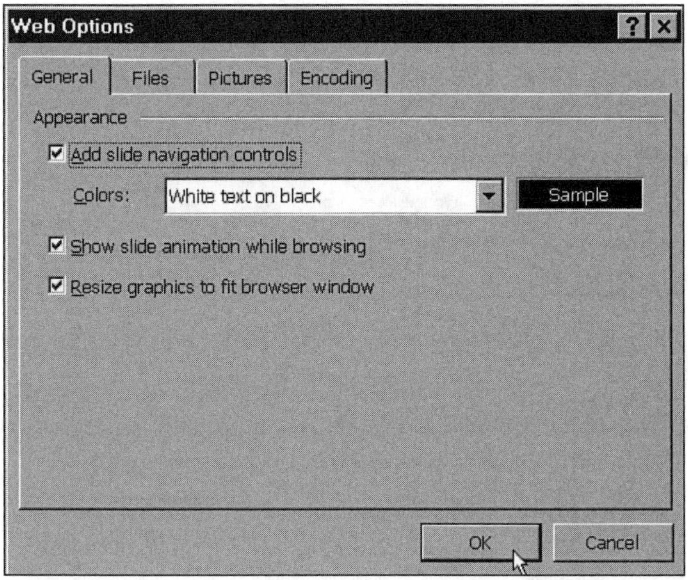

Figure 15.19
General Web options determine how the Web page is to be laid out and whether animations will be active.

Note

The options on the General tab affect only those slide shows prepared for and viewed by Internet Explorer 4.0 or later. However, navigation control color options, even when turned off, do affect the navigational outline in Web pages targeted for Internet Explorer or Netscape Navigator 3.0 or later.

If you click the Files tab in the Web Options dialog box, you see the following options (see Figure 15.20):

- *Organize Supporting Files in a Folder*   Publishing your presentation as a Web page creates several individual files, including the main Web page, pages for the Navigation bar, and other supporting frames, graphics and sound files, as well as a page for each slide. Choosing this option creates a subfolder with the same name as the main Web page file. This makes it easier to locate and move or delete all the files related to your Web page presentation.

- *Use Long File Names Whenever Possible*   If you want to restrict filenames to typical DOS-type filenames (up to eight characters, with a maximum three-character extension), uncheck this option.

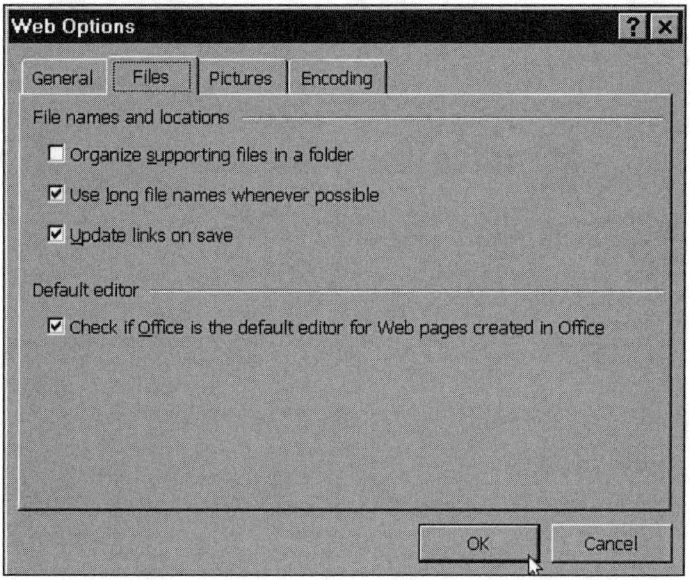

Figure 15.20
File options enable you to specify how files will be named, how they'll be organized, and whether you can edit the resulting HTML files in PowerPoint.

- *Update Links on Save* If you uncheck this box, links from the main page to the supporting pages will remain intact when you save. For example, let's say you want to publish your supporting files to a subfolder where they'll be easy to find and transfer to your Web server, but you want all files to remain in the same folder on the Web server. If you try to view your Web page from your local hard drive, the links will be broken, but when you place them on the server, the links will work again.

- *Check if Office Is the Default Editor for Web Pages Created in Office* This is the option that enables you to save a PowerPoint presentation in HTML and then open it directly from HTML back into PowerPoint without losing any of the special PowerPoint features, such as sounds or animations. Unchecking this option turns off the XML (eXtensible Markup Language) feature, thus allowing only a one-way conversion, from PowerPoint to HTML.

The Pictures tab provides the following options (shown in Figure 15.21):

- *Rely on VML for Displaying Graphics in Browsers* VML (Vector Markup Language) is a method for describing 2D graphics in a text format. VML works only with the latest browsers, such as Internet Explorer 5.0. If your audience might be using other older browsers, do not use this option.

- *Allow PNG as an Output Format* PNG (Portable Network Graphics) is a relatively new Web graphics format that is smaller in size and can have better color and transparency control. Again, however, older browsers (pre-Internet Explorer 4.0) don't support this type of graphic format.

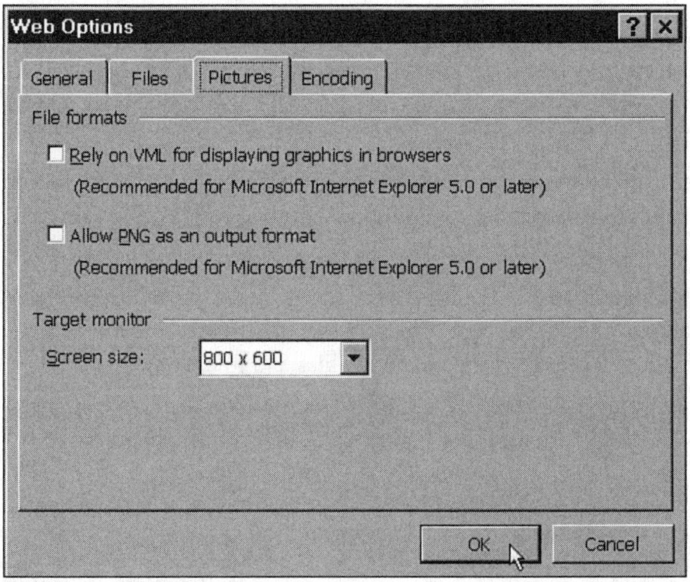

Figure 15.21
Pictures options include advanced graphics display technology options, as well as screen size.

- *Target Monitor Screen Size* If you have chosen the Internet Explorer 4.0 Browser Support *and* the Resize Graphics to Fit Browser Window options, changing this setting has no effect. However, if you publish your presentation for use on older browsers, this option enables you to specify how large the slides should be.

Tip #200 from
Read Gilgen

> Using a screen size that matches the target browser screen settings usually results in a slide that is too small for the available screen. If you want to fill up the browser window with a larger slide, select the next highest resolution (for example, select 1024×768 if the target screen is 800×600).

Finally, the Encoding tab enables you to modify the output for use in browsers that use other languages.

→ For more information on the use of other languages in your presentations, **see** "Using PowerPoint's Foreign Language Capabilities," **p. 733**

TRANSFERRING YOUR WEB PAGE TO A WEB SERVER

Typically, you create your presentation, and save it as a Web page on your local hard disk. Working offline saves time and, in some cases, dial-up connect charges. When you're finally ready to make your presentation available to the rest of the world, you must transfer your files from your own computer to the Web server that will host your Web page.

Tip #201 from

Read Gilgen

If you are connected directly to a company intranet, you may be able to publish your Web page directly to the Web server. Check with your network specialist to find out if this is possible and, if so, how to do it.

Unless you are connected directly to your Web server, you will have to transfer files to your Web server over the Internet, using a file transfer program such as WS_FTP. You need to follow these steps to perform an FTP file transfer:

1. Contact the Web administrator to determine the location and password information you need to connect to the Web server. Typically, the Webmaster will grant you access to a specific area where you can create and delete files and folders.

2. Start your FTP program (for example, WS_FTP) and provide the host computer's name, your user ID, and your password. Figure 15.22 shows a sample connect screen.

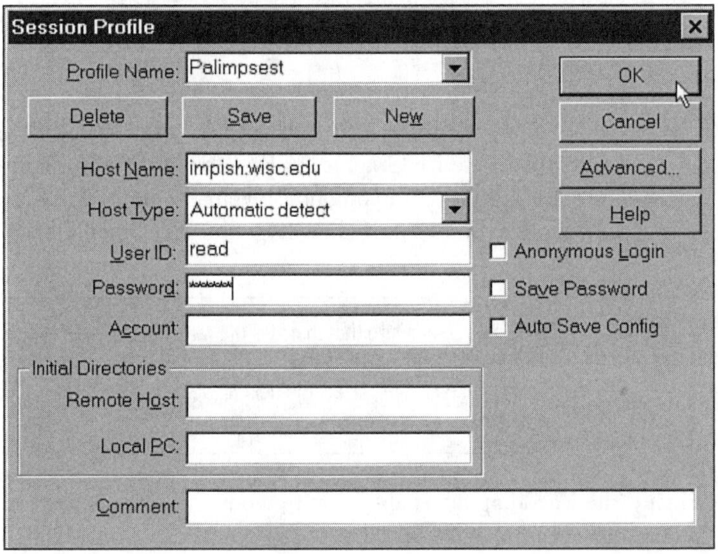

Figure 15.22
If you use an FTP file transfer program, you must know your host computer (Web server), your user ID, and your password.

3. When connected, locate the area on the remote computer where you will store your Web page files.

4. If you published your Web page using a subfolder for supporting files, you must create a corresponding folder on the remote computer.

5. Locate the Web page and its supporting files on your local computer.

6. Transfer the files from your computer to the Web computer, remembering to move files to corresponding subfolders, as necessary. Figure 15.23 shows a sample transfer session.

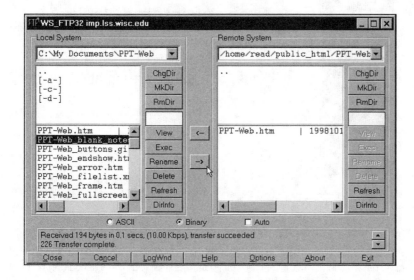

Figure 15.23
A typical FTP session involves moving files from your local computer to corresponding folders on the Web server.

7. Assuming the transfer takes place without errors, close the FTP program. Your Web page is now ready to be viewed by others over the Internet.

Testing Your Web Page

More likely than not, you will test your Web page as you go. At the bottom of the Publish as Web Page dialog box (refer to Figure 15.18), you can check the Open Published Web Page in Browser option so that each time you publish your presentation, your default browser starts and displays the page using files saved on your local computer (see Figure 15.24). If you find something wrong or want to try other options, simply return to PowerPoint and publish the presentation again.

After you transfer your files to your Web server, you should again test your presentation in your browser over the Internet. Some things you should check for are:

- All files should be in their proper place. If you find missing pages or graphics, make sure you have transferred files to folders and locations that correspond *exactly* to the folders on your hard disk.

- Links should be tested individually to make sure they work as you expect them to.

Figure 15.24
A Web page published for Internet Explorer 4.0 or higher includes an outline, the slide, and several navigation buttons.

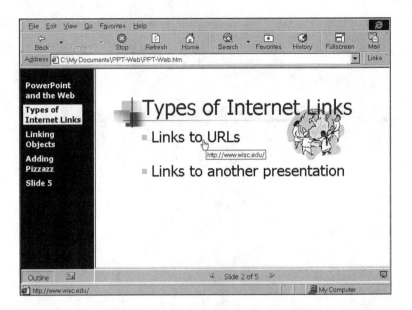

The World Wide Web is a dynamic, constantly changing medium. Links that work today might not work tomorrow. If your Web page contains links, you should periodically check to make sure they're still good.

- If some of your intended audience use dial-up connections, test how long it takes to download your presentation using a modem. You may discover that certain slides simply take too long to download because of large graphics, sound, or even video elements. You have to determine just how important those elements are and consider eliminating them to speed up the presentation.

- Not all browsers are created equal! You should test your Web page using both Internet Explorer and Netscape Navigator, including new and older versions of those programs.

- Not all computers and screen settings are the same, either. Test your pages on standard VGA screens (640×480), on Super VGA (800×600), and on XGA screens (1024×768).

- Test your Web page on Macintosh screens. Screen resolution and colors sometimes are very different on the Macintosh.

If your intended audience uses the same browser and has the same type of computers (for example, in a corporate intranet setting), you may not need to perform such extensive testing. But if you have a wider audience and you want to look good on a wide variety of computer screens (for example, in a university setting), you can't assume everyone uses the same computer and browser that you do.

MODIFYING OR UPDATING YOUR WEB PAGE

If you find during testing that you need to change your Web page, or if at a later date you want to update the information in your presentation, you can still use PowerPoint to edit the presentation.

The easiest way to edit a PowerPoint Web page is to open the main HTML page directly into PowerPoint. Because it uses XML (eXtensible Markup Language) and other advanced HTML processes, the HTML page retains all of PowerPoint's special features, including the use of animations and other multimedia objects.

Tip #202 from	You don't need to keep both a PowerPoint (PPT) and an HTML version of your presentation on your local computer. Keep only the HTML copy, which you can open, edit, and play just as you do any regular PowerPoint presentation.
Read Gilgen	

Tip #203 from	You don't need to ftp your Web page back from the Web server if you retain a copy on your local computer. Simply open and edit the local copy, then ftp the changes to the Web server, replacing the files you sent previously.
Read Gilgen	

After you make the changes you want, simply save the presentation again as a Web page, and, if necessary, transfer the resulting files to your Web server.

TROUBLESHOOTING

Why are some of the image files from my presentation not appearing in the HTML slide show?

If you place your supporting files (such as images) in a subfolder, you must create the same folder structure on your Web server and transfer your files to their correct locations. If you transfer all your files to the same location, without subfolders, your slide show will not work properly.

I have the right folders in the right place on my Web server, but some of my files are still not appearing in the Web slide show. What else can I do?

You must create files and folder names *exactly* as you created them when you published your Web page locally, including upper- and lowercase characters. Using the wrong case in even one character of a file or folder name can prevent your Web page from working properly.

DESIGN CORNER

BEFORE

Linked text in your slide show can make it easy to jump from one place to another, but because the links themselves look markedly different from the text around them, they can also distract from the overall design of your slide. The following figure illustrates how linked text differs from other text in the slide.

Linked text looks different from other text.

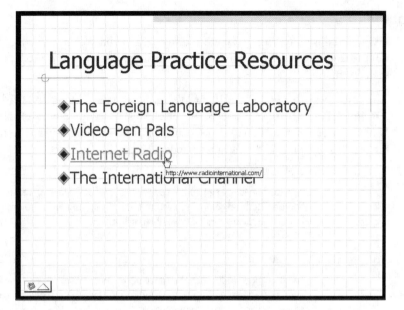

With a little sleight of hand, you can create an invisible link that accomplishes the same purpose as linked text. Simply create an AutoShape, such as a rectangle, that covers the text you want to link, link the AutoShape, and then make the AutoShape invisible.

To create an invisible hyperlinked object, follow these steps:

1. Use the Drawing toolbar to draw a rectangular box that covers the text you want to link.

2. With the AutoShape selected, click the Insert Hyperlink icon (or choose Insert, Hyperlink, or press Ctrl+K).

3. Type the Internet URL in the Type the File or Web Page Name box.

4. Click OK. This creates the link to the AutoShape image.

5. Right-click the AutoShape and choose Format AutoShape; or choose Format, AutoShape. PowerPoint displays the Format AutoShape dialog box.

6. Click the Fill Color drop-down menu and choose No Fill.

7. Click the Line Color drop-down menu and choose No Line.

8. Click OK.

AFTER

An invisible, linked object now appears over the text you want linked, while the text itself has not changed in appearance from the text around it. When you play your slide show, you simply move the mouse pointer to that text area and click when the mouse pointer changes to a hand (see the next figure). To the audience, it appears you are clicking on text, although you are really clicking a linked, invisible graphic shape.

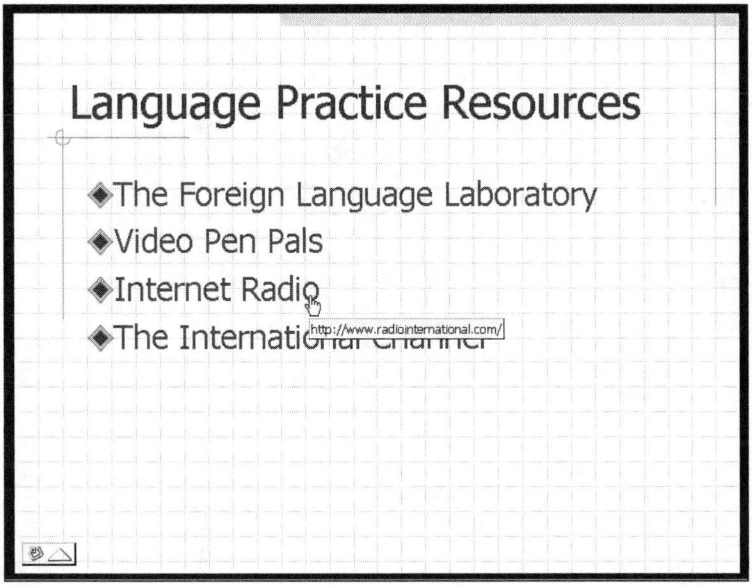

Language Practice Resources

◆The Foreign Language Laboratory
◆Video Pen Pals
◆Internet Radio
◆The International Channel

http://www.radiointernational.com/

The mouse pointer becomes a hand when passed over a hyperlink.

An additional benefit to using an invisible link is that no one except you has to know the link is there. If you choose not to use it, no one will ever know. Text linked in the normal manner, on the other hand, begs to be clicked because the text around it is so obviously different.

CHAPTER 16

WORKING WITH WEB SCRIPTS

In this chapter

by Robert C. Fuller

UNDERSTANDING WEB SCRIPTS

With the new Web functionality of PowerPoint 2000, users now have the capability to save presentations as HTML documents and edit them in the Microsoft Development Environment.

Today's two most popular Web browsers, Microsoft Internet Explorer and Netscape Navigator, have embedded inside them the general-purpose core of a lightweight, object-oriented programming language referred to as both JavaScript—in the case of Navigator—and JScript—in Internet Explorer. Possessing this embedded code allows browsers to read segments of the scripting language that have been written directly into HTML documents. This is referred to as *client-side* scripting.

Understanding the client-side/server-side metaphor can be tricky and has slightly different connotations depending upon its application. For the purpose of this discussion, the *server* is the Web server, where Web pages actually reside. The home PC of a user connecting via the Internet is considered the *client*. This raises a question, however: If the Web page with embedded script is sitting on the Web server, why isn't this a *server-side* script? The answer is that the client home PC and its browser are reading the embedded code and executing it, and it is here where the execution takes place. This is the significant point in terms of the client/server relationship.

Scripting can also be applied on the server-side, when code inside an HTML document points to a script file sitting on the Web server. It is then executed, and the result is sent back to the client. This is especially useful in generating HTML content on-the-fly.

Internet Explorer and Netscape Navigator have slightly different interpretations of the scripting standard. One can assume—this being a book on Microsoft PowerPoint 2000—that most of what follows will refer to Microsoft's JScript and its implementation within this product. A discussion of the problems faced by developers in creating Web content that displays properly across all browsers is a book unto itself. The wars that can break out between fans of Navigator and Internet Explorer are best avoided, as well, but this is not to say that scripting for the Web is a losing proposition and better left alone. In fact, just the opposite is true. Dynamic content and increased functionality are the watchwords of Internet/intranet development and, as with anything else, the more dynamic an effect one tries to achieve, the more complex the route one must take to achieve it.

CREATING AND EDITING WEB SCRIPTS

The Microsoft Development Environment is a powerful new tool for HTML and Web Script editing that provides a high level of functionality and ease of use for the experienced developer as well as the novice. Please note that this chapter is not intended to teach you the VBScript or JavaScript languages, and assumes you already possess some prior knowledge of both scripting and HTML.

The Microsoft Script Editor gives you the capability to view and edit the HTML files you generate when saving your presentation as a Web page. From here you can add scripts, whether they are VBScript or JavaScript.

Thanks to the comprehensive Document Object Model (DOM) supported by Microsoft products, with Script Editor you can create *event handlers* for virtually any element in a PowerPoint presentation. Event handlers are scripts that run in response to actions taken by the user, such as mouse-clicks or the browser's loading of the document.

Editing features are not limited to event handlers. The Microsoft Development Environment can also be used to create independent blocks of script to contain any script you choose. Refer to the Troubleshooting section at the end of this chapter for tips to avoid common scripting errors.

> **Caution**
>
> Use the Script editor to edit only .htm or .asp files. If you edit other files (such as .doc files) in the Script Editor, ID parameters, <SPAN> and <DIV> tags, and some VALUE parameters may be changed when you save or refresh the file.

From PowerPoint you enter the MS Development Environment by following these steps:

1. Save your presentation as a Web page (.htm format) by choosing <u>F</u>ile, Save as Web Page.

2. Name your file and select a folder in which to save it.

3. Click Save.

4. With your presentation onscreen, choose <u>T</u>ools, <u>M</u>acros, Microsoft Script <u>E</u>ditor. This opens the Microsoft Development Environment, as shown in Figure 16.1.

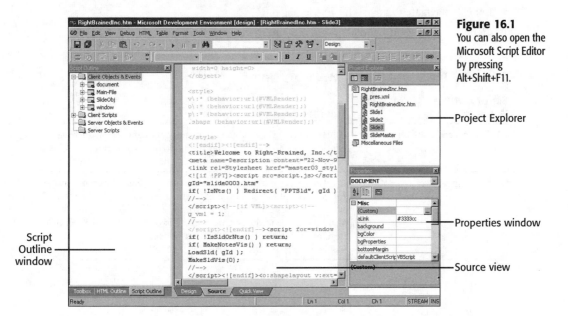

Figure 16.1
You can also open the Microsoft Script Editor by pressing Alt+Shift+F11.

Script Outline window

Project Explorer

Properties window

Source view

The Web page you are viewing in the Script Editor is actually a separate copy of your document. If you make changes to this copy of the Web page while in the Script Editor, the changes are out of sync with the copy of your Web page in PowerPoint. Any changes made to the presentation in PowerPoint while the Script Editor is open are out of sync, as well. To update the unchanged copy of your Web page with the changes you made, be sure to click Refresh on the Refresh toolbar when you return to the unchanged copy.

SCRIPTING IN THE MICROSOFT DEVELOPMENT ENVIRONMENT

The Microsoft Development Environment consists of four primary windows for working with Web scripts: The Script Outline, Source view, Project Explorer, and Properties windows.

The Script Outline window uses a hierarchy tree similar to that seen in Windows Explorer to represent the scripts within a document. The Source view window is the repository of the hard code for the presentation you're working with. Like the Script Outline window, Project Explorer uses the same tree metaphor to display the associated files in a presentation. The Properties window is where certain HTML and scripting attributes are set.

SCRIPT OUTLINE WINDOW

The Script Outline window provides a graphical display of the object model for your presentation (see Figure 16.2). From here, you can

- Display a tree view of all elements in your presentation that have already had their ID or NAME attributes set
- Display the events for each element
- Quickly navigate to any script in the page
- Generate new event handlers for any element in the presentation

TABLE 16.1 THE SCRIPT OUTLINE WINDOW'S NODES

Script Outline Window's Nodes	Function/Use
Client Objects and Events	A hierarchy of the elements that support client scripts or have client scripts attached. Under the node for each element is a list of the events for which you can write handlers.
Client Scripts	A set of nodes for each client script on the page. There is a node for each script block on the page and a separate node for each function or subroutine defined within a script block. There is also a node for inline scripts defined as part of a control definition, as in this example: `<INPUT TYPE="button" NAME="button1" ONCLICK="alert('Clicked!')">`

Script Outline Window's Nodes	Function/Use
Server Objects and Events	A list of nodes for each element that supports server scripts or that has server scripts attached. Under each node is a list of the events for which you can write handlers. The Server Object and Events node also displays the Microsoft Internet Information Server object model, including the Session object, Application object, and so on. In the Script Outline window, these objects do not display events.
Server Scripts	A set of nodes for each server script on the page. Functions and subroutines are identified by name. Inline server scripts appear in a tree, but are not identified by name.

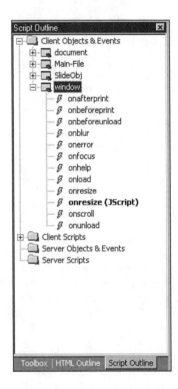

Figure 16.2
The Script Outline window is broken down into folders, or *nodes*, representing the object model of the open file.

> **Note**
>
> The Script Outline does not include elements that are added to a page using an INCLUDE file.

THE SOURCE VIEW WINDOW

The Source view window (see Figure 16.3) enables you to view and edit scripts in the page. Source view is designed for working with the raw code of a Web document, allowing for more precise control over the attributes in a given page. Source view allows you to switch between visual and text representation of all controls on the page using the Design and Source tabs.

Figure 16.3
Edit and view code in the Source view window.

```
</script><![endif]--><script for=window
if( !IsSldOrNts() ) return;
if( MakeNotesVis() ) return;
LoadSld( gId );
MakeSldVis(0);
//-->
</script><![endif]><o:shapelayout v:ext=
  <o:idmap v:ext="edit" data="5"/>
</o:shapelayout>
</head>

<body lang=EN-US style='margin:0px;backg
alink="#3333cc" vlink="#b2b2b2" onclick=
onkeypress="_KPH()">

<div id=SlideObj style='position:absolut
height:400px;background-color:white;clip
hidden'><p:slide coordsize="720, 540" ma
  <p:shaperange href="master03.xml#_x0000
  <![if !PPT]><p:shaperange href="master0
  <p:shaperange href="master03.xml#_x0000
  <p:shaperange href="master03.xml#_x0000
  <p:shaperange href="master03.xml#_x0000
  <![endif]><v:shape id="_x0000_s5122" ty
    left:54pt;top:48pt;width:612pt;height:
    <v:fill o:detectmouseclick="f"/>
    <v:stroke o:forcedash="f"/>
    <o:lock v:ext="edit" text="f"/>
```

Note

Design view is not available for pages created in Microsoft PowerPoint or any other Office application. You can use Source view to modify the script, but design changes must be made in the Microsoft Office program. Design view is available only for pages that are opened from within the Microsoft Script Editor.

To take advantage of Design view's capabilities and having already invoked the Microsoft Development Environment through PowerPoint, close the Source view window and select File, Open File. From here you can navigate to the folder containing the associated files for your presentation in the Open File dialog box.

By enabling Design view in this manner, you are able to extend the WYSIWYG attributes of the editing environment. From here you can more easily attach scripts to individual elements within a page, by right-clicking an object within the page as it is displayed in Design view. Choose Edit Script from the shortcut menu. This switches you to Source view and inserts the cursor at the appropriate position within the code. In addition, a new node is generated in the Script Outline window, as seen in Figure 16.4, enabling all potential event handlers for the object.

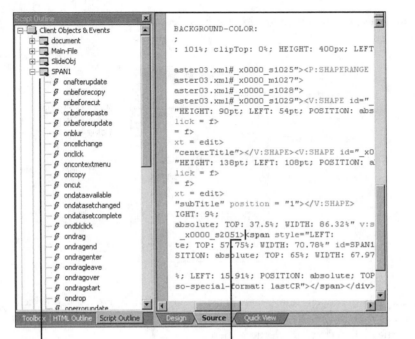

Figure 16.4
To associate a new script with an object in Design view, right-click the desired object.

New node

Cursor active in the code

If you are using design-time controls in your page, Source view allows you to see both the generated scripts from those design-time controls as well as the object information that the design-time control uses to coordinate with other controls.

Caution

In general, you should not directly edit generated script or object information created by a tool (such as a design-time control) because doing so can cause the page to stop functioning properly.

THE PROJECT EXPLORER WINDOW

The Project Explorer displays the associated file in the folder created when you save your PowerPoint presentation. From here, double-clicking on a file's icon opens its source code in the Source view window. You can add the individual .htm files of the presentation you generated by saving the file as a Web page and simply repeating the steps outlined above to enable Design view for your presentation.

THE PROPERTIES WINDOW

The Properties window displays the various HTML and scripting properties within the Web page. From here you can change default settings like Client and Server script types.

This window provides three tool buttons with which to view and edit page attributes, as shown in Figure 16.5.

Figure 16.5
Use the sort buttons to view your attributes.

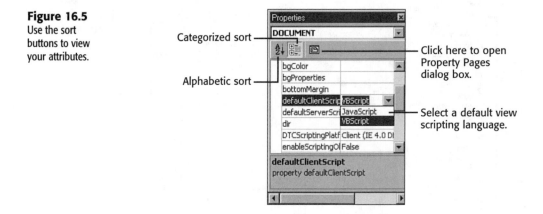

Categorized sort

Alphabetic sort

Click here to open Property Pages dialog box.

Select a default view scripting language.

The Property Pages button opens the Properties dialog box shown in Figure 16.6, which allows you to input your choices. You can also click in the far right column that displays the individual properties and make your selections there.

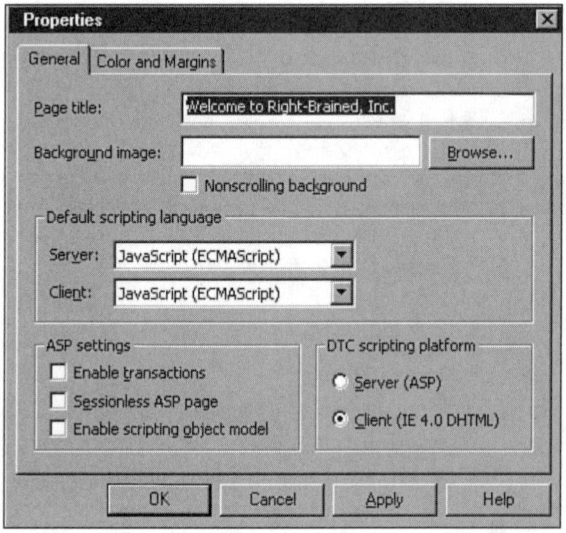

Figure 16.6
The Properties dialog view box allows you to select HTML and scripting attributes.

NAVIGATING TO SCRIPTS

You can use the Script Outline window to move between scripts by clicking the appropriate node to expand the Script Outline tree until you see the script you wish to go to, and then click the script's name. The insertion point in the Source window moves to the script's location in the file.

If you are working on a script in the Source window, you can match up your location in the Script Outline window to see where you are in the context of the overall page.

To synchronize your position with the Script Outline window, right-click anywhere in the Script Outline window (as shown in Figure 16.7), and then select Sync Script Outline.

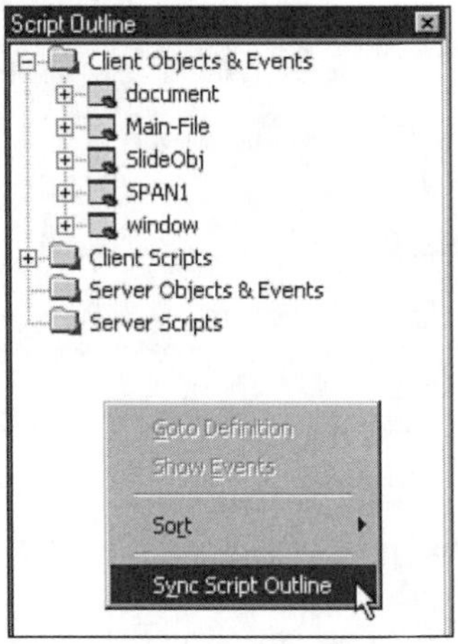

Figure 16.7
You can right-click and select Sync Script Outline or select View, Sync Script Outline to synchronize your position.

ADDING WEB SCRIPT COMMANDS TO YOUR TOOLS MENU

To facilitate scripting in PowerPoint, Microsoft has provided you with three specialized commands you can add to your Tools menu:

- Insert Script
- Remove All Scripts
- Show All Scripts

To insert these items follow these steps:

1. In PowerPoint, choose Tools, Customize. This opens the Customize dialog box, as shown in Figure 16.8.

2. In the Categories box, click Tools.

3. Scroll down in the Commands box until the scripting commands become visible.

4. Drag Insert Script from the Commands box over the Tools menu. From here, drag down to the Macro submenu. When the Macro submenu opens, drag to where you want the Insert Script command to appear, then release the mouse button.

5. Repeat steps 3 and 4 for the Show All Scripts and Remove All Scripts commands.

6. Click Close.

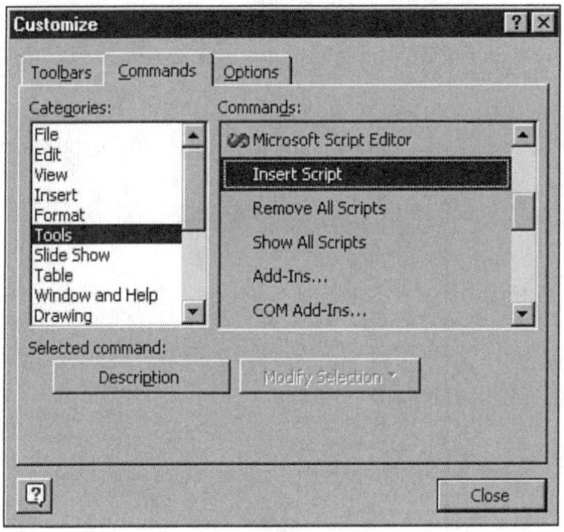

Figure 16.8
From the Customize dialog box, you can drag new tools to your menus.

The Insert Script command invokes the Microsoft Development Environment, placing the cursor at the insertion point you've selected. The Show All Scripts command provides a toggle that displays what Microsoft refers to as a *glyph* to mark the location of a script while still in PowerPoint. As the name suggests, Remove All Scripts removes the scripts from a presentation.

If at any time you wish to remove a command from the Tools menu, simply select Customize and reverse the process by dragging the undesired command off the Macro sub-menu.

CREATING EVENT HANDLERS

The Script Outline window shows you all scriptable elements in your page, and for each element, the events for which you can write handlers. The Script Outline window divides the elements and scripts into those that will run on the client and those that will run on the server.

When you expand an object node in the Script Outline window (as shown in Figure 16.9), a list of potential event handlers for that object is displayed. If the event name is bold, a handler already exists for that event.

To create a new event handler, follow these steps:

1. Expand the appropriate object node until you see the event name for which you want to create a script.

2. Double-click the name of the event. When you double-click the event name, the editor performs the following actions:

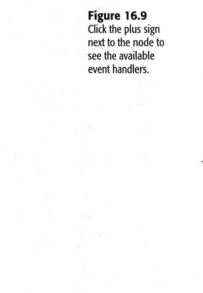

Figure 16.9
Click the plus sign next to the node to see the available event handlers.

- Creates or moves to one of the following script blocks at the top of the document, depending on where the script will run and what language it will be in:
    - clientEventHandlersJS
    - clientEventHandlersVBS
    - serverEventHandlersJS
    - serverEventHandlersVBS
- If the script will be in JavaScript, adds an event attribute (for example, onclick=) to the element.

3. Next, the editor inserts a new script block for the event you selected with a bare handler function that you then must flesh out to suit your needs.

The handler is created in the default language for the current context. For example, if you are creating a server script, the handler is in the default language for the server, as set in the Property Pages dialog box for the current document.

For VBScript functions, the format is

```
Sub elementID_event
{insert code here}
End Sub
```

For JavaScript functions, the format is

```
function elementID_event(){
{insert code here}
}
```

When creating JavaScript event handlers, the editor also adds the following attributes to the HTML element itself:

```
event="return elementID_event()"
```

SETTING THE DEFAULT SCRIPT LANGUAGE

In the Properties window, scroll down until the defaultClientScript and defaultServerScript categories are visible in the bottom-left column, as shown in Figure 16.10. To change the default settings, select the category in the left column and then click on the facing cells of the far right column to display a drop arrow. Clicking this arrow displays the options JavaScript and VBScript.

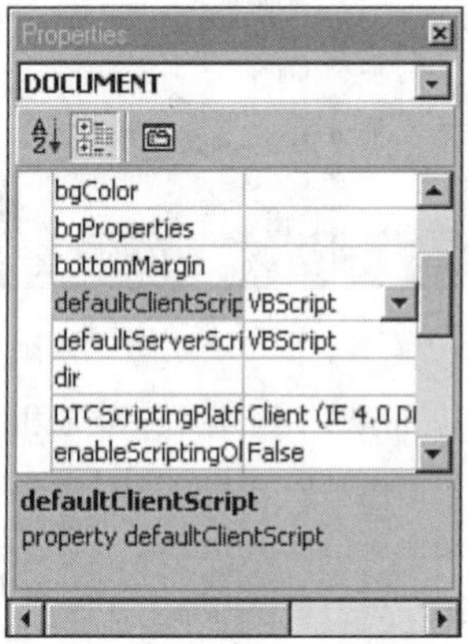

Figure 16.10
VBScript has been chosen instead of the default language, JavaScript.

CREATING STANDALONE SCRIPTS

In addition to creating event handlers, you can create standalone script blocks. This is useful if you want to create procedures (subroutines or functions) called by other scripts, or if you want to create a global script that runs as soon as the browser loads the page.

To create a new standalone script block, follow these steps:

1. Switch to Source view.

2. Position the cursor where you want the new script to appear.

3. From the HTML menu, choose Script Block, Client, or Server.

The Script editor then generates a new <SCRIPT> block. If you choose Server, the script tag contains the attribute RUNAT=SERVER. The script block's LANGUAGE attribute is set to the default language for the client or server.

ARRANGING YOUR SCRIPTS

You can arrange the individual nodes or scripts either by the order in which they are declared in the document or in alphabetical order, by right-clicking anywhere in the Script Outline window. Select So̲rt, and then A̲lphabetically or B̲y Declaration.

When you arrange scripts by declaration, each script block has a node. When you open the node (by clicking the plus sign or double-clicking the object name), it displays the names of individual procedures (functions or subroutines) and public variables. The nodes are arranged according to their order in the page.

If you choose to arrange your script nodes alphabetically, the scripts are displayed as individual nodes by their name. Script blocks that do not contain named procedures are displayed in alphabetical order according to the name of the language in which they are written (for example, VBScript). If a script block contains only one procedure, the procedure name is displayed.

TESTING A WEB SCRIPT

Simple testing of your scripts can be accomplished from within the Microsoft Development Environment by using Quick view, as shown in Figure 16.11. Quick view gives you the capability to view .htm files in a format comparable to the way they will appear in your browser.

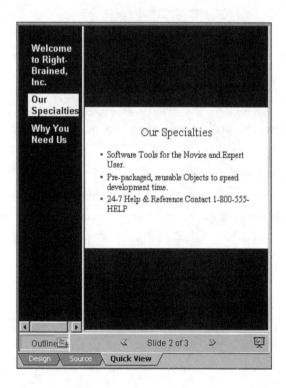

Figure 16.11
To activate Quick view, select its tab below the Source window.

Note

Quick view does not process server scripts, and it may not accurately reflect how .asp files will look in the browser. For example, if a design-time control is created by run-time server script, it will not appear in Quick view.

Quick view allows you to see the changes you've made to your document without saving it and going out to your browser. This allows you to immediately check the status of client scripts as you create them.

Tip #204 from

You cannot edit your page while in Quick view, and the Document Outline view is also unavailable at this time.

Caution

If a file referenced in your document changes while the document is open, the editor does not automatically update your view of the document. To ensure that the most current versions of elements within your document are visible, select Refresh from the View menu.

Quick view is different from Design view in that it is interactive. You can click links or HTML controls and see the results of your actions. In addition, the page is displayed more closely resembling the way it will look in Internet Explorer.

Note

Quick view presents the document formatted for Internet Explorer 5.0, even if you normally use a different browser.

SECURITY IN QUICK VIEW

Because Quick view is not a true browser, it does not possess security elements common to a browser, such as permissions. This makes previewing a page more convenient by not requiring you to respond to messages that are asking your permission to work with objects.

Because Quick view does not participate in browser security, however, you must

- Be absolutely sure that objects on your page are safe for scripting
- Test your page thoroughly by displaying it in the browser exactly as you expect users to view it

TROUBLESHOOTING

Which scripting language is the best to use?

There are places in any programming language where you can get into trouble if you are not careful. Every language has its pitfalls. Microsoft's JScript is no exception. Declaring variables in JScript is a particularly confusing area for anyone with experience in languages like Java, C, or C++. In JScript, variables can be declared more than once, with more than one value, and values of differing types. For example, *var x* could be assigned a string value in its first declaration and be re-declared as an integer later within the same script without causing trouble. This aspect of the language can take some getting used to.

Why won't my simplest scripts work?

Proper syntax is always a concern in programming. Consequently, it is important to pay strict attention to detail when writing scripts. If you mean for a particular parameter to be a string, for example, you will run into trouble if you forget to enclose it in quotation marks when you type it.

Is there a difference in where I put my scripts on the HTML page?

The scripts you write are interpreted as part of your Web browser's HTML parsing process. This means that if the script you create is located inside the <HEAD> tag in a document, it will be interpreted before any of the <BODY> tag is looked at. If you have objects that are created in the <BODY> tag, they don't exist at the instant the <HEAD> is being parsed and, therefore, can't be manipulated by the script.

DESIGN CORNER

Today's Web pages are more than just places to show off someone's favorite new recipes! They can be a way to not only display your company's wares but also an easy way to get to know the most important person to your company: the customer!

In this Design Corner, you can see a standard PowerPoint design template being used to create an interactive Web page.

BEFORE

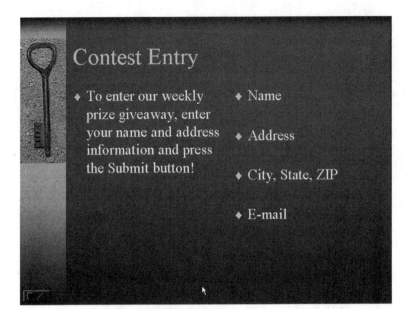

AFTER

Once you master the art of Web scripting, your Web presentations in PowerPoint can become interactive and information gathering, as seen with these new form fields.

CHAPTER 17

USING ONLINE BROADCASTS AND MEETINGS

by Timothy Dyck
timothy-dyck@dyck.org

In this chapter

OK, so you've finished your presentation! It's clear, organized and to-the-point. Your visuals are coordinated, your script is down pat, and maybe you've even added background sound to make the presentation really move.

Now, you've got to deliver on those goods. This chapter is about how to use PowerPoint 2000's presentation broadcast and online meeting tools to do exactly that.

New with this version of the program, PowerPoint can do a live, simultaneous broadcast of your presentation from your PC to tens, hundreds, or even thousands of other PCs tuned in to hear what you have to say. You can also add live audio or video content to the presentation as you make it.

Tip #205 from
Timothy Ryde

Using PowerPoint to do a presentation broadcast is much more convenient than gathering your audience physically into one room and getting the necessary facilities, large-screen computer projectors, and sound equipment organized.

By itself, PowerPoint can transmit a presentation broadcast to as many as 15 other people. For broadcasts to 16 or more people (or for presentations that include video), you need to have access to a specialized server package from Microsoft called NetShow. If you need to make a PowerPoint presentation to a larger group of people, you'll need to contact your IS department to set up a NetShow server for your use.

Tip #206 from
Timothy Ryde

NetShow (or, as it is also called, Windows NT Server Streaming Media Services) is a "streaming media" server. It can take stored video, audio, or other multimedia content (such as your PowerPoint presentation) and "stream" (or send) this information to many client computers at once. NetShow can broadcast this information in real-time (while you're actually doing your presentation), or it can store broadcasts for people to view later.

NetShow is currently available as a free download from Microsoft's Web site (you can get it at http://www.microsoft.com/windows/windowsmedia/). You need a Windows NT Server system on which to run it, however.

Your audience needs to use Microsoft Internet Explorer 4.0 or later to view your presentation. If your audience is using Netscape Navigator or another browser, you should save your presentation as an HTML file, as described in Chapter 15, "Using PowerPoint's Web Features." See the section "Saving a Presentation as a Web Page."

In addition to showing you how to make a PowerPoint presentation broadcast (both with and without NetShow), we'll also cover PowerPoint's other new broadcast feature, online meetings.

Online meetings (p. 402-403) are a nice complement to presentation broadcasts. A broadcast is a one-way connection between you and your audience, whereas an online meeting is a two-way channel. In an online meeting, everyone can communicate with everyone else to brainstorm, hash out a tough decision, or even create a presentation together.

Online meetings also require some software help to work: To use the feature, you'll need to have Microsoft's NetMeeting group collaboration software installed on your computer, and so will everyone else who takes part in the meeting. NetMeeting is included on your Office CD, and if it isn't already on your system, it is installed automatically the first time you try to use it.

Here are some guidelines to help you decide which online presentation approach is right for you:

Choose a presentation broadcast when

- You want to reach a large number of people at once.
- You want to save your presentation broadcast so people can watch it later.
- You want your presentation to be one-way.
- Your audience doesn't have very powerful computers or fast network connections (all they need is Internet Explorer 4.0 or later to see your broadcast).

PART
V
CH
17

Suggested uses for presentation broadcasts are corporate training sessions, general company announcements, and online presentations to business partners or clients.

Choose an online meeting when

- You want to interact with the people to whom you are presenting.
- You don't need to reach many people (say 10 or fewer).
- Your audience has powerful enough computers with fast enough network connections to handle Microsoft NetMeeting (and the computers have the NetMeeting software installed). As a rough guide, everyone needs at least Pentium-class computers with 32MB of RAM and a 56Kbps modem network connection. 486-based PCs are agonizingly slow running NetMeeting.

Suggested uses for online meetings are group brainstorming sessions (especially those now done with videoconferencing equipment), online staff meetings, and one-on-one planning meetings with a colleague.

First, I'll cover how to run a presentation broadcast. Later in this chapter (the "Using Online Collaboration" section), you'll learn how to run an online meeting.

CREATING AND RUNNING AN ONLINE BROADCAST

The first step in starting a presentation broadcast is to schedule the broadcast. This step prepares PowerPoint to broadcast your presentation, and it sets up a special Web page (called a *lobby page*) that your audience will use as an online gathering place before the presentation starts.

As part of setting up a schedule, you can also send electronic mail to people whom you'd like to view the presentation, inviting them to the show and telling them how to view it. We'll give detailed directions on how to do all these things later in the chapter.

CREATING A BROADCAST

The first step is to tell PowerPoint you want to organize a presentation broadcast. Load up the presentation you want to broadcast, and choose Slide Show, Online Broadcast, Set Up and Schedule.

Tip #207 from
Timothy Byok

You can still change your presentation after you've scheduled a broadcast; nothing's chiseled in stone. You can even switch to presenting a whole different file if you want to, without re-doing your broadcast schedule setup. See the "Changing Broadcast Settings Later" section for details on how to do this.

If this is the first time you've tried to run a presentation broadcast, you'll get the message displayed in Figure 17.1 telling you that PowerPoint needs to install some extra software to enable this feature. Choose Yes to enable PowerPoint to install the software.

Figure 17.1
The first time you try to set up a presentation broadcast, PowerPoint will need to install its presentation broadcast modules.

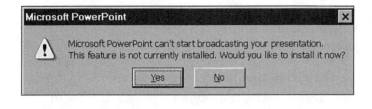

You'll then see a status window (see Figure 17.2) showing you PowerPoint's progress. You can click the Cancel button if you want to stop the install for any reason.

Figure 17.2
Wait while PowerPoint fetches the code it needs from the Office CD or your network server.

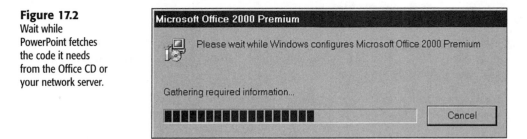

What you'll see next is PowerPoint's main Broadcast Schedule window (see Figure 17.3). Here you can choose to schedule a new broadcast, or you can change the file an already scheduled broadcast is going to use. Because you haven't scheduled this presentation for broadcast before, choose the Set Up and Schedule a New Broadcast option and then click OK to get to the Schedule a New Broadcast window.

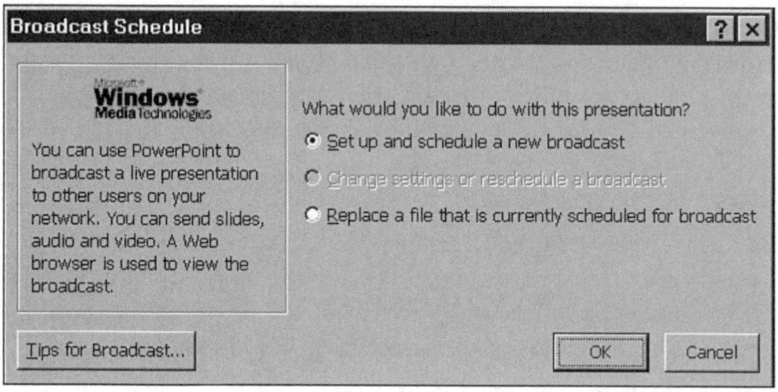

Figure 17.3
Here you can schedule a new presentation broadcast or change the file an already scheduled broadcast will be using.

Tip #208 from
Timothy Dyck

You can schedule your broadcast on a machine different from the one you actually use to make the broadcast. As long as you have your PowerPoint file with you (which contains your broadcast settings inside it), you can use any computer you want to do the broadcast.

Remember, the broadcast computer needs sound and video capabilities if you want to include those features, and it must have PowerPoint 2000 installed and a fast network connection.

The Schedule a New Broadcast window (see Figure 17.4) sets up the basic information your audience will see in the presentation lobby page, and it enables you to configure more advanced broadcast options.

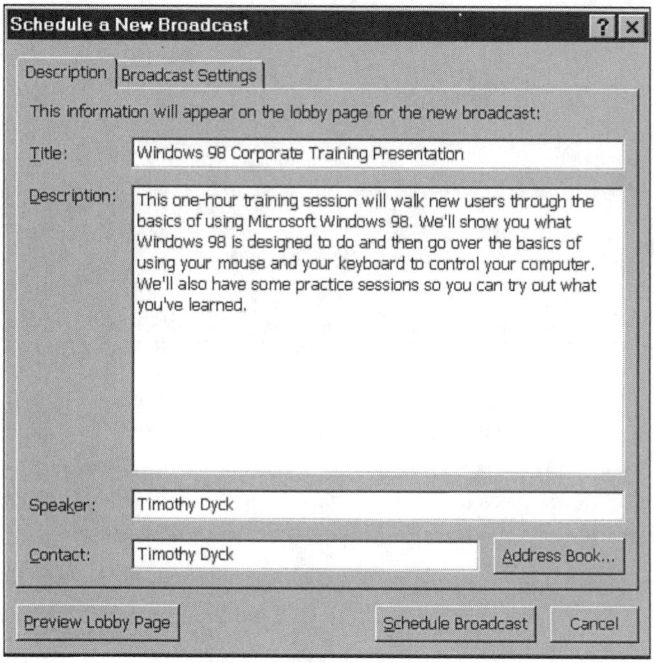

Figure 17.4
Type in a title and description for your upcoming presentation broadcast.

Type in a title and description for your broadcast, as well as your name and, if you want, the email address of the person organizing the broadcast. You should provide enough information here that potential audience members will know what the presentation will be about and for whom it was designed. Putting in the length of the presentation is also a good idea.

CONFIGURING BROADCAST SETTINGS

After you've filled in the information in the Description tab of the Schedule a New Broadcast window, you'll need to set up a few more technical broadcast settings. It's important to do this before you proceed to previewing your lobby page or setting the actual schedule for your broadcast because those features need these settings filled in first.

Click the Broadcast Settings tab of the Schedule a New Broadcast window to see more broadcast options (see Figure 17.5).

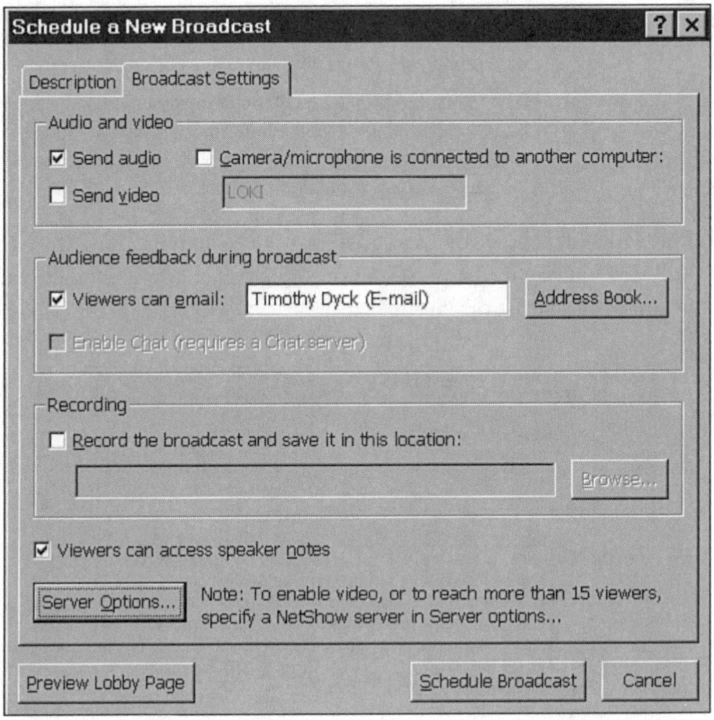

Figure 17.5
The Broadcast Settings tab enables you to set various presentation options, as well as to specify where the presentation should be stored for broadcast.

A lot of options are available on this tab. The first group of options (Audio and Video) enables you to specify if you want to have live audio or video information (or both) broadcast with your presentation. Regardless of what you choose here, audio in the presentation itself (such as a saved narration or slide transition sounds) doesn't get broadcast.

If you want to broadcast audio, you'll need to have a sound card and a microphone set up at your broadcast station. If you want to have video (usually a picture of you talking along with the presentation, although you could also use a VCR as a video source), you'll need to have a video camera and video capture card installed at the broadcast station. Remember that the people tuning into your broadcast need to have audio-capable computer hardware to hear any sound.

Tip #209 from *Timothy Dyck*	If you can't get a broadcast station with this hardware installed (or if your broadcast station is already too busy sending your presentation to your audience members over the network), you can also use another computer as an audio or video input source (click on the <u>C</u>amera/Microphone Is Connected to Another Computer option in the Schedule a New Broadcast window and type the name of the multimedia computer into the box).

You can also add an email address to your presentation so that broadcast attendees will be able to use it later to send in questions during the presentation. You (as the presenter) can put in your email address—or anyone else's.

PART
V
CH
17

Tip #210 from *Timothy Dyck*	If you want to answer questions interactively during the presentation, you might want to put someone else's email address into this box, or let someone check your email for you during the presentation. You'll have your hands full enough giving the presentation!

You can also choose whether to let audience members see your speaker presentation notes by checking off the Viewers Can Access Speaker <u>N</u>otes box.

SETTING BROADCAST SERVER OPTIONS

Finally, you need to specify where you are going to save your presentation for broadcast. Click the Server <u>O</u>ptions button to get to the Server Options window (see Figure 17.6).

When the window opens, type a shared network location into the Step 1: Specify a Shared Location box. PowerPoint will store your presentation files in this location when it needs to start the broadcast. This must be a network shared directory that is accessible to all the members of your audience over the network. Network locations are typed in using the format *servername**sharename* (see Figure 17.6 for an example).

Caution	You need to make sure that whatever you type into the location box is accessible to every member of your audience over the network; otherwise, they won't be able to see the presentation. You must use the *servername**sharename* format to enter this information.

In the lower half of the Server Options window, you have a decision to make. As mentioned earlier, PowerPoint can broadcast presentations in two ways: It can run a broadcast presentation by itself, or it can use NetShow, Microsoft's specialized broadcast server. This window is where you make that choice.

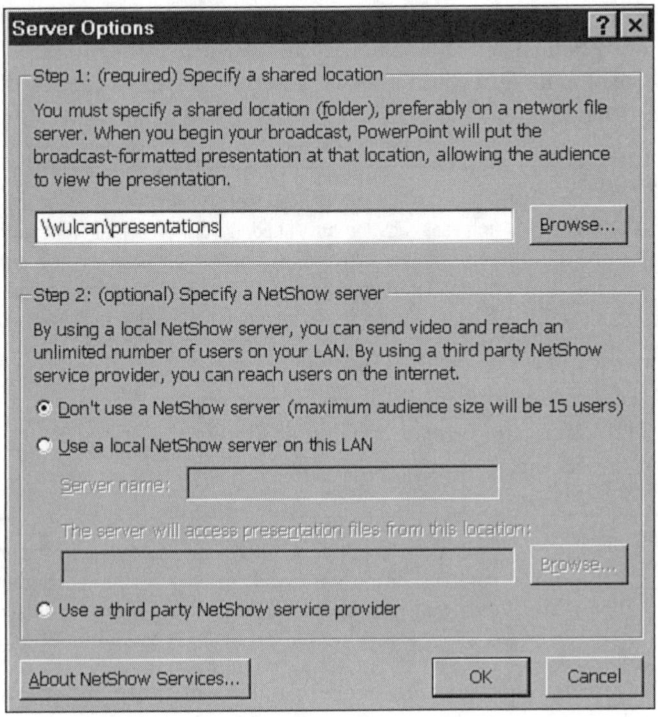

Figure 17.6
Type in a shared
network location that
you and your audi-
ence can both access
over the network.

If you are broadcasting to 15 or fewer people (and if you aren't sending video along with your presentation), you don't need to use NetShow; you can just click OK to finish here (leaving the default Don't Use a NetShow Server option selected). You'll go back to the Schedule a New Broadcast window.

> **Note**
>
> It really doesn't work to have more than 15 viewers if you don't use NetShow—we tried! Viewers after the 15th one don't get their slides updated as you go through your presentation.

On the other hand, if you want to use NetShow to show your presentation, you need to fill in the Step 2: Specify a NetShow Server option.

To do this, click the Use a Local NetShow Server on This LAN option, fill in the name of your NetShow server, and provide the NetShow server with the location of your presentation. For simplicity, this should be the same network location you specified in the top part of the Server Options window. See Figure 17.7 for an example of how to fill in NetShow settings.

After you've got the Step 2 options selected, click the OK button to go back to the Schedule a New Broadcast window.

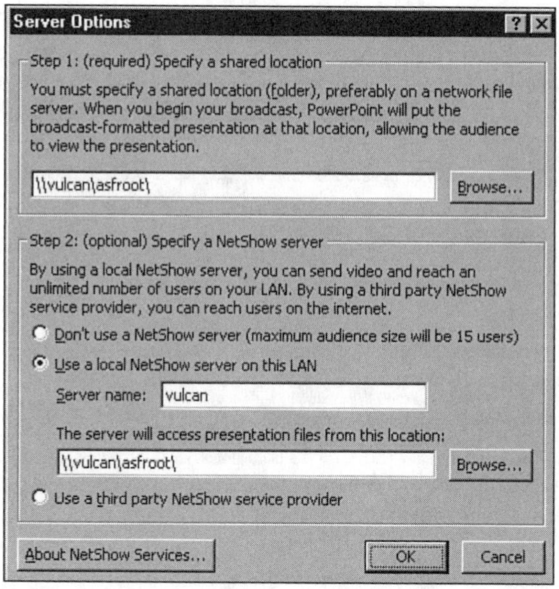

Figure 17.7
If you use a NetShow server to broadcast your presentation, fill in the server's name and the network location where it can access your broadcast presentation files.

PREVIEWING THE LOBBY PAGE

When your audience is ready to view the presentation, they'll use their Web browser to go to a specific Web page, called a *lobby page*, which is specific to your presentation broadcast. There they'll find out how long it is before the presentation actually starts, as well as the presentation title and description you typed in.

If you want to sneak a peek at what the lobby page will look like to your audience, choose Preview Lobby Page while you're back at the Schedule a New Broadcast window. You'll see something similar to Figure 17.8.

> **Note**
>
> The presentation date and time information isn't filled in because you haven't set that information yet. After that's done, your presentation broadcast lobby page will display a running time countdown showing how long until the presentation starts.

> **Tip #211 from**
> *Timothy Pyk*
>
> You can also look at the finished lobby page later (using the Preview Lobby Page button on the Broadcast Presentation window) when you're ready to actually start the broadcast.

SETTING THE BROADCAST TIME

After you've finished entering your broadcast description, broadcast settings, and server options, you're ready to actually schedule the broadcast.

Choose the Schedule Broadcast button to continue.

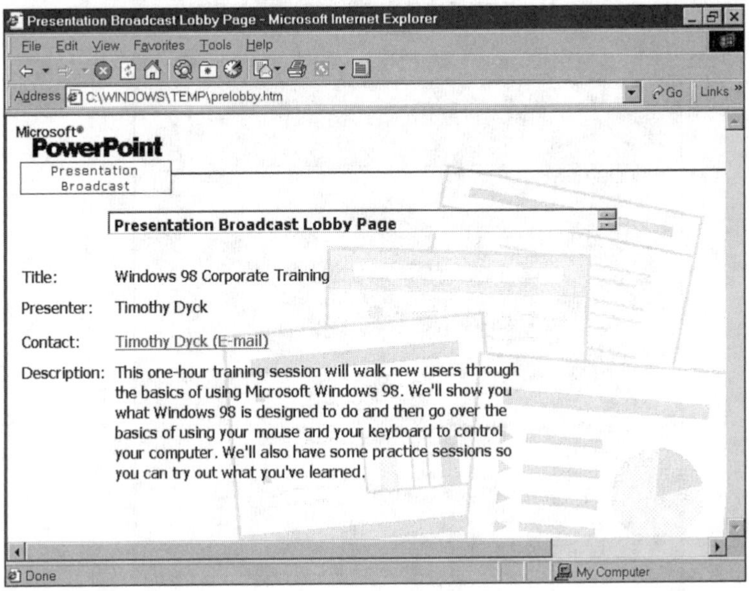

Figure 17.8
The Preview Lobby Page button enables you to get a preview of what your audience members will see when they log on to your presentation lobby Web page.

If you aren't using Microsoft NetShow to broadcast your presentation, you'll be asked to confirm your choice (see Figure 17.9).

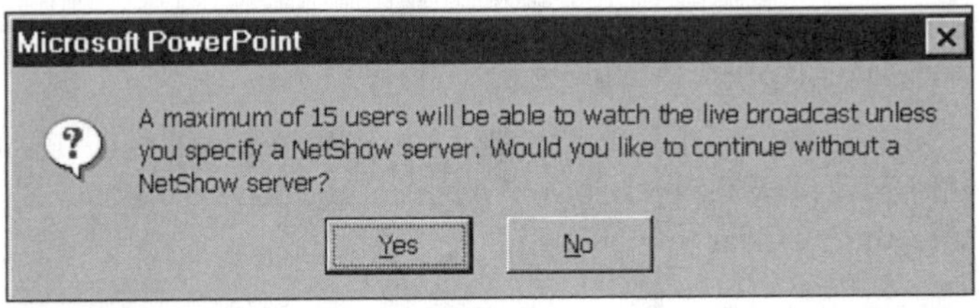

Figure 17.9
Choose Yes to confirm that you won't be using a NetShow server with this presentation.

PowerPoint will then start up your email client to send an announcement to the people you'd like to invite to your presentation. If you are using Microsoft Outlook as your mail client, you'll be able to schedule the presentation using Outlook's group meeting facilities (see Figure 17.10).

Now you're finished scheduling your presentation! PowerPoint displays a confirmation message to let you know your presentation broadcast settings have been saved (see Figure 17.11). Press OK to close the message.

CHANGING BROADCAST SETTINGS LATER

If you decide you want to change the broadcast time or other settings (such as the PowerPoint file you want to broadcast) before the show actually starts, you can modify your settings easily.

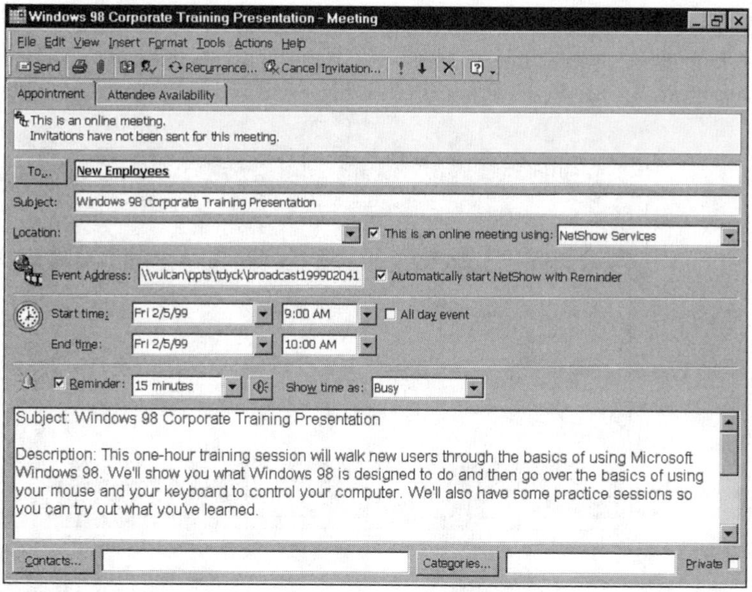

Figure 17.10
PowerPoint can use Microsoft Outlook's meeting scheduling features to book your presentation into your colleague's calendars.

Figure 17.11
Your presentation is now scheduled!

To get to the Broadcast Schedule window, choose Slide Show, Online Broadcast, and Set Up and Schedule, as you did before. You'll notice, however, that the Change Settings or Reschedule a Broadcast option is now enabled (see Figure 17.12).

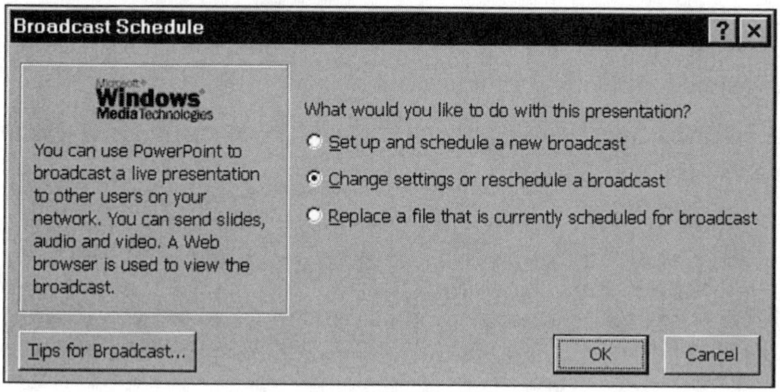

Figure 17.12
Even though you've already scheduled your broadcast, you still can change your mind later.

If you want to change the time the broadcast is scheduled, choose the new Change Settings or Reschedule a Broadcast option, then choose OK. You'll be presented with a list of upcoming presentations for the PowerPoint file you have open (see Figure 17.13).

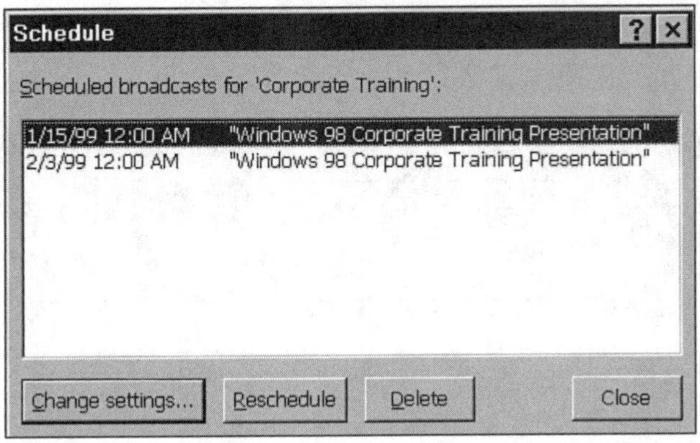

Figure 17.13
You can modify the presentation broadcasts' descriptions or start times from this window.

Choose the presentation you want to modify by clicking its name, and then choose Change settings, Reschedule, or Delete, depending on what you want to do. The Change Settings option enables you to change the presentation broadcast's title or description and broadcast settings; the Reschedule option takes you back into Outlook to send a new meeting notice; and the Delete option cancels that particular presentation.

From the Broadcast Schedule window, you can also change which presentation you'll be broadcasting. Suppose a co-worker mails a modified presentation to you that you want to substitute for your original presentation.

Open up the new presentation (not your original presentation!), and then open up the Broadcast Schedule window by choosing Slide Show, Online Broadcast, Set Up and Schedule, as before. Now choose the Replace a File That Is Currently Scheduled for Broadcast option.

You'll see the Schedule window (see Figure 17.14) open up. Choose the presentation broadcast that you want to modify, and then choose Replace. The presentation broadcast will be changed to use your new, currently open presentation.

You'll now get a reminder from PowerPoint (see Figure 17.15) to save your presentation and lock in your changes.

Tip #212 from
Timothy Pyle

You can schedule multiple presentation broadcasts for the same presentation file if you have to present the same material several times. You'll notice that PowerPoint remembers your presentation broadcast settings so you don't have to re-enter them each time.

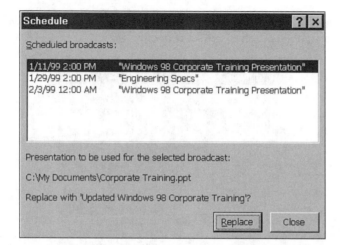

Figure 17.14
Pick the presentation broadcast you want to change and then choose Replace to use a new presentation with a presentation broadcast you've already set up.

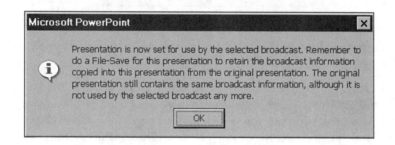

Figure 17.15
After you've inserted a new presentation into a scheduled presentation broadcast, save the new presentation to include the schedule information in the file.

STARTING THE BROADCAST

To get ready to start the actual broadcast, open the PowerPoint file you're going to broadcast and then choose Slide Show, Online Broadcast, and Begin Broadcast. You should do this about 30 minutes before you actually want to get started, to allow time for your presentation to be uploaded to the server and so you'll be able to send messages out to waiting viewers before the presentation starts.

Tip #213 from
Timothy Pyle

> You can tweak your presentation until the moment you give the Begin Broadcast command. After that, your presentation files are copied to the server for broadcast. If you still want to change the presentation, you can close the Broadcast Presentation window by choosing Cancel, making your changes, and then choosing Slide Show, Online Broadcast, Begin Broadcast again.

When you give the Begin Broadcast command, you'll see PowerPoint's Broadcast Presentation window open. PowerPoint verifies that the network locations you typed in earlier are valid; then it checks that your audio and video inputs are working correctly (if you enabled those options when you set up the presentation broadcast). Because real-time audio was turned on in our example, PowerPoint displays a Microphone Check window (see Figure 17.16) to verify that our audio levels are set correctly.

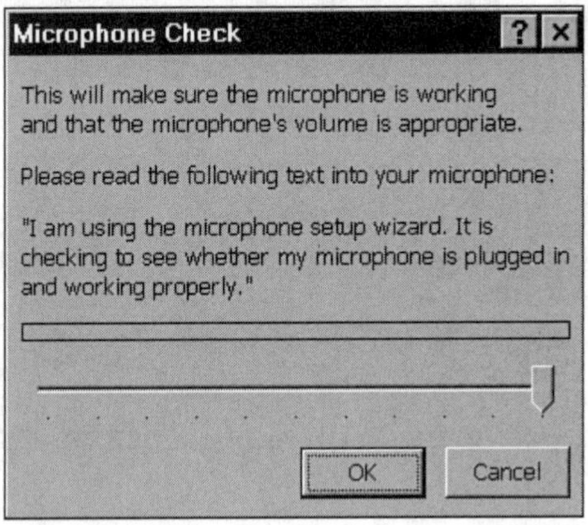

Figure 17.16
Read this window's text into your microphone to check your audio levels.

After you've read the text out loud (and you've seen the horizontal volume bar move), choose OK to continue.

You're now ready to start your presentation! When the Broadcast Presentation window is flashing "Press Start When Ready...", everything is set to go (see Figure 17.17). As you can see, the window displays a countdown to your scheduled start time. You can also click the Audience Message button to send a message to all waiting audience members (handy if you want to announce a brief delay) and preview the presentation lobby page by choosing Preview Lobby Page.

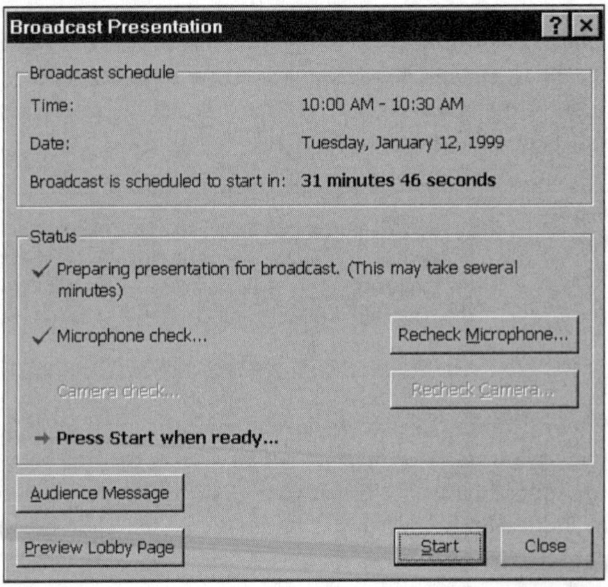

Figure 17.17
Your presentation has been prepared for broadcast and is now ready to go.

Now, you just have to wait (and review your notes, sip from a glass of water, and practice your delivery)! The presentation will ask you if you want to start the broadcast when the countdown timer runs out, or you can just start anytime you want to by choosing Start. Choose Yes when asked if you want to start, and the presentation slideshow will start.

CONDUCTING THE BROADCAST

A broadcast presentation won't look any different to you (the presenter) than if you'd just run a slideshow on your computer. Just move through your presentation as you normally would, but remember to not go too quickly. It takes 10-15 seconds for your clients to download each new page.

Tip #214 from	
Timothy Dyck	You might want to set up a nearby computer and log in as a participant so you can see what your audience is actually seeing. Based on my tests, the time it takes for each slide (and real-time narration, if you're using that option) to reach client systems varies from slow to really slow. Take your time and double-check to make sure you're not getting ahead of your audience.

Your audience will see the current slide of the presentation in the left side of their browser (see Figure 17.18) and some status information on the right. They can also move through your presentation on their own by clicking the View Previous Slides link in the top-left corner of their slide window) and then scrolling through the whole presentation.

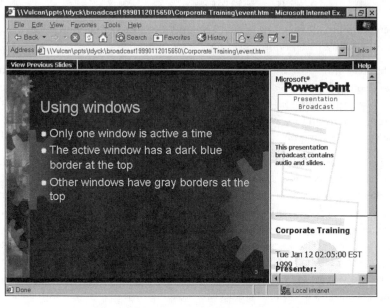

Figure 17.18
Here's what your audience sees in Internet Explorer. They can also view previous slides (if they came in late) by choosing the View Previous Slides option (top-left corner).

Tip #215 from *Timothy Pyle*	Take a look at the presentation lessons in Part VII, "From Concept to Delivery." It's harder to hold your audience's attention when you're not physically in front of them.

What audiences see in a Web broadcast is very close to what they would see if they were actually looking at your screen in person.

PowerPoint's pen and pointer features don't work over presentation broadcasts; if you want to use them, consider switching to an online meeting which does support them. Your audience also won't see any slide build effects (points flying in from the side, and so on). It's best to just go with a simple design and presentation format when using presentation broadcasts.

You can go back and forth through the slides in your presentation using your Page Up and Page Down (or Space and Backspace) keys as you normally would.

ENDING THE BROADCAST

When you've finished your broadcast, just press Esc to end it (if any questions have been emailed in during your presentation, you might want to answer them verbally before you wrap things up). You'll be asked to confirm your decision to end the broadcast. Your audience will be sent back to the presentation lobby page, which will tell them that the presentation has ended.

INTERACTIVE ONLINE MEETINGS

Besides presentation broadcasts, PowerPoint also provides a much more interactive way of sharing your ideas with others: online meetings.

PowerPoint has had interactive meeting features for some time; for example, you can use PowerPoint's Meeting Minder (Tools, Meeting Minder) to jot down minutes and action items while you're presenting to a group of people. Online meetings take the concept of interactive presentations online, where you can bring together a group of people from around the world to present your ideas and then discuss them.

Just as with presentation broadcasts, online meetings enable you to show your presentation to others live, including real-time audio and video commentary (audio and video can be sent to only one other person at a time unless you are using a special group conferencing server). However, online meetings also let your audience in on the action. Instead of passively watching your presentation, participants in a PowerPoint online meeting can jot down ideas on a shared whiteboard; interactively send messages back to you and the group; and even take control of the presentation in midstream, make some changes to the presentation, and then give control back to you so you can continue. Online meetings are much better suited to roundtable discussions and for immediate decision-making than presentation broadcasts are.

In this section, you'll learn how to start an online meeting and how to manage one after you've gotten going.

STARTING AN ONLINE MEETING

The first step in starting an online meeting is to open the presentation you want to present in the meeting. Then choose Tools, Online Collaboration, Meet Now to get started. This starts the program PowerPoint uses for online meetings, a group collaboration tool called Microsoft NetMeeting (it's installed as part of Microsoft Office).

If you've run NetMeeting before, you'll be taken right to NetMeeting's Place A Call window.

If you haven't, you'll be asked to fill in some information about yourself (see Figure 17.19) so the other participants in the meeting will be able to connect up with you. Type in your name and email address (both are required), and choose a NetMeeting directory server in the Server name box. You can choose any one you want from the list, or you can type in your company's private NetMeeting directory server (ask your network administrator for its name). All the people that will be joining this meeting have to log in to the same NetMeeting server, however, so you'll have to let your audience know which server to use ahead of time.

PART

V

CH

17

Tip #216 from
Timothy Dyck

> You don't have to log in to a directory server if you don't want to; it just makes the process of finding the other meeting participants simpler because you can look them up by name. If you don't (or can't) all connect to the same directory server, you can call a person by typing in the Internet Domain Name Server name (for example, `vulcan.olympus.org`) or address (for example, `192.168.0.12`) of their computer. Choose Advanced from the Place a Call window to dial using a hostname or IP address.

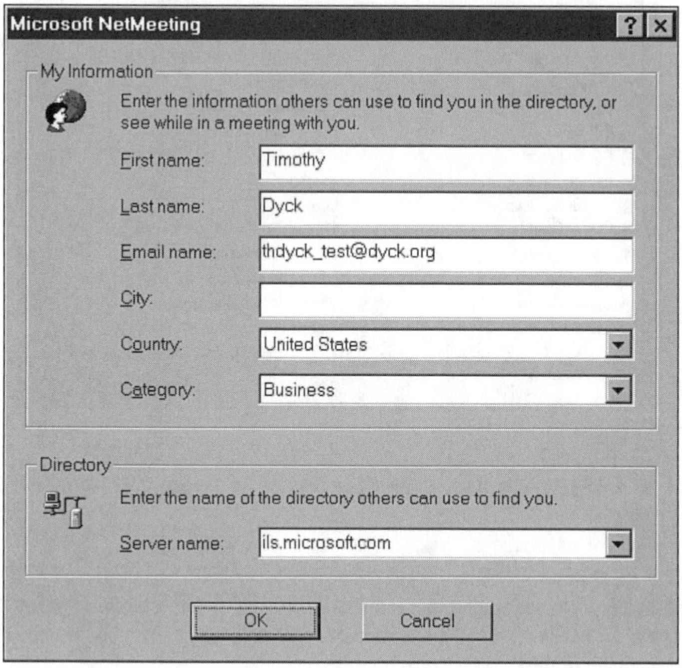

Figure 17.19
When you first start NetMeeting, you're asked to fill out some information about yourself and the server you'll be using to share information with others.

When you finish entering this information (you only have to do it once), choose OK. You might then see the dialog box in Figure 17.20, asking if it's OK to restart your computer to enable NetMeeting application sharing. If you want to use online meetings, you need to do this, so choose Yes. Your computer will restart. After your system has rebooted, restart PowerPoint, load up your presentation, and then choose Tools, Online Collaboration, Meet Now again.

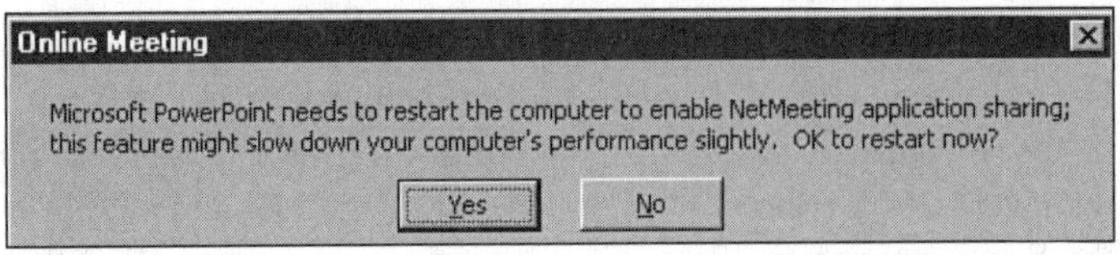

Figure 17.20
NetMeeting needs to install special software on your computer before you can share your presentations with others.

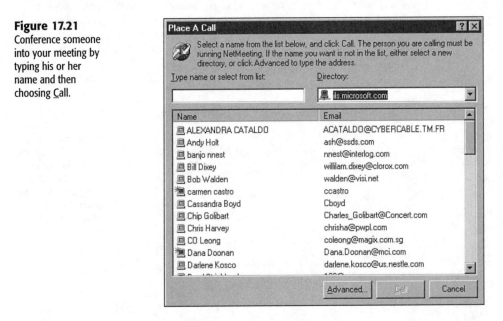

You'll now see NetMeeting's Place a Call window (see Figure 17.21). Setting up an online meeting in NetMeeting is quite different from running a broadcast presentation. Instead of letting your audience come to you, you need to bring in people one-by-one, just as in a telephone conference call.

Figure 17.21
Conference someone into your meeting by typing his or her name and then choosing Call.

The Place a Call window gradually displays a long list of logged-in users as NetMeeting downloads the server user list.

Caution

The most common error at this point is that your selected server is too busy to handle your login request (see Figure 17.22). If this happens, just try to log in again by selecting that server's name from the Directory box.

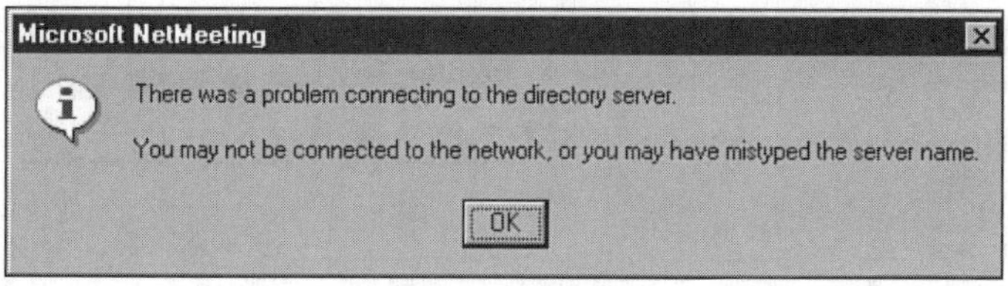

Microsoft NetMeeting

There was a problem connecting to the directory server.

You may not be connected to the network, or you may have mistyped the server name.

OK

Figure 17.22
This kind of error usu-
ally means the server
is actually too busy to
respond to your login
request. Just try again
(or switch to a differ-
ent server).

Type in the name of the person you want to conference in to your online meeting to
quickly jump to his or her name in the list. When you've found the person you want to call,
click that name and then choose <u>C</u>all to give him or her a ring.

NetMeeting tries to make the connection and, if the other person accepts the call, you'll see
the Make a Call window disappear and the Online Meeting toolbar appear (see Figure 17.23).

Figure 17.23
The Online Meeting
toolbar shows you
who's in your online
meeting and also
enables you to open
up a chat window,
open a shared white-
board, or let someone
else edit your
PowerPoint
presentation.

JOINING AN ONLINE MEETING

If you want to have more than two people in the meeting, just call more people by clicking
the Call Participant button (the one with the plus sign) on the Online Meeting toolbar, and
repeat the process. Your guests can also call in on their own using NetMeeting. If they do,
they'll be told that you're in a meeting, but they can join if they want to (see Figure 17.24).

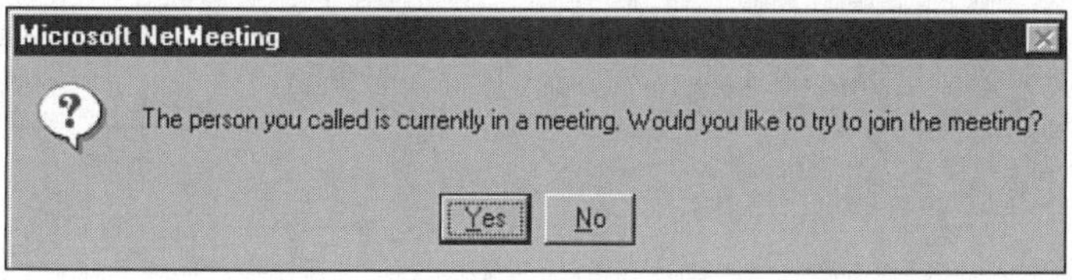

Microsoft NetMeeting

The person you called is currently in a meeting. Would you like to try to join the meeting?

Yes   No

Figure 17.24
Participants calling in
to join a meeting will
be told a meeting is
in progress and asked
if they want to join.
Choose <u>Y</u>es to join.

You, as the meeting host, are then notified of an incoming call and asked if you'd like to
accept it (see Figure 17.25).

Figure 17.25
You have to accept an incoming call before a person can join your meeting. Choose Accept to let him join.

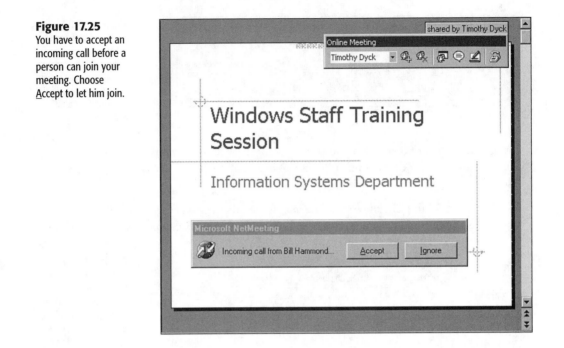

PRESENTING YOUR IDEAS

After you have all the right people connected at the same time (which can take some effort, depending on how busy the NetMeeting servers are), you're ready to start presenting.

Each of the people you've called (or who have called you) now see on their screen an exact duplicate of what's on your PowerPoint screen (see Figure 17.26 for an example of what an online meeting attendee sees). This is a live view, so whatever you do is mirrored on all the meeting attendees' screens: all your menu choices, mouse movements, typing, everything.

> **Note**
>
> Sound is the one exception—any transition sounds you have in your presentation won't be sent over the broadcast because the NetMeeting software is already using your sound hardware for itself. (You might think about using your phone to do an audio conference call along with the online meeting to get around this limitation.)

PART

V

CH

17

Tip #217 from

You can broadcast real-time sound and video (if your computer has the right hardware) to one (and only one) other person in your online meeting, though you can change who that person is at any time.

To enable this option, you'll need to start the NetMeeting software itself (select Start, Programs, NetMeeting from the Windows taskbar) while you're in an online meeting. When NetMeeting opens up, right-click on the name of the person listed in NetMeeting's Current Call window whom you want to have hear you and choose Switch Audio and Video. You'll then be able to talk with him and hear him when he talks back (if he also has a microphone hooked up to his PC).

If you do want to have your voice broadcast to everyone in the online meeting, you can configure NetMeeting (using NetMeeting's Tools, Options, Audio options) to use a special group conferencing server that supports the H.323/T.120 group telephony conferencing standard. Ask your network administrator if an audio teleconferencing server is available.

Figure 17.26
This is what people who join your online meeting see: an exact duplicate of your current PowerPoint window (along with the NetMeeting program PowerPoint uses to provide online meetings).

Only PowerPoint is shared this way: Your attendees won't see any other windows on your system. In fact, if another window—Microsoft Word, for example—covers part of the PowerPoint window, that part of the PowerPoint window will be grayed-out for your meeting attendees.

Right now, with the exception of sound, you've got pretty much the same result as you would have had using a broadcast presentation.

What's really different about the NetMeeting approach is that it allows other meeting attendees to interact with each other.

ONLINE CHAT AND WHITEBOARDING

The easiest way to do this is through NetMeeting's chat window. Click the Display Chat Window button of the Online Meeting toolbar to bring up the chat window (see Figure 17.27). You can send a text message to everyone in the meeting by typing whatever you want into the Message box of the chat window and then clicking the Send button.

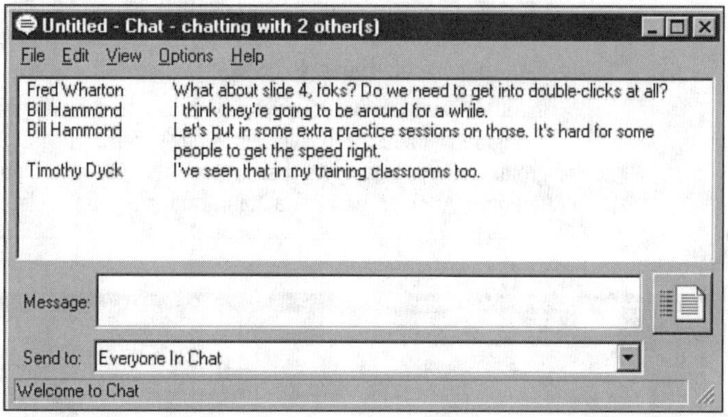

Figure 17.27
A chat window makes it easy to communicate with everyone at the same time in an online meeting.

You can also bring up a graphical whiteboard by clicking the Display Whiteboard button; the whiteboard works just like the chat window (except you can draw on it).

ONLINE GROUP EDITING

The ultimate form of interaction in online meetings goes even further than chat and whiteboard windows, however. With your permission, anyone in the meeting can take direct control of your PowerPoint window and type as if they were sitting at your desk. This is a great way of creating a presentation together—if someone is having a hard time getting across what she'd really like to see, she can take control and drive for a while.

To enable application sharing, you have to tell PowerPoint it's okay for others to take control. Click the Allow Others to Edit button of the Online Meeting toolbar to do so. You'll see the confirmation message shown in Figure 17.28. Choose OK to let PowerPoint know you realize that others will be able to take control over PowerPoint (but nothing else that is running on your computer, of course).

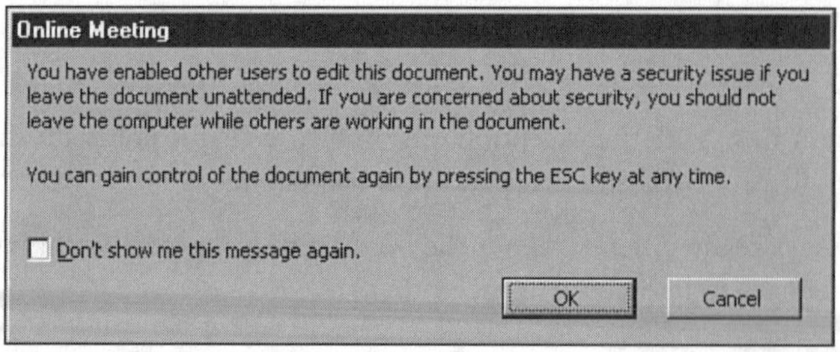

Figure 17.28
When you click the Allow Others to Edit button, PowerPoint double-checks that you really want this to happen. You cancel this permission by clicking this button again.

At this point, the Allow Others to Edit button sticks in a down position and changes to a Stop Others from Editing button.

The other people in the meeting can now double-click the image of your screen (displayed in their monitors) and take control. They'll be able to type right into the presentation open on your computer, add new slides, change slide order, and anything else you could do by yourself.

To take back control, just click anywhere in your PowerPoint window. You might want to turn off the Allow Others to Edit button just so people don't accidentally take control. It can be tricky to know who's in control sometimes.

Note

Note that application sharing doesn't require that anyone but you have PowerPoint installed on your computer. The only software other people need to have is NetMeeting. Pretty neat!

Tip #218 from
Timothy Ryle

You can tell who's in control when using application sharing by looking for their initials in tiny letters at the bottom-right of their mouse pointer.

Your meeting attendees will get a hint (shown in Figure 17.29) to give control back to you by choosing the Tools, Stop Collaborating command.

Caution

This command is not actually in PowerPoint, however (it would be neat if it were), but in the separate NetMeeting program (which will be running on your system, but might be hidden behind some other windows).

To give control back to the online meeting coordinator, switch to NetMeeting using the taskbar or Alt+Tab and choose Tools, Stop Collaborating.

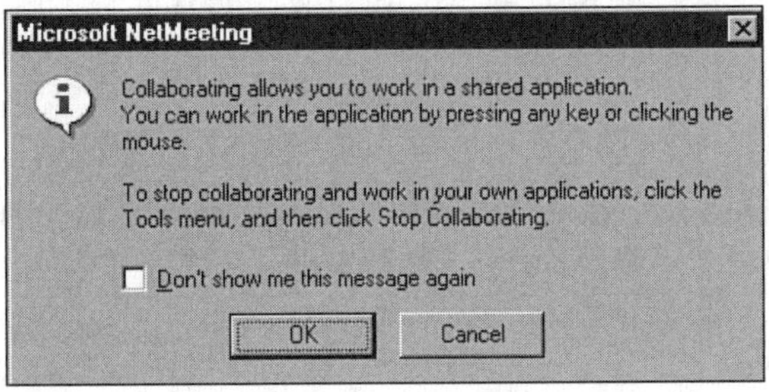

Figure 17.29
The Tools, Stop Collaborating command talked about in this message is actually in the NetMeeting program (pictured at the bottom-right of the image), not in PowerPoint.

ENDING AN ONLINE MEETING

To end an online conference, click the End Meeting button of the Online Meeting toolbar (the one with the picture of a phone). Individual attendees (except you) can individually join and leave as they like during the meeting through you, the meeting host. When you end the meeting, everyone gets disconnected.

SCHEDULING AN ONLINE MEETING

Although the method we've covered here enables you to start an online meeting whenever you want, PowerPoint also has hooks into Outlook that make it easy to schedule an online meeting.

Choose Tools, Online Collaboration, Schedule Meeting. PowerPoint starts an Outlook meeting request, which includes a specified online meeting directory server location and your email address. You can even have Outlook automatically start NetMeeting when the meeting begins.

PARTICIPATING IN WEB DISCUSSIONS

PowerPoint's online collaboration capabilities don't stop with presentation broadcasts and online meetings. You can also access Office 2000's new Web-based discussion forums from PowerPoint (as you can with all the other Office applications).

These forums work like an Internet newsgroup (you may have used one before), and enable you to carry on a discussion with co-workers without all of you having to be present at the same time. Presentation broadcasts and online meetings work in real-time. Web forums aren't real-time; they're there whenever you have a chance to check in to see what's new. It's handy to have the choice between the two approaches.

STARTING A WEB DISCUSSION

To start a new Web discussion (or access a previously created one), choose Tools, Online Collaboration, Web Discussions. The first time you run the command, you'll see the Add or Edit Discussion Servers window (see Figure 17.30), which asks you for the name of your discussion server.

Note

A discussion server is something your network administrator has to set up ahead of time. It's a Web server with special software, called the Office Server Extensions, installed on it.

Type in the server name your network administrator has provided into the top box of this window and, if you want, an easy-to-remember name into the bottom box of the window. Then choose OK to finish this step.

You'll then see PowerPoint's Discussion Options window (see Figure 17.31). Here you can add, edit, or remove Office discussion servers, as well as decide which fields you'd like to see displayed on the discussion server. The default settings are fine, so you can just choose OK to see the server.

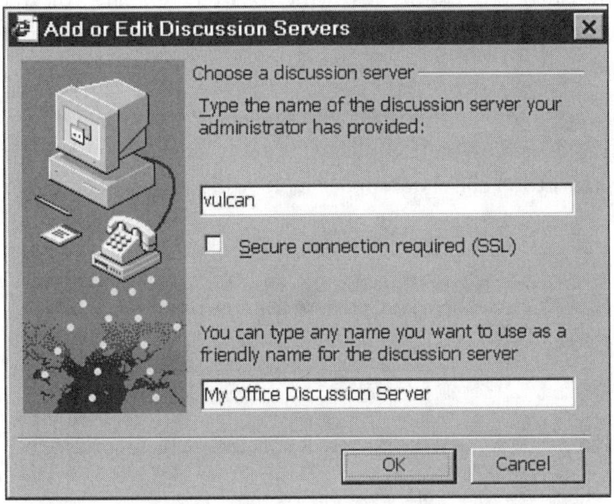

Figure 17.30
You need to type in the server name and, if you want, an easy-to-remember friendly name of your Office discussion server to access a Web discussion.

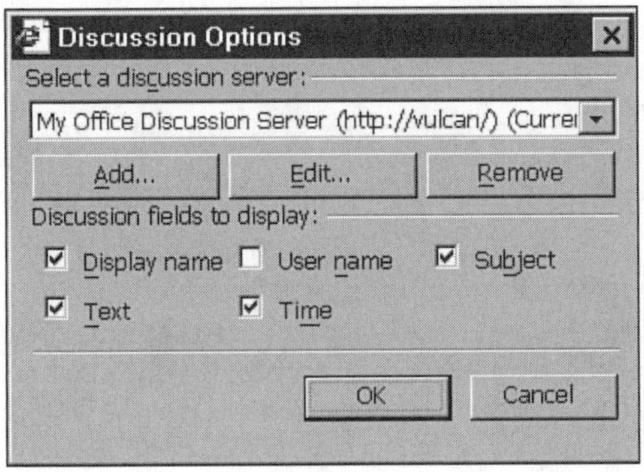

Figure 17.31
You can add new discussion servers here, as well as configure what kind of information you'll see displayed on them.

When the Discussion Options window goes away, it may look as though nothing's happened, but if you look closely, you'll see PowerPoint's Web Discussions toolbar has appeared on your screen (look for it at the bottom of your screen). I've dragged it out onto my presentation (see Figure 17.32) so it's easier to see.

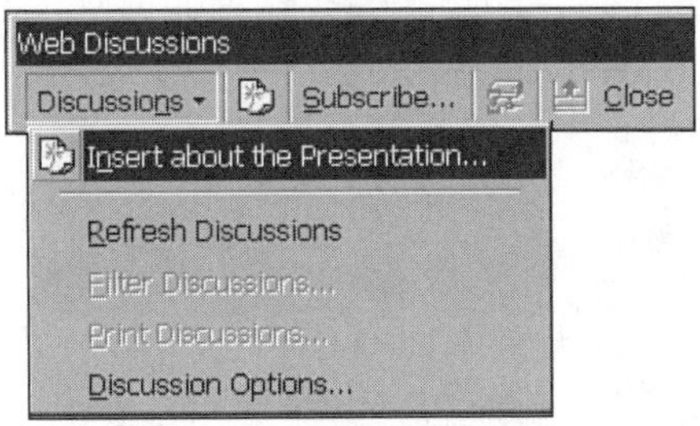

Figure 17.32
The Web Discussions toolbar enables you to add comments to a Web discussion or to be notified by email whenever new comments are added by someone else.

ADDING COMMENTS TO A WEB DISCUSSION

Insert a comment into the discussions database by selecting Discussions, Insert About the Presentation. You'll see the Enter Discussion Text window, which enables you to enter a comment about the presentation. You'll see your comment show up at the bottom of your screen (see Figure 17.33).

The point of Web discussions is that anyone else who opens up the presentation will also be able to see your comment and reply to it. If you want to reply to someone else's comment, you can do so by clicking the little yellow notepaper icon at the end of each comment and choosing Reply.

Figure 17.33
You can enter your own Web discussion comments or reply to other comments by clicking the Insert Discussion About the Presentation button on the Web Discussions toolbar.

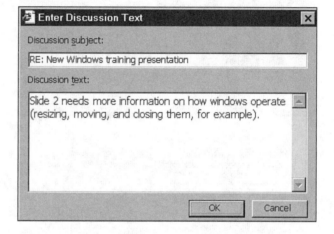

> **Caution**
>
> Web discussion comments are indexed using the exact name of the file you have open. If the file is later moved or renamed, or if you open the file locally from your hard drive and others get at it through a network connection, you won't see the same comments. It's best to put any presentations you want to discuss using Web discussions on a network server and then leave them there.

The Subscribe command on the Web Discussions toolbar is the other big part of Web discussions. When you choose it, you'll see the Document Subscription window come up (see Figure 17.34). Here you can tell the Office Discussion Server you'd like to be notified by email when this document changes or when someone else adds a comment to the discussion database. You can also choose to be notified either right away or less often, such as once a day or once a week.

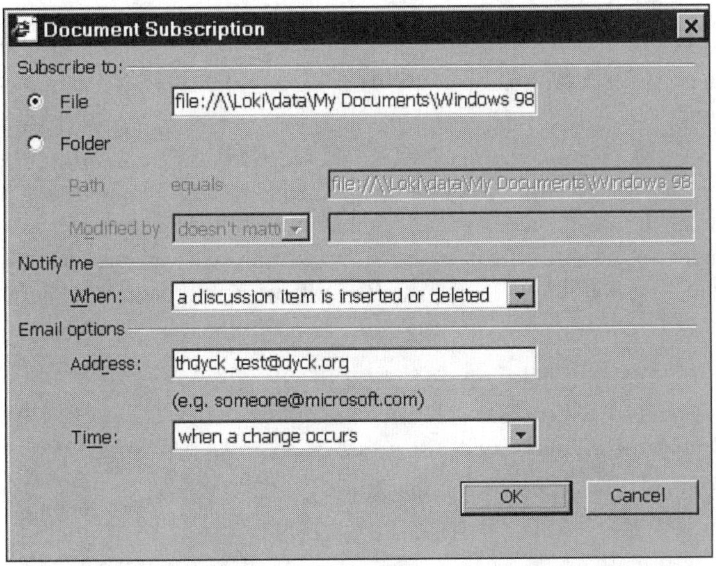

Figure 17.34
You don't have to manually check to see if anyone has added a comment to your presentation. The Document Subscription window enables you to configure the Office Discussion Server to notify you automatically when a change occurs.

Tip #219 from
Timothy Dyck

You don't have to start PowerPoint to view a Web discussion, although it's the most convenient way. You can also start up a Web browser (you need to use Internet Explorer 3.0 or Netscape Navigator 3.0 or later) and go to the Web site `http://discussion_server/msoffice` (where "*discussion_server*" is the name of your Office Discussion Server) to see comments made on any presentation (see Figure 17.35). When you get to the start page, enter the full network location of the presentation you want to load up, and choose Go.

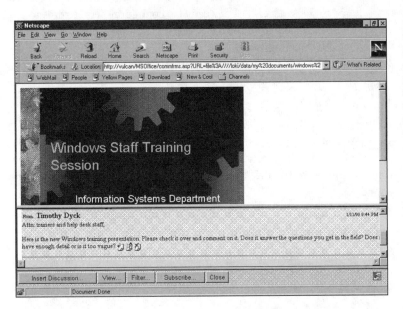

Figure 17.35
You can use a Web browser to see a Web discussion in progress. You can also add, edit, and delete comments the same as you can from within PowerPoint.

TROUBLESHOOTING

People trying to watch the presentation broadcast get a message saying that their computers can't connect to the broadcast.

Make sure that the network location you specified for the location of the presentation broadcast files is accessible by everyone you want to see the broadcast. (People outside the company won't normally be able to access your presentation broadcast location, for example.) If this is happening to the 16th person trying to view the presentation broadcast, you will need to switch to using NetShow. On its own, PowerPoint can't broadcast to more than 15 people.

When people open the broadcast lobby page, they see a mostly empty Web page.

Make sure all your viewers are using Microsoft Internet Explorer 4.0 or later as their Web browser. Netscape Navigator will not display the presentation broadcast correctly.

When I try to start a broadcast, PowerPoint starts the wrong one.

If you have overlapping broadcast schedules defined, PowerPoint always starts the broadcast scheduled to start first. If that was not what you wanted, manually delete the first presentation broadcast using PowerPoint's Slide Show, Online Broadcast, Set Up and Schedule, Change Settings or Reschedule a Broadcast, Delete command. Now begin the broadcast again to see the right presentation broadcast get started.

When I try to call someone using PowerPoint's Online Meeting tools, I get a message saying, "The person you called is not able to accept Microsoft NetMeeting calls."

The person you are calling either doesn't have Microsoft NetMeeting started or hasn't logged in to the same NetMeeting directory server you have. You have to let them know ahead of time that they should have NetMeeting open and be logged in to your chosen directory server so they can get your call. (They can also configure their systems to always have NetMeeting run unobtrusively in the Windows task bar so their computers are always "listening" for incoming NetMeeting calls.)

When I try to log in to a NetMeeting directory server, I get a message saying that there was a problem connecting to the directory server. Also, I try to log in to the directory server and don't get an error message, but the names box in the Place a Call window stays empty.

Any network problem between you and the NetMeeting directory server (or an overloaded server) will cause these kinds of problems. Just reselect the name of the server from the Directory box to connect to the directory server again. If the problem persists, try switching to a different directory server or use the Advanced button to call people using their Internet hostname or IP address.

When I try to join an online meeting, I get a message saying, "The person you called is currently in a meeting and cannot accept your call."

The person you are trying to call is already part of an online meeting. This might happen if you are trying to join a meeting by calling someone other than the conference originator (the person who is hosting the meeting using PowerPoint). That's the only person who can allow you to join an ongoing meeting. Alternatively, he can also call you at any time.

Online meeting attendees can't hear transition effects and sound clips in my presentation.

This is a limitation of online meetings. Because the NetMeeting software has first claim on your computer's sound equipment (in case you want to have an audio conversation with someone), PowerPoint has to operate silently.

Why can't I see other people's comments displayed in the Web Discussions window? I see only my own comments even though I know there are more there.

Make sure everyone that is opening the presentation is opening it from the same place, using the exact same filename. If you open the same file in different ways (from your local hard drive and over the network), PowerPoint thinks the files are actually different and stores comments separately under each filename.

All my comments are suddenly gone from the file!?! What happened?

Did you rename or move the file? That will cause PowerPoint to think it's opening a different file than the one for which you created a discussion. If you need to move the file, you'll need to get a database administrator to edit the Web Discussions database for you.

DESIGN CORNER

BEFORE

PowerPoint's online meeting feature allows you to send images (such as this slide with a chart) to everyone else in the online meeting using a shared whiteboard. However, your colleagues can't do much with the slide after it arrives, because it's been turned into a picture.

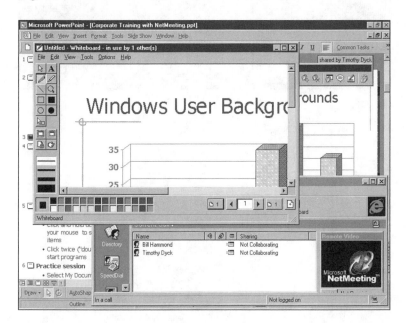

AFTER

By using features in Microsoft NetMeeting not found in PowerPoint's Online Meeting toolbar, you can get more out of online meetings. Once in an online meeting, start NetMeeting by choosing Start, Programs, NetMeeting from the Windows Start menu. You can then send your complete presentation (or any other file you wish, such as meeting minutes) to all meeting attendees using NetMeeting's Tools, File Transfer, Send File command.

You can also utilize an online meeting's "stealth" feature to quickly send out information: Whatever you copy into your Clipboard is automatically copied to the Clipboards of all meeting attendees, who can then paste the formatted information into locally running applications. Be sure you don't copy sensitive information onto your Clipboard without realizing this!

ADVANCED POWERPOINT

CHAPTER 18

INTEGRATING WITH OFFICE 2000

In this chapter

by Laurie Ann Ulrich

In this chapter, you will explore

- *Linking and embedding objects*   Use the Clipboard and Paste Special to insert objects from other applications into your PowerPoint presentation.

- *Building a Word table*   If you need the structure of a table in your PowerPoint slide, add a Word table—and access all Word's table and formatting tools at the same time.

- *Inserting an Excel worksheet*   Build an Excel worksheet in your PowerPoint slide, making all Excel's tools available within your PowerPoint application window.

- *Borrowing PowerPoint content*   Use your PowerPoint slides and slide components to enhance your Word and Excel documents.

One of the primary benefits of working with a suite of programs such as Office 2000 is the interoperability that the suite's programs offer. If it weren't easy to take content from Word and use it in PowerPoint or PowerPoint content and use it in Excel, there'd be little incentive for you to purchase Office 2000.

Because easy and efficient integration and interoperability exist between the Office 2000 applications, you can use all the applications together to build more effective documents. PowerPoint may be the one application within Office 2000 that makes the greatest use of the other applications within the suite—by its nature as a presentation tool, PowerPoint can work with all your other applications, tools, and documents to create a single powerful and effective slide presentation. You can

- Use an existing Excel worksheet or chart on a PowerPoint slide

- Use text and numbers from a PowerPoint datasheet to spawn a new Excel worksheet

- Take a section of an Excel worksheet and use it as a table in Word and/or a table in PowerPoint

- Take charts or drawn objects from a PowerPoint slide and paste them into a Word document to create visual consistency

- Use an entire PowerPoint slide as a graphic in a Word or Excel document

LINKING OFFICE OBJECTS

By now, you've probably used the Clipboard to cut or copy content between and within Office 2000 applications. The Clipboard is one of the most significant tools that Windows offers, and Office 2000 makes it even more powerful by giving you the ability to cut, copy, and paste several objects as a group or one at a time.

For all that power and convenience, however, the pasting process is limited. For example, after you've pasted an Excel chart into your PowerPoint slide, any changes made to the Excel chart or to the data that supports it are not reflected in the pasted copy of the chart in PowerPoint. Simple pasting establishes no connection between the copied chart and its source. To establish such a connection, you must link the source and the target, so that the target can be updated when opened to reflect changes in the source.

USING PASTE SPECIAL TO CREATE A LINK

How is a link between two applications established? By using the Edit, Paste Special command as described in the following steps:

1. In the source document, select the content to be copied to your PowerPoint slide (the target). Figure 18.1 shows a section of an Excel worksheet, selected for copying.

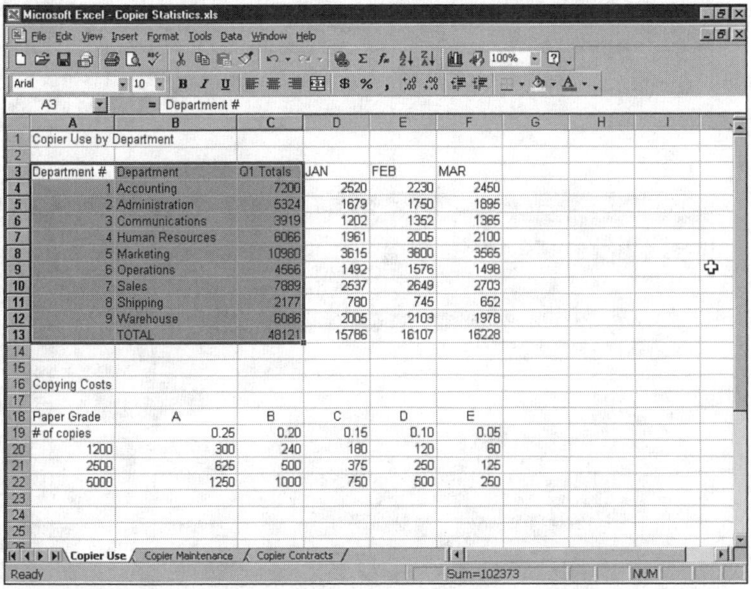

Figure 18.1
When selecting content from another application, imagine it in your slide–will it fit? Does its content effectively communicate your information or message?

2. Choose Edit, Copy.
3. Switch to or open your PowerPoint presentation, and go to Slide View of the target slide.
4. Choose Edit, Paste Special. The Paste Special dialog box opens (see Figure 18.2).
5. Click the Paste Link option. If more than one type of object is displayed in the As box, select the one that most closely matches the source of your content. Figure 18.3 shows the As options for the selected Excel content.
6. Click OK to insert the linked content.

Dimensions of the selected Excel content

Figure 18.2
When pasting Excel worksheet content, PowerPoint displays that object type in the As box.

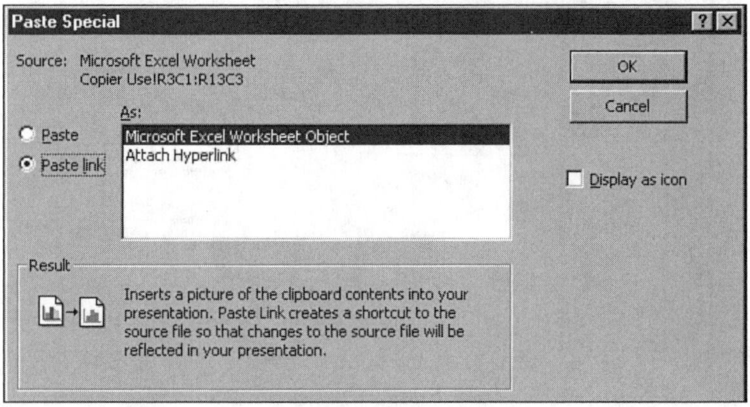

Figure 18.3
PowerPoint correctly assesses the nature of the content to be linked and offers appropriate options.

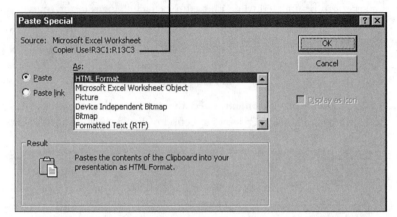

Tip #220 from
Laurie Ulrich

Click to place an X in the Display as Icon check box. Your linked object will appear as an icon, its represented content visible only if you (or a person viewing your presentation) want to see it. To view a link icon, double-click it.

After your linked object is inserted, test the link—go back to the source application and make a change to the content. Switch back to the target slide, and view the updated content—it now reflects the change made to the source.

Tip #221 from
Laurie Ulrich

You can resize the linked object by dragging diagonally from the object's corner handles. Drag inward to shrink the object, outward to increase its size.

> **Caution**
>
> Excel doesn't work properly unless you make sure you save the workbook file before creating the link the first time.

UPDATING LINKS

After a link is established, each time you open the target presentation, you'll be prompted to update the link (see Figure 18.4). This prompt enables you to choose whether to allow any changes that have occurred in the source document to update the linked content in your PowerPoint presentation.

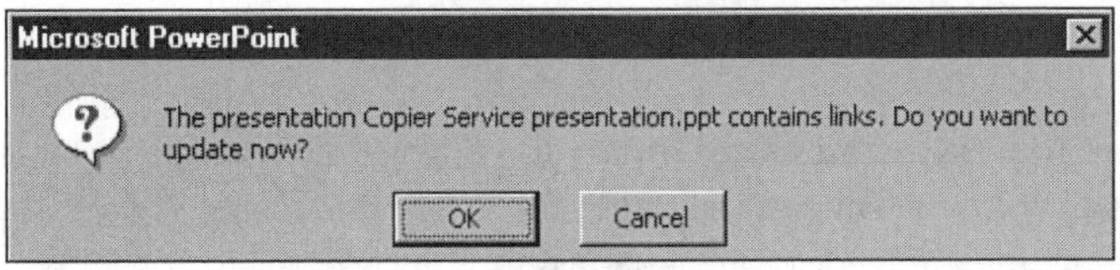

Figure 18.4
Click OK to update the target file with any changes that have been made to the source content.

Why would you choose not to update your target file? Perhaps you need to print the presentation with the older data or save it before changes are made, so that a historical reference will be available in the future. Perhaps your presentation pertains to second-quarter sales, and the source content has been updated with third-quarter data, which you're not ready to use. If for any reason you want to maintain the target data in its current form, click Cancel.

If you choose not to update the links at the time that you open the file, you can always update them later by following these steps:

1. Choose Edit, Links. The Links dialog box opens (see Figure 18.5), displaying a list of files that are linked to your open document.

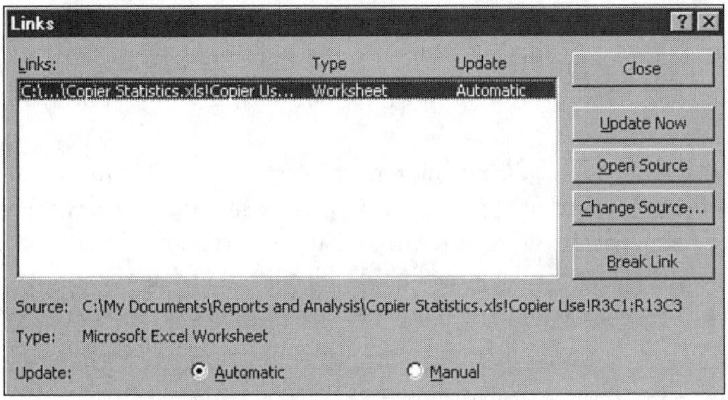

Figure 18.5
Click the Open Source button to view the linked data before updating it.

2. Choose the link you want to update, and click the Update Now button.

3. Click Close to update the target with any changes to the source.

MAINTAINING LINKS

For the most part, links you establish between files with Paste Special require little or no active maintenance on your part. To be sure your links remain intact, simply follow these basic rules:

- Don't rename the source or the target file
- Don't move or delete the source file
- Don't move or delete the target file

If you must move or rename either the source or target file, you will have to reestablish the link through the Links dialog box while in the target file. Click the Change Source button and navigate to the source file's new location, as shown in Figure 18.6.

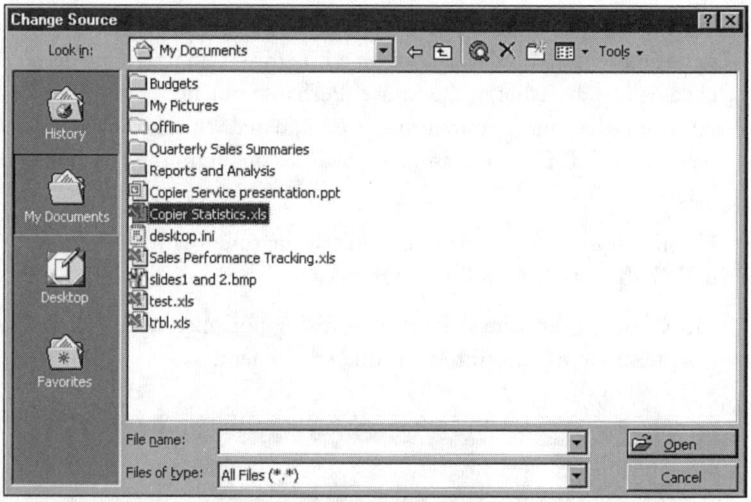

Figure 18.6
The Change Source dialog box allows you to find, select, and reestablish a link between a source and target if one of the files has been moved or renamed.

When making changes to your source document, remember that it is linked to a target file—whether you're editing content or applying formats, make sure that these changes will be useful in the target document. If you need to make changes to the source that won't be appropriate in the target, consider breaking the link. You'll have to update the former target manually (to make content changes), but you won't risk unwanted changes to the target file.

Caution

If you aren't the only person using the source or target files, be sure to alert other users to changes you make to the source that may not be appropriate in the target file. If another user chooses to update a link, he or she may be unhappy with the resulting changes.

REMOVING THE LINK BETWEEN SOURCE AND TARGET FILES

After a link is established, it remains in force (even if updates between the source and target are rarely or never performed) unless one or both of the files are moved or renamed. Moving or renaming either the source or target file breaks the link between the files because the files can't "find" each other anymore.

Although this method technically breaks the link, it doesn't do a very clean job. The target document continues to store a record of a link back to a now-moved or renamed file. To make a clean break, severing all ties and any record between your source and target files, follow these steps:

1. In the target file, choose Edit, Links.
2. In the Links dialog box (see Figure 18.7), select the link you want to break.

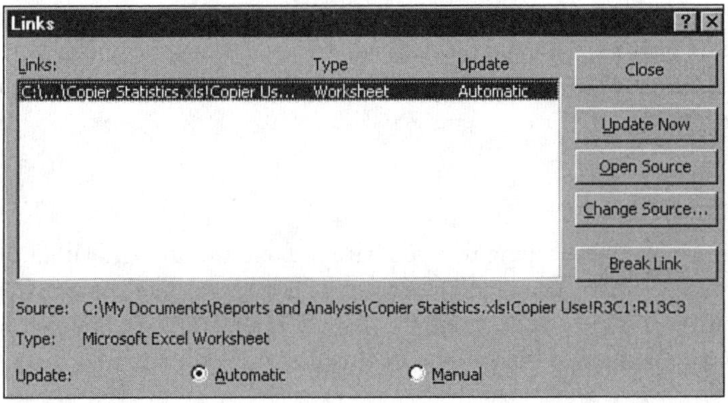

Figure 18.7
Formally sever your link between the source and the target file by using the Links dialog box to break the link.

3. Click the Break Link button.

After the link is broken, the pasted content remains in the target document, but retains no connection to the source data. Changes made to the source are not reflected in the target, and when opening the target file, you will not be prompted to update your link.

> **Note**
>
> A linked paragraph or table from Word or a worksheet section from Excel is seen as an object. After a link is broken, the pasted content is seen as a picture, a simple graphic component of your slide.

> **Tip #222 from**
> *Laurie Ulrich*
>
> One benefit of breaking a link by moving or renaming the source or target file is that the link can be reestablished easily by putting the file back where it was or renaming it to the original filename. Many users use this technique to make a temporary break, allowing changes to the source without the risk of updating the target until it becomes appropriate.

WORKING WITH EMBEDDED OFFICE OBJECTS

Whereas linking connects two applications through a pasted file or a portion thereof, embedding places an entire document and makes the tools of its native application available within another application file. Your choice to embed (rather than link) is based on what you want to do with the object and, in some cases, who will be using the application in which the embedded object resides. The following are two situations that support the decision to embed an object:

- *Limited system resources*   Rather than have two applications open at once, embed one in another by embedding an object. While the object is active, the object's application is also active (and its tools appear in the target application window). The source application can then be closed after any editing of the object is performed, leaving the object in the target file, and freeing system resources for the target application.

- *Simplicity*   Instead of linking (and having to decide when and if to update links), embed an application object and build the content you need, using the embedded application's tools. No need to restrict your moving and renaming of the file because no other files are linked to it.

EMBEDDING NEW AND EXISTING FILES

Embedded objects can be blank—meaning that you have to build the content within the object after it's embedded—or they can be derived from a file with existing content. This latter approach can save you some work because the content is already there. Consider some of these examples of embedded objects in a PowerPoint presentation:

- *Excel worksheets*   Whether you need a block of cells on your slide or need tools for formatting and performing calculations, embed an existing Excel worksheet (if the content of the worksheet will fit on the slide), or start with a blank worksheet and build it within the object.

- *Excel charts*   Build a chart in your PowerPoint presentation, using Excel's formidable charting tools. The object will consist of a worksheet with a Chart tab and a Sheet tab, enabling you to enter data and then watch it turn it into any sort of chart you need. This is an excellent approach for a user who spends more time in PowerPoint than Excel, but needs Excel's superior charting and spreadsheet tools to create an effective chart for his or her PowerPoint presentation.

- *Word text*   If your content is intended only for use in your PowerPoint presentation, you needn't create it in Word first and then copy it to PowerPoint. Instead, create it in PowerPoint through an embedded Word object. Without switching between applications, you're able to take advantage of Word's extensive text formatting tools. You can use this technique to embed an existing Word document as well.

Tip #223 from

Laurie A. Ulrich

You can also embed a PowerPoint presentation in a Word document or an Excel work-sheet. This can be especially useful when sending a presentation and its supporting data to someone for review.

EMBEDDING A NEW OBJECT

A new object is one that has no content and is not based on an existing file. All content will be built within the embedded object, and the object and its content will exist nowhere beyond the slide in which you embed it.

To embed an object in your PowerPoint presentation, follow these steps:

1. Choose the slide that will contain the object, and switch to Slide View.

2. Choose Insert, Object.

3. In the Insert Object dialog box (see Figure 18.8), select the Object Type.

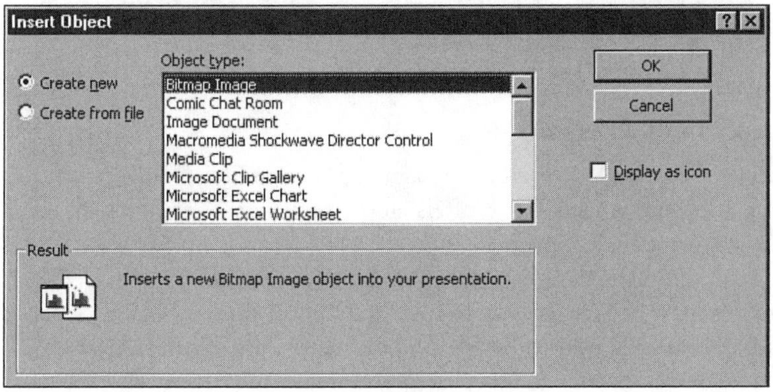

Figure 18.8
Scroll through the list of object types to find the Microsoft Word or Microsoft Excel object that you need.

4. If desired, click Display as Icon. This option is useful when you want to save visual space—the object will only open up for entry and editing (or for simply viewing the content) when the icon is double-clicked.

5. Click OK to insert the object.

When inserted, the object can be edited in terms of content and/or formatting, using the tools of the object's native application. Figure 18.9 shows an embedded Excel chart and the Excel toolbar in a PowerPoint presentation window.

Tip #224 from

Laurie A. Ulrich

When the embedded object's application tools appear, they appear as formatted in the source application. If you turned off the option to have the Standard and Formatting tool-bars share one row, they appear on two rows in the embedded application as well.

Figure 18.9
An inserted object can be selected for movement or resizing, or activated for editing. Double-click the object to activate it and display the tools of the embedded application.

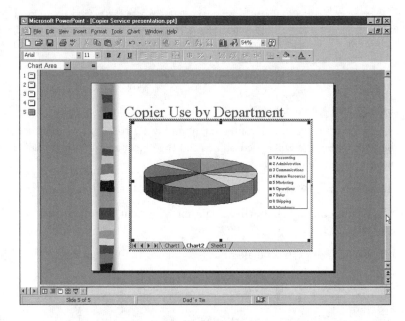

EMBEDDING AN OBJECT FROM AN EXISTING FILE

Embedding an existing file gives you much of the same power as a linked object—your content need only be updated in one place—and offers all the convenience of an object that "lives" within the target presentation. Because the file and its content already exist, you need only edit and reformat the embedded version of the file if or when it's required. When such changes are necessary, you have the source application tools at your disposal without having to open a separate application—the object's application tools appear in the target application window as soon as the object is activated by a double-click.

To embed an existing file in your PowerPoint presentation, follow these steps:

1. In your open PowerPoint application, go to the slide (in Slide View) into which you want to embed the file.

2. Choose Insert, Object.

3. In the Insert Object dialog box, click the Create from File option (see Figure 18.10).

4. Type the path and filename of the file you want to embed, or click the Browse button to find it.

5. If desired, click the Link check box to establish a link between the source file and the embedded object.

6. When the correct path and filename appear in the File box, click OK to insert the object and close the dialog box.

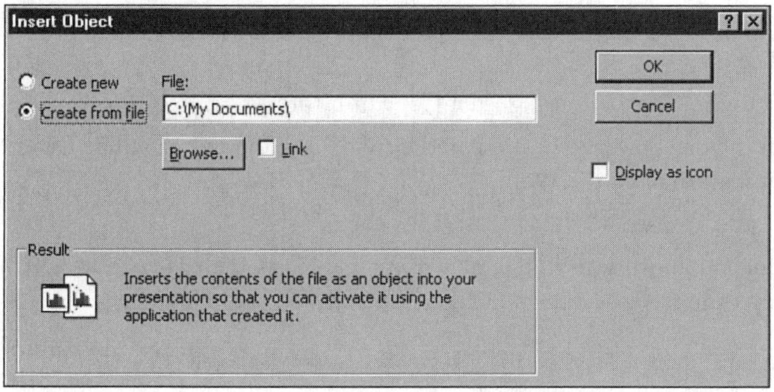

Figure 18.10
Save yourself the time and effort of entering your object's content by embedding an existing file.

Caution

If you choose to establish a link between the source file and the embedded object, be sure to update the link only when you're sure that changes to the source won't conflict with editing that may have been applied to the embedded object. This is especially true when more than one person will be accessing and editing either one or both files.

PART
VI

CH
18

USING WORD TABLES

Just as tables are a powerful feature in Word, they are equally powerful and effective in a PowerPoint presentation. For this reason, one of PowerPoint's slide layouts contains a table (the Table layout), and for inserting tables into a non-table layout, the Insert Table button appears on the Standard toolbar in your PowerPoint application window. If, however, you're more comfortable using Word's table tools (and the complete Table menu found in Word), you can build your table there and paste it into your PowerPoint presentation.

INSERTING A WORD TABLE

A Word table is simple to insert, and with a little forethought (how many columns and rows do you need?), you can add one to any slide in a matter of seconds. You'll use Word's tools to create it, and then bring the table into your PowerPoint presentation with the following steps:

1. Build your table in Word, using your familiar Word tools (found in the Table menu or using the Insert Table button).

2. After building the table, you can enter your content or wait until the table is in your PowerPoint slide.

3. Copy the table to the Clipboard using <u>E</u>dit, <u>C</u>opy or by pressing Ctrl+C.

4. Switch to or open your PowerPoint presentation, and go to the slide (in Slide view) into which you want to paste the Word table.

5. Choose <u>E</u>dit, <u>P</u>aste, or press Ctrl+V to insert the copied table.

6. Edit the content and dimensions of the table using the Tables & Borders toolbar, which appears whenever the table is active (see Figure 18.11).

➔ For more info on the use of these Office table tools, **see** "Working with Tables," **p. 79**

Figure 18.11
Insert an existing Word table or build one in Word to make use of more familiar tools, and then edit it in your PowerPoint slide.

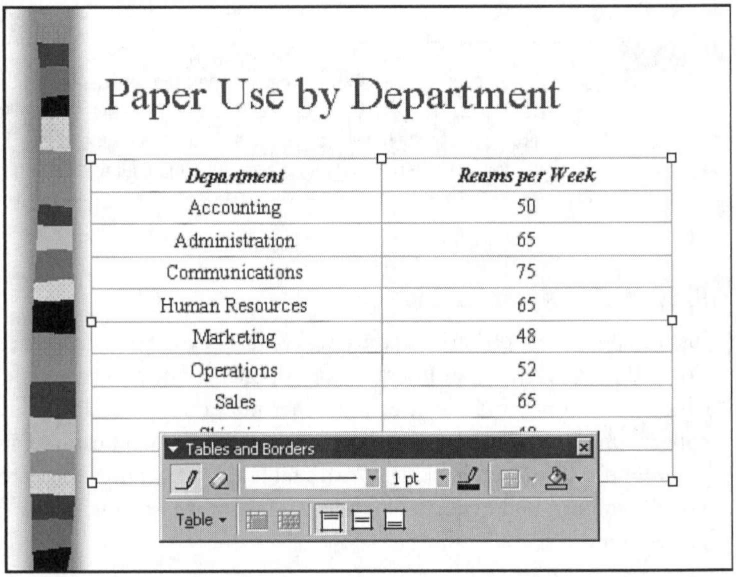

Tip #225 from
Lauren A. Ulrich

If your Word table already exists and you wish to reuse it in a PowerPoint slide, you can link it to your slide so that future updates to the table's content can appear in the PowerPoint version as well.

Tip #226 from
Lauren A. Ulrich

Like any slide component (regardless of its source), a table can be deleted easily. Click the table to select it, and then click its border to disable the cursor in the table's cells. To remove the table from your slide, press the Delete key.

Using PowerPoint Presentations in Other Applications

Throughout this chapter, we discuss bringing content and/or tools from Word and Excel into your PowerPoint slides. Although this is the most common type of Office 2000 integration when working with PowerPoint, you will find that you can use PowerPoint content and slides in Word and Excel as well.

Any PowerPoint slide content—graphics, organization charts, text boxes—can be added to a Word document or Excel worksheet by using the Clipboard to copy the content from the slide and paste it into the target Word or Excel file. The pasted content can also be linked (as discussed previously in this chapter), so that changes to the PowerPoint content are reflected in the Word or Excel target.

Another way to use PowerPoint content in other applications is to use entire slides. You can save an individual slide in virtually any graphic file format (such as .GIF, .TIF, .JPG, .PNG, or .BMP), enabling you to insert it as a graphic in any Word or Excel document.

To save a PowerPoint slide as a graphic file, follow these steps:

1. Choose View, Slide Sorter to view your presentation as an array of thumbnail graphics, or make sure you're in Slide View of the slide you wish to save as a graphic.

2. If you're working in Slide Sorter View, click once on the slide you want to save as a graphic.

3. Choose File, Save As to open the Save As dialog box (see Figure 18.12).

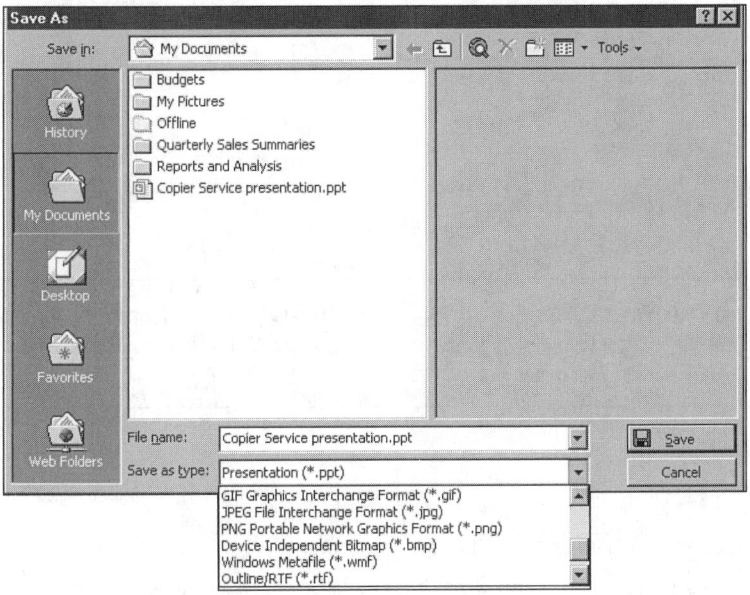

PART

VI

CH

18

Figure 18.12
Before saving the file, it pays to check which formats are acceptable to your target application. Choose the most commonly used formats for greatest usability.

4. In the Save as Type list, scroll through the formats and select a graphic file format such as .JPG, .TIF, .GIF, or .BMP (common graphic formats).

5. Type a name for your file in the File Name box and click Save.

Tip #227 from
Laurie A. Ulrich

If you're working from within Slide Sorter or Slide View as you save your slide as a graphic, a prompt appears, asking you if you want to export every slide in the presentation or just the selected slide. Click No, which exports (saves) only the selected slide.

When saved as a graphic, use the Insert, Picture command in Word or Excel to insert the graphic. The graphic can be sized for legibility and formatted using the Picture toolbar. Figure 18.13 shows a PowerPoint slide in a Word document.

Figure 18.13
If your PowerPoint presentation and your Word document pertain to the same topic and will be distributed to the same audience, use PowerPoint graphics, charts, and slides for visual consistency.

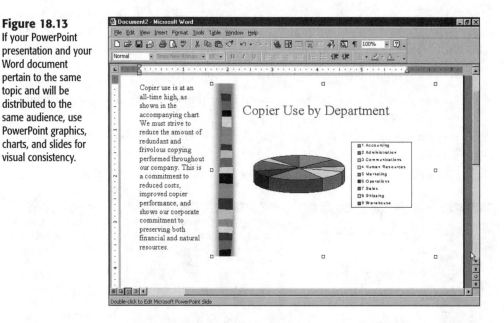

Tip #228 from
Laurie A. Ulrich

If you'll be using the graphic on a Web site, consider saving it in .GIF format. This format is acceptable to most Web design programs and creates small files, which is desirable for creating fast-loading Web pages.

TROUBLESHOOTING

When I paste Excel content into another file, I lose my formatting.

Excel formatting should be retained when worksheet cells or charts are pasted into your PowerPoint slides. If the pasted content looks different than the source content, however, consider these solutions:

- Delete the pasted content and repeat the Copy and Paste procedure.
- If you're using Paste Special to link the content to the PowerPoint slide be sure that you chose the correct object type.

If neither of these options solve the problem, consider embedding an Excel object in the slide, and pasting the content there. You'll be able to edit and format the content in its own application, negating the possibility of lost formatting.

DESIGN CORNER

PowerPoint becomes a natural place to combine the best results of your efforts in Word and Excel for the purposes of creating an effective presentation. Using the Clipboard and OLE tools to reuse existing Word and Excel content as well as to create new slide elements through embedded Word and Excel objects saves time and effort, and assures consistency throughout your Office documents.

BEFORE

The next figure shows a slide that contains an Excel chart object, embedded and undergoing changes within the PowerPoint window. Excel's tools are available through the active object, providing fast access to the requisite tools.

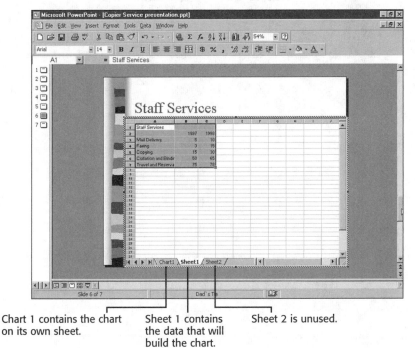

PART
VI
CH
18

Figure 18.4
The entire three-sheet workbook is available, although only part of it (the chart) needs to be shown in the slide.

Chart 1 contains the chart on its own sheet.

Sheet 1 contains the data that will build the chart.

Sheet 2 is unused.

AFTER

The last figure shows the chart as it appears on the slide. To the presentation audience, the tools used to build the chart are invisible, but for the person who developed the presentation, having an entire Excel worksheet available through a simple double-click is a significant convenience, despite any costs due to larger file size and increased use of system resources during editing.

Figure 18.15
While inactive, the chart shows no sign of its roots in an Excel object.

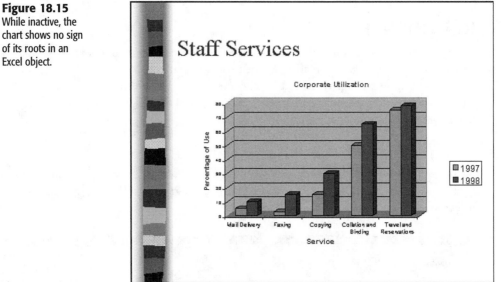

CHAPTER **19**

WORKING WITH POWERPOINT MACROS

In this chapter   *by Laurie Ann Ulrich*

In this chapter you learn how to:

- *Build macros to automate PowerPoint procedures*   Speed up the repetitive tasks in your presentation development cycle by turning them into macros.

- *Edit existing macros to meet changing needs*   Make changes in your macro functions and output through the Visual Basic Editor.

- *Share or not to share: macro security*   Establish who can use and edit your macros to control access and unexpected changes.

- *Run your macros from the toolbar*   Make it faster and easier to run your most frequently used macros by assigning toolbar buttons to them.

The applications found in Microsoft Office 2000 contain so many tools and menu commands that perform such a wide variety of seemingly automatic tasks that it may seem unnecessary for you to ever build your own macros. How could PowerPoint possibly work faster? What tasks require too many steps to be conveniently performed?

Your first impression may be that the software makes it so simple and quick to develop a great presentation that further automation isn't needed. If you spend a great deal of time with PowerPoint, however, or if the presentations you create have many common elements, you'll no doubt benefit from this chapter as you find ways to make repeated tasks simpler, faster, and, most importantly, more consistent in their outcome.

UNDERSTANDING MACROS

Macros are programs that you create by recording a series of tasks which you would otherwise perform yourself. You can record any number of steps in a task, from applying a format to running a slide show, and choose from a variety of ways to run the macro in the future. Macros are simple to create, easy to run, and can be used throughout an office to standardize the development process, as well as the appearance of presentations.

Perhaps you're stumped—you can't imagine how you could use macros to speed up or simplify your use of PowerPoint. Check the following list for some ideas:

- *Getting started*   Your macros can be run as soon as your toolbars appear and the first slide is onscreen. Create a macro to apply a design template and create a series of standard slides for your presentation. After that, all you have to do is add any extra slides that aren't part of your standard presentation, and enter your content. Much of your content entry can also be done with macros.

- *Building an outline*   If you create the same sales or productivity presentations every quarter, don't reinvent the wheel each time, and don't reuse your old presentations and risk overwriting them or leaving old data behind. Create a macro that builds the basic presentation, from choosing slide layouts to entering slide titles. Then, all you have to do is enter the new data and your presentation is complete.

- *Making changes to the master*   Create a series of macros that insert a logo on your slide master, add a slogan to your title master, or change the font of your text on all masters. Any changes that you find yourself making on all or most of your presentations can be automated with macros.

- *Setting up a slide*   If your slide layout needs are not met by any of the installed layouts, simply create a macro that inserts chart objects, tables, text objects, and graphics. The macro can include your placement and sizing of these objects, so that when the macro is run, all you need to do is fill in the blanks—double-click and insert the chart data, edit the organization chart, or type your text—and the layout is done for you.

- *Inserting hyperlinks*   Do all your presentations have links to your company Web site or an internal database? Create a macro that inserts the hyperlink. This includes choosing the linked site or file and entering the text or graphic that serves as the link.

- *Build an organization chart*   With the exception of the names of new or relocated people, the organization charts of most companies don't vary from presentation to presentation. Rather than having to manually copy and paste a chart from a previous presentation, you can record a macro that inserts your company's completed organization chart. After running the macro, all you have to do is edit the names and titles to reflect changes in the roster since you recorded the macro. If, over time, the changes are significant, you can simply edit the source chart so that when the macro inserts it, the majority of the needed changes have already been made.

- *Run a slide show*   Rather than make your audience sit through the process of opening the presentation and starting the show, record a macro that can be run as soon as you open PowerPoint. You'll have rehearsed your show and set any automatic slide timings before recording the macro, so that all the macro needs to do is start the show.

Tip #229 from

Laurie A. Ulrich

Macros use VBA—or *Visual Basic for Applications*—as their programming language. Don't worry, however—recording, editing, and using macros require little or no knowledge of VBA. You can improve your ability to edit and troubleshoot your macros by becoming acquainted with VBA, but many (if not most) users don't interact directly with VBA to create, make simple changes to, or run their macros.

CREATING A MACRO

It's as though you've turned on a video camera that watches your keystrokes, mouse movements, and command selections—the macro recorder notes every move you make and converts your actions to programming code. After you name your macro and perform all the steps you want to automate, you stop the recorder, and by using the name you've given the macro, you can run it at any time. A macro enables you to perform a virtually unlimited series of steps in just seconds.

Note

In earlier versions of Office, the Word, Excel, and PowerPoint programs didn't have features such as AutoCorrect and AutoText. Before these features existed, users created macros to correct common misspellings and turn abbreviations into words, phrases, and paragraphs. As Office evolves, the number of common tasks you'll need to automate yourself will continue to decrease.

RECORDING A MACRO

Before you begin to record a macro, do some planning. Think about where you are in the process of developing or running a presentation when the macro you're about to create is invoked. What situation must exist for the macro to be successful? If the macro formats existing slide content, the content must be displayed and selected before the macro is run. If the macro runs a slide show, the presentation must be placed in the same folder where the macro was recorded. In short, set the stage for your macro to begin, and record it only when the scenario is appropriate.

After you set the stage, record your macro by following these steps:

1. Choose Tools, Macro, Record New Macro.

2. In the Record Macro dialog box (see Figure 19.1), enter a macro name to replace the default name. Your macro's name may not contain any spaces.

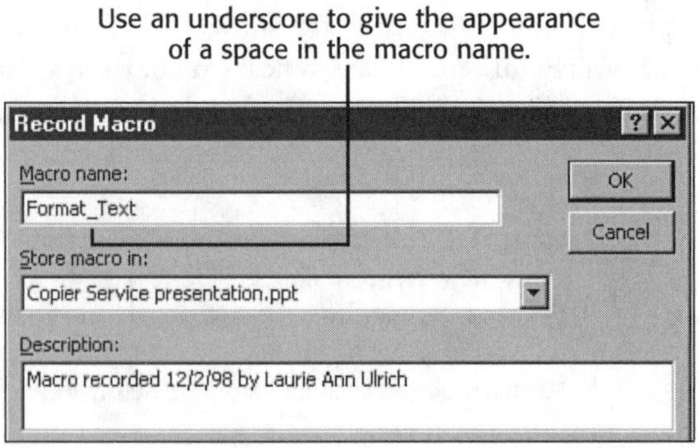

Use an underscore to give the appearance of a space in the macro name.

Figure 19.1
Give your macro a short, yet descriptive, name.

3. As needed, type a description of the macro in the Description box. It's a good idea to leave the name and date text that is already in the box and add your description at the end of that text.

4. Click OK. A floating Stop button appears onscreen (see Figure 19.2).

Stop button

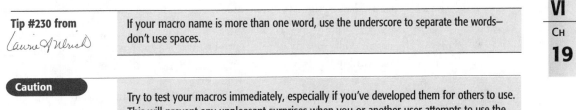

Figure 19.2
As needed, you can move the floating Stop button out of the way by dragging its title bar.

5. Perform the steps you want to record, using the mouse or keyboard to issue commands.

6. When your steps are complete and you reach the end of the procedure you want to automate, click the Stop button on the floating toolbar.

Tip #230 from

Lauune of Ulrich

If your macro name is more than one word, use the underscore to separate the words—don't use spaces.

Caution

Try to test your macros immediately, especially if you've developed them for others to use. This will prevent any unpleasant surprises when you or another user attempts to use the macro, and allows you to edit it as needed while the procedures are fresh in your mind. The process of running a macro is discussed later in this chapter.

PART

VI

CH

19

CREATING A MACRO IN THE VISUAL BASIC EDITOR

If you're familiar with VBA (Visual Basic for Applications), you can build a macro without recording your steps as described in the previous section of this chapter. Instead, you can type the macro programming code directly into an editing window provided by Office 2000's Visual Basic Editor (see Figure 19.3).

Figure 19.3
Even a novice VBA user can learn a lot from building and editing macro code in this window.

To enter the editor, select <u>T</u>ools, <u>M</u>acro, highlight the macro name, and click Edit. The editor window consists of three separate windows, each designed to assist you in the creation and editing of a macro:

- *Project*   The project window shows a hierarchical tree, displaying the various modules of your macro. A simple macro will probably only consist of one module.

- *Properties*   This window again lists the modules involved in the project, but in this window, they're listed alphabetically or by category.

- *Module*   The macro code appears in this central window. Type new or edit existing VBA code in this window.

Figure 19.4 shows the Module window with the parts of a simple formatting macro identified.

To create a macro in the Visual Basic Editor Window, follow these steps:

1. Choose <u>T</u>ools, <u>M</u>acro, <u>V</u>isual Basic Editor.

2. Click inside the Module window to make it active.

3. As needed, choose <u>I</u>nsert, <u>M</u>odule. This creates a blank module for you to begin writing your code (see Figure 19.5).

4. Type **Sub** followed by the name of your macro and press Enter. Your End Sub statement is added automatically (see Figure 19.6).

Name of the macro   Description of the macro

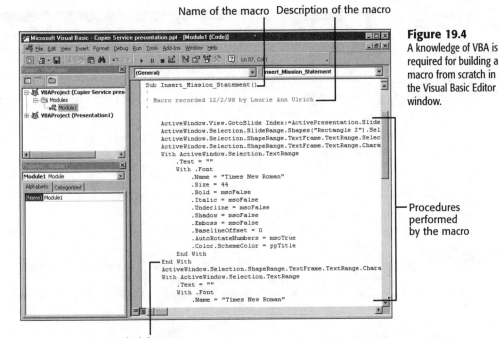

Figure 19.4
A knowledge of VBA is required for building a macro from scratch in the Visual Basic Editor window.

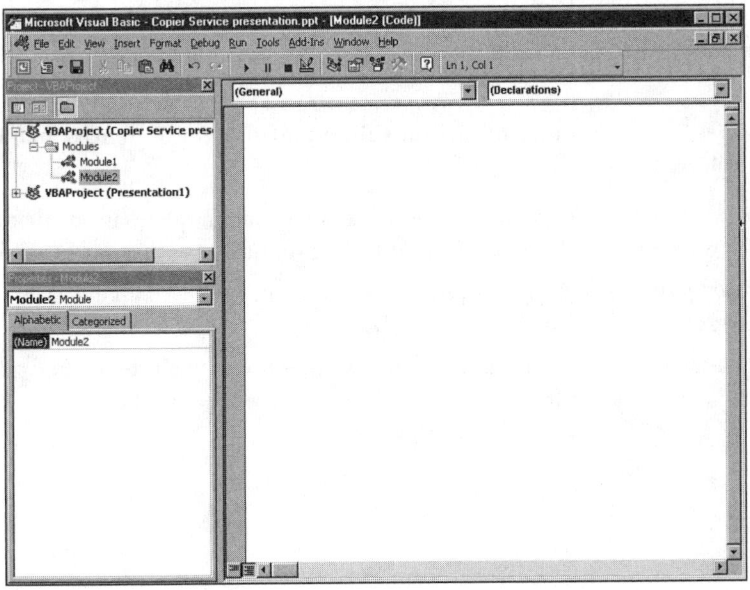

Procedures performed by the macro

End of the macro

Figure 19.5
The Visual Basic Editor opens with a blank module, ready for you to begin creating your macro.

Figure 19.6
If the name of your macro includes spaces, use the under-score character to represent them, as in Format_Title.

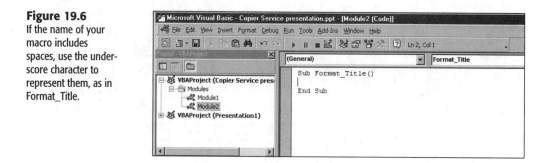

5. Type your lines of code for the steps your macro should perform.

6. Choose File, Close and Return to Microsoft PowerPoint.

Note

If you want to learn more about writing Visual Basic code or using VBA, we suggest *Sams Teach Yourself Visual Basic for Applications in 24 Hours*.

EDITING A MACRO

The Visual Basic Editor is again pressed into service whenever you want to edit a macro. Unless you're familiar with creating macro code in this editor, it's probably a good idea to delete and re-record a macro if it's not working or requires significant changes to work properly.

For simple changes, even a user unfamiliar with VBA can use the editor to make minor modifications such as:

- *Change text entries that the macro inserts* Any text appearing in quotes is text that the macro adds to your presentation (see Figure 19.7). Edit or retype this text as needed.

- *Choose different formats and fonts* Noting the terminology used (see Figure 19.8), change, for example, Times New Roman to Bookman.

- *Select a different element* If your macro currently types text into a title box and you want it to type it into a subtitle box, change the code to redirect the entered text (see Figure 19.9).

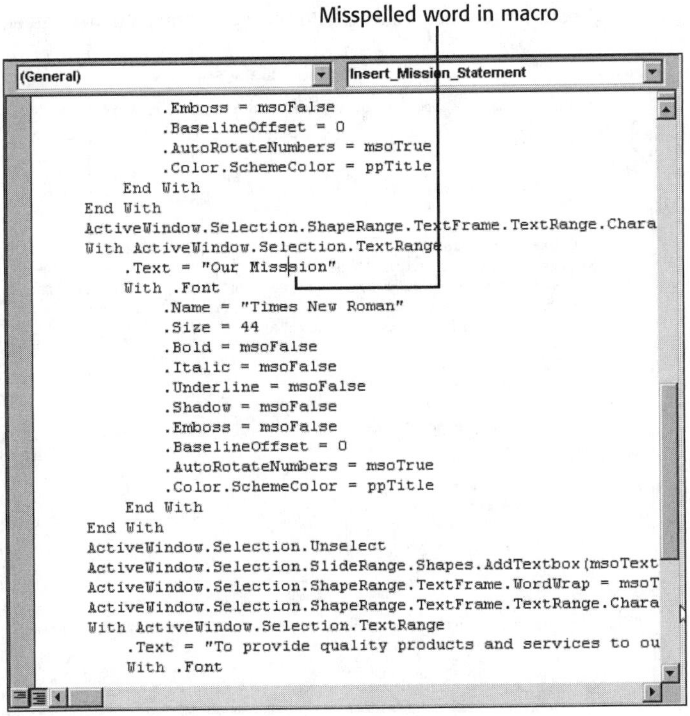

Misspelled word in macro

Figure 19.7
Misspell something while recording your macro? Fix the text in the Visual Basic Editor window.

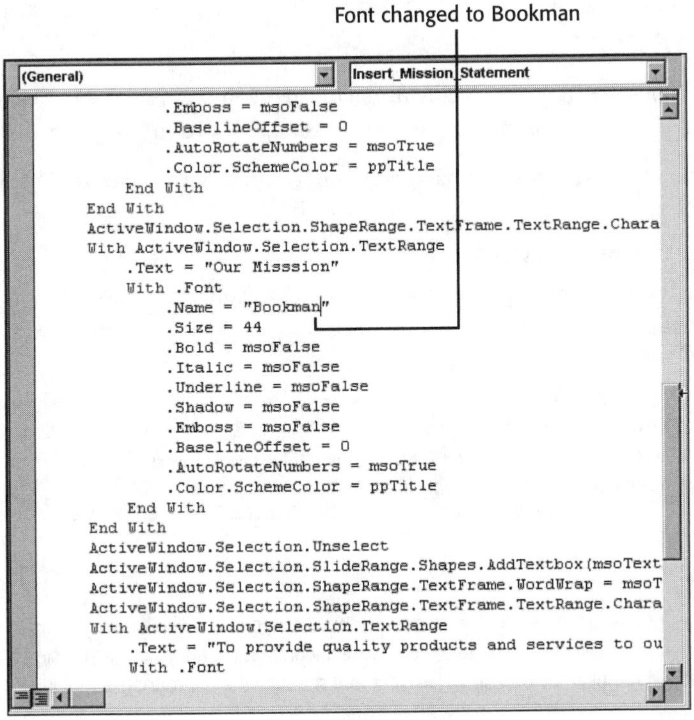

```
                    .Emboss = msoFalse
                    .BaselineOffset = 0
                    .AutoRotateNumbers = msoTrue
                    .Color.SchemeColor = ppTitle
            End With
    End With
    ActiveWindow.Selection.ShapeRange.TextFrame.TextRange.Chara
    With ActiveWindow.Selection.TextRange
        .Text = "Our Misssion"
        With .Font
                    .Name = "Times New Roman"
                    .Size = 44
                    .Bold = msoFalse
                    .Italic = msoFalse
                    .Underline = msoFalse
                    .Shadow = msoFalse
                    .Emboss = msoFalse
                    .BaselineOffset = 0
                    .AutoRotateNumbers = msoTrue
                    .Color.SchemeColor = ppTitle
        End With
    End With
    ActiveWindow.Selection.Unselect
    ActiveWindow.Selection.SlideRange.Shapes.AddTextbox(msoText
    ActiveWindow.Selection.ShapeRange.TextFrame.WordWrap = msoT
    ActiveWindow.Selection.ShapeRange.TextFrame.TextRange.Chara
    With ActiveWindow.Selection.TextRange
        .Text = "To provide quality products and services to ou
        With .Font
```

Font changed to Bookman

Figure 19.8
Change your font by editing the programming code.

```
                    .Emboss = msoFalse
                    .BaselineOffset = 0
                    .AutoRotateNumbers = msoTrue
                    .Color.SchemeColor = ppTitle
            End With
    End With
    ActiveWindow.Selection.ShapeRange.TextFrame.TextRange.Chara
    With ActiveWindow.Selection.TextRange
        .Text = "Our Misssion"
        With .Font
                    .Name = "Bookman"
                    .Size = 44
                    .Bold = msoFalse
                    .Italic = msoFalse
                    .Underline = msoFalse
                    .Shadow = msoFalse
                    .Emboss = msoFalse
                    .BaselineOffset = 0
                    .AutoRotateNumbers = msoTrue
                    .Color.SchemeColor = ppTitle
        End With
    End With
    ActiveWindow.Selection.Unselect
    ActiveWindow.Selection.SlideRange.Shapes.AddTextbox(msoText
    ActiveWindow.Selection.ShapeRange.TextFrame.WordWrap = msoT
    ActiveWindow.Selection.ShapeRange.TextFrame.TextRange.Chara
    With ActiveWindow.Selection.TextRange
        .Text = "To provide quality products and services to ou
        With .Font
```

Redirect the macro to a subtitle box by entering a new number.

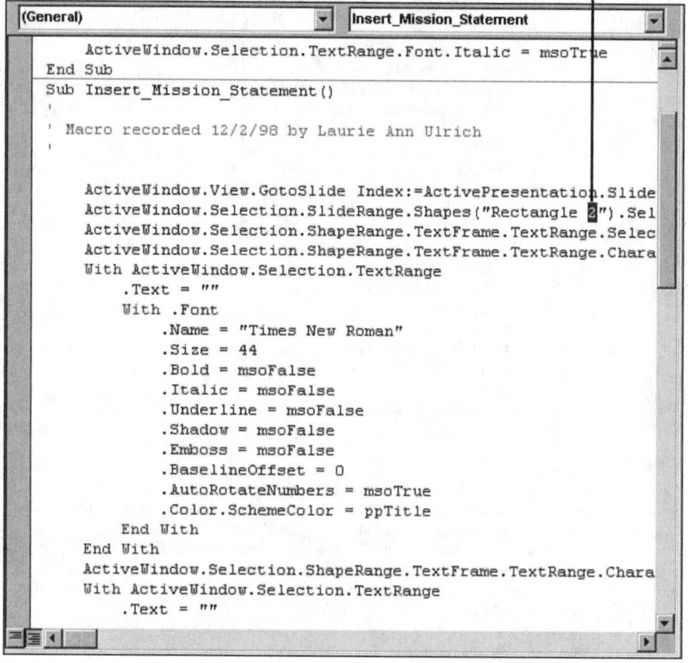

Figure 19.9
Change Rectangle number references to redirect the text that the macro will insert on your slide.

```
(General)                                    Insert_Mission_Statement

            ActiveWindow.Selection.TextRange.Font.Italic = msoTrue
End Sub
Sub Insert_Mission_Statement()
'
' Macro recorded 12/2/98 by Laurie Ann Ulrich
'

    ActiveWindow.View.GotoSlide Index:=ActivePresentation.Slide
    ActiveWindow.Selection.SlideRange.Shapes("Rectangle 2").Sel
    ActiveWindow.Selection.ShapeRange.TextFrame.TextRange.Selec
    ActiveWindow.Selection.ShapeRange.TextFrame.TextRange.Chara
    With ActiveWindow.Selection.TextRange
        .Text = ""
        With .Font
            .Name = "Times New Roman"
            .Size = 44
            .Bold = msoFalse
            .Italic = msoFalse
            .Underline = msoFalse
            .Shadow = msoFalse
            .Emboss = msoFalse
            .BaselineOffset = 0
            .AutoRotateNumbers = msoTrue
            .Color.SchemeColor = ppTitle
        End With
    End With
    ActiveWindow.Selection.ShapeRange.TextFrame.TextRange.Chara
    With ActiveWindow.Selection.TextRange
        .Text = ""
```

DELETING A MACRO

Perhaps your macro is obsolete or has so many problems that you find it easier to delete and start over than to edit it. In any case, deleting a macro is simple if you follow these steps:

1. In the presentation that contains the macro, choose Tools, Macro, Macros. The Macro dialog box opens (see Figure 19.10).

2. Select the macro you want to delete.

3. Click the Delete button. A prompt appears, asking you to confirm your intention to delete the selected macro. Click Yes.

Caution

After a macro is deleted, it cannot be retrieved. Be careful to read the description box for each macro before you delete it, especially if you have several similarly named macros or if your macro names are not terribly illustrative.

Create a Macro Template

If you want to build a series of macros to use in all your new presentations, create a blank presentation template that includes all your macros. Whenever you want to build a presentation that utilizes your macros, simply start the presentation based on that template by choosing File, New, and selecting the appropriate template.

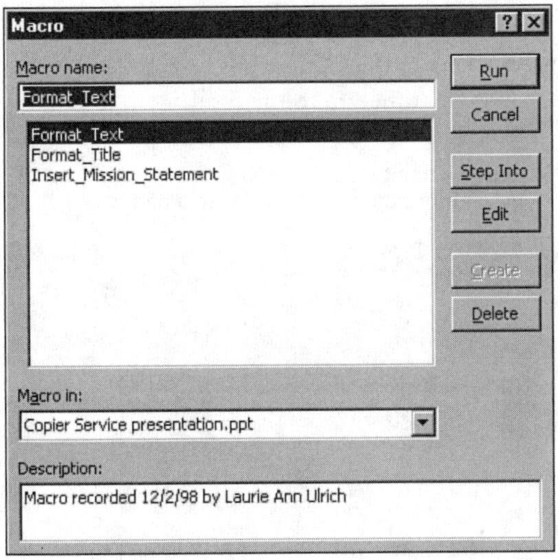

Figure 19.10
See a list of your current macros, created for the open presentation.

RUNNING A MACRO FROM THE TOOLBAR

Macros save time and effort by automating repetitive tasks. The process of invoking a macro, however, can be prohibitive because it requires the use of two levels of menus and a dialog box. To speed up the use of your macros, try assigning them to toolbar buttons with the following steps:

1. In the presentation that contains the macro(s) you want to assign to the toolbar, choose Tools, Customize.
2. Click the Commands tab (see Figure 19.11).

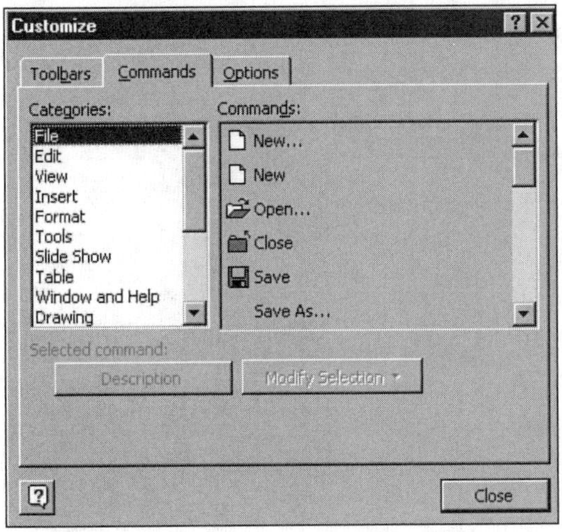

Figure 19.11
The Macros category lists all the macros you've created in the open presentation.

PART
VI

CH
19

3. Scroll through Categories and select Macros.

4. A list of your macro names appears in the Commands box (see Figure 19.12). Click and drag a macro name (one macro at a time) up to the toolbar.

Mouse pointing to new
location for button   Macro name

Figure 19.12
Drag the macro name up to the toolbar. You can drag as many as you want (one at a time) and conceivably assign all your macros to the toolbar.

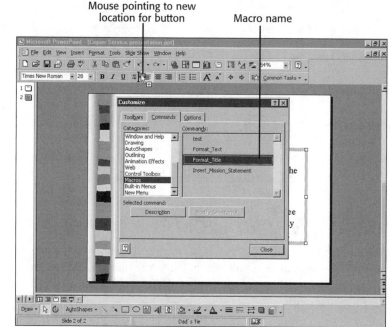

5. When your mouse pointer is on the spot where you want to add the macro button, release the mouse.

6. Right-click the new button (which appears with the macro name on it, as shown in Figure 19.13), and choose Change Button Image from the shortcut menu.

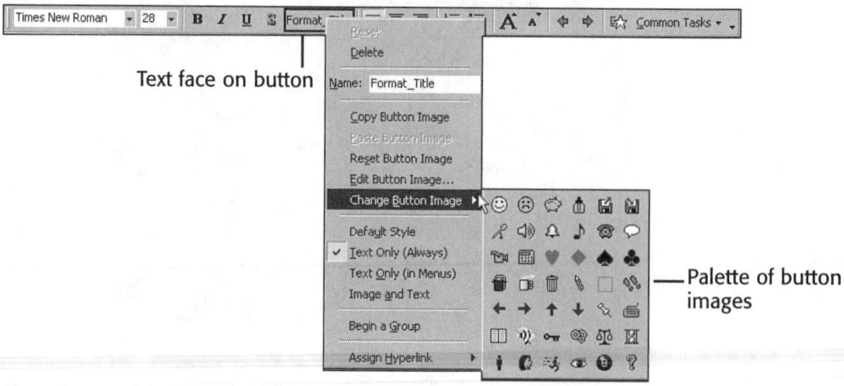

Figure 19.13
If your macro name is long, it may be better to have a picture represent the macro rather than to take up a lot of space on the toolbar.

Text face on button

Palette of button images

7. Click to select one of the graphic images from the palette.

8. Whether your macro name is long (and is wasting toolbar space) or you feel you don't need to see the name to remember which button performs the macro, remove the text portion of the button image. Right-click the button and choose Text Only (in Menus). The text name of the macro disappears, and the graphic image remains.

9. Click Close to exit the Customize dialog box.

Tip #231 from

Laurie A Ulrich

While the Customize dialog box is open, you can move and delete any of the existing toolbar buttons.

TROUBLESHOOTING

The macro I created doesn't work properly, and I'm not sure why.

PowerPoint macros (and macros in any Office 2000 application, for that matter) may not work as expected when the following situations exist:

- Items required by the macro (slides from another presentation, fonts, graphics, sound files) are not available. Once you create a macro that inserts something into your chart, be sure not to rename or delete that item.

- The stage isn't set for the macro to run. If your macro was designed to move from slide 4 to slide 8, it may not work as expected if you invoke it while on slide 5. If your macro will be run during an important slide show, be sure to test it ahead of time and note the circumstances that must be in place for the macro to do its job.

- You've run out of system resources. PowerPoint presentations contain so much graphical content that a machine with marginal resources (memory, speed) may crash or begin to work poorly if your macro opens a presentation or inserts or runs a memory-intensive file. In this situation, it's the hardware, and not the macro, that is at fault. Be sure to close all unnecessary programs before running your slide show so that PowerPoint and the necessary files are all that are open during your show.

DESIGN CORNER

While this chapter has not been intended to teach you to create VBA code from scratch, it can be useful to see the code created by a macro recorded through user actions. The Before figure shows a slide layout created by a macro, and the After figure shows the VBA code created by the recording of the macro.

BEFORE

Create a custom slide layout that you can apply to any slide by invoking your macro. The user of this macro will double-click the charts to enter their data and customize these basic charts for each use.

Charts were added to a Title Only layout.

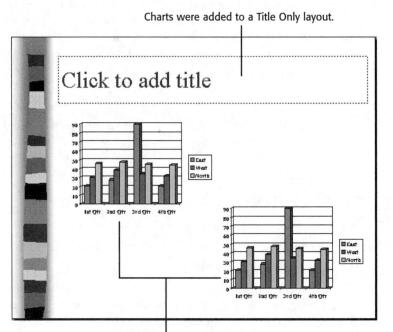

Two chart objects (Microsoft Graph 2000 Chart) can be added and resized as needed.

AFTER

The VBA code includes the name of the macro and the commands issued as the macro was recorded.

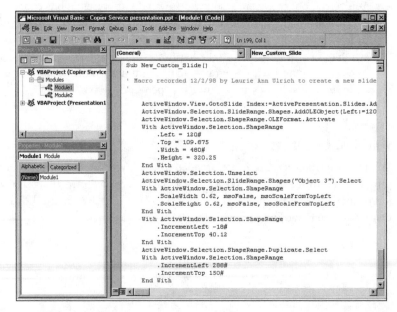

CHAPTER 20

CUSTOMIZING POWERPOINT

In this chapter *by Read Gilgen*

CUSTOMIZING TOOLBARS

The visual element, such as the various icons found on the toolbars, helps make PowerPoint and other Windows programs easy to use. A quick click on a button and you avoid having to search through endless menus to get to the command you want.

PowerPoint has predefined several toolbars, and by default places a few of them at various locations around the screen. For example, the Standard and Formatting toolbars are combined on a single toolbar beneath the menu, whereas the Drawing toolbar appears at the bottom, above the application bar (see Figure 20.1).

Figure 20.1
Toolbars are placed on the PowerPoint screen to help you access commands easily and quickly.

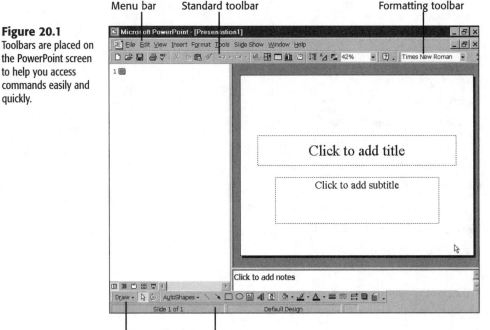

REPOSITIONING TOOLBARS

Typically, you expect a toolbar to appear at the top of the screen. However, you've already noted that the Drawing toolbar is located at the bottom of the screen. Other toolbars—when you select them—may appear vertically along the side of the screen. Toolbars that appear on any side of the screen are said to be "docked," whereas "floating" toolbars can be found in the middle of the screen.

You can reposition any toolbar to any location simply by dragging it to the desired location. For example, to move the Standard toolbar to the left side of the screen, follow these steps:

1. Move the mouse pointer to the Move handle on the toolbar. A four-way arrow appears (see Figure 20.2).

Move handle   Move pointer   Move handle

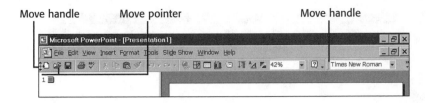

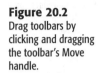

Figure 20.2
Drag toolbars by clicking and dragging the toolbar's Move handle.

2. Click and, while holding the left mouse button down, drag the toolbar away from the edge. PowerPoint displays the toolbar along with a title bar (see Figure 20.3).

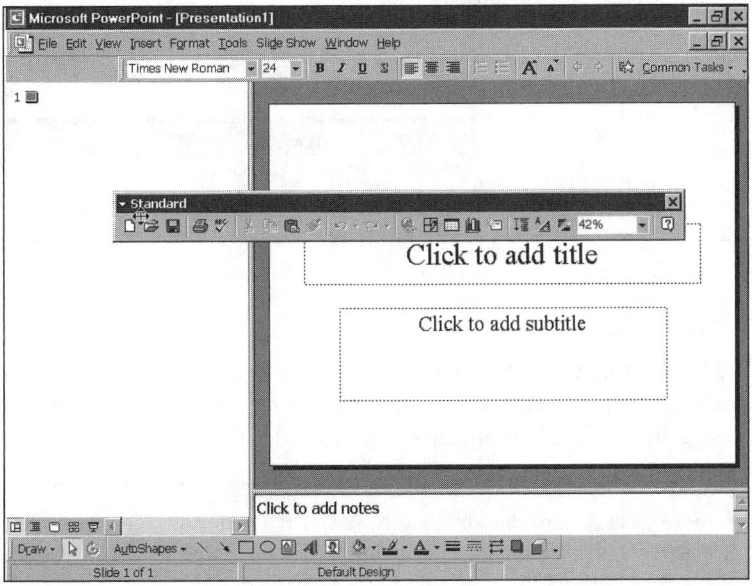

Figure 20.3
A floating toolbar also displays a title bar and can be placed anywhere on the screen.

3. Continue dragging the toolbar to the desired location—for example, along the left edge.
4. When the toolbar's title bar disappears and the Move handle reappears, release the mouse button to dock the toolbar along the edge of the screen (see Figure 20.4).

PART
VI
CH
20

Caution

It's easy to lose toolbars as you drag and drop them. For example, if you accidentally drop a toolbar on top of another one, you may not notice that they've been combined. Use the Move handle to drag one toolbar from on top of another one.

Note

If you drag a toolbar to a new location, it remains there until you move it again, even if you close PowerPoint.

Figure 20.4
Docked toolbars can appear at any side of the screen.

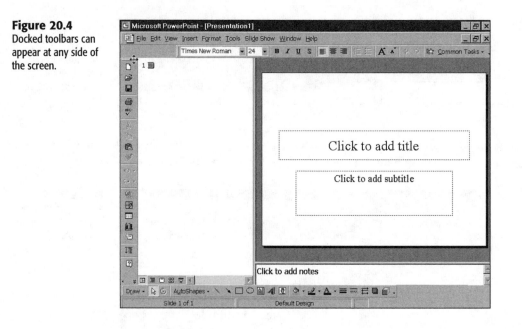

ADDING OR REMOVING TOOLBARS

The Standard and Formatting toolbars contain icons for the most commonly used PowerPoint procedures, such as saving, printing, editing, and formatting. If you need to have other features easily at hand, you can choose additional toolbars for specific tasks:

> **Note**
> Some toolbars appear automatically when you select a feature that is helped by the use of a toolbar. For example, if you select a picture, the Picture toolbar automatically appears.

- *Animation Effects*   This toolbar enables you to quickly add animation effects to text and picture objects and to preview the results without playing the slideshow.

- *Clipboard*   This toolbar enables you to view and selectively retrieve text or other objects you have copied to the Clipboard. You can also use this toolbar to clear the Clipboard memory.

- *Control Toolbox*   This toolbox is handy for building dialog boxes using Visual Basic. Most of you will probably never use it.

- *Outlining*   If you click in the Outline area of the tri-pane view, the Outlining toolbar automatically appears along the left side, ready to help you create or edit the slideshow outline.

- *Picture*   When you click a picture object, the Picture toolbar appears to help you modify the picture's colors, brightness, contrast, lines, and so on.

- *Reviewing* This toolbar assists in collaborative editing of a slideshow. Reviewers can add comments or review comments by others, create Outlook tasks, or send the show as an attachment via email.

- *Tables and Borders* With this toolbar, you can quickly and easily draw or edit freehand tables and borders.

- *Visual Basic* For advanced users, this toolbar assists in the creation of Visual Basic scripts.

- *Web* This toolbar can help you add hyperlinks and search for and link useful information from the Internet.

- *WordArt* Add or modify WordArt objects quickly and easily with this handy toolbar.

You never actually remove a toolbar. Instead, you close it or deselect it. Suppose, for example, that the Web toolbar is displayed, but you really don't need it and want to reclaim the screen space it takes up. Simply choose View, Toolbars, and click Web to deselect that toolbar.

Tip #232 from	
Read Gilgen	Don't forget that you can right-click any toolbar to display the Toolbar menu. You then select or deselect the toolbar from that menu.

As for floating toolbars, you can also close them by simply clicking the Close button at the right side of the title bar.

Note	
	When you close a toolbar that opened automatically, that toolbar no longer automatically opens when needed. You must open the toolbar from the menu to display it, and also to make it appear automatically in the future.

MODIFYING A TOOLBAR

Everyone uses PowerPoint differently. You use some of the buttons on the PowerPoint toolbars on a regular basis, whereas you rarely or never use others. PowerPoint makes it easy to add or remove buttons. Follow these steps:

1. Click the More Buttons button (see Figure 20.5).

PART
VI
CH
20

More Buttons

Figure 20.5
Click the More Buttons icon to reveal toolbar icons that aren't displayed or to add or remove icons from the toolbar.

2. Click the Add or Remove Buttons button. This displays a complete list of currently selected and commonly used buttons associated with that particular toolbar (see Figure 20.6).

Figure 20.6
Select or deselect commands to add or remove icons from a toolbar by clicking the Add or Remove Buttons button.

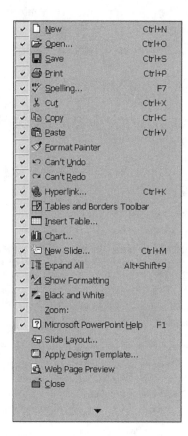

3. Move the mouse pointer to the down arrow at the bottom of the list to scroll down or to the up arrow at the top of the list to scroll up.

4. Click a button to select or deselect the button. PowerPoint automatically adds buttons to the end of the toolbar or removes buttons from wherever they're located on the toolbar.

Note

If you want to go back to the original toolbar, but forget which buttons it contained, simply scroll to the bottom of the Add or Remove Buttons menu and click Reset Toolbar.

These are only a few of the ways you can add, remove, or reposition buttons on a toolbar. At the bottom of the Add or Remove Buttons menu is the Customize option. Alternatively, you can choose View, Toolbars, Customize. Both methods display the Customize dialog box (see Figure 20.7).

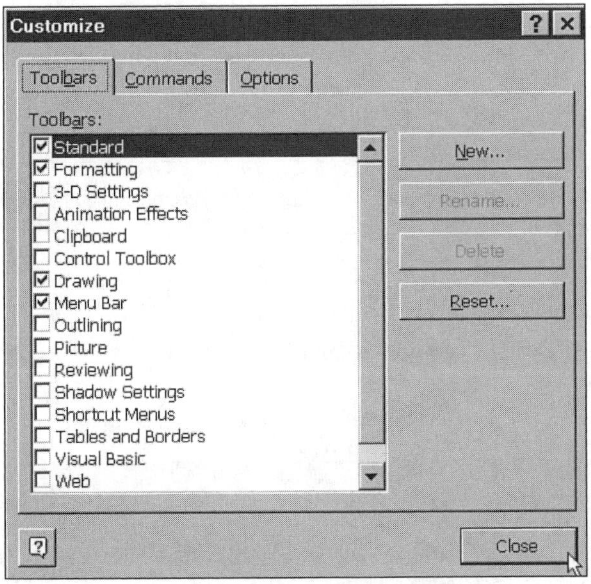

Figure 20.7
Use the Customize dialog box to customize PowerPoint toolbars.

The Toolbars tab displays a list of all standard PowerPoint toolbars, along with any toolbars you may have added. To add, remove, or reposition buttons on a toolbar, follow these steps:

1. Make sure the toolbar is visible. From the Toolbars tab, click the toolbar you want to appear on screen.

2. Click the Commands tab to display a comprehensive list of standard PowerPoint buttons (see Figure 20.8).

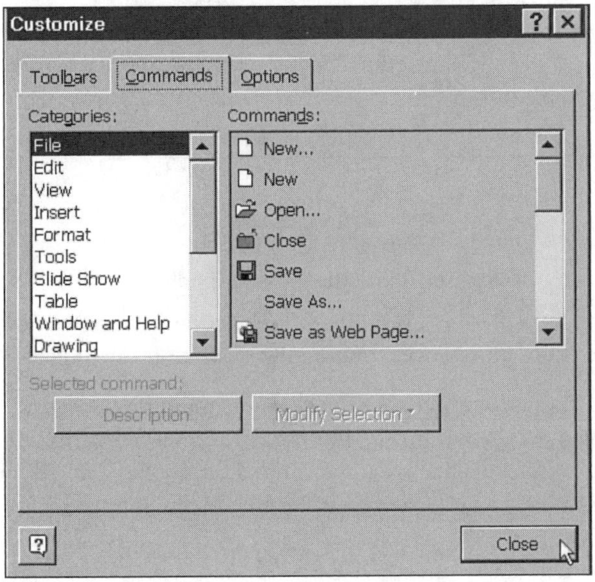

Figure 20.8
The Commands tab displays commands you can add to a toolbar.

3. Locate the command for the button you want to add. For example, if you want to add a button to help you quickly view your color slides in black and white (as they might be printed on a laser printer), first click View in the Categories list, then scroll through the Commands list until you find Black and White.

Tip #233 from

Read Gilgen

If you're not sure what a command is used for, select the command and click the Description button.

---

4. Click and drag the button to the target toolbar.
5. Position the button using the I-beam mouse pointer as a guide (see Figure 20.9) .

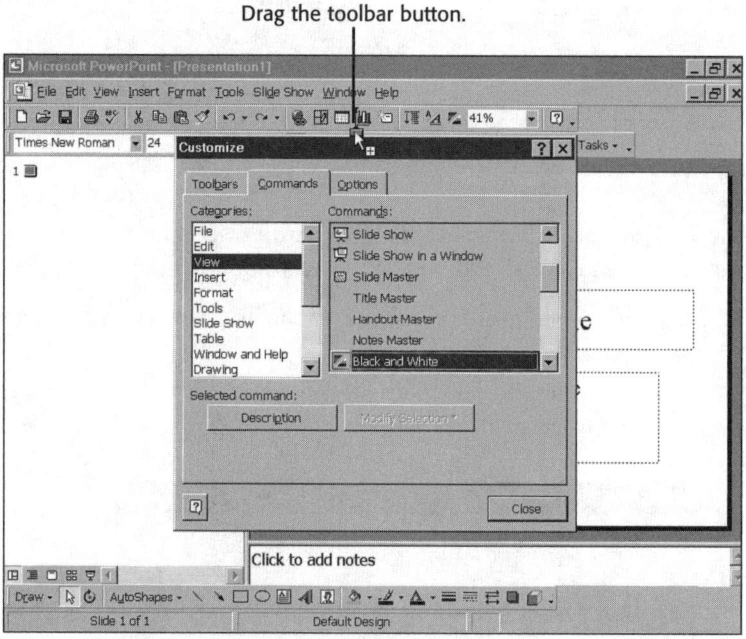

Drag the toolbar button.

Figure 20.9
Drag a command button to the target toolbar and use the I-beam pointer to position it.

6. Release the mouse button to add the button to the toolbar.
7. To save changes to the toolbar, simply close the Customize dialog box.

With the Customize dialog box still open, you can also reposition buttons by simply dragging them to their new location. To remove a button, just drag it off the toolbar.

Some commands are not icon buttons, but are drop-down menu buttons. Instead of executing a command or opening a dialog box, menu buttons provide a drop-down list of additional commands. Adding commands to a menu button is a bit trickier, but still not that difficult. Suppose you want to add a command to an existing menu button. Follow these steps:

1. Click the Commands tab in the Customize dialog box.

2. Locate the first button you want to add to the custom menu (for example, Insert, Duplicate Slide).

3. Drag the command button to the menu you want to change and wait until a menu drops down.

4. As you drag the command button up and down the menu, a horizontal line shows where you are about to insert the button (see Figure 20.10) .

Command is placed here.

Figure 20.10
A horizontal line shows where a command is to be added on a menu.

5. Drop the command on the drop-down menu.

6. Repeat steps 2–5 until you have added all the menu commands you want.

7. Click Close to close the Customize dialog box and to save changes to your toolbar menu.

As you add, move, or delete buttons, you may find that you want to group your buttons so they're more easily distinguished by function. You can do this by adding a vertical line between buttons on the toolbar. To add a group line, follow these steps:

1. With the Customize dialog box open, click the button on the far left in the group you want to separate.

2. Click the Modify Selection button to display a menu of choices (refer to Figure 20.8).

3. Click Begin a Group. PowerPoint adds a vertical line to the left of the selected button.

4. To remove a group line, simply repeat steps 1–3. Clicking Begin a Group a second time deselects the option and removes the line.

PART
VI

CH
20

If you make many changes to a toolbar, you'll find it's nearly impossible to remember which buttons are original to the toolbar and which ones you added. If you decide you want to restore your original toolbar, you can click the Toolbars tab in the Customize dialog box, select the toolbar you want to restore, and click Reset. PowerPoint asks if you're sure you want to do this, and if you're sure, just click OK.

CREATING A NEW TOOLBAR

If you're like many of us, it seems that the buttons we use on a regular basis are scattered about on different toolbars. Perhaps you'd like to create your own toolbar with all those buttons you use the most. Creating your own toolbar also means you won't have to modify PowerPoint's original toolbars.

To create your own toolbar, follow these steps:

1. Choose View, Toolbars, Customize to access the Customize dialog box.

2. Click the Toolbars tab.

3. Click the New button. PowerPoint displays the New Toolbar dialog box (see Figure 20.11).

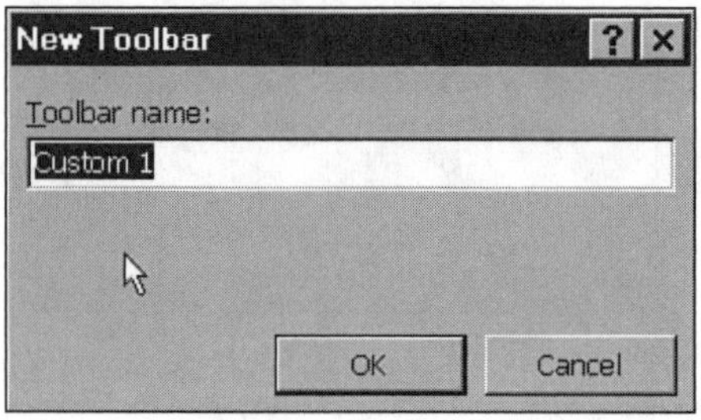

Figure 20.11
Create a new toolbar using the New Toolbar dialog box.

4. Edit the name of the toolbar (for example, "My Tools").

5. Click OK or press Enter, and PowerPoint displays a new floating toolbar (see Figure 20.12).

Figure 20.12
A new toolbar also needs command buttons to make it complete.

6. Click the Commands tab to add and arrange buttons and groups.

→ To learn more about accessing the Commands tab, **see** "Modifying a Toolbar," **p. 449**

7. Dock the toolbar along one of the sides of the screen, or position the floating toolbar where you want it to appear when you access it.

8. Close the Customize dialog box.

CUSTOMIZING TOOLBAR BUTTONS

The power and ease-of-use derived from using toolbars instead of menus depend largely on the ease with which you can visually identify a button and its function. If you find that PowerPoint's standard toolbar icons simply don't convey to you the visual information you need to quickly identify what the button does, you can modify the icon or even create an entirely new one.

To modify a toolbar icon, follow these steps:

1. Access the Customize dialog box by choosing <u>V</u>iew, <u>T</u>oolbars, <u>C</u>ustomize. Select the Tool<u>b</u>ars tab.

2. Select the toolbar that contains the icon you want to change (make sure the toolbar is visible).

3. Click the icon you want to change.

4. Click <u>M</u>odify Selection to display the menu that enables you to modify the icon (see Figure 20.13).

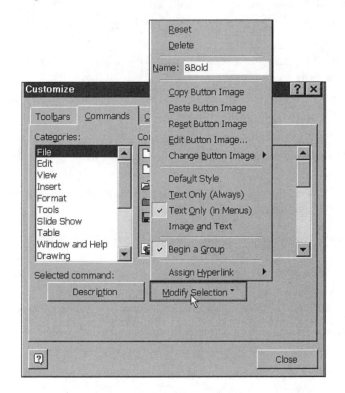

Figure 20.13
The Modify Selection menu enables you to customize a toolbar button.

PART
VI

CH
20

5. Choose the options you want to change.

6. Press Enter and close the Customize dialog box to save the changes.

Among the changes you can make are the following:

- *Reset*   This enables you to restore the icon to its original PowerPoint default. Any changes you have made to the icon will be lost.

- *Delete*   This removes the icon from the toolbar.

- *Name*   This is the text version of the icon that is used if you choose to display text along with or instead of the icon, or if the command appears in a toolbar menu. Also, if you point the mouse at the icon, a text prompt appears to remind you what the icon does. If you add the ampersand (&) before a letter in the name, that letter appears underlined in menus where you can select the command using the keyboard.

Tip #234 from

Read Gilgen

The name you choose can be very important in making it easy to identify the function of a button. Be as descriptive as possible, but also try to keep the name brief because the name may appear in menus as well.

- *Button Image commands*   These are used to modify the appearance of the icon itself.

- *Default Style*   This displays the icon as an image when it appears as a button, and as image and text when it is located in menus.

- *Text Only (Always)*   This ignores the image and displays only text, including the underlined character when appropriate.

- *Text Only (in Menus)*   This displays an image when the command is a button, but ignores the image when the command is located in menus.

- *Image and Text*   This displays both image and text, even when the command is a button.

- *Begin a Group*   This adds a vertical line to the left of the icon, helping to establish the beginning of a group of icons.

- *Assign Hyperlink*   This enables you to add a link to the icon which, when clicked, takes you to the Web or to another document or program.

→ For details on adding links to PowerPoint objects, **see** "Using PowerPoint's Web Features," **p. 337**

CUSTOMIZING TOOLBAR ICON IMAGES

Let's face it. Some toolbar icons simply don't mean anything to you. Fortunately, PowerPoint enables you to change the icon, or even to create your own icon image.

One simple way to change a button's icon is to identify another button that has an image you'd like to use, then copy that image to the button you want to change. To copy a button's image, follow these steps:

1. Access the toolbar Customize dialog box.

2. Locate the icon you want to copy and right-click it to display the Modify Button menu (see Figure 20.14).

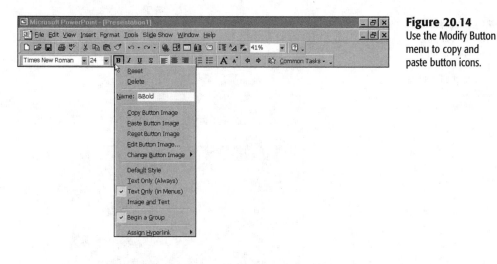

Figure 20.14
Use the Modify Button menu to copy and paste button icons.

You can copy any icon from any toolbar that's visible. You can also temporarily add a button to your current toolbar, copy it, and then delete it.

3. Choose Copy Button Image.

4. Locate the button you want to change and right-click it to display the Modify Button menu.

5. Choose Paste Button Image.

6. Close the Customize dialog box.

Note

Although you can do so, you should avoid having two identical images on the same toolbar. Furthermore, you should avoid using images that are commonly used for other functions (such as Save, Print, and so on).

Don't be afraid to experiment with changing toolbar icons. You want to create icons that work for you, and you can always reset the images if things go awry.

PART

VI

CH

20

You can also change the button icon by selecting an entirely different image or by creating or editing an entirely new image.

To select a new image, follow these steps:

1. Access the toolbar Customize dialog box.

2. Right-click the toolbar image you want to change.

3. Choose Change Button Image from the menu. PowerPoint displays a palette of image icons (see Figure 20.15).

Figure 20.15
If you don't like the current button image, you can choose from a palette of alternative images.

4. Click the image you want.

5. Close the Customize dialog box.

To edit an image, or to create your own, follow these steps:

1. Access the toolbar Customize dialog box.

2. Right-click the toolbar button you want to change.

3. Choose Edit Button Image from the menu. PowerPoint displays the Button Editor dialog box (see Figure 20.16).

4. Use the following tools to make changes to the image:

   - You can view the results of your changes in the Preview area of the dialog box.
   - You can move the entire image up, down, left, or right by clicking the arrows in the Move area of the dialog box.
   - Click a color from the Colors palette, and then click each "pixel" (square) to change its color.
   - Right-click a pixel to "pick up" the color from that pixel. Then continue using the left mouse button to use that color.
   - Click the Erase button and then click pixels to clear color from them.
   - Click the Clear button to erase the entire picture.
   - Click Cancel to abort any editing changes you have made.

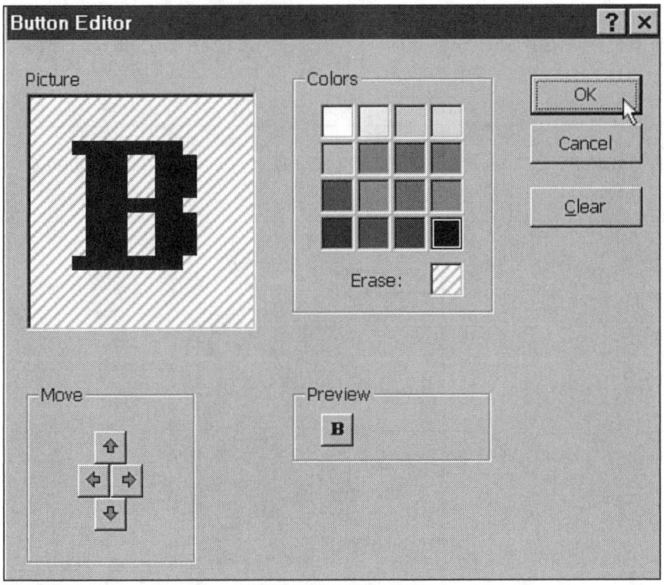

Button Editor

Picture

Colors

Erase:

Move

Preview

B

OK

Cancel

Clear

Figure 20.16
Let your creative side take over as you create or edit new button images.

Tip #237 from

Even if you plan to create your own image, you can get a head start by first changing the image to something that closely resembles what you want to create. You then simply edit that image instead of completely starting from scratch.

5. Click OK to accept your editing changes and to change the icon image on the toolbar.

6. Close the Customize dialog box.

If you decide you want to restore the original image to the toolbar button, follow these steps:

1. Right-click the toolbar and choose Customize.

2. Right-click the icon and choose Reset Button Image.

3. Close the Customize dialog box.

CUSTOMIZING MENU COMMANDS

By default, PowerPoint menus tailor themselves to the way you work. Initially, only the most commonly used commands appear on the menus (see Figure 20.17). If you click the Expand button (the double arrow) at the bottom of the menu or wait a few seconds, the menu expands to include other commands you have used rarely or not at all (see Figure

PART

VI

CH

20

20.18). If you begin to use a command regularly, PowerPoint then adds that command as a regular menu item.

 Although customizing menus is activated by default in PowerPoint, this option can be turned off.

Figure 20.17
By default, PowerPoint displays only the most common menu commands along with recently used commands.

Figure 20.18
Clicking the Expand menu button displays the full range of menu commands.

You can further customize how menus work by changing menu options, by adding or deleting menu commands, and even by adding entirely new menu categories.

Changing Menu Options

You customize menu options using the same dialog box you use for customizing toolbars. Access the Customize dialog box by right-clicking the menu bar and choosing Customize. Then click the Options tab. PowerPoint displays the following options (see Figure 20.19):

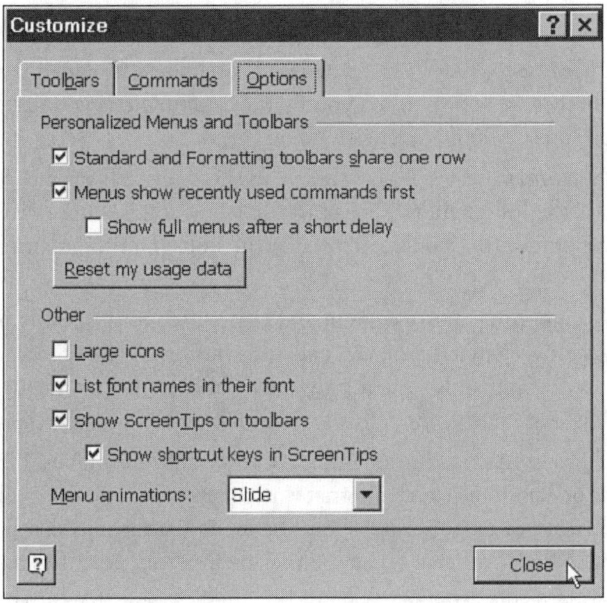

Figure 20.19
PowerPoint offers a wide range of toolbar options.

- *Standard and Formatting Toolbars Share One Row* In an effort to save screen space, PowerPoint displays both toolbars on one row. On high-resolution screens (for example, 1024×768), you may be able to see all of the buttons from both toolbars. On other screens, however, the toolbars are collapsed and you must click the More Buttons button to see and use the entire list of buttons (see Figure 20.20).

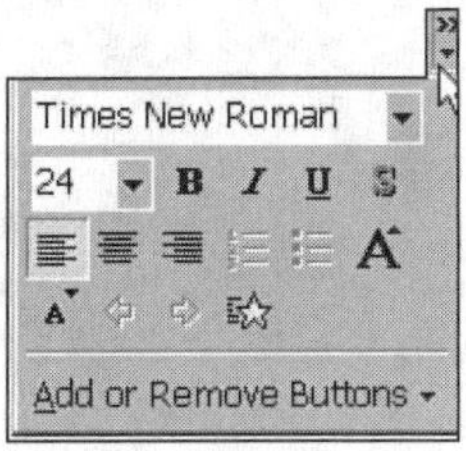

Figure 20.20
Click the More Buttons button if you want to see toolbar commands that aren't displayed but which are active.

This may be confusing or it may require too much effort to constantly access the More Buttons button. If so, deselect this option so that each toolbar appears on its own row (see Figure 20.21).

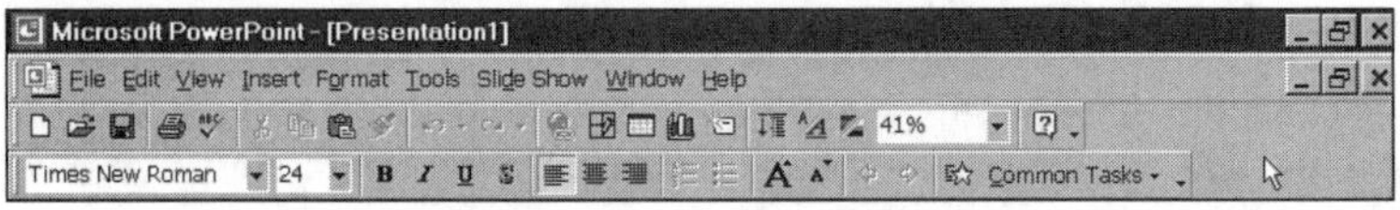

Figure 20.21
The Standard and Formatting toolbars can be displayed separately, but they then take up two toolbar rows.

- *Menus Show Recently Used Commands First*   The basic commands, along with any commands you have used recently, appear when you first click a menu. If you deselect this option, all commands appear when you click a menu.

- *Show Full Menus After a Short Delay*   If you choose to show recently used commands first, this option allows the full menu to appear after a few seconds. Otherwise, you must click the Expand button (the double arrows) at the bottom of the menu to see the entire menu.

- *Reset My Usage Data*   Suppose you use a command quite often for a specific project, but don't otherwise use it very much. You can click this button to reset the history of your use of PowerPoint's commands so that only the default menu commands appear. You then begin establishing once again a history of commands as you use them.

- *Menu Animations*   If you want to add some pizzazz to the way your menus display, choose Unfold, Slide, or Random (which alternates the first two methods). Slide simply slides the menu down from the top. Unfold slides the menu both from the top and from the left. The default is None, probably because either method can be rather distracting.

- *Large Icons*   This option displays the icons about four times larger than usual (see Figure 20.22). You probably won't use this option unless you are visually impaired or you have a very high-resolution screen and have the room required for large icons.

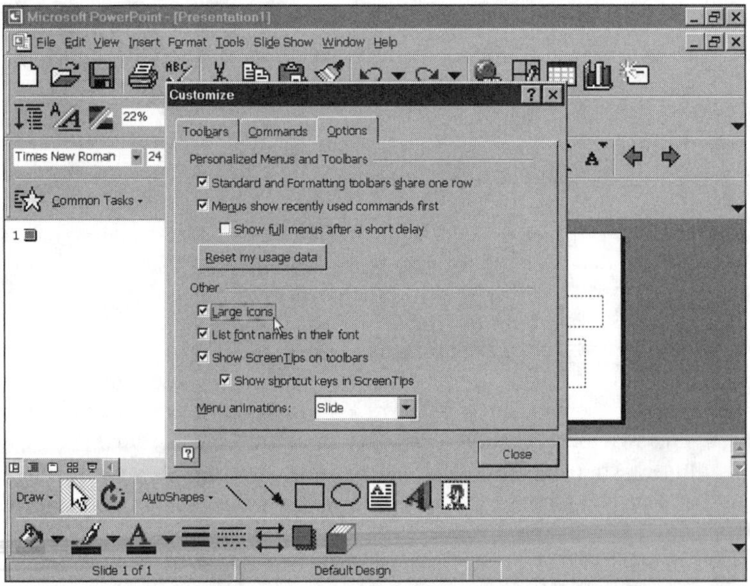

Figure 20.22
Large icons are useful for the visually impaired, but otherwise take up too much of the screen to be useful.

Tip #238 from

Read Gilgen

Although the Large Icons option takes up a lot of space, you can create a custom toolbar with a minimal set of icons that fit on a single row. (See "Creating a New Toolbar" in this chapter.)

■ *List Font Names in Their Font*   By default, PowerPoint displays font names in the toolbar font list using the actual fonts (see Figure 20.23). This may cause the list to appear slowly, especially on older, slower computers. To list them in a standard Windows font, deselect this option.

Figure 20.23
You can display font lists using the fonts themselves or a standard Windows font.

■ *Show ScreenTips on Toolbars*   When you point at a toolbar button, PowerPoint displays the name of the button in a small yellow box. This helps identify the button if you can't discern its use by the icon image alone. If you want to turn off this option, deselect it.

■ *Show Shortcut Keys in ScreenTips*   Believe it or not, lots of people still prefer to use the keyboard whenever possible. This option enables them to see whether a toolbar button command has an equivalent keystroke, such as F5 to View a Slide Show or Ctrl+S to save a presentation.

Tip #238 from

Read Gilgen

Although using the mouse may make it easier to find features and commands you don't often use, usually you can access commands more quickly by using keyboard equivalents. For example, if you're already typing, pressing Ctrl+S to save the presentation is faster than moving your hand to the mouse, then finding and clicking the Save button on the toolbar. Use toolbar button ScreenTips to learn keystrokes that can save you time.

PART

VI

CH

20

CREATING A NEW MENU ON THE MENU BAR

If you find using menus easier than using toolbars, you can create and add your own menus to the menu bar. Suppose, for example, you want your own Quick Stuff menu, using the letter *Q* as the hotkey. On that menu, you intend to add items from the Formatting toolbar because you plan not to display that toolbar.

> **Note**
>
> The menu bar functions and is modified in exactly the same way as toolbars. That is, not only can you add menu items to toolbars, but you can add command buttons or icons to the menu bar. Information in preceding sections about modifying toolbars applies also to customizing menu bars.

To create a new menu and to add items to that menu, follow these steps:

1. Access the Customize dialog box by right-clicking the menu and choosing Customize.

2. Click the Commands tab in the Customize dialog box.

3. Scroll to the bottom of the Categories list and click New Menu.

4. Drag the New Menu button from the Commands list to the menu bar. You can place the button anywhere on the menu bar, not only at the end (see Figure 20.24).

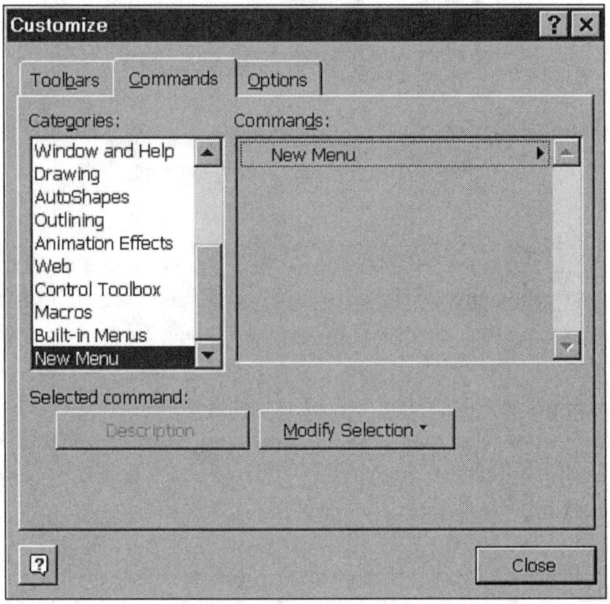

Figure 20.24
Create new menu items and place them anywhere on a menu or toolbar.

5. Click the Modify Selection button. PowerPoint displays the Modify Selection menu (see Figure 20.25).

6. Choose Name and edit the text to change the name from "New Menu" to something more descriptive of the menu's purpose (for example, "Quick Stuff"). If you want to make Q the hotkey, place an ampersand (&) before the letter Q. Press Enter or click anywhere outside of the menu to close the menu.

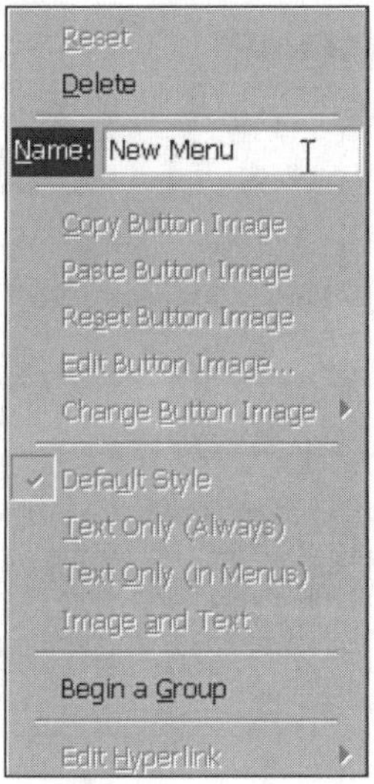

Figure 20.25
The Modify Selection menu enables you to customize new menus.

7. Next, locate the first button you want to add to the custom menu (for example, Format, Bold).

8. Drag the command button to the new menu button (for example, Quick Stuff) and wait until a menu drops down. The first time you do this, the menu consists of nothing more than a blank gray square (see Figure 20.26).

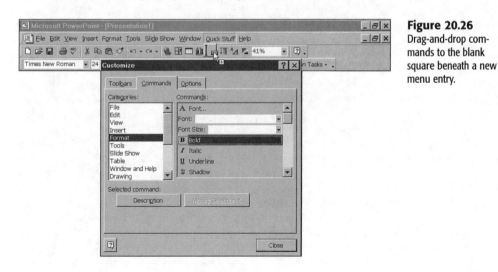

Figure 20.26
Drag-and-drop commands to the blank square beneath a new menu entry.

9. Drop the command on the drop-down menu (or blank square). As you drag the button up and down the menu, a horizontal line indicates where you will drop the button.

10. Repeat steps 7–9 until you have added the menu commands you want.

SETTING POWERPOINT OPTIONS

PowerPoint enables you to change many basic options, such as how screens are viewed and how you edit, save, or print your presentations.

> **Note**
>
> Changes you make in the Options dialog box become your new default settings until you change them again.

> **Tip #240 from**
>
> *Read Gilgen*
>
> Whenever you use a new program or an update to a program, your first inclination is to try to make the program do things the "old way" or the way you're used to doing them. Although it can be tempting to jump right in and make changes to PowerPoint's default settings, you probably should use PowerPoint "as is" for a while, at least, until you decide whether those default settings might actually be better.

To access the Options dialog box, choose Tools, Options (see Figure 20.27).

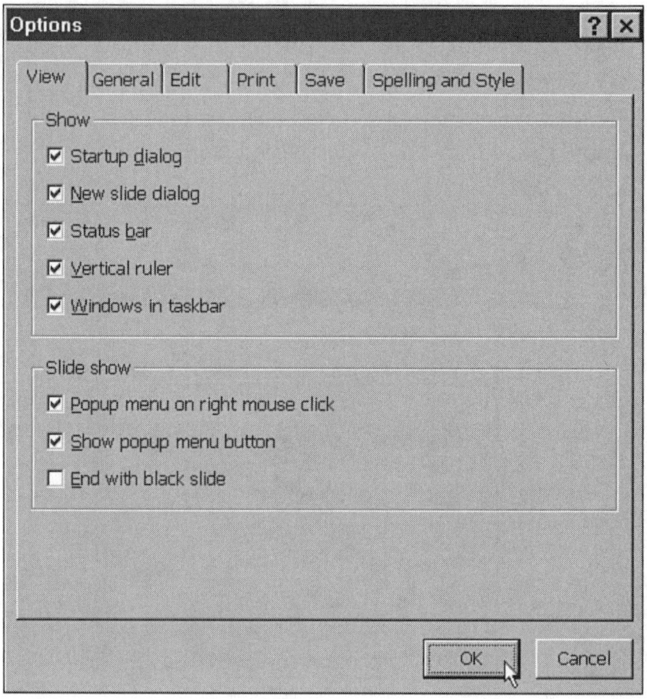

Figure 20.27
The Options dialog box is used to change many of PowerPoint's default settings.

SETTING VIEW OPTIONS

Click the View tab to display options that affect what you see as you create and edit a slideshow, as well as what you see when you play the slideshow (refer to Figure 20.27).

Show options include:

- *Startup dialog* If, when you start PowerPoint, you want to bypass the opening dialog box that prompts you for a template or an existing file, deselect this option.

- *New slide dialog* If you deselect this option, PowerPoint automatically begins a new slideshow with a title slide without asking you first.

- *Status Bar* Although the status bar does take up a bit of territory at the bottom of the screen, it shows you which slide you're editing (when in tri-pane or Slide view), as well as the design you're using. Also, the spelling icon appears with a red "x" if anything on the current slide is misspelled.

Tip #241 from *Read Gilgen*	If you double-click the design name on the status bar, PowerPoint opens the Apply Design Template dialog box, enabling you to quickly change the background template. Double-clicking the spelling icon begins the spelling feature.

- *Vertical Ruler* If you choose to display rulers (View, Ruler), this option displays a vertical ruler along with the horizontal ruler.

Slide Show options include:

- *Popup Menu on Right Mouse Click* When presenting a slideshow, you need an easy way to access navigation and other options. With this option, you can right-click on the slide to display a menu of options.

- *Show Popup Menu Button* By default, when you play a PowerPoint slideshow, PowerPoint displays a small icon at the lower left corner of the slide. Clicking this icon gives you the same menu as the one you get when you right-click the slide. If you don't want this icon on the screen, deselect this option.

- *End with Black Slide* If you deselect this option, PowerPoint returns to the PowerPoint editing screen when you conclude your slideshow. Leaving this option active makes for a cleaner ending.

SETTING GENERAL OPTIONS

Click the General tab to change information about yourself and other items not easily grouped into a specific category (see Figure 20.28). General options include:

- *Provide Feedback with Sound to Screen Elements* To add sound effects for menus, buttons, and other screen elements, select this option.

Note	Changing this option in PowerPoint changes it for all Office 2000 applications. However, you may have to restart Windows for this option to take effect. Also, you may find that other sound schemes take precedence over these sound effects.

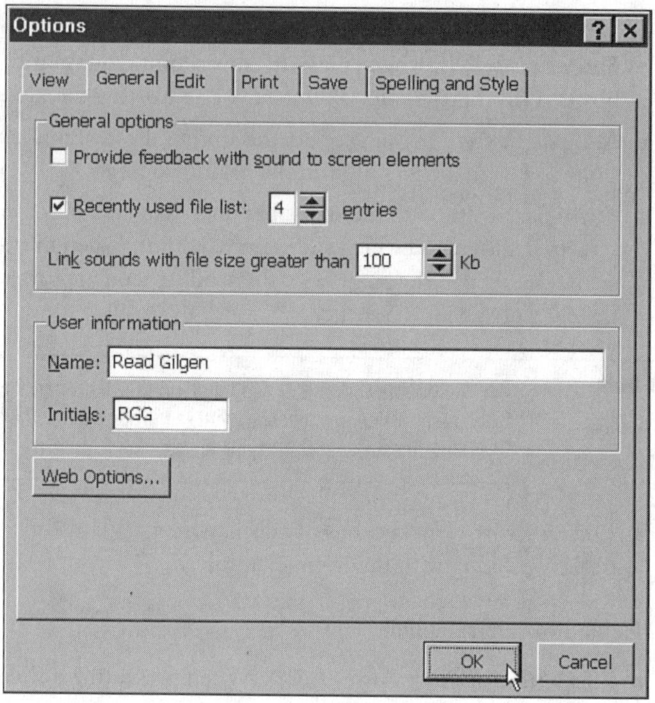

Figure 20.28
The General tab of the Options dialog box offers miscellaneous PowerPoint settings.

- *Recently Used File List:* nn *Number of Entries*   By default, PowerPoint displays the four most recently opened files at the bottom of the File menu. You can increase this number up to nine or reduce it to none.

- *Link Sounds with File Size Greater than* nn *Kb*   PowerPoint normally saves sound files as part of the PowerPoint presentation itself. However, large sound files can make a presentation unwieldy. Selecting this option means that files larger than the size specified are *not* included with the slide show, but instead are linked from their current file location.

- *Name*   Whenever you use options that require your name, such as in the Properties Summary (File, Properties), PowerPoint automatically uses the name found here.

- *Initials*   Whenever user initials are required—for example, during a NetMeeting—PowerPoint automatically uses the initials found here.

- *Web Options*   For details on various Web output options, including formatting, graphic formats, and the like, see Chapter 15, "Using PowerPoint's Web Features."

SETTING EDIT OPTIONS

Click the Edit tab to change options for editing text and charts (see Figure 20.29). These options include:

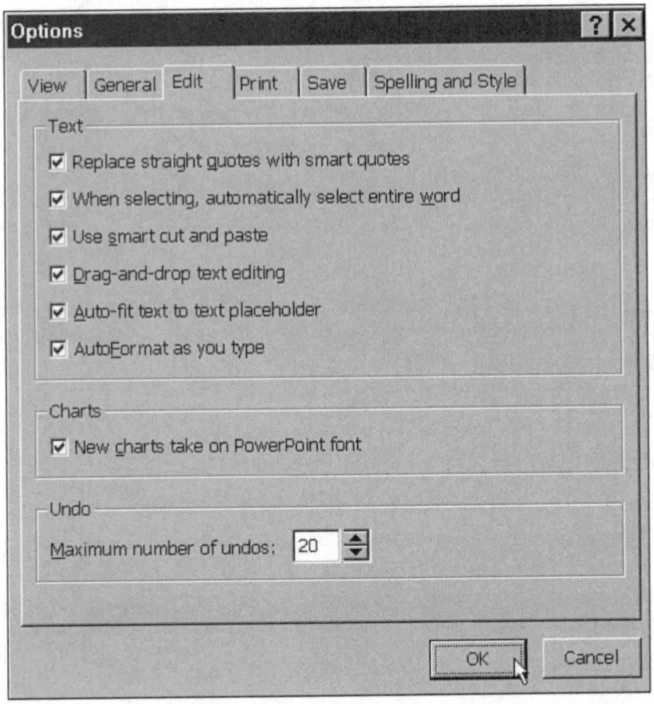

Figure 20.29
The Edit tab of the Options dialog box offers options for text and chart editing.

- *Replace Straight Quotes with Smart Quotes (" ")*   Typographically correct quotes ("") generally look better, but you can use standard, vertically straight quote marks ("") by deselecting this option.

- *When Selecting, Automatically Select Entire <u>W</u>ord*   If you want to select only portions of words when using a mouse, deselect this option.

- *Use <u>S</u>mart Cut and Paste*   The spacing around added or deleted text adjusts to add a space between words or to remove a space before a period, unless you deselect this option.

- *<u>D</u>rag-and-Drop Text Editing*   Clicking selected text and dragging it to a new location is the same as cutting and pasting. If you find this happens accidentally with too much frequency, you may need to deselect this option.

- *<u>A</u>uto-fit Text to Text Placeholder*   Like the option says, checking this will make PowerPoint try to automatically fit text within any text placeholder box on a slide.

- *Auto<u>F</u>ormat as You Type*   See Chapter 3, "Working with Text," for more information on the AutoFormat feature.

- *New <u>C</u>harts Take on PowerPoint Font*   If you clear this option, charts will use a generic default font (for example, Arial) instead of the font and style being used in the current slide.

PART
VI
CH
20

Tip #242 from

Read Gilgen

Although it may seem like a good idea to use the default PowerPoint fonts when creating a new chart, more generic fonts may actually look better. You may want to create test charts using both font methods before actually developing the data or making other modifications.

- *Maximum Number of Undos:* nn   By default, you can undo the last 20 actions. You can decrease the number of undos to as few as 3 or increase it to as many as 150.

Caution

Increasing the number of undos increases the size of your document and also increases the risk of corrupting your document. Unless you really need more, stay with the default number, or fewer.

CHANGING PRINT OPTIONS

To change general printing defaults or to change settings for the current document only, click the Print tab (see Figure 20.30).

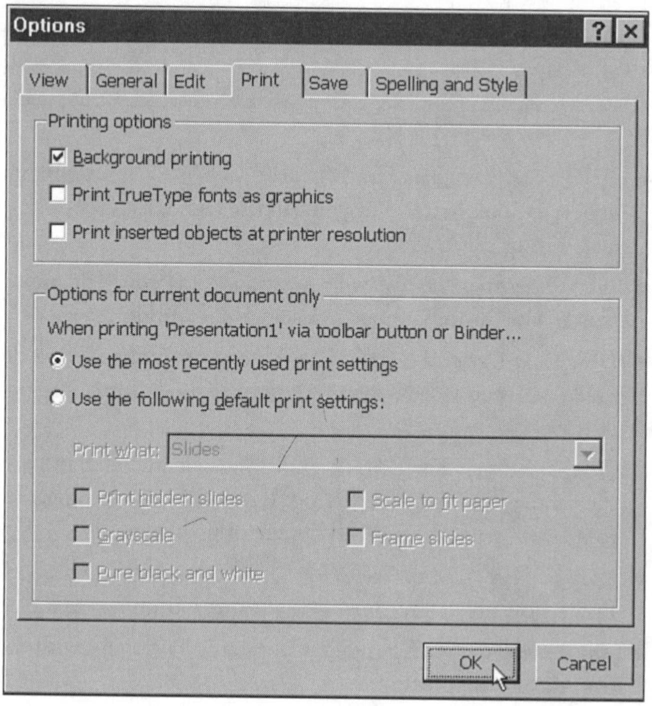

Figure 20.30
The Print tab of the Options dialog box offers several default printing options.

General printing options include:

- *Background Printing*   This option enables you to continue editing your slide presentation while PowerPoint prints slides in the background.

- *Print TrueType Fonts as Graphics* If your printer has trouble printing the fonts used in your presentation, it could be that your printer cannot recognize them or you are using too many fonts for your printer to keep track of. Choosing this option sends text to the printer as graphics, thus bypassing the downloading of fonts to your printer. However, this option generally makes printing much slower.

- *Print Inserted Objects at Printer Resolution* This helps match graphic resolutions to the printer that's printing them. For example, your graphic image might have been created at only 72 dots-per-inch (dpi), but your printer can print at a much crisper 600 dpi. Selecting this option may slow printing.

When you print your current document using the Printer icon on the toolbar or via the Binder, by default you use the most recently used PowerPoint print settings. You can also choose to Use the Following Default Print Settings:

- *Print What* By default, PowerPoint prints slides without animations. However, you can change the default to:
  - Slides (with or without animations) If you print without animations, the entire slide is printed on one page. Printing with animations means that you get several pages, each with successive additions of animated text objects (for example, adding one bullet at a time).
  - Handouts You can print two, three, or six slides per page.
  - Notes Pages This prints a small version of the slide, along with any speaker notes you may have created.
  - Outline View This printout appears exactly as it does in PowerPoint's Outline view.

- *Print Hidden Slides* If you have hidden slides in your PowerPoint presentation, you can choose to include them in the printed version.

- *Grayscale* PowerPoint can automatically convert some of the background colors to various shades of gray, preserving some of the effect of the background design. This option also enables you to print text, especially white text, that is in an Autoshape.

Note

To preview how your printout will look in grayscale, choose View, Black and White. Choose this option again to return to a color view.

PART

VI

CH

20

- *Pure Black and White* If this option prints any background at all, it does so only in black and white, without shades of gray. All text and graphic elements are printed in black and white.

- *Scale to Fit Paper* If you're using other than standard-sized paper, this option enables PowerPoint to scale the slides to fit that size paper.

- *Frame Slides* This option places a single, thin-line border around the entire printed slide.

Don't forget that print options selected from the Options menu apply *only* to automatic printing from the toolbar icon. Choosing File, Print still enables you to choose specific print options before printing.

SETTING SAVE OPTIONS

Click the Save tab to view and change Save options (see Figure 20.31).

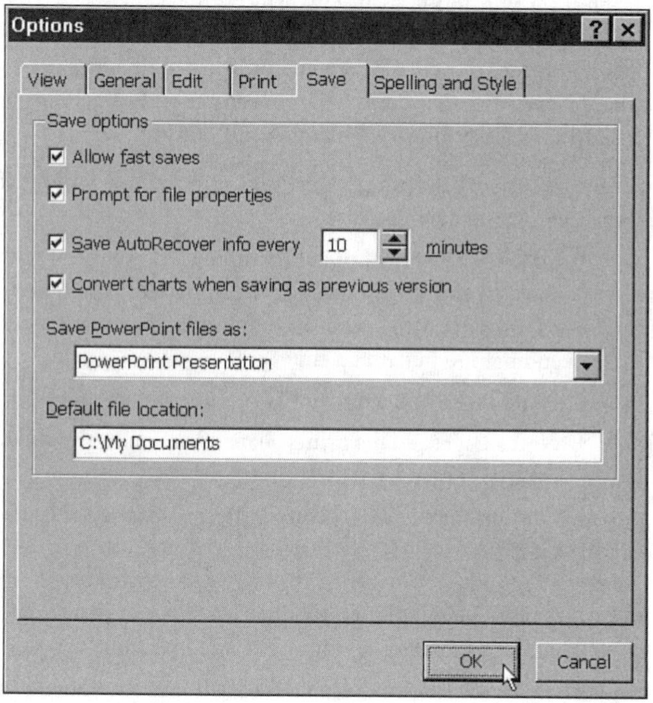

Figure 20.31
The Save tab of the Options dialog box helps change default file saving options.

These include:

- *Allow Fast Saves* — By default, PowerPoint saves only the changes made to a presentation since the last time it was saved, which obviously takes less time than saving the full presentation. However, this also requires more disk space, so if your computer is already fast enough, you may want to consider deselecting this option. Turning this option off also avoids reported problems with file corruption when using Fast Save.

- *Prompt for File Properties* — The Summary, found in File, Properties, helps document the authorship and revision history of your slide presentation. If this is important to you, select this option which automatically brings up the Properties screen the first time the document is saved, or whenever it is saved with a different name.

- *Save AutoRecover Info Every* nn *Minutes* — This is the automatic backup provision that saves a temporary copy of your presentation (typically in the \Windows\Temp folder) as frequently as you specify with this option. If you exit your document properly, the automatic backup file is erased. If you don't exit properly (for example, due to a power failure), PowerPoint automatically opens this file the next time you use PowerPoint so that you can determine whether it contains data you didn't save.

- *Convert Charts When Saving as Previous Version* When saving the presentation to an earlier version of PowerPoint, use this option to convert charts to a format also understood by earlier versions of PowerPoint.

- *Save PowerPoint Files As* By default, PowerPoint saves its files in a PowerPoint 2000 format, which is the same as the PowerPoint 97 format. This format cannot be opened in earlier versions of PowerPoint, such as Office 95.

  However, PowerPoint 2000 can open presentations created in earlier versions. If you work in an environment where not everyone is using PowerPoint 2000, you may need to agree upon a common format to be used by everyone. Then change this option to one of the following formats:

  - PowerPoint presentation, which can be opened and edited in PowerPoint 2000 or PowerPoint 97.
  - PowerPoint 97-2000 & 95 Presentation
  - PowerPoint 4.0 Presentation
  - Web Page

> **Caution**
>
> Be aware that saving a PowerPoint 2000 presentation in an earlier format may result in the loss of certain features available only in PowerPoint 2000.

- *Default File Location* PowerPoint saves your presentations in the folder you specify. Initially this is usually C:\My Documents, but that may vary depending on how PowerPoint was installed.

SETTING SPELLING AND STYLE OPTIONS

Click the Spelling and Style tab to change default spelling and style options (see Figure 20.32). These options include:

- *Check Spelling as You Type* The red hash marks under words indicate that they are misspelled, enabling you to make corrections as you go.

> **Tip #243 from**
> *Read Gilgen*
>
> If you right-click a misspelled word, PowerPoint displays a menu with suggested correct spellings. Simply select the correct spelling to change the word.

- *Hide Spelling Errors in This Document* This option overrides Check Spelling as You Type and hides the red hash marks that indicate misspelled words.

- *Always Suggest Corrections*   Suggested spellings are displayed when you perform a spelling check.

- *Ignore Words in UPPERCASE*   Spelling errors found in uppercase words are ignored. For example, you might use this option if you use a lot of proper names that aren't usually found in the dictionary.

- *Ignore Words with Numbers*   Words with numbers are often correct, but not found in the dictionary.

- *Check Style*   This option enables or disables style checking of such things as case, end punctuation, and visual clarity. For information on Style Options, see Chapter 3, "Working with Text."

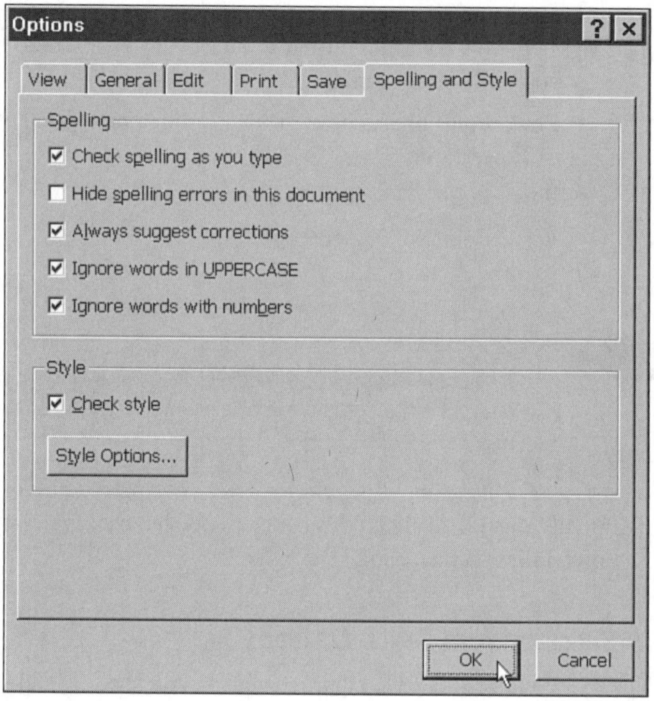

Figure 20.32
The Spelling and Style tab of the Options dialog box customizes correction tool options.

SPECIFYING PAGE SETUP

By default, PowerPoint slides are designed to fit a computer screen when the presentation is played. However, if the presentation's targeted destination is a printed page or a 35mm slide, you can change the *page setup (p. 179–180)* to match that destination.

Tip #244 from
Read Gilgen

If you know ahead of time that your page setup will need to be changed, you can save a lot of reformatting and design time by changing the page setup *before* creating the presentation.

To change the page setup for a PowerPoint presentation, choose File, Setup (see Figure 20.33). Choose from among these options:

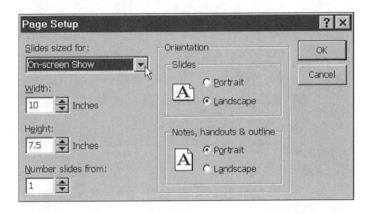

Figure 20.33
Use the Page Setup dialog box to define the shape and size of your slides before you begin creating your presentation.

- *Slides Sized For*   From the drop-down menu, choose the size slide you want: Screen size, regular 8.5"×11" paper, A4 size paper (210mm×297mm), 35mm slide, Overhead transparency, Banner, or a custom size. When you select one of these standard sizes, PowerPoint automatically changes the width and height measurements.

- *Width and Height*   Changing either of these changes the Slides Sized for option to Custom.

- *Number Slides From*   If you use slide numbering—for example, on printed slides—you can specify the number of the first slide.

- *Orientation*   You can choose whether to use landscape or portrait orientation for slides or for notes, handouts, and outlines. By default, slides use a landscape page setup; whereas, the others use a portrait orientation.

SETTING PRESENTATION PROPERTIES

PART
VI
CH
20

As you create and modify your presentation, you automatically change many of the presentation's properties. You can view these properties and also change or add other properties to the document by choosing File, Properties. PowerPoint displays a dialog box with the name of your presentation (see Figure 20.34).

Some of the tabs simply show information about your slideshow. For example, the Contents tab (see Figure 20.35) tells you which fonts you have used, the design template you used, and so on.

The Summary tab (refer to Figure 20.34) enables you to enter custom information about the presentation. This information can be useful when you have to find the file because you can use keywords, for example, even if you can't remember the name of the file.

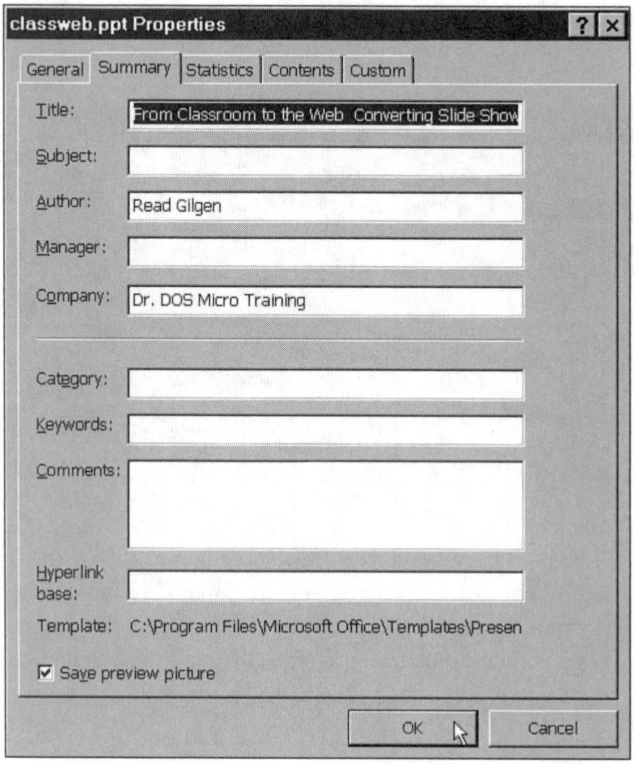

Figure 20.34
Presentation Properties add information to your file that can be used for finding and organizing your presentations.

To customize the presentation's summary, simply fill in the information you think is important. Assuming you created the document and that you supplied your name when you installed PowerPoint, the author's name appears automatically. The title is taken from the first slide of the presentation, but you can change that if desired.

The Save Preview Picture option simply enables you to see a preview of the first slide when you browse the file (see Figure 20.36). If you deselect this option, you cannot preview the file in the Open dialog box.

Figure 20.35
The Contents tab of the Presentation Properties tells you, and others, what kinds of elements the presentation contains.

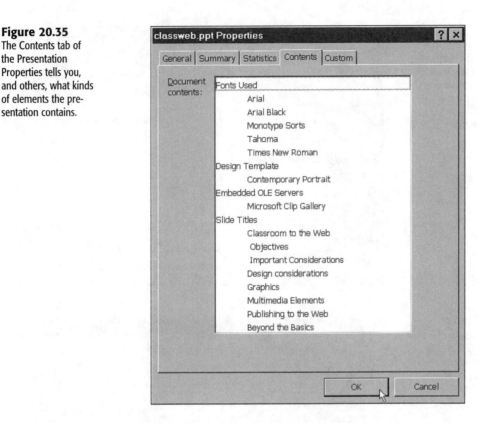

If you choose the Custom tab (see Figure 20.37), you can create a series of customized properties that further categorize your document. Unless you have a great number of presentations that need a high degree of organization, you'll probably never use this option. If you do, refer to PowerPoint's online help for information on how to create a custom property.

PART
VI
CH
20

Figure 20.36
You can use the Save Preview Picture option so that, as you browse for a PowerPoint presentation, you can view the first slide before opening the file.

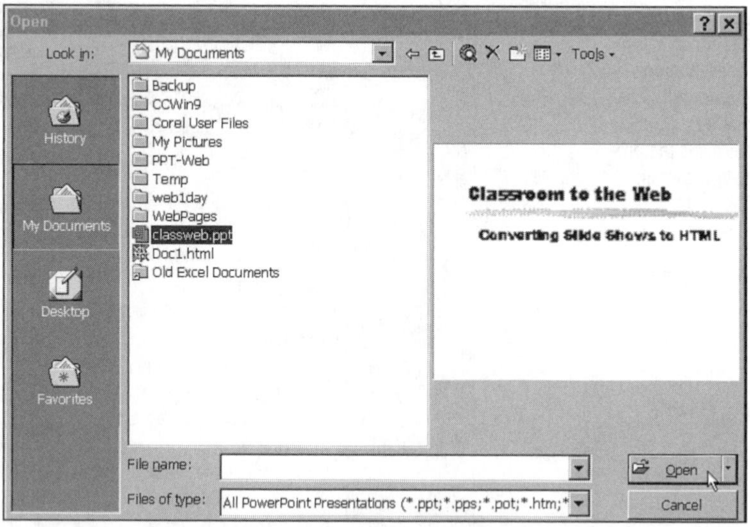

Figure 20.37
Custom properties help you find presentations by searching for unique characteristics you define.

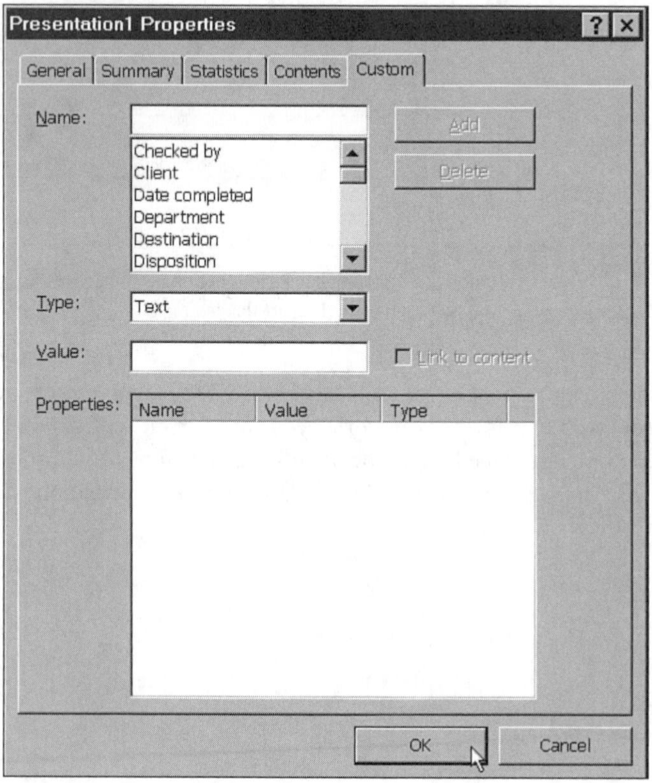

USING ADD-IN PROGRAMS

Add-ins are special supplemental programs, usually provided by third-party sources to extend and enhance the capabilities of PowerPoint. Add-ins range from programs that add multimedia capabilities to those that simply enhance PowerPoint's default menus or toolbars.

Some add-ins are free; others you will have to pay for. You can even write your own custom add-in programs by using PowerPoint's Visual Basic Editor. Also, you can find many add-ins on the Web. Look at the Microsoft Web site for those provided by Microsoft or do a Web search for "addins" and "PowerPoint" to find possible PowerPoint enhancements elsewhere on the Web.

Suppose you find an add-in that enhances the shadow control toolbar. Although not an earthshaking add-in, it does add some helpful controls for dealing with object shadows. To add this, or any other add-in, follow these steps:

1. Choose Tools, Add-Ins. PowerPoint displays the Add-Ins dialog box that lists add-ins that have already been installed (see Figure 20.38).

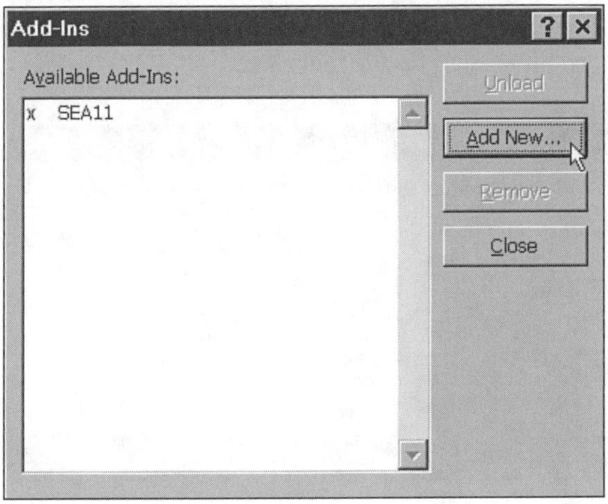

Figure 20.38
Add-ins add powerful functionality to PowerPoint.

2. Choose Add New. PowerPoint opens the Add New PowerPoint Add-In dialog box (see Figure 20.39). By default, PowerPoint looks in the AddIns folder (for example, C:\Windows\Application Data\Microsoft\AddIns) to find add-in programs that have a .PPA filename extension. If the add-in you're looking for isn't in the default folder, browse to its location.

3. Select the add-in you want to install, then choose OK.

PART
VI

CH
20

Note

Some add-ins created for PowerPoint 97 still work in PowerPoint 2000.

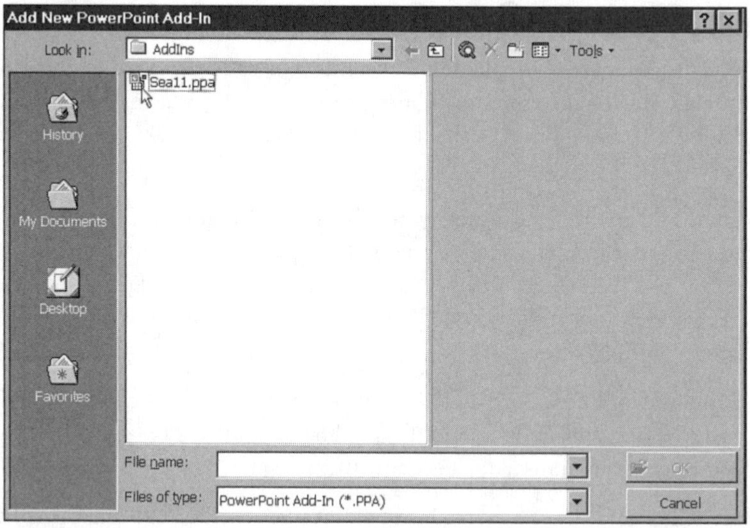

Figure 20.39
PowerPoint add-ins have a .PPA filename extension and usually are found in the Add-Ins folder.

4. If the add-in contains macros, as virtually all add-ins do, a warning message appears that allows you to disable the macros (see Figure 20.40). However, if you want the full functionality of the add-in, you'll need to enable the macros.

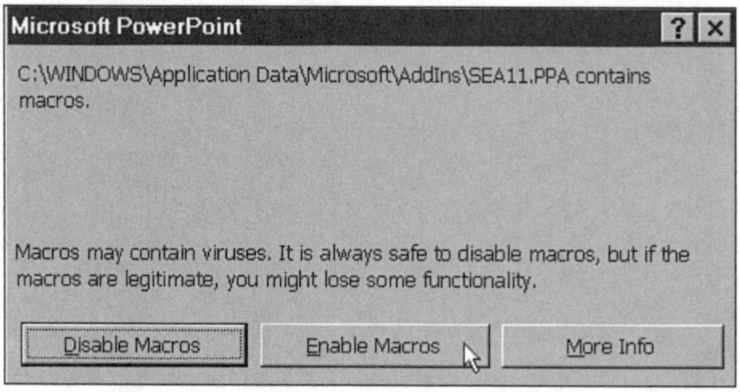

Figure 20.40
Use caution in opening add-ins that require you to run macros because they might carry viruses.

> **Caution**
>
> Macros can contain viruses that in turn can wreak havoc on your computer. You should always exercise caution when enabling macros from unknown sources. Knowing the source of the add-in can help protect you from such viruses. If you're not sure, it's probably best not to use an add-in that contains macros.

5. After the add-in is installed, its name appears in the A̲vailable Add-Ins list (refer to Figure 20.38) with an "x" to the left of it. This means that the add-in is also loaded and ready to use.

6. Choose C̲lose to return to PowerPoint.

You now can use the add-in as you work with your PowerPoint presentation.

WORKING WITH SLIDE MASTERS

PowerPoint is designed to help you achieve a consistent look in your slide presentations. You want your audience to focus on the message and not be distracted by poor and inconsistent design from one slide to the next.

You achieve this consistency by using *templates*, or pre-designed slide presentations, that coordinate background colors and designs, font styles and placement, and other graphic design elements. A good common use for templates is putting a border with your company's name and logo on every slide in the Master layout.

When you first begin using PowerPoint, you should use the templates that come with the program. As you become an experienced PowerPoint user, you may want to experiment by creating your own templates that meet your specific design requirements.

→ For information on using design templates or how to change slide backgrounds and color schemes, **see** "Formatting Slides and Presentations," **p. 117**

CREATING A DESIGN TEMPLATE

Creating your own design template is as easy as modifying the elements of your slideshow and saving it as a template. To save your presentation as a template, follow these steps:

1. Choose File, Save As.

2. In the Save As dialog box, Change the Save as Type to Design Template (*.pot). PowerPoint automatically switches to the template folder.

3. Supply a File Name; for example, MyShow (you do not need to add .pot).

4. Choose Save.

The next time you want to build a slide presentation based on this template, simply choose File, New, and choose the name of your customized PowerPoint template.

MODIFYING THE SLIDE MASTER

Every slide presentation is based on a slide master of some sort. The slide master determines, for example, which font appears on each slide and how it is to be formatted.

PART

VI

CH

20

To modify your slide master, follow these steps:

1. Choose View, Master, Slide Master. PowerPoint displays the Slide Master layout and editing screen (see Figure 20.41).

Figure 20.41
The Slide Master editing screen helps you change the overall look and layout of your custom design templates.

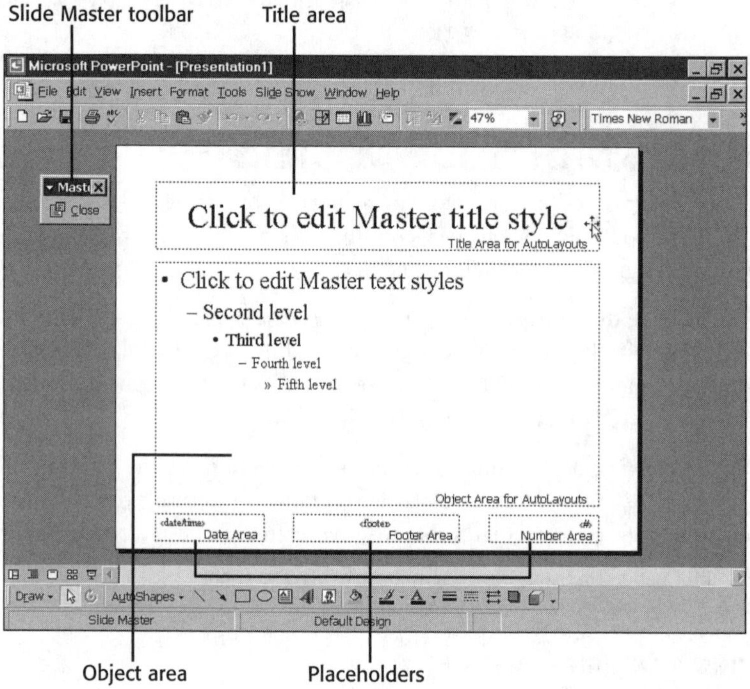

2. Click the Title Area for AutoLayouts box and change the font, style, color, or other properties of the title text.

Note

All changes to the title or other text while in the Slide Master editing screen apply to *all* slides in your slide presentation except those based on the Title Master, thus helping you achieve consistency from slide to slide.

Tip #246 from

Read Gilgen

If you choose to relocate text or other objects, you can use the ruler and guides to help you. Simply choose View, Ruler, and View, Guides to display these aids.

3. Click the Object Area for AutoLayouts box and make similar changes to the font, style, color, bullets, and so on.

4. Click the Date, Footer, and Number Areas and change font attributes as desired.

> **Note** Normally you do not add text here, but instead format only the <date/time>, <footer>, and <#> placeholders. This information is added when you edit the Header and Footer (View, Header & Footer). An exception might be the page numbering where you might add and format "Page" before the <#> placeholder.

5. Choose Format, Background to display the Background dialog box (see Figure 20.42) and to select a preset background color or to create your own custom color combinations or patterns.

→ For more information on customizing background colors, **see** "Formatting Slides and Presentations," **p. 117**

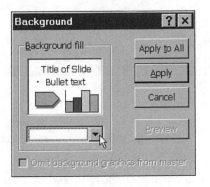

Figure 20.42
Add backgrounds to your custom design templates.

> **Tip #247 from**
> *Read Gilgen*
> Use the Preview button to see the effect of your selections before applying them to the Slide Master. However, even if you do apply the changes and don't like the results, you can still use Undo to restore your colors or other changes.

6. Choose Format, Slide Color Scheme to display the Color Scheme dialog box (see Figure 20.43) and to select a preset or custom combination of text and background colors.

→ For more information on selecting color schemes, **see** "Formatting Slides and Presentations," **p. 117**

7. When you are satisfied with your changes to the Slide Master, click the Close button on the Master toolbar, or choose View, Normal to return to the normal tri-pane view of your slide presentation.

PART
VI
CH
20

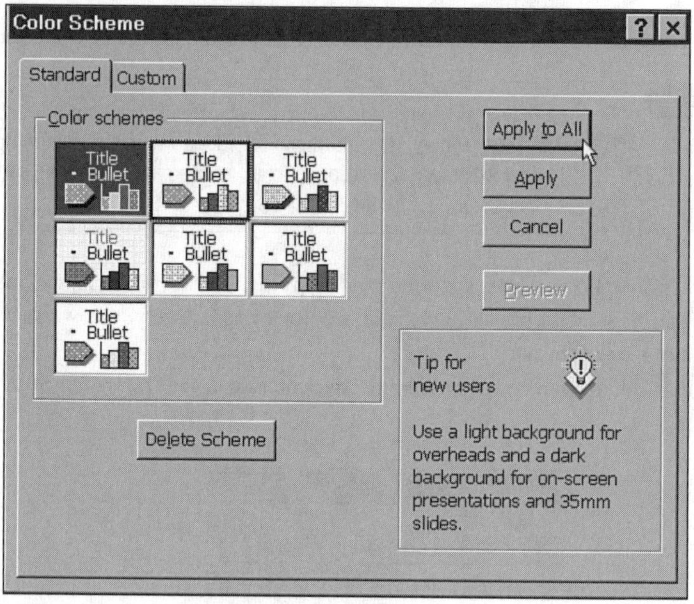

Figure 20.43
Color schemes help you quickly apply coordinating colors to text, graphics, backgrounds, and so on.

MODIFYING THE TITLE MASTER

The title slide often differs slightly from the other slides in a presentation in terms of font size, location of the title slide elements, and so on.

Unless you are modifying a presentation that uses one of PowerPoint's predesigned templates, you must first create a Title Master. The following steps show you how to create one:

1. Choose View, Master, Slide Master to access the Slide Master editing view.

2. Choose Insert, New Title Master; or press Ctrl+M.

If you already created a Title Master or if you are using a predefined PowerPoint template that already contains a Title Master, simply choose View, Master, Title Master. PowerPoint displays the Title Master editing screen (see Figure 20.44).

> **Note**
>
> Make sure you have modified the Slide Master before changing the Title Master. Initially the Title Master uses the same fonts and other attributes as the Slide Master.

If you modified the Slide Master first, perhaps little needs to be changed for the title slide. However, you might make the title font larger, position it differently, or add a graphic object to the screen. Furthermore, you could delete the Date, Footer, or Page area boxes and create a different date or footer for the title slide.

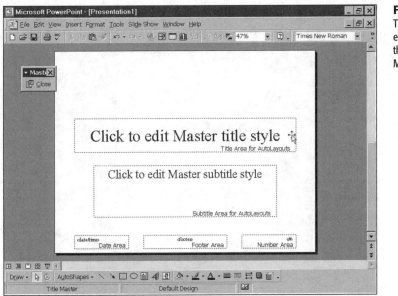

Figure 20.44
Title Masters are edited separately from the general Slide Master.

You don't need to delete the date, footer, or page number placeholders if you don't want them on the title slide. Instead, when you choose View, Header and Footer to display footers for your slideshow, simply check the Don't Show on Title Slide box.

MODIFYING THE HANDOUT AND NOTES MASTERS

In addition to the presentation itself, PowerPoint enables you to modify the Handout and Notes Masters.

To modify the Handout Master, follow these steps:

1. Choose View, Master, Handout Master. PowerPoint displays the Handout Master editing screen (see Figure 20.45).

2. Choose the number of slides (or Outline view) you intend to include on each handout page by clicking a slide positioning button on the Handout Master toolbar.

Note

If the Handout Master toolbar doesn't appear, simply right-click any toolbar when the Modify Master window is open and choose Handout Master from the list.

3. Modify, reposition, or delete the Header, Footer, Date, and Page Area text boxes.

Note

You can easily change the number of slides to be included in the handouts in the Print dialog box when you actually print the handouts.

PART
VI

CH
20

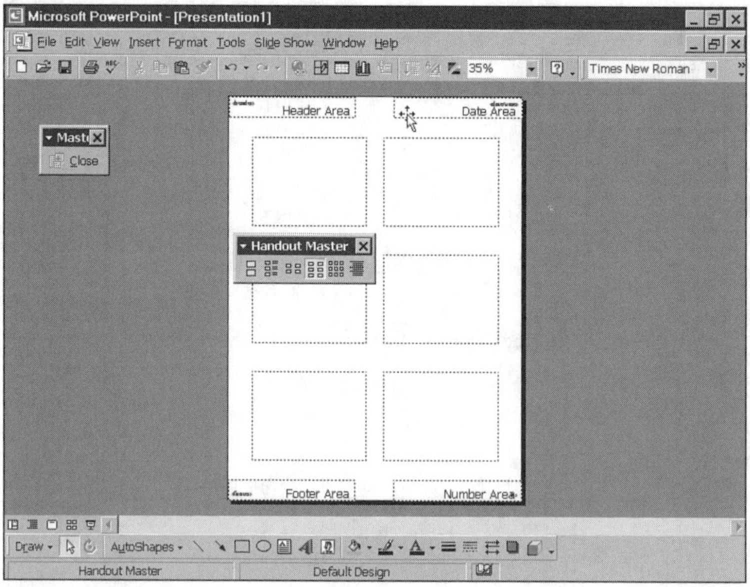

Figure 20.45
The Handout Master defines the default layout for your template's printed handouts.

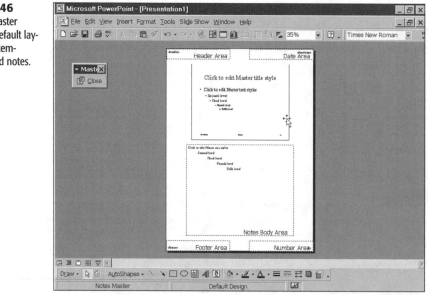

The Notes Master can be changed by following these steps:

1. Choose View, Master, Notes Master. PowerPoint displays the Notes Master editing screen (see Figure 20.46).

Figure 20.46
The Notes Master defines the default layout for your template's printed notes.

2. Reposition or resize the slide area, depending on how much area you want for the text (notes).

3. Reposition or resize the notes area.

4. Modify, reposition, or delete the Header, Footer, Date, and Page Area text boxes.

> **Note**
>
> Although you can change the background colors and color schemes for the Handout and Notes Masters, you probably won't want do so. Handouts and Notes are usually printed, and background colors aren't necessary or desired. You can, however, add a graphic element, such as a company logo, which then appears on each printed page.

TROUBLESHOOTING

After experimenting with customizing my toolbar, I can't remember which icons should be on the toolbar and which ones shouldn't. How do I reset a Toolbar?

PowerPoint makes it easy to return to the original default toolbar settings. Just access the Customize dialog box (View, Toolbars, Customize...), click the Toolbars tab, and click Reset. Be careful, however, because you lose all customizing you may have added to the toolbar.

After working with a presentation for some time, I notice that it takes longer to save or to perform certain tasks that were faster before. How can I make a leaner, faster presentation?

Several things can make your presentation grow unnecessarily, which in turn can slow things down. Try some of the following to reduce your file size, or to otherwise speed up your work with PowerPoint:

- Reduce the number of Undos (Tools, Options, Edit). By default, PowerPoint saves the last 20 changes, but you probably don't need more than 10.

- Turn off the option to save a preview picture with the file (File, Properties, Summary, Save Preview Picture).

- Unload any add-ins you may have loaded (Tools, Add-Ins, Remove).

DESIGN CORNER

Let's face it. When you were a kid, you liked to color outside the lines. Now that you're grown up and have PowerPoint to play with, you still like to do things a bit differently than PowerPoint wants you to.

PART

VI

CH

20

Not only that, you also like to work fast and smart. Let's try something that lets you be creative and also efficient.

Suppose you frequently use a specially modified Autoshape in your slide presentations. Instead of having to re-create the shape each time you use it, you can record a macro to create the shape, and then create a custom toolbar icon to play the macro.

BEFORE

Begin by creating the macro (see Chapter 19, "Working with PowerPoint Macros," for details on recording macros.) For our example, we created a macro named "Nix" that builds the international "No" symbol, changes its fill color to red, and adds a shadow.

Customized Autoshape

You can record a macro to automate the building of a custom Autoshape, like this one.

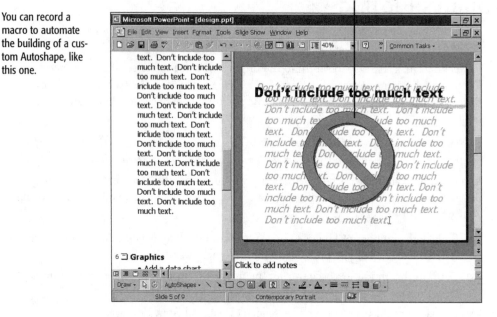

Next, create the toolbar icon for the macro following these steps:

1. Choose View, Toolbars, Customize... and click the Commands tab in the Customize dialog box (refer to Figure 20.8).

2. Click Macros in the Categories list. Available macros, including the one you recorded, appear in the Commands list.

3. Drag the macro you create, for example, Nix, to the desired toolbar. PowerPoint displays a text button on the toolbar.

4. Close the Customize dialog box.

Macro command button

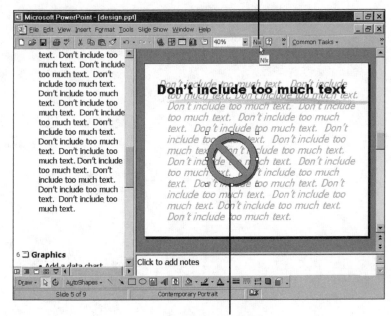

When you add a macro command to the toolbar, it automatically displays the name of the macro.

AFTER

Now, whenever you want your custom Autoshape, simply click the macro button on the toolbar. If you want, you can also create a custom icon for the macro (see "Customizing Toolbar Icon Images" in this chapter.)

Macro command button

PART

VI

CH

20

Automated Autoshape

FROM CONCEPT TO DELIVERY

THE MESSAGE—SCRIPTING THE CONCEPT

EXPERIENCING IDEAS

You know what I like? I like other books. You know, the other books out there that deal with presenting, public speaking, communication—I like them. I figure, anyone who has a plan that works and puts it in writing is probably giving good advice. Of course, that statement may not apply to the pamphlet *Six Easy Steps to Bomb-Making*, but you get the idea. While most advice is mainly subjective, when rooted in something believable, it can be of great value. So I encourage you to investigate the topic of "business presentations" through the eyes of many experts and gather their viewpoints. You can learn a lot from those who have found success.

UNDERSTANDING THE PROCESS

Guess what? There are only three things you have to think about when putting together a presentation.

The first is development of the concept; the second involves the design of the visuals; and the third concentrates on the delivery of the message to the audience. You may be involved in one or more of these stages.

In order to see the big picture, here, you have to understand where you are in the process of presenting. This is a good time to touch on how this chapter relates to the ones that follow as the process is unveiled.

The chapters ahead are separated to cover each part of the process. Chapter 21 examines the *message* and teaches you how to script the concept into a workable presentation. Chapter 22 concentrates on the *media* and offers you advice on designing the visuals. This will help you make the visual expression of the message the best it can be. Chapters 23 and 24 both deal with the *mechanics* of presenting. The presentation skill is separated into two chapters, one covering external *form* and the other concentrating on internal *function*. I arranged these chapters in the order of theory to practice to personal skill. If I were reading this book, I'd skip the theory and practice, jump right to the personal skill, adapt to it, and ask for that raise! But, logic and order must rule our world, so the theory comes first!

Chapter 25 is dedicated to the *environmental* issues concerning a presentation, such as the room, the equipment, the seating arrangements, and other elements that may affect the *performance* of the message.

Chapter 26 applies elements of the presentation process to many different situations including conference rooms, small group meetings, the outdoors, as well as interactive videoconferencing sessions.

PUTTING PEOPLE FIRST

One thing all the experts can agree on is that the success of communication is dependent on the presenter. That would be the person in the front of the room trying to keep the audience awake. The visuals are secondary to the concept, which is subject to the delivery skills of the person. All three elements are important, but without the person, you really can't call it a *presentation*.

If you think the content and the visuals are most important, try this at your next presentation. Get there early and place a chair in the front of the room, right about where you are expected to stand. For added effect, place your jacket over the back of the chair. Now, with a cassette player running a voice recording of your presentation, let the PowerPoint visuals advance automatically for the "audience." Then, using an egg timer, see how long the group remains in the room!

Communication is about people. Competition is so strong that products or services in the same category are starting to look the same. From household goods to cars to electronics— everything seems on par with everything else. The offerings of a company don't make the difference; instead, the people skills used to express those offerings are often what causes us to make a decision. The role of the presenter has taken on new meaning for companies who expect to compete in the next century.

BECOMING A VISUAL PRESENTER

Most people, especially those under the age of 40, are visual creatures. They get their information and stimulation from television, movies, computers, and video games. All of these forms are driven by action. Visual creatures demand action. In fact, they crave it! Think about it! Where do you get most of your news information? TV, right? That's because you like all the little pictures. Who doesn't? We're visual creatures! To be successful, presenters need to match the needs of an audience of visual creatures by becoming visual presenters. A visual presenter embodies a message and delivers it with action, creating a lasting impression on the audience.

My development of the concept, the design, and the delivery follows a consistent set of principles based on over 15 years of experience. The MediaNet approach focuses on messages, media, and mechanics in order to blend concepts and visual support with a person's individual delivery style.

A Method to the Madness
The processes and skills discussed in this book are simply the fundamentals. You can easily advance beyond the basics; one approach to gaining more comprehensive skills is MediaNet's "Presentation Skills Mastery Program," which builds a person's presentation style though four levels: Development, Competence, Achievement, and Mastery. The goal of the program is to master the skills and become a complete visual presenter, capable of delivering a variety of topics across a wide range of media.

This method has proven to be a practical, easy-to-understand, and extremely potent technique for changing ordinary business presentations into very memorable events. The techniques and tactics discussed in this book are designed for a visual presenter. This process advances a personal skill allowing an individual to reach his or her own potential as an expert communicator. The results are immediate and easily applied to new situations. Okay, what if I said you can lose 12 pounds with this method? I thought that would perk you up!

Although this book discusses one method of presenting unlike any other you are likely to encounter, it is not the only way of developing and delivering better presentations; it's just one way. But I really believe if you apply these techniques, you will enhance your proficiency, increase your effectiveness, and develop your own style. Hopefully, your style will incorporate some or all of the skills of a visual presenter, from concept to delivery.

MAKING A LASTING IMPRESSION

People remember people, not data. Very few people will come up to you at the end of your presentation and say, "You know. The third pie chart? The fourth slice? Loved it! The other slices, nahhhh, but the FOURTH slice, wow!"

No way! But a person might say, "You know. The story you told about the young woman and the two kids? I'll never forget that!"

How long after the presentation is your message still memorable? Remember: "Quality" content stimulates thinking and makes a lasting impression.

When you develop content for a presentation, the messages you place in the script should stay with an audience long after the event takes place. It's not about the messages alone; rather, it's about the way those messages are conveyed. People communicate ideas to people. Quality content is only quality content if presented that way. Obviously, if an actor plays Hamlet poorly, the quality of the content is lost.

Now don't over-analyze when you read this chapter; just let the stuff sink in slowly. The messaging issues are broken down to the smallest components so that you can see how to build lasting impressions. The good news is that you probably instinctively know most of this already without even reading it.

People and ideas need to be brought together for content to flourish and for messages to be remembered. To create a lasting impression, you'll need to pay attention to the way messages are created for both the presenter to deliver and for the audience to grasp. The trick is to get this process to the point where you are constantly saying the right things to the right people at the right times! Having said that, the three areas we need to address when scripting a message are

- Constructing the argument
- Qualifying the participants
- Assuring consistency

Note

I chose the development of the message as the starting point. Many believe that the first step in creating content is to analyze the needs of the audience. Then, after meeting those needs, the message is developed. Although I agree these two issues are closely related, the process of creativity dictates that the message needs to be developed before the audience is targeted. You really have to have a reason to say something and have something to say before you can ask someone to listen. Religion, politics, and theatre are everyday examples of how messages need to exist before audiences can be reached.

CONSTRUCTING THE ARGUMENT

Whenever you take on the task of conceptualizing and creating a presentation, you probably have more information at your fingertips than you really need. Sometimes, the sheer quantity of data forces you to try to use every piece of the puzzle at any opportune moment. The problem with that process is the entire presentation becomes a "data dump" on the audience. The visuals become cluttered and the presenter stands there reading the information on each visual to a gradually dozing crowd. Sound familiar? Who has the time to be bored with more stuff than can be remembered?

My favorite test for anyone creating a presentation is to ask, "Would you go to this thing if you didn't have to?"

The good news is that this clutter problem can easily be avoided. You just need to understand that developing quality content is a process, and the more you are involved in this process, the more you will recognize similar patterns and familiar sequences of ideas, intentions, and information. Don't be concerned with details when you begin, just concentrate and focus on the larger issues. In order to collect all the details you need to understand the whole concept.

Zero Out Your Brain

A painter starts with a fresh canvas. You need to clear your mind, relax your brain, and let your inner creative state begin to work. To do this, say the following out loud, "What do I want to talk about?" In fact, sit back in a chair and look up at the ceiling when you say it. You will be amazed at how quickly you'll "zero out" most of the rubble in your head and focus on the development of the message. Of course, there's more to this than a one-sentence exercise, but I want you to understand that the initial creative process is based on very simple actions that take place in a very relaxed atmosphere.

If you just take a step back, look at the bigger picture, relax your mind, and think clearly, you can easily find the simple pattern to a successful presentation. The logical and practical steps to developing a clear message include the following:

- Establishing a purpose
- Capturing ideas
- Creating an outline and storyboard
- Structuring ideas into a flowing script
- Using an opening "hook"
- Allowing for timely grabs
- Understanding non-linear issues

ESTABLISHING A PURPOSE

From an organizational perspective, you really need to start with a reason for creating the presentation in the first place. If you know why you are creating a presentation, you can learn how to convey it most effectively. The key to all communication is action and this is most important to visual creatures who demand constant action to understand information.

Although the word purpose answers the question "why," the word objective adds "to what extent." If you think about your purpose in the form of an objective, you'll get the impression of some action or some intention associated with the word objective.

This action in your message stems from your purpose or objective, and the resulting reaction is what you expect from the audience.

Your expectation is also known as your call to action. If you know what you want the audience to do at the end of the presentation (call to action), you can set an objective (course of action) that will get you to the result.

So, let's say you want your friends to go with you to a comedy club rather than to the museum, as originally planned. Okay, so your call to action (what you want your friends to do) is to get them to choose the comedy club. Your course of action (objective) is to convince them that the comedy club is the only choice. If your argument is convincing, they will see only one choice—comedy club!

ACTION DRIVES CONTENT

In keeping with the approach of developing content for a visual presenter, action-driven concepts are the way to go.

Therefore, your objective must always be stated in terms of action, and you must express your objective actively in the form of "to do something." Whether it is to sell, to motivate, to persuade, or any other action, the entire script must adhere to the chosen objective.

After you state the "To Do" objective using an active verb, it becomes easier to shape the story to fit the objective. For example, if the purpose or objective is "to persuade," then every item in the presentation must, in some way, directly persuade the audience.

If there are components in the presentation that do not directly match the objective, you should remove them. If not, these extraneous bits of information, although indirectly supporting your topic, will become a waste of time for your live audience. This will transform them into a dead audience. It is better to place such additional information and any extensive details in the handout materials.

Tip #249 from	Avoid redundancy and don't be redundant! If you have several ways of displaying similar information, such as a pie chart and a bar chart, don't use both. The test for such wordiness is to examine the sequence of support items and see if you can interchange their order.
	If, for example, you can switch the order of a pie chart and bar chart, then one of them is probably "extra" and can be dropped from the story line.
	Think theatre! Can you simply switch scene one with scene two without messing up the chronology of the play?

When your purpose or objective is clear, it's easier to capture ideas and gather only the relevant supporting information needed to advance the objective.

A well thought-out objective reduces information overload because it takes less data to support a single objective than it takes to support a number of different objectives.

FINE-TUNING THE OBJECTIVE

Sometimes the definition of the objective needs to be stronger. To make the objective stronger, you need to let action act on something or someone. An action verb (to do) needs to act on a noun (to do what) for a more specific result to occur. (You didn't realize how important those fourth grade language classes were, did you?)

For example, the objective "to sell," may not be as emphatic as "to excite and stir emotions." Notice how your approach to the script feels different by adding the noun "emotions." The noun gives you a target. The type of information you'd gather to support the stronger objective would be more extreme or more crucial than otherwise might have been used. Nouns help fine-tune the expression of the objective so you can narrow down the choices of support material.

Consider the expression "to paint detailed pictures." The type of information needed for this objective would contain precise elements that accurately depict the story so that there would be no question in the minds of the audience as to how to interpret the data. Now you know to look for data elements that show detail, such as segmented vertical bar charts showing individual comparisons at specific points in time, rather than line charts which show general comparisons to a trend over time. But that is not all to consider. You might begin to gather stories and examples from real life to continue to support your objective. These may or not be depicted visually but they could be described vividly to help "paint a picture" for the audience.

Here's a good one. The strong or powerful expression "to force a single choice" makes it easier for the audience to agree to your point of view. You could have used this objective for the comedy club mentioned earlier, for instance. This fine-tuned objective tends to make you gather information that is mostly one-sided and not subject to much interpretation or argument. Data elements might include comparative tables or listings, pie charts showing percentages of the whole, and horizontal bar charts which are always used to show items at a single point in time. Stories and analogies will be clearly biased to your point of view to enhance this objective. It is not important right now to know the exact information and statistics buried in your support data. You just have to have an idea of the effort you will need to gather the level of support information you think you might use in your visuals.

The whole point of fine-tuning the objective is to stimulate your brain and get your juices flowing. Compare "to convince" with "to burn an indelible mark on the soul." Which one pushes your creative buttons more?

OBJECTIVE CHARACTERISTICS

The characteristics of the objective may further define the kinds of information required for support of the message. You use an active verb (to do) to express the objective and you may add a noun (to do what) to fine-tune the objective. If you also apply an adjective (by when or for what reason) to the objective itself, you give it character and depth.

Think of being stuck in an airport. Your objective is to get to your destination, right? What if you apply a characteristic of time to that objective? Let's say it's the beginning of your business trip rather than the end. Your objective will not only be more urgent, but the means to your destination might suddenly include a car, train, or boat in order to get there.

The following are examples of characteristics:

- Specific
- Measurable
- Time-based
- Achievable (but not already achieved)
- Relevant

For example, if the objective is to force a single choice, a measurable characteristic such as comparing features and benefits of products will match the objective because forced-choice is a result of measuring comparisons. Later, when you select support information for the presentation, you will know to look for more comparative items that measure differences.

Or, if the objective is to motivate the creative team, a time-based characteristic such as establishing a deadline for a given project will match well with the objective because the motivation for the team is to meet the deadline in order to avoid a consequence. When you select support information, you can narrow your choices to those items that relate to motivating the creative team by a certain date.

When the purpose or objective of the presentation is clearly defined and carefully fine-tuned, the number of required supporting elements will be fewer. This is because a well thought-out objective lets you get to the point quickly without displaying data that doesn't directly support the theme. You are able to focus on gathering the right information to put into the presentation. Less information means less distraction!

Note

> Although you must have an objective, you don't have to fine-tune the objective or even find a characteristic to help shape that objective. But you should consider it as an exercise in reducing data clutter. I've spent the last 15 years showing organizations how the weaknesses in their messages ultimately limit the effectiveness of their presenters. Fine-tuning and identifying characteristics of an objective help to avoid this data overload trap!

When you think about the whole purpose behind the message, you need to come up with a compelling reason to get that message into the minds and hearts of the audience. That's why working with your objective makes sense and why you have to understand the importance of this early phase of the process. After you get your brain thinking in these terms, every script you create will follow a similar pattern, even though the content itself will keep changing.

HOW DO YOU SELECT AN OBJECTIVE?

We covered that an objective must be action-driven and contain an active verb. You've also seen how it helps to fine-tune the objective into a more descriptive expression and even more beneficial to understand certain characteristics of the objective. But how do you make the choice from the start?

Is the objective chosen at random? Is it based on any secret formula? Is it an educated guess? In reality, you can be very accurate in your choice of objective by simply knowing what you plan to say at the very END of the presentation. Your conclusion is critical to your strategy and contains key points that you want to cover.

Think about it. If you tell a joke, you must know the punch line. If you get in a car, you need to know the destination. You prove to yourself all the time that you need to know the END before you know where to START.

DO YOUR CONCLUSION FIRST

The key to selecting your objective is to create your last impression first. This doesn't mean you should present the last visual at the beginning of your presentation; rather, do your conclusion first in order to set the pattern or direction for all of the supporting elements to be presented.

Your last impression, or conclusion, is the verbal description of your overall objective. Think of your conclusion as a dartboard and each of the concepts as a dart. Each concept and support item must be directed at the dartboard in order to be effective. All components of the script MUST point to the "bull's-eye" or the overall objective. You may not always hit the bull's-eye, but if you don't even hit the dartboard—Blllllaaaannnnnppp! Thanks for playing!

Remember that call to action we talked about earlier? Well here it is again.

The call to action that you expect from your audience is directly related to the expression of your objective. For example, if you plan on concluding your presentation with the phrase, "Thank you very much and I hope you will each buy one of our products," then you must have been trying to sell. Each component of your script would then support the objective of SELLING something to the audience, whether it is a product, a concept, or an idea.

If the last thing you plan to say is, "Thank you very much and I hope you learned everything about PowerPoint," then you must have been trying to educate. Every part of your script would have to support the objective of educating the audience, in some direct way, on the features, benefits, processes, or procedures of PowerPoint. Your closing remark summarized your expectation of the group ("I hope you learned") and it was originally expressed as the objective to educate.

Naturally, you can always fine-tune the objective and match a characteristic to the objective to help narrow down your choices of support material. But the original selection process comes from knowing what you want to have happen when the presentation is over.

As Stephen R. Covey, author of *The Seven Habits of Highly Effective People*, says, "Start with the end in mind."

CAPTURING IDEAS

Despite what you may have heard, great ideas are not found on supermarket shelves, they are not a dime a dozen, and they certainly aren't driven by genius. Coming up with truly great ideas usually involves brainstorming, a process that allows the mind to spontaneously bring forth ideas. At times, the development of the message is left strictly to one person; other times that brainstorming process is shared.

The good news is that in both cases the methods by which we capture ideas vary and there is no exact science as to what will produce the perfect script for a presentation. However, several techniques will help you to selectively choose related concepts from the available "pool" of ideas. These tools help narrow your choices so that the next part of the process, the outline and storyboard, can be easier.

The following are four different tools that are used to capture ideas for a presentation:

- Fish-Bone Diagram
- Flow Chart
- Affinity Diagram
- Mind Map

FISH-BONE DIAGRAM

The fish-bone diagram links supporting visuals to a consistent theme (objective). Supporting visuals are linked by like causes while supporting the root cause. Confused yet? A good analogy might be to imagine a highway and the exit ramps off the highway. Then, think of the roads that connect to the exit ramps. That's the picture I'm painting here. Be careful how far you stray from the main highway with supporting information or else the audience may not be able to follow the map to your final destination.

Take a look at Figure 21.1. The end result (call to action) is supported by three categories for grouping your ideas. The most important category is placed closest to the end result because it represents ideas nearest the purpose (objective) of the message. Categories father from the end result represent more supportive ideas for the argument.

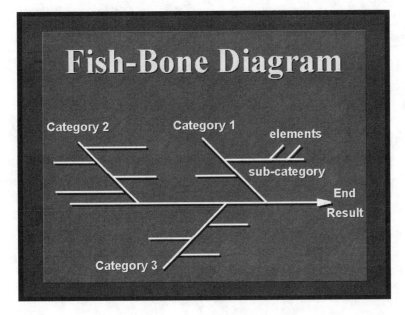

Figure 21.1
This is the layout you can use for a fish-bone diagram. Notice how supporting ideas (sub-category, elements) branch from main (category) ideas.

Tip #250 from

A good rule is to structure about three groups that support the main message and then have no more than three supporting messages beneath each group. If you branch out too far, the audience may not be able to get back on track.

When capturing ideas to a fish-bone diagram, fill in the blank lines where needed with ideas that support the closest or most immediate concept and look for data elements (support information) that match those ideas.

FLOW CHART

A flow chart forces you to think in "stages" of action and tends to show that one step leads to another. Similar to the fish-bone diagram, flow charts, however, are mostly used when showing decision-based branching or interactivity. For example, non-linear electronic presentations may allow a particular subject or issue to be explored further only if the presenter prefers it that way, usually based on some cues or questions from the audience.

If you take a look at Figure 21.2, you'll see how the flow chart helps you place your ideas in sequence, noting any areas where choices might be made to further the message to its conclusion. Maybe after making your first point you check for agreement in the crowd. If they agree, you move on; if not, you bring in more evidence to support your argument. In an electronic presentation, this might mean selecting an object on the visual which contains an action to display another visual, not necessarily in sequence, which hold more information.

→ For more information on how to create interactive elements within an electronic presentation, **see** "Using Action Buttons," **p. 331**

PART

VII

CH

21

Figure 21.2
Here's how you "flow chart" your ideas. This shows how back-up or supplemental data can be used by the presenter only if needed to force a decision at that point.

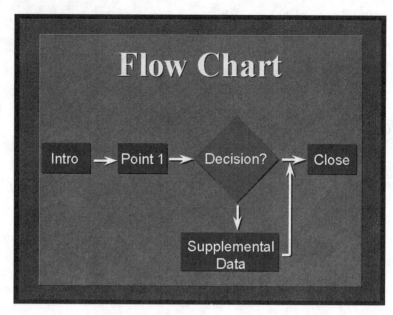

The key to a flow chart is in the logical flow of continuous action. Remove an element and the flow is broken. You can create a flow chart out of a simple day in your life.

If you think about your commute to work, your morning activity, your lunch hour, your afternoon, and your commute home, you have a flow chart. Now, imagine that as a giant flow chart across the wall of your bedroom. But don't lose any sleep over it. The process is a simple one.

The point is to keep it simple, logical and flowing. If you have a process-driven presentation, consider using the flow chart as a tool to capture ideas into the process. You will easily see how some ideas, although seemingly important on their own, actually do not fit the flow chart's process-oriented structure. This will reduce the number of ideas you can squeeze into one continuous flow of information.

AFFINITY DIAGRAM

An affinity diagram helps you sort out your ideas into categories. Think about dropping your ideas into a bunch of different buckets all of which relate to the main theme. If you look at Figure 21.3, you'll see how the categories are decided in advance, before brainstorming the ideas needed to support each of the categories.

By grouping closely related activities, you outline ideas based on agreed-upon categories—or "buckets"—of information. By tossing ideas into these specific buckets, you fill each category with the main points that you know you have to make in order to satisfy the category. The key to this method of capturing ideas is to agree on the categories in the first place.

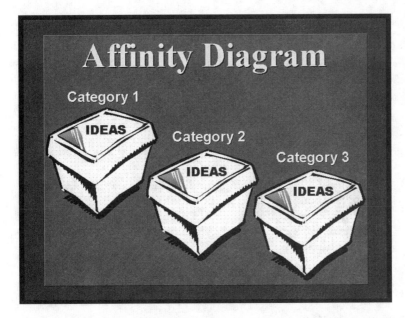

Figure 21.3
The affinity diagram limits your ideas to predefined categories, or "buckets." This helps you focus on the exact message and prevents you from including non-essential information.

For example, Figure 21.4 shows the agreed-upon information buckets to drop ideas into for this presentation. Perhaps this is how the meeting went that day. Someone said, "We have to talk about pricing," and the idea about pricing was placed in the financial category. Someone else mentioned "memory" and the idea of memory was placed under features. But another person said, "We should discuss the service policies of the company." Even though service is an important part of the company, the idea didn't fit any of the categories originally defined. Unless we stretch the meaning of what can be included in a specific category, there won't be any service-talk in this presentation.

Although the service policies are important, it is not the right information to be brought up during this particular presentation. Think of it this way: Ford makes cars and trucks, but they are not shown in the same commercial.

Tip #251 from

Limit your categories to three or four, and limit your ideas per category to about the same number. You'll need at least one item of visual support for each idea. If you have too many categories or ideas within categories, the presentation may drag on too long.

MIND MAP

If Felix Unger is the affinity diagram, then Oscar Madison is the mind map! But don't assume chaos is a bad thing. In fact, when it comes to brainstorming, it's quite the opposite.

PART
VII

CH
21

Figure 21.4
A filled-in affinity diagram showing how the "tossed-in" ideas or discussion points are grouped according to four different predefined categories.

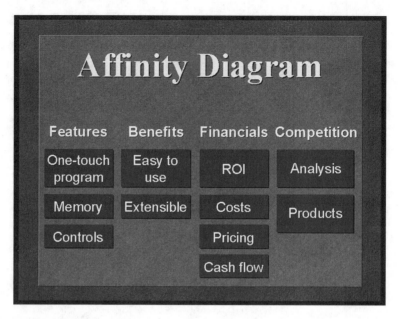

Mind mapping is a technique that starts with a major theme or concept and then looks for immediate supporting issues. After the main issues are defined, additional support can be considered. Each idea you write down may spawn another related idea and so on. The underlying support for each of the main issues ultimately supports the overall theme.

However, as you place ideas farther from the center of the map, you attach a lower importance to the idea, and, as a result, you need less support information for that idea. A mind map template, shown in Figure 21.5, illustrates the placement of ideas in relation to a central theme or core concept.

Although this appears similar to the affinity diagram, the mind map adds a different dimension to gathering ideas. It allows many ideas to make it to the table, and then tries to categorize each idea into a particular mainstream concept. The added dimension is distance. Once an idea is placed on the mind map, you are able to see how close to the center of the map it is and therefore determine its importance in the presentation.

Tip #252 from

Think of the center of the mind map as the core of an apple. To reach the core, you have to bite deeper into the apple. Ideas (items) closer to the core need stronger support or deeper explanation. Knowing the proximity of an idea to the central theme helps you decide how in-depth a concept should be covered when presented.

Since mind maps are usually associated with concepts and concepts are abstract, one supporting idea may be usable in more than one area of the mind map. Where you decide to place the idea will determine the amount of support you'll need for that idea. If, however, you use an idea more than once on the map, then you may need to use different levels of support for the same idea at different points in the script. Is your brain hurting yet?

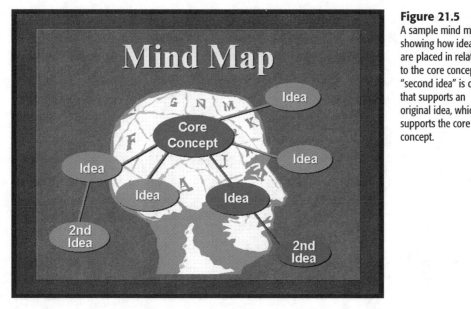

Figure 21.5
A sample mind map, showing how ideas are placed in relation to the core concept. A "second idea" is one that supports an original idea, which supports the core concept.

For example, in Figure 21.6, the idea *Recognize* appears in two areas of the map. It is part of the *Fun Workplace* concept under *Recruiting*, which is one of the issues of *Management Control*. *Recognize* also appears as part of *Motivate*, a subset of *Ownership* which stems from *Authority*, which relates to *Accounting* (yet another issue of *Management Control*). The two ideas are at different distances from the center of the map. So when you look at each idea called "Recognize," you can count the levels each sits from the core. In one area there are two levels to pass through to reach the core; in another area there are four levels to pass through.

In the first instance, the idea of recognition is closer to the core or central theme of management control (count the levels). Knowing this, you should use more support and explanation during the discussion of "recognition" at this point in the presentation than during the other reference. So after seeing where in the map the idea appears and how close to ground zero it really is, then you can gather your support information accordingly.

The other advantage of the mind map is that at a glance you can decide if the ideas are straying too far from the core, causing the presentation to become more drawn out. I suggest you keep the levels to no more than three: main theme (core), supporting issues, and supporting data for those issues. This makes for a shorter, more concise presentation. Remember, a mind map is a terrible thing to waste!

CREATING AN OUTLINE AND STORYBOARD

After you have gathered the main ideas and concepts that support your overall objective, you can create an outline and storyboard. The *outline* is simply a list of headings with some degree of detail attached to a few items. The storyboard is a visual example of the items in the outline.

PART

VII

CH

21

Figure 21.6
A mind map shows
levels of the thought
process.

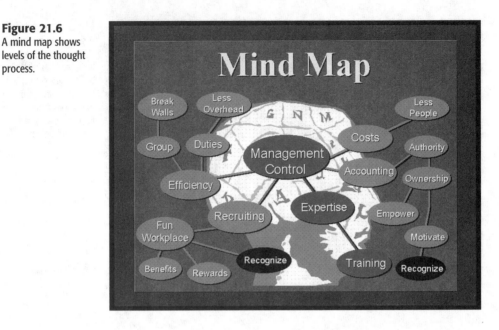

You don't really have to create both an outline and a storyboard, but it helps to see a list of items categorized in sections as well as a visual sketch of those items.

ELECTRONICALLY CREATING AN OUTLINE AND STORYBOARD

PowerPoint simultaneously updates your outline and your storyboard (visuals) as you add content. The good news is that you can move items around quickly in PowerPoint, which is especially useful after all of your ideas have been entered into the outline.

→ For more information about outline and storyboards, **see** "Understanding PowerPoint Views," **p. 16**

Tip #253 from

As you enter each idea or concept into the outline, PowerPoint uses a default "slide layout," typically a bullet chart. If you have support information that you know will be displayed in a different format, such as a data-driven chart, simply change the layout and enter a text description of the visual, plus the type of chart you prefer (pie, bar, line, and so forth). Later, when you create your visuals, you'll know what type of chart you were considering when you entered the idea or concept. Of course, any notes you typed into the layout will have to be removed when you actually begin designing the chart. Otherwise, it will look pretty bad if your final presentation has headings that say things like "A pie chart goes in this space" and "Try a bar chart here".

→ To learn more about working with different slide layouts, **see** "Organizing Your Presentation in Outline View," **p. 101**

When you create an outline or storyboard in PowerPoint, some serious visual design is already happening. The very nature of the software is designed to "multitask" and to do two things at once for you. Let the software do the work and don't worry. Rather than be concerned about the design issues at this point, just try to get your ideas into the outline and then organize those ideas similarly to the way you captured them. Remember, you're not designing the visuals yet, only sketching ideas into a rough visible format.

Manually Creating an Outline and Storyboard

If you are creating a storyboard on paper for later input into PowerPoint, then simply make a rough sketch of how you see each idea visualized. For example, at my company (MediaNet, Inc.), we have created over 1,000 PowerPoint presentations from handwritten notes and sketches sent to us by clients. This is probably a familiar process in your company as well. Lots of people scribble out some rough-looking visuals just to help them visualize the information. Although it is much easier to use PowerPoint for the task of organizing content, you can also tackle the process manually on paper.

On paper, you can create the outline in a hierarchical (first to last) structure. Just remember a few of the outlining rules from school, such as "every A needs a B,"—meaning that you can't have only one supporting point for a major idea—you need at least two. Still wishing you showed up for the fourth grade, huh?

The outline is easy, but the storyboard is a bit more difficult when created manually. The design of the visuals is usually taken from the original sketches in the storyboard. All the information chosen to support the story needs to be presented in a clearly readable format.

Most people belong to the "8$^1/_2$×11 crowd." That is, those who use an entire sheet of paper, squeeze as much information as possible onto it, and then expect to later convert the clutter into a presentation visual. It's true. You take a standard sheet of paper, a magic marker (no one thinks of using a pencil with an eraser!) and you write on both sides of the sheet—and you call it—a visual. The days of the full-page of typewritten text with the little letter "o" for the bullet are gone.

> **Caution**
>
> If you do create a cluttered storyboard with each concept represented by a massive amount of needless information, do not—I repeat—do not invite me to your next presentation! Or, invite me, but allow me to bring a pillow.

A storyboard sketch of each visual should not take up a full, 66-line typewritten sheet of paper. When projected, the final image from that original sketch needs to be clearly seen from a distance. This means the text and any other elements should be large and the only way to insure that is to limit the amount of data placed on the visual in the first place.

The best way to limit what can be placed on a single visual is to take a piece of standard paper and fold it in half before you design anything. Of course this doesn't mean you should write twice as small! But it does force you into a smaller workspace and help you avoid cluttering the image with extensive information that may not be readable for the audience when projected.

Another option is to use 5"×7"index cards to storyboard your ideas. The advantage of index cards is that they can be spread on a flat surface, like a table, and can be moved around as needed to organize your storyboard images into a proper flow. This is the manual version of the slide sorter in PowerPoint. You can probably now see how valuable the software is to the planning process when you consider the alternative of doing this manually.

The goal is to limit the information so the audience can spend more time listening and watching. Studies have shown that people retain only 10% of what they read but 70% of what they see and hear. Use this as hint to stop the data, spare us the details, and save the presentation! Can I make this any clearer! Less words on the screen means more words in your mouth. Remember the KISS principle—Keep It Simple, Stupid!

STRUCTURING IDEAS INTO A FLOWING SCRIPT

An outline and a storyboard help organize captured ideas into a format ready for design. But another issue must be addressed and that is making the presentation presentable. To support the notion of a visual presenter in terms of the script, the strategy is to link ideas so that a person can covey them. The script itself, the story line, must be structured so that the ideas flow easily from paper to people.

Earlier I asked you to think about the big picture when examining the purpose; now you should start thinking about the finer details. When you structure your ideas into some cohesive format, you may think it's easiest to give the audience the big picture and then back that up with the smaller details. That may work in some instances, but you should really consider the opposite strategy, as well.

Our world is complex and we seek simplicity. You will be more effective if you first get right to the immediate issue of the presentation and then offer the larger-than-life view.

One way to look at it is to think of a presentation as a big dinner. The menu is the view of the meal, but the selection is the anticipation of the taste. Then consider how the chosen meal is served: one course at a time. Each course needs to be segmented or cut into bite-size pieces in order to be consumed.

If the courses are the big picture items and the bite-size pieces are the details, from the server's (presenter's) point of view, the order of information should be from bigger to smaller. But, if you look at it from a taster's (audience's) point of view, the food on the fork is more important than the rest of the stuff on the table.

Maybe I've only succeeded in making you hungry, but I want you to begin to see how the details of the argument actually stimulate the anticipation of the audience more than the big picture.

Micro-to-Macro Strategy

Regardless of the method used to construct an argument, each script usually has a mixture of the "small details" and the "big picture." The terms *micro* and *macro* can be used to describe these views of the world. Typically, in a presentation, you separate the macro items (market data, trends, company information, and competition) from the micro items (stories, analogies, specific examples, features, and benefits).

Although the big picture is usually chosen as the starting point for a script, the small details are the qualifiers of the argument. Because time is an issue to a listener, getting to the details is more critical than hearing about the general trends. For example, you would obviously prefer to know whether the route you take to work is clear before you care to know that your city is the eighth most traffic-congested in the country.

When a script is constructed in a micro-to-macro fashion, the unique issues you bring to the table are discussed first and the broad-based marketing data is secondary. The good news is that if you accidentally run out of time in the presentation, the audience only misses the general information. Chances are, they can find that data if and when they choose.

No matter which way you choose to present the information, you still have to develop a pattern or a structure to the script so the information can be absorbed properly.

Think of the structure as the type of script that is used to convey the message. Most presentations follow a linear pattern, which moves from an opening through the body and, finally, into the closing. This open-body-close process is very common and usually expected as the metaphor for receiving information. The good news is that you have a choice of about five types of scripts you can use to convey a message in a linear presentation:

- Matching Ideals
- Main Points
- Question and Answer
- Meeting Needs
- Problem-Solution

Seven "F" Words

From the great works of literature to the trashiest novels, in theatre, movies, or television, you'll find basically seven scripts. No matter what the plot, it fits into one of the seven scripts. Those scripts all begin with the letter F: Fact, Failure, Fantasy, Fear, Fidelity, Freedom, and Fortune. From these scripts all plots are hatched.

The lesson here is that variety stems from simplicity. Consider that only 26 letters make up our alphabet; look at how many words we have, not to mention books! There are only 12 notes on a musical scale (including sharps and the start of the next octave), and yet look at how many songs and musical scores we have!

The writer must master the alphabet first. The singer must master the notes first. Having mastered the subtleties of action within the seven scripts, an actor is able to play many different roles.

Whether it's messages, media, or mechanics, the entire process of creativity is predicated on the notion that simplicity yields variety. When applied to the message, the simplicity in script structure yields a variety of presentations.

MATCHING IDEALS

This structure is really a "set-up" for the audience. The plan is that you describe the ideal product or service, which, of course, you know will closely resemble your product or service. Since the audience accepts your description as the "premise" of the argument, it is quite easy to match your argument to the premise you set up in the first place. This structure is usually used more for products than for services since attributes of a product are more tangible (visible) than qualities of a service.

For example, you selectively mention the ideal attributes of a good car. You say, "The ideal car has front-wheel drive, dual air bags, a rear defrost, and a trunk release." You naturally get the audience's agreement that these are the ideal attributes of a good car. Then you describe your car in terms of the ideal, making sure you only compare to about 90% of the ideal. You say, "Our car has front-wheel drive, dual air bags, a rear defrost, and we're still working on the trunk release." You see, you never want to compare to 100% because that would mean you have the "perfect" product (which no one does), and it would leave you no room for improvement (how do you improve on perfection?).

Nothing is perfect. Ever buy a pair of jeans? Wait, let me rephrase that. Ever buy a pair of jeans that fit? I rest my case. The matching ideals script is designed to lead the audience to an understanding that the product (or service) is the best one for the job, but it may not do the whole job. Sounds like a politician to me!

MAIN POINTS

Typically, this structure is used with information-based presentations such as those dealing with financial results and other historical data. The process follows the familiar pattern of:

Tell 'em what you're gonna to tell 'em

Tell 'em

Tell what you told 'em

One way to identify this structure is the appearance of an agenda early in the presentation and a corresponding summary at the end. This lets the audience know what to expect and then expect what to remember.

The summary at the end is critical because main points can be hard to remember especially when a large number of supporting points are discussed. The audience may get lost unless they are constantly made aware of how the supporting information relates to the main points.

QUESTION AND ANSWER

Question and answer scripting is similar to educational activities of "pre-test" and "post-test." This is useful in training sessions with a lot of unrelated, yet comprehensive, information.

First you pre-test the audience's knowledge of a subject using easy-to-answer questions (true/false, multiple choice). The questions cover all the major points you expect to convey during the session. Then, during the session, you reveal the correct answers using supporting visual elements to explain each answer as you elaborate. Finally, you ask the audience as a group to answer the original questions (post-test).

A question and answer scripting structure can be used in a variety of situations including surveys, polls, and research studies. The important point to remember is that the objective should address how the information is used by the audience toward some result. One way to ensure that the information is more than just a data dump is to repeat key points and summarize conclusions at several stages of the presentation. Repetition will aid in retention of concepts and ideas. Repetition will aid in retention of concepts and ideas. Repetition will aid in retention of concepts and ideas. Any questions?

MEETING NEEDS

Sometimes called the "helping hand" script, this structure starts with the needs of the audience in mind. This is often used in sales presentations where you put the needs of the customer up front and then show how you can address those needs.

But, for business, a first glance at this meeting needs script may seem an easy task. But more often than not, presentations using this format tend to treat all needs on an equal basis. This becomes a problem because if all needs are truly equal, then priorities cannot be set and decisions take longer to reach. If, however, you attach importance to specific needs, you create a sense of gratification by meeting those needs in the order of their importance. This builds value for you in the eyes of the audience.

For example, suppose you are a computer consulting firm specializing in solving Y2K (Year 2000) problems. You are giving a "new business" pitch to a potential client who has the following "needs":

- 24-hour on-site support
- High-level data security
- Detailed reporting
- Expert advice
- Budget constraints

Initially, you might flag "budget constraints" as critical (to you) since it represents your paycheck, so to speak. After all, you do want to get paid for your work. But the meeting needs script structure is meant to place the client's needs up front. In that case, data security and expert advice are more important to the client. But, if you address each of the needs equally, you create equal impact on the last item (the one critical to you). This makes meeting your needs equal to meeting the client needs and makes the client consider budget constraints as strongly as the other issues.

But, if you prioritize the needs and give more weight to the data security and the expert advice issues, you may create an opportunity to build value for your services as the client realizes how well you can meet his primary needs. Less importance will be shifted to the limitations of the budget. This ultimately serves your purpose.

Once you know the priority of the customer needs, you can address those important issues first. Then, you can summarize how you can help with other issues that may not have been verbalized as a "top priority," but may be important to the scope of the project or activity. The point is that many issues are brought into a presentation, some of which can have a negative impact on your objective. By concentrating on primary needs you limit the attention placed on less important and perhaps frivolous needs that could have otherwise stalled the process.

PROBLEM-SOLUTION

Also known as the "divide and conquer" script, the problem-solution structure is one of the most effective scripts you can use, especially for high-level, decision-based presentations. Whereas the meeting needs structure focuses on the goals ahead, the problem-solution structure concentrates on the mistakes of the past. That's why I love this script. It concentrates on failure, it thrives on fear, it accentuates the negative—and it leaves the door open for a hero to save the day! It's like Superman!

The process follows a simple pattern. First, the overall problem is described and presented in a manner that makes it look bleak or negative. Then, you dissect the problem into smaller sections that can be addressed individually. Finally, the solutions to the smaller areas will solve the big problem, as well, and the result will always look positive.

Politicians use the problem-solution scenario frequently. The political candidate announces, "The country is going downhill, crime and inflation are out of control, your children have no future." Immediately you feel depressed hearing the problems at hand. Seconds later, the candidate continues, "...but our party has the solution!" Suddenly you feel better, as if the day has been saved. Okay, it really isn't exactly that way, but you get the idea.

From a business presentation perspective, the problem-solution script can be highly effective because it plays on a very powerful human emotion: Fear. If problems can't be solved, then the consequences may be harmful. This can cause fear and anxiety.

In fact with so many companies touting solutions these days, I keep thinking we're going to run out of problems! Now that is a problem we need to solve. The solution to running out of problems would be to have fewer solutions. Then, we would end up having more problems than solutions. I feel better already, how about you?

Problem-Solution Scenario

Many times I find that presentations are poorly constructed using the problem-solution approach. I usually suggest this pattern. The opening of the presentation should state the case in this order: problem, consequence of inaction, sense of urgency, and solution.

For example, let's say your company markets a software program that keeps track of Internet access. The following italicized text is an example of the conceptual script that might be used.

First, you quickly tell the audience the problem. You state how *employees spend a growing percentage of the workday accessing the Internet for non-business related information.*

Next, examine the consequence of inaction. In other words, what happens if nobody does anything about the problem? You indicate that without action, the *consequence will be a reduction of productivity in the workplace.*

Okay, here's the clincher! Attach a timeframe to action in order to establish a sense of urgency. After all, without urgency there is less need to solve the problem today. In other words, if they do see the problem, how long can they wait to do something about it? You mention that *less productivity from lost time reduces the ability to adapt quickly to constant changes in the industry.*

Finally, you must address the problem with your specific solution. Without a link to your special way of solving the problem, you will only end up educating the audience by increasing general awareness of the problem.

Therefore you show that your software *limits Internet access to non-business information using a unique process, thereby allowing a company to maximize productivity into a competitive advantage.*

This entire scenario—problem-consequence-urgency-solution—should be shared up front with the audience in less than one minute to set the stage for the rest of the presentation.

The problem-solution script positions the presenter as a solution provider for existing problems. Try saying that five times fast! Since most people are cautious and conservative, this kind of script appeals to a sense of urgency.

Of all the structures available, I most prefer the problem-solution type. Any scripts that involve a sense of urgency will always be the most effective because urgency relates to the limits of time, and time, once lost, can never be retrieved.

USING AN OPENING HOOK

We spent a lot of time covering objectives, ideas, and structures, and by now, you should have some grasp on how to construct the argument in order to move an audience to some call to action. But now we have to think about jump-starting the presentation with an opening hook.

Every time I consult on a client presentation, I ask, "What's the hook?" and the response is usually, "What's a hook?" That's when I say, "How long have you worked at the company, not counting tomorrow?" The hook is the very reason the audience wishes to remain in the room for the rest of the presentation.

A hook is used for the purpose of changing something about the way an audience thinks. A hook can be any credible or even doubtful piece of information, which, when presented, causes the audience to immediately react. Whether it be a bit of research, a little known but interesting fact, a revelation, a controversial opinion, a current event, or simply a smile in the face of defeat, the opening hook sets the stage for the rest of the presentation.

I find a statistic can make for a great opening hook. For example, an opening hook I use for my "Electrifying Presentations" seminars is a series of statistics which position the physical "presentation skill," the actual art of delivery, as contributing to over 90% of the communication message. It doesn't mean that content is unimportant; rather, that content needs to be clear and concise since we process more of what we see than anything else.

That hook is important because it forces the audience to make a choice—do they agree or disagree? For those who agree, they spend the rest of the presentation nodding their heads as the evidence to support the hook is presented. For those who disagree, they spend the rest of the presentation tilting their heads looking for more evidence as to why they should change sides. Both groups are forced to change the way they think in order to keep sitting through the presentation.

What happens is this: An audience arrives at the presentation in neutral. Their emotions and thoughts have yet to be swayed. Your goal is to get them in gear—forward or reverse—

PART

VII

CH

21

it doesn't matter, but you must get create a sense of action. Just like the objective is positioned to do something, the audience needs to be pushed to do something, too. Think of them as sitting on a fence and trying to push them to one side or the other. If I'm still on the fence at the end of your presentation, I haven't accomplished anything and neither have you. We both lose. You have to influence the group in some way.

Rarely is this done visually onscreen, as in a before/after comparision. The hook is more of a fact or statement that challenges the status quo or belief system. Even if you displayed a visual of something powerful, such as natural disaster or a victory celebration, you would still have to verbally interpret the hook for the audience. A visual which supports your hook needs to be placed in context and described. Usually, you don't need the visual at all since the description is likely to stand on its own.

The value of the hook is in the timing. When the presentation starts, how long does it take before the group is being influenced by your objective (to sell, to motivate, to convince, or whatever)? How long do you let them sit on the fence in neutral?

The longer it takes you to employ your objective, the harder it gets to arrive at the call to action. However, using an opening hook can instantly affect the audience and get them to make choices about your message.

For example, if you started a presentation by saying, "By the end of the day you will lose all excess weight, look 10 years younger, and add one million dollars to your income!" I'd say that's a pretty good hook. Sign me up!

Note

Don't use a fact for no reason. For example, mentioning that over 83% of all Paul Newman movies have the letter H somewhere in the title may be factual, but is really just trivial, especially because the audience can't control the likelihood that future Paul Newman movies won't have an H somewhere in the title!

The hook can even tap into an audience's sense of urgency for the presentation to be over. One of the best opening hooks I heard a presenter give was to a group of time-starved executives at the beginning of a sales presentation. The presenter said, "This can take five minutes or five hours, but you're going to buy something!" Each person in that room glanced at the clock and was instantly swayed from thinking "Do I want to buy?" to wondering "Do I want buy now or five hours from now? "

ALLOWING FOR TIMELY GRABS

Although an opening hook creates action in the minds of the audience, timely grabs are used to hold the attention of the audience across sections of the script. These grabbers pepper the script at specific points with interesting information, personal experiences, or other stimulating items that relate to or help further the message.

Grabbers include:

- Stories
- Examples
- Analogies
- Statistics
- Interaction
- Questions
- Repetition
- Shock
- Suspense
- Special Effects (animation, sound, video)

Tip #254 from

When using analogies, try to make them as real-world as possible. The advantage of drawing a likeness between something in your content and an everyday activity is that the audience transfers the benefits of the very real experience to your information.

For example, a simple analogy for a maker of digital video cameras might be to specify that a particular model is the Cadillac of the industry. The public impression of Cadillac is one of quality and a transfer is made by the audience to the digital camera as having a high quality.

Typical real-world analogies include references to transportation, household appliances, food, travel, and entertainment. The more the reference applies to everyday experience, the faster the connection is made by the audience.

Grabbers should directly relate to the topic, but can come from nowhere and be completely unrelated to anything you're discussing. It depends on what you want to do with the audience. Unrelated grabbers are used typically to inject life into the crowd. Let's say it's one hour after lunch. You might notice the audience is losing focus, appearing glassy-eyed, getting a bit drowsy. Although it's possible you are boring them to sleep, the head-bobbing is more from the blood leaving the head to travel to the stomach to digest food.

You might have to do something unrelated. I have a full-day seminar/workshop, which has a topic called "Multimedia vs. Multimania." It's one of the eight topics for the day, but it is strategically placed about one hour after the lunch break. In the middle of the lecture is a 10-minute game show on the order of a "Name That Tune" contest. It has less to do with the guidelines for using multimedia than it does to wake the audience up from a low energy point. Plus, it's fun! And you know something, you can have fun and learn at the same time!

UNDERSTANDING NON-LINEAR ISSUES

Non-linear presentations offer the greatest flexibility for a repetitive presentation with a changing audience. With experience, presenters learn where the questions arise and to what extent "back-up," or supporting information, is needed.

PART
VII
CH
21

The technique employed in these presentations relates to features within PowerPoint, specifically Action buttons and hyperlinks. See Chapters 14, "Working with Animation," and 15, "Using PowerPoint's Web Features," for more information on the use of these features.

Using a non-linear structure, you can

- Answer expected or unexpected questions with back-up support information
- Analyze "what if" scenarios by linking to spreadsheets and other data
- Show "generic" presentations to different audiences and use back-up data only where necessary

If you decide to display back-up information based on audience responses, make sure the information is "general" enough to warrant display.

If you decide to do "what-if" scenarios in front of an audience where a software application needs to be used, make sure you know the software well and don't get caught up in details or small changes.

The following situations are some in which a non-linear approach may be effective:

- Show only the "overview" to busy executives and more detailed levels to subordinates
- Adapt to an audience's knowledge level by giving details only where needed
- Respond to different audiences' priorities by showing most important information to that particular audience first

The same way you tell a story based on limited time is the way to think about non-linear access to information. If you have the time, show it. But show limited amounts of information—enough to make the point.

You may have to pre-plan a lot of this "branching" information and you may not be asked to show it all. Usually, a presentation done several times to different audiences tells a presenter where the supporting information belongs.

Make sure you incorporate a "go back" button! Don't leave someone in la-la land wondering how to get back to the original story! Non-linear navigation can be confusing if you don't have a way to get back on track after you've branched off to a supporting item. This is why non-linear presentations are usually meant for an audience of one (like at a kiosk); or, they are thought-out so far in advance to cover every interactive possibility that they end up falling into the pattern of a typical linear presentation. The key thing to remember is not to lose control of the event.

QUALIFYING THE PARTICIPANTS

So what do you really know about the speaker and the listeners? The ability to understand attributes of both the presenter and the audience is critical to the message. The objective and the target audience for that objective are so closely intertwined that you should consider them as coexisting. It's like the Sinatra song "Love and Marriage," where he sings, "…you can't have one, you can't have none, you can't have one without the uhhhhhhhh-uh-uhhh-ther!" (You're trying to sing that right now, aren't you? I thought so.)

The message is buried between the speaker and the listener. In fact, all presentations follow a standard communication model (Sender—Message—Receiver). For visual presenters the model can be described more theatrically as Actor—Action—Audience. Regardless of the terms, the human elements of the process—the sender (presenter) and the receiver (audience)—are key to the presentation process and crucial to message development.

You need to know the following in order to create messages that tap into specific aspects of both the sender and receiver in the communication model:

- Learning the traits of the presenter
- Knowing the particulars of the audience
- Targeting motivators and filters

LEARNING THE TRAITS OF THE PRESENTER

If you are the presenter of your own message, then you already know your own likes, dislikes, habits, and so forth. But if you have to prepare a message or even the visual support for the message for another person to deliver, then the following section can offer you some helpful information.

In order to construct a believable message, it helps if you know certain characteristics or traits of the presenter. The more the presenter is involved in the message, the better the delivery. Of course, I've seen presentations where I've questioned whether the presenter was actually alive during the event. You're not laughing because some of these people work at your company! Okay, so you have to be prepared and you have to get to know your presenters.

Some points to consider for knowing the traits of the speaker:

- Personal attributes
- Delivery style
- Expertise level
- Media preferences

In the real world, you may never have the time to really gather this information. In fact, many of those who create content do so for others to present. In a number of situations, the content providers never even see the presenters. Some actually may feel that's a good thing, but, collaboration is the key to effective messaging. So, you have to find ways of working together with a presenter who may be delivering your content. The goal is to get a dialog going. When a presenter has input, the script becomes more personal and will be delivered more emphatically.

PART

VII

CH

21

Tip #255 from	Send only the outline of the presentation to one or more presenters and ask for suggestions on the order of topics to be covered (not the content, just the order). Wherever a person makes comments, marks, or notes is where the script is more personal and appeals to the presenter.

PERSONAL ATTRIBUTES

One of the things I like to do immediately when working with a presenter is to ask one of three "favorites": I want to know his or her favorite type of movie (action, mystery, romance); favorite type of music (rock, jazz, classical); and favorite type of sport to watch or play (football, golf, tennis). (Sometimes I can even get bank account numbers if I push hard enough!)

For example, let's say I'm coaching you. You tell me that you prefer action movies. I would look for some obvious characteristics about action movies, such as "split-second decision-making, sense of urgency, attention to detail, even a hero who saves the day." Perhaps you have some or all of those traits or at least admire those traits in others.

I then look for parts of the script that relate (or could relate) to decision-making, especially the split-second kind. I would search for other parts that involve sense of urgency or attention to detail. There may even be a part in the script where a problem is solved and the "hero saves the day." At those specific points in the presentation, I would ask you, the presenter, to recount personal experiences (stories), cite specific examples, or use some other informative grabbers for the audience. Your energy and enthusiasm will be greater during any moment that is closer to some attribute of your personality. If you have a greater stake in the details, you will deliver the information with more confidence.

Note	The more personal a message is to you, the more you will express it with conviction. It's not about what the topic means—it's about what the topic means to you.

DELIVERY STYLE

Whenever I am working with someone, I look for special elements in the person's delivery style. Style is an interesting word that can mean so many things. If you need to find out more about a presenter, ask some questions.

For example, is she outgoing? Does she like to interact with the audience? Is she comfortable in front of her superiors? The answers to questions such as these will help you frame the message from a presenter point-of-view.

A presenter who likes to interact and "get in close" with the audience, for example, might be more at ease sharing personal experiences rather than displaying numerous statistics. Someone who loves details and trivia may prefer to point out the hidden meanings by reading between the lines or going inside the numbers.

When you know more about the personality of the presenter, it can make your job easier as a content-provider for a speaker who needs less support data than you may have expected. As you shape the message with a presenter in mind, you may find additional opportunities for unique grabbers, such as humor, simply based on the delivery style of the presenter.

EXPERTISE LEVEL

Knowing how in-depth a presenter understands the topic and the key concepts associated with the message is extremely helpful in your efforts to shaping the quantity of content.

For example, if a presenter has a great deal of expertise, the content can be more visual than verbal, more conceptual than concrete. Ah, but keep in mind that we favor the visual presenter. The script should contain broad concepts and limited data so that the audience spends more time listening, watching, and interacting with the presenter and less time reading the screen.

However, there are times when the expertise leads to wordiness, and the audience is bombarded with too many long-winded explanations. What I've noticed is the greater your vocabulary, the harder it is for you to get to the point. It's true. For some reason, when a presenter has more command of language, the longer it takes for him or her to get to the heart of the matter.

That's why a lot of times when I'm coaching someone I'll say, "You probably write well, don't you?" People who write well tend to speak like they write. They keep adding additional phrases and lengthier descriptions as they deliver the message. They'll say "What's important here, what you really need to understand, what is truly critical to note, in this instance…" Ahhhhhhhh…just get to the point!

I'm not saying that poor language skills make for better presenters; instead, full command of the language needs to be regulated in order to entice an audience to want to know more. If you have presenters that drone on and on, make them move through the script more quickly. Teach them three little words to say as quickly as possible: "You may leave."

MEDIA PREFERENCES

One other trait of the presenter has to do with media preference. You may have to develop the message differently based on a particular media type such as 35mm slides, overhead transparencies, or electronic images. If you know the media preference of a presenter, you can develop support for the message accordingly.

For example, for a 20-minute presentation, a person familiar with using PowerPoint to electronically deliver content will need about 35 electronic images. A person preferring overheads needs about 10 transparencies to cover the topic during the same 20 minutes (see the following note). That's because you can't scale overheads like Frisbees to try to change visuals as rapidly as you might advance an electronic show.

As the creator of the message, you may have to make some adjustments. For the person with the electronic show, you might include several builds as part of the 35 impressions—

PART

VII

CH

21

leaving the presenter some room for stories, analogies, and other grabbers. For the person with the overheads, you may have to fill each transparency with more data—leaving less time for grabbers. Or, you may make the transparencies with limited data, forcing the presenter to have more in-depth knowledge of the topic since fewer visual cues are available during the presentation.

> **Note**
>
> MediaNet has a software utility called Show*STARTER*®, which uses artificial intelligence to help a person plan a presentation. By answering ten simple questions, a ten-page report is available that outlines the visual design, text attributes, proper colors, lead-time, and number of visuals all tied to a selected objective. You can use a free, online mini-version, Show*STARTER*® *Express,* by visiting MediaNet's web site at www.medianet-ny.com.

KNOWING THE PARTICULARS OF THE AUDIENCE

Knowing the audience is the most difficult task imaginable. This is why marketing professionals lose sleep at night! Just when they think they can predict the market, the market changes! Although we want to avoid turning analysis into paralysis on this issue, understanding your target audience is very important to the development of the message.

Here's my take on "audiences." I think people are basically the same. I'm not discounting diversity in any way, but I use the philosophy that whatever is true for me in my own heart is probably true for everyone else on a very basic level. Our similarities allow us to share entertainment, sports, and all types of social activities. Our differences are what business presentations try to isolate and somehow address.

Knowing how to target differences in people is important in building effective messages. We can learn more about an audience in several ways including:

- Direct Contact
- Demographics
- Motivators

DIRECT CONTACT

The difference between learning the traits of the presenter and knowing particulars of the audience is direct contact. You have greater access to the presenters. They work with you! You can call them, email them, fax them, see them. This interaction helps you understand them.

You may have little contact and interaction with your audience until the presentation is starting. This is not uncommon. It happens a lot, especially to those pitching a new business. However, you may have other presentations in which the same group convenes on a regular basis. This might happen with internal presentations or briefings such as those on a monthly, quarterly, or annual basis.

The more direct contact (experience) you have with a particular audience, the easier it is to design a targeted message. Think about your family, friends, or even coworkers. You know how to handle these groups because you see them more often. Of course, in some situations you may prefer not to see them!

DEMOGRAPHICS

Experience through direct contact is getting harder to gain in the real world. Our lives are getting so busy that many of us just don't have the time to get to know a consistent audience. Be honest, aren't you amazed when you actually reach someone on the phone? You might quickly say, "What? No voice message? You're probably not that busy today, are you?" Direct contact is becoming a rare commodity.

When you can't have direct contact with the audience, you still have to try to define them or categorize them in order to look for differences. This analysis will help you design the right message for the right group. You can use demographics to gather certain information including age, gender, expertise, and culture. Note how these measurements are general and not job-specific.

For example, if your audience is primarily individuals who speak English as a second language, your message may have to be designed in very general and conceptual terms, using fewer details and wordy descriptions.

Nostalgia Theory

Knowing the average age of the audience is a significant piece of information that can be used effectively. The nostalgia theory works like this: Experiences and events that occurred during the mid-teen years (near puberty) are memorable for life. In other words, you can remember more things from when you were about 15 years old than almost any other time in your life. You recall specific songs, political issues, sporting events, and even the first person you fell in love with—remember?

So, if the average age of the audience is 43 and it's the year 2000, you know they were 15 in the year 1972. References to events from the late '60s and early '70s will be quickly recognized. The end of the Vietnam war, the last songs of the Beatles, Armstrong on the moon, Nixon resigns, and so on. You can reflect on history to develop examples and analogies to support your message.

MOTIVATORS

Motivators are the emotional elements that induce action. Now we're talking about the juicy stuff! Some of the more basic motivators are pride, profit, love, fear, and need.

> **Note**
>
> Although the basic motivators are general, the type of motivator can be more specific. Need may be refined to necessity, obligation, urgency, requirement, or even compulsion. You can fine-tune the motivator, just as you can fine-tune the objective.

PART
VII

CH
21

Decide which will best motivate your audience and fine-tune your original objective in order to help achieve the emotional response. Stop! You don't change your objective; you only fine-tune it.

How a Motivator Affects the Objective

Let's say your topic is a discussion about sales quotas. The talk is given to different groups such as marketing, senior management, and sales. Initially, you choose the objective "to inform."

You notice your next presentation of this material is at the annual sales conference. You decide that pride is the motivator for this particular audience, the sales force. You fine-tune the original objective, "to inform," and it becomes "to inspire to great heights."

You inspire by reinforcing the group's accomplishments and encourage them to achieve more. You add individual success stories. You use support information including comparisons to last year, growth in market share, perhaps even a testimonial from the president of the company.

Do you see how influential a motivator can be in the development of the message? Your original objective didn't change. It only became more specific.

You might find that more than one motivator moves an audience at different points in the presentation. You just have to match supporting elements in your script to the motivator that targets the type of response you seek. For example, if the best motivator is profit, a less obvious motivator may be fear. Thus, a chart showing the consequences of overspending may tap fear, while still supporting the underlying motive for profit.

UNDERSTANDING FILTERS

People react to information in many ways. What you say and what you show may be quite different from what the audience sees and hears. This happens every day. I say one thing; you hear something different. It's not a matter of who's right—it's a matter of agreement. Since you can't change this about people, don't even try. Just figure a way to deal with it.

Demographics and motivators affect the way an audience filters or classifies information. Each audience member puts his or her own spin on information based on how data is filtered to the brain.

A filter is the slant you apply to a message to make it your own. When someone says, "The way I see it…" you can be sure the person is applying a filter to the information in order to understand it.

The goal is to create a clear message that minimizes the distortion the audience tends to place on information. As we distort messages, we develop barriers because we make personal judgments. For example, when you see a stop sign, you know the message is the same for everyone. When you see a sign that says "Authorized Vehicles Only," you instantly become a member of a distinct group. You then form an opinion about the other group. You begin to question their right to even be authorized! Who are these people and why?

Avoid Clichés

Stereotyping is just one expression of how we filter information. This is a problem in itself because it leads to misconceptions, misunderstanding, and prejudice. Clichés also exist in business, especially when considering organizational duties.

Don't fall into the trap of shaping the message to a job function cliché. A group of accountants do not prefer only numbers. Engineers are not limited to processes. Sales and marketing people can handle details.

If the clichés for business were applied to art or entertainment, then there would have to be separate versions for everyone. Can you imagine *Gone with the Wind* for computer programmers and a different version for financial planners? How about a version of baseball only for doctors called *Medicine Ball*?

The job doesn't make the person. The person makes the job. If you changed your profession or industry tomorrow, would you really be a different person than you are today?

Avoid the job title cliché. If members of the executive team are expected to be in the audience, the message must be still be created for the entire audience. If the entire audience is only the executive team, then the message is still tailored to the needs of that specific group, based on generalities, not specifics. It wouldn't matter if the CEO likes fishing. If you make every reference about fishing, the remainder of the group is likely to miss the boat! Job titles may cause anxiety for the messenger, not the message.

I avoid clichés like the plague. They're old hat. They end up making a mountain out of a molehill.

Since filters exist, a good script finds ways of overcoming those filters. Table 21.1 shows some examples of where filters are used by the audience and the method used to break through the filter.

TABLE 21.1   HANDLING DEMOGRAPHIC FILTERS

Demographic	Method for Breaking Through Filter
Language	Simplify the words
Age	Appeal to generation styles
Gender	Avoid stereotypes
Expertise	Adjust conceptual complexity

For example, in the preceding table, the filters associated with the demographic of age may be addressed by using analogies, references, and other data that earmark a cross section of the audience by generation. You would have less reason to make a comparison of events from the 1950s if the audience is composed of recent college graduates.

Audiences apply their own filters to motivators, too. People put unique slants on emotional responses. After all, who can truly agree on how fear or pride affects any individual? The abstract concepts associated with any motivator leads to very subjective viewpoints for each person experiencing that motivator at any given time. Thus, each person applies a filter to a motivational element based on given circumstances and conditions prevailing at the time. Table 21.2 shows how to handle motivational filters.

TABLE 21.2   Handling Motivational Filters

Motivator	Method for Breaking Through Filter
Pride	Show comparisons and achievement
Fear	Use reassurance and historical data
Profit	Offer reachable goals
Love	Demonstrate teamwork
Need	Meet with urgency

For example, when a company is faced with a crisis situation and the employees are motivated by fear, the initial effort should be to reassure by pointing to how such situations were dealt with in the past, as opposed to immediately suggesting alternatives for the future. Stop the bleeding before you recommend a new brand of bandages.

Assuring Consistency

Until now, we've looked at the micro view of the presentation message. The effort has been to examine all the intricacies and nuances of purpose and people to arrive at a finely tuned message.

Now we have readjust again and take a macro view of the message and examine it according to a much bigger picture. The ultimate objective and the basic philosophy of an organization play a role in the development of the message used for the presentation. We must move beyond words and begin to apply the notion of a visual presenter to the entire organization and its global expression.

The growth of the World Wide Web is enabling any organization, regardless of size, to have a presence. As technology advances, the visibility and reach of an organization becomes more global. We won't be typing to one another to converse; instead, we'll be seeing one another though the eyes of a display device. Electronic communication will be more visual allowing the diversity of our organizations to become the portal to our profits. The heavens will open up as we transgress the universe...sorry, I got carried away!

To assure consistency, you must create presentations that can be delivered by a number of people in your organization to diverse audiences in a variety of settings.

This portability across presenters is easier when you design presentations that are high on conceptual ideas and low on technical information. When designed, the message will need to be scripted for the presenter, either conceptually or literally.

Maintaining the Corporate Image

Companies create and protect their corporate identities by spending millions of dollars on logos, signage, packaging, stationery, and public relations. Likewise, each employee's ability to consistently tell the company story helps establish a verbal corporate image.

Anyone who publicly delivers a message represents his or her company. In fact, the higher you are in the company, the more "you are the company." If you see the president of General Motors presenting poorly, you might instantly have a negative impression about the cars GM produces. These are not related, but in your mind they are. There is no logic to this, but it happens. The leaders are the company. In fact, the higher your level of responsibility, the tougher my coaching sessions. My logic is that if you make the big bucks, then you should present like you deserve the big bucks.

Concepts, visuals, and presenters are each part of the corporate identity. One of the goals of the presentation must be to match the consistency of your company image as demonstrated in other marketing venues. Start taking advantage of those TV ads!

For example, let's take a car company like Volvo. For years the marketing messages for Volvo have consistently stressed safety. Their TV commercials, advertisements, and brochures have always put safety first, as a way to differentiate their product. This doesn't mean Volvo's competitor's cars are not safe; rather, it simply means Volvo has made safety a primary issue. They are spending big advertising dollars to make this point.

Okay, so let's say you are developing the concepts for a new sales presentation for Volvo. One way to assure consistency in theme across other public image venues is to build references to safety into the script. Safety is related to security, protection, and even confidence. If you find stories, analogies, and other grabbers that relate to security or confidence, you will match the existing image portrayed in other marketing endeavors. In other words, you will be supporting the investment the company is already making through its advertising.

The presentation message represents the verbal corporate image, and it should try to support an image that the company is already vested in though other marketing efforts.

One of the ways a company displays its image is through a mission statement. You know, that highly sophisicated document you read through, pause, look up, and say, "We do this? Really? When?" A mission statement is not for the audience. They expect your company to do everything in that statement anyway. They don't count on anything less. The mission statement is really for the employees of the company. If your own presenters don't believe in it, how can you expect the public to buy into it?

Tip #256 from

Examine the company mission statement or the corporate vision. These expressions are designed to set a baseline or tone for all messages. This doesn't mean that every presentation must mention the mission statement. But when the core principles of your company relate to both your objective and your call to action, the impact of your message will be greater.

USING PORTABLE CONCEPTS

Just as the corporate image is expressed in different venues such as advertising and public relations, the same image is also expressed through multiple presenters. When your message is thought all the way through the corporate philosophy, those in the company who've embraced that philosophy will have an easier time delivering the message.

This "through-line of action" takes the traits of the presenter and matches them as closely as possible to the elements within the script as well as to the components of the corporate philosophy. When all three areas—personality, message, and philosophy—are in a direct line, the audience receives the highest communication.

If your personality trait is an appreciation for truthful analysis and the message contains elements about accurate reporting and your company philosophy is built around showing specific details, then a through-line of action exists. It is at these points in the presentation that your energy level and your commitment to the argument will be at its peak.

Tip #257 from

> See if your presenters understand the company philosophy in the same way. Ask your presenters to list the three most important things the company does or provides. Then look at the mission statement and see how many of those things match. Two out of three is good. Anything less means the presenter doesn't "get it." Now if you find that a lot of presenters in your company don't get it, well maybe the executives need to communicate better to those embracing the wrong message!

Concepts need to be portable in the sense that more than one person in the company is able to express those concepts in a variety of circumstances. Naturally, a growing company is likely to have multiple presenters. However, the complexities of the supporting elements for your message may be more difficult for some presenters than others.

Your letterhead may look the same across office locations, but your presenters are all different, even if they all work in the same building. Even though you expect each to deliver your message in basically the same way, it is the individual style that shapes your message for that particular audience.

For example, if you are creating a presentation for a remote sales force and the supporting elements to your objective include several detailed charts and graphs, some of your presenters may be more confident with such details than others. Those who have a better grasp of the material will handle the delivery of the concepts with little problem. Those less certain of their knowledge of the details will present the message with difficulty. Because each presenter places his or her personal spin on the information being conveyed, individual style will breed inconsistency.

To assure a consistency among multiple presenters, consider developing support items with limited details. When faced with less information, a presenter defers to actual experience, personal philosophy, and general concepts to express the verbal corporate message. In essence, they express themselves throughout the presentation, and the result is a more believable statement of knowledge for the audience.

So now I'll add another little twist to the plot! You need to script information conceptually and develop yourself as a visual thinker in order to provide information suitable for a visual presenter. The more conceptual the message, the easier for individual presenters to personalize the message.

Developing Portable Concepts

To enhance your skill as a visual thinker and learn to develop portable concepts, try this exercise. You will need three blank sheets of paper and a candy bar. Place the candy bar away from the paper, but within reach. Now place the sheets of paper in front of you.

On the first sheet, write a one-sentence description of what your company does or what your specific department is responsible for within the company. Imagine this sentence will be part of a press release or be announced on the local news. Be descriptive, but limit your narration to one complete sentence. This is the way you naturally think about the message.

On the second sheet, create three bullet points which cover the one sentence description you wrote on the first sheet. Imagine you are creating a PowerPoint visual using a bulleted list format. This is the way you currently think about designing the visuals.

On the third sheet, reduce the three bullet points to one word for each bullet and, if possible, make each word begin with the same letter of the alphabet. In addition, make sure the structure is the same. If the first one is a verb, they should all be verbs to maintain a parallel structure. This is the way you visually think about developing portable concepts.

If you did this right, your third sheet of paper has three words on it, possibly each beginning with the same letter of the alphabet. Okay, you can have the candy bar now!

Portable concepts offer less experienced presenters an opportunity to appear knowledgeable without sacrificing the consistencies already made public by more experienced personnel. That's a polite, sophisticated way of saying that even the new people can deliver the message when the message is simple.

The disparity between newcomers and seasoned veterans is less obvious when specific details are left to the speaker and not to the speaker support. Save the details for the handouts and spare the clutter on the visuals. Both your presenters and their audiences will be more appreciative!

Providing "Do" and "Say" Scripts

One of the last stages of the scripting process is the actual process of providing the script. At times you may simply provide an outline or you may wait until the visuals are created and provide the presenter a copy of the presentation in print form. In either case you haven't assured a consistency in delivering the essence of the message you've created. You need to provide a script.

There are basically two kinds of scripts, those that do and those that say. Both are designed for the presenter and they normally show the description of each visual (or the actual visuals) and the related message for each visual. The message can be conceptual (driven by actions) or concrete (driven by words).

A do script is conceptual and a say script is concrete. The do script contains suggested actions to convey each element in the presentation. A say script contains the actual words

PART

VII

CH

21

to use during the presentation. A say script is basically a written speech linked to the support material.

For example, you created the message and supporting data for a sales presentation and you expect each of the sales people to deliver the presentation in a local market. You need to provide each person with a script that matches each visual with a related suggestion as to how to deliver the information.

One way to guide the sales force through your message is to provide a do script which suggests actions for each concept or supporting idea. Figure 21.7 is one visual taken from a sample do script. Table 21.3 highlights a segment of the storyboard including the reference to the visuals. The left column shows the sequence, name, and type of visual while the right column describes the action a presenter might take to deliver the information.

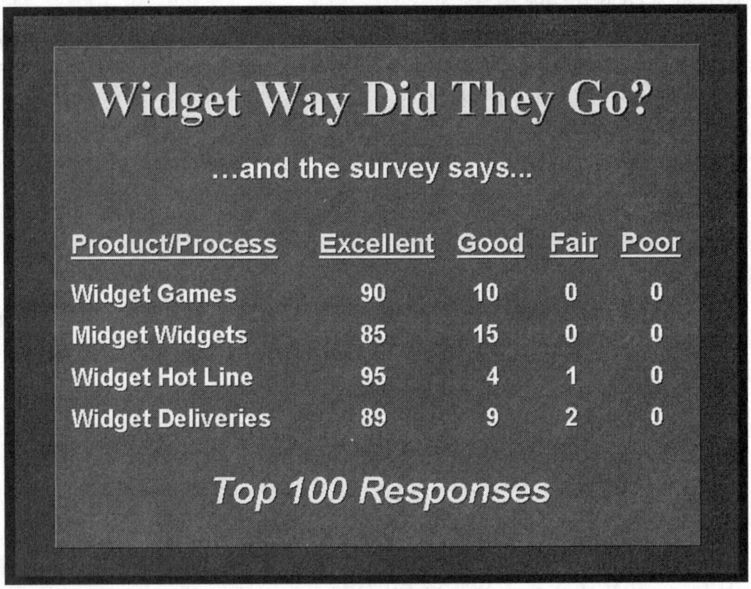

Figure 21.7
A customer survey showing "out of one hundred" satisfaction ratings for a series of products and services. This visual appears as #18 in the storyboard script.

Widget Way Did They Go?

...and the survey says...

Product/Process	Excellent	Good	Fair	Poor
Widget Games	90	10	0	0
Midget Widgets	85	15	0	0
Widget Hot Line	95	4	1	0
Widget Deliveries	89	9	2	0

Top 100 Responses

TABLE 21.3   A SEGMENT OF A DO SCRIPT

Storyboard Visual & Type	Supporting Script
#18—Customer Satisfaction (Survey shown as a table)	Tell a story that describes a personal experience in which you helped solve a customer's problem that resulted in extreme satisfaction and repeat business.
#19—Domestic Locations (U.S. map with dots showing office sites)	Describe your relationship with other sales people around the country and give examples of how you share information and collaborate to achieve sales goals.

Do scripts enhance the authenticity of the delivery and help each presenter develop a unique delivery style. This method requires very little memorization, which reduces the chances for error and inconsistency. Simple visuals that don't lead or confine the presenter are the key to effective conceptual presentations.

Another way to guide the same sales force through your message is to provide a say script that offers the exact wording (speech) for each concept or supporting idea. Figure 21.8 is one visual taken from a sample say script, basically the same example as the do script used earlier. Table 21.4 highlights a segment of the storyboard including the reference to the visuals. The left column shows the sequence, name, and type of visual while the right column gives the actual words a presenter should say when delivering the information.

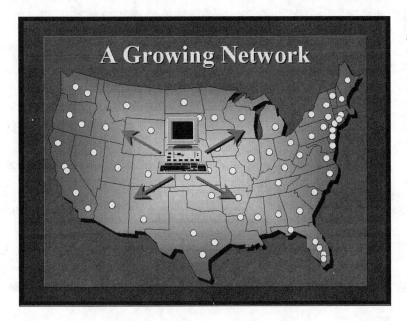

Figure 21.8
A U.S. map showing office locations and demonstrating the concept that the offices are connected by a communications network. This visual appears as #19 in the storyboard script.

TABLE 21.4   A SEGMENT OF A SAY SCRIPT

Storyboard Visual & Type	Supporting Script
#18—Customer Satisfaction (Survey shown as a table)	"As a world class provider of widgets, this survey shows our leadership in building customer satisfaction into every product and process we deliver."
#19—Domestic Locations (U.S. map with dots showing office sites)	"We have sales and service offices in 40 cities in the U.S. alone. Each office is networked through a sophisticated computer system that allows our sales force to expedite orders and share data."

Say scripts seem to offer more consistency than do scripts because all the correct words to support the message have been decided. Sometimes exact wording is necessary, either because someone prefers to work that way and is good at memorization (very rare) or because the person is presenting in a situation where precise timing and complete accuracy

PART

VII

CH

21

are crucial. Examples of these are presentations or speeches prepared for the media, such as TV or videotape.

Say scripts tell a presenter exactly what to say and require that the presenter memorize or read the script word-for-word. Since very few people can memorize a scripted speech, say scripts are usually more effective when using a TelePrompTer. The prompter gives the appearance that eye contact is being maintained as the presenter conveys the message.

Note

> Because the average person can't memorize a speech, he or she will usually read it to the audience. When we see someone reading, we have less faith in that person's knowledge of the subject. In fact, we may even doubt the person's sincerity if the message is emotional.
>
> One way to help someone with a written speech is to have them go through the presentation without the words. The more someone understands the basic flow of information and can them express the ideas and main points in his or her own words, the easier it is to later substitute the words of another.
>
> In the theatre, the actors hear the first reading of the play, then play each scene in their own words (improvisation) to get familiar with actions and intentions. Later, when they learn the lines they are able to make the playwrights words more personal since those words are tied to actions and intentions already experienced.

Otherwise, say scripts become cards or notes delivered from a lectern by a presenter who spends most of the time looking down to catch the next sentence in the script rather than looking up to catch the next response from the audience.

To support the notion of a visual presenter you need to provide the kind of script that offers the best opportunity for the message to be received by the audience. Although do scripts offer the greatest expression of individual style, say scripts conform to a higher expression of consistency.

As you construct the argument and qualify the participants, both presenter and audience, you will seek a consistent expression of the intended message. That message, converted into visual support, must be delivered in an effective manner in order to move an audience to action. Such are the qualities of successful presentation.

I know we covered a lot of information in this chapter and I don't want you to feel overwhelmed. You can't apply everything I mentioned to a presentation you expect to give two hours from now. But, you can start to think more clearly about the message itself.

Maybe you'll be involved in twenty PowerPoint presentations this year at some level. If some of those scripts are in your control at the message stage, then revisit this chapter and find the elements that help you most in designing a clear, concise, and captivating message!

TROUBLESHOOTING

Is there any quick, easy, one-two-three method for scripting a presentation?

Actually there is. It's called a timeline layout. There are three segments in the timeline, based on chronology, following the pattern of past, present and future. Some people use the metaphor of "where we were, where we are, where we're going." You can probably use this process with almost any type of script or situation and it certainly makes it easier to remember your key points when you use the timeline approach.

For example, let's say you have to give a short talk on the progress of a particular project. First, you determine the outcome of the talk (the call to action). You decide you want the group to continue to support the project. Nothing major, just "continued support." People give continued support to things that have a track record of satisfaction. So the objective is to demonstrate satisfactory results. You have an objective and a call to action. Now you need a script. Of the noted types found in this chapter, you select "problem-solution."

Using the timeline layout you apply the problem-solution scenario to the past, present and future using no more than three issues for each segment of the time line. Thus, for the past you mention three specific problems which led to the need for the project and you identify at least one solution that came about to address one of those problems. This begins your journey to providing satisfactory results (remember the objective?).

Next, you focus on current issues (present) and how several initiatives are being used to address the remaining problems from the past. In addition, you show how the solution to some of the problems has opened new concerns, which may develop into problems if left unchecked. For example, you might show that the implementation of a new procedure while streamlining communication has created the need for advanced technology and additional expertise. This is your first indication to the group that you will require their continued support for the increasing scope of the project (remember the call to action?).

Then, you discuss the strategy or plan for the future and the results you expect based on the already demonstrated and satisfactory past performance. You show how the investment in already proven, additional resources will continually improve the specific business function that the project was originally intended to address. You close by showing that without continued support for the project the original problems that created the need for the project will return but the effect of those problems will be magnified based on the current economic and competitive conditions.

Your ability to remember and discuss information is based on your understanding as to where that data fits along the timeline of past, present and future. Just make sure that everything you present matches the objective (satisfactory results) and leads to the call to action (continued support).

How can I maintain consistency in all my messages yet keep them unique?

The easiest way to create and deliver messages with consistency and impact is to find yourself in the message. The closer the message is to your heart and your belief system, the easier it is to be consistent.

But don't confuse consistency with conformity. When you try to conform to the message you make sacrifices and trade-offs in order to fit yourself into the message. This cannot be done with any sincerity because your heart and soul will not allow it. When you are consistent with the message, you make the message conform to you and the message is expressed naturally, through your actions.

If I coached you to higher levels of this presentation skill, I would force you to find where in a given message you have the strongest tie. In other words, what part of the message is closest to your heart? Once you match a core principle (belief) of your life to a particular element in the message, a link is established between you and the message. That is the starting point for developing a consistency. You may have to modify the message by slanting it to your way of thinking. But that's the beauty of shaping a message to your personal and natural style.

For every message thereafter you will use the same process to find the elements in the message which match at least one of your core principles. Messages will change, but you must remain true to your own beliefs. This is why I am able to work with so many different people from such diverse groups. The consistency in the coaching is to simply create the link between the message and the messenger.

And don't think you can't match the message. A message and a corporate philosophy are created by individuals who are part of the the same race—the human race. For all the diversity that exists, we still share basic instincts and characteristics simply by the fact that we are human. So, start from the premise that you are able to find elements of a message or a philosophy that fit you. The consistency in your own heart must be the watermark for all ideas and concepts you expect to support.

In my company, the messages are top-down and the training is bottom-up. This causes a big gap between employees and executives. Who should change?

Change is inevitable for everyone. From a presentation perspective, change is more difficult for those at the top. Technology is a factor. As computers and communication systems evolve, the skills required to deliver information become more visual. Companies that recognize the need to provide presentation skills training usually start from the bottom-up. This approach is incorrect because the newest employees are already visually driven and will adapt naturally to visual communications. The top-level executives need the skills training the most because they are probably not visual presenters. Having coached for more than 15 years I see these problems affecting the bigger companies more than the smaller companies.

For example, I once dealt with the Director of Communications for a major fast food service company—we're talking major with a capital *M*—the leader in the industry. Although many of the mid-level managers had experienced the initial stages of my company's coaching, the director felt that I was not the right fit to coach the top-level executives. When I asked why, the director told me that my personality and my approach would adversely influence the top executives in a way that might affect the corporate message. He was afraid to expose the leaders to the exact skills that others in the company were experiencing and using. This indicated the director's lack of confidence in the executive team's ability to change. In an effort to protect the top-level executives, the director created a gap between management levels. This gap will eventually widen until the mid-level managers move up or until they move on (usually to a competitor).

As a company develops a visual presentation strategy, those nearest the top need the training first. Why? Because they usually deliver the core messages of the company in the most public forums to extremely diverse groups. If the leaders can't change, then the followers will change the leaders!

PART
VII

CH
21

THE MEDIA—DESIGNING VISUAL SUPPORT

BRINGING YOUR STORY TO LIFE

"Image is everything," "Seeing is believing," "You oughtta be in pictures"—you've heard it all before. Well, the look and feel of your visuals will certainly make a difference in your business presentations; you just want to make sure the difference is positive.

For instance, I can look at any presentation and within the first three visuals, I can tell how bad or good the presentation will be, just from a media viewpoint. Want the truth? In most cases, the visuals just su...are pretty bad. Is it that people just don't get it? Is it that they are just not concerned? The trouble with this world is there's too much apathy, but then again, who cares? The point is that some simple techniques can help even a first-time presenter avoid making the most common mistakes.

Face it! A well-conceived script containing a clearly defined objective should be enhanced with good visual support. The features and functions of PowerPoint help bring your outline and storyboard to life, giving you the opportunity to create visuals with impact! This chapter focuses on the effective design of the support elements used to direct your message.

> **Note**
>
> Real-world experience is the best teacher. Since 1985, MediaNet has designed over 3,500 business presentations and conducted over 1,000 seminars on effective presentations. As a presentation skills company, we are involved in all stages of a client's event, from concept to delivery.
>
> Many of the principles, guidelines suggestions, and visual concepts discussed in this chapter are also referenced in MediaNet's original publication *Purpose, Movement, Color* by Tom and Rich Mucciolo (©1994, MediaNet, Inc., New York, NY).

A lot of people take for granted the importance of having well-designed visual support for the presentation. The components of the event, especially those that are most visible, can make or break the moment. If you keep following our notion of a visual presenter, then you can begin to see how the support for your message must be highly visual. The issues concerning the design of the images include

- Choosing a medium for your message
- Controlling eye movement
- Using color

CHOOSING A MEDIUM FOR YOUR MESSAGE

When Marshall McLuhan said, "The medium is the message," he was referring to the power of television and its influence on how we interpret information. Television is one type of media used to express information. Canvas is one type of media for a painter's artistic expression. The medium of expression is basically the link between the message and the mind.

Note

Media is plural and medium is singular, but sometimes media is used as a collective noun to describe a larger set (the newspaper media, for example). Okay, okay. Rather than asking you to consider semantics and form, from here on out, I will refer to everything as simply media, including flip charts, slides, overheads, electronic images, and other related items associated with the visual support used in a presentation.

The media choice represents the physical form of the message. It definitely affects the manner in which the presentation is delivered. For example, using overheads requires a different approach in delivery than an electronic presentation simply because the transparencies need to be handled (touched). Having "one more thing to do" affects the way in which the presenter delivers the message.

Although your delivery style is affected by the media choice, your objective should remain independent of the media. The very definition of visuals as "speaker-support" implies that you should be able to present your message without supporting media. I'm not trying to burst the PowerPoint bubble and suggest not using visuals at all. On the contrary, presentations with no visual support force the presenter to have the most exceptional delivery skills. Think about music. Without the orchestra, a singer is required to have perfect pitch to be a success. Unless you want to be the a cappella presenter, I suggest you stick with visual support.

With that in mind, choosing how you expect to support your message involves the following:

- Understanding media types
- Working with design templates
- Creating handout materials

Understanding Media Types

Presentations involve a number of support options including transparencies, 35mm slides, and electronic visuals. I place them in the order from most to least interactive. Overheads will require changing, slides may involve changing carousels, and electronic presentations are mostly hands-free. *Multimedia (page xxx)* is just an extension of the electronic presentation, although a degree of interactivity does occur when using elements triggered by the keyboard or mouse.

Flip charts and videotapes are omitted to limit this discussion to the most likely media types you would consider when using PowerPoint to design your presentation.

Note

PowerPoint calls the visuals you create "slides." However, in their electronic form (on your PC), they are really "visuals" or "images." If they are produced as 35mm chromes, only then do they become slides. If they are printed to transparency film, they become overheads. In fact, I always describe an electronic presentation as a screen show, not a slide show.

I am not trying to change the software, but throughout this part of the book, I will continue to use the words "visual" and "image" when referencing the media.

Overheads and slides are tangible and require an output device (printer or slide camera) to produce. Electronic visuals, although seemingly intangible, still require an output device (display) to be viewed. In all cases, the support is part of an overall production.

Okay, by now, you're probably aware that I think overheads and slides come in second in the media race. Electronic presentations work best. They offer so much more in the way of variety, interactivity, portability, and flexibility—just to name a few reasons. In fact, as you develop presentations for a visual presenter to deliver to an audience of visual creatures additional components such as sound, animation and video will become considerations in the design of the visuals. The real "power" in PowerPoint is seen in the design of effective electronic events. The electronic presentation is currently the most effective media choice for delivering business presentations.

There, I said it. Right now, the people who make color printers, overhead projectors, and slide imaging devices all hate me. But I'll probably be a keynote speaker at the LCD Projector Convention!

I'm not saying never use slides or overheads, but I am saying that an audience of visual creatures has come to expect more. It used to be that presenting electronically had to be justified in some way. Today, you'll have a hard time explaining why you chose not to present with a computer.

You may even have to explain it environmentally. Electronic presentations are "green"— that is, nothing has to be discarded at a later point that would affect the environment. Slides and overheads are not biodegradable. This is just one of many of the arguments for using electronic presentations.

In keeping with the notion of a visual presenter, you cannot ignore the growing acceptance of electronic presentations over slides and overheads. In fact, black-and-white overhead presentations are the most difficult for an audience to observe and still remain attentive to the message.

The Case for Color

When you watch a black-and-white overhead presentation, it doesn't take long before you start shifting in your seat, updating your daily planner, and checking the stack to see how many overheads are left.

Black text on a white background is called print, and print is meant for an audience of one. That's why you can work at your computer with its paper-white display. You can look away whenever you want and examine information for as long as you prefer.

A presentation is meant for an audience of more than one. An audience of more than one demands color. Color is what real life is made of; black and white is simulated and, therefore, less than real life. When people are faced with less than real visuals, they become distracted. When you present, you want the least amount of distraction possible. Present in color. Enough said.

If you evaluate types of media based on overall impact, color always supersedes black and white. In fact, if you're not using color, then you shouldn't even be thinking about 35mm slides or electronic presentations. Instead, you should stick with overheads. With color, however, the impact is greater, depending on the media type. The more flexibility you have with the media, the better the presentation.

Currently, electronic images offer the greatest flexibility when compared with slides and overheads. If you have several media choices available to you, choose the one with the most flexibility, which I find in most cases is electronic.

If you are already convinced of the benefits of presenting electronically, then you can skip the rest of this section on media types. But, if you need to justify a media choice, take a look at the following comparisons.

Flexibility in media can be examined based on the CCC Model, or Cost, Convenience, and Continuity. These three major considerations can help you decide which media choice to use for your color presentation. To better understand media types, we can apply the CCC Model to overheads, slides, and electronic images.

COST OF OVERHEADS

Sometimes referred to as transparencies, foils, or acetates, *overheads (p. 187–188)* are one of the most commonly used, yet least flexible, media types in business.

Often a company will try to use existing audiovisual equipment before investing in new technology, and the overhead projector is the most common in business. This makes sense. Moreover, for black-and-white presentations, the simplicity of inserting transparency material into a printer makes this choice an easy one with minimal cost.

> **Note**
>
> The easier it is for you to prepare the presentation, the harder it is for the audience to stay attentive to your message. If you quickly create a few transparencies with lots of lengthy phrases, you create a presentation meant to be read and not viewed. Easy for you, tough for us. But, if you take the time to design effective visuals, the audience will find it easier to watch the presentation.

But, when overhead presentations involve color, the cost issues change. After you prepare your presentation in PowerPoint, you can outsource the production of color overheads to a creative services company, or you can use in-house equipment.

The cost of outsourcing the production of the overheads may appear to be higher because the price is reflective of the original investment in equipment, the supplies used, and the time required to monitor the process. In addition, profit is built into the price, as well. However, in-house production has similar "costs" associated with the output.

In-house production of color overheads involves a cost of acquiring a color printer and a recurring cost of supplies. In addition, the cost of time associated with the output process itself is a factor as well.

Note

The factor of time is associated with equipment-related issues and not the time it takes to create the visuals in PowerPoint. That effort is generally the same regardless of the final form of the output. Your investment of five minutes to create a bar chart in PowerPoint doesn't change if you use slides, overheads, or electronic images as the final output.

Let's use the same type of example for the comparisons to slides and electronic images. Say, for example, that a company makes only one 20-minute presentation each week. That's our reference point: one 20-minute presentation per week.

For 20 minutes of presenting, you'll create about 10 color overheads. Over one year, that's 500 overheads. The supplies aren't free. You have to buy them. You can be more exact on supplies cost if you know the actual cost of the transparency material (film) and color cartridge (toner, ribbon, or ink). On average, each color overhead costs about $1.00. If you also factor in the cost of the equipment, even a $500 color printer adds another $1.00 to the supplies cost, if you spread the cost of the printer over a single year.

Ah, but we have one other cost factor. In addition to supplies, you need to consider the cost of time to manage the process of producing the color output. Someone has to do this, whether it is you or some other member of the company. The process includes setup of the printer, maintaining supplies, fixing jams, and waiting for each transparency to print. I've seen people on a Saturday afternoon waiting for stuff to print. What's sad is they actually started the printing on Thursday!

If you count changes, mistakes, setup, and other interruptions, about 30 minutes each week is required for the 10-overhead presentation we've been discussing. Although the hourly wage of whoever is managing the process makes a difference, even a $10 per hour wage adds another $0.50 per overhead to the cost.

So, the cost of producing 10 color overheads, in-house, might be as much as $2.50 each, when you factor in supplies and time. That's $25 a week. And this is assuming you only have one presentation per week.

If you outsource the color overheads by sending a PowerPoint presentation to a service bureau, you'll probably pay twice that or higher, depending on turnaround time. This is something to consider when weighing color overheads against slides or electronic presentations.

COST OF 35MM SLIDES

For *35mm slides (p. 187–188)*, the cost of production also includes investment in equipment, plus the actual cost of developing and mounting the slides. Some companies have in-house equipment to complete the entire process, but many own a slide-imaging device (film camera) from which the 35mm film is sent to a local development lab for processing.

Although the time to maintain the equipment and manage the process is far less than for color overheads, the number of slides needed to make the same points is much higher. If you have 10 overheads in your 20-minute presentation, the same 20-minute presentation using 35mm slides would require you to use about 30 slides. The reason is simple. You use media types differently. Slides in a carousel advance more rapidly than overheads changed manually.

> **Note**
>
> MediaNet designed ShowSTARTER® as a planning tool for a presentation. One of the calculations made by this software utility is to estimate the number of visuals you should have based on the length of the presentation. That's how I know you'll need about 30 slides or 10 overheads for the same 20-minute presentation. The actual quantities, when calculated by the software, are 31 slides and 11 overheads. But it's easier to use more rounded numbers for the example.
>
> You might ask how these calculations are derived. We studied over 1,500 presentations over three years to gather most of the information built into ShowSTARTER. One issue was time. A person usually changes overheads every two minutes or so, because they can't be scaled onto the projector like Frisbees. We noticed that when overheads are printed in portrait style, instead of landscape, there is tendency to add even more text and thus leave each overhead up for a longer time. Slides stay up for less time because the aspect ratio is different (22/35) and less space is available for data. So, to cover the same information, you usually need more slides which means you spend less time on each slide (they change faster).
>
> In addition, builds are used in many slide presentations, which increases the number of slides even though the number of full impressions is the same. A slide with four bullet points, when done as a build, will expand to five separate slides (heading plus four points). Yet those five slides still only deliver one visual impression.
>
> With electronic images the choice of using builds and overlays to reveal information in stages increases the number of visuals beyond that of slides simply because there is no limitation as there is with a slide carousel tray.
>
> This is why the number of visuals is dependent on the media choice, even though the length of the presentation is the same, regardless of the media choice.

Even though film cameras cost more than color printers, the cost per slide is similar to color overheads because you will use more slides per presentation. So, if you produce 30 slides per week for a year, and you invested in a $3,000 slide camera, your cost per slide is about $2.00. Add to that the actual cost of the roll of film and the developing charge, and it's about another $0.50 per slide. So, for about $2.50 per slide you could do it yourself.

If you sent a PowerPoint file to an imaging bureau, the cost of production will be somewhere between $5 and $10 or higher per slide, depending on turnaround time. Obviously, because you are using their camera equipment, their personnel, and their profit margin to image the slides, you will pay a higher cost.

COST OF ELECTRONIC IMAGES

One important advantage with *electronic images* is that they require no additional production output, as with slides or overheads. This is important if you're like me—time-starved! It's true. I know I wait until the last minute to do stuff because there's always too much stuff to do. If I can work on my presentation and fine-tune the images on the plane, that's a better use of my time than sitting around waiting for film to develop!

The good news is that after you complete your PowerPoint presentation, you can use your PC to launch the screen show (slide show) using a display device. Nothing is free, however, and you need to consider the cost factor of the device used to project or display the image. Typically LCD projectors are used with notebook computers to present electronic PowerPoint presentations.

For cost analysis, you should only use the cost of the projection device. Don't add the cost of the PC because the computer has many more business uses beyond presentations. Also, you can't really assign a cost to each image because there is no extra charge to make 10 more electronic visuals in a presentation.

Using ShowSTARTER® to calculate the number of visuals, our 20-minute presentation will require 35 images as compared to 10 overheads and 30 slides. This is because the change from one electronic image to another is a little faster than with slides. Hence, more visual impressions are possible when the duration stays the same (20 minutes).

Looking at cost per presentation, the equipment needed to project the image can be in-house (owned) or outsourced (rented). An LCD projector varies in price depending on feature/function issues, but if we assume owning one requires an investment of about $4,000, your weekly electronic presentation will cost about $80 ($4,000 divided by 50 weeks). Compared to 10 color overheads ($25) or 30 slides ($75), this appears to be the least cost-effective choice, on paper. In fact, if you went out and rented the LCD projector, your costs for that one presentation will be even higher ($200 or more). However, the out-sourced costs are always higher.

Tip #258 from

One way to know if you should buy or rent the display device is to estimate the minimum number of electronic presentations you expect to give in one year. Divide that number into the cost of a projector. If the answer is lower than a typical rental charge for that type of projector, then you might want to consider a purchase.

For example, you plan on giving 50 presentations this year. You set your sights on a shiny new projector that costs $8,000 to buy. $8,000 divided by 50 is $160. If it costs you more than $160 to rent the same kind of projector, then it makes sense to buy the unit.

Use a one year scenario even though your equipment will naturally last longer. To remain current with technology you would have to upgrade every year, so the rent or buy comparison is done against a one-year time frame to take the most conservative view. A five-year comparision would surely make you choose to buy everytime. In fact, most rental prices are based on the equipment paying for itself within one year.

One big issue is that electronic images have no incremental costs per additional visual. Thus, your hard disk can store hundreds of visuals, any of which can be accessed as backup or support information. Electronic presentations offer the flexibility to make changes, updates, create builds and overlays, and even allow for more advanced activity using multimedia and hyperlinks.

From a cost standpoint, that kind of flexibility makes the electronic visuals the better choice.

CONVENIENCE OF OVERHEADS

Convenience is about portability and relevancy. I mention portability because overheads are tangible. You have to carry them around and handle them. The handling factor makes overheads a less attractive media choice.

A three-ring binder of 50 color overheads in vinyl protective sleeves weighs about five pounds. Some presenters carry two or three times this much for certain presentations, which can amount to about 15 pounds of plastic! In addition, overheads can accidentally fall from the "stack," and many a presenter has experienced the "transparency crawl" in an attempt to quickly get everything back into the original sequence.

Another issue of convenience is relevancy, or keeping things current. Many presentations, especially financial ones, rely on the most up-to-date facts to drive home the message. Color overheads limit this timeliness of information to availability of the nearest color printer. In fact, the more specialized the printer you used, the less likely you can find a similar type when you are offsite at a presentation and you want to make changes or updates to several of your color overheads. This media is device-dependent and usually only reproduces consistently when using the same device that made it.

Foiled Again

I was consulting with a group of engineers from IBM several years ago (early 1990s, in case you just picked this book up at yard sale in the year 2015!). At the time, I suggested they present electronically, using an LCD panel and overhead projector. They wanted to present electronically, but hadn't budgeted for the equipment and were headed to six different cities, so renting LCD panels was not an option either. They already owned a color thermal wax-transfer printer, so they went with color overheads.

Now stay with me on this. Tektronix (big company) made the printer and that particular model had 6MB of RAM memory with PostScript features. Think of PostScript as "special fonts." (Yes, this information is important!) IBM's visuals were very "graphic" intensive, with lots of schematics, diagrams and drawings, and, every so often, text on an angle. Thank goodness for PostScript! The visuals took a while to print so the RAM memory was important.

Once prepared, the engineers embarked on the six-city tour with their binder of about 70 color overheads. First stop, Los Angeles. All goes well. But on the afternoon flight to San Francisco, somehow 12 overheads become plastic prunes from a cup of hot coffee! Yep, you guessed it—the important 12 overheads.

Guess what? There was no hotel or public location with a Tektronix color printer. (No surprise there.) Now it's past 5:00 p.m. and the hotel business center is closed. But, after some begging, pleading, and the usual threat of physical harm, they manage to get the hotel manager to open the business center. YES! A color printer! What luck! Oh wait, it's an ink jet, not a thermal. It's a Xerox, not a Tektronix. RAM memory? Don't even go there! PostScript? I don't think so.

They printed the overheads anyway (just to have something), and, of course, they didn't look anything like the other overheads. The audience spent more time distracted than interested, and the presentation pretty much bombed.

Moral of the story: You can't rely on off-site locations to provide consistency with color printed material since that media is device dependent.

One other issue involves the lack of convenience in printing color overheads. After your visuals are created in PowerPoint, you typically have to leave your desk and go to the location of the color printer. In larger settings, this type of printer is not the office printer located a few steps from your desk. Instead, it usually resides in a more central location and may end up being shared by a larger number of users. More people waiting to use the same device will result in longer lines!

CONVENIENCE OF 35MM SLIDES

Here's one for you: There are eight different ways to load 35mm slides into a carousel and only one way is correct. This can pose a problem if you are running out of time.

Tip #259 from

> The fast way to load 35mm slides into a carousel is to face the carousel so the first slot (number one) is to your left. This would be the same as if you were standing in front of the lens looking down at the tray. Take a slide and hold it up to the light so it appears correctly oriented as you look at it. Now simply flip it backward (which will turn it upside-down) and drop it into the slot. This look, flip, and drop process can be done fairly quickly.

Remember that convenience is about portability and relevancy. For slides, the portability issue is not so much that they are heavy (like carrying 100 overheads). Instead, you have some limitations concerning how many you can use.

For instance, the number of slots in a carousel limits slides. When glass-mounted, slides are limited to 80 per carousel tray. With cardboard or plastic mounts, you can use a carousel that holds 140 slides, but the risk of the slides getting jammed increases with the thinner and lighter mounts. Of course you can bring several carousels, but the convenience of portability is affected.

As far as relevancy goes, you actually have less flexibility for making changes when using 35mm slides. It's not that you'll have trouble finding a development lab to process 35mm film; rather, how will you get the slides shot in the first place? The good news is that you can electronically send your PowerPoint file to 24-hour services for processing. But, turn-around time is at least a day if you are out of driving range. The bottom line is that it is not likely you'll be able to make changes to the slides conveniently.

Okay, it's not all negative with slides. (No pun intended.) For certain presentations, the slide's emulsion, a maximum of 5,200 horizontal lines (resolution), offers the best contrast for color and image definition. If you are giving a medical presentation and the audience needs to see the changes in skin tissue to determine a medical condition, the subtle shades and color variations will be most accurate with 35mm slides. Electronic LCD projectors and color printers do not have the resolution (yet) to match slides, so you need to consider the importance of color definition in your support visuals.

High-color definition requirements, such as images rendered in computer-aided design and manufacturing (CAD-CAM) applications, would be another instance where I would recommend 35mm slides over electronic images.

CONVENIENCE OF ELECTRONIC IMAGES

When your images are stored on your notebook computer, you are ready to present! Now that is convenience. When you look at portability and relevancy, electronic images pass those two tests with flying colors.

Portability regarding storage issues for visuals is virtually non-existent. Your notebook computer doesn't weigh more each time you add more images. That would be like saying every time you learn something new, your brain gets heavier and you gain weight. That means the smartest people in the world would be HUGE! Einstein would have weighed about 11,000 pounds!

As far as limitations go, you can store as many visuals as your hard disk can hold. There is no slide carousel to limit you.

But electronic images address portability in a different way. It has to do with transfer. The ability to transfer or disseminate information through other electronic methods makes the electronic presentation more useful. Check out Part V, "Working with PowerPoint on the Web," if you want to stimulate your thinking about information sharing.

Welcome to the Machine

Electronic presentations made today can be delivered in similar form, before and after the actual event. You can reinforce your message to create lasting impact.

For example, you can send a self-running "overview" of your presentation to people in advance. Nothing prevents you from emailing your PowerPoint show to expected attendees, which contains information that helps support your message. This may even prompt better attendance.

After the event, you might have a more detailed version of the presentation available on your Web site, for example, for people to download and reference. The idea of electronic color hard copy takes on a whole new meaning in terms of cost and convenience!

Clearly you don't have the same flexibility with slides and overheads as you do with the electronic form.

I think relevancy is the best quality of this media type. Instant updates, timely changes, and custom versions allow a presenter to tailor current content to more specific audiences. You might have a product presentation for both end-users of your product and your resellers (distribution channel). Many of the visuals are the same, but the end-users aren't going to see the visuals about the "wholesale-pricing model" and the "channel-promotion program." You can either have multiple versions of this presentation on your computer, or simply go to PowerPoint's Slide Sorter view and "hide" the images you don't wish displayed to certain groups.

The electronic presentation format also offers the convenience of instant access. Action buttons and hyperlinks allow easy navigation to back up and support information, including links to other applications on the computer. The capability to do "what-if" scenarios suggests a dimension in presenting that you cannot even consider with more traditional media like slides and overheads.

So, from a convenience perspective, electronic images have too many advantages to ignore.

CONTINUITY OF OVERHEADS

The real clincher when deciding on a media type for the presentation is continuity, which is really about keeping the attention of the audience. If there is any break in the action—any interruption of the flow, any distraction at all—the continuity of the presentation will erode. This reduces the impact of the message.

From a continuity viewpoint, color overheads carry a limitation during the actual presentation process itself.

For one thing, the audience is subjected to the "blast of white light" each time there is a change to the next color overhead.

To overcome the "white light" issue, some presenters may choose to shut off the projector between changes, but that still doesn't eliminate the problem of guessing if the next visual placed on the projector will be straight when the light pops on. If the image is slanted or skewed in any way, the audience is distracted. You have to touch these things and manually place them on the projector, and you don't always get it right.

Even if the transparency is perfectly straight, the presenter, trying to make fast changes, eventually drifts closer to the projector. Soon, the presenter ends up blocking the view of the screen of some of the audience, prompting comments like "I know you're a pain but I still can't see though you!"

Finally, continuity is broken if a presenter has to search for support information. I've seen so many instances where an audience member brings up a specific issue, and the presenter spends a few minutes searching the stack of overheads for the "visual proof" of the point. During all that time, the rest of the crowd is generally distracted and they begin thinking more about dinner than discussion.

CONTINUITY OF 35MM SLIDES

You have fewer continuity problems with 35mm slides simply because there are no handling issues. Yes, slides can get jammed occasionally in a projector, but for the most part, this media type addresses the continuity issue nearly as well as electronic images.

One difference is quantity of images. The carousel is limited (80 to 140) and changing carousels during the presentation breaks the continuity. Of course, you don't want to keep an audience without a break for more than an hour, so 80 slides in a carousel should be more than enough to make it to each break.

The only minor continuity problem that 35mm slides pose is the on/off transition to the next slide. But, audiences get used to the pattern after a while, and it's not really a big deal. In fact, many slide presentations incorporate more than one projector and cross-fade between projected images, which simulates an electronic presentation.

But if you go to that extent, why not use the computer?

CONTINUITY OF ELECTRONIC IMAGES

Certain continuity issues demand the use of electronic images. They include builds and overlays, action buttons and hyperlinks, live applications, and multimedia options.

Builds and overlays, which reveal segments of information (text or graphics), help an audience understand more complex information. These techniques are most effective when done electronically. You can use slides for these effects, but you are limited in the number per carousel. You can attempt a text build with overheads. You know, the magic piece of paper that reveals yet another bullet! Ever notice how the paper always falls off the projector somewhere past the half-way point? Well, as Socrates once said, "Give it up, Crito!" Or, as I used to say, using my old Bronx accent, "Fuh-geddda-bowd-it."

Naturally, action buttons and hyperlinks allow non-linear navigation using the computer. This, by definition, requires electronic presentations. However, the instant access is what maintains the continuity of support information to the central theme.

Live software demonstrations, real-time computer applications, and multimedia presentations can only be done electronically; otherwise, the continuity of the event is completely missing. Imagine showing up to a lecture on using PowerPoint, and the presenter is displaying only screen shots of the software on overheads! Wait—that's this book! Yeah, but a book is not a presentation; it's a book. The media must match the message.

The issues of cost, convenience, and continuity seem to point in the direction of electronic images as being the most effective media choice for business presentations. Selecting the proper media should be your first consideration, before you start designing any visuals.

Let's Back Up!

So, you think we should put an end to slides and overheads? Not so fast! Let me tell you a little story about the need for back-up.

There was this sales event, see, sort of like a tradeshow, see, where makers of "new products" were presenting to potential distributors. It cost $1,000 per minute to present to about 15 potential buyers. But, landing just one deal could be worth millions.

I was brought in to coach the presenters before each would make "the big pitch." I worked with this one guy named Jerry. His product was quite visual. Jerry made some changes to the presentation here and there, and left feeling much more confident.

Thirty minutes before his presentation, he arrived at the conference center, set up his laptop and LCD projector, launched his PowerPoint presentation, and made sure everything was working. As he waited for the audience to arrive, he stepped into the restroom next door for a few minutes. When he returned, his PC and projector had disappeared! No, not disappeared as in "Look, magic!"; disappeared as in "Look, stolen!"

Luckily, he still had his briefcase in which he had about seven 35mm slides from an older presentation on the same topic. Those few visuals along with several of his handwritten sketches using a flip chart helped him secure an order. Sure, they might have "felt sorry" for him for losing his equipment, but he couldn't know that in advance, even if it were true. The back-up media saved him.

Computers can be stolen, but no one wants your slides or overheads! You won't find some guy on the corner opening his jacket while you pass by, saying "Pssst! Check it out—corporate slides!" It just doesn't happen.

So, having a set of back-up materials, whether it be slides or overheads, makes those media types a very viable and important part of the presentation process. They might come in handy someday!

WORKING WITH DESIGN TEMPLATES

You already learned about templates in Chapter 2, "Creating a Basic Presentation," but I want to make a point about the relationship of the template to the readability and to the simplicity of the message.

READABILITY FROM A DISTANCE

A clearly defined purpose needs the support of clearly readable visuals. Will everyone in the room be able to see everything on the screen? Whether you use overheads, 35mm slides, or electronic images, the audience must be able to read your support information or why show it to them? You can use several ways to test whether your images are going to be readable from a distance, even before you consider templates.

For overheads, place a transparency on the floor and stand over it. If you have no problem reading the text, then the audience member in the back of the room will not have a problem reading the information when projected.

For 35mm slides, hold a slide up to the light at arm's length. If you can read all the information clearly, chances are people sitting in the back will be able to read the slide when it is projected.

For electronic images, we use the "8 to 1 rule." The rule states that eight times the height of the image is the maximum viewing distance for the audience to read small-sized text. When I say small, I mean 24 points in size.

So, if your image is 6 feet high, people sitting 48 feet away can read text with a font size of 24 points. If the font sizes are smaller, people will have to sit closer to the screen.

> **Note**
>
> The height is based on the image, not the screen the image is projected on. You may have a 9-foot-high projection screen, but, depending on where you place your projection device, your image may not always fill the screen. In an art gallery, the size of the wall doesn't make the painting any bigger!

You can't control where people sit if you haven't planned the seating in advance. Sometimes you get to an event and the audience looks like they are sitting on another planet! You need to consider the sizes of the elements on your visuals.

> **Tip #260 from**
>
> Run your slide show in PowerPoint and stand back about eight feet from your computer, assuming your screen is about one foot high. Can you read all the text on every visual? Wherever you have trouble, go back and check the font size. You may have to make some adjustments.

Knowing the importance of visibility and readability from a distance, you can examine the use of templates in PowerPoint.

The templates are very helpful because they make choices for you and let you do your real job rather than the job of a graphic artist. But, you may need to make modifications in order for the templates to be effective.

In general, I find the templates in PowerPoint are designed more closely to the media of print than they are truly designed for presentation. I'll tell you why. It has to do with point size. That's the measurement term for a typeface, or font.

> **Note**
>
> PowerPoint calls typefaces "fonts." Actually, a typeface is a family of letter styles (Times Roman, Arial, Courier) and a font is what you do to a typeface, such as bold, italic, underline. But let's not worry about terminology for now.

Figure 22.1 is the slide master from a PowerPoint's Presentation Design (template) called Dad's Tie. I picked it because it reproduces better for this book, but based on the mostly white color scheme, it's obviously meant for overheads, not slides or electronic images. I modified the slide master in Dad's Tie by placing numbers at the end of each text line. Those numbers correspond to the exact font size (point size) used on each line.

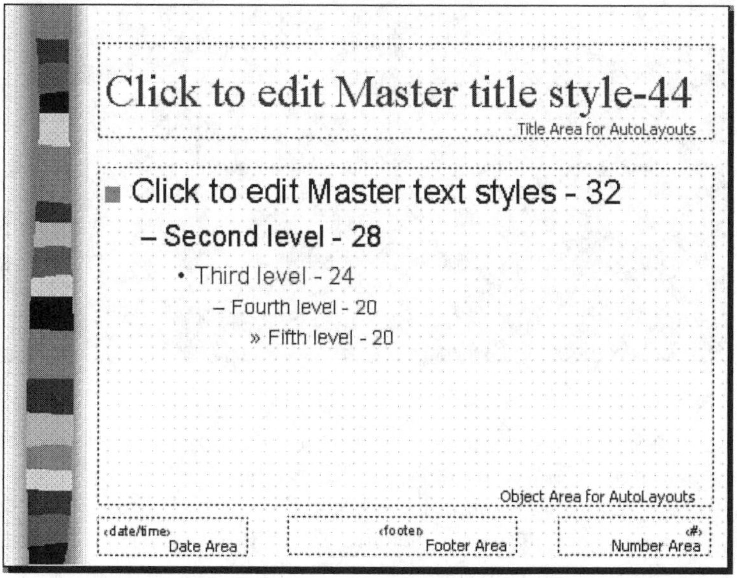

Figure 22.1
The slide master of the PowerPoint template Dad's Tie with the actual font size noted in numbers at the end of each line. The Title Area text box is pre-set to a font size of 44.

The slide layouts that accompany nearly every template in PowerPoint use the same font sizes, from 44 points in the title to as small as 20 points in the body of the layout. From a design standpoint, you don't want to have font sizes less than 24 points on any visual. This should already tell you that any text below the template's third level is unacceptable.

But why dangle over the threshold of 24 points? Why push it? Set your sights on 36 points or higher. Adjust the template before you get started and make the titles 60 points and the first level 40 points. This will force you to use fewer words, making the visuals more conceptual and therefore easier for the audience to grasp and the presenter to deliver.

SIMPLICITY IN DESIGN

The templates offer a variety of graphic elements, geometric shapes, and other interesting components to carry a design theme throughout the presentation.

When you work with templates, see if the design is generic or specific. For example, the Figures 22.2 and 22.3 represent a generic design and a more specific design. The first one is the template Whirlpool and the second figure is the template Tropical. What makes these different?

Figure 22.2
The Whirlpool template. The generic nature of the design makes this template usable for a variety of messages because the artwork makes little suggestion to the viewer.

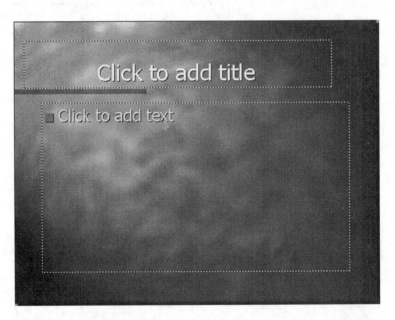

Generic templates contain very simple geometric shapes. Specific templates contain more complex and noticeable designs. Complexity forces the brain to interpret and think. So, when I look at the Tropical template I think of Hawaii, and then of my helicopter ride over Maui with my wife, and the way we just sort of floated right next to a waterfall. Now, as an audience member seeing the tropical template, what are the chances I'll be paying attention to the presentation with a vacation going on in my head?

You don't want the background design in your visuals to get more attention than your message. If you're marveling at the costumes, you can't be listening to the lines!

Over the years, I've learned to simplify themes. For example, at MediaNet, our *Electrifying Templates™ for PowerPoint* is a collection of very simple geometric PowerPoint presentation designs that fit the generic model of almost any topic. When designing so many presentations for so many different companies, it's easier to start with a very simple template and then add the complexity only to the visuals that require it. You can create your own templates using the same logic—simplicity!

Overall, templates should not hinder readability from a distance nor contain specific design elements that cause the audience to be distracted from the message. The presenter delivers the message; the visuals only support it.

Figure 22.3
The Tropical template. The specific nature of the design suggests a place, an atmosphere, and even a mood to the viewer. This reduces usability across different messages.

CREATING HANDOUT MATERIALS

Almost every presentation has some form of handouts. The nature and the timing of these materials are two very important issues. When you decide to give people information to walk away with, you have to think about exactly what they will be given and when they will receive it.

NATURE OF HANDOUTS

The handouts should always be different from the presentation. I know this breaks your heart to think that you now have extra work to do, but you really need to consider this point. Let's think about the relationship between the handouts and the presentation. Typically, you might fall into the trap of printing out a hard copy of your visuals for the audience to take away with them. You can look at this in two ways—conceptually or specifically.

If your presentation is designed for a visual presenter, it is conceptual in nature. The images are clear, readable, easy to understand, and very supportive of the stories and analogies used by the presenter. A copy of these visuals will be useless after a short time. When the event is over, people will not have the presenter available to explain the concepts. Someone will find a copy of the handout about three weeks later under a pile of desk rubble. The person will see a visual with an arrow, a circle, and a big number 11 and have absolutely no clue as to what it means. That is a useless handout.

Same scenario, except the handout reads like a book. Lots of text on each image, very wordy phrases, full sentences, extremely detailed charts, and complex tables of numbers. The handout is designed specifically. Nice handout and useful for a long time, but I pity the person who attended that presentation! It was probably a data dump on the audience with a presenter who simply read from the visuals most of the time. I have seen so many of these that one look at the handouts, and I can pretty much know how the presentation went.

Do you see how you can't win if you try to do two things at once? Handouts must be different from the presentation in the same way a book is different from the movie. How would you feel if you went to a movie and the book was on the big screen? That's right, the entire book—huge pages turning slowly while you gaze in amazement, then turn to a friend, and say, "Wow, look at the size of those fonts!"

Tip #261 from

Use the notes feature (see Chapter 8, "Creating and Printing Presentation Materials") to enter the concept or actual script for each visual. If you print a set of these for the audience, then they can review the comments long after the presentation is ended. This makes the handout more useful.

If you plan on having the audience take notes, then you can consider note-taking handouts. You can make these handouts in PowerPoint (see Chapter 8). They should include a combination of your visuals and an area for note-taking so that the audience can create personal references for later review.

To leave people with supporting documents is better than to bombard them with tons of data on every visual. Specification sheets, detailed charts, advertisements, articles, even free samples are just some of the support items that you can provide to tout your message long after you're gone.

A Pattern to Remember

Hand out more than you say—say more than you show—show it simply!

To hand out more than you say is to provide more material for later review than you verbally cover during the presentation.

To say more than you show means more words are always coming out of your mouth than people are reading on the screen. Remember that the visuals are speaker support, not the speaker. Do not read the visuals to the audience unless you plan to use a white bouncing ball over the text to help people follow along!

To show it simply is self-explanatory. No one ever complains about a business presentation that is clear and easy to understand. Simple visuals force the audience to listen to the presenter's explanation of the intended message.

TIMING OF HANDOUTS

A lot of people ask me, "When is the best time to distribute handouts—before or after the presentation?" I pause, look away for a second, and answer, "Yes." That's not an answer because there is no definite answer, one way or the other. It depends on your objective and your ability to keep the attention span of the group.

I start with a very simple question. Do you think the handouts will distract the audience from your presentation? If the answer is yes, distribute handouts at the end. If the answer is no, you can give them out at the beginning or the end.

For example, one of my seminars, "Presenting Made Easy," is a full-day workshop covering eight different topics. The audience receives a "kit" containing a book, a CD-ROM, additional handouts, and other information about technology discussed during the seminar. Although the handouts are not required to follow along through the topics, the information is provided at the beginning so that the audience can have a reference available during the workshop day. In addition, the scope of the material helps the audience decide how much note-taking is necessary. The more depth to the handouts, the less notes to take. Yes, there is a risk of distraction, but that makes the presenter (in this case, me) work that much harder to keep attention focused on the issue at hand.

Check out the opposite scenario: If I give a two-hour lecture as a keynote speaker, I only provide handouts after the session. I prefer to limit the distraction of people reading ahead and maintain the highest attention for the event. Because my handouts are not copies of each visual, the audience would not be able to "follow along" anyway, so why give them out ahead of time?

You have to examine the handout materials and judge how critical a role they play in the presentation. Can the audience respond to your "call to action" without the handouts in front of them?

Regardless of when you distribute handouts, always announce them at the beginning of the presentation. Let people know what you have, what it covers, and when they can expect to receive it.

CONTROLLING EYE MOVEMENT

We know that eight seconds is the average attention span on any visual. You can leave the visual up as long as you want, but the first eight seconds set the tone for how long someone reads and how quickly that person can begin to listen. Face it, you can't read and listen at the same time. Want to test this? Hand a newspaper article to a loved one. Begin speaking right away. You'll hear, in an angry tone, "How can I read this if you keep talking?" Try it (once).

Given the need to direct the eye quickly, ask yourself some questions. When a visual is displayed, where does a person look first? At what point on the image is the concentration of attention? Where does a person look next? If you can control a physical element of the audience, you will command more attention per visual. You can do this by controlling eye movement. The part of the body most used by an audience member is the eyes. A presentation is mostly watched. You need to find effective ways to direct the eye to the most important element in the visual.

Note

For this discussion, I'll use the word "eye" to mean both eyes. Another way to think about the word "eye" is as a focal point.

When designing the visuals, you need to think about several things to control eye movement. These include

- Establishing anchors
- Choosing typefaces and fonts
- Using builds and overlays
- Creating emphasis

ESTABLISHING ANCHORS

An *anchor* in a visual is really just the solid footing for the brain. It's where we dock our attention to a focal point to begin processing the information. Usually, the starting point is the upper-left corner of the visual because our reading pattern is left-to-right in the English language. But all visuals are not the same. Text changes size, charts are used, artwork appears, lines are drawn, and shapes are placed in varying spots. It can get very confusing.

Figure 22.4 is a simple text chart. The typical way your eye moves on the visual is first you read the word "agenda" in the title. Then you begin reading the numbers on the left side of the visual. Because they look the same, you scan them in a downward fashion. At about the third line (12:00), you say, "Wait, I should be reading this left to right. Let me go back." In the few moments it takes to readjust and start again, you have not been listening to the presenter.

In Figure 22.5, the geometric shape in the background helps guide the eye across instead of down. Text alone cannot guide the eye. Geometric shapes guide the eye.

Geometric shapes are universal. They are not subject to cultural limitations in the way languages are. A square is the same shape in Toronto as it is in Tokyo. We process universal shapes first, and then the language next. So think global!

In Figure 22.6, the list of items covers the basic steps necessary for launching hot air balloons. It is a text chart with no geometric shapes.

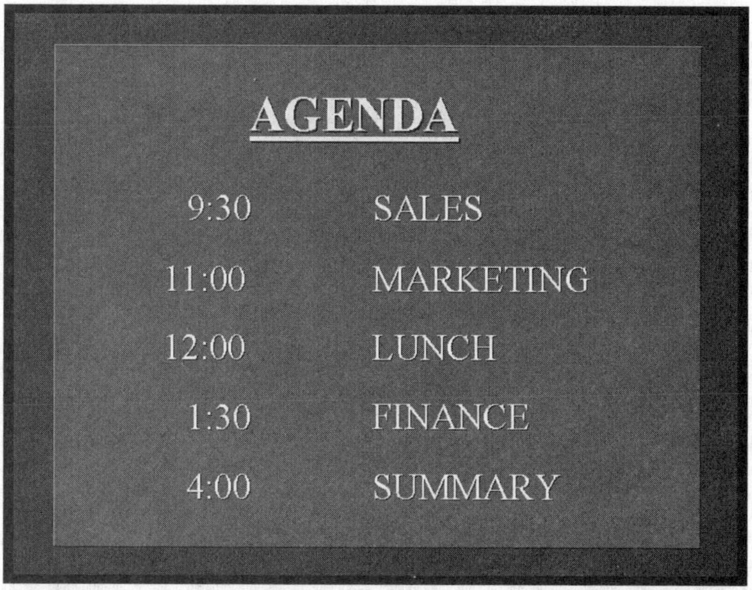

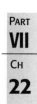

Figure 22.4
Without an anchor, the eye initially scans the text as if it were two separate columns.

Figure 22.5
The geometric shape provides an anchor to guide the eye horizontally, allowing a faster scan of the information.

Figure 22.6
While looking at this visual, your eye will move from top to bottom, as in reading a list.

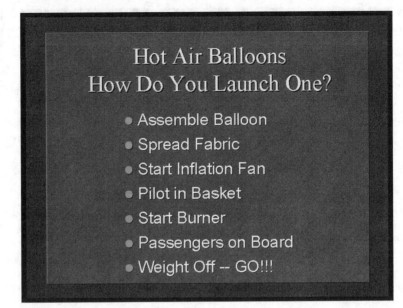

In Figure 22.7, your eye stops after the question mark in the heading and jumps to the tip of the arrowhead. But once you start checking out a geometric shape, you have to finish it to form the image in your mind. So, your eye travels to the end of the arrow at the bottom left corner of the visual to complete the shape. But, you then process the next shape (the bottom balloon) and after that, the text element near it ("Assemble Balloon"). Without thinking, you'll read the steps from bottom to top (backward, technically).

The whole image is designed to redirect your eye. Even the thin diagonal lines on the right side of the visual continue to help your eye move upward. In fact, as the visual forces your eye upward from the bottom, it matches the concept of launching a balloon from the ground.

Parallel Anchors

Another method for anchoring the eye is to keep text parallel, especially in bulleted lists. If you examine only the first word in a list of bulleted items, see if they follow the same pattern. For example, if one word is a gerund (ends with "ing") and another word is a plural noun and another word is a verb, it is not parallel.

If the first word is "Teaches," then each bullet should answer a "What else does this do?" question. Other bullets might begin with "Helps," "Gives," "Makes," "Offers," and the like."

If the first word is "Teaching," then each bullet should answer a "What else is this doing?" question. Other bullets might begin with "Helping," "Giving," "Making," "Offering," and so forth.

Keeping things parallel lets the audience anchor to the pattern and allows them to scan the visual more quickly. A faster visual scan gives the audience more time to listen to the message.

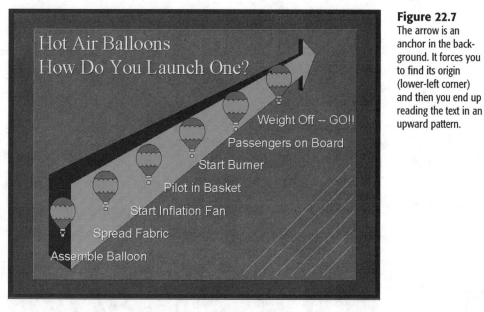

Figure 22.7
The arrow is an anchor in the background. It forces you to find its origin (lower-left corner) and then you end up reading the text in an upward pattern.

CHOOSING TYPEFACES AND FONTS

The eye moves from the simplest shapes to the more complex. Geometric shapes are easiest and text gets more difficult. I mean, when you think about it, the letters of the alphabet are shapes, but because you need to interpret text (language), you can understand why the eye scans text last. That means the design of the letters (the typefaces and fonts) affects the eye movement of the audience.

Basically there are only two kinds of typefaces, *serif* (fancy) and *sans serif* (plain). You can be sure that all the fonts you have on your computer fall into one of those two categories. Fancy typefaces have little curls (or serifs) at the ends of the letters, plain (sans serif) typefaces don't.

The eye slows down on the fancy fonts and speeds up on the plain ones. Think of the font as a road. The more hooks and turns, the longer it takes to travel that road. Fancy fonts have more contours (hooks and turns), so we read them more slowly.

Tip #262 from

If you choose to use two different fonts (please—no more than two!), use a serif typeface for the heading (title) and a sans serif typeface for the body of the chart.

When you make a presentation, you want the eye to slow down while reading the heading (which has the key words), and speed up when reading the body of the chart (where there tends to be more text).

Once the audience locks in on the title, they are more likely to get the rest of the text that follows. The heading is where the emphasis belongs because it's usually the first place the person looks.

The use of fonts and typefaces are the opposite of that in a newspaper. When you see a newspaper, the headlines are usually bold, Helvetica (sans serif), so that you can quickly scan them as you walk past the newsstand. But the body of the paper, Times Roman (serif), takes longer to read and therefore increases comprehension. That's why I keep my email messages in a plain font (Arial). I can't be bothered with comprehension. It might lead to responsibility, and who wants that?

If you look at Figure 22.8, you can see that the contours of the letters themselves cause distraction because the patterns keep changing. Don't you hate it when that happens? The eye travels along the contours of each letter and gets distracted as the different text shapes keep appearing. There should be a law against this!

Note

If you have the entire True Type Font library and feel compelled to use every font on every visual, you may be suffering from CTD, Compulsive Typeface Disorder. Seek help immediately!

Figure 22.8
The heading "NEW PRODUCTS," is a Times Roman font. In contrast, the word "Radios" in the first bullet is Helvetica, which is a sans serif, or plain, font.

Capitalization also affects eye movement. Take a look at Figure 22.9. Did you read it again? It's true. A series of all capital letters makes the text look the same. Our language thrives on ascends and descends as seen in letters like "b" and "g." These extenders give letters character. ALL CAPS leave no room for emphasis or inflection. This causes the eye to read the information again. If the words in all caps were read out loud, the sound would be monotone.

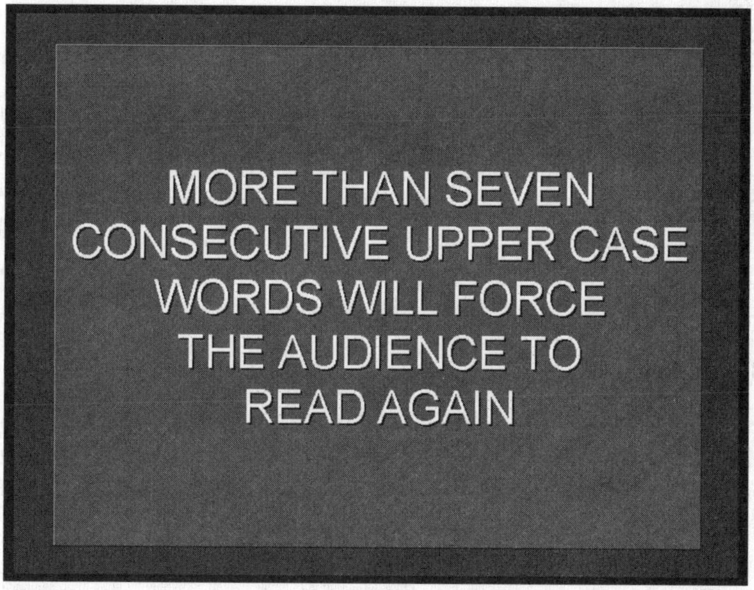

MORE THAN SEVEN
CONSECUTIVE UPPER CASE
WORDS WILL FORCE
THE AUDIENCE TO
READ AGAIN

Figure 22.9
When all the words
have equal weight,
it makes it harder
to know what's
important.

By structuring text phrases similarly to the way we read (uppercase and lowercase), you can then use capitalization to place emphasis at a particular point on the visual. Figure 22.10 shows the verbal inflection. If you read the text out loud in this example, the capitalized words would sound louder than the rest.

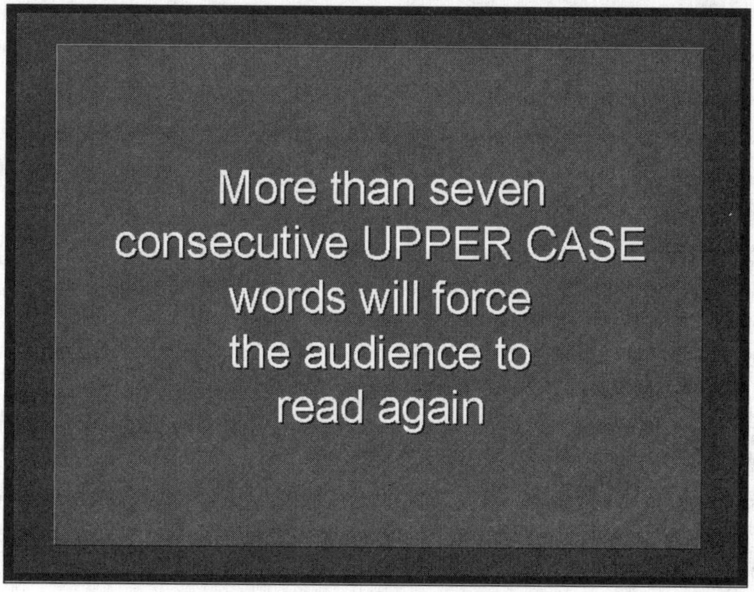

More than seven
consecutive UPPER CASE
words will force
the audience to
read again

Figure 22.10
The proper use of
upper- and lowercase
allows the visual to
"speak" for itself by
indicating the
intended inflection.

One other capitalization issue involves the use of "initial caps" or "first caps," as some refer to it. This is the choice to capitalize the first letter of every "major" word in a given text line to create emphasis. The problem is that there is a lack of consistency on which words to initial cap. After all, what is a "major" word? Is it one with more than four letters? Is it one that is not a preposition? How do you decide? If you are not consistent, the audience begins to get distracted since reading initial caps is not the norm, especially if the pattern in not consistent.

Stick to the natural way we read by initial capping only the first word of a text line, rather than using inconsistent or distracting capitalization methods.

USING BUILDS AND OVERLAYS

Eye movement can be affected by the sheer amount of information the audience is allowed to see on a given visual. Sometimes I look at a visual and think the heading should start with, "It was the best of times, it was the worst of times." You don't want *A Tale of Two Cities* showing up on your visuals!

Obviously, it's easy for me to tell you to reduce the clutter. But the real world doesn't always work that way. The visuals get wordy for one reason or another and maybe you can't be the one to say stop. So what can you do?

One way to soften the blow for the audience is to use the *build sequence (page xxx)*. This simple technique is used to reveal elements of a visual in stages in order to maintain a steady focus for the audience.

Examine Figures 22.11, 22.12, and 22.13. They are shown as three visual impressions, even though only one visual would appear if you look in the Slide Sorter. That's because the build is a transition effect in PowerPoint.

→ For more information about slide effects, **see** "Setting Slide Transitions" **p. 319**

Figure 22.11 shows the beginning of a build sequence with the first line revealed and the remaining information hidden. The presenter is able to concentrate on this element of the visual until the next item is needed.

When ready, the presenter reveals the next bulleted item, as shown in Figure 22.12. I prefer using the *dim-down*—or *gray-down*—approach for a more effective text build sequence. Dimming the color of the prior item—usually to a shade of gray—then revealing the next item allows the eye to focus on the brighter and most current element and still maintains some visibility for what has already been covered. I do this to help all those people who are waking up and want to know exactly what bullet point I'm discussing before they doze off again! I'm kidding, they aren't sleeping—they are usually on their way home by that point!

Figure 22.13 shows the next bulleted item, which is revealed at whatever pace the presenter chooses, allowing direct manipulation of eye movement in a downward pattern throughout the entire visual.

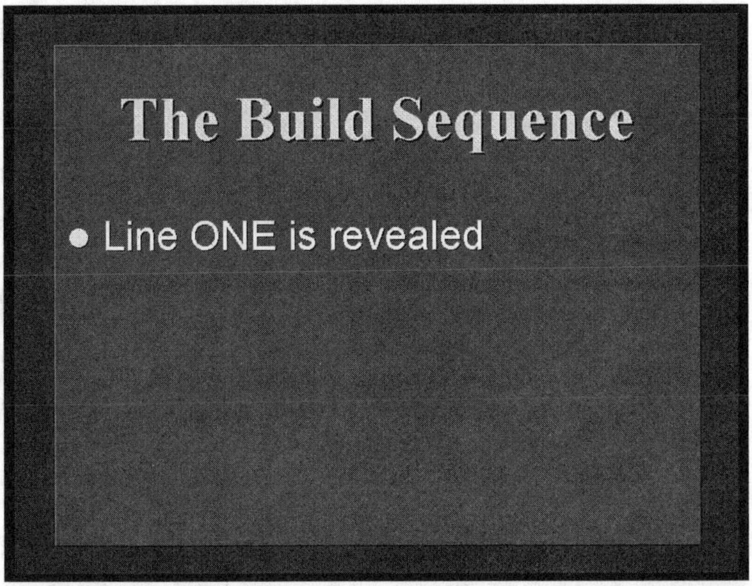

Figure 22.11
The first in a series using builds. One line appears and limits the distraction from additional items to maintain focus.

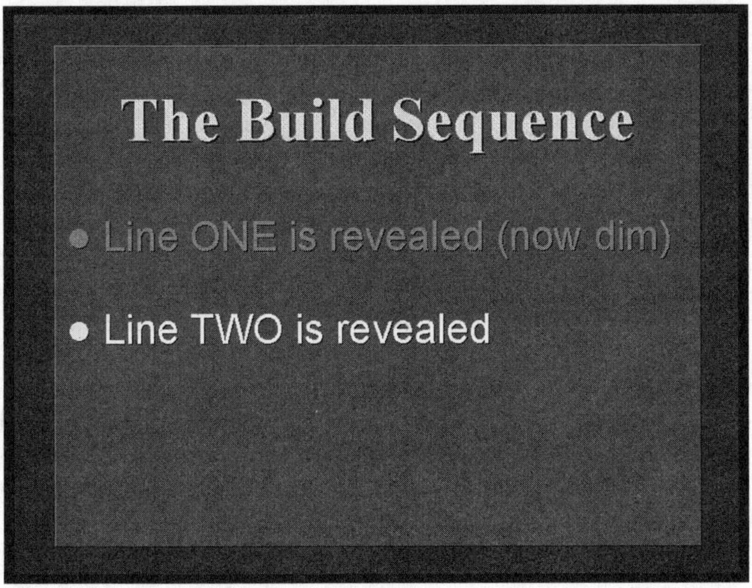

Figure 22.12
The next item in the build sequence is revealed while using the dim-down approach to darken or dim the color of the prior item.

Figure 22.13
The last bulleted point in the build sequence is revealed, and you can still see the dimmed text as a reference to what has been covered.

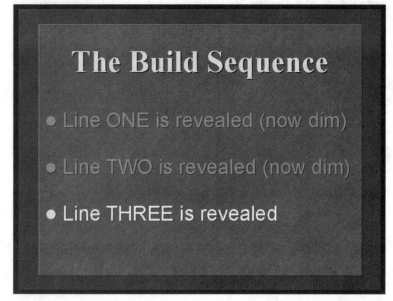

Another sequencing method that helps with data clutter is when you reveal a section of information at a time. Text, data, and graphic elements—each of which contain complete thoughts—are revealed in segments called overlays.

If you show the audience the completed image, too many elements would distract the eye and reduce the effectiveness of the visual. When the eye is bombarded with multiple activities or thoughts, it doesn't know where to look first. If it takes time to design the visual, you have to give the audience time to digest it.

If, however, the audience clearly sees the creative thought process that went into the complete visual, they will not be confused. So, imagine a busy puzzle. If you watch the pieces of the puzzle fall into place, you can appreciate the whole picture. Have you ever put together model or a toy with a lot of pieces? There's always that diagram in the instruction pamphlet that shows the "exploded" view of how all the pieces come together to form the object. Have kids and you'll experience these diagrams constantly! The point is that the exploded view diagram lets you see the pieces spread apart and helps you understand how they fit together.

Figures 22.14, 22.15, 22.16, and 22.17 show the base image and the three subsequent overlays used to show a communications network linking certain office locations in the United States and connected to a central hub. Yet the image can be separated into several little stories or thoughts which, when combined, create the final impression. Consider the amount of information on each of your visuals. Ask yourself if it would be more effective to reveal some of the elements in stages by using overlays.

Figure 22.14
The base image for an overlay sequence. The map of the U.S. appears with only a title above it.

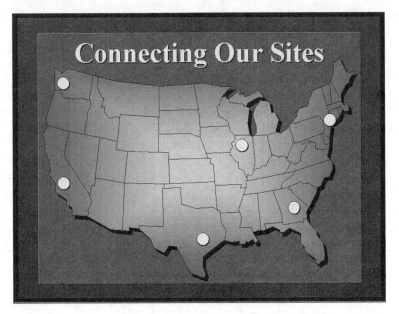

Figure 22.15
The first overlay or "layer" appears showing the office locations (dots) that the communications network will link together.

Figure 22.16
The next piece of the overlay "puzzle" shows the communications network connecting the locations.

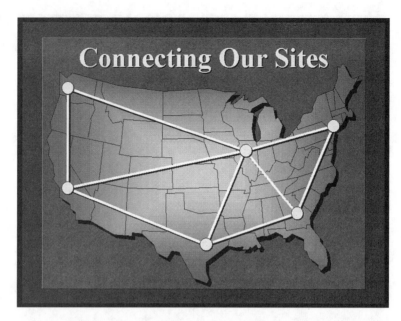

Figure 22.17
The last overlay in the sequence shows the hub or central communication area noted by the "star" in the center of the map (Chicago).

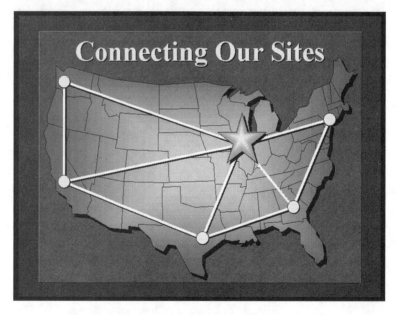

CREATING EMPHASIS

You can control eye movement by designing ways for the audience to immediately know where to look when the visual is displayed. If people are searching around, looking for something on the screen that remotely matches your words, then you have a problem. When people don't "get it," the attention span drops and boredom sets in very quickly. You can guide the eye using words or pictures. Headlines and arrows are both effective when designing guidance into visual content.

HEADLINES

How would you feel if every time you picked up the morning paper the headline read "News"? That's it, just News. Every day the same thing, News. You wouldn't be as interested. I know I wouldn't. Headlines, baby, headlines! That sells newspapers.

So, the best way to direct the eye to the important area of a visual using words is to start with emphatic headlines. Too many visuals have flat titles these days. Quarterly Sales—1st Quarter, Quarterly Sales—2nd Quarter, Quarterly Sales—stop already!

Death from a Pull-Down Menu?

See—a little bit of drama in the headline and you went for it! Face it, we are addicted to headlines. Why do you think the National Enquirer is so popular? That publication thrives on headlines. Actually, it's amazing how Enquirer editors pick their headlines. They have these three cardboard boxes—one with a bunch of famous names, another box full of verbs, and a third box with lots of nouns. Then, each time they need a new headline, they reach into the boxes and pull out one word from each and end up with: Donny and Marie… are…Aliens! And off to the presses they go!

In Figure 22.18, the two charts contain the same data. In the one to the left, I have a 25% chance that the audience will be looking at the exact part of the line chart I will refer to, even before I begin speaking. The heading is flat. However, in the same figure, the chart to the right includes the emphatic headline "Fourth Quarter Sales Post Record Highs!" which directs the eye quickly to the part of the line chart I want attention brought to—the fourth quarter as opposed to the other quarters. In fact, the headline even tells the audience how I feel about the information.

Don't waste the valuable real estate in the heading. If something is important, try to emphasize it in the title of the visual. Okay, you can't do this on every visual, but you can at least review all your headings and see where emphasis can be placed. Used wisely, emphasis in the right areas of a visual can affect both the physical and emotional reactions of the audience.

Figure 22.18
The headline tells a story. On the left, a flat heading doesn't help guide the eye. On the right, the headline quickly gets you to the exact part of the visual to be discussed.

The Laser Pointer and You

You're watching a movie. The killer is lurking in the bushes. Suddenly, a big hand floats over the screen with a finger pointing to a spot near a tree. You'd shout, "Get that thing off the screen!" That's because the visual (camera) has to do the work to guide the eye of the audience.

You should never have to use a laser pointer or any pointing device during a presentation. To use one means you couldn't figure out how to guide the eye with the visual. You needed a prop. Okay, now the laser pointer people hate me.

Face it. You instantly have problems when using a laser pointer. First, no one can hold it steady. And, if you forget to shut it off, you must apologize for searing the eyes out of the people in row three. But mostly you have to spend time directing the pointer to a spot on the screen, which causes you to look away from the audience and interact with the screen. Visual creatures (the audience) demand eye contact. If you're looking at the screen and we're looking at the screen, then who's presenting? You can't interact with things that don't breathe, like the visual.

The only time a pointer makes sense is when the visual is moving, like a video clip. Because the image is in motion, the pointer helps steady the eye to a specific area within the motion. But for still images in presentations, the eye can be directed by creating emphasis.

Don't get me wrong, sometimes pointing to the screen is required in the presentation. You should always do this from a distance and never touch the screen. Touching the screen causes the visual to move or vibrate, and it forces you to step in front of the image. Never block the light source because the visual is designed for a flat surface, and not your backside!

But you can use your voice to target specific areas. You can say, "If you look at the center of the visual…" or "The object in the upper-right corner represents…". You can verbally help guide the eye quickly through very complex information.

ARROWS

The simplest graphic element for controlling eye movement is the arrow. In many instances, using arrows as part of the visual can create the emphasis you need. Arrows not only show direction, but they can also indicate conflict, options, choices, and trends.

But be careful with arrows. Eye movement can easily be distracted when arrows point in too many directions on the same visual. Take a look at Figure 22.19. The eye scans the visual elements and eventually wanders or gets lost. The colors, text sizes, inconsistent capitalization methods, and the variety of geometric shapes add to the confusion. Try to limit the number of arrows used for emphasis on a single visual.

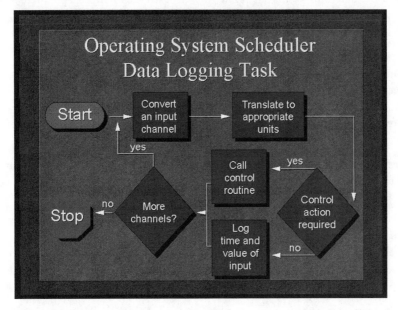

Figure 22.19
This chart uses too many arrows! Your eye movement is actually disrupted rather than enhanced. When this happens it takes longer to scan the image, which reduces attention to the message being delivered.

USING COLOR

I have always been fascinated with color. In 1985, my wife, Joan, worked as a fashion designer for a large sportswear company. She had to do all this research on color theory and the effect of certain colors on the emotions. I waded through several of the library reference books she gathered and said, "This stuff is great! Now when we prepare presentations at MediaNet, we can apply these color theory principles to help shape the story!" She said, "Yes, but think about the cost factor." I said, "What cost factor?" She smiled and said, "Well, it's going to take you a few days to look at all these books and they are already two weeks overdue!"

Over the years I've learned that correct color choices can have a tremendous impact on the success of the presentation. At the beginning of this chapter I pointed out that presentations delivered in black and white are less effective than those in color. We live in world of color and that, in itself, is an anchor to our understanding of information. Consider the following areas when using color:

- Incorporating symbols
- Investigating perception and contrast
- Understanding background colors and emotions

INCORPORATING SYMBOLS

Although geometric shapes are more universal, often you'll find that you need to use actual objects to describe something or make a point. You've heard the saying, "A picture is worth a thousand words." Of course today the saying has changed to, "A videotape is worth a million dollars," but that's another issue. Anyway, the use of imagery in a visual can be very helpful.

Symbols, to me, represent ideas. Clip art is basically a collection of symbols depicted as artistic renderings and available in PowerPoint or from other sources. You've already learned about symbols and graphics in Chapter 11, "Working with WordArt and Clip Art." Let's concentrate on how these elements can be used effectively or, for that matter, ineffectively.

I look for flexibility with symbols. Can I use them in the background of the visual? Can I make them into a silhouette for more utility? Can I avoid the distraction of details?

DEPTH

There is a whole area in the background of each visual just waiting to be used. Sometimes a template is used to fill the background. If the template already contains a lot of elements, you have less chance to use symbols as part of the background. That's why I like simple templates.

Figure 22.20 is a text chart showing how employees spend their time. It's clear, readable, and to the point. The background template is pretty simple. This allows you the option of adding a symbol to support the message.

Okay, so you see the word "time" in the heading and you search the clip art library for a descriptive symbol and you find the stopwatch. As shown in Figure 22.21, if you just use a two-dimensional approach, you'll shift the text to one side and pop the clip art on the other side. This is fine, but the clip art is still pretty small and less obvious from a distance.

But if you think deep into the visual, there is another interpretation available. The percentages could be displayed as a pie chart. A pie chart is round, the stopwatch is round. Instead of making the graphic part of the chart, you can make a chart part of the graphic! Figure 22.22 shows a three-dimensional view of the information. The symbol is now in the background but still retains its meaning. You know it's a hand, even though text covers some of the fingers. You know it's a stopwatch, even though there's a pie in its face! The symbol and the text occupy similar space on the visual, only in layers, and create the illusion of depth.

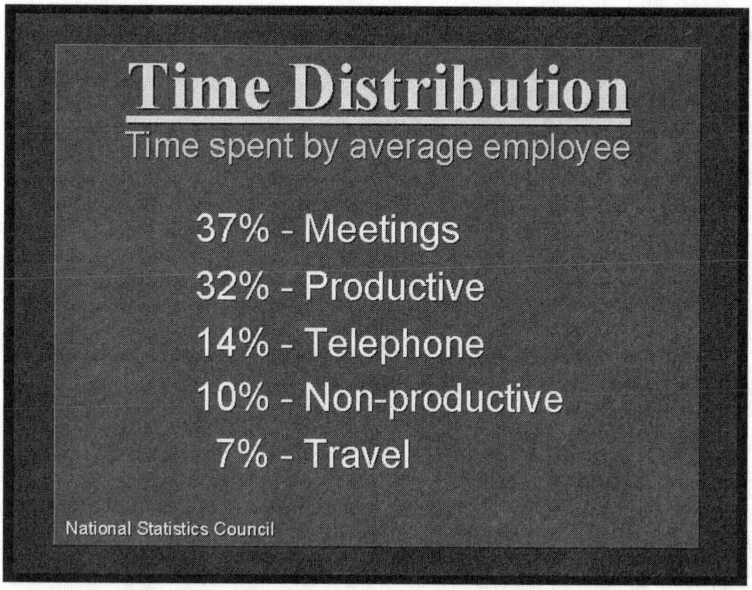

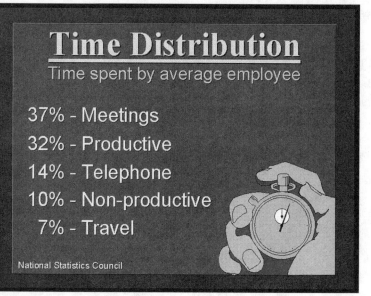

Figure 22.20
This is a simple text chart. A series of percentages, arranged from highest to lowest, shows how employees spend their time during the workday.

Figure 22.21
The hand with the stopwatch (clip art) is added and the text is moved to one side to make room for the artwork. This is a two-dimensional approach.

Figure 22.22
The clip art is sized to fill the background. This three-dimensional approach creates depth while allowing the data to take a more graphical form, a pie chart.

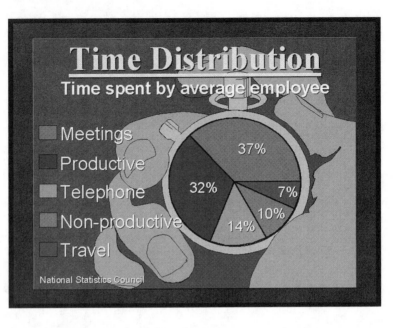

One of the best uses of the background is to incorporate photographs or natural images. A photo is the real-life symbol of an idea. Figure 22.23 is one example of how a photograph of people in a situation adds to the message in a way that clip art just can't. In keeping with our recurring theme of a visual presenter, it makes a lot of sense to use real people in real situations, not only in the message but in the media as well.

Figure 22.23
The photograph in the background is blurred, yet still representative of the "team" concept noted in the title.

Keep in mind that photos usually contain hundreds of thousands of colors in various degrees of brightness. If you add text or other elements on top of a photo, be aware of light and dark spots. Sometimes the foreground information may blend right into the photo and not be as visible. This usually happens with text. You may have to adjust the brightness and contrast of the entire photo in order for lighter text to be readable.

All the Lonely People

Ever notice how many solutions are discussed in presentations but no people are shown using them? I think photographs are really helpful when you are trying to get an audience excited about a product or a process. If you have a "solution" message, odds are the solution is going to help people somewhere along the way. By using photographs of people in the background, you can add the human touch which might be missing among all the charts and tables in your presentations.

I'm not saying you need photos everywhere, but look at your visuals and see where pictures might enhance the story. For example, if you are describing a new project to add facilities for a growing company, photographs or even renderings may be used. But think about using photos of people working in offices, gathering around a water cooler, sharing a cup of coffee, walking through a parking lot, taking the sun with a sandwich, or just burning the midnight oil.

Scenes like these help the message appear closer to reality. Visual presenters and visual creatures are first and always people. The foundation of all communication is people.

SILHOUETTES

I like symbols that translate well across media. Sometimes you have to think about the utility of symbols in a variety of venues. One of the things I look for is the ability to make the symbol into a silhouette. If you fill the symbol completely with black, does it still translate its meaning? Since a silhouette is only two-dimensional, the loss of depth may cause the original object to lose its meaning. For example, a stack of quarters when silhouetted would look like a cylinder. The link to money is gone. But a coffee cup would only lose depth, yet still maintain its shape as a cup.

I find this important when printing in pure black and white. Sometimes, objects in the background end up printing like big blobs and no one knows what they are. Printers today are sophisticated enough to print grayscale images, but what if you have to fax a copy of the printouts to someone? Forget about that grayscale definition you got from your laser jet!

Not every element can or needs to be a silhouette. But if the symbol translates well to a purely solid shape, you can use the shape in a lot of situations. Think about it!

DISTRACTIONS AND DISTORTIONS

Clip art images, if filled with many details, can actually become a distraction when the visual stays in view too long. The audience can get caught up in the artwork and begin to forget about the message. This can happen from the use of hokey-looking graphics that have a cartoonish or silly appearance. It can also happen from very sophisticated renderings that resemble a Rembrandt. The look of something is really up to you. If you don't like it, don't use it, if you don't have to.

But a more obvious distraction is a distortion. This happens when you do something to the symbol to alter its natural appearance. The alteration forces the audience to concentrate on what the symbol looked like before the distortion.

In Figure 22.24, the original bars in the chart are replaced with clip art in the form of pencils, to match the subheading of office supplies. You should always try to match a symbol closely to a concept to help clarify the message.

In this case, the pencils are the proper shapes to substitute for the vertically positioned bars.

Figure 22.24
The pencil symbols (clip art) are sized to match the height of the original bars.

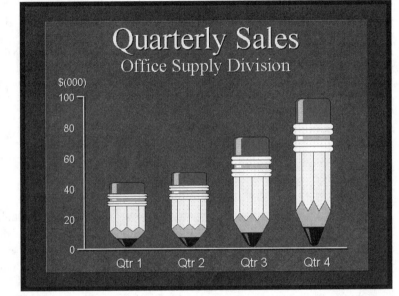

But wait a minute. It doesn't always work out so conveniently. Figure 22.25 shows what happens if the height of the first pencil is not 42. Would you give someone a pencil this little? That deformed, stubby little pencil looks ridiculous. You do stuff like that to your visuals and people will wonder how you make money! Just because you have access to a clip art library doesn't mean you have to incorporate colorful symbols on every chart.

Also, be aware of the geometric shape you replace with a symbol. The bars in the previous examples were all vertical. The choice of pencils made sense. What if you decided to use a stapler as the symbol? Although a stapler is an office supply, it is meant to be viewed horizontally, not vertically. This means you would have to rotate the stapler and stand it on end to fit the vertical form of the chart.

If you have to rotate a piece of clip art, you probably picked the wrong clip art! Why? Because the audience is going to have to re-orient the clip art in their minds just to place it in context. It's even worse when you rotate text. The only people who can quickly read text at any angle are librarians. The rest of us have to tilt our heads!

Avoid distractions and distortions when incorporating symbols into your visuals.

Figure 22.25
Symbols can get distorted! To match the value for the actual data, the first "pencil" is crushed down to the point of being a distraction.

INVESTIGATING PERCEPTION AND CONTRAST

Although numerous studies have shown the beneficial results of using color in presentations, the most important reaction from color is more of a reflex. Perception is a reflex you cannot change. It happens so quickly that you barely notice it.

Try this audio perception test. As fast as you can, spell the following three words out loud and then answer the question. The key is to spell the words out loud. Come on now, you have to spell the words out loud or it doesn't count. Ready?

Spell the word **MOST**.

Now spell **POST**.

Now spell **HOST**.

What do you put in a toaster?

Blaaammmmmp. Wrong, if you said toast! You put bread in a toaster. It comes out as toast, but goes in as bread. If you said toast, it's because you followed the natural reflex of perception to spell the three **O-S-T** words and then blurt out "toast" instead of "bread." You'll try this on the next person you see. You will. I know you too well, now!

Figure 22.26 is a test in content perception. Read each of the phrases in the triangles out loud. Yes, you have to say this out loud, too. Did you read the words in both triangles? Okay, now read the phrase in each triangle, backward, one word at a time. Notice anything different on the way back? In both phrases you'll see a duplicate word.

Tip #263 from

Always proofread your visuals backward, one word at a time. Reading phrases backward lets you spot not only typos, but other mistakes, as well.

If you scanned the visual and didn't notice the duplicate words, it's because you've probably heard the phrases so many times that you perceived your version to be correct. The anticipation happens because the mind moves faster than the mouth! Drink—and you can attest to this!

Figure 22.26
Are you reading too much into these phrases, or not enough?

Color perception works much in the same way. Depending on contrast, some elements may appear closer to the eye, which may or may not enhance the message.

Note

The remainder of this chapter discusses color in a number of situations. Although this book is not in color, the examples I'll use should still translate well using black and white as well as contrasting shades of gray. So, when I mention a color on a visual, you'll be able to tell what I'm talking about from the shading or from the object itself.

Figure 22.27 shows how color can change perception, but it also explains why black-and-white presentations are a problem. The two red squares (the inside dark-color squares) are compared against contrasting backgrounds. The shapes appear to be different sizes but are really the same size.

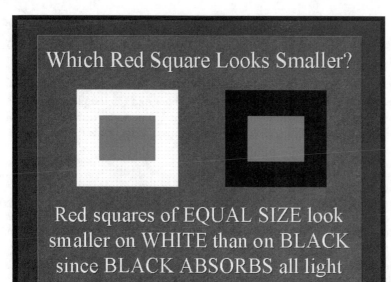

Figure 22.27
The inside (red) squares are set against contrasting outer squares of white and black. Can you see a difference?

A Matter of Contrast

If you want to talk about contrast, remember that black absorbs all light. The darker the color, the more light it absorbs and therefore it seems to push the object away from the eye. White, on the contrary, reflects all light. The lighter the color, the closer the object appears to the eye. In presentations, contrast between background and foreground is critical. The objects in the background should be darker and the ones in the front should be lighter.

This is the major reason why black-and-white overhead presentations are less effective. The contrast is opposite from the norm. The data on a black-and-white overhead is black. It pulls the eye into the visual because the information seems more distant. But, the clear (white) background is reflecting white light into the audience. The problem is that the body cannot handle white light reflected into the eye for very long. It's too distracting. When you use your computer, you can look away whenever you want. But when you watch a presentation, you are being asked to keep your attention fixed for a longer period. Proper contrast is needed to keep attention.

Because too much white light is a distraction, after a while, the eye tries to avoid the conflict and with it, the content of the presentation. Try staring at a fluorescent light for a while or glancing at the sun for a few moments. Your body simply rejects massive quantities of white light.

So the rule of contrast for presentations is to use darker-color backgrounds and lighter-color foregrounds.

This is why I can never understand why anyone using an electronic presentation would choose a bright background and a dark foreground. The only time I can see this option is if you will be in a room with so much ambient light that your visuals are washed out. In that case, the backgrounds would be less visible and wouldn't matter anyway. That's the only time I would recommend dark foregrounds.

Of course, the software is partly to blame. For many years I have been critical of all software programs, not just PowerPoint, for having only about half the templates following the dark background/bright foreground model. Perhaps this is one of the reasons why so often someone presenting electronically ignores effective contrast—they picked the wrong template!

No Room for Black and White?

The white light problem does not mean that black/white overhead presentations are totally useless. (Hey, even poison ivy is useful, to the makers of calamine lotion.) The point is that you may find times when you have to present without color. You just need to be aware of the distraction caused by the amount of white light and consider ways to reduce the impact of the problem.

This may mean designing the visuals more conceptually rather than more technically. Fewer words on each visual would let the audience scan the image faster and concentrate more on the presenter than on the screen.

Reducing the number of black-and-white visuals to be presented may be more effective, as well. To compensate for using fewer visuals, more detailed handouts could be given for later reference. You do have ways you can limit the impact of white light distraction. Awareness of the problem is the first step toward solving it.

Of course, that doesn't change my personal belief that presentations should be in color to be most effective.

RED/GREEN DEFICIENCY

Certain color combinations may pose a problem for some people, particularly men. We just can't do anything right, can we? Yeah, but we still have control of the remote and that will never change. Never! HA ha hahhh! Sorry...where was I?

Some studies show that nearly 15% of men have a red/green deficiency; MediaNet's research has shown that close to 22% of men have some form of this deficiency. Women do not suffer from this problem (in significant numbers), but they should be aware of this fact when selecting colors for visuals.

If you have this deficiency, you might see purple more as blue, or you may mix up brown and green. The effect is not as noticeable with large areas of color as it is with small areas. For example, if a line chart has three lines with one line beige, one line tan, and one line orange, it's possible that someone with a red/green deficiency will not be able to tell the difference between the three lines. The result will be confusion and a loss of attention. Try to avoid red-green color combinations, especially in small areas.

EARTH-TO-SKY COLOR THEORY

When you have related elements in the foreground, arrange them in a darker-to-lighter pattern from the bottom of the chart, upward. This "Earth-to-Sky" pattern is the way we view color naturally, from the earth to the sky. The earth is darker than the trees, which are darker than the sky, which is darker than the clouds. It's the same way a room generally appears as you look from floor to ceiling. It's even a pattern in the way we dress, with darker colors usually toward the bottom.

So, when you have related foreground items that might have different colors, you can choose an order of those colors from darker to lighter.

For example, in Figure 22.28, the segmented vertical bar chart shows the darker-to-lighter Earth-to-Sky pattern used effectively. If the top segment had been the darkest color, the chart would appear top-heavy. The arrangement of colors, done naturally, allows the eye to scan the visual more quickly. A faster scan gives the audience more time to listen to the message. Since the order of the colors can make a difference, why not use it to your advantage?

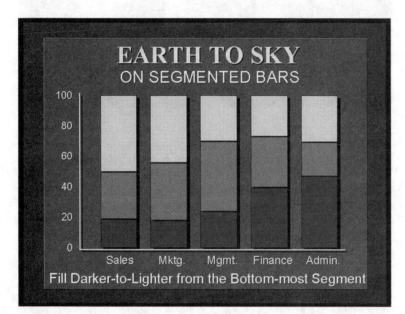

Figure 22.28
The Earth-to-Sky color theory applied to a segmented vertical bar chart. Note the arrangement of colors in a dark-to-light pattern from the bottom upward.

When displaying clusters of bars, as in Figure 22.29, choose a darker-to-lighter pattern starting from the left-most bar in each cluster. Don't use the "piano-key" approach by putting the lightest color between surrounding darker colors. When looking from left to right, the eye scans colors more easily when the arrangement is a dark-to-light pattern, similar to the Earth-to-Sky pattern.

Remember that the Earth-to-Sky theory is for the foreground elements in the visual, not the background color. So, if you choose gradient shading in the background of the visual, it doesn't matter if it's darker at the top, bottom, left, right, or fans out in both directions from the center. Specifically, the theory is most useful in data-driven charts, which usually shows a series of related items distinguished by color.

Figure 22.29
For related elements such as clusters of bars, keep the darker-to-lighter pattern beginning with the left-most bar in each cluster.

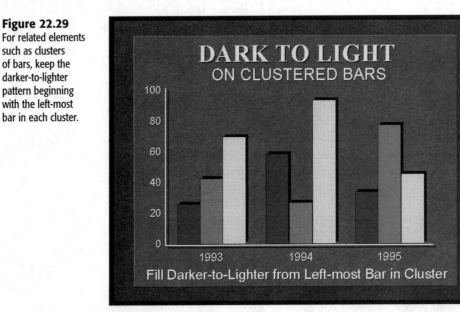

UNDERSTANDING BACKGROUND COLORS AND EMOTIONS

Color affects the central nervous system and the longer you see a particular color, the more it stimulates your emotions. During a presentation, it's best to stay consistent with your backgrounds, so the audience ends up seeing the background more often than each different foreground. The colors in the foreground keep changing and do not really affect the general feeling that the audience gets from the entire event. It's the background color choice that determines the emotional response from the audience.

Note

I always suggest you maintain a consistent background color and template for the entire presentation. But, if you have several different topics to cover, you can switch background colors and even design templates. I have a number of different seminar topics I deliver and the backgrounds are different in all of them, although throughout any one of the topics, the visual template is the same.

Keep in mind that a society makes psychological associations with colors based on appearances or cultural habits. Figure 22.30 shows some of these associations shared in the United States. Green is associated with money, for example. True, it is the color of money in the United States, but does green actually mean money? That would have to be true for all people everywhere. Is green the color of money all over the world? Then it can't mean money. Or else, one hundred years ago in the United States the color gold would have meant money.

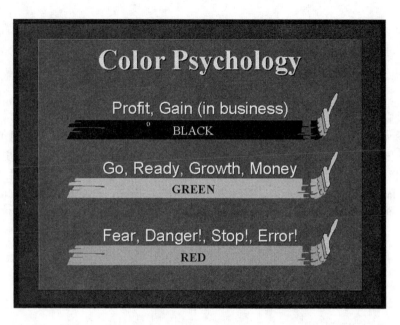

Figure 22.30
The cultural associations made with certain colors are not universal. But it's interesting to see what some colors have grown to signify in our American society.

PART
VII

CH
22

We all live under the same light of the sun. Blue looks the same in Borneo as it does in Bolivia. The effect of color on our emotions is from nature, not heritage. All people, regardless of culture, share a universal range of emotions, such as happiness, sadness, excitement, anxiety, desire, passion, and so forth. The ability to tap into these emotions using correct color choices can increase the effectiveness of the presentation.

Note

Be careful with colors. Don't make the presentation look like a circus. The use of too many foreground colors with a poorly selected background will become a distraction for the eye and result in an ineffective presentation.

Studies have shown that the background color of the visual produces an emotional response from the audience. Although there may be a number of different cultural interpretations of colors, the physical effect of the color is always the same. For example, red is the warmest color in the spectrum and is seen that way, regardless of any cultural associations we make such as negativity or loss (as in, "the company is in the red").

Lots of books and articles are available about color, but the following may help you in choosing a possible background color for your presentation. These recommendations are based on MediaNet's experience in developing over 2,500 presentations.

GRAY

- Neutrality
- Border between directions

- Uncommitted and uninvolved
- Concealment from other emotions
- Escape from anxiety and discontent

Gray represents a neutrality and lack of commitment. Depending on how persuasive you need to be, use of gray backgrounds may be a help or a hindrance. I would avoid using gray backgrounds when displaying any critical business information where you need to sway the audience. However, in situations where the information is left for the audience to make a decision, gray frees the presenter from influencing the audience to respond to the issue.

For best readability, we recommend charcoal or dark gray. Anything brighter than medium gray will ultimately cause glare from the visual, and any brightly colored items in the foreground will be harder to see.

BLUE

- Complete calm
- Increased sensitivity
- Loyalty, security, contentment
- Tied to tradition and lasting values
- Reduces blood pressure and pulse-rate

Blue represents a conservative, secure, yet more vulnerable approach to information. Deep, dark blue is the color of the night sky. At night, when you sleep, you're at peace with the world and most trustful in that vulnerable state.

Blue has a calming effect on the emotions and is useful for situations where you want to create an impression that appears conservative or traditional. You can definitely put critical information on blue backgrounds. The blue helps to develop credibility with the audience, especially when you introduce data based on tested facts and figures rather than speculation.

A blue background also tends to make the statement "This is the worst case scenario." It takes the "hype" out of the information and seeks to elicit an emotion of trust for the argument being presented.

Tip #264 from

When in doubt about colors, choose dark blue backgrounds with yellow and white shadowed text. This combination is the easiest to read from any distance.

GREEN

- Operation of the will
- Resistance to change
- Analytical, precise, accurate

- Opinionated and self-assertive
- Need to impress and exercise control

Green stimulates interaction because it represents the operation of the will. If you want to involve your audience in a discussion of the topic, you should consider using green backgrounds. Green brings out the opinions in people.

In fact, presentations requiring feedback such as management issues or policy decisions may be more effective when green is introduced in the background.

I would choose deep forest green or olive green, or even a teal (blue-green) background in these situations. Avoid very bright green because foreground colors such as yellow or white will not contrast enough to be seen.

Red

- Impact of the will
- Impulse, desire, passion
- Vitality and intensity of experience
- Urge to achieve results and succeed
- Increases blood pressure and pulse-rate

A red background is stimulating. Why? Red is a warm color and warmer colors are linked to an arousal of emotion. In presentations that seek to heighten the emotions of the audience, such as sales or marketing events, or for any situations that strive to motivate the audience to action, you might choose a red background.

Since red is the warmest color of the spectrum, the tendency is for the eye to move toward red more quickly than other colors. This eye movement is most evident with foreground elements, such as a red slice in a pie chart.

From a background perspective, when you look at the color red, your heart and pulse rate increase. You can keep looking at red and keep liking it! You see this in advertising all the time. What color is the fast car, the woman's dress, the uniform of the guy shooting the basket? Typically, it's red. Face it, red backgrounds tend to be stimulating for the audience and can lead to a heightened sense of realism about the topic, even to the point of increasing enthusiasm. Want to pump up that sales meeting? Go red!

The intensity of the red you choose is important. I suggest you stick to the darker shades such as maroon or crimson as opposed to fire engine red or bright cherry red. It's better to tone down the intensity of the red and use a dark contrast for readability.

Black

- Negation of emotions
- Extinction and nothingness

- Surrender and relinquishment
- Powerful, strong, uncontrollable
- Stubborn protest against current state

Black is the absence of all light. This contrast is what makes black such a powerful color (or should I say non-color?) Because black absorbs all light, anything on a black background will appear closer to the eye than the background itself. An object reflecting more light appears closer to the eye than an object reflecting less light.

Because black reflects no light, it offers no emotional stimulus. When the emotional response to a color is removed, the reaction is one of surrender or relinquishment, as in having "no other choice." This can be a very effective tool.

Information on a black background leaves the audience with "no choice" on how to react to the data. It exists, as is, and the audience can do nothing about it. Thus, black is usually associated with things that have already occurred and will not change. Financial presentations, especially those filled with a lot of accounting data, are usually best represented on a black background since the data cannot be changed; it has already happened.

VIOLET

- Mystical union
- Magical and enchanting
- Unimportant and unrealistic
- Irresponsible and immature
- Attempts to charm or delight others

Also called purple or magenta, violet is a color that represents something magical or mystical. Violet is the mixture of red and blue, and the result is fantasy. Why? Because red and blue are opposites in emotional appeal and for those two colors to get along—that has to be fantasy!

Because purple is more charming, it is also adolescent and somewhat childlike. This is a tough background color to use for critical business information. For one thing, the data might be viewed as unimportant or unrealistic and, second, those who suffer from a red/green deficiency would see the violet background color as a washed-out shade of blue—a color that cannot be easily recognized, named, or judged.

If someone can't understand the color, the information carries less importance.

If your objective is to entertain or to amuse, a violet background is great for less critical information such as humor, special effects, or even for the awards dinner presentation at the annual company meeting.

BROWN

- Reduced sense of vitality
- Passive, receptive, sensory
- Establishment of a foundation
- Increased need for physical ease
- Desire for family, a home, solid roots

Pure brown is the search for something permanent to plant your feet on. Brown suggests a need to build a solid foundation that currently doesn't exist. Brown is the mix of red and green, and it actually creates an uneasy physical condition by toning down the sense of energy that red usually gives.

This reduced intensity makes brown seem more passive. For that reason, I would avoid using pure brown as a business background, especially for critical business information. The data on a brown background may be interpreted as "not standing on solid ground," hence, less credible and somewhat unstable. Not the best choice for gaining the support of your audience! So, brown is out as a background!

Now the people at UPS hate me.

KEEPING IT IN PERSPECTIVE

The support of your message with well-designed media provides the springboard to the delivery skills you'll use to inspire the crowd.

A visual presenter constantly strives to stimulate the audience in as many different ways possible. Whether it be background colors, eye movement, or a well-placed graphic, the presenter works with the message through the media in order to get the audience to react.

Although the information in this chapter may appear comprehensive, the good news is that if you simply maintain a consistency in layout and design, you'll end up with clear, concise visuals that do what they are supposed to do—support the speaker, nothing more, nothing less!

TROUBLESHOOTING

How important is it to have the company logo on each visual?

In the past, when presentation visuals were mainly prepared by outside services, some slides and transparencies would get "mixed up" among clients. Sometimes this happened during the mounting of slides or during the printing and collating of the transparencies. Putting the company logo on each individual slide or transparency decreased the likelihood of this production process mistake. However, for electronic images there is no need to identify each image with the company for the purpose of keeping the presentation visuals intact. Basically, a filename and a storage location are all you need to know in order to identify the owner of the visuals. So one approach to this is to decide if your visual content is "hard" (slides, overheads, print materials, flip charts) or "soft" (electronic images, videotapes, Web sites, software applications). If it's hard, put the logo on each component that can be separated from another component, such as each page of a multi-page handout. If the content is "soft," then the logo makes sense on the first visual or at the very beginning of the electronic event.

Some argue that the company logo on every visual acts as a reminder to the audience. Put it this way: If your audience doesn't know what company you're with by the fourth visual, the logo isn't going to save you! The rule is that anything on a visual that doesn't add to its value is a distraction. Some say that after a while the audience doesn't notice the logo. Then that proves it's not necessary. Think about watching TV. How do you feel when the little transparent logo of the TV station stays on the screen, down in the right corner? Annoying? Enough said.

I know PowerPoint comes with so many presentation designs and templates, so why would I ever create my own?

Hey, I'm the first to tell you that you don't have to reinvent the wheel. Many of the designs and templates shipped with PowerPoint can serve your purposes for multiple presentations. In fact, you may decide to use an existing template and then modify it slightly to suit your needs. There is no reason to always start from scratch.

But for many organizations, the desire to create a unique look and feel to each presentation usually requires a "from-the-ground-up" process. Some organizations will not invest in off-the-shelf clip art because the same artwork might be used by a competitor which would reduce the chance of presenting a one-of-kind image. In fact, some companies create "standard" templates and designs for use within the company and they sometimes specify a group of images to be associated with certain presentations. For example, a sales presentation may require a certain template plus five or six visuals containing company information.

Because electronic presentations can be reproduced in other forms such as print or even publishing to a Web site, companies need to maintain a consistency across different media. So the use of predesigned templates may or may not be the choice of every company, depending on how unique they want their presentations to look.

CHAPTER 23

THE MECHANICS OF FORM—DEVELOPING EXTERNAL PRESENTATION SKILLS

In this chapter

by Tom Mucciolo

UNDERSTANDING THE OUTSIDE

"It's not what you say, it's how you say it!" We've all heard that before. And it's especially true when making a presentation.

A study of intimate relationships found that 55% of everything you say is what you look like when you say it. Another 38% is how you actually deliver the information. And only 7% is what you say. Only 7%! You might say this is a measurement derived from personal relationships and not business ones. I say our personal and business lives are so interrelated that it's hard to separate them. To me, this says that the biggest part of communication is nonverbal.

> **Note**
>
> The referenced study is from work done by Albert Mehrabian, PhD, and Professor Emeritus of Psychology, UCLA. Dr. Mehrabian is known for his work in the field of nonverbal communication, particularly body language. His findings on communication are described in his book, *Silent Messages*, which deals with all facets of nonverbal communication and with combinations of verbal and nonverbal messages. The book contains reviews of Dr. Mehrabian's own and others' research findings on important elements of subtle or implicit communication. Communicators, leadership trainers, and political campaign managers often make use of these findings.
>
> Dr. Mehrabian specifically notes, "The equations regarding differential importance of verbal and nonverbal messages were derived from experiments dealing with communications about feelings. Unless a communicator is talking about (his) feelings or attitudes, these equations are not applicable."
>
> In our discussions, feeling is definitely an issue. From a visual presenter's perspective, the *emotional* link to an audience is critical for an effective delivery of nearly every message and makes this study especially relevant to what is covered in this section of the book. Thank you, Dr. Mehrabian!

Here's more proof: You can speak up to 150 words per minute, but you can listen to over 700 words per minute. Do the math and you'll find that more than 75% of the time you are processing nonverbal cues. These cues are important.

Regardless of the exact percentages, the bottom line is that delivery skills make or break the moment. This is not to say that content needs to be ignored, of course. We just spent two chapters on content! That would be like saying a playwright's words are meaningless. Not at all. But it is true that the success of the spoken lines depends on the actors. And yes, bad Shakespeare does exist—I've seen it. (Unfortunately, I've even been part of it.) Poetry can easily be ruined by a poor performance.

A Delicate Balance?

I work on a theatre principle called "off-balance" perspective. I apply this view to the message, the media, and most often to the mechanics of a presentation. The off-balance approach is a one-sided push for consistency. If I can shift your position to one side (off-balance), then I've made some change in you.

Your "position" might be your stance on a message. It might be your way of looking at visual content on the screen. It might be your view of the presenter in the room.

It actually matches the rule of thirds in photography. If you look at a framed image in three vertical sections, you should use the outer sections for the subject. In other words, when you take pictures, try not to center your subject. The image is more interesting because a bigger picture emerges for the viewer's eye to complete. This is not always done, but if you glance through magazine photos, you'll notice that most shots of people have them positioned more to one side than the other.

This off-balance approach is very effective. I use it often in developing, designing, and delivering presentations.

The actions of the presenter, from a physical and vocal standpoint, can add value to the visuals and make the entire event more effective. During a presentation, the brain must process a large amount of content. Therefore, the presentation needs to be as streamlined and effective as possible; that is, clear, concise, and to the point.

Okay, now you know that the greatest percent of your communication effort is physical. It is a combination of your visual and vocal delivery. So, you need to develop the related skills to become a more visual presenter. But visual and vocal skills are directly linked to the way you think and feel. Your mind and heart play a significant role in your delivery style, just as your body and your voice do.

Through all of this, don't forget to smile. If you're not having a good time presenting, how can anyone have a good time watching? This doesn't mean that you have to tell jokes all the time, but the presenter has more impact with an inside smile. It's called energy. Without this energy, your speaking will be flat, uninteresting, and definitely less effective. It only takes two muscles to smile. Try it.

The mechanics of delivery are partly external (form) and partly internal (function). That's why two chapters are dedicated to these mechanical skills.

Let's start with the external skills, the mechanics of form, because your form is the first impression processed by the audience. The skills covering external form involve

- Conquering fear
- Using your body
- Using your voice

CONQUERING FEAR

According to the *Book of Lists*, the number one fear is the fear of public speaking. This eclipses even the fear of death! Wait a minute—if the number one fear is public speaking and not death, it means you'd rather be in the coffin than give the eulogy!

Call it nervousness, call it stage fright, call it whatever you want. If you can't speak in front of a group, you won't get very far in the business world. I'm probably not the first to tell you that. Now, if you have no problem speaking in front of people, then skip this section. But, if you have some anxiety when it comes to presenting to groups, pay close attention. Some powerful techniques can help you deal with being scared speechless.

So what gives? Does your fear increase as the next person enters the room? Why does the anxiety level rise in proportion to the number of people in the audience? What really causes this fear? You might think it's a simple lack of confidence. That, however, is just a symptom of a disease for which we need a cure! The fear is actually rooted in your physical presence in the situation. Think about it! If you didn't have to be there, you wouldn't have any fear!

Suppose you split communication into three types: written, spoken, and face-to-face. Match those with the way you work. You create documents such as letters, faxes, and emails for the written word. You use telephones and voice mail for conversational correspondence. You have meetings and presentations for the face-to-face method of communicating. Only one of these (face-to-face) requires your complete presence. The other two physically hide you from the receiver of the information.

When you write, you have time to edit and restate your words until you are ready to send them out for response. When you speak on the phone, you have less time to edit, but you are free to sit comfortably, and it doesn't matter how you may be dressed or how you appear. In fact, the telephone demands very little effort, especially now that you can screen calls, invent interruptions and use the ever-handy hold button. Even voice mail gives you a chance to plan your response in advance. So these two methods of communicating are less stressful simply because we can't be seen for who we really are at the moment and we get more time to collect our thoughts. When we are less visible, we have less fear. It's that simple. This protection from people helps you get through the communication effort with ease.

So let's take a look at the major problems associated with your physical presence in a situation. You can conquer the fear of presenting in two ways:

- Attacking the causes
- Learning to relax

ATTACKING THE CAUSES

Over the years I have found four main reasons why people fear public speaking. Looking foolish, being judged, appearing boring, and wasting the listener's time. Possibly hundreds of other reasons exist, but these four usually cover most people's fears.

When you examine these reasons, do you see what they have in common? Each is a result of being self-conscious. It becomes a question of "What will they think of me?" The focus of the problem is internal. It is self-directed.

So here is a good rule to remember: When the problem is internal, the solution is external. You need to concentrate on things outside of yourself in order to remove the doubt. This concentration always involves some type of action. Let's examine the four problems I mentioned earlier and see what solutions—or actions—can be used to combat the dreaded fear of presenting in public.

FOOLS RUSH IN

"I'm afraid that people will think I'm stupid!" I hear this one a lot when people discuss their anxiety concerning public speaking. Well, first I ask, "Are you stupid?" And only the really stupid people take a moment to think about that one. Hey, everyone is stupid, at times. Look at me. I'm one of the stupidest people I know. There are hundreds of people who will testify to that. But, then again, I hang around with a lot of stupid people who can't tell the difference. Then, when I'm with the really smart people, all ten of them, I use the skills in this section of the book to mask my ignorance!

PART
VII
CH
23

Forrest Gump said that "Stupid is as stupid does"—whatever that means. Actually, it's a brilliant statement about actions speaking louder than words. If you do something crazy, others might think you really are crazy!

For many people, the typical uneasiness of speaking in public comes from this fear of looking foolish. What would cause that? Are you poorly dressed? Have you prepared your information? Are you speaking from a script you honestly believe has merit? Looking foolish is a feeling you get when you don't have control of the content as well as you hoped.

It's no different from the feeling you had in school when the teacher called on you and you didn't give the correct response. You were embarrassed. You didn't have the answer and you looked stupid! But if you knew the content—and, hence, the answer—you felt exactly the opposite. So, your first action is to get control of content. If you do this, your fear will begin to disappear.

Although you might think that content is controlled though memorization, that is not the case at all. The best way to get control of content is to first conceptualize your information, then visualize the manner in which that information will be delivered.

→ To learn about conceptualizing and visualizing information, **see** "Providing Do and Say Scripts," **p. 529**

You need to script your message using concepts which link together to form the discussion or the argument. Normally, written scripts, or Say scripts, force you to simply read back the content without really knowing it. Conceptual scripts, or Do scripts, are those that segment the topic into main ideas, each of which has some associated action. The action helps you remember the concepts and allows you to present without any notes.

How Actors Learn Lines

I know you've heard the phrase "Places everyone!" Ever wonder how the actors know exactly where to be on any given line? In the theatre it's called blocking. It's the director's job to make sure everyone who paid for a seat can see all the action. Line of sight is very important, especially to folks who shelled out 80 bucks to watch the show! Blocking also helps the actors learn lines.

Here's the way it works. At the first rehearsal, the actors sit around a big table and read the script—once. At the second rehearsal, the actors are up on the stage with scripts in hand learning the blocking. The director might say to an actor, "Okay, now cross to the middle of the stage and pick up the letter from the second drawer in the desk." The actor moves to center stage, with script in hand, and stops at the yet-to-be-built set piece (the desk) and says the line, "I have the proof right here!"(or whatever). The point is that the actor remembers the line because it is linked to an action, the act of finding the letter in the desk drawer.

Obviously not every line has physical movement attached to it. But the lines become associated very quickly with the surrounding action, making it easier to memorize the words. You can learn a lot from this theatrical process.

When you link action to your words, you visualize the concept for the audience. The typical responses are, "It looks like she really knows her stuff," or "He appears to have a handle on that." Once you have obvious control of content, you won't be singing the "I'm feeling foolish" theme anymore.

JUDGMENT DAY

Another reason you might dread public speaking is the belief that the audience is judging you in some horrible, vindictive way. Let's look at that. What could possibly motivate a group of people to dislike you the moment you step in front of them? Why would such a group suddenly unite in the hopes of squashing you like a bug? What would they gain? Always remember that the audience is made up of people, people like you. The key to that statement can be found by changing the emphasis. People like you. They do. Ask Sally Field.

When you meet someone for the first time, don't you hope the meeting is positive? You're basically the same as everyone else in the world, and everyone wants to make a positive impression with each new person he or she meets. Before you open your mouth, the audience starts off by liking you.

Of course, some pre-existing situations can cause the audience to not like you. If the circumstances are hostile, negative, or life threatening, then the audience is preconditioned to feel a certain way before seeing you. But barring any pre-existing negative conditions, the audience is on your side. They want you to be effective.

Tip #265 from

Here's a test you can use to see if the way you judge others has merit: Every time you make a subjective statement using the word "they" or "people," simply substitute the word "I" and see if the statement is still true. Try it.

Say the phrase, "People just don't understand this business." Now substitute "I" for "People" and say it again. Notice a difference? Try the phrase, "They don't care about anything," then change "They" to "I." Using "I" changes your perception and, hence, the acceptance of the statement as being true. You can't separate yourself from the world. You are an integral part of it, just as I am.

Think of yourself as a mirror and you will get back what you project to others. In theatre, acting is reacting. The same is true in life. If you offer a positive, nonjudgmental attitude it truly does come back to you.

So, to reduce the fear that people are judging you, just believe in people as you do yourself. Approach an audience with the belief that they are just like you and that they just like you. This will begin to reduce the anxiety of feeling that you are being judged in a bad way.

Okay, time for a reality check. Unfortunately, it is very difficult to completely remove the fear of being judged by simply believing the audience likes you. This may work during the 15 minutes prior to your stepping onto the platform, but what happens when you look out into the room and see all of those expectant faces?

To overcome the inner feeling of being judged, you'll have to concentrate on something outside of yourself, some action or activity, to get your mind off the anxiety. To avoid being judged you need to become a judge. You can do this by focusing on the anchors in the audience.

Simply select a few people in the room to focus your attention on while speaking. These friendly faces, or anchors, are points of concentration that you must continually seek. This removes the feeling of being judged and puts the judgmental responsibility on you as you present. You are forced to judge whether those anchors are staying attentive, still interested, and still maintaining eye contact with you. In other words, your action is to judge others as to their attentiveness to the message. This will push you to make the effort to keep them awake! If you're doing the judging, then the fear of being judged is transferred to the audience.

THE BORED-ROOM

"The stuff I have to talk about is so boring." I get this a lot, especially from accountants. Well, I used be a public accountant. I found it to be the best training for a life of crime. That's a lie. Political science is the best training for a life of crime. Accounting is the best training for a life of full employment! But that's another story.

The fear is that the talk will be boring, because the topic is boring. Stop for a moment. That might be true depending on your topic. After all, not every topic needs to be delivered. However, the topic is usually not the problem when it comes to lulling the audience into a false sense of excitement. When you finish the talk, if the audience responds with a nice round of indifference, chances are you were the problem, not the content.

To combat a boring topic, you need to find significance. The action, for you, is to convey the importance of the topic. Look for the sense of urgency. The more you identify the critical components of your script, the more determined you get to discuss those components and get reactions from your audience. Reactions reduce boredom. Reactions give the audience something to do.

I'll use the accounting example. A budget report given monthly may seem a bit mundane. Yeah, it probably is. But let's say you linked some budget information to ways that money will be allocated to make some specific task easier for everyone. Maybe the budget for computer networking has been increased. No big deal, unless you make it a big deal. What if you pointed out that faster file transfers will reduce lag time and waiting time and give everyone more free time. In one sentence, you went from lowly accountant to giver of free time! You can't do this all the time, but if you can connect parts of your message to the needs or desires of the audience, boredom will not be your problem.

TIME FLIES

"I think I'm just wasting everyone's time when I'm up there!" This is another anxiety-producer.

The feeling of wasting time may come over you more often during the presentation rather than before it. Suddenly, you have this instant loss of confidence and you can't find a compelling enough reason to ask a group of people to continue taking the time to watch you present.

Do you see the problem here? Wasting time can only happen if there is time to waste. Get it? It's the opposite problem of being boring. People get bored by monotony and hearing too much of the same thing. Wasting time is when you don't have enough relevant stuff to say!

Believe it or not, the structure of your script might cause you to try to fill up the time. Just because you have an extra 15 minutes doesn't mean you must fill it with poor content. You have to make the best use of time in order to reduce the fear of having wasted it. In some cases, that may even mean letting people leave early. Perish the thought!

The easiest way to make the best use of time is to use a form of action known as interaction. You can manage your time better by involving the audience throughout the presentation. This requires you to plan ahead, think quickly on your feet, ask questions, stir discussion, and even create controversy. Naturally, this shifts the concentration from yourself to your audience because you have to monitor their involvement. Activities that help audiences experience new things are seen as positive and not perceived as wasted time.

Now, instead of just planning time for the audience to ask questions, plan the time for you to ask your audience questions. Be proactive. Come up with thought-provoking ideas to stimulate discussion. Not only do you involve people in the topic, you learn from the experience, too. This type of involvement helps reduce the fear that you are wasting the listener's time.

If you can't fill the time with enough information of your own, then maybe the audience can help you. Again, you need to redirect the fear inside of you by placing the problem outside of yourself. Hand the task of not wasting time over to the audience. Believe me, they'll perk up.

LEARNING TO RELAX

Some say the nervousness before a performance is both natural and necessary. I say it might be natural, but it is certainly not necessary. If you can reduce a case of the jitters before a presentation, you will be able to deliver your message more effectively. One way to do this is to learn to relax physically. Of course, a limber body is always more relaxed under any pressure. Stretching exercises and other aerobic activities will, among many other benefits, definitely help you relax when giving a presentation.

How It All Falls Apart

Fear affects you physically. Your body "talks" to you right before the big moment. It works something like this:

Your heart starts pounding, pumping precious blood from your belly to your brain. Your stomach gets queasy as the knot tightens and the butterflies begin to bounce. Your nervous system sounds the alarm and chemistry gets the call.

Helloooo, Adrenaline! On the street they call it speed.

The slick little stimulant marinates your muscles, weakens your knees, and races to your extremities. The friction of its fury lights a fire under your flesh.

You call it nervous energy. On the street they call it sweat.

Your heart beats faster and you take deeper breaths to assault the adrenaline rush. Oh no! Too much oxygen! You picked the wrong time to fill those lungs, pal!

Wham! The aerated blood in your brain begins to pulse as the rich, red river rolls through your head, suddenly giving you the power to think quickly. Your thoughts are progressing faster than your mind can contain them. What's coming out of your mouth is making no sense at all as you stand there slobbering in your shallow shell.

You've been reduced to a hyperventilating, babbling blob of Jell-O, shivering in your own skin, as you pathetically preach to the people who pay you!

You call it presenting. On the street they call it shame!

Kinda makes the point, doesn't it?

As I mentioned, one way you can help yourself prepare for those opening moments is with some kind of physical exercise such as stretching or even something more strenuous beforehand. Another way to reduce the adrenaline rush and rapid heartbeat is create other activity (action) for yourself. For example, you can slowly tak a few deep breaths before you begin. Yes, this increases the amount of oxygen in the system, but it reduces the heart rate before the adrenaline kicks in. More important, the taking of a few deep breaths gives you something to do (action), which takes the focus away from thinking about your presentation.

Once you start speaking, you may still experience some jitters. You can still create an external action—something to do to reduce the nerves—without the audience being aware of it. You might try wiggling your toes in your shoes. No one sees this and your concentration again becomes focused on some physical action. Maybe your mouth becomes dry. No you can't take a drink of water, but you can slightly bite down on the outer edges of your tongue or on the insides of your cheeks to create saliva and keep your mouth moist.

Again, you simply need to do something physical to reduce the internal nervousness, anxiety, and fear by using external means. When the problem is inside, the solution is outside. The goal is to redirect your attention away from the internal workings of the mind onto things that are external to you.

The more you concentrate on actions, the less chance you have of being self-conscious, which ultimately creates nervousness. So take a few deep breaths, wiggle your toes, and start talking!

USING YOUR BODY

Keep in mind that eliminating the fear doesn't mean you automatically will present well. That's the same as being unafraid to sing, but not knowing how to hit the right notes. (At that point, the fear is with the audience, who wonders if you will ever stop!)

Face it! You can't present well because you haven't learned the rules. You don't know how to play the game because no one taught you how. This is completely understandable. I was the same way. Then I learned to play the game.

The skills I want to share with you are based on the theatre. I was lucky enough to get exceptional acting training that very few others have ever experienced. I now apply those skills to presentations and guess what? They work! If I can make 1,500 people react to a playwright's intention, I can easily teach you a method that makes you a better communicator no matter what the topic, where the opportunity, or how big the audience. After reading this section, you'll be able to start using these skills tomorrow!

The only way to develop a method or systematic approach to any skill is to agree on the parameters that make that skill achievable. In this section, you learn to build a concrete foundation from which to work. With a core set of guidelines, you remain consistent from one presentation to the next, regardless of the content. I want you to concentrate on the basics—on things external to you. The things external to you always involve some type of action or activity and include

- Positioning and moving
- Making eye contact
- Using gestures
- Mastering the lectern
- Avoiding problems

POSITIONING AND MOVING

The first thing you have to learn is your relationship to the room. The physical space you occupy must be subject to your control. Like the home-field advantage in sports, if you know the space and feel comfortable within it, you can achieve your goal and deliver a more effective message.

For presentations, understanding the layout of the room, especially the size, distance from the group, and placement of the screen (visuals) is very important. All that stuff will change from place to place, and you may have to make certain adjustments to get the room situated comfortably for you and your audience.

But you want to develop a consistent behavior, regardless of the physical attributes of the room. These universal concepts will help you in every presentation situation because you can control all of them, at any time.

ESTABLISH AN ANCHOR

When presenting with visual support, you need to set an anchor for the audience to watch and read. Anchor your body to the same side as the starting point to read the language (that is, left-to-right or right-to-left).

For presentations in English (and many other languages), you must stand on the left side of the room; that is, the left side from the audience's point of view. In the English language, we read words from left to right. The eye is less distracted if it sees the presenter speaking from the left (in the anchored position), then glances slightly to the right to read the visual (left-to-right). The eye then naturally returns to view the speaker again as in the act of reading.

PART
VII
CH
23

If you stand on the opposite side of the room (the audience's right), the audience has to look at your face, then navigate backward and across the visual just to find the reading anchor and then "read" just to get back to you again. This extra step is a distraction. It is a waste of time. Listening is delayed and effectiveness is reduced.

Now if you were in Israel, you could be on the other side; in Greece, stand in the middle; in China, on your head—I don't know. But in the United States, we read words from left to right, so stand on the audience's left when presenting. This is the way to establish an anchor for the audience, because it matches the reading pattern (anchor) they've grown accustomed to all their lives.

> **Note**
>
> If you have no visuals for the audience to view, it doesn't matter which side of the room you present from, as long as people can see and hear you. However, it is always better to choose a side and remain in that area.
>
> Off-center is always a good choice because a centered presenter ends up having to work twice as hard by shifting and moving to both sides of the room. The one-sided approach sets a positioning anchor for the audience, which, if constant and unchanging, is less distracting.

You want to present from the side of the room that matches the reading pattern of the language. But, don't worry if you get stuck on the opposite side of the room. While you should try to avoid it, but you never know what you might be faced with when you haven't set things up yourself. If you have to present from the wrong side, just make fewer references to your visuals during the presentation to limit the distraction for the audience. Naturally you won't be the most effective you could be, but you won't necessarily walk away a failure, either.

BUILD A TRIANGLE

You want to know the biggest problem for most presenters? Moving! That's right, moving. They have no idea where they are going! They never really think about it!

Can you imagine if the actors had no idea where to go? The actor playing Hamlet would say, "To be or not to be...whoops...oh...sorry, Dave...didn't see your foot!" as he pulled himself from the floor.

The only way to know how or when to move is to know where to move first. An easy way to learn this is to design an area in front of the audience in which you can move. It's called the *Presenter's Triangle*™. It's imaginary because you must create it!

Figure 23.1 shows the triangle. Here's how you build it. While standing at a fixed distance from your display equipment, construct an imaginary line from the eyes of the person sitting on your far right, to the left edge of the screen. This line becomes the long end of the triangle, an angled wall. From each end of this angled wall, draw two lines meeting at a 90-degree angle to complete the shape behind you. Now you are standing inside an imaginary triangle.

The most important point to remember is that the angled wall is a boundary you cannot penetrate. If you step through the wall, people on your right will not be able to see the screen.

Note

Naturally, the illustration suggests you position yourself at a fixed distance from any display equipment. If you are using transparencies or seated at a keyboard, the triangle option is limited to those times when you take a position that does not block the view of anyone. This is another reason why presenting with overheads is so difficult. The line of sight from the audience to the visual is broken for some people.

Figure 23.1
A top-down view of the Presenter's Triangle. You create this imaginary space in which to present so that you don't block the view of anyone in the audience.

Okay, here's the good news. There are only three positions of the triangle that your body ever has to occupy. That's it —only three spots—the front, the middle, and the back!

Figure 23.2 shows a close-up view of the triangle with the three positions noted. The front is closer to the audience; the middle is where you should be most of the time; and the back is much closer to the screen. Now you will never use the full area of the triangle, unless you feel like hiding in the far corner (the shaded area) for some reason. Actually, you are really presenting inside a corridor within the triangle. You simply move along this little hallway, which follows the path of the angled wall.

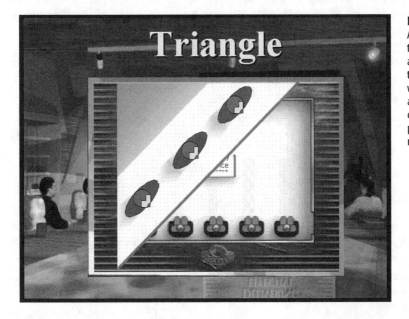

Figure 23.2
A close-up view of the triangle. You can use any of the three positions along the angled wall, but you want to avoid using the far corner (the shaded portion) when you move.

So why are there three positions? Because you have to move! You need to change the position of your body every so often or people won't watch you. If your body is not adding value for the audience, then they have less reason to watch you present the information. If you don't move, then it's talk radio. The audience will spend less time looking at you and more time updating their daily planners!

All forms of communication require some type of change to be effective. The change takes place in writing, in speaking, and in delivering. When you write, you skip lines and start new paragraphs. That's form in writing. When you speak, you pause between thoughts. That's rhythm in speech. When you're face-to-face, you create action in a defined space. That's movement in delivery.

Does Size Matter?

You rushed to read this one! We know each other too well! It's the size of the triangle I'm referring to!

The dimension of your space is based on the distance from the screen to the first row of chairs. At times you may have a 25-foot area to move around in. Other times, you may have only a few feet between the first seat and the screen.

For example, in a conference room you may only have a few steps between both ends of your triangle. But there is always a triangle, even if the only way to change between positions is to shift your weight. Your body must make visible changes based on the available space in order for the audience to pay attention.

So size doesn't matter for the triangle to exist. However, the more area available to you, the longer it will take to get to different spots. This will have some effect on your delivery. You'll want to make your key points when standing still for more impact. Thus, a larger triangle will force you to create additional words or phrases between those key points to naturally fill the moments needed to move to a new position

From that perspective, when it comes to using different positions, size really does matter! Hmmm...where have I heard that before?

All you have to do is treat the three positions of the triangle like peg holes or stopping points. You move to these points periodically, but with authority, remembering to stop and remain in a particular position for a while as you speak. You don't want to appear to be running back and forth, meandering aimlessly, drifting from place to place for no apparent reason. Just as you don't add paragraphs after every sentence or pauses after each word, you don't want to overdo and have constant movement while you present.

You might be wondering when to use the front, middle, and back of the triangle. Here's a guide. Choose the back of the triangle when the visual is complex. A busy visual forces the audience to keep looking at it. If your body is closer to the screen (the back of the triangle), then there is less distance for the audience to look between your visual and your voice. You don't want people moving their heads back and forth like they're at a tennis match!

Choose the middle of the triangle for the majority of the talk. Think of the middle as the launching pad to move in either direction. The middle is like the...well...it's the middle! It's the midpoint between two extremes.

Use the front of the triangle when your visuals are less busy and you want to be closer to the audience. A simple visual allows the audience to reference it fewer times. This means you can be a farther distance from the screen.

Here's one more point to consider about position. If you want to convince an audience with a key point, which do you think would be most effective—to be in the front, middle, or back of the triangle? Obviously, the front, where you're closer to people. Well now you have learned one of the most valuable lessons of all—choreography drives content! It's not the other way around. Decide where you want to be at certain points in the presentation and then look at the visual. Does it allow you to be in that spot based on its format? If not, then change the visual.

If you know you want to emphasize an important point when you move to the front of the triangle, your visual content needs to be simple enough to allow your body to navigate to the front of the triangle. Or is the image so cluttered that half the audience is still reading while you're addressing the major issue? Change the visual to suit your movement.

Don't let content be your guide! Simply decide where you want to be on a given visual and adjust the complexity of the image according to your position in the triangle.

The triangle is important because it represents part of your physical plan of action. Without some definite planned movement, you end up wandering aimlessly, giving the audience no reason or logic for the direction. (Don't forget that the audience is processing your body language more than your visuals or your voice.)

Play the Angles

While there are only three places to move in the triangle, there are only two body positions you have to worry about! See? It's getting easier!

You're going to find that all the power in your presentation rests in your shoulders! The angles of your body enhance communication. Figure 23.3 shows the two body positions or angles used in presenting, rest and power. For most of your talk, you should be at a 45-degree angle to the room. To create the angle, point your shoulders to the opposite corner of the room. This is a rest position. It's a nonthreatening stance, which opens your body to both the audience and the screen when you need to gesture or move.

After you establish the rest position, you can use the power of your left shoulder. The shoulder farthest from the audience is always your power shoulder. Because you are on the left side of the room, the power comes from what you do with your left shoulder.

To get power, simply square your shoulders to the back wall of the room. Each time you turn your left shoulder toward the audience, you move into a power position. This signals that the information being communicated is of greater importance. But don't stay in that stance too long or the effectiveness of your words and actions will diminish. Constantly staying in the power position is the body's way of yelling. That's why the rest position is so important.

So, if you plan it right, you can choose the exact moments to add impact to the presentation by switching to the power position from any of the three places in the triangle.

For example, let's say you have 20 minutes to present. You start off in the middle of the triangle in a rest position. On a particularly busy visual, you navigate to the back of the triangle, closer to the screen, but still in a rest position. From that same spot, you square off to a power position just long enough to make a key point, and then you revert back to the rest position as you continue. Maybe later in your presentation you navigate to the front of the triangle to get a little closer to the crowd. You're telling an experience related to the topic and at a high point in the story, you square off for impact.

Wait…relax…calm down…you don't have to plan a move for every spoken word! But, if you practice, just like an athlete, the "moves" of your body will develop automatically. If you can get used to being a visual presenter, using the positions of the triangle and angles of the body will add enormous value to your presentation.

Figure 23.3
You should only be concerned about two positions (angles) of the body: rest and power. The 45-degree angle is a rest position and the squared-off move puts you in a power position.

MAKING EYE CONTACT

So how do you please the crowd? You look at them! Yes, you look at them. It is so easy to do. Effective presenters look at people and make eye contact. This is critical to the communication process, especially to a group of visual creatures—the audience. The less time you spend looking at people, the less effective you are going to be.

The Eyes Have It!

When you watch TV, you are constantly exposed to eye contact. Think about it. The newscasters are looking right at you, with the help of a TelePrompTer®, of course. I don't understand why they have to use a TelePrompTer®. Why can't they just memorize the news the day before?

Anyway, they make constant eye contact. Characters on TV shows (sitcoms, dramas, or whatever) don't look at you, but they look at each other. Here again you are watching eye contact, only not directed at you.

Let's face it. We all watch a lot of movies and TV and are used to the idea of continual eye contact. As a visual presenter, you must not fight the expectation that a group is mostly made up of eye-contact hounds.

So, throw 'em a bone and look at 'em!

DIRECT EYE CONTACT

Direct eye contact is easier in a smaller group, simply because you have less faces to find. In a conference room with 10 people, for example, it will be easy to look at every person in the room at one time or another during your presentation. In a large audience, say 50 or more people, you can make direct eye contact with several people, but probably not everyone.

Now suppose you're afraid to make direct eye contact. You just don't like looking right into someone's eyes. Here's a trick for you: You don't have to look directly into a person's eyes.

Instead, you can look between the eyes and, from a distance, it looks like you're making eye contact. Just look at the spot on a person where the bridge of the nose meets the eyebrows, and it will seem as if you are looking directly into that person's eyes. It works with everyone, every time—but it doesn't seem to work with a spouse…hmmmm.

ANCHORED EYE CONTACT

Let me ask you: What's your limit? You know, the highest number of people you feel comfortable presenting to? Is it like 5? Or 15? Or 50? Maybe 100 or more? Usually there's a number. Suppose your number is 25. Then let's say that one more person walks in the room. Do you suddenly stop, throw your hands in the air, and shout, "Hey, hey you—out. Yeah, you, out! 25 is my limit, pal!" (I don't think so.)

The point is that although the limit is in your imagination, it still doesn't change the fact that a larger group may intimidate you. The reason your "crowd-alarm" goes off is because you haven't established anchors in the audience with whom to make eye contact.

Here's what can happen: During a presentation, your eyes occasionally leave the audience, perhaps for a quick glance to your visual. When your eyes look away and then return to the audience, you suddenly see thousands of eyes staring back at you and—zap!—you lose your trend of thought. You forget the next phrase because the group—not any individual, the group—temporarily distracted you.

But, if you have identified specific people in the crowd, say a few friendly faces in separate areas of the audience, then you have a better chance of staying focused. If you look away for a moment, on your return trip to look at the crowd, you will be able to seek out those individuals and make anchored eye contact with any one of those friendly faces.

The anchors you select in the audience should be far enough apart so that it looks as if you are speaking to whole sections, even though your eyes are fixed on one person within that section. So split the audience up into a few big areas, maybe two on one side, two on the other, one down the middle—and pick out a single face inside each area as your anchor. Then, when your head turns away, the next look back to the crowd will have you finding an anchor instead of having the entire group overwhelm you. (Think of it as presenting to a just few people who happen to have lots of other people sitting around them.) This way, you maintain your concentration and you don't feel intimidated.

After you have found your anchors, any direct eye contact with other selected individuals is even more effective. If you've been looking into sections of the audience, and then suddenly lock your eyes onto one particular person (not one of your anchors), it will be extremely powerful, especially for that person. It's as if you made personal contact with that individual; in other words, you singled out someone in the audience, making that person feel special.

You may have experienced this yourself if you've ever gone to a play or a concert and the performer, while entertaining the crowd, suddenly makes direct eye contact with you, it's something you never forget. So, the more eye contact you make with people, the more involved in the presentation they become.

USING GESTURES

What do dance, ballet, mime, and most every sport have in common? With the exception of bobbing for apples, they all require the use of the hands. Presenting is no different because the hands control the eyes of the audience. What you do or don't do with your hands when you present makes a huge difference. Unfortunately, most presenters simply don't know what to do with those things at the ends of their wrists.

At times during your presentation, you'll have to guide the eyes of your audience toward your visual. Letting the audience look where they want is one thing—it's more effective if they look where you want.

Never hide your hands behind your back or inside your pockets. Avoid putting your hands together in front of you for more than three seconds. When your hands stay together for even those few moments of time, the audience tends to look at them and not at your face. Always remember, the eyes travel wherever the hands go. Keep your hands apart, yet always visible.

> **Note**
>
> When you're nervous, your hands tend to join together or marry. In others words, they end up folded in front of you, doing nothing. Because you're a mammal, you have no skeleton in the center of your body, so you tend to protect that area by letting your hands rest together in front of you. You never see anyone with his hands on top of his shoulders saying, "Boy, am I nervous!" No way! Hands clasped in front or even locked behind your back, indicate nervousness and reduce your effectiveness.

If you aren't making any gestures, then return to a simple position with your hands at your sides. Or if your hands are up, waist high, then just avoid bringing them together.

If you are not elevated on a stage or standing on platforms (risers) when you speak, gestures are harder to see for everyone except the people in the front seats. For those viewing you from the waist up, keep your wrists higher than your elbows so that the gestures are visible. Always be aware of those sitting behind others and the view they might have of you while you speak. Gestures with your wrists lower than your elbows will generally go unnoticed and create little impact or meaning.

If used properly, the hands can orchestrate the eyes of the audience. Casual or emphatic gestures made to the screen or to the audience can create visual inflection. This helps the group recognize what is important. You can use a number of gestures with your hands and with your body that can help make your message more meaningful.

REACHING OUT

The best gesture you can make as a presenter is reaching out. When the palm of your hand faces up as your arm extends out to the audience, it is a very friendly move and can be done with one or both hands. When you reach out to the audience, you appear as if you want the group involved in the event. The palm-up and the arm-out gesture is generally pleasing to the eye and indicates a warmth of expression for the presenter.

Think about your everyday actions in business. When you greet a person in business you shake hands by extending your arm out with your hand open (an exposed palm). You are reaching out to that person. You might shake hands as a greeting, a parting, or as a result of an agreement.

You can shake hands with the audience by reaching out to them. You reach out to the group as a way of greeting them, parting with them, or bringing them into agreement with you. Just because there's more than one person in the room doesn't mean your personal interactive skills suddenly disappear. When you reach out to the audience, you become more approachable and ultimately more effective.

The reaching out gesture also works best when you interact with the audience, especially in a question-answer situation. If someone asks a question, reach out to acknowledge that person. But don't stop there! You must keep your arm outstretched with your palm up until the person begins to speak, and then you can casually pull your arm back, almost as if catching the first syllable in your hand.

If you don't leave your arm extended until you get the beginning of a response, you end up with the opposite effect, a gesture that suggests insincerity or indifference. It's called the "Like I Care" gesture. You've seen it. The presenter flings a hand at a person while asking a question, as if to say, "Yeah right, like I care about your answer!" Don't start tossing your limbs at people and then expect interaction.

Tip #266 from	The reaching out technique works best for the first question asked. After you set the stage for a nice way of interacting, the audience will be more inclined to ask additional questions.

THE LEFT HAND FOR GUIDANCE

Your left hand does the majority of the guidance for the audience. If you recall, the screen is always to the presenter's left for languages that read left to right. So, if you want to guide the eye to the screen, simply lift your left arm and use your left hand to motion slowly in the general direction of the visual. This indicates that the image should be glanced at by the group, but they should remain more focused on you. However, if you raise your left arm and dart your left hand quickly toward the screen, the more emphatic movement tells the audience that the content has more importance.

In both examples the key is to make your movements with authority. Do not make half-hearted gestures or the impact diminishes. Would you have a few images appear which were not bright enough to be seen? Would you casually whisper a few phrases that few could hear? You wouldn't make less of an effort with your visuals or your words, so don't use half-hearted moves when delivering the story.

Tip #267 from

> Use your head! If you gesture to the screen and keep looking at the audience, the group has a choice to either stay focused on the screen or return their focus to you. This is because you are facing them and, technically, so is your visual. But if you turn your head to look at the screen as you gesture toward it, you force the audience to focus more on the visual than on you. Even if they look back at you, they see you looking at the screen and realize that's where the concentration should be. Both of these methods should be used to help shift emphasis on and off you from time to time. This variation is important.

THE LEFT HAND FOR MOVEMENT

The left hand can help you move through the triangle. That's right! You can walk toward the audience with no gestures, but you can't walk backward without an excuse. The audience needs a reason for any movement away from them. If the body retreats, it is a sign of distrust; the body language indicates that you are not telling the truth or that you are unsure of your accuracy. You appear to be "backing away" from the issue.

So you might wonder, "How will I get from the front of the triangle to the middle or back if I can't retreat?" You can retreat—with a reason—by using your left hand. If you gesture to the visual while navigating backward through the triangle, the audience accepts the movement because you are gesturing. They allow your retreat using the logic or excuse that you had to back up because you had to gesture to the screen.

Tip #268 from

> The only way to understand this is to try it. Stand in one spot. Start describing one of your best qualities while you move backward a few steps without making any gestures. How does it feel?
>
> Okay, now pretend a screen is behind you. Stand in that spot again, use the same description and use your left hand to gesture back to the imaginary screen as you move backward. Notice the difference? It's as if some key support information exists to help make your point.

As you've just seen, only gestures can get you backward through the triangle, which is why it's so important to link your movements to your visual content. Make sure when you're directing attention to the screen (as you navigate away from the audience) that what you're saying relates to the visual to which you're gesturing. If it doesn't, you'll create even more confusion.

Justifying Movement

The audience needs a reason for your moving away from them. Your gesture to the screen is that reason. But only you need a reason to move toward the audience. Typically, this requires no gestures, just movement. Your reason is to get closer to them. In both cases you have justification for the movement in either direction.

But what if you had to move sideways? What if you had to break the triangle and cross to the other side of the room? The only reason to do this must be to get to a visible reference. Most likely that reference is a prop. You cross the room to get something you need to incorporate into the presentation at that exact moment.

Of course, if you don't require the item, you can gesture to it without crossing the room. However, if you know you are going to need a prop, you should place it closer to you before you begin your presentation so you don't have to cross the room to get it.

You may also want to move sideways and cross the room to interact with a person. This is not a valid reason to break the triangle; a reaching out gesture is the way to interact with anyone in the audience.

Use the rationale that a break from the triangle requires carrying something back with you from wherever you are tempted to go. You'll find few reasons, if any, to ever drift from the anchor of the triangle. But if you do, there better be a clear reason as to why.

THE LEFT HAND FOR HELP

You can only look at each visual one time! That's it, one time until it changes or something on the visual changes. If you look at the same visual more than once, the audience thinks you don't know the information. They wonder why you have to keep looking back at the visual simply to make the next point.

You might think the easy way out of that problem is to use builds. Why not? The next bullet point pops up (a visual change) allowing you an opportunity to look at the image and quickly get the next thought. Nice try, but the audience will know you're using the visual for help when you don't speak until after you read a bullet point. They'll know you're reading the stuff—maybe for the first time!

Okay, so what can you do? Yep, you guessed it—use your left hand! You already know that you can look at your visual once without a gesture. To look at the same visual again, add a gesture to the screen. It's the old "give-them-a-reason" move. The audience forgives your extra glance to the screen, silently saying to themselves, "Well, of course you had to look at the screen again. You had to gesture and be sure of the spot you were referencing."

Now suppose you have to look at the same visual a third time? With the first glance, you need no gesture. The second glance, you gesture—ahhh, but this time you leave your hand in the air. Don't drop your arm, keep it extended. Then, when you look at the visual for the third time, you only have to change the angle of your hand. Just a slight tilt of your wrist, up or down, moves your hand and creates another gesture or another excuse for the audience. You can even look for a fourth time as long as your hand changes position again. I know some presenters who haven't the slightest idea what's on each visual; but, by leaving an arm extended and glancing toward it a couple of times, the audience thinks, "What brilliance!"

Tip #269 from

Leaving your left hand in the air can help with the pacing of the presentation. How? When you gesture toward the visual and leave your arm extended, the next time you glance back at the image, you can turn your wrist slightly until the face of your watch is visible as you look over the top of your hand. Now you'll know what time it is, and you may have to adjust your pacing, depending on how much time is left in the presentation. Of course, your watch must be on your left arm for this to work. It's also best to wear an analog watch with a contrasting face and visible hands. Digital display watches may not be as easy to read, especially if the lighting in the room is dim.

SHIFTING YOUR WEIGHT

When you are not making gestures, your hands should be at your sides and always visible. The eyes travel wherever the hands go so never hide your hands from the audience. Without gestures, your feet should be shoulder-width apart, your elbows and knees unlocked, and your weight evenly distributed. That's the position to use when you are not making gestures.

When your elbows and knees are unlocked, you have your best opportunity for movement. When you stand still, the tendency is to lock your knees and even your elbows. If your limbs are locked, you lose energy. If your limbs are unlocked, you unleash energy.

Center of Gravity

Men and women are different. I mean, in terms of the way they stand. Men have a higher center of gravity than women, located in the middle of the chest. A man tends to stand with his feet wider than his shoulders, for balance. Invariably, for some strange reason during the presentation, his feet will get farther apart, little by little. When his feet are spread too far apart, he is less likely to move and ends up in the same spot for the entire presentation. So a man should stand with his feet at the same width as his shoulders in order to make movement more likely.

Women have a lower center of gravity, closer to the hips. A woman tends to stand with her feet closer together, sometimes with the heels touching, for balance and posture. Men—don't try this stance or you'll tip over like a bowling pin! However, during a presentation a woman will often establish this posture-position and lock into that one spot for the duration of the talk. If a woman keeps her feet shoulder-width apart, she is more likely to move at some point.

So, don't mess with gravity—it's the law!

Movement is necessary and gestures are important. You know this by now. But, if you want to use your hands and make all your gestures look natural, you need to shift your weight.

You see, if your heels are both touching the floor, you can't make gestures that look natural. Instead, they appear stiff. Stand up and try it. Rest your weight evenly on each foot with both heels on the floor. Now lift your left arm to gesture. Stop! Take a look in the mirror—you look like a flagman on a highway or the person directing the plane into the gate! You look stiff. It's because your heels are touching the floor at the same time and your weight is evenly distributed on each foot.

Okay, so you have to learn to shift your weight. But first you must know the limits of your own body to do the weight-shift thing properly. Try this. Stand up and place your feet at the width of your shoulders. Both heels should be on the floor and your weight distributed evenly between both feet. Now take a half-step to your left, just far enough for the opposite heel to lift off the floor. Feel that weight shift to your left foot? Okay, now shift your weight back onto the right foot until your left heel lifts off the floor. Now you know the limits of your body to make gestures look natural. The weight must be on one foot or the other for the gesture to look smooth.

Tip #270 from

> The easiest way to know if you are shifting your weight properly is to keep the base of your neck lined up with the same foot you're placing your weight on (you could also line your chin up with your knee). Now you can gesture and it will look natural.
>
> If the nape of your neck is not lined up with one of your feet, then your weight is probably evenly distributed and you are most likely resting on both heels. If you gesture from this position, it will look unnatural.

Leaning Can Have Meaning!

Weight shifting combined with gestures can help make your message stand out. Depending on the direction you shift your weight, the effect can be quite dramatic.

For example, if you shift your weight to your left foot–toward the visual–while gesturing with your left hand, you are silently saying to the crowd, "Come with me and let's inspect this information." If you shift your weight to your right foot–away from the visual–while gesturing with your left hand, you are saying, "This information proves the point." It's like the magician who leans into the trick and then leans back to reveal the magic!

So, if you have a problem-solution script, you might want to lean toward a visual when identifying a specific problem and, later, lean away from the visual when the related solution is shown.

MASTERING THE LECTERN

A lectern is what you stand behind and a podium is what you stand on. However, people use both these terms to mean the same thing—a big box between you and the audience! Imagine if you wore a lectern to work each day! But you don't. It would make interpersonal communication so difficult—not to mention trying to squeeze past people in the hall!

The actors don't have lecterns. How would you feel if they did? You would think they didn't learn the lines! Why should they be forced to memorize the words of a writer? But politicians giving speeches and use lecterns. Aren't they, too, actors using the words of a writer? Hmmmmm. Where do you draw the line on this one?

The problem is that visual creatures—you know, the ones under 40—expect eye contact. They get a lot of information from body language, gestures, and movement.

That's why the most difficult prop to overcome is the lectern. It covers 80% or more of your body and allows for little mobility. Although the lectern is a convenience to the speaker for reading a speech or for referring to notes, it allows for much less direct eye contact with an audience.

Lecterns are for losers! I despise lecterns! There should be a ban on them! There! I said how I really feel. I vented my anger and shouted my opinion for all the world to know! As far as I'm concerned, lecterns have no place in the life of a visual presenter.

Having said that, lecterns are still used quite a lot. So, how can you master the lectern if you get trapped behind one? You have a few options to help minimize your losses.

First, place the lectern at a 45-degree angle to the room if you can, matching the non-threatening rest position (discussed earlier in this chapter). From that angle, both your hands can rest on or touch the lectern and you'll still be in a rest position. You can easily switch to a power position with just a turn of your upper body, leaving only your left hand resting on or touching the lectern.

If the lectern can't be angled but remains fixed and facing directly to the back wall (like a pulpit), you can still use the rest and power positions. Assume the rest position (45-degree angle) while behind the lectern. Only your right hand touches or rests on the lectern until you switch to the power position (by squaring-off to the back wall), at which point both hands can rest on or touch the lectern.

Make sure the audience sees your hands as much as possible. If you hide your hands, the interpretation is that you're hiding something. Don't let your hands disappear for too long, even if it is just to turn a page.

Even though you are stuck behind the lectern, the three positions of the triangle still exist for you to use. The middle of the triangle is when your weight is on both feet. The movement to the front or to the back happens by shifting your weight to one foot or the other. These slight changes in body position may help to keep the audience looking at you from time to time. Naturally, the lack of mobility and the fact that you are probably reading your speech or your notes limits effective communication.

Typically, the reason you use a lectern to begin with is when you are giving a speech. The lectern supports the pages of the script while you deliver (read) the speech. When you read, you make less eye contact. The following is a guide for maintaining good eye contact.

Every 20 seconds (or about 50 words) you are allowed to look away from people, but only for about one second. That means, for every one minute of speaking (or about 150 words), you're allowed just three seconds to look down and read the next group of words. In effect, you should be spending 95% of the time looking at people and only 5% of the time checking the script.

Unless you are using a see-through teleprompter, as is done on TV, the more you read from the script, the less amount of eye contact you have with the audience. Concepts are the solution. Build a conceptual script around key phrases, and you'll spend more time delivering a personal version of the topic directly to people because you won't have a lot of words to read, just concepts. Doesn't this sound like a Do script? (See Chapter 21, "The Message—Scripting the Concept.")

Don't get caught behind a lectern just reading a bunch of statistics to the audience. Think eye contact—and avoid facing the facts!

AVOIDING PROBLEMS

When the audience can't interpret your physical actions, they become preoccupied trying to figure out how the words link to the movements. The audience can't ignore these body distractions and, therefore, they need to be eliminated. If you work on removing these distractions, your message is easier to convey.

UPSTAGING

Sometimes the audience is prevented from hearing your words simply because they can't see your face or your expressions. When a part of the body passes between the speaker's face and the audience, the result is called upstaging.

Turning your back to the audience is the most obvious example of upstaging and is depicted in Figure 23.4. If you're facing the screen and the audience is facing the screen, then who's presenting? When you turn your back to the group, you can't see them and they can't see you. You lose valuable eye contact and the chance to use facial expressions. In addition, your voice is projected away from the audience and is therefore less audible, unless you have a microphone.

Figure 23.4
Don't turn your back to the audience. You lose all the face-to-face benefits of communication when no one can see your face!

If you have to turn your back to the audience, do it for as short a time as possible. At the same time, increase your volume so the group can still hear what you're saying. Avoid walking into the audience. This happens a lot when you have a U-shape seating arrangement. You might think that it's more personal to penetrate the "U" to get closer to the person you are interacting with at the moment. Not true. Your effort to get closer to one person puts your back toward everyone else you walk past as you penetrate the group. Don't alienate one person for the sake of another. You can still make eye contact and reach out to anyone in any part of the room while maintaining your position. The bottom line is that when your back is to the audience, you're least effective.

Tip #271 from

One easy way to keep from turning your back is to make sure the person seated to your far right can always see the front of your right shoulder. This technique keeps your body facing out to everyone in the crowd as you speak.

Crossing the upper body with your right hand is another example of upstaging, as shown in Figure 23.5. Whenever you gesture to the screen, use your left hand rather than your right. If your right hand goes across the front of your body, it causes a visual distraction that limits your effectiveness.

Figure 23.5
Don't cross your body with one of your arms. The gesture to the screen in this example should have been done with the left hand, not the right.

Tip #272 from

Use your left foot as a guide. To gesture to anything left of your left foot, use your left hand. Use your right hand to gesture to anything to the right of your left foot. This forces you into a more open stance when presenting and allows you to add impact to your delivery style with correct gestures and movements.

THE GUNFIGHTER

One stance to avoid is what I call the gunfighter position where your arms are locked at your sides as if your elbows were sewn to your rib cage! This limits the gestures you can make with your hands. So, don't press your elbows to your sides as you batter your arms about shouting "Danger, Will Robinson! Danger!"—it looks ridiculous. To avoid the gunfighter position when presenting, pretend that you must be able to touch your hands to the top of your head without bending down. This would be impossible with your elbows still attached to your sides.

THE HEAD WAITER

Be careful about folding your arms in front of you. This head waiter position not only upstages you by putting your arms across your upper body, but it also indicates that you are hiding something from the group. With your hands locked under your arms, your gestures are completely limited.

THE THIRD BASE COACH

Do not clasp your hands together behind your back. This position, the third base coach, forces you to use your shoulders and your chin to create gestures. You'll end up throwing your chin or shoulder forward to acknowledge a question and the reaction from the audience will be far from positive.

THE HAND TALKER

Avoid conversationalizing your gestures. This happens when you move your hands in the rhythm of your speech. It ends up looking like you have a gesture for every syllable. The trick with gestures is to keep them still and not have them bounce around on each word. The audience takes more time to process gestures than it does to process words. Gestures should freeze to add impact to a phrase.

Try this exercise. Say the phrase, "This is very, very, very important," and move both your hands up and down on as many words as you can. Then, say the phrase again, but this time just let your hands come down once and lock them in mid-air as you finish the rest of the phrase. Did you feel a difference? When a gesture stops moving, it is more powerful.

BLOCKING THE LIGHT

The image is meant for the screen! Sometimes you make the mistake of trying to point to something on your visual and you walk in front of the projector. Never block the light source with your hands or body unless you intend to make shadow puppets for the audience. When you block the light source, the audience finds it difficult to view the distorted image depicted on your clothes.

PINKIE COUNTING

Who started this habit anyway? Pinkie counting is simply counting on your fingers in front of the audience. The action occurs when you hold out your left hand, palm up, and use your right index finger to count on the left pinkie, then ring finger, and so on. The obsession plagues almost everyone from time to time. The audience has no idea when you plan to stop, although five seems to be the limit.

The reason you pinkie count is to keep track of the order of things by giving yourself tactile feedback as you count through the items you relay to the audience. This distraction can be avoided by dropping one hand to your side and simply touching your index finger to the thumb of same hand to maintain the tactile feedback. You don't need to switch to different fingers. Just touch your index finger to your thumb to click softly by your side, and you can keep track of many things. By inconspicuously using just one hand to count with, the audience is not distracted.

If, however, counting is really important to making your point, then raise your hand above your shoulder and count so that everyone can see. This will force you to limit those times that you count obsessively and it will add impact to those times that you need to count emphatically.

USING YOUR VOICE

I've been at events where some rude, inconsiderate moron in the crowd stands up, holding a chocolate donut in one hand and a buttered roll in the other and shouts "Hey—I can't hear you!" Well, at least that's one way to know if you should speak up. But—you can't always rely on me being in the audience, unless you're serving donuts and rolls!

Although I am the first to say that actions speak louder than words, your vocal delivery plays the role of interpreter for the message. If the visual media is truly the content and the body is definitely the delivery, then the voice is a combination of both. Words carry information and action. In order to develop the action in your voice, you have to consider a few issues such as:

- Breathing properly
- Phrasing and pausing
- Avoiding problems

BREATHING PROPERLY

Sometimes your choice of where to take the next breath can disrupt the flow of your words. By breathing between phrases, rather than during phrases, you get an opportunity to vocalize better. The key to this is having enough air in your lungs to sustain a longer phrase. For example, I have been known to deliver very long phrases with volume and emphasis. I believe that's from knowing how to breathe properly. Some say it's because I'm so full of hot air that the Gettysburg Address would be a cinch—but, I pay no attention to insults from family members!

When you don't have enough air, you may end up rushing through your words, and then they run together from speaking so quickly. Chances are that your emphasis and inflection will be lost. In any case, by having enough air, you can say longer phrases more slowly, which helps to make the message clear.

First, let's find out if you are breathing properly right now. Try this. Stand up and take a deep breath. Did your shoulders go up? Did your chest expand? Are you still holding the air in your lungs as you read this sentence while you turn blue? Okay, okay breathe again, please. Let the air out! Whew, that was close!

If your shoulders went up, you filled your chest with air. Unfortunately, that's not the way you naturally breathe. The air normally goes into the lower abdomen. Try this test. Lie down on the floor, face up, with a book on your stomach. No, not this book—I want you alive at the end of this exercise! Breathe normally and watch the book. Notice it moving up and down? That's your diaphragm at work. The muscles in your stomach, not your chest, control breathing. Now take a deep breath and force the book upward—it should be easy once you concentrate on the correct muscles to do the job.

Next, remove the book, stand up, and take the same deep breath, but don't expand your chest or raise your shoulders. Your stomach should expand. This is the proper way to breathe between your phrases when speaking.

PART

VII

CH

23

Tip #273 from

> Try breathing through your nose and it will be easier to expand your stomach (diaphragm). Of course, when speaking, the tendency is to also take in air through your mouth because it is already open. It's not where the air enters but where the air reaches that makes for better vocal control.

Again, the key is having enough breath to complete long phrases or sentences without running out of air. This is important for languages such as English, in which the major points are made at the end of phrases, not at the beginning. Without enough air, your voice might trail off and the audience will not hear the key part (the end) of the sentence. The beginning of the next phrase will be less connected to the important part of the prior one. The result is confusion for the audience.

The following is an exercise for breath control. You should be able to say this entire passage in one breath.

> What a to-do, to die today, at a minute or two to two
> A thing distinctly hard to say, yet harder still to do
> For they'll beat a tattoo at twenty to two
> A rah-tah-tah-tah-tah-tah-tah-tah-tah-too
> And the dragon will come at the sound of a drum
> At a minute or two to two, today,
> At a minute or two to two.

When you develop truly excellent breath control, you will be able to say the above passage two times with one breath.

If you can't remember the above phrase, here's another breathing exercise you can try. In one breath say, "One by one, they went away." Pretty easy, right? Okay, add another to the count, like this, "One by one and two by two, they went away." Try adding another to the count and in one breath say, "One by one and two by two and three by three, they went away." Don't forget that each of these segments have to be done in one breath. You should shoot for as high as "twelve by twelve," and, with practice, fifteen or higher is possible, as you get more control of your breathing.

PHRASING AND PAUSING

Take natural pauses between your sentences. Say a phrase, pause, then say a phrase and pause, and so on. By using this technique, you can control the pacing of the presentation. Natural pauses give you a chance to make eye contact, to breathe, or even to think. You end up with smooth transitions and a more consistent delivery.

FILLERS ARE KILLERS

The funny thing about getting up in front of people is you have an altered sense of time. You think you're going too slow and you begin to pick up the pace, not so much with your speech, but more with your thoughts. You begin to think more quickly and between one phrase and another phrase the audience hears "uhhhhhh," "ummmmm," "errrrrr," "ahhhhh," and the like—you know—the fillers. The sounds you make in between the words you say. Fillers are not language. They are grunts and groans. The audience can't process fillers. In fact, if you have a lot of them in your presentation, the audience becomes preoccupied with the distraction and they end up concentrating on your fillers, not on your phrases!

Fillers can even be whole words, such as "okay," "right," "you know," "again," and "see," to name a few. Fillers are evidence that you are thinking out loud. You're letting the audience hear you think. To counter this problem, use silence as filler and it appears that you are taking natural pauses when you speak.

THE OPENING PAUSE

When I'm coaching a person, I always suggest the opening two-second pause. Right after the first phrase, such as "Good morning," you should take a two-second pause. That's right! Complete silence for two seconds. It can seem like an eternity, but it gives you the chance to establish two important things: pacing and anchors.

From a pacing perspective, the opening pause sets up the audience. They get to know right away who is in charge of the momentum. People have to know that you are in control. That's the role of the presenter—to control the flow. The role of the audience is to be controlled. If you don't appear rushed, the audience settles into the presentation at the pace you have set.

Those two seconds of silence help you in another way. In our earlier discussion of anchors, we talked about identifying the friendly faces to focus on. Unfortunately, you can't establish anchors in the audience until you first take the stage because that's when almost everyone is seated. You can't look out in the audience 40 minutes before the presentation, see a few people, and shout, "Hey—you three—you, you, and you—don't switch seats on me—I need you to be my anchors later!" (I don't think so.) No, you'll have to find your anchors during the opening pause. Don't worry, though, it will only take you about two seconds to scan the crowd for those friendly faces. Typically, those sitting under the most light are the easiest to spot.

WHEN IN DOUBT—PAUSE FIRST

Have you ever been asked a question during your presentation and you didn't know the answer? Well, don't blurt out the ignorance right away! Instead, pause for a moment. Here's what happens: Someone asks you a question and you don't know the answer. You stop, you pause, you look to the heavens for some revelation—you get none—you look back at the person and say, "I'll have to get back to you on that." The audience will be thinking, "Ohhhh mannn—you were sooooo close. If you only had the knowledge, you would have known!" That's a lot better than saying, "I don't know—blue?" Then the audience thinks, "Blue?—and you call yourself a doctor?" I've seen this happen plenty of times. You don't want to leap into the fire with a very quick, and likely incorrect, response. Remember that the audience is on your side. They want you to be right.

The pause maintains whatever level of credibility you had before the question was asked. By pausing for a moment, the audience actually believes that you could have answered the question, given enough time (yeah, like about a month). The point is that the group watches you search your mind for an answer, even though you never come up with one. It's politics at its best!

So, when in doubt, pause first. It buys you time and credibility. Of course, don't stop there. The words "I'll get back to you on that" indicate your intention to follow up at a later point with an answer. Make sure you do!

TARGETING PHRASES

Once you have control over your voice, you can direct your phrases for more impact. You can target your words to entire sections of the audience or simply to one person.

It's a given that everyone in the room has to be able to hear you. Sometimes a microphone will be needed for the entire audience to hear every word you say. But, because you can't count on having a microphone in every situation, you'll have to learn to project your voice.

Although proper breathing is important to voice projection, you should also target your phrases toward the back of the room to be sure everyone hears what you say. One way to do this is to play to the back third of the audience. In the theatre, it's called "playing to the cheap seats." The farthest one-third of the audience is where most of your phrases should be targeted because if they can hear you, everyone can hear you.

You never have to worry about the people in the front. They took those seats. They'll give you their wallets! But the people in the back—the troublemakers! Pretend that they are never sold, never convinced, never in agreement with your message. This forces you to target your phrases to them. The good news is that this causes your chin to lift slightly higher in the air, opens your throat, and makes your voice clearer. In addition, you'll find yourself facing forward more often in order to project to the back of the room. The intensity of your phrases, no matter how calm or soft-spoken, become more audible and your facial expressions more visible!

Voice projection helps when fielding responses from the audience. Sometimes an audience member speaks so softly that only you and a few other people hear the person. Make sure you repeat the question or comment so that the entire group can hear it. If you fail to do this, then your response will make sense only to those who heard the original question or comment in the first place. Also, by repeating a question, you get more time to formulate your answer.

You can also target your phrases directly to a specific person. You can do it with just a look, but you get more impact if you know the person's name. People love to hear their name. Watch a TV commercial. If it has your name in it, you love it!

A name is so important! How you would feel if you raised your hand to ask a question and the presenter knew your name but chose to identify you by your seat number instead! Names add a personal touch to presentation.

When you reference a person by name, only the first name is needed. This makes it a little easier for you because last names can sometimes be difficult to remember or even pronounce. Of course, if you are speaking to an audience that you have never met before, it will be difficult to identify people by name. During interaction, you could ask that people identify themselves to the audience before they speak. Then, you'll know a person's name and be able to use it in your response.

Targeting your phrases to an entire section or to a specific person makes the audience more conscious of each other and more respectful of your caring to take the time to treat people as individuals when possible.

TRANSITIONING

Transitioning is having something to say during changes in your presentation. Those changes can be as a result of movement or can be from the visuals themselves.

Movement in the triangle, from place to place, can be very obvious when your space is bigger. It may take several steps to get from the middle to the front, for example. You should not be moving on a key phrase. The words have more impact when you are still. Suppose you want to say the words "It saves money" in the front of the triangle. If you are in the middle of the triangle and a few steps away from the front, you have to add a transition or some extra words to allow you time to get to the front. Once there, and not moving, you can say the key phrase, "It saves money." Perhaps your entire phrase turns into: (said from the middle while walking to the front) "One of the most important advantages of this new product is that (now you stop at the front) it saves money." The transitional text allows you to move to the next space and deliver the key words while standing still.

Transitions are also useful whenever the visuals change, although this is less of a requirement when using slides or electronic images because they change more rapidly. But a more traditional medium, such as overheads, requires verbal transitions.

Here's what happens. The time it takes to remove one transparency from the overhead projector and replace it with the next can take several seconds. Don't let that time be filled with silence. Have a transition—something to say as you approach the equipment, as you change the visual, as you set the next visual, and as you move away from the equipment. Even in the world of state-of-the-art electronics, a pause to press a remote control is just as obvious as changing an overhead if you leave too big a gap with nothing to say.

Don't confuse silence with timed pauses. A timed pause lasts about one to three seconds and is useful to get the audience to think or to ponder a question. Dead silence lasts longer and tells the audience you can't really think of anything to say at the moment.

RULE OF THREES

People remember things in sets of threes. Our system of government is based on the number three, many religions are based on three, even the family—mother-father-child —is based around the number three. You can find this rhythm in many political or religious speeches. Key concepts or arguments are constructed around three references. For example, a politician might make the statement: "We'll be more prosperous, we'll pay less taxes, and our children will have a future." Notice the use of three references in the phrasing to make a point. Many references include a triad of some sort, such as Julius Caesar's "Veni, vidi, vici" ("I came, I saw, I conquered") and the courtroom oath of "…the truth, the whole truth, and nothing but the truth…." Even the Olympic Games grant three medals, Gold, Silver, and Bronze.

Try to incorporate the rule of threes when presenting your next topic. It's easy, it's simple and it works like a charm!

AVOIDING VOCAL PROBLEMS

Just as with the body, distractions can occur when using the voice. Most of the time, the vocal problems can be corrected, but sometimes our natural speech will sound different to diverse audiences. Accents are an example of natural speech to some, but unique speech to others.

If you have an accent, as most of us do, it means that you will sound different from what the audience may be used to hearing. My grandmother, who came from Italy, once said to me in broken English, "Don't laugh at people with accents. They speak one more language than you do!" Of course, accents from speaking a foreign language are no less noticeable than regional accents. When I delivered a seminar in Mississippi the person who introduced me ended the opening remark with "at least you'll like his New York accent." Just as I began to speak, I looked at him and said "Wait a minute. I thought you had the accent."

The point is that if you have a well-rehearsed presentation and you can be understood when you speak, your accent should not reduce your effectiveness.

Some believe in eliminating regional or foreign accents, but I think they constitute diversity in voice and help make the individual stand out for an audience. If you can be understood, then don't worry about an accent. However, some other vocal issues can become major problems if not corrected.

THE MUMBLER

The mumbler is the person who does not enunciate clearly. The lips stay so close together that the audience can't even see the words forming. When the mouth stays very closed, volume decreases and the words are barely audible. Remember to loosen those lips and articulate!

Tip #274 from	Place a pencil across your mouth between your teeth. Push it as far back as you can, which stretches your lips. Bite down a little on the pencil and begin to talk. Say a couple of phrases for about 30 seconds up to a minute. Take the pencil away and notice how flexible your lips are and how much better you enunciate every syllable.

THE GARBLER

Another person with an enunciation problem, the garbler is the person who speaks so quickly that the audience can't hear the end of one word before the next word arrives. To correct this problem, try saying a short phrase very slowly by stretching out each and every syllable in every word. This helps to reduce the speed of speech.

Tip #275 from	Find a newspaper article and read the first two sentences out loud. Read them again out loud and you'll probably go even faster. Okay, now read the words in the sentences backward, one word at a time. Hear how slowly you must read and try to match that speed when you speak. Although in practice that pace is definitely too slow, your habit of speaking too quickly will offset the slow speech and the result will be a closer-to-normal speed.

THE DRONER

The droner has a constant, monotone, expressionless voice and is the closest known cure for insomnia! The problem is from little or no inflection. This is often prevalent among presenters who have limited interest in the topic or those who have been presenting the same information in the same way for too long. They are simply bored with the stuff they deliver. The voice reflects the boredom, gets lazy, and eventually becomes monotonous.

One solution to this problem is to practice placing stress on different words in a sentence. For example, the following list uses ALL CAPS to show the changing emphasis in the same phrase:

> And WE offer the best service.
>
> And we OFFER the best service.
>
> And we offer the BEST service.
>
> And we offer the best SERVICE.

Try saying these phrases out loud and note the difference in the stress of the capitalized words. Placing emphasis in this way forces the voice into a higher and lower pitch within a phrase by adding vocal variety to an otherwise droning tone.

THE DROPPER

The dropper is the person who starts out with a lot of volume and then gradually drops off to the point where the audience is straining to hear the disappearing words. This problem is definitely related to improper breathing. The exercises mentioned earlier can help with sustaining longer phrases. But, sometimes, the words drop off because you are not completing one thought for yourself before introducing the next. Basically, you become anxious to get to the next part of the argument. The key to avoiding this problem is to maintain volume through the end of every phrase.

PART

VII

CH

23

Tip #276 from

In addition to breathing exercises, you can also try adding a question at the end of every sentence. Keep in mind that this is only for practice. Don't do this while presenting. For example, add the question, "Is that statement clear?" to every sentence. The question forces a slight raise in pitch and volume. Plus, the extra words make the sentence even longer, forcing you to plan for more air to get to the end. When presenting, you can still silently say the question to yourself if you feel you are dropping off in volume as you present.

When a vocal problem becomes a distraction, you need to take steps to eliminate it. When your voice becomes trained to the point where you can control it effectively, you gain another advantage in conveying the message you intend for the audience.

TROUBLESHOOTING

How do these external skills apply to small group meetings with just a few people sitting around a conference table?

Actually the skills are the same. The room is just smaller. Good presentation skills work everywhere. This is the same as writing or speaking. Would you tolerate poor grammar or poor enunciation if the crowd were only eight people in a conference room? The key difference is in how you express yourself to fit the size of the group. You are not going to make wide, sweeping gestures, but you would certainly reach out to any size group. You would still use the three positions of the triangle, even though the space is smaller. You would still use the rest and power positions to add emphasis. The point is that your "body language" is expressed all the time, regardless of the number of people observing you.

If possible, stand up when presenting. This doesn't mean you can't control a meeting while sitting; rather, you get more power when your head is higher than people. That's why kings sit high on thrones, judges sit up high, even pharmacists fall into the pattern—they're up on those platforms—it's a power thing!

If you are sitting, you can still create rest and power positions with your body by simply turning in your chair and angling your shoulders to the group. Gestures should be done with your elbows above the edge of the table and your fingertips can still be used to reach out to include one or more people in the conversation. The actions of your body are always available. All in all, small group meetings still require a physical plan in your delivery style just as large groups do.

Is there a such thing as too much eye contact?

Obviously, in large groups the chances for direct eye contact are not as great as with smaller groups. Fewer faces for you to look at means more time to look at each face. So it seems that when there are fewer people in the room, the eye contact with each one should be greater. Not exactly. Too much eye contact tends to backfire.

Let's use the smallest "group" scenario: one other person in the room with you. Let's call the other person Debbie. If you are talking with Debbie and you make constant eye contact with her as you speak, after a short time she will have to look away. She won't be able to stare into your eyes continually so the eye contact between you will be broken. That means another object is likely to catch her attention when she looks away. At that point she is no longer listening to you because her attention is diverted to something else.

However, if you break the eye contact from time to time, while you are speaking, Debbie will have no choice but to remain fixed on your eyes, even as you glance away. You will have greater control of her attention if she is busy fighting for your eyes instead of you fighting for her eyes when you speak. And you really don't look at anything specific when you break the eye contact because you are still talking and your eyes are only wandering on occasion in order to keep her more attentive.

When you are listening you should always maintain eye contact. But when you are speaking, especially to fewer people, you should break the eye contact from time to time to keep the attention of your listeners. In presentations you allow the audience to look away by giving them a chance to glance at the visual on your display screen. The object of their attention, the visual, is still part of your message. In smaller groups the visuals can be just as useful. But if the interaction is mostly one-to-one without much visual support, then allow for occasional breaks in your eye contact with your listeners when you are speaking.

CHAPTER 24

THE MECHANICS OF FUNCTION— DEVELOPING INTERNAL PRESENTATION SKILLS

In this chapter   *by Tom Mucciolo*

PUTTING YOURSELF FIRST

Okay, now it's time for you to get real. Read this chapter only if you are interested in developing the best presentation skills possible. If not, then avaunt, begone, cease to be! This is where we separate the presenters from the pretenders!

Okay, now I'll get real. You're going to find that this is really a fun chapter because it takes you to another level of presenting—a level that gets the audience to react to how you think and feel about your message.

Teaching about the body and the voice is somewhat easier because they are tangible and very measurable parts of the delivery skill. Hey, if you're not moving or no one can hear you, it doesn't take a rocket scientist to figure out the problem. But if you're not focused or you don't have enthusiasm—well, people notice that something is not right, but they're not sure what it is they're really missing. The audience sees external distractions, but they only sense internal ones. The external problems make them not want to look at you at the moment. The internal distractions make the audience not want to watch you again. So, the mechanics of function are what keep them coming back for more!

Perhaps sometime you've gone to a movie or a play and you left with an empty feeling, maybe unsure as to why you felt that way. This happens because you might not have the expertise to analyze the problems in the performances, but you have the experience to know what good performances should be. Well, everyone in the audience has been to a presentation before and they have the experience of both good and bad events. This is what leads people to arrive at the presentation with an expectation.

The good news is that the average audience member at a business presentation expects boredom and talking heads. You can exceed that expectation with the well-planned *mechanics of form*, the external presentation skills using the body and the voice. People are always appreciative of your having given them more than anticipated. But, if you can take the time to prepare on the outside—you know, dress the part, plan the movements, and work the voice—then you need to make the effort to prepare the inside. The inner plan is your character, shaped by thoughts and feelings.

If you truly want your message remembered and linked directly to your personal delivery of that message, you'll have to use the *mechanics of function*, the internal presentation skills. The components of these skills include

- Using your mind
- Using your heart

USING YOUR MIND

In acting, it takes someone with a lot of intelligence to play the part of ignorance. Take Carroll O'Connor and Jean Stapleton, brilliant people who played Archie and Edith Bunker on TV's *All in the Family*, a '70s sitcom. Each played ignorance in a special way. But to know all the intricacies of ignorance, a high level of knowledge is required. How would one know what is stupid unless one were smart enough to understand the difference?

The point of this is that your mind is one of your most powerful assets. As a presenter, you can think on your feet, sway the audience with reason, and persuade people with your logic. In essence, you can use your mind effectively by

- Linking intention to content
- Working with detailed data
- Selecting focal points
- Using virtual space
- Handling distractions

LINKING INTENTION TO CONTENT

This sounds more difficult than it is. The fun in this process is using your imagination to create connections between your actions and the supporting elements in your message. In other words, for every major section of information you are sharing with the audience, you need to identify the intention or sub-text that goes along with that information. The intention follows the same pattern as the objective. Based on action and described in the form of "to do" something, it isn't a feeling, although a feeling will always arise out of action. It's like a little objective.

For example, let's say it's your next presentation. The overall objective is to persuade the group to take action on a new budget item. So, at the beginning of the talk, you plan to bring up a comparison to a similar budget decision that was made in the prior year. Stop. What is your inner intention as you go through the comparison? You know you have to persuade, but use your imagination for a moment. How many ways are there to persuade? Probably a million. Pick one.

Let me pick one for you: You show the absurdity in bringing up what happened a year ago. You stress that this is like comparing apples to oranges, and the data from last year is meaningless to this issue.

Let me give you another one: You proclaim the validity of the comparison to last year. You stress the decision was made by the same management team evaluating the current project and their track record on these issues is impeccable.

Your intention is different in each case, yet the visual support looks the same. The angle of your approach is going to change depending on your inner intention.

In other words, you've got a whole bunch of little things to do inside the big thing you have to do. Just like a wedding when there are a million little details, each with an intensity, an action, an outcome. Then, you have to consider the scope of the entire event—the wedding. Details exist in so many things you do. Why would your presentation be any different? It's attention to detail that will make it successful.

To do this, dissect your presentation into smaller segments and see what is going on in your mind as you cover each segment. If a few charts are displayed in one part of your talk, what is your subtext, what are you really thinking? Is your intention to distract the audience with the details? Is it to drive home the point? Is it to set the stage for the next section of the presentation?

Don't chop the presentation into such tiny segments that you try to find an intention for every moment. This will result in the analysis-into-paralysis problem! Typically, your intentions cover a group of visuals. Maybe you'll have about six to eight different intentions for a 20-minute talk. You might use an intention more than once for repetitive items such as humor or storytelling. For example, the intention in each of three different stories might be to teach a lesson.

If you just concentrate on the major sections and the related intentions, the tiny moments take care of themselves. How? They happen as a result of your natural thinking pattern to accomplish tasks. Trust yourself and give yourself more credit. You wouldn't even be reading this book if you didn't have the ability to express yourself and your intentions. You've been doing this all your life. You just have to apply the process to presenting. If you understand the big segments, then the little things under every single moment will become so natural, you won't have to think about them.

Your inner intentions are buried in your brain and you have to identify them so that you can be sure that the way you offer the information is the way you expect the audience to understand it. This is what I mean by linking intention to content.

Playing the Stakes

In theatre, the actor must "play the stakes" in each scene. The actor searches for the most important moments to make clear in each scene.

The same is true in presenting. Look at any piece of information in your script and decide on its priority to the whole story. The closer it is to being essential, the higher the stakes get if you don't present it well.

You might not convince your audience if you fail to deliver the key information. So if you fear your talk will be boring, find the importance in the information and allow the audience to discover the importance with you.

You can play the stakes in a section of the presentation or even on a single visual. If you have a visual that displays several bullet points, you need to decide which of those points is most important to the story at that moment.

Although you may cover all the points anyway, you may find yourself discussing one point in much more detail. This is probably the critical element in the visual, and you should focus more of your attention on delivering that point as clearly and directly as possible. This doesn't mean the rest of the material is unimportant; instead, it helps you use the surrounding information as support for the more important item.

By playing the stakes in each visual you will add the sense of urgency to the topic that otherwise may appear to you as too boring for others to experience. In addition, the physical actions you use to play the stakes will heighten the importance of the information.

WORKING WITH DETAILED DATA

Sometimes your visuals contain detailed information. Typically this happens with data-driven charts (bar, pie, line, area, and so on). Most presenters display these charts for the audience and discuss the obvious items, usually the biggest slice, the tallest bar, the upward moving line—the easy stuff. Although nothing is wrong with this, it adds little value to the audience if they could have figured it out for themselves.

But a visual presenter (there's that term again!) reads between the lines and makes the detailed information come to life. It's a process of identifying the means inside the extremes.

Think of the means as internal causes for the extremes. The extremes are the external data elements that are different enough to force a comparison or a discussion.

For example, Figure 24.1 is a vertical bar chart. It contains four selected months of data showing the time (in seconds) it takes to connect to the Internet from home and from business. Wait—don't start calling your Internet service provider and complaining. I made these numbers up just for the example!

Okay, back to the example. Let's say you select one particular set of extremes related to the home group. You might point out that the connect time in February is so much faster than in December. You picked two data elements different enough to stimulate a discussion.

Now you have to stress the means of those extremes. You identify the causes of the difference. An obvious one would be a seasonal issue. The reason it takes longer to connect in December is because of the holiday season and the online calls to friends and family. Maybe you dig deeper into the means. You might bring up a recent article you read that mentioned how the home sales of digital cameras seem to peak in mid-November because people want to have holiday pictures in advance of the holiday season. The effect of more digital photos is their later transmission in December over the Internet. These photos are much larger files resulting in more traffic over the Net and, hence, slower connect times. None of this extra stuff appears on the chart—it's all in your head.

PART
VII

CH
24

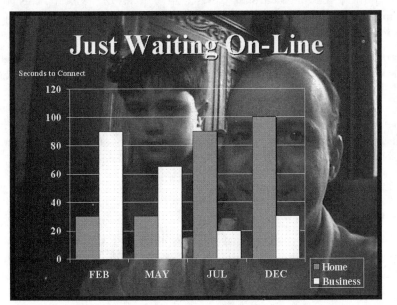

Figure 24.1
A simple bar chart showing selected months of activity. You can choose to discuss from eight different items. Look to compare the extremes; that is, any items that are different enough to warrant an explanation.

Want to try another? Let's use the same example, but pick two other extremes. Compare home to business in the month of July. What are the means inside those extremes? You could point out that more employees take vacations during the month of July than any other time during the year. Not being at the desk in the office results in fewer connections to the Internet, hence less traffic from the business group. However, vacation doesn't always mean travel away from home, and you might mention that with kids home from school, an increase in Internet activity from home results in more traffic on the Net. Maybe you dig deeper into the means. You cite a statistic from the National Education Extension Outreach Foundation (whatever) that shows a sharp increase in the number of online college-level courses being taken during the summer months when classroom sessions are fewer. The students in these electronic programs are participating from home, which is another reason for the rise of Internet activity in July and the longer connect times from the home group. Once again, the audience gets none of this from the chart on the screen.

By identifying the means inside the extremes wherever possible, you create a lasting impression on the audience. You become the critical bond for the audience between data and description. Without you as that link, anyone could have presented the topic. And a visual presenter would never allow that!

SELECTING FOCAL POINTS

We've talked about anchors a lot in the past few chapters. The audience needs anchors and so do you. Anchors don't really move during the presentation. That's why they're called anchors! The anchors are usually big—standing on the left side of the room, five friendly faces in the audience, geometric shapes to help guide the eye—these are all anchors.

But another type of anchor is called a *focal point*. It's more of a temporary anchor, but something you can use at various times during the presentation. Many of the focal points you'll use are less apparent, if at all, to the audience. But focal points are visible and fixed objects that help you target your attention as you speak.

Have you ever just stared off into space while you were thinking about something? Well, you probably weren't always looking at the night sky when you zoned out. You might have been at your desk or at home and you were looking at something, but you were not focused on the attributes of the object. You were busy thinking. The best example of this is talking on the telephone. Next time you see someone talking on the phone, watch how many places they look when talking, almost none of which are required for continuing the conversation. You do this a lot yourself. Your focal points change and vary depending on what your brain is doing.

As a presenter, you need to be aware of these temporary anchors and you need to use them to your advantage!

You can use two kinds of focal points: primary and secondary. Primary focal points include the screen, the display equipment, and the audience. Secondary focal points include the floor, the ceiling, the walls, the furniture, the fixtures, the exit sign, and any other decorative or noticeable objects you might glance at during the presentation.

Primary focal points are referenced a lot in the presentation and you'll find yourself gesturing to them and interacting with them constantly. The primary focal points help you concentrate your attention and they are very apparent to the audience.

Secondary focal points are less obvious to the audience. Yet, these focal points also help connect your thoughts to physical objects in order for your delivery of information to appear more natural.

You can't stare off into oblivion or space-out during the presentation, even though you do it in real life. But the very act of staring can be so effective for the audience because they can see you thinking, pondering, and struggling to make information important. Without an object to focus attention on, you can't show the audience that you're thinking. Ahhh, but focal points make thinking a reality!

PART

VII

CH

24

For example—finally, an example! You're presenting in front of a group of 40 people. You're getting ready to start and you take note of several objects in the room that catch your attention. On the back wall is a painting of a snow-covered mountain. On the ceiling is a row of track lighting with spotlights facing the side-wall. On the other side-wall is a thermostat and, next to it, a wall telephone. All of these are usable secondary focal points.

Let's say that during the presentation you are telling of a work-related experience where you had to lead a team of people to accomplish a task. During the story you are reflecting about the experience, and your eyes glance to the painting on the back wall. It only takes a few seconds of your attention on that painting to give the impression to the audience that you are reflecting on the experience. They see you staring into space and believe you are explaining to them what you see in your mind's eye. Without an object to focus on, you might recount the story too quickly and lose some of the impact. The painting gives you a visible focal point that helps demonstrate your thoughts and makes the telling of the story look more natural.

So, you can't just look off into space; no, you need something to look at, like the painting. And, because you looked at it before (prior to the presentation), you are not distracted by the details in the painting. That's why you glance around the room before you begin the presentation. You have to know your focal points in advance. You don't want to be surprised by anything you glance at while speaking.

Sometimes the attributes of a focal point can help in your description. Okay, let's use the same example. It's later in the presentation. You're displaying a line chart and commenting on the rising costs of a current project. You glance at the thermostat briefly and you describe the skyrocketing costs as reaching the boiling point, ready to burst. The thermostat as a focal point created a heat-related image in your mind, helping you build a better description for the problem.

Of course, this means you can never present unless you're in a room with a painting and a thermostat!

Creating Distance

Focal points have a *near* or *far* nature, similar to a camera lens. If the focal point is closer to you, the background blurs; if the focal point is more distant, the foreground blurs.

You can try this by holding your index finger up in the air at arm's length, about the height of your eyes. Look at your finger and everything behind your finger is blurry. Look past your finger at some distant point and your finger (even your hand) is blurry. In fact, you can almost see through your finger by focusing on the background. Don't close one eye or you'll lose all depth perception and your finger will become a solid mass, blocking your view of the background. Okay, okay, try it, I'll wait... .

The near or far focus is helpful when describing people or things that are not visible to the audience but need to be more real for you. You might stretch your arm out and focus directly on your palm as you describe items from an invisible contract that you're holding. You could be relaying two parts of a conversation, and the face of the invisible other person is the picture frame on the far wall, making it appear that you are conversing with that person.

In both cases, creating distance requires a focal point or something to look at to help you make it appear real.

Focal points are extremely useful, and the more you can selectively use these temporary anchors, the easier it is to show the audience what you're thinking!

Using Virtual Space

Virtual space (p. 690) is the most fun you can have in front of people with your clothes on! Okay, I just thought you needed a break from all this reading! But it doesn't take much to distract you, does it?

Just as focal points help you connect your thoughts to visible objects, virtual space helps you connect the audience to invisible objects. You use virtual space to show the audience how your mind is visualizing the concepts you're explaining.

At times during a presentation, you will mention several related concepts to the audience and not really know if the group is following along. You already see the concepts in your mind, but the audience has no idea how to distinguish among them.

For example, you mention to the group that three separate departments will be involved in a decision: marketing, sales, and finance. The instant you name the three groups, you have a visual image in your head of each of those departments. You can see where in the building the departments are, you see the faces of people who work in each area, and you are visualizing three distinctly unique departments.

Now you have to get the audience to see three different departments. You do this with virtual space. You physically place the departments in the air for the audience to reference. As you say "marketing," your right hand places the word in the air to your right. As you say "sales," your left hand places the word in the air to your left; as you say "finance," you place the word in the air in front of you, using both hands. In all three moves, your palms would open out to the audience without blocking your face.

The point is that the three departments are floating in virtual space and you can immediately reference any of the three by physically retrieving it from its floating position. If you say, "The marketing department is going to…," you can gesture to the space occupied by the word marketing, to your right, where you placed it. If instead you use the space to your left, the audience would say, "No, no—that's the sales department over there!" The audience remembers where you placed the references because they have been given focal points to reference. The concepts are floating in virtual space for the audience to see.

Use virtual space to identify concepts as separate and distinct from one another. Don't just use virtual space and then do nothing with the floating anchors you handed the audience. When you place the items in the air for the audience, immediately reference one of them to begin noting the distinction.

Other ways of using virtual space include showing timelines and distance. For example, if you are describing several events from 1990 through the present, you might use your right hand to place 1990 in the air as the beginning of the timeline. Then use your left hand to stretch an invisible thread from your right hand to a place in the air to your left to show the length of the timeline. For showing distance, you might gesture, with your left arm fully extended, to a point at the far corner of the room while you mention an office location in another state. The group would realize you are referencing a place in the distance and not somewhere nearby.

PART

VII

CH

24

Keep in mind that the moment you change physical space, virtual space falls to the floor and disappears. For example, you're in the front of the triangle and you use virtual space to distinguish three items. You reference one item, but then you navigate to the middle of the triangle. Because you moved to another physical space on the floor, the virtual references disappear. Those little anchors or focal points for the audience can't float in space if your body is not around to support them! This means that whenever you move in the triangle, you get another opportunity to use virtual space.

HANDLING DISTRACTIONS

When I talked about the mechanics of form in the last chapter, I mentioned some body and voice problems that the audience might find distracting. Sometimes it's the other way around, and you can get distracted while presenting. In almost every distraction, the result is a loss of concentration. Your mind loses the focus on the objective in the presentation. You usually get sidetracked because you were not prepared for the diversion. The following are some of the external forces at work that may challenge your attention to the message.

THE SLACKER

Activity in the audience is a very common distraction for a presenter, and this usually happens at the beginning of a presentation. It's called tardiness. A latecomer can cause a break in the flow for you while you speak. This is more apparent as the tardy person takes a seat closer to the front because more people have to watch the person get settled.

I think the solution for lateness is a public beheading. Now, now—relax—stay with me on this. It seems a bit cruel to do this to the person who shows up late, but I suspect the laggards will be fewer once the heads begin to roll. Actually, beheading is not a popular solution because you can't fit a guillotine in the overhead compartment of the plane, so you'll have to rent one. That just isn't cost-effective!

Okay, seriously, the best way to handle the distractions caused by someone who arrives late is by finding a way to repeat or recap as much of the story necessary for the person to catch up. What? Catch up? But the slacker was late. The actors don't recap what's happened after the play begins. True, but this is not like theatre where the ticket has already been purchased. The one who is late may be critical to your planned call to action. The tardy person may be the one making the final decision! You never know what role the latecomer plays. Don't chance alienation. Bring that lost sheep back into the fold.

In addition, the distraction of a latecomer usually messes up your current point anyway. Because you'll have to repeat what you just covered for everyone else's benefit, you can sneak in a quick sentence to recap for the slacker.

THE ATTACKER

Sometimes a hostile audience member can distract you. Hostility in the audience usually relates to the content in some way. It's simple: You counter hostility with friendliness.

Sometimes political or market forces are at work causing frustration for some people and the reactions are negative. I've seen this hostility at employee meetings right after a downsizing takes place. It happens at shareholder meetings if profits take a hit.

If you are faced with hostility, agree with your adversary as quickly as you can. Then, look at the source of the conflict and ask yourself, "Can I fix this?" Be honest. If you can address the issue, do it. If you can't, then try turning it around. Ask the person, "Do you have a suggestion?" The key to this is that your attempt to solve or ask for help in solving a problem is viewed as a friendly way of working with your adversary.

You usually can't win if you fight back in a public forum. The reason is that the audience believes you know more than you reveal and fighting back suggests you don't have an answer nor will admit to being wrong. That's why agreement helps soften the blow. I realize this approach can't cover every hostile situation, but it works in most cases.

THE KNOW-IT-ALL

Another distraction is caused by the ego of the know-it-all. Counter the conceit with fellowship. The know-it-all appears more in small group presentations because the chance to speak out is more readily available. Regardless of the venue, the know-it-all can cause you to lose your concentration.

Like the attacker, you need to side with the know-it-all right away (if possible). For example, you are discussing the tax benefits of a new copy machine for a client. In the meeting is a person from the client's accounting department. We'll call him "Zeno." Now Zeno pipes up very early in your talk and says, "Are you considering this a Section 1231 Asset for depreciation purposes?" The rest of the group rolls their eyes, having seen Zeno openly destroy others in the past! No one escapes his deadly wrath. But, for you to be discussing tax benefits, you already understand enough accounting details to easily handle Zeno. You address his concerns and respond with enough information to satisfy his hunger. Yet, you also know this is only the beginning. Zeno lives for these moments!

This is when you form the Fellowship of Accountants where you and Zeno are the charter members. Minutes after responding to Zeno, at the very next accounting issue, you look right over to Zeno and say, "And as Zeno can tell each of you, the equipment...." In other words, you make an ally. Zeno becomes your constant resident expert to support nearly every financial point that even remotely sounds confusing.

By making that person your support for complex issues, you always have a very effective way to neutralize the smart-aleck. If you fight the know-it-all, you may gain some sympathy from the rest of the group, but you'll be diverted from your topic and end up being less effective with your message.

PART
VII

CH
24

THE TALKER

This is the person who distracts by talking during your talk. Usually, talkers travel in pairs, unless they're crazy. In that case, they are probably senior executives and we know there is no cure for them! So how do you handle people talking when you're talking?

You do nothing. That's right, nothing. Believe it or not, the audience handles them for you. Try this. Go to the movies with a friend. Start talking with your friend. It won't take long before someone (usually someone big) whirls around, stares at you, and says, "Hey, shut up!" In a play, a ballet, or an opera—anywhere people paid money—fear not, they will quiet down the talkers.

Well, people pay "good money" to attend a meeting. It's called their time. And time is good money. So trust the crowd to help you out on this one because the talkers not only disrupt the speaker, they distract the listener, too.

THE BOSS

Of all the distractions in the world, this one can stop a presenter cold. "Oh, no. My boss is watching! I'm really in trouble now!" How do you deal with a superior in the crowd? You usually freak out. The reason is that your effort to impress becomes greater, and you simply try too hard. In the theatre it's called overacting, and it usually happens when the actor knows a critic is in the audience.

You may find yourself making more eye contact and directing more of the information to your boss at the expense of the rest of the audience. This is a big mistake because you lose on two counts. First, the audience is slighted from your true attention, and second, your boss may feel singled out during every moment. This is frustrating. When a presenter pays a lot of attention to one person, that person feels obligated to listen even more attentively, almost out of courtesy. It's like being at a family function and having to sit and listen to that one relative who won't let you leave the table until the story is over. You know the type. Every family has at least one of these characters. I believe it's the law of nature!

So the solution of presenting to a superior is to treat that person as equal to all the others in the room. Don't pay any more or any less attention than you would to anyone else in the room. A boss gets dressed, eats food, travels, works, and plays just like everyone else in the audience and should not be presented to in a special way. If you deliver the talk with sincerity and you follow the objective through to the call to action, the existence of your boss will have gone unnoticed by both you and your boss. The key here is to neutralize the superiority with equality.

All in all, the distractions you might face can break your concentration if you are not prepared to handle the diversion. Typically, you don't fight fire with fire in these cases. You usually play to counter or neutralize the offender. If you stay focused, you remain in control of the presentation, and you hold the attention of your audience as you deliver the message.

USING YOUR HEART

You go to a play and the actor comes to the edge of the stage and he's crying. If you say, "Wow, look at that! Real tears!" you saw technique. But if he's crying and you're crying— you are in the moment. You are sharing the emotion, not watching it happen.

You can't limit your skill set to the physical or even the physical and mental. You have to use your heart. The reason for this is you. You're a whole person—body, voice, mind, and heart. You present with your whole being.

I once had a colleague who had the potential for complete mastery of this skill. She had so much going for her. She perfected the physical movement and developed excellent voice control; she used her head, linking intentions with content to effectively convey messages. But she failed to take the last step and use her emotions. This limited her use of humor, as well, and it restricted her growth as a consummate communicator. By not committing herself to her own feelings, a gap of emptiness will always be between her and her audiences.

The use of emotion is what separates presenting from performing. As a visual presenter you will have to create the emotional link between you and your audience. You can use your heart in your delivery by

- Understanding motivation
- Adding stories and personal opinions
- Using humor
- Developing your own style

UNDERSTANDING MOTIVATION

Think of all the means at your disposal to express your feelings to an audience. Your eyes, facial expressions, voice, and gestures—your whole body emits feeling in order to make words have meaning. But without your personal commitment, your belief and your motivation, the audience doesn't react as well as expected. Motivation requires inner energy to deliver the information with conviction.

That energy starts with you. You're the catalyst. You have to give an emotion to get an emotion. You have to be motivated before you can expect the group to be motivated. This is one of the most obvious problems I find in working with presenters. They fail to "get into it," but they expect the audience to "get it." Come on, get with it! If you can't psyche yourself up for the moment, then why should the audience be expected to do so? You have to work on yourself to get your heart into it. But before you build the desire (the motivation) to tell the story, you have to believe in your message.

SENSE OF TRUTH

The chance to stir the feelings of a group to truly believe what you believe is the essence of your skill. Your ultimate challenge is that they believe in your belief in the message. People can't have faith in the message without believing in the person representing the message. People believe in other people. The audience wants, above all, to believe what you are telling them. It is that simple. But that belief starts in your own heart because if you don't buy it, they don't buy it! You have to have a sense of truth about your message. This becomes your motivation to deliver that sense of truth with clarity and enthusiasm.

So, ask yourself, "What in the message do I really believe is true?" Everything, something, nothing? Remember that in life, truth is what you know. In presenting, truth doesn't exist until you demonstrate it. Using action, you must show your version of the truth to an audience. But if you can't justify your actions, then the truth is less obvious. Truth and belief are inseparable. So you must believe something to show its truth. It reminds me of the saying "Practice what you preach." So, in almost every coaching session I say, "Yeah…but do you believe it?"

The best way to develop a sense of truth in your message is to play the devil's advocate with the argument you constructed for the audience. Can you convincingly play both sides of the issue? Can you be the prosecution and the defense? Naturally, the side that wins has more of your sense of truth because it has more of your heart. Truth is in the heart, not the mind. So the more the message appeals to you, the more evidence you look for to support it. If you love what you do, you'll love doing it!

Your sense of truth in your topic is directly related to your belief in that topic. Whatever appeals to you most in that truth will be delivered with the most conviction.

THINKING, FEELING, WANTING

Your sense of truth in the message justifies your presenting it. Motivation makes it happen. The motivation to speak is measured by your will, your desire, and your determination. Your feelings and your intellect are both supported by your will. They all work for one another and can hardly be separated. If you use your intellect (mind) to decide on some action, you must call upon your feelings (heart) and your desire (motivation) to make the action happen. You can't separate these. They all work together synergistically. Although action drives emotion, you have to "want" to create the action in the first place.

For example, let's say you must make a presentation to a group of people about a new product. You know how you will present the message because you've planned it. The planning involved a thinking process. But, it doesn't stop there. How do you feel about the plan to present the product? How do you feel about the product itself? How about the people you'll be speaking to, and even the place you'll be presenting in? And, considering those feelings, what motivates you to deliver the information at all?

You might say, "My paycheck!" Believe it or not, money can motivate only in as much as what it gives you—security, luxury, power, and so on. The point is that if the motivation is only from a need to present (to get paid), then it is not being driven by desire. It becomes one of those presentations you have to do, but would skip if you could. This, unfortunately, is the case with over 95% of all presentations.

You've heard the excuses. "I just don't have it today," or "I'm not into it right now," or, "This doesn't interest me." You've used these expressions yourself, at times.

When the motivation—the desire—the will—is missing, the feelings disappear and the mind is left alone to direct the body and the voice. When this happens, the presenter appears to be "going through the motions," and the effect of the message is usually lost.

People Make a Difference

Motivation is a key element to making presentations more effective. I have been giving the same basic skills seminar for a number of years. Often people come up to me who've seen my "show" more than once and say, "I keep getting more and more out of this seminar; what have you added?" I say, "I've changed nothing!" The response is typically, "But something is different."

True. There is one difference. Can you guess? I'll tell you in a minute.

I've had others ask, "How can you give the same seminar, over and over again, and not be totally bored with the topic?" I respond, "The same way in the theatre an actor can play the same role, six nights a week for two years, and deliver the same part with enthusiasm— because every night is different!" It's the same reason why my seminar appears "different" each time.

The answer is different people. When the people change, the event changes. That's because the event is by people, for people. It's a completely new presentation for each new audience. That's the secret behind the motivation. It's the desire and the will to share anew. Whether it's the same information for different people or even new information for the same people, the motivation is a result of change.

Never look to your content to stimulate your will. Look to the people who will be stimulated. It's not the joke that's funny; rather, it's the reaction. Your anticipation of the laughter motivates you to tell the joke! The inspiration you need to present the topic with conviction comes from the simple fact that people are willing to give you moments of their time. If that's not enough to get you excited about your delivery, then consider yourself one of the average communicators—one of the talking heads that people expect to see each time a presentation takes place.

Always visualize the effect of your words on the group and you will understand your motivation. Think of infecting rather than affecting the audience, and your desire to deliver the message will increase.

ADDING STORIES AND PERSONAL OPINIONS

In a world of parity products, where everything looks the same, the one difference is you. That's what being a visual presenter is all about—you! That's how companies differentiate. Not with products, but with people. So, if people make the difference, then you can bet your bottom dollar that individual experience and personal opinion count for something. And guess what? Experience means you've "been there" and have probably formed some philosophy over the years. You've learned some lessons over the course of time. So, talk about them. About the lessons. You know, the stuff you learned and about the way you see it. Talk about the way it was and you'll convince people about the way it should be. Come on, tell a story!

The best presenters tell stories. I can't stress that enough. The advantage of good stories is that they are unique. No one can copy, duplicate, reiterate, reproduce, retransmit, or recount your stories. They are personal references that allow a group of people to know something about what you have been through. Stories and personal experience are ways to share your character with an audience.

TIME, PLACE, AND CIRCUMSTANCE

The rules of storytelling are simple. The audience has to know when it happened, where it happened, and what conditions existed while it happened. If you don't establish time, place, and circumstance, you have less chance of keeping the audience attentive to your story.

For example, several years ago I was at a big conference and everything was hectic. That's the beginning of my story. But how involved are you at this point? I mean, what do you really know so far? More important, what do you visualize about the event compared to what I remember about it? Let's break it apart. "Several years ago"—whatever year you might be thinking of may not be the one I am referencing, so we are not together on that issue. I mentioned "a big conference"—but you are probably visualizing a completely different event in a much different place. Finally, I said, "everything was hectic"—to you, maybe hectic means chaotic, or confused, or frenzied, or simply wild. Adjectives are tough for everyone to agree on, you know.

Clearly my story doesn't put us on the same page so far. Our references are different. A story works best when we all share a common set of parameters. I need to establish time, place, and circumstance for you, very quickly, to pull you into my story.

…So here it was, August 12, 1996. I'm inside the San Diego Convention Center at the Republican National Convention, escaping the 100-degree heat. But, I'm with a few thousand people crammed into this one closet-of-a-room, and suddenly—no air conditioning. Oh man, everything was hectic!

Do you see what a big difference those details made? Sure, it takes about 20 more seconds to add the description, but you are definitely with me in the story. You know the time (August 1996); you know the place (San Diego, Republican Convention); you know the circumstance (no air conditioning). We both can agree on what hectic means now!

When you specify time, place, and circumstance, you help the listener see what you are recalling in your mind. When you detail with adjectives (crammed, closet-of-a-room, and hectic), you let the listener feel what you are recreating in your heart.

Storytelling is about attributes and attitudes. Keep that in mind every time you tell a story, and you will be more descriptive of both the facts and the feelings associated with the experience.

PERSONAL OPINIONS MATTER

It's one thing to tell good stories, whether they happened to you or to someone else. It's also important to editorialize. You have to voice your opinion every so often so that people know you're involved in the message. The editorial is the slant on the topic that the audience expects to hear from you. It's the emotional hook that keeps them coming back for more. Just don't be afraid to say the word "I" when you speak.

For example, let's say you're giving a presentation, and you bring up a bullet chart with a list of services your company provides. You may find yourself reciting the list and maybe adding more explanation here and there. But how do you feel about any one of these services? The audience would love to know. So maybe you say, "What I really find helpful about…" or you state, "One of my favorite ways to use this…"—these are personal opinions. Your own views tell the audience so much more than your reviews. So don't be afraid to show them your take on life.

Hey, that's why we watch talk shows! We love reading those letters to the editor. We are addicted to the unsupported assertions of people we will never meet! If a schoolteacher in West Podunk, Ohio, calls in to "Larry King Live" and criticizes a comment from a state senator out of Texas, I'll sit there mesmerized while I dig deeper into my half-gallon of vanilla-fudge swirl. Why? I have no idea, other than I have to hear an opinion on anything by anybody, anywhere! Okay, so maybe you're not that bad. You have a half-gallon of Rocky Road, instead. The point is that we are fascinated by other people's opinions and stories. It's part of the intrigue of being human.

The bottom line is that you can be so much more effective when you break the pattern of the presentation with stories and personal opinions. It gives the audience an image of a real person who knows how to share real information in a really interesting way.

USING HUMOR

A traveling salesman walks into a local bar and orders a beer. The bar is crowded, but it's pretty quiet.

Suddenly a voice shouts out, "72!" and everyone just bursts into laughter. The salesman looks puzzled.

The crowd settles, again another voice yells, "114!" and people are just doubling over in hysterics.

The salesman leans to the bartender and says, "What's the deal with the numbers and the laughs?"

The bartender replies, "Oh, this bar has been here for years. Same crowd all the time. Well, they know all the jokes, got tired of telling them, so they numbered them all. When you want to tell a joke, you just yell the number. It's pretty simple!"

The salesman whispers, "Hey, do you mind if I try?"

The bartender says, "Give it a shot."

The salesman clears his throat, waits for a lull, and yells, "84!" Nothing! No response, not even a chuckle. He tries again, even louder, "84!" Dead silence. One more time he shouts, "84!" Blank stares. A funeral would be funnier.

Frustrated, he turns to the bartender and says, "What's up? Why don't they laugh? Is something wrong with number 84?"

The bartender shakes his head and says, "Hey, pal, face it. Some people just can't tell a joke!"

I think you get the point. If you aren't funny now, you probably won't be funny when you present. This doesn't mean you can't learn things about timing and rhythm, but humor is exactness, it's preciseness, it's accuracy! You can miss with tragedy and have some people in tears while others sniffle, but comedy is different. They either laugh or they don't. Smirks and chuckles don't count.

I don't want you to shy away from using humor; rather, I want you to realize how effective humor can be in a presentation. In a world of visual creatures, entertainment ranks high on the list of "what they want." Humor is the best entertainment you can add to an event, because it relaxes people and makes them realize that the whole world isn't coming to an end after all. The use of humor, at the right time with the right inflection, can be extremely effective.

OPENING LINES

"I just flew in from New York. Boy, are my arms tired!" That's fine if you are a stand-up comic. A comedian is expected to be funny. But are you expected to be funny? When someone says, "I want to start off with a joke," I ask why? What makes you think the audience expects an opening joke? For that matter, why not sing? If they expect a joke, surely they expect a song, maybe even a dance! If they've seen you present before and they know you for your humor, then yes, tell the joke. But if they don't know your style, the joke better be really funny. No, I mean really funny. If it's not, it will probably bomb.

Bombs Away!

One January, I was in Boston, coaching a group of sales executives during their annual sales conference. The CEO of the company wanted 30 minutes to work with me, early in the afternoon. He came into the room, holding a few index cards and he said, "I just want you to help me with some jokes. I was roasted at dinner last night by the senior management team and I want to get back at them. So I came up with my own jokes." I looked at him and said, "So Dan, let me get this straight, you wrote the jokes, right?" He nodded and I asked him to begin.

He told the first joke and I didn't react. I prompted him to continue and the second and third jokes were worse than the first. I helped him reword a few things. We worked a few minutes on rhythm and delivery. Still—nothing. I looked at him and said, "Forget it, Dan. These won't work. You're not funny." He looked shocked and I continued, "You're not a funny guy. You have no timing, no sense of rhythm, and the jokes stink! Other than that, you're fine!"

He insisted on using the jokes and I said, "If you do, you will bomb, big time. I am telling you the truth. Don't do it!" Sure enough, later that evening I saw him in the hotel lobby and he came right up to me, put his hand on my shoulder and said, "You were right. Not a single laugh. I stunk up the place."

I looked at Dan, glanced at his hand resting on my shoulder, smiled a little and said, "Dan, keep the day job." And we both laughed.

Dan wasn't funny because he was never funny to those people in the first place. They had no expectation or frame of reference for his humor. Dan also wasn't used to telling jokes, so his delivery style didn't fit the situation. You have to develop a skill for humor, just as you would for any other form of entertainment.

Don't just tell an opening joke for the sake of the joke. Whatever opener you choose, make it relate to the topic, the industry, the specific business, or even to a general characteristic about the group, like the fact that they are all in sales or marketing.

I was the keynote speaker at an annual meeting for a global travel agency. My opener was a Henny Youngman joke: "So, I got to the airport, walked up to the ticket counter and said, 'I have three bags here. I want one bag to go to Rome, one to Detroit, and the third one to Dallas.' The attendant said, 'We can't do that!' I said, 'Why not? You did it last week!'" For this group, the joke fit the industry.

STRETCHING THE RUBBER BAND

When I prepare my own presentations, I structure the key issues around the jokes. This is very important because it uses a theatre principle called "stretching the rubber band." Think of the emotions of the audience as a simple rubber band. One side is serious; the other side, humorous. When the rubber band is stretched, the distance between the two sides is greater. If you let go of one side, the impact from the other side is bigger. An unstretched rubber band creates less impact. (I think I read that in a fortune cookie once.)

Applying this principle to presentations, the humor offsets the serious tone of the talk. The timing is the trick. When the humor is at its peak, when you are delivering the funniest line—that's when the rubber band is stretched the most. Immediately following that moment is when you can get the greatest effect from being serious! That's right. The seriousness of the message is greater when the audience least expects it. If they are relaxed from a lighthearted comment, then they are vulnerable to the importance of an issue. The timing of your humor can effectively heighten the importance of your message.

INDICATING AND APOLOGIZING

Don't indicate your humor. If you begin to laugh before the audience does, then the effect of the joke diminishes. This is because you indicated or telegraphed the result (laughter) before it could happen for the audience. If you laugh for the crowd, then they won't have to. One other way of indicating humor is by stating, "That reminds me of a joke…," or "Here's a really funny story…." When you say things like that, you raise the expectation of the group. In that case, it better be funny!

The best way to develop your delivery of humor is to practice telling jokes or funny stories to those closest to you. Family and friends will be the first to tell you if your jokes are funny. But make sure you find the jokes funny, as well, or you will not tell them with commitment.

Finally, if a joke falls flat, keep going. Never apologize and never comment on the failure of humor. It's done. Move on. Only a comedian has to worry about being funny all the time. If you bomb out, it only makes the audience relieved that you don't tell jokes for a living!

That reminds me of the two construction workers who…

DEVELOPING YOUR OWN STYLE

Probably the most important issue in the whole skill of delivery is the development of your own style. Think of style not as fashion, but as character.

The audience evaluates your character in relation to the message, the media, and the mechanics. All of these elements are part of the event. If you have developed your own natural way to deliver consistent messages, your style will emerge. People will remember your kind of presentation. Your style will show each time you deliver, regardless of the content.

LEVELS IN YOUR STYLE

One way of assuring your own style is to match three levels of objectives in this order: the objectives for your life, for your role within the organization, and for your current presentation.

The way this works: Start with your life. Let's say one of the objectives or goals you have in life is to attain great wealth. You want to be rich! Okay, fine. Then look at your role in your current company. Is there an objective in your job description that can possibly match your life goal of attaining great wealth? Well, maybe not great wealth, but possibly a raise or a promotion—the steps to greater wealth. Finally, is there anything in the presentation that has to do with the attaining of great wealth, even if not directly for you but for the company? Look for it.

For example, perhaps part of the presentation discusses company growth. More revenue for the corporation might just increase the budget for payroll. That could mean a nice fat raise for you! The extra cash might be what you need for the mortgage payment on that piece of property you've been looking at recently. Since they're not making any more land, you know that property appreciates in value and it would be so nice to have the land as an investment for the future. The road to great wealth is paved with real estate tycoons!

The point is that during the presentation, the discussion of company growth is in direct line with your goal of attaining great wealth. Chances are you will cover this topic with more enthusiasm because it matches something that appeals to you—in your heart. That's important in the development of your own style.

Many things in your life appeal to you. If any of them exist in your work and through the presentations you give because of your work, all the better to identify them and use them! Link the little objectives of your talk through the larger objectives of your work and into the even bigger objectives of your life.

THROUGH LINE OF ACTION

Paying attention to everything that comes before, during, and following your presentation develops your character or style. It is one continuous process, which is called a through line of action. This is important in the event because it lets you link all of the elements in the presentation with the reality of the way things are.

For example, you are giving a presentation on a Monday morning to a group of people. You begin at 9:00 a.m. and plan to finish at about 11:00 a.m. There will be one 15-minute break scheduled at 10:00 a.m. Okay, pretty simple. Let's make your through line of action for this example run from the time you woke up until after lunch.

Run through the details of those moments and you'll see a range of events from the very consistent to the very unique. The wake up routine is probably the same. Depending on where the presentation takes place, locally or out of town, the commute to the event may be more or less familiar. The arrival at the event will be as unique as however many times you've done this same presentation for the same people in the same space. The event itself will have some information you've mentioned many times and some new information you are presenting for the first time. You can see how just the examination of the continuous action will show you a combination of daily habits and one-of-a-kind activities.

The habits are already a part of your personal style. Don't worry about them at all. The one-of-a-kind moments are part of this through line of action, which eventually may add to your personal style, depending on how often they repeat. The more you can pinpoint and control the unique moments, the more likely they will recur the next time you present.

DON'T EVEN THINK ABOUT IT!

The examination of your through line of action—that is, the connecting points along the way—is how you develop good habits. Although habits are hard to break, the good ones last forever. You don't even need to think about them after a while because they are part of your natural way of doing things.

Tip #277 from

> Look back on all the segments in Chapters 21 through this chapter and put a check mark next to those sections you believe are already part of your style. Put a question mark next to the parts that you think you can achieve for yourself with some effort. Cross out any section that you feel is totally impossible for you to ever accomplish, regardless of how hard you try.
>
> For the check-marked items, they're already yours and you need not think about them. The question marks represent the work you have to do to make them into check marks.
>
> My guess is that you won't cross out anything because there is nothing you can't accomplish, if you try hard enough!

You know, there was a time in your life when, for a few weeks, all you did was spend every single waking moment of your day trying to accomplish a task that, today, you take for granted. It's called walking. At one time, it was a rare privilege; now, it's just part of the way you move.

When your presentation skills evolve from a rarity to a routine, your own style becomes second nature. This is the result of putting as much of yourself into the mechanics of function—the inner life of your delivery—so that no one else can copy, reproduce, or mimic your personal skill set in any way.

Your body, voice, mind, and heart combine to form the foundation of your skill as a visual presenter. Once developed, your own style will be evident in the message, the media, and the mechanics as you perform your presentation for an appreciative audience. Every move you make, every word you utter, every thought you express, and every feeling you have will be part of your natural style. You'll finally be able to trust your own skills whenever you are truly being yourself in the presentation.

So next time you present, relax, wiggle your toes and break a leg!

TROUBLESHOOTING

What's the best way to do a product demonstration for a group?

Whenever you have to focus the attention of the audience on a prop (a tangible object), you should be concerned about physical perspective. If your physical perspective of the object—your viewing angle—is different from that of the audience, the communication is lost. Many product demonstrations fail because the presenter and the audience do not share the same perspective during the demonstration.

For example, let's say the product you need to demonstrate is small enough to rest on top of a table and light enough that you can hold it up to show people. If you are standing and the audience is sitting, any reference to the object as it rests on the table will be viewed from different angles. Your angle is from above and each person in the audience, by virtue of his or her seat, has a different viewing angle to the object. That should be your first indication that you need to change the perspective. You might decide to hold the object in the air so people father back can see. But you still end up with a variety of viewing angles. What can be done to equalize the perspective?

PART

VII

CH

24

One solution is to reproduce the demonstration for view on the screen. The display screen is the "great equalizer" of perspective. You can use a still photograph of the object or you can play a videotape of the object in use. You can even use a document camera connected to your projector to show the live demonstration on the big screen. There are many ways you can create a visual impression of the object so everyone has the same perspective. This is why movies are so entertaining. The camera is doing all the work for you.

I go to presentations as part of a team. Sometimes two or three of us present different parts of the big picture. Do you have any advice for "team" presentations?

Teams are very common in high level sales presentations, initial public offerings (IPOs), and other events where several experts are required to deliver a single message. Whatever the venue, the point is that more than one person is presenting and that fact alone changes the dynamics of the event.

The mechanics of function, as discussed in this chapter, play a very important role in the relationships established by the team for the audience. The better the team members know each other, the more cohesive the team appears. So I would first suggest you get to know the players on your team. Find out likes, dislikes, hobbies, interests, opinions, concerns, fears, aspirations, and anything else that will help you understand the characteristics of your team members.

Let's put this into perspective using a husband/wife analogy. Even if you aren't married, this can apply to any two partners who know each other very well. You and your partner are at a dinner with several friends. A suggestion is made to commit to doing something the following Saturday night. You look at your partner and you can sense, within seconds, his or her interest in the plan. This is because you understand how each of you thinks, feels, and behaves in similar situations. You share a personal history.

When I coach teams, I use exercises to build a personal history to be shared by all team members. I suggest you look for that history in your team members, as well. Have they been through this type of presentation before? Have they experienced a similar turn of events?

Another important element in team presenting is what I call "the exchange." This is the transition between presenters—you know the awkward moment when one person finishes a section and introduces the next person to continue with the presentation. It is during that moment that an audience looks for a relationship between the two individuals. Do they like each other? Are they friends? Do they get along? Most presenters will simply leave this moment blank. There are no words spoken, no dialog planned, no exchange.

You should develop a small bit of business, or banter, so the audience gets an immediate impression that the two presenters have a good, healthy relationship. Maybe you plan a humorous story where one person comments on the driving habits of the other "on the way to the presentation." Perhaps you mention a personal hobby or sport that the other person likes. The whole point is about letting the audience see that a relationship exits. If they think you work well together, they will feel more confident in the organization that supports you, as well.

Team presenting is about demonstrating relationships and relationships can only be built from sharing personal information that can be used to help the team function as a unit.

CHAPTER 25

TECHNIQUES AND TECHNICALITIES

In this chapter *by Tom Mucciolo*

DEALING WITH THE CONDITIONS

Beyond the message, the media, and the mechanics, the event itself adds another dimension to the planning process. The environment plays a significant role in how the presentation is received by the audience.

For example, when you go to a movie, the lobby, the concession stand, the seats, the size of the screen, and the general conditions of the place will affect how much you enjoy the movie. These environmental elements won't really change from day to day, so they become issues you can learn about in advance of going to that particular theatre.

Now, the audience will also make a difference in how much you enjoy the event, but you can't predict the crowd, unless you already have experience with the general group that frequents that theatre. You have less control (if any) over the audience than you have over the environment.

So, you want to be ready for anything when you present and, believe me, anything can happen, even at the most well-planned events. This chapter looks at the external factors that can impact your performance. I will show you a few techniques and make you aware of some technicalities concerning the conditions of the presentation. These circumstances include

- Dressing the part
- Setting the stage
- Using technology

DRESSING THE PART

Yes, you must be dressed when you present. Even if you tried the old trick of picturing the audience naked, I doubt you really want them looking at you the same way. Come on, with that body? I don't think so!

So, the first external element to deal with involves what to wear when presenting.

When you're not presenting, anything goes based on corporate or social standards. You're all grown up so you know what you can or can't wear. But in front of a group, I suggest you stick to something *BASIC*: A Believable Appearance is Simple and the Image is Conservative.

So, try for that classically conservative look with a dash of personal style. When you dress more conservatively, the audience accepts you more quickly. You will reduce those "first impression" biases. If the costumes are very noticeable by the audience, then the actors are upstaged! Period pieces will naturally catch your eye because the context of the play is out-of-date. But a business presentation is contemporary and the clothing must not overtake the message. A few points to keep in mind to make the outfit go unnoticed are

- Focusing on the face
- Working with accessories

- Wearing business outfits
- Choosing a formality

FOCUSING ON THE FACE

Your face is looked at the most because it carries the message through your voice and your expressions. Nothing should distract the audience from seeing your face. Usually, your clothes can cause a distraction, but in some cases the items around and even on your face can lessen the impact of your expressions. Let's take a look at what it takes to keep the focus on the face.

THE SKIN

My first bit of advice is to the guys—Shave! Let me try this one more time—Shave! A clean look is an advantage because it lets all your facial expressions show, especially your smile. Now, my advice to the women—Shave! (Just seeing if you were still with me). Actually, women have the advantage of using make-up to accent their features and make expression more visible from a distance. With make-up, be aware of lighting and how the brightness may wash out your features; if possible, apply make-up in the same type of lighting you'll be in while presenting. Cosmetics, like clothing, change style with the seasons, so avoid the make-up time warp. If you have or know of a beauty consultant, it never hurts to get advice. For both men and women, if presenting under bright lights, use pressed powder to reduce the shine, mostly caused from the heat. This is important as the lighting gets closer.

THE HAIR

Your hair must be well-trimmed, so that it enhances, not hides, your facial expressions. If you wear your hair long, try to keep it pulled back. Or else, when you turn your head, your hair might block much of your face. The audience needs to see at least one eye. With your head turned toward the visual, most people only get to see one of your eyes. If it's covered by your hair, it's like having your back to the audience.

Long hair on men is still not generally accepted in all the ranks of presenting, and depending on the audience, may generate an undesirable reaction. That's why I wear my hair in a style I call missing. Actually, if you are balding—I mean follically challenged—you have a presentation advantage. You have the added expression of the brow, and of making all your facial features appear more dominant. In any case, the hair should not make a statement or the focus will not be on the face.

THE EYEWEAR

If eyewear is required, you should first opt for contact lenses because they don't hide eye expressions. If you must wear glasses, try to find ones with a non-glare finish. This will reflect less light and the audience will be able to see your eyes better. Usually, in conference rooms and most rooms with average-height ceilings, the glass-glare is most noticeable. When you stand and people sit in this type of room, the angle of reflection from the overhead light breaks right at your eyes, regardless of your height. No one knows why this is so, but it is. You could try to raise the earpieces to tilt your glasses forward, but make sure they don't fall off. Otherwise you'll be crawling around on the floor, and I can guarantee the focus will not be on your face!

WORKING WITH ACCESSORIES

Collars and necklines should be kept conservative. You can add a little more expression with ties and scarves. These accessories are great because they naturally draw attention to your face. Bow ties typically get associated with a character trait, and unless the audience already knows you and your bow-tie look, they may not take you seriously. For ties, learn to make a square knot (Windsor knot) so the tie looks symmetrical at the neck. Don't wear those big cartoon ties or the ones with pictures of dead presidents. And avoid the scarves with artistic images of who-knows-what-it-is-or-cares. All these styles distract the audience.

Pins, tie clips, pocket squares, beads, cuff links, and earrings can add polish and style, but wear them sparingly and make sure they don't distract by being reflective or noisy. A watch is your most important presentation accessory because you probably need to keep track of the time. Choose a watch face that has enough size and contrast for you to easily sneak a look at the time as you gesture.

Tip #278 from

Wear your watch on your left arm when you present, even if you normally wear it on your right. The left hand is the one that gestures to the screen and can be lifted higher than your shoulder. The glance to the face of the watch is easiest from that angle and because your face is turned away, the audience can't see you look slightly downward to see the time. If you had your watch on your right arm and then tried to look at it, your glance to your wrist would be more obvious to an audience member who is looking directly at your face.

WEARING BUSINESS OUTFITS

If the suit fits, wear it! The look, comfort, and style all depend on how well a suit fits and drapes your body. Suits that fit well make you feel better. A suit that is too baggy will look sloppy as you move, and one that's too tight will restrict your movement. Choose a suit that is well constructed and use that suit often. In fact, if you present a lot, I suggest investing in a presentation suit that you reserve for events.

Once again, think conservative! Solid colors or subtle patterns are best. Plaids and large houndstooth patterns tend to "vibrate" and can be quite distracting. As for color, it's best to be traditional and subtle. Dark blue and dark-to-medium gray are the most conservative and traditional choices. Women have more opportunities with color choices than men, but that doesn't mean trendy selections will always work. Choosing the right clothing colors for your complexion can make you seem vibrant and energetic whereas the wrong colors can make you look tired and gloomy. Color can also compliment your figure. In fact, dark colors minimize the figure; light emphasizes the figure. Based on your body type, choose accordingly.

ON THE TOP

Shirts and blouses should be fitted for movement and comfort. You don't want very tight outfits, and you should avoid short sleeves while presenting. The reason is that a short sleeve makes the arms look choppy right around the elbow because of the change from cloth to skin. Your gestures are harder to follow because they don't look smooth.

For men, the shirt should be lighter than the suit, and the tie should be darker than the shirt. When in doubt, white is never wrong. For women, the color contrast can vary a bit more, but if you plan on wearing a lavaliere microphone, make sure you wear a blouse that buttons up the front or a v-neck top so that the microphone can be clipped in the center and not to one side. Centering equalizes the sound pick-up.

Jackets and blazers, like suits, should be fitted for movement and comfort. Watch out for pairing separates of contrasting colors. Think of making a solid line of color from the floor to the neck to draw attention up to your face. A lot of people wonder whether the jacket should be buttoned or unbuttoned. Men must wear jackets unbuttoned, if they plan on moving and gesturing. This eliminates double-breasted styles because they are meant to be buttoned all the time. If a man buttons a single-breasted jacket and gestures to the screen, for example, the jacket will gape and pucker because men's jackets are cut in a boxy manner. But women have the choice to leave their jackets buttoned or unbuttoned because women's jackets are cut to fit the curves of the female frame and tend to move naturally with the figure. However, usually the jackets look better when buttoned.

TOWARD THE BOTTOM

Men will wear trousers, but women have the choice of a skirt or trousers when presenting. Trousers allow for easy movement and are generally accepted in the corporate setting when part of a suit. Avoid separates, because they tend to be less formal and more contrasting. With both skirts and trousers, pay attention to hems, making sure the length is tailored and conservative. For both women and men, socks must coordinate with trousers and be long enough to cover the calf. There may be times when you are part of a panel on a platform stage. When you sit, your pants ride up and you don't want the skin on your leg showing. Longer socks prevent this. Women should choose stockings that minimize attention to legs and create a solid look, drawing the eye from the floor to the face.

IT'S GOTTA BE THE SHOES

Footwear is a sound investment because good shoes tend to look and feel good. Of course, the funny thing is that people judge one another by the shoes. It's true. People look at your feet and decide on your grooming habits and even how much money you make! So, all things being equal, if you can't present, at least polish your shoes!

Specifically for women, heels are a symbol of authority and highly recommended for boosting your credibility (no pun intended). However, heels that are too high affect balance and breathing, so stick to one-inch or two-inch heel heights. Just remember, if you hear the word "platforms," it's probably in reference to the stage and not footwear from the '70s.

Then again, add a leisure suit and a rotating mirrored ball and that might not be a bad way to present! Move over, Travolta!

Actually, platforms are a big trend in footwear right now, mostly among teens and the 20-something crowd. So when you're out shopping for shoes and hear the word "platforms," think youth, before you think presentation. Obviously, lower heels will allow for easier movement when you navigate backward in your triangle. Although the heels today that are usually worn with business suits are thicker than in the past and fairly comfortable, I have talked with some women who've worn heels for most of their careers and they say that totally flat shoes are actually uncomfortable because their calf muscles are stretching more than with heels. Well, you be the judge on this one. But like my dad always says, "When your shoes wear out, you'll be on your feet again!"

CHOOSING A FORMALITY

Just think—dress-down Fridays have caused a 20% drop in business for the pantyhose makers! Lots of companies have a business casual day at least once a week, and many offices have adapted a relaxed dress code throughout the week. In fact, with the growing number of telecommuters and people working in other non-office-like settings, casual attire is becoming more and more accepted. This definitely puts a strain on presenters who aren't sure what to wear and when. I mean, do you always wear the power suit when presenting, or do you match the corporate culture?

Here's the way to look at this issue: When in doubt, wear your suit. Otherwise, try to dress one "level" above your audience. For example, if they are wearing jeans and chambray shirts, wear khaki trousers and a sweater vest. If they're wearing khakis, wear dark wool trousers and a blazer. If they're wearing blazers, you wear the suit. Your goal is to maintain a sense of authority over your audience. A "one-level-above" in formality will help you look the part.

This whole "what-to-wear" thing is more about sincerity than anything else. Take a long look in the mirror or even ask a friend to be blatantly honest. But, it's too easy to find the flaws. Focus on what looks right and make it better. If you ever get unsolicited compliments, build on them. The problem with this world is there's too much vanity. But enough about what I think of me—what do you think of me?

Seriously, don't be afraid to consult with professionals. Lots of books cover this topic in depth, and I encourage you to read some of them. From the view of a visual presenter, the focus must be on the face, and from that point outward the gestures and movement will create the action in the presentation. The clothing should not take the attention of the audience because the outfit cannot deliver the message.

SETTING THE STAGE

You might spend a lot of your time getting prepared for the presentation, but when you arrive at the place to deliver the topic, all your difficulties may just be starting. It seems the only things that go according to plan are the problems. I know. I've been there many times.

A whole bunch of things can happen that make the audience uncomfortable, distracted, and even disinterested. Lots of these things can be dealt with in advance. Of course, experience is the best teacher. Hundreds of presentations have taught me that well thought-out logistics (the planning and coordinating) of an event make a world of difference for everyone involved, especially me.

The bottom line is that YOU are ultimately responsible for your presentation and the conditions of the event for the audience. If the group expects coffee and there is no coffee, then consider it your fault. It's certainly not the audience's fault. They did their jobs; they showed up. The rest of the event is in your hands. Even if you delegate tasks to others, the responsibilities are still yours.

If you plan ahead, you can set the stage for a great event by paying attention to some of the logistics, including

- Using risers
- Working with lighting and sound
- Choosing a display screen
- Deciding on seating arrangements

USING RISERS

Well, if you've already dressed the part, then it makes sense that everyone be able to see as much of your outfit as possible. If you use the Hollywood principle of "more face, more body, and more screen" when planning the room layout, you'll realize a good starting point is to consider risers or stage platforms. I'll use the terms interchangeably, even though a riser is typically lower than a platform.

Remember that ballrooms are designed for dinner and for dancing but not for discussion. So, the plan to make such a space "presentable" must be well thought-out. Line-of-sight is critical: If the audience can't see you or your support information, then they can't grasp the entire message.

Usually, when you stand on the same level as the chairs, most people see only the top third of your body. In larger settings, always look for the opportunity to use platforms to raise yourself one or two feet from the floor. The platforms give those sitting in the back a chance to see more of you. It is more difficult to communicate when less of your body is visible. So, when you are on the same level as the audience, I suggest that you at least keep your wrists higher than your elbows when gesturing, so that everyone has a better chance of seeing those gestures.

But, if given the chance to place yourself at a higher level than the floor—take it! The audience will get to see more of you, and thus get more of your physical expression of the message. Stage platforms or risers can give you that little lift you need to be seen.

Risers can range from as little as 6 inches high to large platforms that adjust from 18 to 24 inches. You can even use a fixed stage, if available, which is usually 36 inches from the floor.

In some corporate auditoriums, the seating is fixed, as well, and the rows are sometimes built up on an incline (raked), similar to a playhouse or movie theatre.

Well, you won't be able to make any changes to fixed structures or stationary seating, but in most hotel situations, you can request platforms. Platforms are usually 6'×8'designs, which can be rolled into the space and locked together for stability. In some cases, the platforms are 4'×8'. In addition, most of these platforms have extension supports which can change the height from 18 inches to 24 inches.

For audiences of about 50 to 100 people, 18 inches should be the minimum. For more than 100 people, use the 24-inch height setting for maximum visibility. Of course, if the best you can get are 12-inch risers, take them. Any opportunity for the audience to see you better is worth it.

Most platforms are covered with material, like carpeting, to dull the hollow sound from your footsteps when you move. If the staging is not carpeted, you'll have to place less of your weight on your heels as you move, or simply take smaller steps to minimize any distractions.

Tip #279 from

Check for the creaks! If possible, walk around the entire "stage" before the presentation and take note of any creaks or squeaking sounds you hear when stepping in certain areas. If you know that a part of the staging makes a noise when you walk over it, you should avoid that area as much as possible. The last thing you want is a loud squeak just as you say a key phrase. Many creaks in staging happen where the platforms meet. Some heavy-duty tape can usually eliminate the problem.

Of course, when you are up on risers, avoid leaning forward when you are in the front of the triangle. For people in the front row of the audience, this can appear intimidating. It's best to keep your weight shifted back or stand straight. Depending on platform height and proximity to the first row, the angle of your face gets distorted when you get too close to the edge of the stage.

WORKING WITH LIGHTING AND SOUND

If you can choose only one thing during a presentation, it should be good lighting followed closely by good sound. The whole notion of a visual presenter revolves around being seen and heard. When an audience watches your presentation, they are getting a lot from your physical delivery, and a tremendous amount of emphasis is given to your facial expressions, including your voice. Bad lighting masks your expressions and poor acoustics make the message difficult to hear. So, lighting and sound become important issues.

LIGHTING

Good lighting is the key to a good presentation. The audience should see as much of the presenter's face as possible. The goal is to create an unequal distribution of light, with most of the light on the presenter, some light over the audience for note-taking, and no light on the screen (other than from the projected image, of course).

The good news is that you need only two stage lights to cross-light the presenter effectively. Add a dimmer pack, and you can adjust the light level so that the presenter can still see the audience while speaking.

I recommend using two Leiko lights on trees. A Leiko light is a stage light of 500 to 750 watts (or more) and has four adjustable shutters for directing (cropping) the light into a specific area without spilling onto another area, specifically the screen.

The light is hung from a "tree," a big metal pole that sits in a round heavy base with a smaller metal pole across the top that holds one to four lights. When you use stage lights, it's best when the ceiling height is 15 feet or higher, and free from obstructions such as low-hanging chandeliers. The lower the ceiling, the lower the lights hang from the tree. Low-hanging lights usually spill into the first few rows of the audience, and you end up with shadows of people in your triangle. You don't want a bunch of big-headed silhouettes all over your body as you move around, which happens when the angle of the light is too low. Higher ceilings allow the light to cast down on you and not spill onto the audience. Use the shutters to crop the light from the bottom if the angles are too low.

Tip #280 from

In the case of low ceilings, position the light trees closer to the riser on opposite sides of the room and direct the light just a little higher (using a little bounce light from the ceiling). Be sure to keep all light from spilling onto the screen. Depending on the angle, this will be more difficult for the light positioned on the side of the room where the presenter stands. In addition, you may need to arrange a few seats differently so no one's view is blocked by light poles.

A dimmer pack can be a small switch with a round knob or it can be a complete lighting board with moving levers to reduce the intensity of the lights.

If you are not used to lighting and you stand on a stage with even one light at 100% (full intensity), you'll be seeing orange spots for about a week! If you are working with stage lights, make sure you can handle the bright light without excessive blinking or squinting. That's why a dimmer pack is important. Typically, you'll drop the level to about 60% or lower, depending on how much of the audience you need to see. The brighter the lights, the less chance of your seeing a hand raised for questions. Hmmm…maybe this could be your plan—super bright lights so you can't see anyone!

Tip #281 from

One way to test how bright the lights should be is to bring them up until you see a glare off your cheeks in the lower peripheral of your eyes. The point at which your skin reflects the light into the bottoms of your eyes is the maximum brightness setting.

Two lights are needed to provide cross-lighting. Just a single light from one side creates shadows on your face on the opposite side. But cross-lighting allows light to reach you from each direction and eliminates any shadows, regardless of whether you stand in the rest or power position.

You might think it costs a lot of money to have lighting set up as I just described, but we're only talking about $250 for everything. Obviously, that's an average price and it may be higher, but it's worth checking into when planning the event.

Creative Lighting!

If lighting isn't available, you have some inexpensive options, especially if you're at a hotel or conference center. One approach is to rent two 35mm slide projectors and position them at opposite sides of the room on high stands. You can adjust the size of the projected light to fill the presenting area.

You may need a blank CLEAR slide to let the light pass through the lens, although some slide projectors will project light without a slide in the carousel. To make a blank, simply take any 35mm slide and punch out the film to make a clear opening.

Another lighting option is to rent two overhead projectors. Place them on opposite sides of you on high stands, keeping in mind that you'll have to place them much closer than slide projectors. But, you can tape sheets of paper to the overhead projector to shape the light to your exact space, similar to the way shutters work for stage lights.

In smaller venues, such as a conference room, incandescent lighting works best. These are the recessed lights that usually have a dimmer control. Avoid fluorescent lights whenever possible because they are the least flattering and least controlled, and they cast an equal amount of light around the room. When the light is equal, the audience could be distracted by wall hangings, furniture pieces, and worst of all, a clock! But, by creating an unequal distribution of light, you keep the audience's eyes focused on you and minimize other distractions in the room.

SOUND

What? Did you say sound? I couldn't hear you! Sound is especially important for groups of 50 or more. A wireless *lavaliere* microphone (one that clips to the tie or blouse) is always preferred to allow you the most mobility. The microphone, or *mic* as it is commonly called, should always be clipped in the center—not on the lapel—because most lavaliere microphones pick up sound from only one direction to eliminate background noise. So, if the microphone is on your lapel, when you turn your head away, you'll be less audible.

You have a couple of ways to select a microphone, and without getting technical, here are some things to think about.

The environment makes a difference. Directional mics are best when you don't want anything but the voice from one direction picked up by the mic. Typically, for presenting, this is what you will use. The microphones found on lecterns tend to be omni-directional (nondirectional), which means they pick up nearby sounds, including your voice. That's why you may hear pages turning or thumping sounds when the hands hit the lectern as you speak into the mic.

Tip #282 from	If you are picking up sound from vibration while at a lectern, try taping another micro-phone to the existing microphone on the lectern. Shut the lectern mic off and use the other similar-type microphone instead. Then, any vibration caused by your hands bumping the sides of the lectern will be very muffled or completely eliminated.

Mics also fall into one of two basic types, *dynamic* or *condenser*. Dynamic mics are very durable and usually of the handheld or lectern type. They are very versatile and handle most any sound. They don't require batteries because they are directly connected to some audio power source.

Condenser mics are smaller and more sophisticated. Usually found on those wireless lava-lieres, these are best for picking up the richer tones in the voice. But these mics are more breakable, especially where the cable meets the mic.

They need power, usually supplied by batteries.

Tip #283 from	If you plan on using a wireless mic for a full-day event, change the battery at lunch time to ensure quality sound for the rest of the day.

The key to any microphone setup is to make sure the mic is far enough away from your mouth so there is no distortion. For the lavaliere microphone, keep it clipped one hand's width below your neck. What? One hand? That's right, one hand. Put your thumb at the base of your neck and lay your hand flat so it rests on the top of your chest. You'll feel your heart beating below your palm. Well, right past your hand, below your bottom knuckle, is where to clip the mic.

Finally, because the transmitter clips to your belt, place it on your left side, more toward your back, away from your hip bone. It will have less of a tendency to fall off. If you place it on your right side, a gesture you make with your left hand toward the screen is higher and usually tilts your body down to your right. This can then lift the transmitter off your right side and possibly make it fall off.

Naturally, a belt helps, but for some women's form-fitting suits, the clipping on the side may create a slight bulge through the jacket, so you can just as easily clip the transmitter behind you, near your backbone. If your suit jacket is less restrictive, you can even place the transmitter in the inside or outside left pocket, depending on where it looks least distract-ing. The point is that if you know you are going to be wearing a mic and transmitter, plan an outfit that will accommodate the wearing of this equipment with the least problem.

Choosing a Display Screen

You have two considerations regarding the display screen. One has to do with the physical characteristics of the screen, and the other has to do with the placement of the display. Both involve visibility issues.

SCREEN TYPES

The most versatile displays are those that allow for the best viewing from all angles. For projection screens, I recommend a flat, non-glare, matte-white screen. The image will be just as bright from the sides as from the center. Conversely, glass-beaded screens tend to be very bright when viewed from the center, but gradually look dimmer when viewed from wider angles.

Rear-screen projection will be less bright than front-screen, but viewable from the same angles. This is good for situations where people may be crossing in front of the screen, as in an awards ceremony. You, as the presenter, should never cross in front of the screen, whether the image is projected from behind or from the front.

In addition, the screen should be *keystone-correcting*. An image "keystones" when the projector is positioned lower than the projection screen. The greater the angle, the more the visual appears like the letter "V," wider at the top and narrower at the bottom. Usually, a tripod screen has an extension bar at the top. When the bar is extended, the screen is able to hook onto the bar at any of several tabs or notches depending on how far forward you want the screen to lean. The more you tilt the screen toward the projector, the more the image becomes square (less like a V).

Sometimes presentations take place using a monitor or TV. The difference is that a monitor takes computer input directly, whereas a TV needs to change the computer signal using a device known as a *scan converter*. Usually, the more you pay for these converters, the closer the image looks to the original.

Tip #284 from

> Typically, converters increase the size of the computer's image, and the edges of your visual will be cut off. If you plan to present on a TV using a converter, check your images in PowerPoint's Slide Show view. Then, place your thumb up to the first knuckle on each side of any visual where you think information is close to the edge. Usually, the headings and the right side are the problem areas. Anything under your thumb may be missing when the image is sent through the scan converter. If you pretend you have this border or safety zone when creating the visual, you can be sure it will be seen through nearly any scan converter.

A monitor or TV has a light source from within, and therefore the lighting in the room can be quite bright and the image will still be visible. But the size of these displays is usually limited to about a 35-inch diagonal or less, which limits the number of people able to view the presentation. In addition, monitors are usually set in a wall or mounted in some other fixed position, which makes connecting another piece of equipment pretty difficult. You may have to hire a body builder to pull out one of these monster 100-pound monitors so you can get to the connectors on the back. Go for the projection screen whenever possible!

SCREEN PLACEMENT

Look at where the bottom of your visual is in relation to the floor. The bottom of your visual should be higher than your shoulder as you stand on the floor; this way, people seated behind other people will probably be able to see the entire visual. To be sure this is the case, try to get the bottom of the visual to be at least six feet from the floor.

Check this out at the next presentation you attend. Sit behind someone and you probably can see only the top two-thirds of the image, unless your view is clear. Usually, only the people in the front row have the full view of the screen. In a conference room, the views are usually fairly good for most people, but larger events are the ones with the most problems.

If only the top two-thirds of your image is viewable and you have any data-driven charts showing progress over time, chances are the comparison points are at the bottom. If the content is financial data and the audience can't see the changing dates along the bottom of the visual, how can they understand the chart? For example, Figures 25.1 and 25.2 compare the way a visual can appear, depending on your seat. Figure 25.1 shows a vertical bar chart viewed when sitting in the front row. It is completely visible.

Figure 25.2 is the same visual, but note the way it appears from about row six! From this view, you can't see the lower third of the image, and the heading makes little sense because you don't know which are the best four months. Comparisons are more difficult when the people have to make an effort to see the entire image. The harder your audience works to see the full screen, the less effective you will be.

Figure 25.1
A simple bar chart showing activity for selected months in the year. If you sit in the front row, you can see the entire image.

What happens when you can't raise the screen so that the bottom is at shoulder height because the ceiling is too low? As I mentioned before, look for a ceiling 15 feet or higher. In hotels, a ballroom is typical of such height. For example, if you can get a room with a ceiling height of 16 feet, you can use a nine-foot-high screen and place the bottom of the screen six feet from the floor, leaving a foot to spare!

Figure 25.2
The same bar chart seen from a few rows back. When the bottom of the image is not high enough, you have to look around people to see things on the screen.

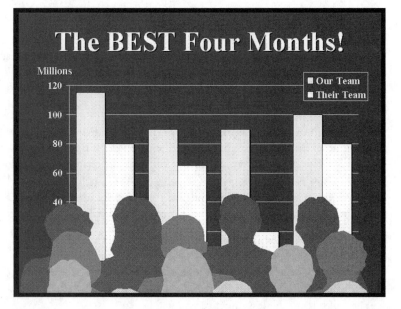

If your ceiling height is too low, then you can try shrinking the overall size of your image so that the bottom of it is higher. If you can get the bottom to a height where anyone can see the entire image from any seat, then the only other thing you have to check is text readability from the back row. Don't shrink the image so that it is totally unreadable from a distance. That's like being able to see from a distance that a letter has a stamp on it, but not being able to see what's actually on the stamp. I'd rather lose some of the visual at the bottom in order for the rest of it to be readable.

DECIDING ON SEATING ARRANGEMENTS

You can use several different styles of seating , but they generally fall into one of two categories, theatre or classroom. The difference? Tables!

Theatre style, no matter how you arrange the chairs, does not include tables. This style is typical for large groups, and when the seating is not fixed, flexibility improves. You will probably use theatre-style seating for groups of 50 or more, and for events of short duration (no more than a half-day). Figure 25.3 is MediaNet's suggested room layout for theatre-style seating. This diagram, along with more complete setup advice, appears on MediaNet's Web site at www.medianet-ny.com/layout.htm. You can print out these layout considerations and use them to help set up your own event.

But if the event is more than a half-day, you should provide tables for a classroom-style approach. Although this reduces the number of people the space can hold by about 60%, the comfort of your audience will be greatly enhanced.

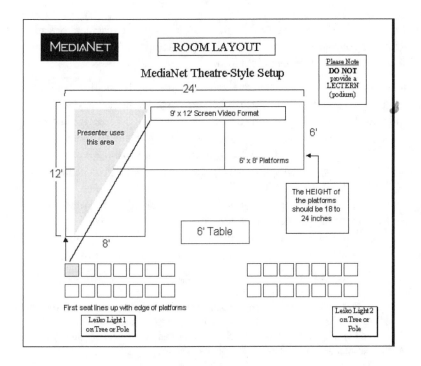

Figure 25.3
A suggested room layout with theatre-style seating. Note the two Leiko lights, the platform staging, and the presenter's triangle. As you can see, the setup does not call for a lectern because it limits mobility of the presenter.

Classroom-style seating can have all the tables facing straight to the front, as the theatre setup would be. Classroom style can also have variations. Angling the tables toward the center of the room, called *chevron* seating, can help increase the interaction among audience members because people can see more of one another with the tables on an angle. Interaction is increased even more when you use a *u-shape* arrangement because almost everyone can see everyone else in the room. The u-shape is like a big conference table without the table.

Tip #285 from

> Don't make a perfect u-shape. Leave off the front-end table on the side you present from, the left side, so that you have more room for your triangle.

The smaller the group, the more likely your setting will be in a conference room or in a training room with ten-foot or lower ceilings, limited lighting options, and less area for you to move. When you are faced with a lot of limitations, arrange the seats with more people facing one another. This shifts the focus more toward discussion and allows you to play the role of both lecturer and facilitator.

SEATING AND DISTANCE

The size of the text displayed should relate to the distance people are seated from the viewing screen. You learned about this in Chapter 23 with the "8 to 1 rule." To recap, eight times the height of the visual (not the screen) is the maximum viewing distance to read 24-point size text. So, if your visual is 6 feet high, then people seated 48 feet away should be able to read text that is as small as 24 points in size.

Just for your reference, when you type a letter to someone, the text is usually 12-point size. The cell of a spreadsheet is about 10-point size. The pull-down menu bar on your computer screen (you know, File, Edit, View, and so forth) is about 8-point size. If you do the math, you can see that presenting software or demonstrating a Web site to an audience is going to be a lot harder than running a PowerPoint presentation. With the software program or Web page, you likely will be displaying 12-point type at best (if you're lucky). If the point size is 12 rather than 24, the "8 to 1 rule" becomes the "4 to 1 rule"! This means everyone has to sit twice as close. Using a six-foot-high image, people will have to sit no more than 24 feet from the visual (instead of 48 feet) in order to be able to read your screen. Unfortunately, when the room is set up, the hotel staff doesn't think about point size. Now you'll have to ask people in row 14 to move up to row 7. (I don't think so!)

Calculating the Distance

If you want a simple formula for calculating how far away a person can sit and still be able to read your information, use these three letters, T, V, and D. T for the type size, V for the height of the visual, and D for the maximum distance to sit. The formula is $(T/3) \times V = D$. (The type size T divided by 3, then multiplied by the visual height V equals the maximum seating distance D to read that type size).

Find your smallest point type size on any visual you intend to display. Divide that point size by three. Multiply that answer by the height of your image. The result is how far away people can sit and still read your visual.

Try this example. The smallest type size in your presentation is 18 point, and your visual is 4 feet high. How many feet away can a person sit and still be able to read your image easily?

Why do type size and distance make a difference? Think about the number of people attending your presentation. When you know the maximum viewing distance, you figure out if the room you plan to present in is big enough. In fact, the arrangement of the seats will make a difference as to how many people you can accommodate.

For example, using theatre-style seating (no tables, just chairs), how can you figure out the number of people that can fit in the room? First, the typical space between rows—that is, from the back of one chair to the back of the chair in the next row—should be about three feet. This leaves enough room for people to pass by. But keep in mind that to display your image, the projection equipment will take up room in the front. So, the first row of chairs is usually set up a distance away from the screen, usually about 25% of the maximum seating distance from the visual. Wait a minute—that means the audience can only occupy the space in the remaining 75% of the maximum distance.

Let's say you have a six-foot-high image containing 24-point type, which allows a 48-foot maximum seating distance. That means the first 12 feet (one-fourth of 48) is cleared so that the projector can be set up to cast that six-foot-high image. You end up with only 36 feet of available depth for the audience. So, because you need about three feet of space between rows, you now have room for about 12 rows of chairs.

Based on approximately 16 people across each row separated by a middle aisle, you have room for as many as 120 people, give or take a few.

Tip #286 from

Set up one middle aisle and limit the width of any row on either side of the aisle to no more than 10 chairs. In this way, no one need pass in front of more than five people to exit any row into the middle or side aisle.

Another way to set up the rows is to double the height of the visual. For example, if you have a 6-foot-high image, seat no more than 12 people per row. With a middle aisle, you'll have six chairs on each side.

Figure 25.4 is a section taken from the table "MediaNet Seating Calculations for Distance and Capacity." This chart is helpful in determining what changes you may have to make to your font sizes or your visual height in order to accommodate your audience. The rounded-off calculations allow for empty seats and extra rows here and there, but the general results are useful when planning your event. The entire table can be seen by visiting MediaNet's Web site at www.medianet-ny.com/seating.htm.

PART
VII
CH
25

MediaNet Seating Calculations for Distance and Capacity

Visual Height (in feet)	Smallest Font (in Point-size)	Distance to Last Row (in feet)	Theatre-Style (Chairs only)			Classroom-Style (Tables and Chairs)	
			Total Rows to set	Max. People in each row	Seating Capacity to expect	Total Rows to set	Seating Capacity to expect
6	12	24	4	12	41	1	16
6	18	36	8	12	82	3	33
6	24	48	12	12	122	4	49
6	32	64	17	12	177	6	71
6	38	76	21	12	218	7	67
6	44	88	25	12	259	9	103
6	48	96	28	12	286	9	114
7	12	28	5	14	56	2	22
7	18	42	9	14	111	3	44
7	24	56	14	14	167	5	67
7	32	75	20	14	241	7	96
7	38	89	25	14	296	8	118
7	44	103	30	14	352	10	141
7	48	112	33	14	399	11	155
8	12	32	5	16	73	2	29
8	18	48	11	16	145	4	58
8	24	64	16	16	218	5	87
8	36	96	27	16	363	9	145
8	42	112	32	16	435	11	174
8	44	117	34	16	459	11	184
8	48	128	37	16	508	12	203
9	12	36	6	18	92	2	37
9	18	54	12	18	184	4	73
9	24	72	18	18	275	6	110
9	32	96	26	18	398	9	159
9	38	114	32	18	490	11	196
9	44	132	38	18	581	13	233
9	48	144	42	18	643	14	257
10	12	40	7	20	113	2	45
10	18	60	13	20	227	4	91
10	24	90	20	20	340	7	136
10	32	107	29	20	491	10	196
10	38	127	36	20	604	12	242
10	44	147	42	20	718	14	287
10	48	160	47	20	793	16	317

Figure 25.4
A section of MediaNet's seating table, showing calculations for visual heights of 6 to 10 feet and selected font sizes. If you know the height of your image and the smallest font size you used, you can get an idea as to how far back the chairs can be placed and how many people can fit in the room.

When seating people classroom-style, the presence of tables reduces the available seating space. Typically, fewer than half the number of people seated theatre-style can be seated classroom style because you have about five to six feet of space between the rows of chairs to allow for the table.

For example, suppose you have an 8-foot-high image. If you use six-foot-long tables and place two rows of tables on each side of a middle aisle, you'll probably end up with six people on each side or just 12 across (as opposed to 16 across in theatre-style seating). Not only do you have fewer rows, but you have fewer people per row. So, when using classroom seating, estimate no more than 40% the audience capacity of theatre-style seating to be safe.

Visibility from a distance and the seating arrangements are important considerations when you design your support visuals. If you can't get the room set up the way you want, you may have to change the appearance of some of your visuals. Of course, the more control you have over the room conditions, the fewer changes you'll need to make to your content.

Most presenters ignore the importance of the room. They take what they get when they get there, and then wonder why the event failed. As a presenter, it is YOUR job to provide a room layout diagram to a meeting planner, a hotel A/V group, or even a major presentation service in order to get what you want.

USING TECHNOLOGY

It seems any mention of technology is obsolete before you finish reading the sentence! However, you should be aware of some generalities when you use different devices, especially from a technical perspective. As a visual presenter, you should be adept at using different pieces of equipment, although you will probably get comfortable using one particular device for most of your presentation needs. In any case, here are a few things to consider in regard to equipment:

- Handling projectors
- Working with laptop presentations
- Incorporating multimedia

HANDLING PROJECTORS

If you recall, Chapter 23 covered the "cost, convenience, and continuity" issues related to overheads, 35mm slides, and electronic images. The traditional devices—overhead and slide projectors—are not difficult to work with from an operational standpoint. Typically, the big technical question is, "How do you turn this thing on?" But for electronic presentations, you have to know a bit more than the on/off switch when you work with the current crop of LCD (Liquid Crystal Display) projectors.

→ For more information about projectors, **see** "Understanding Media Types," **p. 539**

First the good news: These devices are getting easier and easier to set up, but until personal computers are a cinch to work with, these electronic projectors will carry a bit of intimidation along with them. But don't worry. If you haven't used one of these devices, chances are someone is available who has.

I don't want to get into a long list of specifications, except to tell you that the LCD projector connects directly to your PC and depending on the features of your PC, the projected image may or may not need to be adjusted.

BRIGHTNESS

The brightness of the image is a big issue when you can't control the lighting in the room. You'll probably hear the word *lumens* bandied about when people talk of a projector's brightness. Just think of lumens as a measure of brightness. The more lumens, the brighter the projector. Sure, there's more to it than that, but that's why there are professionals out there who sell these things! Audiovisual companies (A/V dealers) are excellent sources for learning more about the unique features and benefits of electronic projectors.

In a room with only fluorescent lights, go for a projector with at least 500 lumens so that your image remains visible, even with the light spilling onto the screen. Of course, if you have less light hitting the screen, the image will look even better.

RESOLUTION

Think of resolution as the quality of the image. I like to use the comparison of a chain link fence, some chicken wire, and a screen on a door. The sizes of the holes are different in each. If you took a paint brush and painted the word "resolution" on the fence, the wire, and the screen, which would be easiest to read? The screen, because the holes are closer and smaller, making the letters in the painted word appear less broken up and of higher quality. Now, if you hear "640×480 resolution," pretend that's the chain link fence. "800×600 resolution" is the chicken wire and "1,024×768" is the screen door. The higher the resolution, the closer the holes, and the better the quality of the image. That's because the *pixels*, or little dots (holes), that make up the image are closer together!

PART

VII

CH

25

PORTABILITY

Naturally, if you don't have to carry anything to the presentation but your PC, then you don't need to be concerned about the portability of the projector. Why care about weight if you're not toting it? Well, these devices are getting lighter—most are around ten pounds, but some are as light as five pounds. The convenience of bringing the device with you is that you are confident of the image you will get. If you carry the light source to the event, you have more control of the display. I have made plenty of presentations when I did not have the quality image I was used to and had to overcompensate on my delivery to make up for the poorer image. Thus, a lighter projector means more likelihood of your taking it with you to the event.

MULTIPLE CONNECTIONS

Having options for more than one input and output is helpful, especially if you plan on using a variety of media including video and audio. Some projectors even allow hookups for two computer sources. This can be helpful in an event with more than one presenter, each of whom has his or her own PC. The capability to connect a VCR or even a video camera or other device can add value and flexibility, as well. In my full-day "Presenting Made Easy" seminar, I use my computer and play a videotape as well, using the same projector by simply switching sources when needed. Typically, to switch between different inputs, a press of a button on the projector is all that's required.

Note

When a projector allows for multiple sources, it usually lets you set up each source independently. For example, when I switch from my PC to my video source, the video settings on the projector change. So, I can control volume, brightness, contrast, and so forth separately for each input because they are usually different.

Of course, not every piece of equipment works perfectly when connected to another piece of equipment, as may happen with some projector-to-computer hook-ups. Sometimes, one person's notebook PC works fine with a projector, but the next person's PC does not for a variety of reasons. And changing the settings on projectors varies among models and types, so it is best to arrive at your presentation early enough to make sure that everything works properly.

The worst moment in the world is when you start playing with menu options on the projector two minutes before the show is supposed to begin!

Many projectors have multiple outputs, as well. Outputs for video and audio can be very valuable when presenting. For example, if you plan on using sound during your presentation, having an external audio feature on the projector is very helpful. When you have a larger group of people, the tiny speakers of a projector can't disperse sound evenly to everyone in the room. It sounds louder for those who sit closer. But, in some places such as in a hotel, you can connect the projector to the sound system used for your microphone, which is typically connected through the speakers in the ceiling. *House sound*, as it is called, distributes the audio evenly to the audience.

WORKING WITH LAPTOP PRESENTATIONS

Chances are, if you use an electronic projector, you are probably connecting a laptop or notebook computer to it. You'll have some limitations with laptop systems, but I don't want to get too technical on the subject. The good news is that the laptop is a fully functioning office, complete with backup information and tons of other stuff, literally at your fingertips! You need to know a few things about computers and projectors, especially when it comes to laptop presentations.

REMOTE CONTROL

Okay, let me say this again. Remote Control. Wait, let me try one more time. Remote Control. Am I getting through yet? Anyone who stands in front of a group of people and advances the PowerPoint presentation with the keyboard doesn't get it! If you are one of those people—snap out of it! You're losing it! Touching the spacebar when you present with a laptop is like pushing your car to make it go. I'm sorry, but I won't even budge on this one!

Face it! A remote control offers you incredible freedom of movement and enhances your presentation skills accordingly. Please buy a remote control for the PC. I beg you. In fact, it doesn't even have to be a remote mouse because 98% of all presentations are linear (forward or backward) and do not require any interaction with a mouse pointer. Just get a two-button remote control that can advance your visuals while you stand inside your triangle and present.

Pro Presenter

Many types of remotes are available on the market right now, and, although I normally avoid endorsing products, I've got to say that I've been using the same remote control for years now. It's the perfect device for delivering linear electronic presentations. In fact, when I coach people, they are using it within seconds–that's how easy it is to control. It's called the Pro Presenter.

It's a flat, infrared wireless, handheld remote control for the PC or the Mac. The remote can be used with or without its software. It's the same size as a credit card, it fits snugly into the palm of your hand and operates from up to 35 feet away from your computer. It's a $99 wonder that frees you from ever touching the computer while you present. At the risk of sounding like I'm selling you something, visit MediaNet's Web site (www.medianet-ny.com) to learn more about this little product, which is manufactured by Varatouch Technology out of California (www.varatouch.com).

Some remotes also have the capability to control the mouse pointer, as well. So, it's like having the left/right mouse buttons and the pointer all in your hand at the same time. The only thing to worry about is accidentally moving the mouse pointer while you present; and, without your knowing it, the audience sits there wondering what the heck you're pointing to on the visual!

Some remotes are RF (radio frequency) rather than infrared. This just means that you don't have to point them at the receiver while you advance the visuals. Unfortunately, these remotes tend to be larger in size. When a remote cannot fit comfortably into the palm of your hand, it becomes more obvious that you are using one.

When you think of the amount of money invested in a computer and a projector—not to mention the presentation and your time to deliver it—the cost of adding a remote control is insignificant. Think of this: A 65-cent key gets you into a Mercedes! Need I say more? Buy a remote!

SIMULTANEOUS DISPLAY

This is a very big advantage to any speaker, but particularly to a visual presenter. Think about overheads and slides for a minute. You have to turn your head back toward the screen just to glance at information. If your visuals are busy, you end up doing this even more often. But a laptop offers you a unique advantage called *simultaneous display*. The image the audience sees on the big screen appears on the display of your PC at the same time. If this feature is not already set up in your PC, you normally can send the display signal "out the back door" by pressing a combination of keys on your keyboard. Look at your notebook computer and you may see a graphic symbol that looks like a PC and a screen on one of the function keys, usually F5. This is like a toggle that can be set in three positions. One keeps the image on your notebook screen; another sends the image out the VGA (monitor) port on the back while removing it from your notebook screen; and the third setting sends the image out the back, but leaves it on the notebook screen at the same time. This is called simultaneous display.

It's like a little TelePrompTer, except you don't have any speech to read. In fact, if your visuals are less busy, the text displayed on your notebook screen will be larger and should be readable from however far away you are standing from the computer as you present.

In addition, if you look back to Figure 25.3, you can see how your equipment (computer and projector) are centered in the front of the room. When you glance at your notebook screen, it will appear as though you are making eye contact with the section of the audience sitting beyond the table but still in your line of sight. It takes only a slight shift of your eyes downward to catch the information on the screen. Although some may notice the movement, it certainly is not as obvious as the complete look back to the screen done constantly with overheads and slides.

Depending on your computer and the projector, the simultaneous display option may not be available, however. This is a constantly evolving issue with both the computer and projector manufacturers, but in any case, what you need to be concerned about is this: In most cases, when the resolution of the projector is lower than the resolution setting on your PC, the projector compensates for the higher signal coming from your PC and drops bits of the image. This makes smaller text appear choppy. The solution is to lower the resolution setting on your PC to match the projector. However, with some computers, that's still not enough. You may have to disable the simultaneous display feature so that the projector can project a full and clear image at the lower resolution. This is not always the case, but you'll have to try it to be sure.

On the other hand, if the projector has a higher resolution than the computer, you should have no problem, for the most part, because the projector should be able to handle the lower-resolution signal coming from your computer. But, I haven't tested every combination of notebook and projector, so you'll have to make sure for yourself. Once again, the advice of an A/V professional can be of immense help and save you a lot of headaches.

TRANSITIONS

Electronic presentations allow the use of transition effects between visuals. Rather than use transitions randomly, you should consider the way the next image will appear to the audience. The most consistent approach is to try to use a transition that matches the eye movement pattern for the upcoming visual, not the current visual. In other words, transition effects are designed for the visual yet to appear, not for the visual already displayed.

For example, let's say you're displaying a text chart with several bullet points, followed by a horizontal bar chart and then a pie chart. You could use a "horizontal blinds" transition into the text chart because the lines of text are separated by horizontal space. Then you might use a "wipe right" transition from the text chart to the bar chart because the eye will be moving from left to right when the bar chart appears. Then, from the bar to the pie chart, a "box out" transition could be used. The circle of the pie centers the eye in the visual, and the transition opens from the center matching the circle.

So, check the general geometric shapes in the next visual when planning the transition to assure a consistency in eye movement from one image to the next.

Screen Savers, Reminders, and Navigation Issues

One of the things you should do with your laptop is turn off any screen savers you may have. If you stay on one visual too long and your screen saver comes on, it may knock out the signal going to the projector. Then, suddenly, the audience is left staring at a blue screen! Check that you disable the screen saver in Windows and any time-out functions set in the computer itself. A run through your PC's diagnostics or setup screen will tell you if any system savers are enabled.

Some contact-management programs offer reminders, such as alarms, that pop up when the task is due. When you present, don't load software that has the task reminders, unless you want the audience to see just who it is you're having dinner with that night!

Finally, in PowerPoint under Tools, Options select the View tab and make sure all three check boxes in the Slide Show area are unchecked. First, you don't want the pop-up menu to display on the right mouse click. When you leave this box unchecked, then your right mouse button will do what it is supposed to do—navigate the show backward one visual. If you need to navigate to different images or you need to get other help during the presentation, you can simply go to the keyboard and press F1, and the menu of choices will pop up. Second, you don't want the pop-up menu button to show in the corner of each visual as you present. Unless you have a remote mouse, you won't be able to click this transparent icon anyway. Third, you don't want to end your presentation with a blank slide, especially if you've been using a consistent background throughout. Instead, under the Slide Show menu, choose Set Up Show, and check the box "Loop Continuously until 'Esc'," so that your show loops back to the beginning. This allows your presentation to "end" with the same image you started with, if you so choose.

Incorporating Multimedia

You know, nothing you can do with a laptop computer—using animation, sound, video, or any special effects—even comes close to what you see in the movies. We are all accustomed to seeing incredible special effects, and we have Spielberg and Lucas to thank for it. No one walks out of a business presentation and runs home saying, "Honey, you won't believe this, but at this presentation today—well, I don't know how—but the computer—well, it played music and a voice came out—a real voice!" Face it! It's hard to impress people with technology these days. Your only resort is to set yourself on fire as you speak—a real attention grabber, but tough to repeat.

Although much has been said about multimedia, all I can add is this: Beware of multiMANIA. Multimania is the overuse of technology to the point that the audience is enamored by your special effects, but can't remember the plot! One word—*Waterworld*—you paid how much? I think you get my drift.

The point is that you should be concerned when you think about adding elements in your presentation that go beyond your delivery. For example, playing a video clip during your presentation introduces another character to the audience, another presence—basically, another messenger. This isn't wrong, anymore than it's wrong to introduce another presenter. But elements that simulate or mimic real-life forms (speech, movement, real people in action) reach the audience in different ways than traditional visual content.

So, you just need to understand the particulars of animation, sound, and video as unique multimedia elements and their effect on the audience.

ANIMATION

This effect is simply an object in action. However, it should never be text in action. Objects can move, but text should stand still. Take this test. Move this book up and down and try to read it. I rest my case. You can't read moving text until it stops or at least slows down enough for you to anchor on it. Ever try reading the weather warning as it crosses the bottom of your TV? You can't read each word as it appears from the far right; no, you have to wait for a few words to make it to the far left of the screen so you can anchor and read left to right.

So, text should never move. All those transitions you picked with the animated bullet points—out. Just because a programmer can make it happen doesn't mean it's useful. Animated text lines can't be read until they stop. This means the only effect was the animation, the movement. If an action serves only itself, it is useless because the audience takes interest only in the action, not the information. Eventually, people will watch your text flying in from different points and begin to take bets on where the next line will enter from and when!

Note

If the text you are animating is part of a logo or is to be treated as a standalone item, then it is really more like an object and probably contains very little *anchor-and-read* requirement. In those cases, you can animate the text object.

Objects can be animated, but apply a sense of logic. Don't have a clip art symbol of an airplane floating from the top of the visual downward. Airplanes don't do that—at least not more than once! Yet, animated bars or moving lines showing a procedure can help the audience understand growth or flow and make the visual come alive to express an idea. Animation is not a bad thing, as long as it is not overdone to the point that only the effect is noticed.

SOUND

The first sense you experienced was hearing. Before birth you could hear the soft echo of your mom's tender voice as she carried you from place to place. Sound is one of the most important senses throughout our lives and can dramatically affect our perceptions.

Sound can either be used or abused during a presentation. Typically, you might want to add sound at certain points to highlight a key phrase or to add value to some information.

The main thing is to be consistent with sound. The audience not only looks for anchors; they listen for them as well. Your voice becomes an anchor as people adjust to your volume, pitch, and tone. Other sounds placed in the presentation need justification and sometimes repetition to become anchored. But don't just make a noise because your software program has this great library of sounds that you feel compelled to use.

Sounds linked to elements on the visual are usually ineffective. Examples of these are the cash register sound linked to a symbol of money; the sound of applause signifying achievement; the shutter of a camera releasing each time a photo of a person appears on the visual; and, the worst of all sound effects—the typewriter sound linked to animated text and possibly to each letter on each text line!—Please, shoot me NOW—in fact, use the machine gun effect when you do! In all these cases, the sounds are one-time effects that when repeated can become phony or even obnoxious.

Don't get me wrong, sound can play a major role in the presentation if done right. Music is a good example of this. The movie *Jaws* wouldn't be the same without music. *The Omen* wouldn't be as scary. *Ishtar*? Nothing could save that one! The nice thing about music, particularly instrumental music, is that you can talk over it and the audience can blend your words with the background music. In addition, if the music track is long enough or loops continuously, the audience gets the benefit of repetition and will anchor to the music as it plays.

PART
VII
CH
25

Tip #287 from	Even if you don't incorporate music during the presentation, consider playing some tunes as people are coming into the room or perhaps closing off with music as people leave.

You don't even need to have the music clips stored on the computer because the files can be quite large. You can simply use your computer's CD-ROM drive (if you have one) or bring a portable CD player and connect it directly to the projector.

→ To see how to use sound effectively with the Nostalgia Theory, **see** "Knowing Particulars of the Audience", **p. 522**

For example, let's say you are giving a presentation in 1999 to an audience, the average age of which is 31. That means they were 15 years old in 1983. Michael Jackson's "Beat It" will be a more popular sound clip for this crowd than his 1970 tune "ABC," when the majority of this group wore diapers!

You get the idea. Continuity in sound is better than periodic or intermittent sound. You can process continual sound just like listening to the radio while driving a car. But hear a siren or horn beep (noncontinuous sound), and your attention is immediately diverted.

Video

Multimedia takes on a very different flavor when you incorporate video. The multimedia issues with video come in two flavors, full-screen and full-motion. The goal is to have them both, but the technology you currently own may not allow either. Full-screen video is easy to envision. The video fills up the whole screen just like a TV. Many video clips in presentations today are half, one-third, or even one-quarter the size of the screen, depending on the computer system used to deliver the video.

Full-motion video is what you get when you watch TV—30 frames per second. That speed is fast enough for the images to appear lifelike, which is why TV is such a powerful medium. Much of the video shown through laptops is not full-motion, but about half-motion or 15 frames per second. At times, especially during longer computer or digitized video clips, you can get synchronization problems with voice and video after a while. That's when the video and voice get out of sync, and it looks like one of those foreign films with poor dubbing—you know, the ones where the character's mouth moves as if saying eleven words, but you only hear "So, Hercules…".

Out of the Mouths…
When my company's CD-ROM *The Art of Presenting* first came out, my son Peter was about 6 years old. I was playing one of my video clips through the PC, but outside the CD program so that only the clip appeared on the screen. My son was standing next to me as I played the little movie file on the screen of my notebook computer.

"Hey Dad! You're on TV!" he shouted. "Make it big. As big as the screen!". I laughed a bit and said, "Well, I can't make the video bigger or it will get all messed-up and won't run right. It has to be this size because of the computer."

He then asked me, "How much does that computer cost?" I replied, "About $5,000, why?" He looked at me and then into the living room and said, "Wow, then how much did the TV cost?"

I said, "Well, the TV was only $300…" and then I just sat there, puzzled, wondering how to explain THAT one! I mean, here's my son looking from the PC to the TV and back to the PC, both made by the same company, wondering why the one that costs more gives you less of a picture! You can see how visual creatures expect full-motion and full-screen video, simply because of TV.

But, with most laptops, we sacrifice full-motion and full-screen for the sake of storage and speed. Naturally, the storage required for video is much greater than for still images or even clip art, for that matter. I won't go into the technical details of file sizes, but if you've ever loaded a video clip on your PC, you know that it takes up a lot of disk space. For example, a one-minute clip that plays in a window only half the size of your screen might be about 10 megabytes. Of course, one minute is a long time for a video clip when you consider that TV commercials are averaging 15 to 30 seconds. The point is that storage and speed are issues for video and you should limit the length of the clips.

So, the goal is full-screen, full-motion video. And, believe it or not, the speeds of computers are getting faster and faster so this will soon not even be an issue. But not everyone uses the most current technology, and I suspect it will be a few years before video is a breeze to watch through a PC in a presentation.

Regardless of speed, another issue with video concerns movement and direction. If your video clip is not full-screen, you may be including it as part of a visual. If the visual has text and the video clip shows something moving in one direction, make sure that direction matches the way the text reads. For example, a visual in English would have a left-to-right reading pattern. So, if your clip shows a car moving from right to left, you'll have an eye movement clash. Try to match the direction whenever possible.

IMAGE MAGNIFICATION

You may find times when your presence on stage is also reproduced on screen. This might happen if you present in a large venue where people are sitting so far back that they cannot get a good view of you or your expressions. *Image magnification* can be used to make you visible from a far distance. The way this works is that a separate screen is set up, a camera focuses on you, and the video signal is projected on the big screen. Suddenly, you're on TV! The good news is that everyone can see you as if they were in the front row. However, some problems can occur when the camera frames you for the audience. Whenever a camera is used, you should be concerned about what the framed image looks like to the audience. Figure 25.5 shows how different the perspective is when the presenter is viewed from the audience and through the eye of the camera. The banner hanging behind the presenter looks fine when viewed from the audience, but the close-up shot as framed by the camera clips some letters from the company name "Lawe Losetta, Inc." showing only the last two letters of "Lawe" and the first four letters of "Losetta"; through the camera it reads "we Lose."

Figure 25.5
To the live audience, the banner in the background presents no problem. However, when the presenter's image is magnified, the close-up view from the camera frames the presenter and the background suddenly tells a very different story.

In Figure 25.6, the banner is hung vertically and the framed image doesn't reveal any surprises. Always check the viewing angle when using a video camera to frame the presenter.

Figure 25.6
When image magnification is used, the framed view through the camera crops the image of the presenter and the background. A vertical banner behind the presenter remains in the framed image and allows the full company name to appear from the audience view and the camera angle.

GLITCH HAPPENS!

It goes without saying that you should practice your presentation. In fact, the more multimedia effects you have planned, the more need for a technical run-through before the event. But, let's face it. Sometimes computers cause problems and usually at the worst moments. Whether the video clip moves in a jerky motion or the sound effect doesn't play or the system just "locks up" for no apparent reason—the thing to remember is not to panic. We have all been there before, and it's not unusual for things to go wrong every so often.

If you know how to fix a problem, then fix it. At the same time, explain to your audience what you are doing. Don't just turn your back and say, "Pay no attention to that man behind the curtain!" The real issue is time. If you can fix it within three minutes, fine. But, if you think the problem will take longer to fix, then give the audience an opportunity to take a short break.

For practice, run your presentation and somewhere in the middle of it, turn off or reset the computer. Time how long it takes to reboot your PC and get it back to the exact spot where you turned it off. If it takes more than three minutes, you'll know to give the audience a short break the instant you know you may have to reboot the computer during your presentation.

Overall, if you keep calm and collected during technical difficulties, you have a better chance of keeping the attention of the audience. Of course, the more command you have of the message and the more effective your delivery skills, the easier it will be for you to overcome any technical problem.

Remember that the technology only carries the speaker support material. You are the speaker, and your delivery embodies the message. The audience will constantly look to you for guidance and direction. Never forget that YOU are in control!

TROUBLESHOOTING

Do you have any advice for the best time and place to conduct a presentation?

Usually, a "presentation" happens as part of a meeting, seminar, or some type of planned event. Regardless of the size of the group, you do have to consider the location and the calendar when planning the event. The bottom line is to develop a plan that "captures" your audience when it is most attentive. You can do this by conducting the event at the right location, on the right day of the week, and at the right time of day!

Regarding location, you should try to find a spot that contains the fewest distractions. This usually is offsite (not in your building). Most people, if close enough to their desks, will find opportunites to do a few work-related tasks and before they know it—the presentation is over! If you want the full attention of a group, keep them away from their desks by holding the event at a neutral spot (hotel or conference center) which is an easy drive, but just too far away to walk. You don't want people sneaking back to their desks at each break.

For timing, you should consider the best day of the work week for getting the most people to attend. Having conducted over 1,000 seminars, I can tell you that Tuesdays are best, followed in order by Thursdays, Wednesdays, Fridays, and, finally, Mondays. I have met other presenters who agree with the order. So, if Tuesday is open for your next meeting, chances are more people will be available than on Monday. Check it out in your own environment and see if it's true for you.

Finally, consider the time of day. Early morning, between 9 a.m. and 11 a.m., seems to be the best time of day for getting the highest attention span from a group. One hour after lunch is the worst time of day because people are digesting. When you digest food, the blood goes from your head to your stomach, your eyes get heavier and before you know it—you doze off! So, the morning is better than the afternoon. In fact, in some sales presentations when you have a choice to present first or last to a prospect, knowing your competitors are presenting on the same day to the same prospect, try to go first. Some say the last presentation is the only one remembered. In reality, it's the one the audience hopes will end most quickly. If you go first, you have the most attention from the group and you become the "tough act to follow."

If I want to use music or video in my presentations, do I need to be concerned with copyrights?

Copyrights protect intellectual properties. The rule I live by is simple: When in doubt, ask permission. However, you may already have indications as to what extent you can use certain multimedia elements without infringing on someone's rights. For example, let's say you wanted to buy a CD-ROM that contained a collection of instrumental musical selections. If the CD packaging contains a statement such as "royalty-free" or "unlimited use," it doesn't mean there is no copyright; rather, it indicates that you can probably use the selections in your presentations and you won't have to pay a fee each time you use a clip. On the other hand, it doesn't mean you can repackage the selections on a new CD and sell it.

I have been at tradeshows, for example, where the movie *Top Gun* (with Tom Cruise) is playing in someone's booth. Without permission, this would be an illegal use of the movie, especially because it is being used in a selling process. How? The movie is entertaining and the value of that entertainment brings people into the booth, at which point sales opportunities arise. Thus, the playing of the movie increases the prospects. The selling process is enhanced through the use of an intellectual property (the movie) with no payment (royalty) made to the property owner. A phone call to the copyright holder of the movie may be all that is needed to get permission to play the movie, for that one tradeshow, without infringing on the copyright.

The same applies to popular music. If you want to play some songs from a CD during your presentation, perhaps as background filler while the audience is arriving, you should get permission to use the material.

One exception I found to the copyright law involves "educational use." If you are commenting on the actual copyrighted material for educational purposes, you may not need permission. For example, Siskel and Ebert are movie critics. They are educating the public on the quality of the films they review. They do not need permission for the clips they use, even though the show, "At the Movies," is making money from advertisers. If the two critics needed permission then only the movies that get good reviews would allow their clips to be shown!

Surely any point of law can be argued and interpreted in different ways. This educational use issue may not always be interpreted the same way. I have a lecture called "Multimedia vs. Multimania" in which I use several popular music tracks from different CDs. To be safe, I received permission from the copyright holders and I even run "credits" at the end of the lecture to acknowledge the owners of the material. So, I insist you research any use of copyrighted material and get permission, in writing if possible, to reduce the chances of a lawsuit.

CHAPTER 26

PRESENTING IN A VARIETY OF SETTINGS

In this chapter

by Tom Mucciolo

ADAPTING TO EVERYDAY ENVIRONMENTS

Not every performance takes place on the big stage. The majority of business presentations are done for smaller groups, and sometimes those talks take place in unique settings. So, you have to learn to adapt to different circumstances. The good news is that the skills we've been discussing translate well to the variety of situations you may encounter when delivering your message.

I always laugh when someone tells me, "Oh, the meetings I speak at are so informal that you don't really need great presentation skills to make your point." My response is something like, "I guess you don't need to wear clean clothes on those days, either!" Don't underestimate the power of the moment. If the meeting really is unimportant, then your time is wasted. Do you really have that luxury? Yet, given that the meeting is important, you want your voice to be heard and remembered. Presentation skills are universally adaptable to almost every circumstance in which you speak and someone else listens.

The goal is to use the same skills that work in a more controlled setting and apply them to the given environment. Most of your presentations are likely to take place close to your everyday work area. Believe it or not, these environments are the ones you least prepare for and take most for granted. At other times you may find yourself in situations that challenge even the most basic of your skills. In fact, one of the biggest challenges will be in the way you use your skills in a highly visual setting, such as TV.

The good news is that the external and internal skills discussed in Chapters 23, "The Mechanics of Form—Developing External Presentation Skills," and 24, "The Mechanics of Function—Developing Internal Presentation Skills," apply to a variety of situations. In this chapter, we examine the use of these skills in various situations.

GETTING UP CLOSE AND PERSONAL

The most likely scenario you'll encounter is a presentation to a small group. I find that more than 80% of presentations are given to groups of fewer than ten people, usually in conference room settings. Typically, the fear factor is reduced when fewer people are in the room, so these up close and personal situations are easier for most presenters. Perhaps that is what makes small group presentations more common. Another reason is probably scheduling: It's easier to convene a smaller group of people in a local setting than it is to gather a crowd for a larger event.

Regardless of how these situations develop, the common fallacy among presenters is that less formality exists when the group is smaller and people know one another. Be careful! Just because everyone knows one another doesn't mean your presentation has automatic impact. Remember that it gets more and more difficult to impress a person after the first date! When presenting in those informal settings, your skills must be better, especially if you think the formality is unnecessary.

Who can really define just what "formality" means in the context of a presentation?

Moreover, who can say which presentations merit formality and which do not? Use the logic that every presentation is formal in the sense that your skills must be as sharp as ever to make an impact with your message.

Your goal is to maintain consistency of style in all presentation settings. For the up-close and personal moments, you should consider the following:

- Understanding the conference room and U
- Handling one-to-one situations
- Socializing your skills

UNDERSTANDING THE CONFERENCE ROOM AND U

In Chapter 25, "Technicalities and Techniques," we discussed theatre-style and classroom-style seating in relation to the room setup. Yet, the traditional conference room offers some important seating opportunities that are a bit different from the others. This is also true of another common room setup, the U-shape. Both conference room and U-shape settings share the same seating dynamics. Because many conference room tables are longer than they are wide, most of the people at the table face one another. The same is true with the U-shape.

Tip #288 from

Increase the size of your triangle. You can give yourself more room to maneuver in the small group setting by moving or removing some seats. In the conference room, the first, and possibly second, seat immediately to your right can be eliminated. This makes your triangle longer (from the screen to the first available seat). When you have more space, your movements within the triangle are more distinct, and you can create more impact as you change positions during your presentation.

In a U-shape, consider removing the first table on your right (the one closest to you) to create a larger space in which to move. The U-shape starts to resemble a J-shape when the first table is taken away.

If some care is taken to properly arrange the seating of your "guests," the results of your meeting may be more successful. As the presenter, you have three different audiences: There are people to your far side and your near side, as well people seated straight ahead of you toward the middle. These three seating areas or positions are referred to as the Power, Input, and Observer seats. Depending on where people sit, an interesting dynamic may be added to the discussion.

Note

I'm assuming that you are standing to the left of the screen, from an audience perspective. Even without a screen for visual support, you should still anchor to one side, preferably to the left, to maintain the same seating dynamics throughout the talk. Moving around to different sides is not recommended, because it disrupts the original perspectives of those in the audience.

POWER SEATS

Those who sit diagonally opposite you as you speak are in the *power seats*. Because these seats mirror the presenter, an implied power is given to those occupying these seats. Figure 26.1 shows the location of the power seats. In a typical conference room or U-shape, these seats are grouped in the corner. Depending on the size of the table, or the U-shape, two or more people may occupy the power seats. Keep in mind that these people assume power whenever they make comments or interact in some way. Even though they are not standing when they speak, the dynamics of the room create the effect of the seating importance to the rest of the group simply because those in the power seats mirror you.

Figure 26.1
From the presenter's view, the power seats are diagonally opposite. People in these corner or near-corner seats actually "mirror" the presenter.

You can take most advantage of your rest and power positions with those occupying the power seats, because people in those seats tend to face you more than they face the other people in the room. In addition, you can stimulate more group interaction by directing your attention and targeting your gestures toward those in the power seats. Your efforts to include those opposite you will automatically spread the interest to either side, thereby including the entire group.

INPUT SEATS

As you present, the *input seats* are the ones along the far side of the conference table or U-shape. Because you normally stand to the audience's left when you have visual support, the input seats are to your left. Figure 26.2 show the location of these seats. Those sitting in the input seats have an unobstructed view of you, and they typically interact only when prompted. When they do interact, it is usually to provide input in the form of support information or to offer some type of agreement to a suggestion.

Figure 26.2
From the presenter's view, the input seats are to the far side. People in these seats have a good view and tend to interact more than those seated across from them.

Those occupying the input seats will normally interact more often with the people sitting across from them. The constant challenge of conference-room and U-shaped seating is that many people in the room are distracted because they can see and interact with one another, which diminishes their attention to your words. But the input seats still offer a direct view of you and your support visuals (if any). These factors raise the importance of the input seats.

OBSERVER SEATS

The people sitting on the near side to you as you present are in the *observer seats*. Because you normally stand to the audience's left when you have visual support, the observer seats are to your right. Figure 26.3 shows the location of the observer seats. These are the worst seats in the house. People usually have to shift their chairs on angles or lean over just to make eye contact with the presenter. More than likely the people in these seats will have to give up the convenience of the table to position their chairs to see you as you speak. This means they lose a writing surface to take notes effectively, and they just can't reach for the all-important coffee cup without making the effort obvious to the rest of the group.

One of the main reasons these seats are referred to as "observer" seats is that the people in these seats tend to spend more time observing the group than they do the presenter. When you think about it, these people have to work harder just to see you in action, and this decreases their attentiveness to your message. If you're going to lose any of your conference room crowd, it will most likely be the observers.

PART

VII

CH

26

Figure 26.3
The observer seats are along the near side of the table, from the presenter's viewpoint. People in these seats have the poorest view of the presenter, and they tend to be the most distracted.

PUTTING PEOPLE IN PLACE

It would be great if you could assign seats for people based on the Power, Input, and Observer seating positions. But as a meeting comes to order, people usually take seats on a first-come, first-served basis. There are exceptions to this, of course, but for the most part the seating in any presentation is left unplanned. You can balance the scales in your favor, however, by subtly forcing people to take certain seats.

For example, let's say you want to hold one of the power seats for a key person you expect at the presentation. Of course, you have no idea when they will arrive in relation to the others in the meeting. So how can you increase the chances that the key person will occupy a power seat? You pray for luck or hope for the best. Nah! You just have to bend the rules a little.

The strategy is simple, assuming you arrive in the room before anyone else. As soon as you can, place a folder or small stack of your papers on the table, right in front of the power seat that you want to "hold" from being taken. You could also use a briefcase or jacket on the chair itself, but a chair can be moved out of place more easily.

Then, as people come into the room, be ready to greet them at the door. This helps you spot when the key person approaches. As the room fills, there is less chance anyone will take the power seat you've "held," because most people will assume the seat is already taken. People don't like to touch other people's stuff, unless of course no other place is left.

Now, as soon as you greet the key person you start a conversation as you both move into the room. If you are saying something of real value, the person will naturally follow you to keep listening. You casually meander to the open seat where your folder or papers are resting on the table. Just as you get there, you break the conversation and offer the seat while apologizing for having left your "stuff" on the table. Or, you can actually have planned a moment in the discussion where you need to refer to something in the folder. Either way, the excuse to remove your things makes the seat available. As you gather your papers, you pick up the conversation right where you left off, and the person will naturally take the seat as they continue listening.

Note

This is not to suggest that you will be more attentive to only one key person during your presentation. Instead, you must treat everyone the same. The difference is that the key person occupies a seat that offers the best opportunity for attention to your message. This seating strategy only plays to your advantage if you present with the same energy to everyone in the room without singling out any individual.

You'll have to practice this strategy a few times to make the transition look smooth and unnoticeable. Otherwise your intended "guest" may become wary of your intentions. Even with practice, this effort may not work every time. For that reason, your presentation skills must be at their peak under all conditions.

SEATING YOUR TEAM AND THEIR TEAM

Sometimes you may attend a presentation along with one or more people from your department or organization. These people are part of your "presentation team," even though some or all of them may not present information. Teams are common among many of the sales forces I coach, especially those in financial services and real estate. The "seller-buyer" relationship is very clear when representatives of two companies meet.

That same relationship exists within organizations where, in many meetings, several coworkers from one department present information to a team of workers from another department. One group is usually "selling" an idea, while the other group is asked to "buy-in." The seller-buyer relationship typically involves a persuasive argument.

I don't want to condense every possible presentation situation into a seller-buyer theme, but usually, whenever a clear separation of duties exists among the groups, some type of persuasive argument is being presented. Otherwise, what is the point of gathering members from diverse departments if not for consensus? Hey—even the holiday party meets this test. Everyone is supposed to agree that they are having fun!

Regardless of the reason members of your team are involved, you can strategize a seating plan before everyone has taken their chairs in the room. Let's separate the teams by using the simple terms *their team* and *your team*. Figure 26.4 shows how you might seat some of the attendees of the meeting.

PART
VII
CH
26

Figure 26.4
Try to have some of your team in the observer seats and some of their team in the power/input seats. Avoid stacking everyone on your team on just one side of the room.

Obviously you want the power seats to be taken by members of their team, especially for a persuasive presentation. If you can identify key players from their team, try to get a few of them into the power seats. Following that, any of their team's subordinate decision-makers or support staff should occupy some of the input seats. Naturally, you want your team to blend in, so use the remaining input seats for members of your team, specifically those who are not presenting at the meeting.

Finally, save some of the observer seats for your team, especially for those who will be presenting during the meeting. Then, when they are ready to speak, they've had the opportunity to glance at others during your presentation to notice key reactions, interest level, and so forth. Awareness of any details about the group's reactions to information is invaluable to each presenter.

In addition, members of your team occupying the observer seats are probably familiar with your presentation. They don't need to be as attentive to your words at every moment. Come on—they've seen your act before! The target of attention for the observer seats is the rest of the group in an effort to gain insight.

Following the presentation, you should regroup with your team and discuss the behavior observed during the meeting. Someone may have noticed a perplexed look when a certain subject was covered. Another member of your team may have observed someone taking notes as soon as a specific chart was presented. Believe it or not, the observers can also notice people nodding off. Maybe the presentation is longer than it should be! In any event, the feedback from those in the observer seats can be very helpful in preparing for your next presentation.

Sit-Down Scenarios

Okay, let's scale down the setting to the times when you are just sitting down. In these meetings, typically in conference rooms, you might spend a few minutes standing and giving a presentation and then take the remaining time to sit and continue the discussion. The seating positions can still be used effectively.

Keep in mind that when seated, the position of your shoulders still controls the rest and power positions discussed in Chapter 23 (refer to Figure 23.3 for a visual example). When your shoulders match the shoulders of another person, you are in a power position in relation to that person (as they are with you). When your shoulders are at an angle to another person, you are in a rest position. Your goal is to be in a seat where the angles of your body can be used effectively with the greatest number of people in the room.

For example, avoid putting yourself in a center-seating situation at a conference-room table. Take a look at Figure 26.5. Let's say that the man in the center of the group, at the head of the table, is leading the meeting. You might think he is in a power position in relation to the others on his right and left. However, he can only take a power position with the person directly opposite, at the other end of the table (not shown in the photo).

Figure 26.5
The man at the head of the table is limited by his center-seating position. He can only create a power position with one other person at the table, namely, the one opposite him (not shown in the photo).

PART

VII

CH

26

The seat at the head of the table is not as effective, unless you are facilitating a meeting rather than leading it. When facilitating, you represent a neutral position. This is similar to an arbitrator or mediator. If you are playing such a role, then consider a center-seating position in relation to the group.

If you want to lead and control a meeting, you have a better chance from one of the corner seats. Look at Figure 26.6. It's the same group of people shown from a different camera view. The woman wearing the eyeglasses has a power seat in relation to the others at the table. She is able to square her shoulders or angle them to many different people by swiveling her chair or shifting the upper part of her body.

Figure 26.6
The woman wearing the eyeglasses occupies a power seat. She can create rest and power positions with a number of people at the table. All the corner seats are the most effective in these conference room settings.

This "off-center seating" strategy allows you to gain a wider perspective of the entire group. In addition, any props such as documents or other items will be easier to angle for view when you take one of the corner seats.

HANDLING ONE-TO-ONE SITUATIONS

Okay, what happens when you are faced with one or two people in the room with you? You can still have a seating strategy to help your message along. For one-to-one meetings, use your rest and power positions in the same way as you do in conference room settings. The smaller the group, the easier it becomes to use body angles to your advantage.

CREATE ANGLES

The most common situation to avoid is the "head-on collision" where you are directly opposite the other person and your shoulders match each other. The goal is to avoid having your shoulders parallel to the other person in what is called a "squared-off" position. Angling your body or your chair is the easiest way to avoid squaring-off to the other person. Look at Figure 26.7. In the background of the photo you see two people standing and having a conversation. Because their shoulders match, they are both in a power position in relation to each other. This is a less effective way to communicate. When two people square off like that, it's as if their bodies are yelling at one another. In the foreground of the same image, the two women are seated, but they are at angles to one another. Communication works better when your shoulders are angled to the other person.

Figure 26.7
The people standing in the background are squared-off to one another, and the two people seated are at angles. Communication is more effective when people are at angles to one another.

You can put yourself into an angled position in relation to another person in a number of ways. When seated, you could choose a corner of a table, or, if you are standing and someone else is sitting, you could lean on the edge of a desk (half-standing) and keep your shoulders angled to the person seated.

SHARE PERSPECTIVE

When two people look at something from completely different angles, they are not sharing a common perspective. This is not really a problem when the object in view is large enough to be seen from a distance, such as a projected image on a screen. But if the object is meant for an audience of one, then perspective becomes an issue.

The most common object for one person to look at is a document. If you are opposite a person when you hand over a document, you immediately lose a common perspective. The person is looking down at the piece of paper and you are looking upside-down at the same object. The perspective is different for each of you. It will be more difficult for you to point our specifics in the document from your perspective. You'll probably end up stretching your neck and rotating your head at some weird angle. Trust me, this looks ridiculous. Try to get the same perspective on the object as the other person.

Figure 26.8 shows a man standing next to a woman seated at a table. Both of them share a common perspective on the document in view. When people have the same point of view (literally) on something, the message is easier to convey and interpret.

The photo is merely a captured moment in time. Once equal perspective is achieved regarding the document, the man can return to his original position at the other side of the table and continue the discussion, meeting, or presentation.

Figure 26.8
By standing to the side, the man shares the same perspective on the document as the woman. A shared perspective makes communication more effective.

The same perspective can also be achieved when two people are sitting. In Figure 26.9, the two men have the same perspective looking at the papers in front of them. It will be easy for one of them to point to information on the sheets, if necessary, to facilitate the discussion. Imagine how difficult it would be if one of them was standing opposite and looking over the top of the papers to point out something specific.

Naturally, you can't always put yourself in a position to share the same perspective with another person. Yet, when an opportunity arises, you should take advantage of it, if possible.

Tip #289 from

Don't make your effort to get a common perspective so obvious that the other person wonders what you are doing. For example, if you are in a conference room with one other person and the table is long enough to hold 20 people, don't sit right next to the person. Instead, take a corner seat, if you can. Then, when you need to share a document, you can always get up and stand to the side of the person to point out information in the document.

SCAN THE EYES

A lot of information stored in your brain is in the form of pictures. It's true. These visual references are tucked away neatly in your brain waiting for retrieval. For example, if you think about your high school biology teacher, a visual image pops into your head, and you see that person in your mind's eye, so to speak. You even visualize situations that haven't happened. If I ask you to think about your own road to success, you create a little picture in your brain as you "see yourself" in some type of successful moment. The point is that everyone uses visual references. Whenever one of those references is retrieved, the eyes move in some direction to see the image in the brain.

Figure 26.9
Two people, sitting side by side, share the same perspective when looking at documents.

PART
VII
CH
26

Therefore, in many one-to-one situations, the eyes of the other person can offer you some interesting clues as to what they might be thinking. As an observer, you can scan the eye movement of a person whenever you say something thought provoking. To interpret the other person's reaction, however, you need to learn how they personally look for the images they create.

The easiest approach is to probe for a timeline. Figure 26.10 shows how you place an imaginary timeline in front of the person's face. The timeline is always from your point of view. Start with the assumption that the person's past is to your left, and their future is to your right.

By asking a question involving reflection or something in the past, the person normally shifts their eyes in one direction to physically "look up" the visual image of the experience. You can observe which direction the eyes travel as the person recalls the experience. Not everyone glances in the same direction to look up an image, but for most people, that direction is up and to their right. Whatever the direction, it represents their past. Figure 26.11 shows how a person's eyes might move when they reflect on a past experience. You look at them through an imaginary timeline, with the past to your left and the future to your right. In this example, the direction of their eyes matches your timeline.

Figure 26.10
When scanning the eyes of another person, place an imaginary timeline in front of them. The timeline is viewed from your perspective, with the past to your left and the future to your right.

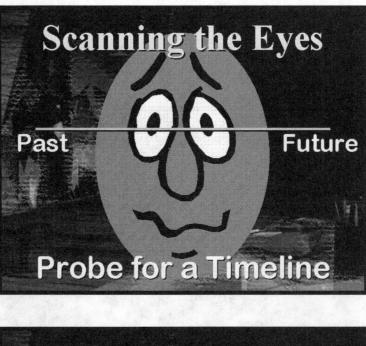

Figure 26.11
When a person reflects on the past, their eyes move in some direction. In this example, the eyes shifted up and to the person's right. In this case, the shift matches your timeline.

If their eyes shift the opposite way of your imaginary timeline, then reverse your timeline and realize they look up their past differently (to your right). The point is that you first have to notice how the person recalls past experiences to establish the end points of your timeline. Whatever the direction of their eyes, it represents "the past" on your timeline.

After you know the person's past, whenever you prompt a thought-provoking glance in the opposite direction, the person is likely indicating anticipation of something in the future. Figure 26.12 shows an already established timeline with a glance to the person's left indicating a vision of the future.

Figure 26.12
After a timeline is established and you know the person's past, a shift of their eyes in the opposite direction indicates anticipation.

I have always taken the position that, whenever a person paints a picture of their future, it is always positive, unless they have some specific reasons to expect something negative to happen. Using the assumption that a person's view of the future is ultimately optimistic, a shift of a person's eyes to the "future" on the timeline you established may be the most opportune moment for you to close the deal, so to speak. After all, if the person appears to be "looking forward" to using your product or service, take that eye movement as a hint and go for it—close the deal, ask for the order, complete the call to action!

The eyes give other hints, as well. For example, if the person is staring directly at you and not shifting their eyes at all, there's a good chance that they are not listening. They are likely giving you the courtesy of direct eye contact, but they are probably drifting away in their thoughts. Break the eye contact with them and they will be attentive again. Take a look at the Presenter's Corner at the end of Chapter 23, for more comments about eye contact.

SOCIALIZING YOUR SKILLS

Never underestimate the power of a coffee break! When you think about it, lots of business is conducted in a social setting such as lunch, dinner, the cocktail hour, or even a golf outing. For example, I speak at many conferences, and in many cases there is usually some type of opening reception for the attendees to walk around with little nametags and get to know one another. This is commonly called networking. The objective of the typical "cocktail hour" is to use a relaxed atmosphere to establish lasting relationships. We used to do this in college. Of course, we called it "bar-hopping." The objective was the same—to use a relaxed atmosphere to establish lasting relationships—only the effort did not require little nametags.

Anyway, these casual get-togethers are a great way to create business opportunities. During those moments, the physical positions you take can make a difference. Body angles and gestures will be your most effective communication tools. When standing and conversing, for example, you can establish a 45-degree angle to the other person and, when necessary, make important points by squaring your shoulders to face the person directly. You can use virtual space to visually explain concepts and ideas.

→ To learn more about virtual space, **see** "Using Virtual Space," **p. 630**

Tip #290 from

> Some say to always keep a beverage in your left hand so the right hand is free to shake hands, and it won't be cold or damp from having held the glass. The truth is that in most social situations where people are mingling, there isn't a lot of hand shaking going on as introductions are made. Most people just nod their heads to greet others. So, if you are holding a glass while speaking to another person, always hold it in the hand closest to them. This may be the left or the right, depending on where the other person is standing. By keeping the glass closer to the person, your other hand is free to use a wider area for virtual space.

In all situations, hand gestures work well. Reaching out when referencing someone or hanging a gesture (keeping it still) when making a point is always effective, even during meals. These settings are also a great place to practice your gestures and get comfortable with how your hands move when you speak. For example, if you are eating dinner with a group of people and you say, "Pass the bread, please," you should take note as to how your arm extends and how your hand opens (reaches out) for the bread. The same natural flow of that gesture used at dinner should be the same as the one used on stage. Social gatherings help you with your natural delivery skills. The more you practice your one-to-one skills, the easier it will be for you to maintain those skills in more formal presentation settings.

In addition to body positions and hand gestures, one of the best communication skills for social events is storytelling. Whether the reference be fact or fiction, comedy or tragedy, the ability to use stories to augment a discussion is very useful. You can even use social settings to work on specific areas of your delivery style, such as humor. I always test new jokes or humorous comments with small groups of people, most of whom I don't really know. I work on timing, rhythm, phrase selection and I'll even try different "punchlines" with different groups to see which is most effective.

If you keep the notion that every moment with others is a presentation skill learning experience, you will increase your effectiveness each time you interact with others. You are your own best teacher (assuming you're willing to learn).

WORKING IN REMOTE LOCATIONS

Not every presentation offers you the convenience of a roof over your head. In fact, sometimes you may find yourself presenting in harsh environments or in settings that make it nearly impossible to keep an audience attentive for more than a few minutes. Many business presentations take place in remote locations much different than the typical conference room. Let's take a look at some of these situations including:

- Presenting outdoors
- Dealing with extreme conditions
- Delivering tradeshow presentations

PRESENTING OUTDOORS

When someone talks about presenting "out in the field," don't be surprised if they are referring to a stretch of land that yields wheat! A number of companies have to conduct business in outdoor environments because of the nature of what they need to discuss or show. The reasons you might conduct a presentation outdoors are for convenience or display. In some cases, you are forced to present yourself at the location of your listeners, thus making it convenient for your audience to evaluate your message. In other cases, you ask your audience to attend your presentation so that you may display some product that would otherwise have been difficult to bring to the listeners.

For example, it is not unusual for a company that manufactures heavy construction equipment to demonstrate a large piece of machinery to a group of interested prospects outdoors. You won't find too many hotel ballrooms able to accommodate a 150-foot crane. Even if they could get one into the hotel, think of the marks on the carpet!

Naturally, there are many ways to show products in a presentation using photographs and line art. A picture of the crane or a schematic drawing of its unique functions can be inserted directly into a PowerPoint presentation. There is nothing wrong with this as a way to discuss feature and benefits.

But the most effective way for someone to grasp the entire picture is to experience the real thing, in real life. If you were considering purchasing a building, you could look at photos or renderings, but you would benefit most by going to the location and walking through the space itself. It is during these moments that presenting "outdoors" takes place.

DEMONSTRATING LARGE OBJECTS

Okay, so you're presenting outdoors, and you have a product to show or demonstrate. One of the first things to consider is the size of the "object" in relation to the group. Because you picked the outdoor venue for a reason, let's assume the object is bigger than you are. This being the case, you won't be able to pick it up and hold it. You can't pass it around for the group to examine. You won't even be able to move it, without creating an obvious effort. This is really no different than the conditions you have when you present visuals on

PART
VII
CH
26

a screen. You won't ever attempt to move the screen and the good news is you don't have to. You leave it stationary and use your own movement and gestures to reference it.

So the first thing you do with a large object is to anchor it for the audience. Leave it in the same spot for as long as you can while you present. This gives your audience a single perspective on a stationary object. If you need to change the viewing angle, decide if it is easier to reposition the object or reposition the audience by having them move in one direction or another.

For example, let's say your company manufactures cars and you want to "present" the latest model to a group of car dealers who sell your products. You decide to hold the meeting at an outdoor venue, such as a racetrack, and you gather your group in an open space to show the vehicle. To make sure everyone can see, you have the group stand on a series of raised platforms with each row higher than the row in front. The long side of the car faces the group, and you can describe features of the vehicle by moving slowly from one end of the car to the other. It doesn't matter which side you start from because there is nothing for the audience to read. Only when the visual content contains text do you have to anchor to the side of the visual where the reading normally starts.

The key to showing a large object is to create a linear path for the audience to follow. Don't move back and forth to different points. Try to plan your movements to navigate in as straight a line as possible from your starting to your ending point. This reduces distraction.

Walking and Talking

Sometimes you may have to give your presentation as you lead your audience through a defined space. A number of businesses encounter these situations all the time. You can be selling real estate or conducting guided tours—the fact is that you are walking and talking with a group as you point out specific items. When the audience is moving, the dynamics of the presentation change in relation to the perspective.

Think about what happens when people are moving. They have to focus attention on where they are going, first, before they even begin to concentrate on something else. This means that attention span is shorter when the group is moving. Thus, when the group is standing still, attention is greater. As a presenter, your goal is to make your key points at times when the group has stopped moving. The more you can control the movement of your audience, the more effectively you can direct their attention.

While you are moving, especially in situations where you are walking as you guide the group through a space, you must be aware of your ability to be heard. Each time you turn your face away from the group (perhaps to see where you're going), you have to speak louder for your voice to carry. In fact, anytime you are looking away and still speaking, try directing your voice toward a hard surface rather than a wide-open space. A hard surface reflects sound. This helps your voice bounce back and return in the direction of the listeners.

To help the group focus on objects more quickly, use vocal directions prior to describing the item. For example, if you are guiding a few people through a workspace in a building and you want to point out certain objects along the way, phrases such as "to your left" or "along the floor to your immediate right" to indicate direction before a description. When what you are describing is already in view, a person can relate to your description more attentively.

When walking and talking you may also be gesturing toward things. Try to maintain a consistency with your gestures and with the direction you turn your body. Choose a repeating pattern such as using your right hand to gesture whenever your body turns to your right. The goal is to reduce distractions with a smaller variety of movements. Keep in mind the audience may be looking in three different places: at something you are pointing to, at where they are walking, or directly at you. You may be looking in three different places as well based on what you are doing at the moment. You can clearly see how a moving presenter and moving audience limit the chances to establish anchors. At least a consistent pattern of movement will not add to the confusion.

DEALING WITH EXTREME CONDITIONS

Believe it or not, circumstances occur that may make it nearly impossible to conduct the presentation in the manner that you expect. I'm not talking about a projector bulb burning out. I'm talking about extreme conditions that test the limits of your ability to deliver the message. Think of an extreme condition as one that reduces your chances of either being seen, heard, or even understood by the audience. In each of these cases the strategy is to focus your energy on the parts of the presentation that are of greater importance to your audience.

Keep in mind that the components of communication involve your body, your voice, and your visual support. The audience concentrates on each of these elements while the message is being delivered. When one of those elements is restricted, the audience places more focus on the remaining elements to get the most from the message. Knowing this helps you put more emphasis on the more obvious components of the communication. Let's take a look at some extreme conditions that can hinder your efforts to deliver a message with impact.

PART

VII

CH

26

DARK SHADOWS

When people can't see you, that's a problem. You already know how important it is for the audience to see your body and, more specifically, your face. Expressions help a listener understand your intent behind the message. Therefore, lighting is a critical element to your being seen by everyone. Poor lighting or no lighting at all can be a major obstacle in your effort to deliver your story with impact.

We already talked about lighting in Chapter 25, including some "creative" techniques to illuminate you as you speak. But what happens when you end up presenting in the dark? Well, some people say that when there is very little light the audience falls asleep. That's a fallacy. People don't just fall asleep when the lights go down. After all, some of the most exciting moments in our lives happen in the dark. It's not the lack of light that puts people to sleep—it's lack of visible action! Come on, if lack of light induced sleep in every situation, then people would be snoring though every movie! Okay, *2001, A Space Odyssey* might be an exception. Oh, you haven't seen it? Don't worry, as we change over to the next millennium, it will be on TV about 2001 times. You can count on it!

→ To learn more about creative lighting techniques, **see** "Working with Lighting and Sound," **p. 652**

Because lack of visible action reduces attentiveness and interest, you need to work around poor lighting conditions as best you can. The best way to do this is to get your body in a position where it is most visible, namely, closest to any available light source. In a very darkened room, you already know that the greatest concentration of light will be on the screen displaying your visuals. The screen, then, is your closest light source. The amount of light bouncing off the screen determines how much of you the audience sees. Proximity to your screen or light source is the strategy to consider.

For example, under poor lighting conditions, you have to limit the movement in your triangle. You have to make your available space smaller and confined to those areas with the most light reflecting from the screen. Naturally, this forces you to play more of the action toward the back of your triangle where the light is brighter from the screen.

Another thing you can consider is reversing your color scheme. I normally suggest dark background and bright foregrounds, but poor lighting conditions are not "normal." So, you'll have to trade off some of the impact from your visuals to gain some value from your physical presence. If you use lighter backgrounds and darker foregrounds, you'll have more white (bright) light emanating from the screen. This gives you a better chance of being illuminated by the spillover of reflective light, especially as you get closer to your visual. You won't be so visible that people can see your facial expressions, but your gestures will make more sense even if the light from the screen casts you only as a silhouette for the audience to see.

From an audience perspective, when your body language and facial expressions are less visible, the concentration of attention shifts more to the two components of your content: your voice and your visual support. From a vocal standpoint, realize that the audience can't see your mouth moving when you speak. This means you'll have to speak more slowly, enunciate your words better, and use pauses more often. Pretend you are in a phone conversation with your audience where the greatest percentage of the message comes from your tone, not just from the words you say.

When referencing your visuals, use vocal directions. These are lead-in phrases such as "the second bar labeled 1999," or, "the two largest slices on the right side of this pie chart." Actually, vocal directions help guide the eye in all presentation settings, not only when you find yourself in poor lighting conditions.

THE SOUNDS OF SILENCE

Sometimes the audience may have difficulty hearing you. Microphones are great tools for allowing people to hear your voice from a distance. But in many situations, for one reason or another, a microphone is not available. Depending on the size of the space and the distance to the last row, making yourself heard might become a real challenge.

Part of the problem may be that you aren't speaking loud enough. In Chapter 23, you learned several techniques to enhance your vocal delivery. However, even if you can raise the volume of your voice, it may create more problems than you think. For example, if you have to shout so that people in the back of the room can hear you, then imagine what effect your voice has on the people in the front! As you examine the glaring evil stares of those whose eardrums have been ruptured, you will most likely begin to lower your voice. Of course, the people in the back will strain to hear you once again. You can easily see how distance creates a sound imbalance for your audience. So what can you do?

→ For more information on vocal delivery techniques, **see** "Breathing Properly" **p. 614**

First find a volume level that is at least audible from the back, even though it is not at the level those people prefer. Because your words have less impact, you need to show more and say less. Remember that when a component of the communication is restricted, the remaining components draw more attention from the audience. If your voice is barely audible, then your gestures, your movements, and even your visuals are more apparent.

From a physical perspective I'm not suggesting you run around flapping your arms to create more attention. But you should emphasize your words with descriptive gestures by using virtual space more often to explain things. When your words are harder to hear, your actions speak that much louder. You'll have to "act out" your thoughts. The ability to express yourself without words is important for those times when you are less audible as well as for all other times when you want to add more impact to your message above and beyond what your voice is able to do.

→ To learn more about virtual space, **see** "Using Virtual Space," **p. 630**

PART
VII
CH
26

Tip #291 from	Play a visual game like Charades in which you have to act out a phrase without speaking. Or give directions to someone who doesn't speak your language. Or simply spend a little time entertaining an infant. In each of these situations you will have to rely more on your nonverbal skills to communicate a message completely.

Another way to compensate for your inability to be heard well is to add more visual support to your presentation. Naturally, you'll have to plan ahead for this because you can't create a whole bunch of extra visuals at the last minute. Additional content on the screen gives the audience a more visual reference for the words they may not hear. You can use builds and overlays to reveal information in stages so that the audience knows exactly where you are on a given visual. You can even create a series of additional images to support what normally might have been displayed as a single visual.

For example, suppose you have a map of the United States with three defined regions: west, central, and east. Under normal conditions you planned to cover information about all three regions without changing the visual. But because you are barely audible, you can help the audience through the topic by adding three more visuals, one for each region. On each of these subvisuals, you can add bulleted text to highlight some of the key points you are discussing. So, even if it is difficult to hear everything you are saying, the audience is "reading" more of your visual content to get a better understanding of the message.

Overall, whenever you find yourself "vocally challenged," realize that your audience will rely more heavily on the components of your presentation that are easiest to grasp. In situations where you can't be heard well, increase your movements in the triangle, add more emphatic gestures to the screen, use virtual space more often to describe things, and consider adding extra visual content to help tell a more complete story.

CULTURE SHOCK

In the growing world of global communication, it is not unusual to find yourself facing audience members who may have trouble understanding you, because they are less familiar with your language. Whether you present locally or abroad, you are likely to encounter language barriers with some people in your audience from time to time. In fact, you may present in another country where not only are your words difficult to understand, but your visual support is too. When an audience views cultural differences as distractions, your presentation is less effective.

In these situations, your best bet is to put the majority of your effort into the physical delivery. After all, body language is universal; spoken language is not. You can test this theory at home. Find a TV station broadcasting in a language you barely understand. If you watch for awhile, there will be enough visual clues and details for you to get some semblance of what is happening. This is because you can see the action. Now, turn your back to the TV so you can't see the screen. Because you can't understand the words, notice how little information you can get. It's obvious that observable action is a big contributor toward understanding.

Your physical actions and your visual support play the major roles in overcoming language barriers when you present. Regarding your content, consider creating images that are more graphical. Embed more photographs in the backgrounds of your visuals. Use arrows, colors, and geometric shapes to help tell your story. Avoid showing too many text charts. In fact, numbers and other data-driven charts (bar, pie, line) may be easier for the audience to understand than heavy text-based visuals.

Your physical actions are important, but presenting in a foreign country can be challenging. Gestures and movements you make may be considered distracting, rude, or even offensive without you knowing it.

Tip #292 from	You may want to investigate this reference regarding this topic: *Cross-Cultural Communication: A Practical Guide,* by Gregory Barnard. Also, take a look at the Web site: *The Web of Culture,* cross-cultural communication, at www.worldculture.com.

You never know what certain actions might mean. The last thing you need is to accidentally scratch your right ear while your left elbow points at a 45-degree angle to the northwest corner of the room and, immediately, some military extremist in the middle of the crowd leaps up and declares that you've just insulted their leader! Hey, these things can happen! That's why it's always best to check with a resident about local customs and cultural issues.

And That Translates Into…

There may be times where your words have to be translated for an audience to understand. I experienced that situation recently in Sao Paulo, Brazil, where the native language is Portuguese. My visuals were in English, but my words were simultaneously translated for the audience. It was interesting to look at 300 people wearing headphones. It felt like I was at a convention of radio broadcasters!

I learned a few things that day about simultaneous translation. First of all, it's not simultaneous. There's a delay between the time your phrase ends and the time everyone else hears it translated. I noticed this after my first joke. I delivered the punchline and everyone laughed—about 10 seconds later!

I also had the chance to practice with the translator before the seminar started. Now if you've ever seen me present, you know I have a high energy level. Unfortunately, the translator had no energy level. His voice was low-key and relatively flat. So the audience was watching me deliver an action-packed presentation while a symphony of monotone phrases played through their headphones!

But perhaps the most embarrassing moment of the day happened at the very end of my three-hour session. It was time to field questions, and now I had to put the headphones on to listen to the translator convert the audience questions into English. I scan the crowd and gesture to a man sitting about ten rows back. He stands and proceeds to ask his question, in Portuguese, of course. Being the great listener that I am (just ask my wife), I stood there, attentive to every word—nay—to every syllable directed at me during this rather lengthy question. It took about 30 seconds for me to finally realize that I was listening to the man in the audience and not the translator. The bad news is that I don't speak nor understand Portuguese!

By the time I started listening to the translator, the only words I heard were from the end of the man's last phrase, "…wondering does that cause confusion?" I appeared calm, but inside my head I was in a panic. I asked myself, "Wondering does what cause confusion? What did this guy just say? Why am I even on this planet right now?"

I settled into my best presentation stance. I looked away, briefly, as if pondering the numerous possible answers to this important question. Realizing I was lost, I looked directly at the gentleman, still standing there clutching his tethered cap and tilting his head toward me like an innocent child waiting for permission to have a cookie. In a calm voice I broke the silence and said, "I'll tell you the real cause of confusion—headphones! That's right, headphones cause confusion!" The man, the rest of the audience, even the translator had no idea what I was talking about.

So I told the truth. I admitted that I wasn't listening to the translator during most of the man's question, and I really didn't know what he asked. That's why I related the word confusion to the headphones. Well, after everyone heard that, they all just laughed—about 10 seconds later!

PART

VII

CH

26

DELIVERING TRADESHOW PRESENTATIONS

Many companies participate in tradeshows. Presentations at these events range from simple demonstrations to full-blown theatrical wonders! Regardless of all the hoopla and the hype, these events need to be planned and organized effectively.

The typical tradeshow involves a bunch of people from the company standing on their feet about ten hours a day for almost a week. During this time these brave souls are fielding questions, spouting out theories, running for coffee, eating junk-food, listening to arguments, shaking hands, smiling at strangers, reading badges, handing out literature, gathering business cards, and praying for the end of the show! Sound familiar?

Regardless of the excitement surrounding a tradeshow, the bottom line is that the interaction among participants is either from conversations or presentations. Conversations are the one-to-one spontaneous discussions with passersby and booth visitors. Presentations are more planned topics delivered several times a day, usually from a dedicated space inside the booth, to small groups of spectators. You can spot these setups right away. Just look for a bunch of chairs facing a screen and maybe a sign displaying something like, "The next presentation begins at…" or words to that effect.

To get the most from your tradeshow event, you should understand the underlying objective or purpose behind every moment of your "delivery," whether it is conversation or presentation. The purpose is to enlighten. The purpose is not to survey, not to brag, but to enlighten. This means that everything you say, in one form or another, must enlighten the listener with new or different information. Remember the reason people go to tradeshows—to see something new and different, something wonderful, something exciting, and something—dare I say—enlightening! So, give people what they want, and they will remember you.

Tip #293 from	One way to add value to your offerings at a tradeshow is to appeal to the most important part of an attendee's body—the feet! People walk for hours at a tradeshow, and they remember the booths with the softest carpeting! In my marketing days when I had to design our tradeshow booth, I always spent extra dollars for the thickest carpeting available. I also tried to get space nearest the restrooms. I believe these were additional reasons for people to hang around a bit longer in our booth and hear more of our enlightening stories!

INFORMAL CONVERSATIONS

Earlier in this chapter we discussed one-to-one situations and all the same rules apply to tradeshow conversations. The big difference between conference rooms and tradeshows is the underlying sense of urgency for both parties involved.

Naturally, you want to cover information quickly, and the listener wants to gather information quickly. Well, at least you each agree on the result—quick, concise data. One of the informal studies we conducted at MediaNet was a random sample of tradeshow attendees to see the average stay at any booth location. We found the average stay to be 2 minutes and 14 seconds at those booths where the attendee actually stopped to have a conversation. During that time, the attendees focused attention mostly on items directly in view while they listened to the person talking with them. If you figure on people staying only a short time, then by all means—get to the point!

That's why conversations at tradeshows should be no more than short descriptions containing key words about the product or service on display. We call these brief phrases *sound bites* (or *bytes*, if you prefer). The sound bite should be the capsule summary of a somewhat lengthier statement, which, given the extra time, you would have said. You should create a whole library of these little pieces of enlightening facts and then use them at the appropriate times during the conversation. Most people working tradeshow booths are never taught to use sound bites. That is why conversations end too quickly or drag on for too long about unimportant issues.

Sound bites are important for controlling the flow of traffic around you. Let's say you are standing in your booth and talking to one person about a new product that your company is introducing. You already know this person may walk away after a minute or two, so you use your strongest sound bites first. Your mention the top three "enlightening" features as soon you can. In the meantime, other people are passing by, eavesdropping, as they should. Before you know it, a new listener, hearing a sound bite instantly joins the small discussion. Now you have two people seeking enlightenment. Well, you can't repeat the same features for the new person because the first listener gets no added value and probably walks away. So you add a new sound bite and perhaps rephrase one of the original ones, as well. This keeps both listeners attentive a bit longer. The point is that you have to keep the enlightenment going in some small way as each new listener joins the group.

After you run out of new things to say, you will begin to lose the people who were there the longest. But if you got two minutes out of them, you made a successful contact. Even though the person received only a brief impression, it gives them the choice of either moving on or seeking even more information from you or others in the booth. Of the hundreds of people who stop and listen, many will move on, but some will stay longer, and a few of those will actually conduct some business. Just think of a tradeshow as a live version of a newspaper ad in the Sunday circular. There are lots of things to look at, only some of which you can take the time to consider buying.

One other interesting thing about conversations is the likelihood of joining one. In other words, most people would rather join an existing conversation than initiate one. Think about it. It is less work for you to approach two or more people engaged in open conversation than it is for you to approach someone and just start up a discussion from scratch. At a tradeshow, the more sound bites you have, the longer you can keep your first listener attentive. It follows that the longer a listener stays attentive, the greater the chances of another listener joining the existing conversation. As you continue to enlighten, the crowd around you grows. Even from a distance others will be attracted to see what is so interesting. Little do they know—it's just a bunch of really attractive sound bites!

PLANNED PRESENTATIONS

For many companies, the tradeshow venue includes a short presentation. Typically, these little "shows" are delivered a couple of times each day. They normally span 20 to 30 minutes, and the audience is usually seated in some theatre-style arrangement. I have trained many different groups of tradeshow presenters over the years, and the one point I make early on is that the presentation must be first and foremost entertaining. Second, the entertainment must directly relate to what your company does or sells, or else you can't make a lasting impression. This is why the magician at the tradeshow booth is a big waste of time, unless your product is truly magical! After all, if the entertainment is simply to draw a crowd, then how will you know who in the crowd is a potential customer?

I remember one company, a manufacturer of network switching equipment, insisted on using a live rock band in their booth. In addition, they decided to raffle a sports car at the end of the show. They must have gotten 10,000 leads—people that liked rock music and liked to drive sports cars—not exactly the profile of their current customers. The issue is not quantity of leads, but quality. If quantity is the goal then open the phone book—all your customers are in there.

So, just follow the principle of "entertainment with direct relevance" to build a more effective tradeshow presentation. If you can provide an enlightening and entertaining experience, you will create a lasting impression with your audience.

The best way to provide a memorable show is to concentrate on a few logistics. First of all, rehearse the presentation so that you know it lasts the 20 or 30 minutes you planned for it to last. Second, make sure your visuals are extremely simple. Don't use a lot of text; use plenty of graphics and photos. Visual presentations attract people from a distance to get closer and keep those seated from being distracted by the constant activity in the surrounding area. If you are presenting software or a Web site or anything that requires a computer-looking interface, keep in mind that readability from a distance will be more difficult. It is best to concentrate on key features and benefits, rather than teaching unique details that are difficult for an easily distracted audience to grasp.

Regarding the position of your "stage," try to face out to a cross-aisle. In other words, if you anchor your presentation area to a corner of your booth, perhaps you can be seen from two different aisles at the same time. This will increase the chances of attracting people walking from two different directions. When presenting, make sure your eye contact, your voice, and your gestures reach to the back of the group and beyond to increase the chances of others stopping to listen to your story.

Some of the most distracting elements at a tradeshow are light and noise. Without a canopy or enclosed space, the light from the exhibit hall can wash out your display screen. To offset this, your visuals should have a lot of contrast between backgrounds and foregrounds. When it comes to noise, expect a lot of it. Get used to the noises immediately around your booth. Sometimes you can detect a pattern from other presentations or activities. If your timing is good, you can make your key phrases heard at the least distracting moments.

Finally, make sure you get your captured audience to do something at the end of the presentation. You must get their contact information because they represent a more qualified opportunity. After all, if the average person stays two minutes at a booth and these people sat for twenty minutes, you can safely assume they have greater interest—unless, of course, they only sat there to get a prize. In that case, you made the mistake of attracting the wrong people for the wrong reason at the wrong time. Anyway you look at it—you're wrong! My son seems to mention that to me more and more often as he gets older, hmmmm…

The Wrong People

I remember one of the tradeshows I coordinated back in the early 1980s. The show, Comdex, was a week long gathering of manufacturers displaying their wares to mostly resellers and some corporate end-users. We had about 20 people working our booth—our entire national sales force of 15 people and the rest from marketing and engineering. Just from sales quotas alone, I think we had over 1 million dollars of employee time value in that 40×40 booth!

The night before the show officially opened, I decided to walk around the tradeshow floor and take a look at some of the other booths. Some call this spying; I call it market research! I walked up and down several aisles and then it hit me. I was dumbfounded by what was staring me in the face. It was the booth of death to anyone even remotely involved in marketing. I could only gaze with my mouth open as I glanced at a 60×60 booth space filled with about 25 computers on pedestals. Next to each pedestal was a life-size cardboard cutout of a person in a business suit, holding a printed sign with the words "Our salespeople are out selling. Where are yours?"

It turned out that by using a booth full of computers running repeated demos of accounting software and staffed by a few marketing people who could answer most questions, that company had a cost-effective way of gathering the necessary leads from the show. You can't always do something like that, but it makes you think about the right people to staff a tradeshow.

I certainly knew who the wrong people were. I realized we made a big mistake by taking our sales force out of action. From that show on, we only brought local sales people in to support the show, locally. Any leads generated from a national perspective were sent to the salesperson responsible for the area.

I learned that to enlighten people with information at a tradeshow, you don't need your entire national sales force. You just need people who know the sound bites and people who have rehearsed their presentations.

Tradeshow interaction needs to be planned and practiced. Whether you are in a conversation or presentation, if you focus on working around the distractions at a tradeshow, you can make the time spent on your feet worthwhile. The only thing that doesn't change is that after you work your first big show, you never look forward to working another one!

PART

VII

Ch

26

Tip #294 from

If you ever have a tradeshow in Las Vegas, be careful! In Vegas the food is cheap, the air is dry, there are no windows or clocks, and everywhere you turn there's another machine waiting to eat your paycheck. So you might end up eating, drinking, staying up late, and emptying your pockets. By the third day, you will be useless to everyone, including yourself. My advice is to wear a watch, eat a full meal before 7:30 p.m., and walk past the casinos. Go back to your room, and I guarantee that after standing on your feet all day, the minute your head hits the pillow you will be out! That is the only way to keep your energy level high for the rest of the show in a city like Vegas that offers a wealth of entertaining distractions. I'll lay you seven to one odds that I'm right!

Picturing Yourself on TV

Before your career ends, you will not be typing to people anymore. You will be seeing them, just like you see people on TV. It won't exactly be face-to-face, but it will be very close. One reason communication will have to be more visual is the fact that the baby boomers are past the age of 50. As our bodies get older, the dexterity in our fingers diminishes. As a maturing society we will demand an easier way to electronically converse than using a verbal banter of email messages. This evolution is inevitable. To prepare for the new age of visual communication, you need to have a better understanding of:

- Playing to the camera
- Using videoconferencing technology
- Interacting in a visual world

PLAYING TO THE CAMERA

Maybe you're already communicating on camera…for occasional teleconferences, to produce videotapes, for image magnification at large conferences, or even when speaking to the media. When on camera, you need to reinforce your message using your voice, positioning, and movement.

VOICE

When you are on camera, you have to learn to relax and breathe normally. When you talk through a lens, even though you feel rushed and think you're speaking too slowly, fight the tendency to speed up. You must learn to phrase and pause naturally. Enunciate clearly and be careful to pronounce every syllable. When you're on camera, chances are you are wearing a small lapel microphone. These microphones are sensitive devices that pick up every sound in your voice. Be aware that certain consonants may cause problems. For example, the letter *P* can create a popping sound, and the letter *S* can cause a hissing sound. The microphone will pick up a lot of distracting sounds. Avoid mumbling, sniffing, clearing your throat, or using fillers (such as um, er…). Just be sure to keep your all your comments directed at the camera. If you make minor mistakes, keep going. Don't add unnecessary information by apologizing or by whispering some short, frustrated phrase insulting yourself for not being perfect.

POSITIONING

Positioning yourself to the camera and your audience has as much to do with your physical presence as it does with your personal image. You just have to be yourself. Even though you are under the scrutiny of the camera, you should feel comfortable and act appropriately in everything you say and do. It's easy to forget this when you are alone in front of the lens without a live audience watching you. You need to present yourself as credible and confident.

Given the choice, standing is preferred to sitting because it is easier to breathe when standing. In addition, being on your feet tends to keep your more alert. Sitting may be necessary for longer sessions. Keep in mind that when the camera projects your image, any movements you make look much more pronounced to the viewer. So, when seated, choose a solid chair that doesn't swivel. If you wear a jacket, sit on the back hem and you'll actually sit up straighter. This also keeps your coat from bunching up in front. If you tilt your head slightly downward or slightly to one side every now and then, you will appear more relaxed.

Naturally, in well-planned environments, someone will play the role of stage manager or production director and make sure the set looks "just right." But you need to be prepared for the local communication that becomes visual. You will play the role of producer, director, and actor—in much the same way that you play the role of publisher, editor, and author when you create your own email messages. Before the cameras start "rolling," check directly behind you. Pay attention to your backdrop. Is a disorganized bookshelf or a left-over lunch plate the image you want to portray? Assume the camera is always running and don't show or say anything that distracts from your message. Don't be distracted by items or other people in the room; you'll appear detached and uncertain.

Movement

Remember that we've been talking about the triangle since Chapter 23. The basic choreography used for stand-up presentations, whether in large or small settings, applies to working on camera—the smallest setting of all. The real difference between the environments is the proximity of the audience. In live situations you tend to be farther from the audience when you speak, and your movements need to be bigger to be seen from a greater distance. Through the camera, especially when the image is a close-up, the triangle is magnified for the viewer, and the movements need to be much smaller. You establish the triangle positions with a slight tilt of the head rather than full body movement. Take the basics of body movement and translate them to the sensitivity of the camera.

The three positions of the triangle are still used. You can establish intimacy with the audience by tilting your head forward. Technically, you are in the front of the triangle. You can create neutrality by not tilting your head at all, and you will be in the center of the triangle. You can tilt your head back to reach the back of the triangle and appear to present the larger view of the topic. On camera, the simple tilting of your head creates movement, inflection, meaning, and interest. Former U.S. President Ronald Reagan was a master at using subtle head movement to communicate his views. He was a film actor before he was politician. He knew how to take advantage of the camera.

You can also make adjustments in the angle of your body. Position your shoulders at a 45-degree angle to the camera to establish a "rest" position. By doing this, you can, when necessary, shift the upper part of your body and "square off" to the camera to evoke power and emphasis.

One of the other issues unique to the camera is the degree to which you exist in the frame. In a live event, your view of the presenter is a function of where you sit. Obviously the camera has the ability to zoom in or pull back to create a completely different view for the audience. That is why you need to know how close the camera is set at any particular moment. If you know your "frame" of reference, you can decide what movements, if any, are available to you. Depending on the camera setting, you may have to limit your expressions and gestures.

You'll have to learn to concentrate on both your topic and your movements. If you accidentally move out of the frame, those watching won't be able to see you. If you're operating the camera yourself, you will make the choice to change the zoom level or the camera angle. In many videoconferencing sessions, either you or someone sitting with you in the conference usually controls the camera. If someone else is controlling the camera, you should talk with that person in advance and discuss any movements you expect in which the camera will have to be adjusted. In fact, if your presentation hits a particularly emotional point, you may want to cue the camera to move to a close-up.

Now, unless the event is highly choreographed, chances are the camera will stay in a relatively fixed position and capture you from the waist up. In a videoconference, the technology can usually be preset to certain angles, and many systems are voice activated so that the camera automatically shifts to the person speaking. As technology evolves toward more sophistication, you will be less concerned about the technical aspects of the visual communication. But for now, the camera angles and close-ups are controlled decisions. The timing of those decisions influences the viewer because the camera lens is the link between the presenter and the audience.

USING VIDEOCONFERENCING TECHNOLOGY

Technology is driving communication. The power of telecommunication and personal computers will soon have us all videoconferencing with the same ease and confidence that we currently use to pick up the phone. Okay, maybe not that easy, but video as the vehicle will be more the norm than the exception.

The current evolution in visual communication is toward videoconferencing, whether it is personal or group. When the videoconference is personal, it is conducted from your desktop. When a group delivers the session, it takes place in a larger setting like a conference room. In either case, this technology is ever changing. From the moment I write this to the time you read it, there will have been several changes to the systems available and already in use. Such is the nature of our fast-paced world. I don't want to talk a lot about features or limitations; instead, I want to cover the challenges posed by the nature of the technology itself.

Note

Personal Videoconferencing, by Evan Rosen, is an excellent reference on this topic. Although personal videoconferencing refers to the individual desktop, many of the same issues apply to group videoconferencing, as well.

I think the best way to explain videoconferencing is to think of it as combining the power of television with the intimacy of face-to-face communication while bridging the gaps of distance, time, and relationships. How's that for a mouthful? It's important to understand the challenges of distance and time, especially to a growing world of visual creatures.

THE DISTANCE FACTOR

Face-to-face meetings require your physical presence. Although a lot can be accomplished through email and voice, the ability to be in the presence of another person is the highest form of communication. Sometimes you have to travel to create a face-to-face meeting. When you think about attending meetings that require travel, distance influences your plans. For example, if you work in San Francisco and need to attend a meeting in Atlanta, you already know that much of your time will be spent travelling to and from the meeting. Typically, you'll try to arrange other appointments to help "justify" the trip, the expense, and the inconvenience of being away from the office for so long. However, if the meeting were on site you would not create additional activity with nearby departments just because you happen to be going all the way to the other side of the building. But when travel distance is involved, the need to get other things accomplished while in the area becomes a priority.

So, as you plan your trip to Atlanta, you call two other contacts in the Atlanta vicinity, and you request a brief meeting because you plan "to be in the area." The others may agree to meet with you but more likely out of courtesy rather than real need. After all, they didn't call you, and they may not be as ready as you are to discuss things or make decisions. Some meetings are called because distance dictates the availability of one or more of the parties involved.

Videoconferencing tries to bridge the gap of distance while offering some of the benefits of face-to-face. It may be easier to coordinate mutually convenient schedules for a videoconference meeting if all parties need only travel a short walking distance to the visual meeting. You may be able to offer the other people two or three optional times, rather than let the airlines dictate the time and place for the event.

THE TIME FACTOR

Although convenience of scheduling is time related, the real factor here is length of time for a meeting. Today, most meetings take place in company conference rooms are based around the convenience of the clock. Typically, conference room charts are filled with one-hour meetings, even though these meetings may not really need to be one hour. But, it is not feasible to schedule a 23-minute meeting and then another 18-minute meeting and so on.

But our other forms of communication are much more to the minute, especially when you think of phone conversations. Even a telephone conference call among distant parties offers a start time, but rarely a stop time other than an approximation. Why? Because the parties involved are private phones, separated from one another. If some of the people on the call were occupying a conference room to place the call, then the time for the call may be more limited to make the conference room available for others.

Today, videoconferencing equipment is not on everyone's desk as is a telephone or a personal computer. So the availability of the technology from a time factor is still limited by appointment. However, when the technology is on each desktop, the length of meetings will be determined by the objectives of the conversation, not the availability of space.

PART

VII

CH

26

Current videoconferencing technology has a higher cost of connect time than a simple voice phone call. From an expense standpoint, companies need to limit the length of each call. This has a benefit because when you pay "by the minute," you will likely make more prudent use of the time during a videoconference session than you might in a typical face-to-face meeting in the conference room.

THE RELATIONSHIP FACTOR

Many projects involve assembling a team of experts from within an organization or even across organizations. Too often, people in different departments, in different companies, and even in different cities don't have the time or resources to meet face-to-face and yet, they somehow are required to complete a task as a team. When face-to-face meetings are not possible, it is more difficult to get a group of diverse personalities to perform as a team.

A lot of our time during business communication is spent imagining what the people we haven't met really look like. Every moment we interact without seeing a person, we are communicating with the mental image of the person, which we create. This is a natural process. The beauty of face-to-face communication is the chance to meet and greet others. This is how relationships are formed. Relationships are a huge part of the team concept.

Videoconferencing gives separated parties the chance to see and hear others who may be brought together for only a short time to accomplish a task. Although everyone can't shake hands, at least they can remove the task of imagining what the other people look like because they can see and interact through the technology of videoconferencing.

THE POWER OF TELEVISION

Television. Chances are that you grew up on it. How much money would you have if you were paid $5 dollars for each hour of TV you watched in your life? Even if you averaged 40 hours a week, and you've been watching TV for 20 years, you would have amassed more than $200,000 by now—and that's assuming you never put the money in any investment plan!

Regardless of how much TV you really do watch, the point is that no one can deny the influence of TV over the generations of the past 25 years. Figure 26.13 summarizes the most obvious features of television that keep us glued endlessly to a variety of channels sometimes offering little content.

Television is a highly produced, action-driven medium. You thrive on visual images, and you have become highly critical of those writing, producing, and performing for television. Although you are comfortable with the media as you watch the screen or talk into the lens of a home video camera, you have much higher expectations of those performing profes- sionally on TV. It doesn't take a great stretch of the imagination to wonder what your expectations will be of those who communicate using videoconferencing technology. Maybe you won't expect TV personalities, but you might expect talent to be something better than what you have recorded on your home video camera!

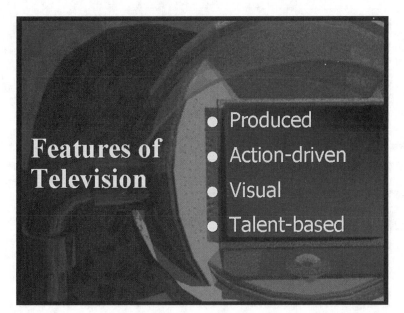

Figure 26.13
The major features of television are what really keep us entertained. Without these instantly available attributes, TV would not be as powerful a presence in our everyday lives.

From a business perspective, the power of television is used most often as a "store and forward" medium, rather than a real-time one. You may have been asked to view tapes in the workplace for training, informational, or motivational reasons. This is more private and mostly one-sided—you are receiving information but not interacting. The good news is that these video productions are usually done well. They are produced using professional talent, and they are highly visual. You don't read a lot when experiencing video. We are content to use the medium of TV to serve our purposes both in business and at home. Until television is two-way and more interactive, it will continue to serve a much more passive and entertaining role in our daily life.

THE BEAUTY OF FACE-TO-FACE

Television has its place in business, similar to home, but it can't compete when a situation requires a face-to-face encounter.

Figure 26.14 summarizes the aspects of face-to-face communication. The ability to engage in real-time conversation in the same room with another person is clearly important to all of us. But the whole interpersonal experience is a very natural one when it comes to using your five senses. Just the handshake as a greeting tells you so much about another person. A casual stroll past a freshly brewing pot of coffee can change the perspective of almost any conversation.

PART

VII

CH

26

Figure 26.14
The attributes of face-to-face communication support the need for personal contact. With its real-time intimacy and natural interaction, the face-to-face meeting is the essence of interpersonal communication.

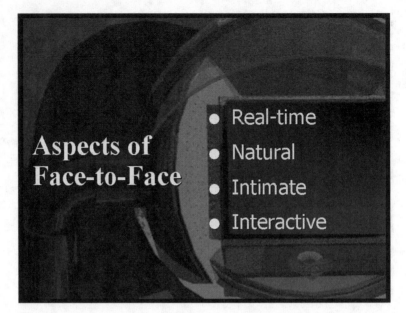

A heightened level of intimacy or closeness exists when people share face-to-face communication. The fact that people share the same moments at the same location allows them to cement a memory beyond what any other form of communication can offer. It's that closeness, that friendship, which helps develop business relationships over the course of time. Even the degree to which you can be truly interactive in a meeting makes you want to use the face-to-face process wherever and whenever you can. After all, you can tell right away if you need to change direction in a discussion or bring up additional data to support your point. In many cases you know these things by simply being in the same space as the other person.

THE IDEAL COMMUNICATION CHANNEL

If any medium could harness the best of both television and face-to-face communication, it would be the ideal communication channel. Figure 26.15 shows the elements of the ultimate medium, if it really existed. Even at this stage in the development of this technology, videoconferencing possesses many of these attributes and comes close to being the ideal communication channel.

When you think about it, videoconferencing is definitely action-driven and highly visual. Videoconferencing happens in real-time, give or take a second for transmission of the signal. In addition, it's intimate and interactive.

But of the eight elements of the ideal medium, videoconferencing falls short in some areas. Figure 26.16 shows where the technology misses, specifically in the areas of production, talent and naturalness.

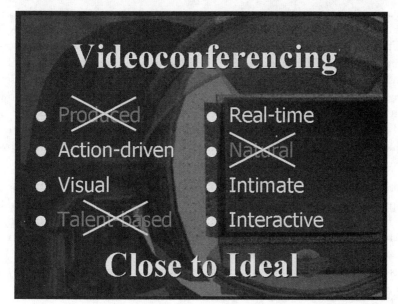

Figure 26.15
By combining the features of television and the aspects of face-to-face, you can create the ideal communication channel.

Figure 26.16
Although it certainly offers a lot, video-conferencing currently falls short of meeting all the requirements of the ideal communication channel. Yet there are ways to work on some of the deficiencies.

As far as being produced and talent-based, videoconferencing requires specific skills to make the event and the participants more effective. Acquiring these skills will put you on the fast track for decision making, problem solving, and getting noticed. You can't escape the eventual need to become a video communicator and screen-to-screen collaborator.

Note

Evan Rosen, author of *Personal Videoconferencing*, uses the term *collabicator* to identify those "collaborators who use video as well as application sharing and document conferencing." In the near future, we will all be called upon to "collabicate" at one time or another.

As far as the technology allowing completely natural interaction, just like face-to-face—well, let's just say that kind of virtual reality is getting closer but it is far from here. So let's take a look at what you can do to make videoconferencing look more produced and more talented than it is now.

THE PRODUCTION ASPECT

The only way to make videoconferencing more like TV is to produce a simple production. Videoconferencing allows you to incorporate a few of television's powerful elements. The effectiveness of TV stems from its capability to tap emotions. The medium leaves little to the imagination as images, graphics, voices, and music provide every detail of the stories it tells. You can enhance the visual effectiveness of videoconferencing through your setting, screenplay, and special effects.

One thing you can do is control the setting by enhancing the layout of the room where you conduct your conferences. Whether you are using personal or group videoconferencing, pay attention to the positioning of the equipment in relationship to the seating and doorways. In a group setup, the camera and codec (coding/decoding or compressing/decompressing) unit usually sit on top of the monitor to allow for the most meaningful eye-contact between the sites. Make sure the distance between the equipment and seats allows for a complete group shot, as well as appropriate close-up views of the individuals. The system's microphone should be equidistant from all participants and, if possible, positioned on a separate table to eliminate noises from shuffling and vibrations. Doorways should allow for people to enter and exit the room with minimal distraction in front of the camera.

Backdrops allow you to manipulate the audience's perception of you and your environment. The backdrops you see on television are chosen to provide details in the story being told. They are used to create an effect. This approach may be overkill for the business world, but remember that your image is everything and understanding the power of the visual image can give you an edge. For best results, choose a backdrop (or wall paint) that is about 17% gray. This ensures a flattering and smoothly transmitted backdrop.

The typical conference room is lit with fluorescent and incandescent lights. These are unflattering and provide little control. If you are creating a videoconferencing room, rely on professionals to design a lighting system that highlights each seat with quality lighting. If you will be conducting a lot of videoconferencing from your office, pay attention to how your face is lit and consider aiming a couple spotlights at your chair.

When choosing the clothes you'll wear on camera, you need to consider both technical and personal image issues. From a technical standpoint, avoid white because it washes out the picture and reflects harshly to the viewers on the other side of the video transmission (also known as the "far side"). Also avoid narrow stripes and houndstooth prints because they tend to "vibrate" on the screen. Large prints and plaids also tend to distract from the communication because there are more colors and patterns that need to be transmitted through the system. Your best choice is solid blue or gray, but make sure you don't become camouflaged by your background. These colors evoke credibility and authority. Lavender and yellow are also good choices, but be careful with light pink because it tends to transmit as white and it becomes too bright from the far side view.

Another way to make a videoconference appear more "produced" is to write a screenplay. Like meetings, effective videoconferences require a bit of advance planning and a shared set of assumptions as to who does what and what rules are followed. Remember, the more the videoconference is structured around some type of plan, the better it will be for everyone.

An agenda is crucial and should be shared in advance with both parties so that the participants can be prepared for the discussion and tasks at hand. The agenda should note any visual presentations and video that may be used and which site will be responsible for the delivery. In addition, make sure that both sites are equipped and prepared to use the videoconference technology. You don't want to waste valuable meeting time teaching people how to work with the equipment.

Decide who will be facilitating or leading the meeting and who at your site will be taking responsibility for the equipment and any media used. If you divide these responsibilities in advance, the meeting will run more smoothly, and if any troubleshooting is necessary, it can be addressed quickly. With the latest advancements in videoconferencing equipment, one person can easily manage to lead the discussion while controlling the technology through a simple remote, with a few touches of a button!

Before you begin, make sure the first-time users understand that there might be a slight delay in the audio transmission. Naturally, as the bandwidth increases, the transmission of audio and video signals will be closer to the broadcast levels we get with TV. For now, the equipment may have some limitations. Just let everyone know that their brains will adjust quickly to any sound delays and that, after a while, they will learn to pick up the cues of a video conversation. At the start, introduce everyone at each site. If someone has to leave in the middle of the conference and the camera doesn't make their departure apparent to the far side, be sure to let them know that someone left the room. In a face-to-face meeting this would not be necessary, but in a videoconference the only view you have to the other side is through the eye of the camera.

The fact that you have control of the camera can add value to the production aspect of the event. Your equipment probably allows for the camera to pan and zoom, giving you a unique ability to change the perspective on the meeting. With a little practice (or a system that can program preset camera positions) you can bring the camera in close when you want to make a strong point or pan the room for individual reactions.

In fact, some systems allow you to control the camera in your room as well as that at the far side. You can pan around the room on the far side, zoom in on individuals as they speak,

PART
VII

CH
26

and pull back to view a group reaction. Just be aware that a picture-in-picture function on the far side may allow them to see what you're seeing!

Your system may also allow you to incorporate an electronic presentation, videotape, or dataconferencing into your remote meeting. You can even audioconference outgoing and incoming phone calls if you need to access the expertise of a colleague. If you choose to use these media, be sure that you rehearse the order and switching to ensure that you can move smoothly between the different devices. The power of these tools can be diminished when you begin fumbling with the technology. No matter how simple the equipment is to operate, take the time for a technical run-through.

Finally, keep in mind that a videoconference can also be videotaped for archival or review purposes. All it takes is a VCR connected to the videoconferencing system. Although the replay will only be the action from the far side, the audio will be two sided, similar to what it may have looked like had you attended the meeting. The only thing you won't see is any interaction that may have happened in the room on your side of the conference. Keep in mind that if your interactive sessions are archived, there will be compelling visual evidence available in case you change or need to defend your position on a particular topic. This is true of email and voice mail messages, but a videotape is much more impressive. Of course, a videotape recording can be blessing or a curse, depending on the nature of the content.

Those are just some of the things you can consider if you want a videoconference to appear more like a TV production. This is not much different than the effort it takes to make an average presentation look extremely professional. The more you become aware of what to work on, the easier it becomes to accomplish the task.

BOOSTING YOUR TALENT

It goes without saying that a talent-based medium requires talent. The people embracing videoconferencing are developing a unique set of skills that is setting them apart as communicators. The skill set goes beyond the ability to write well and speak comfortably in public. This technology is quick, interactive, and intimate. It requires that you constantly assess what your saying, how you are saying it, and what you look like all the while.

Earlier in this chapter we talked about playing to the camera, and a videoconference is a prime example of a situation in which your voice, positioning, and movement are most noticeable. Some other unique issues related to videoconferencing also come into play.

From a vocal standpoint, avoid the rudeness of side conversations. People may see you whispering but may not hear your comments. However, in negotiations, asides can be your ally. Many videoconferencing systems have a "mute button" on the microphone that allows you to pause the audio transmission temporarily. If you first get an agreement that both parties will be using this function to discuss items among themselves, negotiations can proceed more quickly. Just be aware that the video may still be running, allowing the other party to read your expressions and body language.

As I mentioned before, when you are using a system that has a slight audio delay, it's important to wait until an individual has completely finished a sentence before replying. Because in normal conversation, we tend to interrupt each other a lot, many experts believe that the patience required by videoconferencing users may finally teach us to wait for the other person to finish. This more "formal" timing will actually put us in line with the communication styles of our European and Asian partners and could lead to more effective communication overall. Of course, after all systems are up to real-time broadcast quality speed (like telephones), there won't be any audio delays. Then we'll go back to stepping on each other's sentences again. Some things just never change!

From a physical delivery perspective, facial expressions are critical to the communication process. By reading the faces of the other party, you may be able to tell if they are confused or supportive, eager or bored, trustworthy or lying. Likewise, your face will communicate information about how you are thinking and feeling. Remember that even though you may not be the person speaking, you are still on camera and, therefore, are still communicating. Try to manage the messages you are sending through body language, and you will be much more effective.

Note

How to Read a Person Like a Book, by Gerald Nierenberg and Henry Calero (Pocket Books), offers some interesting insights into the role body language plays in interpersonal communication. Understanding nonverbal cues can be extremely useful in any small group environment, including a videoconference.

Eye contact is still a dilemma in videoconferencing. You can't make direct eye contact with the camera and the person on the screen simultaneously, unless you are sitting back far enough from the camera lens that you appear to be looking directly back at someone. Figures 26.17 and 26.18 demonstrate this line of sight issue. As I was typing this I decided to take some quick photos of myself with my small digital camera attached to my PC. Imagine you are looking at me during a videoconference. Figure 26.17 shows how I appear to you when I look directly into the camera lens. Notice I am looking right at you. But, if I wanted to look at your image on my end of the conference and my viewing screen is set much lower than the position of the camera, then Figure 26.18 shows how I appear to you. The only reason you notice this is because I am so close to the camera. I would have to sit farther back from the camera to give you the appearance of direct eye contact as I look at your image on my screen.

Figure 26.17
If you were watching me over a videoconference and I looked straight into the camera lens mounted on top of my viewing screen, it would appear as if I am looking directly at you.

Figure 26.18
So it doesn't seem that I'm looking down all the time, I need to be sitting farther from the camera to make the eye contact appear more direct.

That is why most videoconference systems use a 27-inch or 32-inch TV screen with the camera mounted on top of the set and the participants seated about 10 to 12 feet away. From that distance you really can't tell that the person you're looking at is really looking slightly below their camera lens at your image on their screen. Of course, if the camera could be mounted into the middle of the TV screen then you would always appear to be looking into the lens regardless of how close you were to the screen.

If you were on TV, you would always be looking directly into the camera lens because it's still a one-way communication tool. This line-of-sight problem between where the camera is mounted and where the display screen is situated is most apparent in personal videoconferencing and close-up views. Until the technology is perfected (and many solutions are being researched), you must learn to look into the camera when speaking or adjust to any differences.

Look at Me When I Talk to You!

When you watch television, there is no reciprocal eye contact. The transmission of the signal is one-way. As the viewer, you are are not sending your image back to the person in the studio, so that person only has to look into the camera lens and know that eye contact is being made with you watching from home.

Unlike television, group and desktop videoconferencing systems, today, face the challenge of absolute direct eye contact. Videoconferencing is interactive, and the two-way communication means eye contact is important on both ends of the transmission. Because the lens is outside the viewing area of the screen, maintaining absolute eye-to-eye contact is impossible. To reduce this distraction, experts suggest reducing the angle by which the eyes are averted from the lens. Adjusting the distance people sit from the screen (TV or monitor) and/or using a smaller screen size can help with direct eye contact issues.

As the screen size gets larger, you must increase the distance participants sit from the screen. The goal is to have the angle between the camera lens and the person's foveal point (the spot focused on with the eyes) to be 10 degrees or less. 10 degrees…you'll need to use your handy protracter! Oh, you don't carry a protracter? Neither do I. Okay, so here's a suggestion. Mount the camera on top of the monitor and center it. Then, make sure the monitor is at a height such that when you're sitting you're looking straight into the top third of the monitor. This reduces the angle that those on the other end (looking at you) have between your image and their camera lens.

To minimize the angle between your camera and the image of those you are looking at on your monitor, frame the shot of the other people so there is only a small amount of "unused space" above their heads. This way, your eyes have to drop down only a short distance when you look at them on your monitor, and it appears you are looking more directly into the camera lens.

Of course, the simplest way to know if your eye contact is a distraction is to ask those on the other end if it seems like you are looking directly at them or somewhat downward. If you appear to be looking down, from their perspective, then sit farther back from the monitor to reduce the distraction.

PART

VII

CH

26

If you plan to move around at all, one way to stay within the frame of the camera is to test the camera positions in advance and plan your movement. If your videoconferencing equipment allows you to preset camera positions, you'll also be able to change from a wide shot to a close-up with the touch of a button.

Of course, real talent develops with experience. The more you use videoconferencing, the less your viewers notice the technology, and the more comfortable and natural you'll feel. Be an early-adapter and as the technology becomes more common, you can share your expertise to introduce others to the power of the media. In the beginning, it may feel like the technology is controlling you, but eventually you will use videoconferencing with the ease that you currently use your computer, fax machine, and phone.

NOT QUITE NATURAL

Although videoconferencing falls short of being the ideal communication channel, the efforts on your part concerning production and talent can bring the technology much closer to the ideal. Figure 26.19 lists all the components of videoconferencing that can be achieved, with some degree of effort—with the exception of one element: naturalness.

Figure 26.19
With effort you can bring video-conferencing to nearly match the elements of the ideal communication channel, with the exception of the one element circled here. As close as it might get to being a relationship medium, videoconferencing still can't attain the total natural qualities of face-to-face contact.

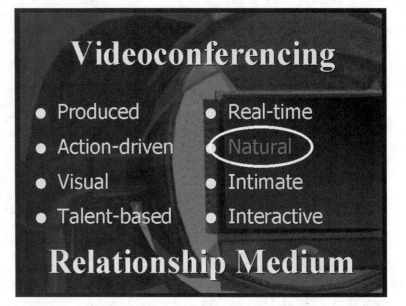

Current videoconferencing cannot duplicate the natural aspects of face-to-face communication. You still can't fill the coffee cups of the person at the far side. You can't smell colognes or shake hands. You can't see the subtle expression in their eyes or hear the faint pronunciation of their words. You can't casually notice the small actions of the group unless the camera picks it up for you. You can't do these things because you aren't there, on site. This limitation of videoconferencing may never be overcome.

But technology advances as we speak and perhaps, over the course of time, virtual reality will allow for seamless workplaces that simulate very real and natural interactions among people. Regardless, it is more likely that we will sacrifice the five senses for the sake of just two or three, rather than not use videoconferencing as the new age communication medium.

INTERACTING IN A VISUAL WORLD

I really think the shift to a more visual society is already upon us. Look around—the evidence is everywhere, from the workplace to the home. We have met the visual creatures, and they are us! The next century can be dubbed the Visual Age, and its effect will be massive.

Note

> There has been much research about the relationship between people and media. A superb source is *The Media Equation*, by Byron Reeves and Clifford Nass (Cambridge University Press). The book is about how people treat computers, television, and new media as real people. The studies done by the authors suggest that the design of media technologies, including computer devices, applications and Web sites, be considered from a social perspective. I highly recommend this book.

The Visual Age will bring us closer together as a global society because we will be able to see one another on a more frequent basis. Realizing that, here are my forecasts for the new millennium regarding the effect a visual way of life will have on individuals and society.

THE EFFECT ON INDIVIDUALS

Let's look at the age groups in the year 2000. Anyone under 10 probably already has the words "visual creature" stamped on the inside of their head. That age group will not have any problem adapting to an interactive and visual world. When they finally begin working for a living, I expect them to one day walk through a flea market, pick up a computer mouse, and ponder what its use might have been!

Those between 10 and 20 years old are still well developed visual creatures. When they finally embark on their journey into the business world, using visual communications will be as simple as touching a keyboard. People between 20 and 30 will be on the cusp of the changing technology. The good news is that this age group already knows that to adapt is to succeed and being in their high-spirited 20s, this crowd will lead the way to a host of major technology changes in the workplace.

Okay, now lets discuss the problem groups. Those between 30 and 40 will accept the new world of visual communications, but will resist direct participation mostly for vanity reasons. After all, knowing the camera adds ten pounds will not appeal to the Generation Xers at all. These are the people that cut their teeth on Internet chat rooms where remaining anonymous was the standard level of interaction. It is unlikely to believe this group will welcome a visual conversation while sitting around in a bathrobe eating a Pop Tart.

People between 40 and 50, the tail end of the baby boomers, will mostly resist all forms of visual communication, some for vanity reasons and others because they will be fed up with the years of email and voice mail inundation. People in this age group are already growing tired of being accessible through every other form of communication and will see the visual process as a real intrusion into the only remaining personal space in their lives. Little do they know that by adapting to a more visual world, this age group holds the life experience and maturity to lead the up and coming companies of the future. Expect only those who adapt to the new technology to come out ahead and the rest to lag behind or fall by the wayside.

PART

VII

CH

26

Age Before Beauty?

Believe it or not, those over 50, the original baby boomers, will adapt to the world of visual communications because their biggest priority will involve nurturing. That's right. After 50 you begin to think about winding down your career, even though you may still work another 20 years. The point is that when you start thinking about retirement you wonder who will take care of you when you get older. It's not all you think about, but it certainly becomes an issue. Therefore, when a huge segment of the population ages toward retirement, long-term care becomes a priority. Women hold an advantage because they have played the role of both nurturers and decision-makers in our society. Over the past 25 years, women have proven they can handle nearly every pressure situation, whether at home or in business.

For these reasons, expect women to gain a much stronger hold on key business leadership positions in the future. Why? Because the "nurturer" will place more emphasis on the needs of the aging population, and the "decision-maker" will appeal to the financial goals of the same group—which, by the way, will control the vast amount of the wealth in the nation.

Invariably, the over 50 age group will welcome visual communication with open arms because, as people age, they are more honest about adopting new habits that reduce stress on the body. Visual interaction will allow for less travel and less wear and tear on the body. Remember that these people grew up on face-to-face communications, and the visual technology will help simulate that experience more than a phone conversation or an email ever could. The good news is they won't have to travel to make the face-to-face interaction happen.

So there you have it! The very young and the very old adapt, and the middle groups have some big decisions to make. I believe that anyone between 30 and 50 years old in the year 2000 will truly have no choice but to adapt to the most current visual technology. If not, they will find themselves unable to adjust to the younger crowd sneaking up from behind and the older crowd looking back for support.

This doesn't mean people will lose their jobs, but it does mean that by avoiding the changes in the workplace, some people will experience limited advancement. It's hard to see just how rapidly things advance, but here's an interesting piece of information. High school graduates in the year 2000 will have virtually no frame of reference to a TV set without a remote control. Some of us still remember getting up to change the channel! The technology changes as you sleep! I'm 44, so I happened to be one of those who already realizes the world of visual communication is inevitable, and I have been embracing the concept for several years. I expect to be changing as rapidly as the technology—and only for my own sake!

THE EFFECT ON SOCIETY

You also have to look at the social benefits of a more visual world. You will be seeing people of different cultures and backgrounds more visually and more frequently than ever before. There will be a greater acceptance of diverse audiences. You can expect a more visual world to be one that welcomes our visual differences.

I really think that when you see another person, any fears, inhibitions, prejudices, concerns, ignorance, or other negative feelings can disappear faster. It's when we can't experience the whole person that we sometimes create false impressions. I was lucky enough to grow up in New York City where interaction among many cultures was the norm. No matter what the prejudices, you still had to interact with different people on a daily basis. When you ride the bus and subway with different people every single day, you just learn to get along. You don't have much choice. I'm not saying we lived in perfect harmony, but to this day I find it easy to accept people whose lifestyles and backgrounds are much different than my own. If I can't, then it's my problem, not theirs.

A world of visual communicators will offer more direct contact with more people, more frequently, resulting in a greater acceptance of diverse opinions. The good news is that a more visual world will be better for our children. After all, kids aren't born with a natural fear or dislike of others. They can only learn it. A visual world will provide more evidence as to why those who look or think differently have so much in common. Okay, so you can tell I grew up in the sixties. The point is that, the more we see one another, the more we understand one another. Visual interaction will bring us closer together, globally.

The growth of visual communications will place you in view, mainly through the eyes of a camera. The more you adapt to the changing technology, the better the chances of your success. But keep in mind that to prepare for the visual changes ahead, you will have to develop your current skills and become a more visual presenter. Everything we discussed in the earlier chapters—from messaging to media to mechanics—consistently follows the path of a visual presenter. After you add-in the latest technology, you'll be able to demonstrate your skills to the world.

So, what are you waiting for? Get used to picturing yourself on TV and before you know it you'll be staring straight into the camera lens saying, "I'm ready for my close-up, Mr. DeMille!"

TROUBLESHOOTING

Regardless of the setting, are there any general recommendations that you have for covering all the bases when preparing presentations?

Maybe the best way to approach this is to provide a presenter's checklist. These are some of the more important questions you might ask yourself when preparing for a presentation. Of course, not every question applies to every situation, but this is a pretty good list to check.

Presenter's Checklist:

- ❑ What is the topic of the presentation?
- ❑ How long is the presentation?
- ❑ What is the format? Lecture? Panel? Q&A?
- ❑ Do you need an outline of the presentation in advance of the event?
- ❑ What is the objective of the meeting? Call to action?
- ❑ When is the meeting scheduled? Date? Time?

- ❏ Where will the meeting be held? Directions?
- ❏ Is the event sponsored by an individual or an organization? Do they need to be recognized?
- ❏ Who will be attending?
- ❏ What is the anticipated size of the audience?
- ❏ What is the average age of the audience? Gender ratio?
- ❏ What cultural issues (language, customs, humor) exist?
- ❏ What is arranged for staging and A/V?
- ❏ Is the proper media (overhead, slide, or LCD projector) available?
- ❏ Is a microphone necessary and available?
- ❏ When are rehearsals and A/V checks scheduled?
- ❏ Will the meeting be video- or audiotaped?
- ❏ Is a speaker's lounge or "ready room" available?
- ❏ Will any other speakers be sharing the platform? Names? Topics?
- ❏ Who will be making introductions?
- ❏ What are the arrangements for housing and travel?
- ❏ What are the arrangements for hotel check out and return travel?
- ❏ Are any additional events planned on-site? Dress code?
- ❏ Can arrangements be made to sell/distribute support materials on-site?
- ❏ Will evaluation forms be used, and will results be available?

If you present outdoors and you still want to do a PowerPoint presentation, how do you cope with the elements of nature?

Sometimes presenting outdoors can involve the use of a screen and visual support. Assuming it's not inclement weather, lighting and sound become the major issues. Ambient (natural) light as well as background noises are controlled by nature when you present outdoors, so you have to cope with what nature provides you at the moment. I have found that most outdoor presentations that use visual support are linked to a greater outdoor activity or event. The presentation itself is the not the main component of the day.

I remember designing a presentation for the president of a company to deliver at the company picnic. It was a short presentation supported by a few visuals. The visual content was really required to help the president of the company remember everything. But let's not go there!

The presentation took place inside a big tent and all the sides of the tent were open, so there was a lot of light spilling into the space. With a lot of light hitting the screen, any dark color backgrounds tended to wash out and the related foreground elements were hard to see. The only way to create contrast was to reverse the normal design of the visuals. I had to consider light-color backgrounds and dark foreground elements. In fact, because the sun was shining so brightly, pure black and white ended up being my only choice for best readability from distance.

Another issue I had to deal with was sound. Because the sides of the tent were open, there were no walls for sound to bounce off. The microphone setup was adequate for the size of the space, but a number of background noises were drowning out the sound as I tested the microphone. It was breezy that day, and the wind was causing the hanging edges of the canvas tent to flap. Outside the tent, there were lots of kids running around, playing games and making noise, as you would expect at a picnic.

Before the presentation started, I suggested to the president of the company to invite some of the people standing at the back to move up along the sides. This created a "wall" of people in a sort of semi-circle around those seated. The "people-wall" helped localize the sound by keeping it inside the tent. In addition, those standing reduced the amount of ambient light giving the visuals higher contrast. The semi-circle of people also cut down on the wind and the noises from outside the tent.

All in all, the outdoor presentation was easier to see and hear after coping with the elements of nature that seemed like huge obstacles from the beginning.

PART

VII

CH

26

APPENDIXES

TROUBLESHOOTING POWERPOINT

by Laurie Ann Ulrich

DEALING WITH ERROR MESSAGES AND PROMPTS

Problems may arise with your PowerPoint presentation during the development, editing, printing, or saving process, and the goal of this appendix is to give you some ideas for what to expect and how to handle these problems if and when they occur.

Many PowerPoint problems announce themselves in the form of an error message that appears when you attempt to issue a command or perform some task. Others are more subtle—the command you want to use is dimmed, the graphic you want to rotate won't. When an error message occurs—although frustrating—it does give you more information about the nature and cause of the problem. Take advantage of this additional information, and react to it logically and cautiously. When an error message appears onscreen in PowerPoint or any application, read it carefully, and make a written note of when it happened and what you were doing at the time.

The following suggestions can help you resolve your problem and, if necessary, assist you in describing the problem to a technician or help-desk attendant.

- *Use Print Screen* This key, located above your Insert key on a standard keyboard, may appear as PrtScn or Print Screen. Pressing this key takes a snapshot of your screen and places the image on your Clipboard. You can then paste the image into an email message (to send to your company's technical staff) or WordPad document for printing. The image contains the exact message that appeared. Because what was going on in the background is clearly shown, the technical staff sees the error message in context.

- *Try again* As best as you can, attempt to perform the task again that resulted in the error message. If the process works with no problem, you may be out of the woods and can continue working. If the error appears again, you might want to find out what's going wrong before you continue to repeat the error-inducing procedure.

- *Call for help*   If you don't know what happened or why, don't try to fix the problem yourself. If you don't know the source of the problem, you're likely to cause more trouble by tinkering. Call your company's technical staff, or call Microsoft.

Note

Call for Help. If you're running a properly licensed copy of PowerPoint, you may be entitled to free support at 425-635-7145. If you are not able to take advantage of free support, you can also get help at 900-555-2000 for $35 per question/problem. The fee is a flat rate—whether it takes you one call of five minutes in length or five calls of an hour each to resolve the problem, the cost is the same.

RESOLVING PROBLEMS

Some problems you can solve yourself, by determining the cause of the problem and eliminating any contributing factors. Most problems you encounter in PowerPoint will probably be memory-related, even if you have a great deal of memory (RAM) on your computer. In addition, because PowerPoint is a graphical application and most of your slides contain several graphical elements (pictures, textures, and colors), printing and display can also be problem areas, if your printer doesn't have enough memory or your video card isn't powerful enough.

When you consider solving a problem yourself, be honest with yourself—do you feel confident changing your computer's configuration? Are you fluent with the Control Panel? If you begin tinkering in one dialog box or another, do you completely understand the nature and ramifications of all the changes and settings with which you're working? If the answers to these questions are not Yes on all counts, don't try to solve the problem on your own—call for help.

Note

If you want to try a possible solution on your own, try to exit without saving or choose File, Save As and save the file under a new name and restart PowerPoint. You may lose any work (in your original file) done since your last save, but if the last batch of changes was what caused your problem, you've also lost *them*!

DISPLAY PROBLEMS

Most display problems, if they occur suddenly, are memory-related. Typical complaints include the following:

- Ghosts of previous slides or dialog boxes appear behind your current slide, or even on top of it.
- Text on your slides changes to a choppy, sans serif font.
- Graphics don't fully appear, appear grainy or choppy, or appear as though a pattern is placed on top of them.

- Ornate graphics or background elements take a long time to refresh as you move from slide to slide.

If any of these problems occur, save your work and exit PowerPoint. If you have other programs running, shut them down, too. You may even consider restarting your computer to empty your memory and start with a clean slate. Most of the time, however, simply restarting PowerPoint resolves the problem.

If the problem is chronic, you might consider upgrading your video card to one that has more memory and is therefore capable of displaying and handling more complex graphic and multimedia content.

Tip #295 from	If your slide's background or object fill colors display in stripes or just don't look as smooth as you think they should, check your zoom level. Choosing 100% should smooth out the display, removing any distortion. You can also try viewing the offending slide in Slide Show View, which allows you to see the entire slide.
Laurie Ulrich	

TROUBLESHOOTING DRAWN OBJECTS

Problems with objects you draw on your PowerPoint slides usually occur as you try to draw the object or when you attempt to move, resize, or recolor it. Depending on the nature of the problem, your solutions will vary. Problems you may encounter:

- *Curved lines or shapes look jagged*   First, make sure it's not your monitor's display. Print the slide to see if the object looks jagged on paper. If your slide is to be viewed onscreen only, try viewing the offending object in Slide Show view. If the enlarged image (full screen) still looks jagged, revert to Slide view, select the object and choose Draw, Edit Points. Increase your zoom, and begin adjusting the vertexes (you may have also heard them called *nodes* in illustration software programs). Drag them up, down, left, right, reducing any jagged edges on your curved lines and shapes. You can also delete vertexes to eliminate jagged edges or changes in a line's direction.

- *Freeform shapes won't align properly*   If the Draw, Align or Distribute command doesn't produce the desired effect on your shapes, try moving them manually. Select one of the items and depress the Ctrl key. Tap your arrow keys (in the direction you wish to move), moving the selected shape in 1-pixel increments. When the desired location is achieved, move the other object in the same way. By using this *nudge* feature, you know exactly how far you're moving an object.

Tip #296 from	When moving or resizing objects, control placement and alignment by choosing Draw, Snap, to Grid. Once on, you can toggle this feature off as needed (for drawing freeform shapes or moving objects freely) by pressing the Alt key as you drag.
Laurie Ulrich	

APP

A

WORKING WITH GRAPHICS

Graphics—clip art and scanned photographs—can be significant elements in a PowerPoint presentation. Their complexity, however, can cause problems during your presentation's development stages. Be on the lookout for these common difficulties:

- *You can't rotate or flip your image*   Only PowerPoint drawings can be rotated or flipped. This needn't prevent your applying these effects to your clip art from other sources, but you have to convert it to a PowerPoint object first. Select the object and choose <u>D</u>raw, <u>U</u>ngroup. A prompt warns you that you're about to turn the object into a PowerPoint object. After the object is ungrouped, you can regroup it (to keep from inadvertently disassembling it) and then rotate or flip it as you would any PowerPoint drawn shape.

- *You can't select the object with your mouse*   If you're in Slide view, the object must be part of the slide master, and therefore only available for selection while you're in Slide Master view. Choose <u>V</u>iew, <u>M</u>aster, <u>S</u>lide Master, and then select the object. When you're ready to go back to working with your non-master items, return to Slide or Normal view.

- *You can't ungroup a graphic picture*   This is most likely because the picture is a bitmap. Use another program, such as Microsoft Photo Editor or Adobe Photoshop to edit the image, and then import it into your PowerPoint presentation.

Tip #297 from *Laurie Ulrich*	When working with your Slide Master, be sure to place any graphic or text objects so that they don't visually interfere with the content of your individual slides. Place logos, slogans, or any other object that will appear on all slides in an out-of-the-way place, such as a corner or along the bottom of the slide. If the object must be large, consider giving it a light or muted fill so that it can appear behind your slide content without reducing legibility.

Tip #298 from *Laurie Ulrich*	If you need to, you can save just the text portion of your presentation. In the Save As dialog box, choose Rich Text Format (.rtf) in the Save as <u>t</u>ype list box. Your graphic content is to be saved, but your text is saved in a universally acceptable format, enabling you to use your presentation text in any word processing program or as the outline basis for another presentation.

PRINTING PROBLEMS

Printing problems are generally related to your printer and are usually transient—don't rush out and take your computer in for repairs just because a print job doesn't come out as expected! Some common printing problems include the following:

- The whole page doesn't print—about a third or half-way through the page, the image appears "chopped off."

- Text objects are missing.
- Nothing prints, or only a few pages of random characters and symbols print.

Not to oversimplify, but most of the problems you'll encounter when printing will probably be due to a "confused" printer, a printer with too much input from too many people (if you're on a network) or too much data to handle in your particular presentation. If the same presentation with the same content printed fine before on the same printer, this is further evidence that the current environment—other printer traffic—is the culprit.

If you're on a network, contact your company's network administrator or technicians. They may suggest printing the presentation at night or early in the morning before other workers come in and use the printer. If possible, direct your print job to another printer that is used by fewer people.

If you don't have the luxury of delaying your print job because of a tight deadline, you can always take the presentation on disk to a local printing and photocopying store. Many rent time on their computers, and you can print it out there.

To reduce the amount of information that your printer must handle for your presentation, try printing in black and white (use the Print dialog box setting).

If all quick-fix or workaround options fail or are inappropriate for your immediate needs, you can take a more direct approach and check your printer's settings. Each printer's settings are a little different, being based on the printer's specific capabilities, its connection to your printer and/or a network, and your system configuration. To access your printer's settings, choose Settings, Printers from the Start menu, and double-click the icon for the printer in question. The resulting dialog box will show you the current settings for your printer's connection to the computer, speed, resolution, and other options, again, depending on your printer. If you're working with someone else's computer (the computer on your desk at work, for example), it's a good idea to ask for assistance from a technical resource before making any changes.

App

A

Also not advisable if you're dealing with a computer at work (where you're probably not supposed to do your own repairs), you can try changing or updating the driver for your printer to solve printing problems. Check the manufacturer's Web site for the latest driver, and after downloading it, install it by double-clicking the Add Printer icon in the Printers window. When asked, direct the installation program to the folder where you have stored the driver, and a new printer icon will appear, based on that driver file. Attempt your print job again, and if the previous driver was the culprit, your print job should be successful.

TROUBLESHOOTING PROBLEMS WITH POWERPOINT FEATURES

PowerPoint is loaded with effective and normally efficient tools to enhance your presentations, and most of the time, these features work perfectly. When they don't, however, they can truly be more trouble than they're worth. Before starting your next presentation, familiarize yourself with these situations and their resolutions:

- *AutoCorrect isn't correcting*   Make sure it's on. Choose <u>T</u>ools, AutoCorrect, and check to see that a check mark is next to Replace <u>t</u>ext as you type and any of the other AutoCorrect options that you wish to use.

- *AutoCorrect is working when you don't want it to*   In your presentation for the law firm of Tidwell, Evans, and Havilland, you need to type TEH and not have it converted to THE. You don't want to remove the AutoCorrect entry from the list, and you don't want to turn off AutoCorrect altogether. What to do? As soon as AutoCorrect converts TEH to THE, choose <u>E</u>dit, Undo or press Ctrl+Z. Resume your typing after TEH and continue to work. You can also go back and select the word THE and retype it as TEH. As long as you don't press the Spacebar or Enter after the H, it won't be AutoCorrected.

- *Your hyperlinks don't work*   The most common cause of this problem is that the target file or Web location is no longer valid or has been moved. It's a good idea to maintain your links by checking them periodically, especially an intranet or Web pages on the Internet. If the hyperlink fails, right-click it and choose <u>H</u>yperlink, Edit <u>H</u>yperlink from the shortcut menu, and in the Edit Hyperlink dialog box, click the <u>B</u>rowse button to find your targeted link.

- *An error message tells you that you don't have enough memory to create an Organization Chart*   This error occurs primarily in cases where the computer running PowerPoint has more than 200 fonts in the Fonts folder. Cut and Paste your excess fonts (be sure to leave your system fonts in the Fonts folder) to a spare folder (call it Fonts2 or something similar) and when you've reduced the number of fonts in the Fonts folder to 200 or less, retry creating your Organization chart.

- *Drag and Drop editing doesn't work*   If you've ruled out that your mouse skills are the cause of the problem—not having text properly selected can often be the culprit—make sure that the drag-and-drop feature is turned on. Choose <u>T</u>ools, <u>O</u>ptions, and in the Edit tab, look for a check mark in the <u>D</u>rag-and-drop text editing option. If it's not checked, click the option box.

Tip #299 from
Laurie A Ulrich

If your hyperlink works but takes a long time to get to the target Web site, the server on which the target resides may be busy. Try to reach the site later, or try during times of the day that are less likely to be busy—early in the morning or very late at night.

SLIDE SHOW PROBLEMS

If you're having a problem with your slide show, the problem is likely that the show is too slow or your animations don't work as expected. In the case of speed, your computer's memory may be the problem, or if you're using graphic files, if they were scanned at a high resolution (600 or 1200 dpi), this may slow down your show as well. To see if memory is the problem, close any other programs that aren't essential, and try restarting PowerPoint. If the show is still too slow and you are using graphic files in your presentation, consider rescanning it at a lower resolution (if you have access to the original artwork), or opening the file in a program that allows you to edit and resave the image at a lower resolution.

If your animations aren't working as expected, try the obvious first—go back to the slides and make sure your settings are correct. If it turns out that they are, try deleting the offending object (a piece of clip art that doesn't fly in as desired or a title that doesn't appear at all during the show) and reinserting it. Then, reapply the animation effects. Years of using PowerPoint and helping hundreds of students create presentations has proven this method; although not technically elegant, it is the most effective and expeditious way to solve such problems.

Note

When any PowerPoint problem occurs in printing, running a slide show, or editing your slides, try the Help menu. From the Help menu, choose Microsoft PowerPoint Help, and then pose your question to the Office Assistant by typing it into the box as directed. If you type "Printing," for example, the topics that the Office Assistant will find for you include "Troubleshoot printing."

APP

A

USING POWERPOINT'S FOREIGN LANGUAGE CAPABILITIES

by Patrice-Anne Rutledge

UNDERSTANDING POWERPOINT'S MULTIPLE LANGUAGE FEATURES

Office 2000, including PowerPoint, includes many new features that simplify creating multilingual documents and presentations. Some examples of these features are

- *A single worldwide executable* This enables you to use one version of the application in multiple languages including most European, Asian, and bi-directional languages such as Arabic and Hebrew.
- *Language AutoDetect* PowerPoint automatically detects the language you're using based on the keyboard and applies the appropriate proofing tools.
- *Multiple language editing* PowerPoint 2000 enables the use of multiple languages in a single document, including the capability to check spelling and apply special formatting in the languages you enable.
- *Text editing in right-to-left languages* If your system supports right-to-left languages, such as Arabic or Hebrew, PowerPoint displays these languages correctly and enables editing.

UNDERSTANDING THE MULTILANGUAGE PACK

The Microsoft MultiLanguage Pack for Office 2000 provides user interfaces and online help for more than 25 languages. The MultiLanguage Pack also includes the Microsoft Proofing Tool Kit, which provides fonts, templates, and spelling/grammar checkers for 37 languages. Additionally, this kit includes IMEs required for Asian languages. An IME is an Input Method Editor, which enables you to create documents and presentations in Asian languages by translating what you type into Asian characters.

The MultiLanguage Pack comes on a separate CD—not the one you use to install Office 2000. Install the Language Pack CD if you want to use multiple languages in PowerPoint.

Caution

Even if you install the MultiLanguage Pack to enable multilingual features in Office 2000, you still need to verify that your system supports the language you want to use. Windows NT 5 is the best platform for extensive multilingual use—it supports all languages. If you use Windows 95, 98, or NT 4, you may need the corresponding language version of this software for full support of languages such as Chinese, Japanese, Korean, Thai, Vietnamese, Arabic, or Hebrew.

CHANGING THE USER INTERFACE AND ONLINE HELP LANGUAGE

You can change the language of both the user interface and the online help from the Microsoft Office Language Settings dialog box, which displays when you install multiple language support. From the Start menu, choose Programs, Office Tools, Microsoft Office Language Settings to open this dialog box, shown in Figure B.1.

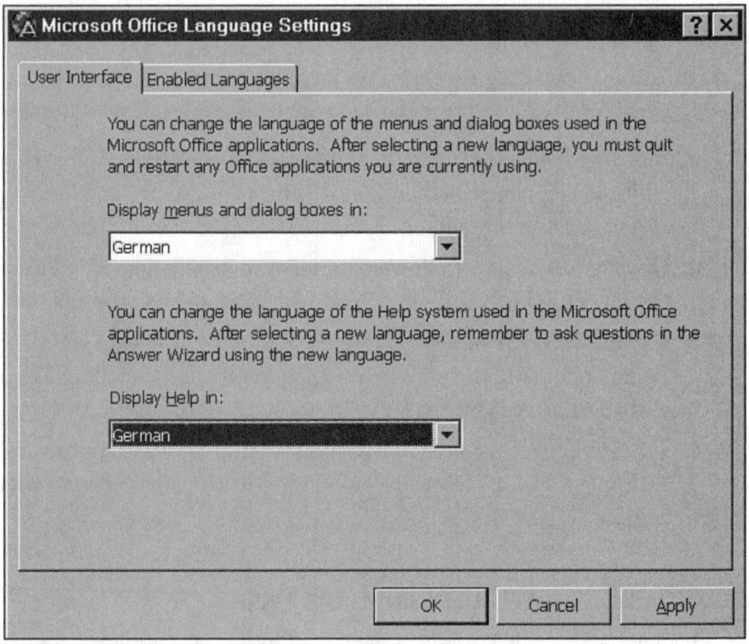

Figure B.1
You can choose the language of both the interface and help in PowerPoint.

> **Can't find the Microsoft Office Language Settings dialog box?** See the Troubleshooting section at the end of the chapter.

On the User Interface tab, you can specify the language in which you want to display the user interface—such as menus and dialog boxes—as well the language of the online help. This affects all Office applications, not just PowerPoint.

From the Display Menus and Dialog Boxes In drop-down list, choose the language in which you want the user interface to appear.

From the Display Help In drop-down list, choose the language in which you want to view online help.

You need to restart all open Office applications for the language change to take effect (see Figure B.2).

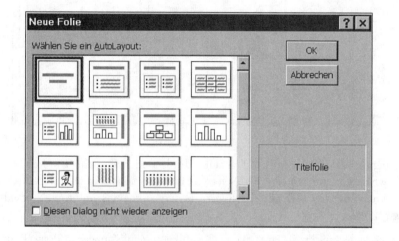

Figure B.2
You can change PowerPoint's user interface to another language, such as German.

ENABLING MULTIPLE LANGUAGE EDITING

On the Enabled Languages tab of the Microsoft Office Language Settings dialog box (see Figure B.3), you can enable PowerPoint (and other Office applications) to edit additional languages.

APP

B

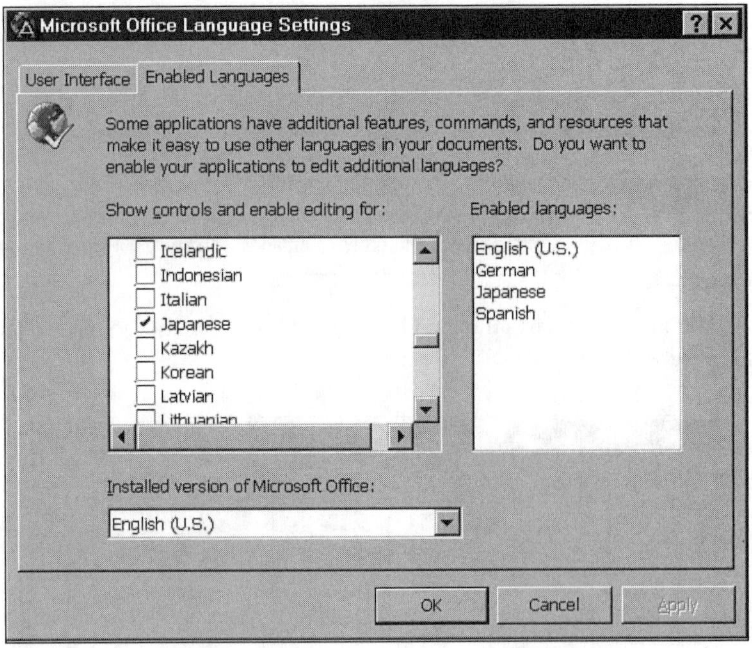

Figure B.3
Enabling a language activates special menus and dialog boxes related to it.

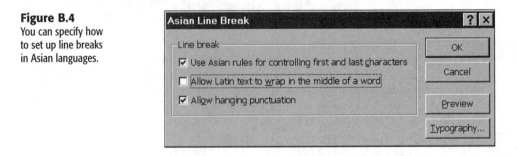

In the scroll box beneath Show Controls and Enable Editing For, place a check in front of each language in which you want to edit. The selected languages appear in the Enabled Languages box. When you click OK, additional features and commands are installed based on your language choices.

For example, if you enable editing in Japanese, new menu commands appear in PowerPoint such as Format, Line Break, which opens the Asian Line Break dialog box, shown in Figure B.4.

Figure B.4
You can specify how to set up line breaks in Asian languages.

Can't find the menu options you need? See the Troubleshooting section at the end of the chapter.

This dialog box enables you to set line break rules for Asian languages.

Note

Office 2000 doesn't automatically enable all languages for editing, in order to avoid adding unnecessary options. You must manually enable editing in any language in which you create a PowerPoint presentation.

Tip #301 from
Patrice-Anne Rutledge

Be sure to have your Office 2000 CD set available when you enable a new language for editing. Depending on the language, you may be prompted to insert a CD to install additional features.

Even if you enable editing in certain languages—such as many Asian, right-to-left, and Central European languages—you must also meet certain system requirements before you can truly edit in those languages. For example, for some languages you need to use Windows NT 5 to gain full support.

In other cases, you can simply install the appropriate keyboard layout to edit in that language. To do this, choose Settings, Control Panel from the Windows Start menu and double-click the Keyboard icon in the Control Panel dialog box. Depending on your operating system, you can add a new keyboard layout on either the Language tab or the Input Locales tab. Figure B.5 shows the Language tab from Windows 98.

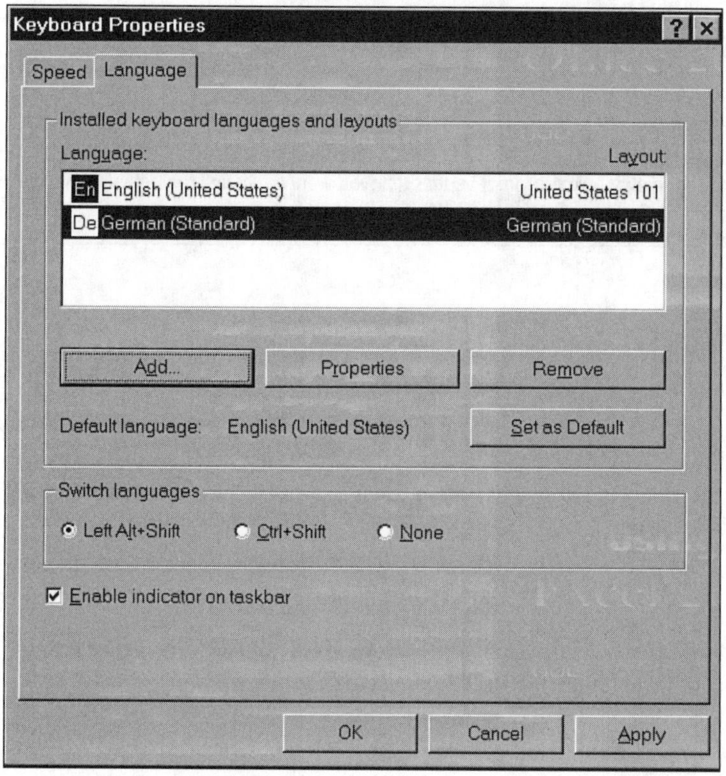

Figure B.5
Adding keyboard layouts makes it easier to work in another language.

APP

B

CHECKING SPELLING IN ANOTHER LANGUAGE

To check spelling in another language, follow these steps:

1. Select the text you want to spell-check.

2. Choose Tools, Language to open the Language dialog box, shown in Figure B.6.

Figure B.6
You can spell-check
in multiple languages
in PowerPoint.

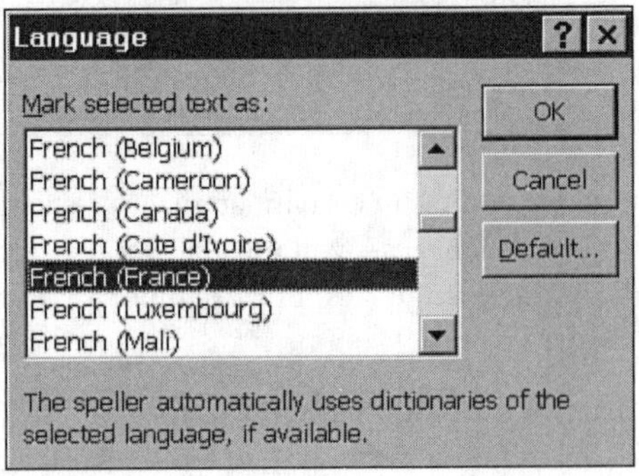

3. In the scroll box under Mark Selected Text As, choose the language whose dictionary you want the spelling checker to use.

4. Click OK to close the dialog box.

5. Click the Spelling button on the Standard toolbar to check the spelling in this language.

Tip #302 from
Patrice-Anne Rutledge

You can change the language of the default dictionary by clicking the Default button in the Language dialog box. A prompt verifies that you want to change the default language for this and future presentations to the language you selected.

TROUBLESHOOTING

I can't find the menu options to edit in a certain language.

You must enable a language for editing before you can view related menu options. To do so, choose Programs, Microsoft Office Tools, Microsoft Office Language Settings from the Start menu. Go to the Enables Languages tab in the Microsoft Office Language Settings dialog box to enable the language you want to use.

I can't find the Microsoft Office Language Settings dialog box, or I can find it but certain tabs don't appear.

You must install the Microsoft MultiLanguage Pack in order to view this dialog box and all its tabs. Install this from the Language Pack CD.

WHAT'S ON THE CD?

by Patrice-Anne Rutledge

Special Edition Using Microsoft PowerPoint 2000 includes a companion CD-ROM that provides electronic books, samples, templates, and other software to enhance your experience using PowerPoint 2000. The following sections offer a brief description of some of the things you'll find on the CD.

Browsing this CD via the CD-ROM interface is easy. If you have AUTOPLAY turned on, your computer will automatically run the CD-ROM interface when you insert the CD in the drive. If AUTOPLAY is turned off, follow these steps:

1. Insert the CD in your CD-ROM drive.
2. From the Windows desktop, double-click the My Computer icon.
3. Double-click the icon representing your CD-ROM drive.
4. Double-click the icon titled START.EXE to run the interface.

ELECTRONIC COPY OF *SPECIAL EDITION USING MICROSOFT POWERPOINT 2000*

Although it's not a complete substitute for a printed book, an electronic version can definitely come in handy. We included a full electronic version of *Special Edition Using Microsoft PowerPoint 2000* in which you can perform searches for any text located in this book. You'll find it in the \EBOOK folder on the CD. It's also a useful tool when you have your computer with you, but don't want to carry your printed version of the book.

Caution

Please note that this electronic copy is for your use only. You may not copy it to a network, another CD-ROM, or the Internet for others to use. The print capability of this version has also been disabled (you already have a printed copy of the book so you shouldn't need to print this) and you cannot copy and paste material from this electronic book.

Special Edition Using Microsoft PowerPoint 2000 is delivered in Adobe Acrobat format. If you don't already have Acrobat software, you'll find it on the CD in the \3RDPARTY\ADOBE folder.

QUE'S *SPECIAL EDITION USING MICROSOFT OFFICE 2000* SHOWCASE

This PDF showcase, located in the \SHOWCASE folder, provides content from our best-selling *Special Edition* series. It features additional electronic coverage of other books in this series and more, including:

- *Special Edition Using Microsoft Office 2000* by Ed Bott and Woody Leonard (ISBN: 0-7897-1842-1)
- *Special Edition Using Microsoft Word 2000* by Bill Camarda (ISBN: 0-7897-1852-9)
- *Special Edition Using Microsoft Excel 2000* by Patrick Blattner and Laurie Ulrich (ISBN: 0-7897-1729-8)

GRAPHICS PACK

The Graphics Pack is a unique graphics library that will help you customize your projects and presentations. You'll find it in the \GRAPHICS folder on the CD.

THIRD-PARTY SOFTWARE

The CD includes several additional third-party software programs, located in the \3RDPARTY folder, which will enhance your experience using PowerPoint and other Office products. These include

- **Adobe Acrobat Reader by Adobe Systems, Inc.** The reader enables you to view files in Acrobat format on this CD.
- **Colorful Business Templates for Microsoft PowerPoint by Tektronix.** This series of templates will help enhance the use of color in your PowerPoint presentations.
- **SourceCheck 2000 by GPP Software.** SourceCheck checks the source code for potential year 2000 date compliance problems.
- **WinZip by Nico Mak Computing, Inc.** This utility program makes zipping and unzipping your files easy and convenient.

Caution

Some of these programs may require you to transfer files to a folder other than the software installer default. Please see the installation notes following each product for more details.

WEB RESOURCES PAGE

The Web resource page lists the Web site addresses for productivity tools and commercial vendors, as well as helpful tips on the Office 2000 suite of products, including PowerPoint. You'll find it in the \WEBRESOURCES folder.

INDEX

Symbols

3D effects
adding to presentations, 289-292
troubleshooting, 296

3D Settings toolbar, buttons, 291-292

3D view charts, 218-219

3D View command (Chart menu), 218

3D View dialog box, 218

35mm slides
continuity, 548
convenience, 546
cost, 542-543
creating, 187-188
Genigraphics Wizard, 187

A

accents, 619

acetates. *See* overheads

action buttons, 331-332

Action Buttons command (Slide Show menu), 331

Action Settings, 329
hyperlinks, 348-350
inserting, 329-330

Action Settings command (Slide Show menu), 329

Action Settings dialog box, 329, 348

action-driven concepts, 498-499

Add Clip to Clip Gallery dialog box, 305

Add to Favorites button, 158

Add Trendline command (Chart menu), 219

Add Trendline dialog box, 220

add-ins, 479-481

adding
charts, 201
AutoLayouts, 199
menus to menu bar, 463-465
slides, 118
text, 58-59
toolbars, 448-449
Web discussion comments, 408

affinity diagrams, 504-505

alignment
formatting organization chart text, 234
objects, 293-294
table text, 85-86

Allow Others to Edit button, 404

anchored eye contact, 603

anchors, 556-597

angles, creating, one-on-one presentations, 684-685

animation, 318-319, 668
customizing, 323-327
chart effects, 325-327
multimedia settings, 327-328
setting ordering and timing, 323-324
special effects, 324-325
preset animation, 322-323
troubleshooting, 333
slide transitions, 319-322

Animation Effects toolbar, 332-333, 448

appearance. *See* physical appearance

applications
Office, integrating with PowerPoint, 427-428.
See also Office 2000
PowerPoint. *See* PowerPoint

Apply Design Template dialog box, 127

area charts, 202

arranging scripts, 379

arrows, 569
adding to presentations, 269-271

assistants, adding to organization charts, 231

audience considerations, 522-524
defining motivators, 523-524
demographic considerations, 523
direct contact with an audience, 522
how an audience filters information, 524-526

audio. *See also* media clips; sound
broadcasts, 388
playing a CD audio track, 313

audioconferencing, 712

AutoContent Wizard, 36-39, 58

S

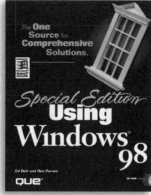

Get **FREE** books and more...when you register this book online for our Personal Bookshelf Program

http://register.quecorp.com/

 Register online and you can sign up for our *FREE Personal Bookshelf Program...*unlimited access to the electronic version of more than 200 complete computer books—immediately! That means you'll have 100,000 pages of valuable information onscreen, at your fingertips!

 Plus, you can access product support, including complimentary downloads, technical support files, book-focused links, companion Web sites, author sites, and more!

 And, don't miss out on the opportunity to sign up for a *FREE subscription to a weekly email newsletter* to help you stay current with news, announcements, sample book chapters and special events including sweepstakes, contests, and various product giveaways.

 We value your comments! Best of all, the entire registration process takes only a few minutes to complete...so go online and get the greatest value going—absolutely FREE!

Don't Miss Out on This Great Opportunity!

QUE®is a product of Macmillan Computer Publishing USA—for more information, visit: *www.mcp.com*

SPECIAL OFFER

The OfficeReady™ templates you're using are just a selection from the 650 templates offered in the complete version of OfficeReady.

If you're enjoying the time-saving benefits of these professionally designed, ready-to-use templates, just imagine having templates for nearly every task you perform using Microsoft® Office.

It's easy. All of the additional templates are already located on your *Special Edition Using Microsoft PowerPoint 2000* CD-ROM. You'll immediately be able to use them for all of the work you do using Microsoft Office. Even better, you'll have all 650 templates for only $19.95. That's 50% off the normal retail price!

Ordering is easy. Just call 1-(800) 385-2155. All of the additional templates are already located on your CD-ROM. You'll be issued a password to unlock the templates.

Designing documents in Microsoft Office can take up hours of your valuable time. Now, for only $19.95, you can save that time, and devote it to something that makes sense – like your business.

Offer subject to availability. Prices subject to change without notice.